BROOKE COUNTY

VIRGINIA/WEST VIRGINIA
LICENSES AND MARRIAGES

1797-1874

Compiled by
Renee Britt Sherman

HERITAGE BOOKS
2009

HERITAGE BOOKS
AN IMPRINT OF HERITAGE BOOKS, INC.

Books, CDs, and more—Worldwide

For our listing of thousands of titles see our website at
www.HeritageBooks.com

Published 2009 by
HERITAGE BOOKS, INC.
Publishing Division
100 Railroad Ave. #104
Westminster, Maryland 21157

Copyright © 1991 Renee Britt Sherman

All rights reserved. No part of this book may be reproduced or transmitted in any form or by any means, electronic or mechanical, including photocopying, recording or by any information storage and retrieval system without written permission from the author, except for the inclusion of brief quotations in a review.

International Standard Book Numbers
Paperbound: 978-1-55613-534-7
Clothbound: 978-0-7884-8087-4

TABLE OF CONTENTS

Foreword	v
Abbreviations	vii
Marriage Licenses & Marriage Records 1797 - 1874	
Books 1A,2A,3A,4A	1
Marriage Records 1853 - 1874	
Book 1	133
Marriage Record Notes	303
Religious Denominations	305
Marriage Officials	309
Districts, Towns, Townships & Place Names	315
Map of Brooke & Hancock Counties, VA./WV	317
Bibliography	321
Index Marriage Book 1	323

FOREWORD

Brooke and Hancock Counties, VA./WV. Licenses and Marriages 1797 To 1874

The area of Brooke Co., Virginia was settled in about 1744, created May 1797 from Ohio Co., Virginia, became Brooke Co., West Virginia on 20 Jun 1863, when the new state of West Virginia was formed. In 1861, western Virginia was organized under the name of Kanawha, and two years later it became the state of West Virginia. Brooke Co. today is located between Hancock Co. and Ohio Co., in the panhandle of West Virginia. Hancock Co., Virginia, created 15 Jan 1848, was originally part of Brooke County. The records are included in the book to the year 1848.

The book is based on 66 years (1797-1863) of Brooke Co., Virginia, and 12 years of (1863-1874) Brooke Co., West Virginia, a total of 78 years of marriage history. Records were kept in Virginia, West Virginia, Ohio and Pennsylvania, as there were many boundary disputes during the time period.

A unique area because of its location in the panhandle of West Virginia, it borders Pennsylvania, Ohio and the Ohio River. Many travelers of the time went by way of the Ohio River to travel west and south, primarily to settle the states of Ohio, Kentucky, Kansas, Indiana, Illinois, Missouri and Arkansas.

Marriage records and licenses from the county clerks "Register of Marriages" and "Marriage Licenses" cite references to book and page number for easy location of the original handwritten documents. Over 5000 persons are listed, brides and grooms, parents and ministers. Reference was made to about 1500 marriages and 600 marriage licenses.

It covers persons from Canada, Delaware, England, France, Germany, Holland, Ireland, Kentucky, Maine, Maryland, Massachusetts, New Hampshire, New Jersey, New York, Ohio, Pennsylvania, Prussia, Scotland, Vermont, Virginia, West Virginia, etc.

Licenses and Marriages (Book 1A, 1797 to 1815) are shown in a two line alphabetical format, showing bride and groom, date of marriage, state, marriage official and record location.

Marriage records (Book 1, 1853 to 1874) are shown in an alphabetized and paragraphed format, listing such personal information as bride and groom, parents, age, single, widowed, divorced, where the couple was married and when, place of birth, residence, occupation of the groom, marriage official and religious denomination, and any remarks. Colored marriages are also listed. Reference is given to book, page and line number of the original handwritten documents.

Licenses and Marriages (Book 2A, 1815 to 1854) are shown in a two line alphabetical format showing bride and groom, date of marriage, state, marriage official and record location.

Marriage records (Book 2A*, 1848 to 1854) are shown in a two line alphabetical format showing bride and groom, date of marriage, state, marriage official and record location. Seventeen pages of marriages not listed on any of the clerks indexes. Some marriages have corresponding licenses in Book 3A.

Marriage licenses (Books 3A and 4A, 1852 to 1874) are shown in a two line alphabetical format, listing the bride and groom, date of license, state, recorder, reference to book and page number of the original handwritten documents. Marriage licenses were first recorded in 1852 as a separate document.

FOREWORD

The book is alphabetical in all sections, listing males and females by maiden surname and married surname. Each section provides a quick reference to all persons listed with the same surname. The paragraphed section (Book 1 Marriage Records) has a separate index for parents and other persons. The special sections list county clerks, ministers and their denominations, churches, towns, districts, and place names of Brooke and Hancock counties, with a location map.

The records were all handwritten and sometimes difficult to read, with poor copy. Every possible effort has been made to give an accurate representation of the information listed. Every name was also checked with the clerks indexes.

The town of Wellsburg (created 17 Jan 1791) celebrated their "200th Anniversary" on 17 Jan 1991. Brooke County will celebrate their "200th Anniversary" in May 1997." This book provides a valuable tool for the person researching the above areas.

ABBREVIATIONS AND SYMBOLS USED

Alabama	AL.		Vermont	VT.
Alaska	AK.		Virginia	VA.
Arizona	AZ.		Washington	WA.
Arkansas	AR.		West Virginia	WV.
California	CA.		Wisconsin	WI.
Colorado	CO.		Wyoming	WY.
Connecticut	CT.			
Delaware	DE.			
Dist. of Columbia	DC.		Allegheny Co.,	Allegh. Co.,
Florida	FL.		Belmont Co.,	Bel. Co.,
Georgia	GA.		Brooke Co.,	B.C.
Hawaii	HI.		Christian Co.,	Christ. Co.,
Idaho	ID.		Columbiana Co.,	Col. Co.,
Illinois	IL.		Fayette Co.,	Fay. Co.,
Indiana	IN.		Hancock Co.,	Han., Co.,
Iowa	IA.		Hampshire Co.,	Hamp. Co.,
Kansas	KS.		Harrison Co.,	Har. Co.,
Kentucky	KY.		Hollidays Cove	H. Cove
Louisiana	LA.		Jefferson Co.,	Jeff. Co.,
Maine	ME.		Lancaster Co.,	Lanc. Co.
Maryland	MD.		Marshall Co.,	Mars. Co.,
Massachusetts	MA.		Montgomery Co.,	Mont. Co.,
Michigan	MI.		Muskingum Co.,	Musk. Co.,
Minnesota	MN.		Ohio Co.,	OH. Co.,
Mississippi	MS.		Philadelphia	Phila.
Missouri	MO.		Pittsburgh	Pitts.
Montana	MT.		Rappahannock Co.,	Rappa. Co.,
Nebraska	NE.		Steubenville	Steuben.
Nevada	NV.		Somerset Co.,	Som. Co.,
New Hampshire	NH.		Washington Co.,	Wash. Co.
New Jersey	NJ.			
New Mexico	NM.			
New York	NY.		Canada	CAN.
North Carolina	NC.		England	ENG.
North Dakota	ND.		France	FRA.
Ohio	OH.		Germany	GER.
Oklahoma	OK.		Ireland	IRE.
Oregon	OR.		Scotland	SCT.
Pennsylvania	PA.		Wales	WLS.
Rhode Island	RI.			
South Carolina	SC.			
South Dakota	SD.			
Tennessee	TN.			
Texas	TX.			
Utah	UT.			

ABBREVIATIONS AND SYMBOLS USED

Alexander	Alex.		January		Jan.
Andrew	And.		February		Feb.
Archibald	Arch.		March		Mar.
Augustus	Aug.		April		Apr.
Benjamin	Benja.		May		May
Catharine	Cath.		June		Jun.
Catherine	Cath.		July		Jul.
Charles	Chas.		August		Aug.
Christopher	Christ.		September		Sep.
Daniel	Dan'l.		October		Oct.
Edward	Edw.		November		Nov.
Elisabeth	Elisa.		December		Dec.
Elizabeth	Eliza.				
Franklin	Frank.				
Frederick	Fred.				
George	Geo.		book		bk.
Jackson	Jack.		county		Co.
James	Jas.		official		off.
John	Jno.		page		pg.
Joseph	Jos.		unknown		unk.
Margaret	Marg't.		unknown information		- -
Michael	Mich'l.		unknown surname		(...)
Montgomery	Mont.				
Mortimore	Mort.				
Nathaniel	Nath'l.				
Nichodernus	Nichod.				
Patrick	Pat.				
Richard	Rich'd.				
Robert	Rob't.				
Samuel	Sam'l.				
Thomas	Thos.				
Virginia	Virg.				
Washington	Wash.				
William	Wm.				

BROOKE COUNTY
VIRGINIA / WEST VIRGINIA
LICENSES AND MARRIAGES
1797 - 1874

BOOKS
1A,2A,3A,4A,

BROOKE CO., VA./WV. LICENSES & MARRIAGES, 1797-1874   1

ABEY			and		UBY	VA.	bk. 3A	pg. 110
Mary P.		25 Dec	1861		Alexander C.	off. J.	OXFORD	
ABRAHAMS			and		KIMBERLAND	VA.	bk. 2A	pg. 067
James		30 Oct	1838		Prudence	off. A.	YOUNG	
ABRAHAMS			and		KEMP	WV.	bk. 3A	pg. 130
Mort. Benton		12 Aug	1863		Ann Elizabeth	off. H.	SHEPHERD	
ABRAHAMS			and		JACKSON	VA.	bk. 2A	pg. 049
Robert		27 Dec	1827		Matilda	off. S.	REED	
ACKERMAN			and		CLOSE	VA.	bk. 01	pg. 003
Elizabeth Jane		08 Nov	1855		Peter	off. E.	QUILLEN	
ACKINSON			and		BROWN	VA.	bk. 1A	pg. 005
James		02 Jan	1799		Nancy	off.	UNKNOWN	
ACKINSON			and		OWENS	VA.	bk. 1A	pg. 079
William		22 May	1813		Amelia	off. J.	PRITCHARD	
ADAMS			and		MOREN	VA.	bk. 2A	pg. 090
Agnes		13 Jan	1848		John T.	off. J.	MONROE	
ADAMS			and		HALES	VA.	bk. 2A	pg. *02
Benjamin F.		08 Apr	1849		Amity	off. I.	DALLAS	
ADAMS			and		BUCKALEW	WV.	bk. 4A	pg. 060
Eli		20 Mar	1869		Lydia Jane	off. W.	WHITE	
ADAMS			and		WYLIE	VA.	bk. 2A	pg. 060
Elisabeth		24 Mar	1829		John	off. S.	REED	
ADAMS			and		RICHARDSON	VA.	bk. 1A	pg. 074
James		13 Jan	1815		Catharine	off. L.	BROWNING	
ADAMS			and		KEITH	WV.	bk. 4A	pg. 128
James A.		21 Oct	1873		Clara Jane	off. W.	LATIMER	
ADAMS			and		WARD	WV.	bk. 4A	pg. 080
James M.		14 Dec	1870		Mary A.	off. W.	WHITE	
ADAMS			and		PARK	VA.	bk. 2A	pg. 058
Jane		07 Nov	1829		William	off. T.	BEEKS	
ADAMS			and		GUNION	WV.	bk. 4A	pg. 037
John A.		08 Jan	1868		Margaret	off. H.	MELVIN	
ADAMS			and		WELSH	VA.	bk. 2A	pg. 085
Josiah		25 Sep	1844		Elizabeth	off. J.	SCOTT	
ADAMS			and		ATKINSON	VA.	bk. 2A	pg. 011
Malinda		06 Apr	1819		Thomas	off. G.	BUCHANAN	
ADAMS			and		HOLLINGSWORTH	VA.	bk. 1A	pg. 039
Mary		22 Nov	1802		Joshua	off. J.	DODDRIDGE	
ADAMS			and		MURRY	VA.	bk. 1A	pg. 039
Nancy		26 Jul	1802		Nicholas	off. J.	DODDRIDGE	
ADAMS			and		NUNEMAKER	VA.	bk. 2A	pg. *09
Richard		09 Oct	1851		Catharine	off. H.	SNYDER	
ADAMS			and		HUKILL	WV.	bk. 4A	pg. 076
Richard		14 Sep	1870		Matilda	off. W.	WHITE	
ADAMS			and		SMITH	WV.	bk. 4A	pg. 010
Ruth A.		-- Sep	1866		Isaac Y.	off. R.	NICHOLLS	
ADAMS			and		GREEN	VA.	bk. 2A	pg. 060
Samuel		06 Oct	1828		Elisabeth	off. E.	SMITH	
ADAMS			and		CAMPBELL	VA.	bk. 2A	pg. 083
Susan		26 Sep	1839		William	off. R.	WHITE	
ADAMS			and		CREAL	VA.	bk. 2A	pg. 054
William		22 Jan	1828		Rachael	off. L.	BROWNING	

ADRIAN		and		PRITCHARD	VA. bk. 2A pg. 013
Mordicai	31	Aug	1820	Mary	off. J. PRITCHARD
AGNEW		and		TALBOTT	VA. bk. 2A pg. 069
Ann	29	Oct	1839	Richard	off. M. TELCHENELL
AGNEW		and		HARTFORD	VA. bk. 2A pg. *03
James M.	22	Jan	1850	Rachel	off. T. NEWELL
AGNEW		and		MARSHALL	VA. bk. 01 pg. 005
James M.	25	Mar	1857	Rebecca C.	off. E. QUILLEN
AIKEN		and		RUSSELL	WV. bk. 4A pg. 032
Anne A.	12	Oct	1867	George W.	off. H. MELVIN
AKERS		and		MC KEE	VA. bk. 2A pg. 080
Alexander	15	Feb	1828	Harriet	off. S. LAUCK
ALBAN		and		COX	VA. bk. 2A pg. 038
George	22	Dec	1825	Nancy	off. T. BEEKS
ALEXANDER		and		CALDWELL	VA. bk. 2A pg. 041
James	25	Apr	1826	Fanny	off. W. WYLIE
ALEXANDER		and		JOHNSON	VA. bk. 2A pg. 060
John	18	Sep	1828	Isabella	off. S. REED
ALEXANDER		and		ROBERTS	VA. bk. 2A pg. 022
Joseph	30	May	1822	Nancy	off. G. BUCHANAN
ALEXANDER		and		KERNS	WV. bk. 3A pg. 152
Samuel H.	24	Feb	1865	Ann Rebecca	off. H. SHEPHERD
ALEXANDER		and		PERRY	WV. bk. 3A pg. 152
Samuel H.	24	Feb	1865	Ann Rebecca	off. H. SHEPHERD
ALISON		and		WHITE	VA. bk. 2A pg. 052
Charles	30	Aug	1827	Sarah	off. G. SCOTT
ALISON		and		PUGH	VA. bk. 2A pg. 060
Jonathan	28	Sep	1828	Lena	off. S. REED
ALISON		and		PUGH	VA. bk. 2A pg. 057
Samuel	14	Jan	1830	Fanny	off. G. SCOTT
ALLEN		and		TARR	WV. bk. 4A pg. 113
Edwin T.	04	Jun	1872	Mary Belle	off. W. LATIMER
ALLEN		and		CALENDINE	WV. bk. 4A pg. 069
Elizabeth	19	Feb	1870	George	off. W. WHITE
ALLEN		and		ANDERSON	VA. bk. 1A pg. 036
Jackamiah	07	Mar	1809	Jane	off. J. HUGHES
ALLISON		and		PUGH	VA. bk. 2A pg. 084
Christina	15	Nov	1843	Moses	off. R. WHITE
ALLISON		and		MORROW	VA. bk. 2A pg. 082
Eleanor	20	Feb	1839	James	off. R. WHITE
ALLISON		and		WORK	VA. bk. 2A pg. 082
Elizabeth	24	Jan	1839	Amos	off. R. WHITE
ALLISON		and		VAUGHN	VA. bk. 2A pg. 084
Elizabeth	19	Sep	1844	Jacob	off. R. WHITE
ALLISON		and		PUGH	VA. bk. 2A pg. 056
James	25	Nov	1830	Sarah	off. G. SCOTT
ALLISON		and		FOWLER	VA. bk. 2A pg. 084
James	05	Jan	1844	Mary	off. R. WHITE
ALLISON		and		MC MILLAN	VA. bk. 2A pg. 083
Jane	18	Feb	1841	William	off. R. WHITE
ALLISON		and		CARIENS	WV. bk. 4A pg. 018
John	04	Jan	1867	Mary	off. H. MELVIN

Name		Day	Mo	Year	Spouse	Reference
ALLISON	and				MARTIN	VA. bk. 2A pg. 086
Lucinda	25	Sep		1845	Allison	off. G. SCOTT
ALLISON	and				DANIEL	VA. bk. 2A pg. 083
Nancy	28	Oct		1841	Frederick	off. R. WHITE
ALLISON	and				WILCOXON	VA. bk. 2A pg. 082
Robert	18	Jul		1838	Blanche	off. R. WHITE
ALLISON	and				WYLIE	VA. bk. 2A pg. 077
Samuel	31	May		1842	Elizabeth	off. J. SCOTT
AMICK	and				FLEMING	VA. bk. 2A pg. 061
Catherine	29	Sep		1832	James	off. G. MC CASHEY
AMOLA	and				LINDSAY	VA. bk. 2A pg. 051
Elisabeth	17	Oct		1827	John	off. J. CAZAD
AMSPOKER	and				WHEELER	VA. bk. 01 pg. 003
Elizabeth Ann	15	Feb		1855	Zachariah C.	off. J. THOMAS
AMSPOKER	and				BURT	VA. bk. 1A pg. 030
Martha	04	Dec		1806	William	off. J. HUGHES
AMSPOKER	and				DONOVAN	VA. bk. 3A pg. 060
Mary Ann	21	Dec		1858	Asa O.	off. J. NAYLOR
ANDERSON	and				ANDERSON	VA. bk. 2A pg. 046
Alexander	18	Jan		1827	Anne (...)	off. G. BUCHANAN
ANDERSON	and				WYCOFF	VA. bk. 2A pg. 026
Andrew	13	Jan		1823	Hannah	off. G. SCOTT
ANDERSON	and				ANDERSON	VA. bk. 2A pg. 046
Anne (...)	18	Jan		1827	Alexander	off. G. BUCHANAN
ANDERSON	and				HELM	VA. bk. 2A pg. 086
Catharine	31	Dec		1845	George K.	off. W. LEMON
ANDERSON	and				SUTER	VA. bk. 3A pg. 086
George	14	Jul		1860	Mary C.	off. J. NAYLOR
ANDERSON	and				MC ELHANY	VA. bk. 1A pg. 021
James	01	May		1806	Martha	off. UNKNOWN
ANDERSON	and				ALLEN	VA. bk. 1A pg. 036
Jane	07	Mar		1809	Jackamiah	off. J. HUGHES
ANDERSON	and				CRAIGHTON	VA. bk. 2A pg. 028
Lydia	20	Mar		1823	John	off. J. CAZAD
ANDERSON	and				BROWN	VA. bk. 2A pg. *13
Mary	03	Mar		1853	James B.	off. A. MYERS
ANDERSON	and				WELLS	VA. bk. 3A pg. 126
Rebecca Eliza	21	Feb		1863	John Dusty	off. J. NAYLOR
ANDERSON	and				CONN	VA. bk. 2A pg. 049
Robert	24	Apr		1827	Margaret	off. S. REED
ANDERSON	and				ORR	WV. bk. 4A pg. 031
T.F.	21	Oct		1867	Maggy B.	off. H. MELVIN
ANDREWS	and				SPURVIER	VA. bk. 2A pg. 059
Elizabeth	24	Jun		1830	Owen	off. G. BUCHANAN
ANDREWS	and				JENKINS	VA. bk. 2A pg. 071
Elizabeth	03	Jun		1841	David	off. J. GALLOWAY
ANDREWS	and				WATT	VA. bk. 1A pg. 010
Ester	29	Apr		1802	William	off. J. HUGHES
ANDREWS	and				STRAIN	VA. bk. 2A pg. 081
Mary	13	Mar		1845	John	off. D. THOMPSON
ANDREWS	and				MC CURDY	VA. bk. 2A pg. 056
Nancy	11	Mar		1830	William	off. G. SCOTT

4   BROOKE CO., VA./WV. LICENSES & MARRIAGES, 1797-1874

ANDREWS		and		EDIE	VA. bk. 2A pg. 073
Rebecca	24	Mar	1842	John	off. J. HERBERT
ANNY		and		CRAFT	VA. bk. 2A pg. 080
David S.	01	Mar	1838	Harriet	off. S. LAUCK
ANTILL		and		MAYHALL	VA. bk. 2A pg. *02
Elizabeth	24	Jul	1848	John	off. I. DALLAS
ANTILL		and		NELSON	WV. bk. 3A pg. 149
Rebecca V.	28	Dec	1864	John M.	off. H. SHEPHERD
ANTILL		and		GREEN	VA. bk. 3A pg. 053
Sarah E.	19	May	1858	William L.	off. J. NAYLOR
APPLEGATE		and		PARISH	VA. bk. 2A pg. *13
Andrew	09	Dec	1852	Ellen	off. E. QUILLEN
APPLEGATE		and		LOCKHART	VA. bk. 2A pg. 082
Eda	05	Apr	1838	Jeptha	off. R. WHITE
APPLEGATE		and		BERNARD	VA. bk. 2A pg. 082
Eleanor	12	Sep	1839	Dennis S.	off. R. WHITE
APPLEGATE		and		ST. CLAIR	VA. bk. 2A pg. 076
Elizabeth	11	Jun	1843	John D.	off. C. BEST
APPLEGATE		and		MACKEY	VA. bk. 2A pg. *14
Moses	16	Jun	1853	Elizabeth	off. S. NESBITT
ARBAUGH		and		BICKERSTAFF	VA. bk. 2A pg. *16
Abigail	22	Jan	1854	Enos	off. S. DUNLAP
ARBAUGH		and		FERREL	VA. bk. 2A pg. 067
Catharine	07	Feb	1839	William	off. A. YOUNG
ARBUCKEL		and		FOWLER	VA. bk. 2A pg. 082
Isaac	16	Aug	1838	Verlinda	off. R. WHITE
ARCHBOLD		and		COX	VA. bk. 2A pg. 061
Benjamin	18	Apr	1832	Nancy	off. R. HOPKINS
ARCHER		and		FRESHWATER	VA. bk. 2A pg. 057
Eleanor	21	Sep	1830	Philip	off. G. BUCHANAN
ARCHER		and		ORR	VA. bk. 2A pg. 083
Elizabeth	09	Nov	1841	George G.	off. R. WHITE
ARCHER		and		GOURLEY	VA. bk. 2A pg. 021
Nancy	12	Feb	1822	William	off. G. BUCHANAN
ARCHER		and		LEE	VA. bk. 2A pg. 020
Samuel	08	Mar	1821	Mary	off. E. MACURDY
ARCHER		and		GORRELL	VA. bk. 1A pg. 030
William	09	Apr	1807	Margaret	off. J. HUGHES
ARMSTRONG		and		PRICE	VA. bk. 2A pg. 001
Betsy	20	Aug	1815	John	off. E. MACURDY
ARMSTRONG		and		MELVIN	VA. bk. 2A pg. 068
Ebenezer	07	May	1840	Sarah	off. G. SCOTT
ARMSTRONG		and		RIZER	VA. bk. 2A pg. 007
George	19	Feb	1819	Catharine	off. E. MACURDY
ARMSTRONG		and		ORR	VA. bk. 2A pg. 020
Martin	29	Apr	1821	Margaret	off. E. MACURDY
ARMSTRONG		and		HARRIS	VA. bk. 2A pg. 060
Nancy	26	Mar	1829	Jacob	off. S. REED
ARMSTRONG		and		JONES	WV. bk. 4A pg. 129
Robert	04	Nov	1873	Hannah	off. W. LATIMER
ASHBROOK		and		CRIDER	VA. bk. 2A pg. 038
Mary Ann	11	Apr	1830	Frederick	off. D. MERRYMAN

ATEN Elizabeth	16	and Mar	1815	PROSSER Abraham	VA. bk. 1A pg. 063 off. G. SCOTT	
ATEN Jacob	19	and Jun	1823	BROWN Elizabeth	VA. bk. 2A pg. 029 off. G. SCOTT	
ATEN John	20	and May	1819	HART Sarah	VA. bk. 2A pg. 008 off. G. SCOTT	
ATEN John	22	and Jun	1822	MYLAR Mary	VA. bk. 2A pg. 023 off. G. SCOTT	
ATEN Mary	17	and Apr	1827	WITHERS James	VA. bk. 2A pg. 049 off. S. REED	
ATEN Richard	09	and Apr	1840	PETERSON Ann	VA. bk. 2A pg. 083 off. R. WHITE	
ATEN William (Jr.)	14	and May	1846	PITTINGER Elizabeth	VA. bk. 2A pg. 087 off. G. SCOTT	
ATKINS Sarah	28	and Sep	1830	RUSSELL James	VA. bk. 2A pg. 055 off. R. HATTEN	
ATKINSON Alexander	21	and Jun	1853	CAMPBELL Rebecca	VA. bk. 2A pg. *15 off. J. GALLOWAY	
ATKINSON Ann	25	and Aug	1825	RALSTON Alexander	VA. bk. 2A pg. 033 off. G. BUCHANAN	
ATKINSON Flora A.	26	and Jan	1870	CALDWELL Robert	WV. bk. 4A pg. 066 off. W. WHITE	
ATKINSON James	06	and Feb	1823	SWEARINGEN Matilda	VA. bk. 2A pg. 025 off. G. BUCHANAN	
ATKINSON James	22	and Oct	1841	GRIFFITH Jane	VA. bk. 2A pg. 072 off. S. FULTON	
ATKINSON Joseph	14	and Feb	1839	GRIFFITH Margaret Ann	VA. bk. 2A pg. 065 off. G. BUCHANAN	
ATKINSON Margaret	25	and Dec	1858	BLAYNEY James F.	VA. bk. 3A pg. 061 off. J. NAYLOR	
ATKINSON Mary Ann	26	and Apr	1842	HUPP Isaac	VA. bk. 2A pg. 075 off. G. BUCHANAN	
ATKINSON Miss.	--	and --	1809	FOWLER Mr.	VA. bk. 1A pg. 048 off. J. DODDRIDGE	
ATKINSON Nancy	16	and Mar	1826	MC KIM Thomas	VA. bk. 2A pg. 040 off. G. BUCHANAN	
ATKINSON Narcissa	29	and Mar	1827	SHARPE John F.	VA. bk. 2A pg. 051 off. G. BUCHANAN	
ATKINSON Richard	22	and Jan	1824	SWEARINGEN Elenor	VA. bk. 2A pg. 029 off. G. BUCHANAN	
ATKINSON Samuel W.	29	and Oct	1868	SNEDIKER Clarinda L.	WV. bk. 4A pg. 052 off. S. QUEST	
ATKINSON Sarah Ann	25	and Oct	1827	MARSH James	VA. bk. 2A pg. 048 off. G. BUCHANAN	
ATKINSON Thomas	06	and Apr	1819	ADAMS Malinda	VA. bk. 2A pg. 011 off. G. BUCHANAN	
ATWELL Mervin Richard	13	and Oct	1863	FLEMING Amelia F.	WV. bk. 3A pg. 132 off. H. SHEPHERD	
BACHELL Jennie	19	and Sep	1871	GREEN Marshall S.	WV. bk. 4A pg. 095 off. W. WHITE	
BACHELL Mary Elizabeth	30	and Dec	1871	ROBINSON A.W.	WV. bk. 4A pg. 103 off. W. LATIMER	

Groom	Day	Month	Year	Bride	Reference
BADEN		and		BROWN	VA. bk. 1A pg. 039
Mary	31	Aug	1802	Stephen	off. J. DODDRIDGE
BAIL		and		WILLIAMSON	VA. bk. 2A pg. *11
Elizabeth	12	May	1852	Mackwright	off. D. HERVEY
BAIL		and		TAYLOR	WV. bk. 3A pg. 161
Thomas W.	27	Mar	1866	Alice	off. H. SHEPHERD
BAILE		and		RALSTON	VA. bk. 2A pg. 087
Ellen	29	May	1845	Rezin	off. J. GALLOWAY
BAILEY		and		JARRETT	VA. bk. 2A pg. 004
Robert	26	Dec	1816	Nancy	off. G. SCOTT
BAILEY		and		WATKINS	VA. bk. 2A pg. 090
William T.	21	Nov	1847	Mary	off. J. MONROE
BAILEY		and		BLAIR	VA. bk. 01 pg. 003
William T.	26	Oct	1854	Evaline	off. C. HOLMES
BAILEY		and		KIMBERLAND	WV. bk. 4A pg. 079
William T.	08	Nov	1870	Harriet	off. W. WHITE
BAILEY		and		WATKINS	WV. bk. 4A pg. 079
William T.	08	Nov	1870	Harriet	off. W. WHITE
BAIR		and		MC INTIRE	WV. bk. 4A pg. 029
Sarah E.	02	Sep	1867	Robert (Sr.)	off. C. MELVIN
BAIRD		and		WILLSON	VA. bk. 1A pg. 072
Esther	22	Dec	1812	Aaron	off. J. PRITCHARD
BAKER		and		WILCOXON	VA. bk. 1A pg. 023
Christiana	25	Mar	1806	Samuel	off. J. PRITCHARD
BAKER		and		FOWLER	VA. bk. 1A pg. 073
Elizabeth	21	Apr	1814	Richard	off. J. PRITCHARD
BAKER		and		BRANDON	VA. bk. 2A pg. 030
Elizabeth	26	Feb	1824	John	off. G. BUCHANAN
BAKER		and		HAWLEY	VA. bk. 2A pg. 078
Elizabeth	27	Mar	1842	Andrew	off. J. HARRISON
BAKER		and		WILCOXON	VA. bk. 2A pg. 016
Fanny	17	Oct	1820	John	off. G. BUCHANAN
BAKER		and		BEALL	VA. bk. 2A pg. *17
Levin H.	07	Sep	1853	Clara A.	off. S. NESBITT
BAKER		and		GAMBLE	VA. bk. 2A pg. 016
Mary	01	Feb	1821	Allen	off. J. PRITCHARD
BAKER		and		WHITE	WV. bk. 4A pg. 081
Mary	02	Jan	1871	James M.	off. W. WHITE
BAKER		and		CAMPBELL	VA. bk. 1A pg. 080
Morris	26	Oct	1815	Mary	off. J. PRITCHARD
BAKER		and		GRAFTON	VA. bk. 1A pg. 054
Nancy	04	Dec	1807	William	off. J. PRITCHARD
BAKER		and		WARTENBEE	VA. bk. 1A pg. 043
Otho	11	Mar	1802	Margaret	off. J. DODDRIDGE
BAKER		and		GRIFFITH	VA. bk. 2A pg. 003
William	12	Nov	1818	Rebecca	off. G. SCOTT
BAKEWELL		and		BARCLAY	WV. bk. 4A pg. 023
Emma C.	28	Feb	1867	Robert J.	off. H. MELVIN
BAKEWELL		and		CAMPBELL	VA. bk. 2A pg. 059
Selina	31	Jul	1828	Alexander	off. E. SMITH
BALLENTINE		and		CRUTH	VA. bk. 3A pg. 051
James	24	Feb	1858	Jane	off. J. NAYLOR

BROOKE CO., VA./WV. LICENSES & MARRIAGES, 1797-1874   7

Surname	Given	Day	Mo	Year	Spouse Surname	Spouse Given	Officiant / Reference
BALLETT	Edward	11	Sep	1865	GILBERT	Bridget	WV. bk. 3A pg. 160 off. H. SHEPHERD
BAMBRICK	Thomas	01	Sep	1825	KEENAN	Ann	VA. bk. 2A pg. 034 off. G. SCOTT
BANE	Amanda	19	Apr	1854	WILSON	Adam	VA. bk. 01 pg. 003 off. E. QUILLEN
BANE	Hugh	09	Feb	1829	HANSON	Louisa	VA. bk. 2A pg. 058 off. T. BEEKS
BANE	Jane	04	Nov	1815	BLACKBURN	Samuel	VA. bk. 1A pg. 064 off. G. SCOTT
BANE	John	28	Oct	1852	COLEMAN	Mertine	VA. bk. 2A pg. *14 off. S. NESBITT
BANE	Margaret	17	Mar	1808	SMITH	William	VA. bk. 1A pg. 036 off. J. HUGHES
BANE	Margaret	28	Mar	1854	WILSON	Andrew J.	VA. bk. 01 pg. 002 off. E. QUILLEN
BANE	Mary	06	May	1827	HUKILL	William	VA. bk. 2A pg. 046 off. C. MURRAY
BANE	Sarah Jane	17	Mar	1873	WILSON	Joseph B.	WV. bk. 4A pg. 124 off. W. LATIMER
BANE	William	18	Oct	1852	LAZEAR	Maria W.	VA. bk. 3A pg. 005 off. J. NAYLOR
BANNON	Bridget	08	Jan	1869	DOWNEY	Patrick	WV. bk. 4A pg. 056 off. W. WHITE
BANNON	Catherine	01	Jan	1859	MC GEE	Charles	VA. bk. 3A pg. 061 off. J. NAYLOR
BARBER	Abraham	08	Feb	1849	HINDMAN	Margaret	VA. bk. 2A pg. *05 off. J. STOCKTON
BARBER	Mary (Mrs.)	12	Sep	1856	COGAN	John	VA. bk. 01 pg. 004 off. W. GAMBLE, JR.
BARCLAY	John J.	04	Apr	1863	CAMPBELL	Decima H.	VA. bk. 3A pg. 127 off. J. NAYLOR
BARCLAY	John Rowan	05	Dec	1843	ROSE	Mary Hooper	VA. bk. 2A pg. 078 off. S. WORTHINGTON
BARCLAY	Robert J.	28	Feb	1867	BAKEWELL	Emma C.	WV. bk. 4A pg. 023 off. H. MELVIN
BARCLAY	W. C.	02	Dec	1852	KUHN	Emily M.	VA. bk. 2A pg. *13 off. E. QUILLEN
BARCUS	Ebenezer	14	Apr	1808	VANMATRE	Elizabeth	VA. bk. 1A pg. 035 off. W. WILLSON
BARCUS	Nancy	30	Dec	1838	WABLE	George	VA. bk. 2A pg. 067 off. A. YOUNG
BARNES	Alexander	20	Mar	1822	WORSTELL	Mary	VA. bk. 2A pg. 080 off. S. LAUCK
BARNES	Lydia M.	09	Feb	1859	MITCHELL	William H.	VA. bk. 3A pg. 064 off. J. NAYLOR
BARNES	Mary E.	03	Nov	1866	LONG	James	WV. bk. 4A pg. 014 off. R. NICHOLLS
BARNES	Rebecca	18	Jul	1861	ROSE	Wm. Henry	VA. bk. 3A pg. 103 off. S. NAYLOR
BARNES	Shepley	28	Dec	1867	NICHOLLS	Mary Eliza.	WV. bk. 4A pg. 039 off. C. MELVIN

8   BROOKE CO., VA./WV. LICENSES & MARRIAGES, 1797-1874

BARNES		and		BLAYNEY		VA. bk. 01 pg. 003
Walter D.		-- --	1855	Sarah		off. A. ENDSLEY
BARNET		and		CRAWFORD		VA. bk. 1A pg. 041
George	10	Jun	1800	Polly		off. J. DODDRIDGE
BARNET		and		LYON		VA. bk. 1A pg. 033
Susannah	26	Sep	1809	Andrew		off. J. DODDRIDGE
BARNS		and		CRAFT		VA. bk. 1A pg. 071
Alexander	29	May	1815	Mary		off. W. WILLSON
BARTH		and		LETZKUS		VA. bk. 01 pg. 009
Hugh	26	Nov	1860	Frances		off. S. HUBER
BARTHOLOMEW		and		BRIGGS		VA. bk. 3A pg. 088
George K.	08	Aug	1860	Elvyn Jane		off. J. NAYLOR
BARTHOLOMEW		and		SHRIMPLIN		W.V. bk. 4A pg. 042
Samuel D.	18	Feb	1868	Ella		off. H. MELVIN
BAUER		and		JOHNSTON		VA. bk. 1A pg. 072
Nancy	03	May	1812	James		off. J. PRITCHARD
BAUSMAN		and		CARTER		VA. bk. 2A pg. 007
Edward	26	Sep	1816	Prudence		off. S. LAUCK
BAUSMAN		and		MC CONNELL		VA. bk. 2A pg. 044
James	25	Jan	1827	Jane		off. J. CAZAD
BAXTER		and		GIST		VA. bk. 1A pg. 014
Ann	01	Jul	1804	Samuel		off. J. PRITCHARD
BAXTER		and		BUTLER		VA. bk. 1A pg. 027
Charity	09	Sep	1807	Henry		off. UNKNOWN
BAXTER		and		WILLIAMS		VA. bk. 2A pg. 083
Elizabeth	25	Nov	1841	Henry		off. R. WHITE
BAXTER		and		BROWN		WV. bk. 4A pg. 042
Ellen V.	18	Feb	1868	John L.		off. H. MELVIN
BAXTER		and		WALTERS		VA. bk. 2A pg. *03
George	17	Dec	1846	Louisa		off. J. GOODWIN
BAXTER		and		JACOB		WV. bk. 4A pg. 026
George A.	08	Jun	1867	Alice W.		off. H. MELVIN
BAXTER		and		MILLS		VA. bk. 2A pg. 080
John		-- --	1844	Eliza. Jane		off. R. SIMONTAIS
BAXTER		and		LANE		VA. bk. 1A pg. 055
Martha	04	Jan	1810	Dutton		off. J. PRITCHARD
BAXTER		and		HEDGES		VA. bk. 1A pg. 037
Mary		-- --	1799	Elijah		off. J. DODDRIDGE
BAXTER		and		WILLIAMSON		VA. bk. 3A pg. 111
Mary Ann	31	Dec	1861	James		off. S. NAYLOR
BAXTER		and		WELLS		VA. bk. 2A pg. *03
Nancy	15	Jul	1849	James		off. J. GOODWIN
BAXTER		and		BRADY		VA. bk. 2A pg. 078
Ruth	15	Jul	1841	John		off. J. HARRISON
BAXTER		and		BRANDON		VA. bk. 2A pg. 077
Ruth	14	Oct	1843	John		off. S. GRAFTON
BAXTER		and		MC DUGAN		VA. bk. 01 pg. 002
Sarah	26	Oct	1854	James		off. F. GUTHRIE
BAXTER		and		BUCKINGHAM		VA. bk. 1A pg. 053
William	31	May	1810	Mary		off. J. PRITCHARD
BEAL		and		JESTER		VA. bk. 2A pg. 059
Elizabeth	25	Aug	1828	A.O.		off. E. SMITH

BROOKE CO., VA./WV. LICENSES & MARRIAGES, 1797-1874   9

BEAL		and		CAMERON		VA. bk. 2A pg. 057
Philip	15	Apr	1830	Jane		off. G. BUCHANAN
BEAL		and		STILL		VA. bk. 1A pg. 066
Ruth	05	Apr	1816	Samuel		off. UNKNOWN
BEALL		and		GIST		VA. bk. 2A pg. 059
Bazel	14	Feb	1828	Louisana		off. E. SMITH
BEALL		and		BAKER		VA. bk. 2A pg. *17
Clara A.	07	Sep	1853	Levin H.		off. S. NESBITT
BEALL		and		MAXWELL		VA. bk. 2A pg. 067
Elizabeth	28	May	1839	Robert		off. J. GALLOWAY
BEALL		and		DAVIS		WV. bk. 4A pg. 073
Ellen	01	Aug	1870	Augustus		off. W. WHITE
BEALL		and		WATSON		WV. bk. 4A pg. 113
Leanna	19	Jun	1872	Green		off. W. LATIMER
BEALL		and		PARISH		WV. bk. 4A pg. 109
Lillie	30	Mar	1872	John D.		off. W. LATIMER
BEALL		and		SIMPSON		VA. bk. 2A pg. 051
Nancy	22	Mar	1827	William		off. G. BUCHANAN
BEALL		and		WYLIE		VA. bk. 2A pg. 062
William (Jr.)	22	Mar	1832	Martha		off. C. BEATTY
BEARD		and		BONER		VA. bk. 1A pg. 078
Andrew	05	Apr	1814	Rebecca		off. W. WILLSON
BEATER		and		BEATER		WV. bk. 3A pg. 143
Agnes (...)	30	Aug	1864	Casper		off. H. SHEPHERD
BEATER		and		BEATER		WV. bk. 3A pg. 143
Casper	30	Aug	1864	Agnes (...)		off. H. SHEPHERD
BEATTY		and		RISHER		VA. bk. 2A pg. *07
Elizabeth	07	Nov	1850	Asa		off. C. JACKSON
BEATTY		and		MC KIM		VA. bk. 2A pg. *09
Martina A.	25	Sep	1851	John		off. C. JACKSON
BEATTY		and		LEE		VA. bk. 2A pg. *04
Nancy M.	14	Mar	1850	William D.		off. E. NICHOLSON
BEATTY		and		COLEMAN		VA. bk. 01 pg. 005
Sarah A.	02	Oct	1856	David O.		off. J. CARVER
BEATY		and		ROGERS		VA. bk. 1A pg. 005
Catherine	01	Nov	1798	Hugh		off. J. HUGHES
BEATY		and		TENCK		VA. bk. 2A pg. 067
Lucinda	03	Mar	1839	William		off. A. YOUNG
BECK		and		BROWNING		VA. bk. 2A pg. 080
Caroline	15	Feb	1825	Lemuel		off. S. LAUCK
BECK		and		CROUCH		VA. bk. 1A pg. 030
James	05	Feb	1807	Cornelia		off. W. WILLSON
BECK		and		GILES		VA. bk. 2A pg. 017
Lenore	22	Jun	1820	Samuel		off. S. LAUCK
BECK		and		MILLER		VA. bk. 2A pg. 007
Sarah	31	Oct	1816	Joseph		off. S. LAUCK
BECKWITH		and		WELLS		WV. bk. 4A pg. 060
Oscar J.	15	Mar	1869	Josephine		off. W. WHITE
BEDILLION		and		CONANT		VA. bk. 3A pg. 050
Joseph	13	Feb	1858	Abigail		off. J. NAYLOR
BEDWELL		and		DARLING		VA. bk. 2A pg. 080
Jane	05	Jun	1838	Joseph		off. S. LAUCK

10 BROOKE CO., VA./WV. LICENSES & MARRIAGES, 1797-1874

BEDWELL		and		BONER	VA. bk. 1A pg. 078	
Samuel	15	Dec	1814	Elizabeth	off. W. WILLSON	
BEERBOWER		and		NOBLE	WV. bk. 4A pg. 104	
Elizabeth	09	Jan	1872	Westley	off. W. LATIMER	
BEHIN		and		MC GEE	VA. bk. 01 pg. 003	
Margaret	19	Feb	1855	Felix	off. J. BRAZILL	
BEITER		and		LETZKUS	WV. bk. 3A pg. 151	
Mary Ann	20	Jan	1865	Ambrose	off. H. SHEPHERD	
BELL		and		RAMSAY	VA. bk. 2A pg. *03	
Adeline	24	Oct	1849	Basil	off. J. IRWIN	
BELL		and		STEWART	VA. bk. 2A pg. 063	
John	05	Dec	1832	Mary	off. G. SCOTT	
BELL		and		CASH	VA. bk. 1A pg. 081	
Mary Ann	02	Apr	1812	William	off. UNKNOWN	
BELL		and		HAMMOND	VA. bk. 1A pg. 047	
Miss.	--	--	1803	Henry	off. J. DODDRIDGE	
BELL		and		HAMMOND	VA. bk. 1A pg. 047	
Mr.	--	--	1809	Suky	off. J. DODDRIDGE	
BELL		and		LEWIS	VA. bk. 3A pg. 060	
Sarah Adaline	16	Dec	1858	Hezekiah	off. J. NAYLOR	
BELL		and		WILSON	VA. bk. 1A pg. 012	
William	27	Jun	1803	Jean	off. E. MACURDY	
BENCE		and		MC KIM	VA. bk. 3A pg. 095	
Casper	05	Oct	1860	Mary J.	off. J. NAYLOR	
BENCE		and		FOSTER	VA. bk. 3A pg. 082	
Cidonia	27	Mar	1860	James Jacob	off. J. NAYLOR	
BENTZ		and		KLINE	WV. bk. 4A pg. 106	
Barbara .	27	Apr	1872	Charles	off. W. LATIMER	
BENTZ		and		EASTERDAY	VA. bk. 3A pg. 119	
Josephine	10	Nov	1862	Martin	off. J. NAYLOR	
BERNARD		and		APPLEGATE	VA. bk. 2A pg. 082	
Dennis S.	12	Sep	1839	Eleanor	off. R. WHITE	
BERRY		and		WELLS	VA. bk. 2A pg. *15	
Thomas V.	18	Oct	1853	Michael	off. A. MYERS	
BERTRAM		and		STIETZE	VA. bk. 01 pg. 004	
Henry	08	Sep	1856	Wellhemine	off. E. QUILLEN	
BICKERSTAFF		and		ARBAUGH	VA. bk. 2A pg. *16	
Enos	22	Jan	1854	Abigail	off. S. DUNLAP	
BICKERSTAFF		and		COX	WV. bk. 4A pg. 098	
Isaac C.	25	Oct	1871	Julia C.	off. W. LATIMER	
BICKERSTAFF		and		REEVES	WV. bk. 4A pg. 098	
Isaac C.	25	Oct	1871	Julia C.	off. W. LATIMER	
BICKERSTAFF		and		BUCHANAN	VA. bk. 2A pg. *08	
John	14	Aug	1851	Sarah Jane	off. C. JACKSON	
BICKERSTAFF		and		MILLER	WV. bk. 4A pg. 017	
Nancy	18	Dec	1866	Samuel	off. R. NICHOLLS	
BIER		and		SUTER	WV. bk. 3A pg. 146	
Henry A.	02	Nov	1864	Clarinda	off. H. SHEPHERD	
BLACK		and		MATTHEWS	VA. bk. 3A pg. 001	
Catherine	--	--	1852	Oscar L.	off. J. NAYLOR	
BLACK		and		ROGERS	VA. bk. 2A pg. 048	
Elizabeth	22	May	1828	Hugh	off. A. CAMPBELL	

BROOKE CO., VA./WV. LICENSES & MARRIAGES, 1797-1874   11

Name				Spouse	Reference
BLACK		and		JOHNSON	VA. bk. 2A pg. 060
James	18	Sep	1828	Mary	off. S. REED
BLACKBURN		and		BANE	VA. bk. 1A pg. 064
Samuel	04	Nov	1815	Jane	off. G. SCOTT
BLACKMORE		and		BANE	VA. bk. 1A pg. 064
Samuel	04	Nov	1815	Jane	off. G. SCOTT
BLAIR		and		MC KEEHAN	VA. bk. 1A pg. 008
Elizabeth	14	Apr	1803	Samuel	off. J. HUGHES
BLAIR		and		BAILEY	VA. bk. 01 pg. 003
Evaline	26	Oct	1854	William T.	off. C. HOLMES
BLAIR		and		KERR	VA. bk. 2A pg. 018
Mary	19	Aug	1817	Alexander	off. S. LAUCK
BLAIR		and		HERFORD	VA. bk. 2A pg. 063
Robert	05	Apr	1833	Ann	off. G. ROBINSON
BLANKENSOP		and		MERRYMAN	VA. bk. 3A pg. 085
George	16	Jun	1860	Angeline	off. J. NAYLOR
BLANKENSOP		and		HESSEY	WV. bk. 4A pg. 084
George	01	Mar	1871	Kate	off. W. WHITE
BLANKENSOP		and		CAMPBELL	WV. bk. 4A pg. 105
James	17	Jan	1872	Anna	off. W. LATIMER
BLANKENSOP		and		GOUDY	WV. bk. 4A pg. 033
John	24	Oct	1867	Mary R.	off. C. MELVIN
BLANKENSOP		and		MARKLY	VA. bk. 2A pg. 058
Peter	21	Jan	1830	Susanna	off. D. MERRYMAN
BLANKENSOP		and		HEDGES	VA. bk. 2A pg. 064
Rosett	04	Mar	1838	Thomas	off. A. YOUNG
BLANKENSOP		and		MILLER	WV. bk. 4A pg. 122
Sallie	10	Feb	1873	Frank	off. W. LATIMER
BLAYNEY		and		ATKINSON	VA. bk. 3A pg. 061
James F.	25	Dec	1858	Margaret	off. J. NAYLOR
BLAYNEY		and		BARNES	VA. bk. 01 pg. 003
Sarah	--	--	1855	Walter D.	off. A. ENDSLEY
BLOTTAN		and		PICKLEMAN	WV. bk. 4A pg. 086
John A.	10	Apr	1871	Julia A.	off. W. WHITE
BOLES		and		WRIGHT	WV. bk. 4A pg. 094
S.P.	17	Aug	1871	Amelia	off. W. WHITE
BONAR		and		HEDGES	VA. bk. 2A pg. 075
George	12	Jan	1843	Nancy	off. C. WEIRICK
BONAR		and		CLENDENEN	WV. bk. 3A pg. 148
Mary Jane	24	Nov	1864	Edward W.	off. H. SHEPHERD
BONAR		and		SMITH	WV. bk. 3A pg. 158
Sallie/Sarah	02	Sep	1865	James Pursel	off. H. SHEPHERD
BOND		and		HAVELIN	VA. bk. 2A pg. 093
Elizabeth	20	Apr	1848	John	off. J. MONROE
BOND		and		BUCKALEW	VA. bk. 2A pg. *15
Mary A.	08	Sep	1853	Garrett	off. G. LOWMAN
BOND		and		MC CORMACK	VA. bk. 1A pg. 029
Richard	07	Dec	1807	Catherine	off. J. PRITCHARD
BONE		and		WELLS	WV. bk. 4A pg. 016
Russell	19	Nov	1866	Emma B.	off. R. NICHOLLS
BONER		and		BEDWELL	VA. bk. 1A pg. 078
Elizabeth	15	Dec	1814	Samuel	off. W. WILLSON

12 BROOKE CO., VA./WV. LICENSES & MARRIAGES, 1797-1874

BONER Jane	and 04 Jul 1815	KEACH James	VA. bk. 1A pg. 070 off. UNKNOWN
BONER Rebecca	and 05 Apr 1814	BEARD Andrew	VA. bk. 1A pg. 078 off. W. WILLSON
BONER William	and 29 Dec 1814	GORRELL Sarah	VA. bk. 1A pg. 078 off. W. WILLSON
BONSALL Mary Jane	and 01 Nov 1853	KISSINGER John A.	VA. bk. 3A pg. 029 off. J. NAYLOR
BONSALL Thomas	and 04 Jul 1839	GRAFTON Christiana	VA. bk. 2A pg. 066 off. W. SCULL
BOON Nelly	and 02 Jul 1805	PUMPHREY John	VA. bk. 1A pg. 021 off. W. WILLSON
BORING Elizabeth	and 28 Oct 1821	KAY John	VA. bk. 2A pg. 019 off. J. PRITCHARD
BORING Elizabeth	and 17 Sep 1851	RUSSELL Oliver G.	VA. bk. 2A pg. *09 off. C. JACKSON
BORING George W.	and 01 May 1858	STARKEY Mary	VA. bk. 3A pg. 052 off. J. NAYLOR
BOSLEY James	and 14 Feb 1859	CAIRNES Ruth E.	VA. bk. 3A pg. 064 off. J. NAYLOR
BOSLEY Samuel	and 26 Apr 1855	WILLIAMSON Mary	VA. bk. 01 pg. 003 off. E. QUILLEN
BOSMAN Happuck	and 29 Dec 1827	WHEELER Ignatius	VA. bk. 2A pg. 059 off. E. SMITH
BOSMAN Sarah	and 31 Oct 1811	MAGERS Elias	VA. bk. 1A pg. 057 off. J. PRITCHARD
BOSMAN William	and 04 Sep 1828	WHEELER Elisabeth	VA. bk. 2A pg. 059 off. E. SMITH
BOTHWELL John H.	and 02 Oct 1858	SNEDIKER Elvira Virg.	VA. bk. 3A pg. 056 off. J. NAYLOR
BOUGHER John M.	and 11 Apr 1833	MARKS Amanda	VA. bk. 2A pg. 063 off. G. SCOTT
BOUNDS John	and 04 Jul 1799	DUNLAP Rebekah	VA. bk. 1A pg. 009 off. UNKNOWN
BOWERS Adam	and 30 Oct 1856	ORAM Nancy	VA. bk. 01 pg. 005 off. E. QUILLEN
BOWLES John W.	and 16 Dec 1868	MURCHLAND Elizabeth	WV. bk. 4A pg. 054 off. S. QUEST
BOWMAN Caroline	and 09 Nov 1857	WHARTON Gipson	VA. bk. 3A pg. 044 off. J. NAYLOR
BOWMAN Cecelia M.L.S.	and 05 Nov 1861	MILLER David B.	VA. bk. 3A pg. 108 off. S. NAYLOR
BOWMAN Dora	and 05 Mar 1874	ROBINSON Gilbert E.	WV. bk. 4A pg. 137 off. J. LATIMER
BOWMAN Henrietta M.	and 13 Jun 1850	DOBBS George W.	VA. bk. 2A pg. *04 off. J. IRWIN
BOWMAN Jacob	and 08 Aug 1827	HOOD Sarah	VA. bk. 2A pg. 048 off. S. BROCKUNIER
BOWMAN Jane	and 14 Nov 1872	BUCY Darwin E.R.	WV. bk. 4A pg. 119 off. W. LATIMER
BOWMAN John	and 28 Dec 1854	CARSON Mary	VA. bk. 01 pg. 003 off. F. GUTHRIE

BROOKE CO., VA./WV. LICENSES & MARRIAGES, 1797-1874   13

Name				Spouse	Reference
BOWMAN John (Jr.)		03 Aug	1861	FRANK Amanda E.	VA. bk. 3A pg. 105 off. S. NAYLOR
BOWMAN Marietta		15 May	1851	RICE Edward W.	VA. bk. 2A pg. *08 off. J. MC GAN
BOWMAN Sarah		27 Sep	1869	WHITE James	WV. bk. 4A pg. 064 off. W. WHITE
BOWMAN Sarah		23 Feb	1870	GREEN Thomas Hood	WV. bk. 4A pg. 069 off. W. WHITE
BOWMAN Sarah E.		04 Oct	1855	THOMPSON Joseph	VA. bk. 01 pg. 003 off. J. MEANS
BOWMAN Susan		11 Feb	1846	PERRY Oliver	VA. bk. 2A pg. 086 off. W. LEMON
BOYCE Robert		28 Nov	1819	WILHELM Christiana	VA. bk. 2A pg. 015 off. G. SCOTT
BOYCE Timothy		06 Feb	1812	HAMBLETON Mary	VA. bk. 1A pg. 062 off. J. PRITCHARD
BOYD Mathew		06 May	1828	FARQUER Elisabeth	VA. bk. 2A pg. 059 off. E. SMITH
BOYD Robert		15 Aug	1850	MURCHLAND Nancy	VA. bk. 2A pg. *05 off. J. STOCKTON
BOYD Robert		25 Mar	1867	WILLIAMSON E.A.	WV. bk. 4A pg. 025 off. H. MELVIN
BRACKEN Caleb H.		03 May	1869	EVERETT Maggie V.	WV. bk. 4A pg. 061 off. W. WHITE
BRADLEY Thomas		07 Mar	1857	CHAMBERLAIN Sarah	VA. bk. 01 pg. 005 off. E. QUILLEN
BRADY Anne		14 Oct	1862	SMITH Robert N.	VA. bk. 3A pg. 119 off. J. NAYLOR
BRADY Bernard		26 Oct	1850	CULBERTSON Elizabeth	VA. bk. 2A pg. *06 off. R. WHITE
BRADY Hannah J.		25 Nov	1872	WILSON John	WV. bk. 4A pg. 119 off. W. LATIMER
BRADY John		15 Jul	1841	BAXTER Ruth	VA. bk. 2A pg. 078 off. J. HARRISON
BRADY John D.		07 Nov	1871	MC CLEARY Sallie	WV. bk. 4A pg. 098 off. W. LATIMER
BRADY Mary A.		06 Apr	1853	POWER Joseph C.	VA. bk. 3A pg. 017 off. J. NAYLOR
BRADY Permelia		03 Oct	1844	RAY Joseph	VA. bk. 2A pg. 085 off. S. WORTHINGTON
BRAFFORD Noah		12 Sep	1838	SLY Lucinda	VA. bk. 2A pg. 065 off. A. YOUNG
BRANDON John		26 Feb	1824	BAKER Elizabeth	VA. bk. 2A pg. 030 off. G. BUCHANAN
BRANDON John		14 Oct	1843	BAXTER Ruth	VA. bk. 2A pg. 077 off. S. GRAFTON
BRANDON Marg't Cecelia		09 Dec	1863	OWEN George	WV. bk. 3A pg. 134 off. H. SHEPHERD
BRANNON Margaret		20 Oct	1829	ROBERTS Samuel	VA. bk. 2A pg. 056 off. G. BUCHANAN
BRANNON Maria		01 Jun	1819	COLLINS Joseph S.	VA. bk. 2A pg. 008 off. G. BUCHANAN

Name		Day	Month	Year	Spouse	Reference
BRANNON	and				GUNION	VA. bk. 3A pg. 094
Rebecca		20	Sep	1860	Wilson	off. J. NAYLOR
BRASHEARS	and				ROBINETT	WV. bk. 4A pg. 078
Calvin B.		28	Sep	1870	Catharine M.	off. W. WHITE
BRASHEARS	and				KENEDY	VA. bk. 2A pg. 067
Mary		14	Nov	1838	Garlan B.	off. A. YOUNG
BRASHEARS	and				NANGLE	WV. bk. 3A pg. 136
Mary		02	Jan	1864	Samuel G.	off. H. SHEPHERD
BRENNEMAN	and				MAHON	OH. bk. 2A pg. 065
Barbara		07	Dec	1837	John L.	off. G. HOLMES
BRENNEMAN	and				BROWN	VA. bk. 2A pg. 065
Jacob		29	Mar	1838	Margaret	off. J. BEATTY
BRENNEMAN	and				HEWIT	VA. bk. 2A pg. 044
Nancy		04	Jan	1827	Thomas	off. J. BROWNING, JR.
BRIAN	and				FRAZIER	WV. bk. 3A pg. 148
Elizabeth		07	Dec	1864	John Wesley	off. H. SHEPHERD
BRICE	and				LOGAN	VA. bk. 2A pg. 063
Margaret		25	Apr	1833	William	off. R. BROWN
BRICELAND	and				EDGINGTON	VA. bk. 1A pg. 060
James		20	May	1810	Rachel	off. E. MACURDY
BRICELAND	and				COX	VA. bk. 2A pg. *02
John M.		16	May	1849	Nancy B.	off. I. DALLAS
BRICELAND	and				CREAL	VA. bk. 2A pg. 054
Josiah		04	Dec	1827	Margaret	off. L. BROWNING
BRICK	and				RAMSEY	VA. bk. 3A pg. 002
Robinson		11	Mar	1852	Jane E.	off. J. NAYLOR
BRIDGET	and				CULLIN	VA. bk. 2A pg. 082
Emily		16	Aug	1838	Matthew	off. R. WHITE
BRIERLY	and				HOWLET	VA. bk. 1A pg. 026
Thomas		04	Mar	1807	Elizabeth	off. UNKNOWN
BRIGGS	and				MORLEY	WV. bk. 4A pg. 117
Alice U.		16	Sep	1872	Evander	off. W. LATIMER
BRIGGS	and				COULBURN	VA. bk. 3A pg. 087
Caroline A.		31	Jul	1860	Thomas L.	off. J. NAYLOR
BRIGGS	and				HANEY	WV. bk. 4A pg. 027
Clara E.		19	Jun	1867	Henry	off. H. MELVIN
BRIGGS	and				BARTHOLOMEW	VA. bk. 3A pg. 088
Elvyn Jane		08	Aug	1860	George K.	off. J. NAYLOR
BRINDLEY	and				HELMS	VA. bk. 01 pg. 003
Zachariah		--	Nov	1854	Luisa	off. E. QUILLEN
BROTHERS	and				MC CONNELL	VA. bk. 2A pg. 058
Susanna		25	Feb	1829	William	off. T. BEEKS
BROWN	and				HYATT	VA. bk. 1A pg. 016
Benjamin		16	Aug	1804	Margaret	off. W. WILLSON
BROWN	and				LINDSAY	VA. bk. 2A pg. *12
C.T.		03	Jun	1852	Elizabeth	off. W. SUMMERS
BROWN	and				CONCKLIN	VA. bk. 2A pg. 068
Christiana		05	Dec	1839	Daniel T.	off. J. GALLOWAY
BROWN	and				CRAWFORD	VA. bk. 1A pg. 025
Elisabeth		10	Feb	1807	Archibald	off. E. MACURDY
BROWN	and				WYLIE	VA. bk. 2A pg. 020
Elizabeth		26	Mar	1821	Robert	off. E. MACURDY

BROOKE CO., VA./WV. LICENSES & MARRIAGES, 1797-1874   15

Surname	Given	Day	Month	Year	Spouse Surname	Spouse Given	Reference
BROWN	Elizabeth	19	Jun	1823	ATEN	Jacob	VA. bk. 2A pg. 029
BROWN	Elizabeth	16	Aug	1827	POLSLY	Daniel	VA. bk. 2A pg. 047
BROWN	Elizabeth	09	Sep	1833	WILLIAMS	John	off. L. BROWNING
BROWN	Elizabeth				BURT		VA. bk. 2A pg. 063
BROWN	Elizabeth P.	10	Apr	1856	Samuel Wm.		off. R. BROWN
BROWN	George W.	16	May	1871	MORTON	Amanda J.	VA. bk. 01 pg. 004
BROWN	Jacob	19	May	1871	YOUNG	Caroline	off. E. QUILLEN
BROWN	James	19	Nov	1829	WILHELM	Hannah	WV. bk. 4A pg. 089
BROWN	James	05	Jun	1802	HUTSON	Sarah	off. W. WHITE
BROWN	James B.	03	Mar	1853	ANDERSON	Mary	WV. bk. 4A pg. 090
BROWN	John	30	Mar	1848	MARKS	Elizabeth	off. W. WHITE
BROWN	John	12	Sep	1797	GLASS	Ann	VA. bk. 2A pg. 056
BROWN	John	--	--	1802	GRANT	Eleanor	off. L. BROWNING
BROWN	John L.	18	Feb	1868	BAXTER	Ellen V.	VA. bk. 1A pg. 008
BROWN	Joseph	23	Dec	1819	HOOD	Rachel	off. J. HUGHES
BROWN	Leondas	11	Nov	1861	DAUMONT	Clara A.	VA. bk. 2A pg. *13
BROWN	Leondas	11	Nov	1861	GIST	Clara A.	off. A. MYERS
BROWN	Margaret	29	Mar	1838	BRENNEMAN	Jacob	VA. bk. 2A pg. 092
BROWN	Margaret	21	Mar	1811	CAMPBELL	Alexander	off. T. NEWELL
BROWN	Mary Ann	09	Sep	1852	COUNSELMAN	David F.	VA. bk. 1A pg. 004
BROWN	Nabby	18	Jun	1797	WITHERS	Robert	off. J. HUGHES
BROWN	Nancy	02	Jan	1799	ACKINSON	James	VA. bk. 1A pg. 045
BROWN	Robert	10	Apr	1817	LEADLIE	Sarah	off. UNKNOWN
BROWN	S. Turner	06	Nov	1858	LLEWELLYN	Jane L.	WV. bk. 4A pg. 042
BROWN	Sally	15	Nov	1797	COLWELL	Robert	off. H. MELVIN
BROWN	Samuel	01	Feb	1803	DOTTY	Betsy	VA. bk. 2A pg. 017
BROWN	Stephen	31	Aug	1802	BADEN	Mary	off. S. LAUCK
							VA. bk. 3A pg. 107
							off. S. NAYLOR
							VA. bk. 3A pg. 107
							off. S. NAYLOR
							VA. bk. 2A pg. 065
							off. J. BEATTY
							VA. bk. 1A pg. 072
							off. J. PRITCHARD
							VA. bk. 2A pg. *12
							off. H. SNYDER
							VA. bk. 1A pg. 001
							off. J. DODDRIDGE
							VA. bk. 1A pg. 005
							off. UNKNOWN
							VA. bk. 2A pg. 004
							off. G. BUCHANAN
							VA. bk. 3A pg. 057
							off. J. NAYLOR
							VA. bk. 1A pg. 002
							off. J. DODDRIDGE
							VA. bk. 1A pg. 011
							off. E. MACURDY
							VA. bk. 1A pg. 039
							off. J. DODDRIDGE

Name		Date		Spouse	Reference
BROWN	and			ORR	VA. bk. 3A pg. 015
William	14	Mar	1853	Margaret	off. J. NAYLOR
BROWNING	and			HOGG	VA. bk. 2A pg. *12
Clinton	16	Jun	1852	Hannah	off. W. SUMMERS
BROWNING	and			HARRIS	VA. bk. 3A pg. 066
Jasper	24	Mar	1859	Sarah J.	off. J. NAYLOR
BROWNING	and			BROWNING	VA. bk. 2A pg. 021
John F.	11	Oct	1821	Mary (...)	off. L. BROWNING
BROWNING	and			BECK	VA. bk. 2A pg. 080
Lemuel	15	Feb	1825	Caroline	off. S. LAUCK
BROWNING	and			JENNINGS	WV. bk. 4A pg. 127
Margaret A.	04	Sep	1873	John	off. W. LATIMER
BROWNING	and			MAHON	VA. bk. 3A pg. 042
Margaret C.	01	Oct	1857	William B.	off. J. NAYLOR
BROWNING	and			BROWNING	VA. bk. 2A pg. 021
Mary (...)	11	Oct	1821	John F.	off. L. BROWNING
BROWNLEE	and			WEST	WV. bk. 4A pg. 118
Elizabeth	21	Sep	1872	Elisha	off. W. LATIMER
BROWNLEE	and			CORBIN	VA. bk. 2A pg. 013
James	08	Apr	1819	Ann	off. L. BROWNING
BROWNLEE	and			ROSS	VA. bk. 2A pg. *14
James	15	May	1853	Susan	off. S. NESBITT
BROWNLEE	and			KEITH	WV. bk. 4A pg. 101
James	04	Dec	1871	Sallie	off. W. LATIMER
BROWNLEE	and			HAMILTON	VA. bk. 2A pg. *06
Joseph	28	Aug	1850	Sophia	off. R. WHITE
BROWNLEE	and			DOWDLE	WV. bk. 4A pg. 102
Martin V.	16	Dec	1871	Daisy	off. W. LATIMER
BROWNLEE	and			TOWN	VA. bk. 2A pg. *02
Mary J.	07	Mar	1849	Eli C.	off. I. DALLAS
BROWNLEE	and			MAXWELL	VA. bk. 2A pg. 060
Nancy	01	Jan	1829	Henry	off. E. SMITH
BROWNLEE	and			PALMER	VA. bk. 01 pg. 002
Nancy	05	Oct	1854	Francis	off. S. NESBITT
BROWNLEE	and			SMOTE	VA. bk. 01 pg. 002
William E.	26	Feb	1854	Elizabeth Jane	off. S. NESBITT
BROWNLEE	and			SWINER	VA. bk. 01 pg. 003
William J.	27	Dec	1854	Mary Ann	off. S. NESBITT
BRYCOFF	and			SNEDIKER	VA. bk. 1A pg. 018
Arthur	21	Feb	1805	Anne	off. W. WILLSON
BUCHANAN	and			COX	VA. bk. 1A pg. 083
Elisabeth	25	Mar	1813	Joseph	off. UNKNOWN
BUCHANAN	and			HEADINGTON	VA. bk. 3A pg. 063
Rebecca	03	Feb	1859	Nicholas	off. J. NAYLOR
BUCHANAN	and			LEWIS	WV. bk. 4A pg. 065
Richard W.	29	Nov	1869	Micha	off. W. WHITE
BUCHANAN	and			CHENEY	VA. bk. 2A pg. 047
Robert	22	Feb	1827	Julia	off. C. MURRAY
BUCHANAN	and			BICKERSTAFF	VA. bk. 2A pg. *08
Sarah Jane	14	Aug	1851	John	off. C. JACKSON
BUCHANAN	and			WELLS	VA. bk. 2A pg. *12
Sarah Jane	18	Sep	1852	William C.	off. H. SNYDER

BROOKE CO., VA./WV. LICENSES & MARRIAGES, 1797-1874

Name		Date		Spouse	Reference
BUCHANAN Thomas	and 05	Oct	1848	HAMMOND Sarah	VA. bk. 2A pg. 094 off. T. NEWELL
BUCKALEW Ann Elizabeth	and 30	Oct	1856	ROBERTS Marcellus	VA. bk. 01 pg. 005 off. W. GAMBLE, JR.
BUCKALEW Garrett	and 08	Sep	1853	BOND Mary A.	VA. bk. 2A pg. *15 off. G. LOWMAN
BUCKALEW Josephine	and 31	May	1862	MURCHLAND David H.	VA. bk. 3A pg. 116 off. J. NAYLOR
BUCKALEW Lydia Jane	and 20	Mar	1869	ADAMS Eli	WV. bk. 4A pg. 060 off. W. WHITE
BUCKEY George	and 08	Jan	1829	WHEELER Henrietta	VA. bk. 2A pg. 060 off. E. SMITH
BUCKEY John	and 14	Jan	1869	FISHER Mary	WV. bk. 4A pg. 057 off. W. WHITE
BUCKEY Kate C.	and 03	Jan	1860	JESTER David E.	VA. bk. 3A pg. 081 off. J. NAYLOR
BUCKEY Mary L.	and 18	Jan	1869	GEORGE James	WV. bk. 4A pg. 057 off. W. WHITE
BUCKEY Sarah E.	and 05	Sep	1868	MC CREARY George W.	WV. bk. 01 pg. 019 off. W. BROWN
BUCKINGHAM Absalom	and 11	Sep	1826	CONKEL Margaret	VA. bk. 2A pg. 037 off. N. HEADINGTON
BUCKINGHAM Mary	and 31	May	1810	BAXTER William	VA. bk. 1A pg. 053 off. J. PRITCHARD
BUCY Darwin E.R.	and 14	Nov	1872	BOWMAN Jane	WV. bk. 4A pg. 119 off. W. LATIMER
BUKER Mary	and 24	Oct	1863	HILL Salathiel	WV. bk. 3A pg. 132 off. H. SHEPHERD
BUKEY Robert	and 18	Sep	1851	VIERS Rebecca Ann	VA. bk. 2A pg. *10 off. W. SUMMERS
BULLOCK Ann	and 02	Jun	1856	KUHN John	VA. bk. 01 pg. 004 off. A. ENDSLEY
BUNN Benjamin	and 16	Aug	1804	HYATE Marjerit	VA. bk. 1A pg. 016 off. W. WILLSON
BUNN Elizabeth	and 05	Sep	1802	ORAM Thomas	VA. bk. 1A pg. 039 off. J. DODDRIDGE
BUNTING Samuel	and 21	Mar	1838	GORRELL Mary	VA. bk. 2A pg. 082 off. R. WHITE
BURGESS John	and 23	Apr	1851	RUTHERFORD Marian	VA. bk. 2A pg. *08 off. R. WHITE
BURGESS John S.	and 10	Dec	1862	TAYLOR Anne	VA. bk. 3A pg. 120 off. J. NAYLOR
BURGOIN Joshua	and 04	Jun	1840	MAHAN Sarah	VA. bk. 2A pg. 069 off. S. BABCOCK
BURGOYNE Rebecca J.	and 09	Nov	1870	HELMICK Andrew S.	PA. bk. 4A pg. 080 off. W. WHITE
BURK Surrilla (Mrs.)	and 13	Nov	1856	KEMP Adam	VA. bk. 01 pg. 005 off. E. CHRISTIAN
BURK William	and 30	Mar	1816	DRAKE Rebecca	VA. bk. 2A pg. 009 off. J. DODDRIDGE
BURKE Ann	and 28	Apr	1825	SALMON Cutler	VA. bk. 2A pg. 033 off. G. BUCHANAN

BURKE		and		KLINE	VA. bk. 2A pg. 036
Sarah	26	Jan	1826	Joseph	off. G. BUCHANAN
BURNS		and		GIST	WV. bk. 4A pg. 063
Callie	08	Sep	1869	William H.	off. W. WHITE
BURNS		and		PORTER	VA. bk. 1A pg. 031
Catherine	17	Mar	1807	Thomas	off. W. WILLSON
BURNS		and		WELCH	VA. bk. 1A pg. 009
John	08	Apr	1800	Rebekah	off. UNKNOWN
BURNS		and		CRALY	VA. bk. 3A pg. 074
Rosanna	14	Sep	1859	James	off. J. NAYLOR
BURRIS		and		DAVIDSON	VA. bk. 2A pg. 079
Elizabeth	11	Jan	1844	David	off. S. WORTHINGTON
BURSLEY		and		SMITH	VA. bk. 3A pg. 105
Gilbert E.	03	Sep	1861	Kate P.	off. S. NAYLOR
BURSON		and		CHANEY	VA. bk. 2A pg. 058
Ann	--	--	1830	Henry	off. N. HEADINGTON
BURSON		and		CHANEY	VA. bk. 2A pg. 053
Tamar	--	--	1826	William	off. N. HEADINGTON
BURT		and		EVERET	VA. bk. 1A pg. 030
Elisabeth	20	Oct	1807	James	off. J. HUGHES
BURT		and		DANNER	VA. bk. 3A pg. 106
Mary Jane	20	Sep	1861	Berhart	off. S. NAYLOR
BURT		and		BROWN	VA. bk. 01 pg. 004
Samuel Wm.	10	Apr	1856	Elizabeth P.	off. E. QUILLEN
BURT		and		AMSPOKER	VA. bk. 1A pg. 030
William	04	Dec	1806	Martha	off. J. HUGHES
BURTON		and		PEARCE	VA. bk. 2A pg. *08
John	06	Feb	1851	Matilda	off. R. WHITE
BUTLER		and		BAXTER	VA. bk. 1A pg. 027
Henry	09	Sep	1807	Charity	off. UNKNOWN
BUTLER		and		OWEN	VA. bk. 1A pg. 022
Nicholas	20	Nov	1806	Phebe	off. J. PRITCHARD
BUXTON		and		NOAH	VA. bk. 3A pg. 111
James	03	Dec	1862	Marg't Ellenor	off. S. NAYLOR
CAIN		and		GORDON	WV. bk. 3A pg. 159
Catherine	05	Sep	1865	Anthony	off. H. SHEPHERD
CAIN		and		ORAM	VA. bk. 1A pg. 040
Nancy	06	May	1802	Smallwood	off. J. DODDRIDGE
CAIRNES		and		CARTER	VA. bk. 3A pg. 098
Margaret E.	08	Jan	1861	Joseph J.	off. J. NAYLOR
CAIRNES		and		BOSLEY	VA. bk. 3A pg. 064
Ruth E.	14	Feb	1859	James	off. J. NAYLOR
CALDERWOOD		and		FRAZIER	WV. bk. 4A pg. 111
D.W. (Rev.)	04	Apr	1872	Laura A.	off. W. LATIMER
CALDWELL		and		ALEXANDER	VA. bk. 4A pg. 041
Fanny	25	Apr	1826	James	off. W. WYLIE
CALDWELL		and		FRESHWATER	WV. bk. 4A pg. 021
Martha	25	Jan	1867	John	off. H. MELVIN
CALDWELL		and		COWLE	VA. bk. 2A pg. 008
Mary	30	Mar	1819	Alpheus	off. G. SCOTT
CALDWELL		and		ATKINSON	WV. bk. 4A pg. 066
Robert	26	Jan	1870	Flora A.	off. W. WHITE

BROOKE CO., VA./WV. LICENSES & MARRIAGES, 1797-1874   19

Name					Spouse	Reference
CALENDINE			and		MILLER	VA. bk. 2A pg. 060
Catharine	17	Mar	1829		John	off. E. SMITH
CALENDINE			and		WARTENBY	VA. bk. 1A pg. 028
Catherine	29	Sep	1807		Francis	off. UNKNOWN
CALENDINE			and		DOUBLAZIER	VA. bk. 01 pg. 002
Edward	02	Nov	1854		Susan Eliza.	off. W. DAVIDSON
CALENDINE			and		ALLEN	WV. bk. 4A pg. 069
George	19	Feb	1870		Elizabeth	off. W. WHITE
CALGORE			and		LYONS	VA. bk. 1A pg. 012
Nancy	12	May	1803		Mathew	off. E. MACURDY
CALLENDINE			and		FOWLER	VA. bk. 1A pg. 040
Elizabeth	29	Apr	1802		William	off. J. DODDRIDGE
CAMBLE			and		JAMISON	VA. bk. 1A pg. 022
Alexander	08	May	1806		Easter	off. UNKNOWN
CAMERON			and		SCOTT	VA. bk. 2A pg. 021
James	16	Jan	1822		Jane	off. G. SCOTT
CAMERON			and		BEAL	VA. bk. 2A pg. 057
Jane	15	Apr	1830		Philip	off. G. BUCHANAN
CAMERON			and		DAWSON	VA. bk. 2A pg. 055
Jane	22	Mar	1831		Thomas	off. G. SCOTT
CAMERON			and		SWEARINGEN	VA. bk. 2A pg. 036
John	05	Jan	1826		Rebecca	off. G. BUCHANAN
CAMERON			and		MONTGOMERY	VA. bk. 2A pg. 062
Lucinda	29	Nov	1832		Robert	off. G. BUCHANAN
CAMERON			and		DUNGAN	VA. bk. 1A pg. 061
Margret	02	Apr	1811		Levi	off. E. MACURDY
CAMERON			and		CUMMINS	VA. bk. 2A pg. 084
Matilda	28	Apr	1842		James	off. R. WHITE
CAMERON?			and		QUINN	VA. bk. 2A pg. 004
Peggy	27	Mar	1817		William	off. G. SCOTT
CAMP			and		DOUBLAZIER	VA. bk. 2A pg. 071
Chester	14	Feb	1841		Nancy	off. T. STEIRSHCOMB
CAMPBELL			and		BAKEWELL	VA. bk. 2A pg. 059
Alexander	31	Jul	1828		Selina	off. E. SMITH
CAMPBELL			and		BROWN	VA. bk. 1A pg. 072
Alexander	21	Mar	1811		Margaret	off. J. PRITCHARD
CAMPBELL			and		BLANKENSOP	WV. bk. 4A pg. 105
Anna	17	Jan	1872		James	off. W. LATIMER
CAMPBELL			and		MURRAY	WV. bk. 01 pg. 020
Anna B.	08	Jul	1870		James A.	off. A. CAMPBELL
CAMPBELL			and		HENDRICKS	WV. bk. 4A pg. 118
Barclay	30	Oct	1872		Mary E.	off. W. LATIMER
CAMPBELL			and		MC CLURE	VA. bk. 2A pg. 032
Catherine	30	Dec	1824		Robert	off. G. BUCHANAN
CAMPBELL			and		BARCLAY	VA. bk. 3A pg. 127
Decima H.	04	Apr	1863		John J.	off. J. NAYLOR
CAMPBELL			and		STEWART	VA. bk. 2A pg. 014
Elizabeth	26	Jun	1820		Joseph	off. G. SCOTT
CAMPBELL			and		TOLAND	VA. bk. 2A pg. 082
Elizabeth	13	Sep	1838		James	off. R. WHITE
CAMPBELL			and		SNEARY	WV. bk. 4A pg. 049
Elizabeth	11	Aug	1868		Stewart	off. S. QUEST

Surname/Name		Day	Month	Year	Spouse	Reference
CAMPBELL Ellen M.	and	17	Nov	1862	HOLTON Thomas F.	VA. bk. 3A pg. 121 off. J. NAYLOR
CAMPBELL George W.	and	27	Sep	1842	HINDMAN Eliza Jane	VA. bk. 2A pg. 077 off. J. SCOTT
CAMPBELL Greer McIlvaine	and	16	Mar	1864	MORTON Elizabeth	WV. bk. 3A pg. 139 off. H. SHEPHERD
CAMPBELL Isabella	and	16	Jan	1828	TARRISON Joseph	VA. bk. 2A pg. 059 off. J. CAZAD
CAMPBELL Isabella Jane E.	and	17	Sep	1839	HENDERSON Andrew	VA. bk. 2A pg. 067 off. J. GALLOWAY
CAMPBELL Jane	and	04	Feb	1865	STANSBERRY Daniel Bosley	WV. bk. 3A pg. 151 off. H. SHEPHERD
CAMPBELL Jane	and	29	Oct	1811	SMITH Job	VA. bk. 1A pg. 057 off. J. PRITCHARD
CAMPBELL Jane C.	and	26	Apr	1866	DAWSON William C.	WV. bk. 3A pg. 162 off. H. SHEPHERD
CAMPBELL John	and	24	Jan	1828	EVERETT Elisabeth	VA. bk. 2A pg. 052 off. G. BUCHANAN
CAMPBELL Mary	and	26	Oct	1815	BAKER Morris	VA. bk. 1A pg. 080 off. J. PRITCHARD
CAMPBELL Mary	and	09	Sep	1851	WYLIE James	VA. bk. 2A pg. *10 off. J. GALLOWAY
CAMPBELL Rebecca	and	21	Jun	1853	ATKINSON Alexander	VA. bk. 2A pg. *15 off. J. GALLOWAY
CAMPBELL Robert	and	19	Mar	1829	YOUNG Elenor	VA. bk. 2A pg. 060 off. S. REED
CAMPBELL Robert	and	06	May	1830	PURDAY Margaret	VA. bk. 2A pg. 057 off. G. BUCHANAN
CAMPBELL Susanna	and	03	Sep	1828	MC MILLEN Joseph	VA. bk. 2A pg. 060 off. S. REED
CAMPBELL Virginia A.	and	26	Oct	1863	THOMPSON William R.	WV. bk. 3A pg. 133 off. H. SHEPHERD
CAMPBELL William	and	26	Sep	1839	ADAMS Susan	VA. bk. 2A pg. 083 off. R. WHITE
CARDEHAM Bridget	and	21	Jan	1874	DUNN Hugh	WV. bk. 4A pg. 134 off. W. LATIMER
CARIENS Amanda	and	08	Mar	1865	ELSON John R.	WV. bk. 3A pg. 154 off. H. SHEPHERD
CARIENS Elizabeth	and	04	Jan	1849	PROSSER John A.	VA. bk. 2A pg. *03 off. J. GOODWIN
CARIENS Mary	and	04	Jan	1867	ALLISON John	WV. bk. 4A pg. 018 off. H. MELVIN
CARIENS Narcissa	and	23	Jan	1866	LATIMER John H.	WV. bk. 4A pg. 006 off. H. SHEPHERD
CARMICHAEL Catherine A.	and	12	Mar	1872	PLANTS David	WV. bk. 4A pg. 108 off. W. LATIMER
CARMICHAEL James W. M.	and	07	May	1861	FORBES Mary	VA. bk. 3A pg. 101 off. J. NAYLOR
CARMICHAEL Nancy E.	and	08	Aug	1866	FORBES Thomas	WV. bk. 3A pg. 167 off. R. NICHOLLS
CARR Joshua	and	09	Dec	1808	SRIMPLIN Mary	VA. bk. 1A pg. 037 off. J. DODDRIDGE

BROOKE CO., VA./WV. LICENSES & MARRIAGES, 1797-1874

Surname	Given	Day	Mo	Year	Spouse Surname	Spouse Given	Location
CARR	Rebecca	14	Jan	1854	MURPHY	Benjamin	VA. bk. 3A pg. 038
CARREL	Thomas M.	31	Mar	1840	COMBS	Elizabeth M.	VA. bk. 2A pg. 070
CARRIER	John	05	Sep	1844	GEER	Hannah	off. D. THOMPSON
CARSON	Mary	28	Dec	1854	BOWMAN	John	VA. bk. 2A pg. 084
CARTER	Edith	03	Mar	1814	HEDGES	Ephraim	VA. bk. 01 pg. 003
CARTER	Elisabeth	08	Jun	1812	NOLAN	Sampson	off. F. GUTHRIE
CARTER	Ewing T.	23	Jan	1868	MONTGOMERY	Mary E.	VA. bk. 1A pg. 078
CARTER	Joseph J.	08	Jan	1861	CAIRNES	Margaret E.	off. W. WILLSON
CARTER	Juliana	11	Sep	1814	LEWIS	Ephraim	VA. bk. 1A pg. 081
CARTER	Lewis Wash.	13	Oct	1863	PUNTNEY	Isabelle	off. UNKNOWN
CARTER	Martha Louisa	10	Jan	1870	HEADINGTON	John	WV. bk. 4A pg. 058
CARTER	Mary	15	Nov	1866	HINDMAN	Samuel B.	off. W. WHITE
CARTER	Mary Anne	30	May	1827	GREEN	Hugh	VA. bk. 3A pg. 098
CARTER	Prudence	26	Sep	1816	BAUSMAN	Edward	off. J. NAYLOR
CARTER	Rebecca Ann	23	Sep	1817	LEWIS	Samuel	VA. bk. 1A pg. 078
CARTER	Samuel	21	Jan	1844	WELLS	Michel	off. W. WILLSON
CARTER	Stephen	06	Sep	1855	FISHER	Catharine	WV. bk. 3A pg. 131
CARUTH	Rachel B.	02	Dec	1874	HASLETT	William K.	off. H. SHEPHERD
CASH	William	02	Apr	1812	BELL	Mary Ann	WV. bk. 4A pg. 067
CASNER	Cora	27	Aug	1870	MILLER	George	off. W. WHITE
CASNER	Elizabeth	19	Oct	1848	KLEIN	Christopher	WV. bk. 4A pg. 014
CASNER	John C.	06	Nov	1858	SMITH	Rose V.	off. R. NICHOLLS
CASNER	Scintha M.	24	Jun	1859	GRANDFIELD	Dennis M.	VA. bk. 2A pg. 046
CASSIDY	Joseph N.	23	Oct	1871	HEADINGTON	Maggie E.	off. J. CAZAD
CATHCART	Sarah	17	Jun	1841	STEWART	Joseph	VA. bk. 2A pg. 007
CAUGHEY	Josiah	24	Apr	1838	MALONE	Elmira	off. S. LAUCK
							VA. bk. 2A pg. 018
							off. S. LAUCK
							VA. bk. 2A pg. 079
							off. S. WORTHINGTON
							VA. bk. 01 pg. 004
							off. J. MEANS
							WV. bk. 4A pg. 146
							off. J. LATIMER
							VA. bk. 1A pg. 081
							off. UNKNOWN
							WV. bk. 4A pg. 074
							VA. bk. 2A pg. *02
							off. I. DALLAS
							VA. bk. 3A pg. 058
							off. J. NAYLOR
							VA. bk. 3A pg. 070
							off. J. NAYLOR
							WV. bk. 4A pg. 097
							off. W. LATIMER
							VA. bk. 2A pg. 083
							off. R. WHITE
							VA. bk. 2A pg. 082
							off. R. WHITE

CAVANAUGH	and			DOWNEY		VA. bk. 3A pg. 103
John	22	Jun	1861	Susan		off. S. NAYLOR
CEATH	and			BROWNLEE		WV. bk. 4A pg. 101
Sallie	04	Dec	1871	James		off. W. LATIMER
CHALLENCE	and			MENDEL		VA. bk. 01 pg. 004
Elijah B.	11	Aug	1856	Clarinda E.		off. A. CAMPBELL
CHAMBERLAIN	and			STEWART		WV. bk. 4A pg. 001
Ellen	21	Oct	1865	John Gibson		off. H. SHEPHERD
CHAMBERLAIN	and			BRADLEY		VA. bk. 01 pg. 005
Sarah	07	Mar	1857	Thomas		off. E. QUILLEN
CHAMBERS	and			SWEARINGEN		VA. bk. 2A pg. 047
James	31	May	1827	Mary		off. G. BUCHANAN
CHAMBERS	and			WYLIE		VA. bk. 2A pg. 083
James	21	Jun	1841	Emeline		off. R. WHITE
CHAMBERS	and			SWEARINGEN		VA. bk. 2A pg. 013
John	29	Aug	1820	Ann		off. J. PRITCHARD
CHAMBERS	and			PATTERSON		VA. bk. 1A pg. 051
Margaret	--	--	1809	Andrew		off. J. DODDRIDGE
CHAMBERS	and			PENTECOST		VA. bk. 2A pg. 066
Nancy	14	Mar	1839	George W.		off. G. BUCHANAN
CHAMBERS	and			KELLY		VA. bk. 1A pg. 067
Sarah	15	Jun	1813	Samuel		off. UNKNOWN
CHANEY	and			BURSON		VA. bk. 2A pg. 058
Henry	--	--	1830	Ann		off. N. HEADINGTON
CHANEY	and			BURSON		VA. bk. 2A pg. 053
William	--	--	1826	Tamar		off. N. HEADINGTON
CHAPLINE	and			RICHARDSON		WV. bk. 3A pg. 160
Albert W.	26	Sep	1865	Mary B.		off. H. SHEPHERD
CHAPMAN	and			GREGORY		VA. bk. 2A pg. 056
Elisabeth	22	Apr	1830	William		off. L. BROWNING
CHAPMAN	and			WEAVER		VA. bk. 3A pg. 019
Elsa	20	Apr	1853	Robert		off. J. NAYLOR
CHAPMAN	and			ROBINSON		VA. bk. 3A pg. 109
Jacob	25	Nov	1861	Mary		off. J. NAYLOR
CHAPMAN	and			THOMPSON		VA. bk. 2A pg. 021
Joana	21	Jan	1822	Giles S.		off. G. SCOTT
CHAPMAN	and			PERRY		VA. bk. 2A pg. 086
Margaret	03	Dec	1845	John		off. W. LEMON
CHAPMAN	and			RALSTON		VA. bk. 2A pg. 031
Mary	14	Dec	1824	Robert		off. G. SCOTT
CHAPMAN	and			GRAFTON		VA. bk. 2A pg. 091
Rachel	20	Jan	1848	Nathan B.		off. E. REGAL
CHAPMAN	and			CHAPMAN		VA. bk. 1A pg. 038
Susana (...)	29	Dec	1802	William		off. J. DODDRIDGE
CHAPMAN	and			CHAPMAN		VA. bk. 1A pg. 038
William	29	Dec	1802	Susana (...)		off. J. DODDRIDGE
CHARLTON	and			ROBSON		VA. bk. 3A pg. 059
Edward	08	Dec	1858	Margaret		off. J. NAYLOR
CHEEK	and			COX		WV. bk. 4A pg. 008
James	04	Sep	1866	Rebecca		off. R. NICHOLLS
CHENEY	and			BUCHANAN		VA. bk. 2A pg. 047
Julia	22	Feb	1827	Robert		off. C. MURRAY

BROOKE CO., VA./WV. LICENSES & MARRIAGES, 1797-1874   23

Surname	Given	Day	Month	Year	Spouse Surname	Spouse Given	Location
CHENOTH			and		EASTINGHOUSEN		VA. bk. 1A pg. 023
	Sophia	16	Apr	1807		Lewis	off. J. PRITCHARD
CHESTER			and		JEFFERS		WV. bk. 4A pg. 126
	Callie	10	Jul	1873		Harvey	off. W. LATIMER
CHESTER			and		STEWART		WV. bk. 4A pg. 070
	Georgianna	29	Mar	1870		James Clinton	off. W. WHITE
CHESTER			and		GASSAGE		VA. bk. 2A pg. *02
	John	13	Sep	1849		Mary Ann	off. J. IRWIN
CHESTER			and		RUSSELL		WV. bk. 3A pg. 142
	Mary E.	30	Jun	1864		Travilla A.	off. H. SHEPHERD
CHESTER			and		WALDRON		WV. bk. 3A pg. 157
	Sarah Elizabeth	14	Aug	1865		Joseph	off. H. SHEPHERD
CHRISTIAN			and		ELLIOTT		VA. bk. 3A pg. 043
	Edmund	13	Oct	1857		Jemima	off. J. NAYLOR
CHURCHMAN			and		PERRY		VA. bk. 2A pg. *17
	Joseph	08	Nov	1853		Elizabeth	off. S. NESBITT
CHURCHMAN			and		LUCAS		WV. bk. 4A pg. 089
	Joseph	17	May	1871		Nancy	off. W. WHITE
CHURCHMAN			and		PATTON		VA. bk. 2A pg. 087
	William	14	Nov	1845		Eliza Jane	off. S. WORTHINGTON
CLARK			and		MORROW		VA. bk. 2A pg. 083
	Jane	03	Mar	1842		Aaron	off. R. WHITE
CLARK			and		SHEPARD		VA. bk. 1A pg. 007
	Samuel	05	Apr	1801		Ruhanna	off. UNKNOWN
CLARK			and		INGLEBRIGHT		VA. bk. 3A pg. 089
	William A.	21	Aug	1860		Elizabeth J.	off. J. NAYLOR
CLAYTON			and		PUNTNEY		VA. bk. 2A pg. 050
	Charlotte	29	Jun	1826		John	off. N. HEADINGTON
CLAYTON			and		CRIDER		VA. bk. 2A pg. 035
	George	11	Mar	1824		Melinda	off. N. HEADINGTON
CLAYTON			and		HEDGES		VA. bk. 01 pg. 004
	Nancy	07	Sep	1856		Otho	off. E. QUILLEN
CLAYTON			and		PUNTNEY		VA. bk. 2A pg. 058
	William	--	--	1830		Elizabeth	off. N. HEADINGTON
CLEARY			and		ROBINSON		VA. bk. 2A pg. 071
	Margaret E.	02	May	1841		Israel	off. T. STEIRSHCOMB
CLELAND			and		RAMSEY		VA. bk. 2A pg. 059
	Jane	05	Jun	1828		Robert	off. E. SMITH
CLELAND			and		HINDMAN		VA. bk. 2A pg. 068
	Robert	11	Oct	1839		Elisabeth	off. J. GALLOWAY
CLELAND			and		RAMSEY		VA. bk. 2A pg. 039
	William	14	May	1825		Rachael	off. J. CAZAD
CLEMENS			and		DENINGEN		WV. bk. 4A pg. 130
	Sarah	06	Nov	1873		Hugh	off. W. LATIMER
CLENDENEN			and		BONAR		WV. bk. 3A pg. 148
	Edward W.	24	Nov	1864		Mary Jane	off. H. SHEPHERD
CLENDENEN			and		SHARRON		VA. bk. 1A pg. 009
	John	15	Apr	1799		Anna	off. UNKNOWN
CLENDENEN			and		YOUNG		VA. bk. 1A pg. 081
	Margaret	15	May	1814		William	off. UNKNOWN
CLENDENING			and		MC CORMACK		VA. bk. 1A pg. 083
	Polly	24	Jun	1813		George	off. UNKNOWN

24 BROOKE CO., VA./WV. LICENSES & MARRIAGES, 1797-1874

Name					Spouse	Location
CLERKIN		and			DORSEY	VA. bk. 3A pg. 085
Bridget	20	May		1860	John	off. J. NAYLOR
CLINTON		and			HAMILTON	VA. bk. 1A pg. 083
Sarah Ann	02	Nov		1815	Daniel	off. UNKNOWN
CLOSE		and			SHADE	VA. bk. 2A pg. 075
Peter	16	Feb		1843	Margaret	off. S. GRAFTON
CLOSE		and			ACKERMAN	VA. bk. 01 pg. 003
Peter	08	Nov		1855	Eliza Jane	off. E. QUILLEN
CLOSEN		and			HITCHCOCK	VA. bk. 2A pg. 075
Sophia	03	May		1843	Josiah	off. C. WEIRICK
CLOUGH		and			DARNALL	WV. bk. 4A pg. 005
Wm. Overton	22	Dec		1865	Henrietta R.	off. H. SHEPHERD
CLOW		and			CONANT	VA. bk. 01 pg. 006
William	30	Jul		1857	Jane	off. E. QUILLEN
COATES		and			DUNWELL	WV. bk. 4A pg. 081
William B.	26	Dec		1870	Mary Ann	off. W. WHITE
COBB		and			TEALIN	VA. bk. 2A pg. 049
Samuel	04	Jan		1827	Jane	off. S. REED
COCHRAN		and			SNYDER	VA. bk. 2A pg. 065
Jabez H.	10	Jan		1839	Huldah	off. G. BUCHANAN
COCHRAN		and			RALSTON	VA. bk. 1A pg. 080
James	02	Nov		1815	Mary	off. J. PRITCHARD
COCHRAN		and			LANE	VA. bk. 1A pg. 067
Margaret	04	Jan		1816	William	off. E. MACURDY
COCHRAN		and			JOHNSTON	VA. bk. 2A pg. 034
Mary J.	01	Sep		1825	William	off. G. SCOTT
COCHRAN		and			DURBIN	VA. bk. 2A pg. 082
Nancy	10	Apr		1838	John	off. R. WHITE
COCHRANE		and			PRATHER	VA. bk. 01 pg. 002
Mary	24	Aug		1854	Elbert	off. E. QUILLEN
COCKER		and			CRAWFORD	VA. bk. 1A pg. 052
James	--	--		1809	Christiana	off. UNKNOWN
COGAN		and			BARBER	VA. bk. 01 pg. 004
John	12	Sep		1856	Mary (Mrs.)	off. W. GAMBLE, JR.
COGAN		and			THORP	VA. bk. 01 pg. 004
John	12	Sep		1856	Mary	off. W. GAMBLE, JR.
COLE		and			GRIFFITH	VA. bk. 3A pg. 104
Rebecca M.	26	Sep		1862	Jacob B.	off. J. NAYLOR
COLE		and			HARRIS	VA. bk. 1A pg. 071
Sarah	06	Jun		1815	James	off. W. WILLSON
COLE		and			JONES	VA. bk. 2A pg. 061
William	09	Oct		1832	Catherine	off. G. ROBINSON
COLEMAN		and			NELSON	VA. bk. 1A pg. 005
Ann	18	Sep		1798	Joseph	off. J. HUGHES
COLEMAN		and			MORGAN	WV. bk. 4A pg. 021
Clara B.	31	Dec		1866	McCullough	off. H. SHEPHERD
COLEMAN		and			BEATTY	VA. bk. 01 pg. 005
David O.	02	Oct		1856	Sarah A.	off. J. CARVER
COLEMAN		and			LEWIS	VA. bk. 3A pg. 107
De Witt C.	13	Nov		1861	Elizabeth	off. S. NAYLOR
COLEMAN		and			ROBERTS	WV. bk. 4A pg. 020
Emma D.	31	Dec		1866	William	off. R. NICHOLLS

BROOKE CO., VA./WV. LICENSES & MARRIAGES, 1797-1874   25

Name		Day	Month	Year	Spouse	Reference
COLEMAN	and				YATES	WV. bk. 4A pg. 013
Mary		10	Oct	1866	Elijah M.	off. R. NICHOLLS
COLEMAN	and				BANE	VA. bk. 2A pg. *14
Mertine		28	Oct	1852	John	off. S. NESBITT
COLEMAN	and				CROUCH	VA. bk. 1A pg. 030
Polly		20	Aug	1807	James	off. J. HUGHES
COLEMAN	and				HEDGES	VA. bk. 2A pg. 064
Sarah		19	Oct	1837	John M.	off. A. YOUNG
COLEMAN	and				MC CORMACK	VA. bk. 1A pg. 021
Sarah		--	--	1806	John	off. UNKNOWN
COLGRAVE	and				LYONS	VA. bk. 1A pg. 012
Nancy		12	May	1803	Mathew	off. E. MACURDY
COLLINS	and				LINTON	VA. bk. 2A pg. *10
Augustus		25	Dec	1851	Susanna	off. H. SNYDER
COLLINS	and				BRANNON	VA. bk. 2A pg. 008
Joseph S.		01	Jun	1819	Maria	off. G. BUCHANAN
COLLINS	and				MURPHY	WV. bk. 4A pg. 130
Timothy		04	Nov	1873	Bridget	off. W. LATIMER
COLWELL	and				MC FERRAN	VA. bk. 2A pg. 005
Abigale		04	Nov	1816	William	off. E. MACURDY
COLWELL	and				BROWN	VA. bk. 1A pg. 002
Robert		15	Nov	1797	Sally	off. J. DODDRIDGE
COLWELL	and				MACURDY	VA. bk. 2A pg. 008
Sarah (Mrs.)		30	Mar	1819	Elisha (Rev.)	off. O. JENNINGS
COLWELL	and				STEVENSON	VA. bk. 1A pg. 036
William		15	Sep	1808	Mary	off. J. HUGHES
COMBS	and				CARREL	VA. bk. 2A pg. 070
Elizabeth M.		31	Mar	1840	Thomas M.	off. D. THOMPSON
CONANT	and				BEDILLION	VA. bk. 3A pg. 050
Abigail		13	Feb	1858	Joseph	off. J. NAYLOR
CONANT	and				CLOW	VA. bk. 01 pg. 006
Jane		30	Jul	1857	William	off. E. QUILLEN
CONAWAY	and				RUNNELLS	VA. bk. 2A pg. *17
Evan		14	Nov	1853	Jemima	off. S. NESBITT
CONAWAY	and				MILLIGAN	VA. bk. 3A pg. 077
Evan		22	Nov	1859	Mary Ann	off. J. NAYLOR
CONCKLIN	and				BROWN	VA. bk. 2A pg. 068
Daniel T.		05	Dec	1839	Christiana	off. J. GALLOWAY
CONE	and				CUNNINGHAM	WV. bk. 4A pg. 038
Michael		21	Dec	1867	Anne	off. H. MELVIN
CONGLETON	and				FITZ-RANDOLPH	VA. bk. 2A pg. 010
Julianna		13	Mar	1819	Cornelius	off. A. CAMPBELL
CONGLETON	and				GOOD	VA. bk. 2A pg. 019
Maria		12	Oct	1820	Thomas	off. A. CAMPBELL
CONKEL	and				BUCKINGHAM	VA. bk. 2A pg. 037
Margaret		11	Sep	1826	Absalom	off. N. HEADINGTON
CONN	and				MACKDANIEL	VA. bk. 1A pg. 071
George		21	Jan	1814	Ester	off. W. WILLSON
CONN	and				ANDERSON	VA. bk. 2A pg. 049
Margaret		24	Apr	1827	Robert	off. S. REED
CONN	and				SANDERS	VA. bk. 1A pg. 069
Samuel		28	Jan	1815	Linney	off. UNKNOWN

CONNELL Charles H.	14	and Dec	1847	MENDEL Sarah		off. J.	VA. bk. 2A MONROE	pg. 090
CONNELL Ellen E.	--	and --	1867	MC NALLY Arthur F.		off. C.	WV. bk. 4A MELVIN	pg. 028
CONNELL Harrison	11	and Sep	1838	RUSSELL Elizabeth		off. A.	VA. bk. 2A YOUNG	pg. 065
CONNELL James	08	and Oct	1844	WELLS Martha Ann		off. S.	VA. bk. 2A WORTHINGTON	pg. 085
CONNELL James S.	22	and Oct	1826	MENDEL Elizabeth		off. J.	VA. bk. 2A BROWNING, JR.	pg. 044
CONNELL John	14	and Mar	1802	SWEARINGEN Eleanor		off. J.	VA. bk. 1A DODDRIDGE	pg. 044
CONNELL Polly	--	and --	1802	MARSHALL Samuel A.		off.	VA. bk. 1A UNKNOWN	pg. 044
CONNELL Sarah	07	and Nov	1843	FOGG Thomas P.		off. J.	VA. bk. 2A HARRISON	pg. 078
CONNELL Solomon	31	and Jan	1808	MAGRUDER Sally		off.	VA. bk. 1A UNKNOWN	pg. 050
CONNELLY Bridget	22	and Jan	1868	DAVIN Dusty		off. H.	WV. bk. 4A MELVIN	pg. 040
CONNELLY Jonathan	12	and May	1825	DAVIS Selah		off. T.	VA. bk. 2A BEEKS	pg. 038
CONNER Margaret	25	and Dec	1853	COOK William C.		off. E.	VA. bk. 2A QUILLEN	pg. *17
CONNERS Margery	09	and May	1871	O'HARA Bernard		off. W.	WV. bk. 4A LATIMER	pg. 087
CONOWAY Elisabeth	14	and Aug	1805	JONES Joseph		off. J.	VA. bk. 1A PRITCHARD	pg. 019
COOK Elizabeth	02	and Nov	1848	PERKINS James		off. T.	VA. bk. 2A NEWELL	pg. *01
COOK Nancy	03	and Mar	1831	SCOTT Robert		off. G.	VA. bk. 2A SCOTT	pg. 057
COOK Samuel	01	and Feb	1869	SNEDIKER Clay		off. W.	WV. bk. 4A WHITE	pg. 058
COOK Thomas	09	and Jun	1800	HIBBIT Nancy		off. J.	VA. bk. 1A DODDRIDGE	pg. 041
COOK William C.	25	and Dec	1853	CONNER Margaret		off. E.	VA. bk. 2A QUILLEN	pg. *17
COOK William H.	29	and Apr	1847	RICE Mary Cath.		off. G.	VA. bk. 2A JONES	pg. 093
COOK William J.	02	and Feb	1830	PUMPHREY Drusilla		off. T.	VA. bk. 2A BEEKS	pg. 058
COOPER John M.	19	and Sep	1860	HEDGES Sallie B.		off. J.	VA. bk. 3A NAYLOR	pg. 093
COOPER Nancy	14	and Nov	1871	WELLS Bazil (Jr.)		off. W.	WV. bk. 4A LATIMER	pg. 099
COOPER Valinda J.	07	and Mar	1871	TILTON Joseph		off. W.	WV. bk. 4A WHITE	pg. 085
CORBIN Ann	08	and Apr	1819	BROWNLEE James		off. L.	VA. bk. 2A BROWNING	pg. 013
CORBIN Joseph	26	and Aug	1841	WALTERS Mary Ann		off. J.	VA. bk. 2A HARRISON	pg. 078

CORNELIUS		and	JOHNSON	VA. bk. 1A pg. 059
Elizabeth	21	Aug 1810	Joal/Jacob	off. J. PRITCHARD
CORNELIUS		and	MORTON	VA. bk. 3A pg. 037
John	07	Jan 1854	Mary	off. J. NAYLOR
CORNELIUS		and	SMITH	VA. bk. 3A pg. 108
Sarah	09	Nov 1861	George F.	off. S. NAYLOR
CORRIEGYS		and	HARRIS	VA. bk. 2A pg. 074
Sarah	18	Aug 1841	Benjamin F.	off. W. STEVENS
CORY		and	RAY	VA. bk. 2A pg. 016
Elijah D.	30	Nov 1820	Lydia	off. G. BUCHANAN
COTINGHAM		and	WHELAN	WV. bk. 4A pg. 091
Mary	29	May 1871	Michael	off. W. WHITE
COULBURN		and	BRIGGS	VA. bk. 3A pg. 087
Thomas L.	31	Jul 1860	Caroline A.	off. J. NAYLOR
COULTER		and	FILSON	VA. bk. 2A pg. 029
Hannah	27	Jan 1824	Joseph	off. G. BUCHANAN
COULTER		and	JAMES	VA. bk. 2A pg. 055
James	08	Jul 1831	Matilda	off. G. SCOTT
COULTER		and	SILVERTHORN	VA. bk. 2A pg. 029
John (Jr.)	24	Jun 1823	Jane	off. G. SCOTT
COULTER		and	SNEDIKER	VA. bk. 1A pg. 021
Mary	--	-- 1806	John	off. UNKNOWN
COULTER		and	OWINGS	VA. bk. 2A pg. 018
Olivia	02	May 1821	John	off. G. BUCHANAN
COULTROUGH		and	PARKINSON	VA. bk. 1A pg. 036
Benjamin	19	Dec 1808	Martha	off. J. HUGHES
COUNSELMAN		and	BROWN	VA. bk. 2A pg. *12
David F.	09	Sep 1852	Mary Ann	off. H. SNYDER
COUNSELMAN		and	LINDSAY	VA. bk. 2A pg. 060
Elisabeth	05	Mar 1829	Joshua	off. E. SMITH
COUNSELMAN		and	ZINK	VA. bk. 2A pg. 043
George	22	Mar 1826	Emma	off. C. MURRAY
COUNSELMAN		and	ZINK	VA. bk. 2A pg. 042
Phrania	04	Apr 1826	John	off. C. MURRAY
COWAN		and	DINSMORE	VA. bk. 3A pg. 048
Patrick	20	Jan 1858	Gracy	off. J. NAYLOR
COWLE		and	CALDWELL	VA. bk. 2A pg. 008
Alpheus	30	Mar 1819	Mary	off. G. SCOTT
COX		and	TEAL	VA. bk. 1A pg. 038
Elizabeth	02	Jun 1803	Nicholas	off. J. DODDRIDGE
COX		and	MILLER	VA. bk. 3A pg. 080
George	26	Dec 1859	Unity (Mrs.)	off. J. NAYLOR
COX		and	MUNCY	VA. bk. 3A pg. 080
George	26	Dec 1859	Unity	off. J. NAYLOR
COX		and	REEVES	VA. bk. 01 pg. 004
James W.	29	Nov 1855	Cornelia K.	off. A. ENDSLEY
COX		and	WRIGHT	WV. bk. 4A pg. 018
Jonathan	16	Jan 1867	Nancy J.	off. H. MELVIN
COX		and	BUCHANAN	VA. bk. 1A pg. 083
Joseph	25	Mar 1813	Elisabeth	off. UNKNOWN
COX		and	HEDGES	VA. bk. 2A pg. 038
Joseph	25	May 1825	Sarah	off. T. BEEKS

28   BROOKE CO., VA./WV. LICENSES & MARRIAGES, 1797-1874

Surname	Given	Day	Month	Year	Spouse Surname	Spouse Given	Location
COX	Julia C.	25	Oct	1871	BICKERSTAFF	Isaac C.	WV. bk. 4A pg. 098 off. W. LATIMER
COX	Nancy	--	--	1803	MC MAHAN	John	VA. bk. 1A pg. 047 off. UNKNOWN
COX	Nancy	22	Dec	1825	ALBAN	George	VA. bk. 2A pg. 038 off. T. BEEKS
COX	Nancy	18	Apr	1832	ARCHBOLD	Benjamin	VA. bk. 2A pg. 061 off. R. HOPKINS
COX	Nancy B.	16	May	1849	BRICELAND	John M.	VA. bk. 2A pg. *02 off. I. DALLAS
COX	Rebecca	04	Sep	1866	CHEEK	James	WV. bk. 4A pg. 008 off. R. NICHOLLS
COX	Sally W.	17	Jan	1861	HUKILL	Martin	VA. bk. 3A pg. 098 off. J. NAYLOR
COX	Sarah	12	Aug	1800	DUNLAP	Josiah	VA. bk. 1A pg. 009 off. UNKNOWN
COX	Serina	29	Dec	1842	WRIGHT	Jonathan	VA. bk. 2A pg. 075 off. C. WEIRICK
COX	Susannah	06	May	1828	HARRIS	Mathias	VA. bk. 2A pg. 059 off. E. SMITH
COX	Wylie	14	Oct	1868	DOW	Mary	WV. bk. 4A pg. 051 off. S. QUEST
COXTON	Miss.	--	--	1809	HULFORD	John	VA. bk. 1A pg. 048 off. J. DODDRIDGE
CRAFT	Alexander	14	Dec	1843	WRIGHT	Jane	VA. bk. 2A pg. 078 off. S. WORTHINGTON
CRAFT	Charles H.	16	May	1821	NEWLAND	Rebecca	VA. bk. 2A pg. 080 off. S. LAUCK
CRAFT	Charles H.	24	Oct	1859	WAUGH	Sarah Ann	VA. bk. 3A pg. 075 off. J. NAYLOR
CRAFT	Clara C.	20	Aug	1868	SCHELL	William H.	WV. bk. 01 pg. 019 off. J. DARSIE
CRAFT	Harriet	01	Mar	1838	ANNY	David S.	VA. bk. 2A pg. 080 off. S. LAUCK
CRAFT	Mary	29	May	1815	BARNS	Alexander	VA. bk. 1A pg. 071 off. W. WILLSON
CRAIG	Absalom	25	Oct	1826	SILVERS	Matilda	VA. bk. 2A pg. 045 off. J. CAZAD
CRAIG	Maranda A.	12	Jun	1841	DAVIES	David	VA. bk. 2A pg. 072 off. S. FULTON
CRAIGHTON	John	20	Mar	1823	ANDERSON	Lydia	VA. bk. 2A pg. 028 off. J. CAZAD
CRALY	James	14	Sep	1859	BURNS	Rosanna	VA. bk. 3A pg. 074 off. J. NAYLOR
CRANE	Sarah	30	Sep	1826	MC GLAUGHLIN	William	VA. bk. 2A pg. 043 off. C. MURRAY
CRAW	Joseph	13	Jun	1826	CRAW	Mary (...)	VA. bk. 2A pg. 042 off. C. MURRAY
CRAW	Mary (...)	13	Jun	1826	CRAW	Joseph	VA. bk. 2A pg. 042 off. C. MURRAY
CRAWFORD	Ann	02	Jul	1806	HANSON	James	VA. bk. 1A pg. 021 off. UNKNOWN

BROOKE CO., VA./WV. LICENSES & MARRIAGES, 1797-1874   29

Surname	Given	Day	Mo	Year	Spouse	Reference
CRAWFORD	Ann	13	Apr	1826	JONES Lewis	VA. bk. 2A pg. 043 off. C. MURRAY
CRAWFORD	Ann	09	Feb	1815	JONES Ellis	VA. bk. 1A pg. 078 off. W. WILLSON
CRAWFORD	Archibald	10	Feb	1807	BROWN Elisabeth	VA. bk. 1A pg. 025 off. E. MACURDY
CRAWFORD	Christiana	--	--	1809	COCKER James	VA. bk. 1A pg. 052 off. UNKNOWN
CRAWFORD	George	21	Jul	1841	MOREN Harriet	VA. bk. 2A pg. 072 off. D. HERVEY
CRAWFORD	John	03	Jul	1821	LEADLIE Nancy	VA. bk. 2A pg. 019 off. G. BUCHANAN
CRAWFORD	Lewis	13	Sep	1814	WILLIAMSON Rachel	VA. bk. 1A pg. 077 off. J. PRITCHARD
CRAWFORD	Mary Ann	18	Apr	1844	TARR Jackson	VA. bk. 2A pg. 081 off. J. GALLOWAY
CRAWFORD	Polly	10	Jun	1800	BARNET George	VA. bk. 1A pg. 041 off. J. DODDRIDGE
CRAWFORD	Thomas	16	Jun	1842	DAVIS Sarah	VA. bk. 2A pg. 078 off. J. HARRISON
CRAWFORD	William	20	Aug	1806	MC CORMICK Sarah	VA. bk. 1A pg. 022 off. UNKNOWN
CREAL	Ann	12	Sep	1839	HUNTER John V.	VA. bk. 2A pg. 067 off. G. BUCHANAN
CREAL	Margaret	04	Dec	1827	BRICELAND Josiah	VA. bk. 2A pg. 054 off. L. BROWNING
CREAL	Rachael	22	Jan	1828	ADAMS William	VA. bk. 2A pg. 054 off. L. BROWNING
CREE	Hamilton	07	Oct	1846	SCOTT Catharine	VA. bk. 2A pg. 088 off. R. HOPKINS
CRIDER	Daniel	14	Jan	1854	DOWLER Melinda	VA. bk. 3A pg. 039 off. J. NAYLOR
CRIDER	Frederick	11	Apr	1830	ASHBROOK Mary Ann	VA. bk. 2A pg. 058 off. D. MERRYMAN
CRIDER	Melinda	11	Mar	1824	CLAYTON George	VA. bk. 2A pg. 035 off. N. HEADINGTON
CRIDER	William	20	Jan	1858	HEDGES Permelia	VA. bk. 3A pg. 048 off. J. NAYLOR
CRISS	Hanna	22	Feb	1868	STANSBERRY Hudson R.	WV. bk. 4A pg. 043 off. H. MELVIN
CRISS	Jacob P.	26	Mar	1865	HESSEY Caroline	WV. bk. 3A pg. 154 off. H. SHEPHERD
CRISS	Rebecca W.	04	May	1861	MC CONNELL George	VA. bk. 3A pg. 101 off. J. NAYLOR
CRISWELL	Patty	10	Oct	1815	MC CAMMON Samuel	VA. bk. 1A pg. 079 off. J. PRITCHARD
CRISWELL	Thomas	23	Aug	1838	FLANEGAN Margaret	VA. bk. 2A pg. 082 off. R. WHITE
CRITZER	Nancy	31	Dec	1818	WILHELM George	VA. bk. 2A pg. 001 off. G. SCOTT
CROTHERS	Hugh W.	12	Aug	1847	DUVALL Ann Hooper	VA. bk. 2A pg. 090 off. T. NEWELL

30 BROOKE CO., VA./WV. LICENSES & MARRIAGES, 1797-1874

Name		Date			Spouse	Reference		
CROTHERS	and				WOLCOTT	WV.	bk. 4A	pg. 114
Sallie H.	24	Jun	1872		William M.	off. W. LATIMER		
CROUCH	and				VANMETER	VA.	bk. 1A	pg. 081
Anna	27	Aug	1812		John	off. UNKNOWN		
CROUCH	and				BECK	VA.	bk. 1A	pg. 030
Cornelia	05	Feb	1807		James	off. W. WILLSON		
CROUCH	and				CROUCH	VA.	bk. 1A	pg. 075
Henrietta (...)	29	Oct	1812		John	off. J. MEEK		
CROUCH	and				COLEMAN	VA.	bk. 1A	pg. 030
James	20	Aug	1807		Polly	off. J. HUGHES		
CROUCH	and				CROUCH	VA.	bk. 1A	pg. 075
John	29	Oct	1812		Henrietta (...)	off. J. MEEK		
CROWLEY	and				GOODWIN	VA.	bk. 2A	pg. 022
Elizabeth	17	Feb	1820		John	off. J. LAWS		
CRUSON	and				MC ELROY	VA.	bk. 2A	pg. 074
Coleman	05	Jan	1842		Elizabeth	off. W. STEVENS		
CRUSON	and				WILSON	WV.	bk. 4A	pg. 019
Mary E.	28	Dec	1866		George A.	off. R. NICHOLLS		
CRUTH	and				MC CONNEL	VA.	bk. 01	pg. 005
Alexander	17	Feb	1857		Mary Jane	off. E. QUILLEN		
CRUTH	and				MC HUGH	VA.	bk. 3A	pg. 109
Andrew	11	Nov	1861		Mary Ann	off. J. NAYLOR		
CRUTH	and				BALLENTINE	VA.	bk. 3A	pg. 051
Jane	24	Feb	1858		James	off. J. NAYLOR		
CRUTH	and				HASLETT	WV.	bk. 4A	pg. 146
Rachel B.	02	Dec	1874		William K.	off. J. LATIMER		
CULBERTSON	and				BRADY	VA.	bk. 2A	pg. *06
Elizabeth	26	Oct	1850		Bernard	off. R. WHITE		
CULLEY	and				SCOTT	VA.	bk. 2A	pg. 007
Hannah	12	Dec	1816		Charles	off. S. LAUCK		
CULLIN	and				HALE	VA.	bk. 2A	pg. *15
Alexander H.	07	Nov	1853		Emma S.	off. G. LOWMAN		
CULLIN	and				MARSHALL	VA.	bk. 2A	pg. 082
Isaac	15	Feb	1838		Elizabeth	off. R. WHITE		
CULLIN	and				PETERSON	VA.	bk. 2A	pg. 084
Israel	25	Oct	1842		Rebecca	off. R. WHITE		
CULLIN	and				BRIDGET	VA.	bk. 2A	pg. 082
Matthew	16	Aug	1838		Emily	off. R. WHITE		
CUMMINS	and				CAMERON	VA.	bk. 2A	pg. 084
James	28	Apr	1842		Matilda	off. R. WHITE		
CUMMINS	and				IRWIN	VA.	bk. 2A	pg. 014
Martha	06	Sep	1820		Joseph	off. J. CAZAD		
CUMMINS	and				STEWART	VA.	bk. 2A	pg. 028
Mary	20	Aug	1823		William	off. J. CAZAD		
CUMMINS	and				GRATIGNY	VA.	bk. 2A	pg. 076
Mary E.	01	Feb	1843		Cyrus	off. C. BEST		
CUNNINGHAM	and				CONE	WV.	bk. 4A	pg. 038
Anne	21	Dec	1867		Michael	off. H. MELVIN		
CUNNINGHAM	and				MILLER	VA.	bk. 3A	pg. 038
Cyrus H.	11	Jan	1854		Jane	off. J. NAYLOR		
CUNNINGHAM	and				VERMILLION	WV.	bk. 4A	pg. 023
Ella I.	30	Jan	1867		C. A.	off. H. MELVIN		

CUNNINGHAM		and		STEEN		VA. bk. 2A pg. 071
George	01	Jul	1841	Elizabeth		off. D. HERVEY
CUNNINGHAM		and		VESY		VA. bk. 2A pg. 068
James	19	Dec	1839	Susan (Mrs.)		off. W. SCULL
CUNNINGHAM		and		MORROW		VA. bk. 2A pg. 088
Nancy	12	May	1846	James		off. J. GALLOWAY
CUNNINGHAM		and		STEWART		VA. bk. 2A pg. 084
Nancy Ann	20	Jun	1844	John		off. R. WHITE
CUNNINGHAM		and		LETZKUS		WV. bk. 4A pg. 090
Rebecca J.	26	May	1871	Pierce		off. W. WHITE
CUPPLES		and		MC ELFRESH		VA. bk. 3A pg. 114
James	11	Mar	1862	Mary A.		off. J. NAYLOR
CUPPY		and		SUNDERLAND		VA. bk. 1A pg. 042
Anne	18	Nov	1800	Francis		off. J. DODDRIDGE
CUPPY		and		WHINN		VA. bk. 2A pg. 052
Jane	29	Mar	1827	Joshua		off. G. SCOTT
CURRAN		and		MC HENRY		VA. bk. 01 pg. 004
Joanna	30	Mar	1856	Joseph		off. A. ENDSLEY
CURRAN		and		ORR		VA. bk. 3A pg. 068
Margaret	09	May	1859	Edward		off. J. NAYLOR
CURTIS		and		RALSTON		VA. bk. 2A pg. 060
Alexander	23	Apr	1829	Catharine		off. S. REED
CURTIS		and		RODGERS		WV. bk. 4A pg. 125
George C.	10	Apr	1873	Mary		off. W. LATIMER
D'FOSSIT		and		NANGLE		VA. bk. 3A pg. 063
John A.	08	Feb	1859	Elizabeth		off. J. NAYLOR
DAILY		and		HANEY		WV. bk. 3A pg. 156
Elizabeth	28	Jun	1865	John		off. H. SHEPHERD
DANIEL		and		ALLISON		VA. bk. 2A pg. 083
Frederick	28	Oct	1841	Nancy		off. R. WHITE
DANNER		and		BURT		VA. bk. 3A pg. 106
Berhart	20	Sep	1861	Mary Jane		off. S. NAYLOR
DARE		and		STRINGER		VA. bk. 01 pg. 004
Edmund	08	Nov	1853	Ruth Jane		off. G. CRANAGE
DARLING		and		DARLING		VA. bk. 1A pg. 083
John	07	Jan	1813	Polly (...)		off. UNKNOWN
DARLING		and		BEDWELL		VA. bk. 2A pg. 080
Joseph	05	Jun	1838	Jane		off. S. LAUCK
DARLING		and		DARLING		VA. bk. 1A pg. 083
Polly (...)	07	Jan	1813	John		off. UNKNOWN
DARLING		and		MOUNTS		VA. bk. 1A pg. 081
Sarah	29	Aug	1811	Providence		off. UNKNOWN
DARNALL		and		CLOUGH		WV. bk. 4A pg. 005
Henrietta R.	22	Dec	1865	Wm. Overton		off. H. SHEPHERD
DARRAH		and		KELLY		VA. bk. 3A pg. 067
Thomas J.	02	Apr	1859	Elizabeth		off. J. NAYLOR
DAUGHERTY		and		YOUNG		WV. bk. 4A pg. 138
Abram M.	23	May	1874	Lucy A.		off. J. LATIMER
DAUGHERTY		and		WHICKERLY		WV. bk. 4A pg. 117
Charles W.	10	Sep	1872	Mary		off. W. LATIMER
DAUGHERTY		and		KELLY		WV. bk. 4A pg. 124
George	20	Mar	1873	Susan Ann		off. W. LATIMER

32 BROOKE CO., VA./WV. LICENSES & MARRIAGES, 1797-1874

Name					Spouse	Reference
DAUMONT		and			GIST	VA. bk. 01 pg. 005
Alfred A.	03	Sep	1856		Clara A.	off. G. CRANAGE
DAUMONT		and			BROWN	VA. bk. 3A pg. 107
Clara A.	11	Nov	1861		Leondas	off. S. NAYLOR
DAVIDSON		and			BURRIS	VA. bk. 2A pg. 079
David	11	Jan	1844		Elizabeth	off. S. WORTHINGTON
DAVIDSON		and			SMITH	VA. bk. 2A pg. *01
James	15	Apr	1849		Juliana	off. J. MOFFITT
DAVIDSON		and			PERKINS	WV. bk. 4A pg. 143
Samuel M.	08	Oct	1874		Minnie	off. J. LATIMER
DAVIES		and			CRAIG	VA. bk. 2A pg. 072
David	12	Jun	1841		Maranda A.	off. S. FULTON
DAVIN		and			CONNELLY	WV. bk. 4A pg. 040
Dusty	22	Jan	1868		Bridget	off. H. MELVIN
DAVIS		and			BEALL	WV. bk. 4A pg. 073
Augustus	01	Aug	1870		Ellen	off. W. WHITE
DAVIS		and			HINDMAN	VA. bk. 1A pg. 031
Catherine	23	Jun	1808		Samuel	off. J. PRITCHARD
DAVIS		and			FREEMAN	VA. bk. 1A pg. 015
David	04	Sep	1804		Patty	off. J. PRITCHARD
DAVIS		and			THOMAS	VA. bk. 2A pg. 041
Irvin	27	Dec	1825		Jane	off. J. BROWNING, JR.
DAVIS		and			ROBINSON	VA. bk. 3A pg. 077
Isaac L.	17	Dec	1859		Eliza. Jane	off. J. NAYLOR
DAVIS		and			SMITH	VA. bk. 1A pg. 062
Jacob	11	May	1815		Sally	off. L. BROWNING
DAVIS		and			RIDGLEY	VA. bk. 3A pg. 042
John	12	Oct	1857		Rebecca E.	off. J. NAYLOR
DAVIS		and			PROSSER	VA. bk. 2A pg. 083
John S.	23	Feb	1841		Elizabeth	off. R. WHITE
DAVIS		and			MAY	VA. bk. 2A pg. 064
Margaret	05	Dec	1837		Jacob	off. A. YOUNG
DAVIS		and			ROBINSON	VA. bk. 3A pg. 099
Mary Jane	20	Feb	1861		Jesse	off. J. NAYLOR
DAVIS		and			WELLS	VA. bk. 1A pg. 042
Miss.	04	Sep	1800		Jesse	off. J. DODDRIDGE
DAVIS		and			WRIGHT	VA. bk. 2A pg. 059
Peggy	24	Jun	1830		Jacob	off. G. BUCHANAN
DAVIS		and			WOODY	VA. bk. 01 pg. 004
Rachel	04	Oct	1856		Tarlton	off. UNKNOWN
DAVIS		and			HAINES	WV. bk. 4A pg. 120
Rachel	28	Nov	1872		Thomas J.	off. W. LATIMER
DAVIS		and			MORROW	VA. bk. 1A pg. 037
Ruth	28	Dec	1802		James	off. J. DODDRIDGE
DAVIS		and			PROSSER	VA. bk. 2A pg. 083
Samuel L.	07	Sep	1841		Rachel	off. R. WHITE
DAVIS		and			CRAWFORD	VA. bk. 2A pg. 078
Sarah	16	Jun	1842		Thomas	off. J. HARRISON
DAVIS		and			CONNELLY	VA. bk. 2A pg. 038
Selah	12	May	1825		Jonathan	off. T. BEEKS
DAVIS		and			ERVIN	WV. bk. 4A pg. 132
Susan	26	Nov	1873		James	off. W. LATIMER

BROOKE CO., VA./WV. LICENSES & MARRIAGES, 1797-1874   33

DAVIS		and		GREEN		VA. bk. 01 pg. 006
Thomas M.	11	Aug	1857	Miriam		off. E. QUILLEN
DAVISON		and		HAWKINS		VA. bk. 1A pg. 072
William	14	Oct	1812	Sarah		off. J. PRITCHARD
DAWSON		and		MENDEL		VA. bk. 2A pg. *01
Augustus M.	24	Jul	1849	Mary		off. J. IRWIN
DAWSON		and		SMITH		VA. bk. 2A pg. 071
John	07	Jan	1841	Matilda		off. T. STEIRSHCOMB
DAWSON		and		EBERLINE		VA. bk. 3A pg. 071
Mary A.	24	Jun	1859	John		off. J. NAYLOR
DAWSON		and		MARSHALL		VA. bk. 2A pg. 018
Robert	07	Sep	1820	Mary		off. A. CAMPBELL
DAWSON		and		WESTBROOK		VA. bk. 2A pg. 074
Sarah	14	Oct	1841	Alexander		off. W. STEVENS
DAWSON		and		CAMERON		VA. bk. 2A pg. 055
Thomas	22	Mar	1831	Jane		off. G. SCOTT
DAWSON		and		CAMPBELL		WV. bk. 3A pg. 162
William C.	26	Apr	1866	Jane C.		off. H. SHEPHERD
DECAMP		and		SPEER		VA. bk. 1A pg. 022
Jacob	27	May	1806	Sarah		off. UNKNOWN
DECAMPS		and		DUVALL		VA. bk. 2A pg. 072
T.J.	02	Nov	1841	Julia A.		off. S. FULTON
DEFFENBACH		and		GOOD		WV. bk. 4A pg. 131
N. Lee	12	Nov	1873	Elizabeth I.		off. W. LATIMER
DEFFENBAUGH		and		HINDMAN		VA. bk. 2A pg. 093
William H.	04	Mar	1848	Harriet		off. G. BUCHANAN
DEGARMO		and		KELLY		WV. bk. 4A pg. 120
Amanda	08	Jan	1873	William F.		off. W. LATIMER
DEGARMO		and		MC CLELLAND		WV. bk. 4A pg. 132
Anne	28	Nov	1873	George		off. W. LATIMER
DEGARMO		and		DEULEY		WV. bk. 4A pg. 121
Margaret	08	Jan	1873	George		off. W. LATIMER
DEIGHTON		and		MAYHALL		WV. bk. 4A pg. 082
Isabella	11	Jan	1871	William A.		off. W. WHITE
DEIGHTON		and		SAUNER		WV. bk. 4A pg. 083
John M.	23	Feb	1871	Hannah		off. W. WHITE
DEIGHTON		and		ROBERTS		VA. bk. 3A pg. 047
Margaret V.	26	Dec	1857	Richard T.		off. J. NAYLOR
DEIGHTON		and		MACKEY		WV. bk. 3A pg. 143
Millie	30	Aug	1864	Robert		off. H. SHEPHERD
DEIGHTON		and		HAPNER		VA. bk. 3A pg. 112
Ophelia	13	Feb	1862	Charles Wm.		off. J. NAYLOR
DEIGHTON		and		NASMITH		WV. bk. 4A pg. 005
Ralph	02	Jan	1866	Mary		off. H. SHEPHERD
DEIGHTON		and		ROBERTS		VA. bk. 01 pg. 003
Rosetta	01	May	1855	Andrew J.		off. E. QUILLEN
DEIGHTON		and		WILKINSON		VA. bk. 3A pg. 050
Sarah	16	Feb	1858	James		off. J. NAYLOR
DEMPSEY		and		TIERMAN		VA. bk. 01 pg. 005
Margarett	02	Oct	1856	Thomas		off. J. BRAZILL
DENER		and		WELLS		VA. bk. 3A pg. 097
Franklin	25	Dec	1860	Susan A.		off. J. NAYLOR

Name		Date		Spouse	Reference
DENINGEN	and			CLEMENS	WV. bk. 4A pg. 130
Hugh	06	Nov	1873	Sarah	off. W. LATIMER
DERBYSHIRE	and			KING	VA. bk. 2A pg. *15
Emily T.	23	Aug	1853	Jacob	off. E. QUILLEN
DEULEY	and			DEGARMO	WV. bk. 4A pg. 121
George	08	Jan	1873	Margaret	off. W. LATIMER
DEULEY	and			WAY	WV. bk. 4A pg. 094
Mary E.	30	Aug	1871	William	off. W. WHITE
DEVINNEY	and			O'HARA	VA. bk. 01 pg. 005
Charles	15	Oct	1856	Margarett	off. J. BRAZILL
DEVORE	and			INGRAM	OH. bk. 3A pg. 164
Ruth Ann	03	May	1866	Charles W.	off. R. NICHOLLS
DILL	and			THOMAS	VA. bk. 2A pg. 078
John	03	Nov	1842	Mary	off. J. HARRISON
DINSMORE	and			MC FADDEN	VA. bk. 3A pg. 008
Elenor	09	Nov	1852	John	off. J. NAYLOR
DINSMORE	and			COWAN	VA. bk. 3A pg. 048
Gracy	20	Jan	1858	Patrick	off. J. NAYLOR
DINSMORE	and			MORRIS	VA. bk. 3A pg. 029
Mary	04	Nov	1853	Micheal	off. J. NAYLOR
DOAK	and			WILCOXON	VA. bk. 2A pg. 057
Robert	21	Jan	1830	Elizabeth	off. G. SCOTT
DOBBS	and			BOWMAN	VA. bk. 2A pg. *04
George W.	13	Jun	1850	Henrietta M.	off. J. IRWIN
DODDRIDGE	and			MUSSER	VA. bk. 1A pg. 045
Benjamin	--	--	1802	Sophia	off. UNKNOWN
DODDRIDGE	and			GANT	VA. bk. 1A pg. 043
Eleanor R.	25	Apr	1801	John	off. J. DODDRIDGE
DODDRIDGE	and			KLEIN	VA. bk. 2A pg. 060
John	20	Nov	1828	Catharine	off. E. SMITH
DODDRIDGE	and			RAMSAY	VA. bk. 2A pg. 067
Julia Adeline	02	Oct	1838	Benjamin	off. A. YOUNG
DODDS	and			WAUGH	VA. bk. 3A pg. 040
Thomas	15	Sep	1857	Jane	off. J. NAYLOR
DODGE	and			PATTERSON	VA. bk. 2A pg. 028
John	18	Sep	1823	Nancy	off. J. CAZAD
DONAHUE	and			MARSHALL	VA. bk. 2A pg. 061
James	29	Mar	1832	Elizabeth	off. G. MC CASHEY
DONALD	and			MC DOWELL	VA. bk. 2A pg. 046
Daniel	08	Feb	1827	Nancy	off. J. CAZAD
DONNAL	and			LEE	VA. bk. 2A pg. *13
Eleanor	14	Apr	1853	Elias M.	off. H. SNYDER
DONNELLY	and			MC FADDEN	VA. bk. 3A pg. 036
Catherine	03	Jan	1854	Charles	off. J. NAYLOR
DONNELLY	and			KINDRICKS	VA. bk. 3A pg. 091
Catherine	05	Sep	1860	James	off. J. NAYLOR
DONNELLY	and			MC NALLY	WV. bk. 4A pg. 033
Margaret	26	Oct	1867	John B.	off. H. MELVIN
DONOVAN	and			NICHOLLS	VA. bk. 2A pg. 059
Absalom	28	Feb	1828	Elizabeth	off. E. SMITH
DONOVAN	and			GARDNER	VA. bk. 2A pg. 011
Ann	10	Feb	1820	David	off. J. PRITCHARD

BROOKE CO., VA./WV. LICENSES & MARRIAGES, 1797-1874   35

Name			Date	Spouse		Reference
DONOVAN		and		AMSPOKER		VA. bk. 3A pg. 060
Asa O.	21	Dec	1858	Mary Ann		off. J. NAYLOR
DONOVAN		and		HINDMAN		VA. bk. 2A pg. 048
Cornelius	08	Nov	1827	Mary		off. G. BUCHANAN
DONOVAN		and		REDICK		VA. bk. 1A pg. 074
Eleanor	13	Jun	1815	David		off. J. PRITCHARD
DONOVAN		and		JEFFERS		VA. bk. 2A pg. 012
Henrietta	03	Dec	1818	John		off. J. PRITCHARD
DONOVAN		and		OWINGS		VA. bk. 2A pg. 057
Ruth	04	Feb	1830	Asa		off. G. BUCHANAN
DONOVAN		and		RUSSELL		VA. bk. 3A pg. 067
Ruth C.	12	Apr	1859	Charles P.		off. J. NAYLOR
DONOVAN		and		STEPHENSON		VA. bk. 1A pg. 066
Sarah	20	Apr	1815	John		off. UNKNOWN
DONOVAN		and		OWINGS		VA. bk. 2A pg. 053
Thomas	19	Oct	1826	Catherine		off. G. BUCHANAN
DORLAND		and		LANDIS		VA. bk. 3A pg. 088
George S.	08	Aug	1860	Martha A.		off. J. NAYLOR
DORSEY		and		PARISH		WV. bk. 4A pg. 123
Drusilla	19	Feb	1873	Thomas B.		off. W. LATIMER
DORSEY		and		CLERKIN		VA. bk. 3A pg. 085
John	20	May	1860	Bridget		off. J. NAYLOR
DORSEY		and		TOSTEN		VA. bk. 2A pg. 019
Joseph	04	Apr	1820	Hannah		off. A. CAMPBELL
DORSEY		and		FOSTER		VA. bk. 2A pg. 036
Owen	29	Sep	1825	Elisabeth		off. N. HEADINGTON
DORSEY		and		ZINK		VA. bk. 2A pg. *17
Rebecca Ann	29	Dec	1853	John F.		off. W. LONG
DORSEY		and		ZINK		WV. bk. 4A pg. 015
Rebecca Ann	10	Nov	1866	William		off. R. NICHOLLS
DOTTY		and		BROWN		VA. bk. 1A pg. 011
Betsy	01	Feb	1803	Samuel		off. E. MACURDY
DOTY		and		SMITH		VA. bk. 1A pg. 076
Peter	03	Apr	1813	Mary		off. E. MACURDY
DOUBLAZIER		and		CAMP		VA. bk. 2A pg. 071
Nancy	14	Feb	1841	Chester		off. T. STEIRSHCOMB
DOUBLAZIER		and		CALENDINE		VA. bk. 01 pg. 002
Susan Elizabeth	02	Nov	1854	Edward		off. W. DAVIDSON
DOUBLE		and		ROBERTS		VA. bk. 2A pg. 067
Susanna	29	Oct	1838	Samuel		off. A. YOUNG
DOUGHERTY		and		WHITE		VA. bk. 2A pg. *16
George	05	May	1853	Caroline		off. J. DAWSON
DOUGHERTY		and		WHITE		VA. bk. 2A pg. *02
Grace	22	Jan	1849	Isaac		off. I. DALLAS
DOUGHERTY		and		JONES		VA. bk. 2A pg. 069
John	16	Jan	1840	Sarah Eliza		off. M. TELCHENELL
DOUGHERTY		and		LYONS		VA. bk. 01 pg. 004
Matilda	15	Sep	1855	David		off. J. BRAZILL
DOUGHERTY		and		MC GROUERTY		VA. bk. 3A pg. 068
Patrick	30	Apr	1859	Martha		off. J. NAYLOR
DOUGLASS		and		FOWLER		VA. bk. 2A pg. 094
Robert N.	29	Dec	1848	Mary Jane		off. T. MC CLEARY

36 BROOKE CO., VA./WV. LICENSES & MARRIAGES, 1797-1874

DOW		and		MILLER		WV. bk. 4A pg. 072
Isaac	21	Jul	1870	Rosann		off. W. WHITE
DOW		and		COX		WV. bk. 4A pg. 051
Mary	14	Oct	1868	Wylie		off. S. QUEST
DOW		and		SHIELDS		VA. bk. 3A pg. 124
Samantha	12	Jan	1863	Henry T.		off. J. NAYLOR
DOWDEN		and		MC CAMICK		WV. bk. 4A pg. 133
Frances P.	16	Jan	1874	Nathan		off. W. LATIMER
DOWDEN		and		PALMER		VA. bk. 2A pg. *10
Mary	14	Dec	1851	Samuel		off. H. SNYDER
DOWDEN		and		SPENCER		VA. bk. 2A pg. 071
Thomas	08	Jun	1841	Priscilla		off. J. GALLOWAY
DOWDLE		and		BROWNLEE		WV. bk. 4A pg. 102
Daisy	16	Dec	1871	Martin V.		off. W. LATIMER
DOWLER		and		PARSONS		VA. bk. 3A pg. 041
John F.	23	Sep	1857	Sue G.		off. J. NAYLOR
DOWLER		and		HALL		VA. bk. 01 pg. 003
Mahala	09	Nov	1854	David		off. C. HOLMES
DOWLER		and		CRIDER		VA. bk. 3A pg. 039
Melinda	14	Jan	1854	Daniel		off. J. NAYLOR
DOWNEY		and		LUCAS		VA. bk. 2A pg. 038
John	01	Dec	1825	Elisabeth		off. T. BEEKS
DOWNEY		and		TURNER		VA. bk. 2A pg. 091
Louisa	05	Dec	1847	Matthew		off. T. NEWELL
DOWNEY		and		BANNON		WV. bk. 4A pg. 056
Patrick	08	Jan	1869	Bridget		off. W. WHITE
DOWNEY		and		O'HARE		VA. bk. 3A pg. 096
Rosanna	04	Dec	1860	John		off. J. NAYLOR
DOWNEY		and		CAVANAUGH		VA. bk. 3A pg. 103
Susan	22	Jun	1861	John		off. S. NAYLOR
DOWNING		and		HEWIT		VA. bk. 1A pg. 073
James	14	Feb	1816	Nancy		off. G. SCOTT
DRAKE		and		BURK		VA. bk. 2A pg. 009
Rebecca	30	Mar	1816	William		off. J. DODDRIDGE
DUFFY		and		GILMORE		WV. bk. 4A pg. 133
Anne	02	Dec	1873	F.H.		off. W. LATIMER
DUKE		and		WELLS		VA. bk. 2A pg. 043
Alexander	07	Jun	1826	Elizabeth		off. C. MURRAY
DUKE		and		GROVES		VA. bk. 2A pg. 060
Catharine	29	Jan	1829	Andrew		off. E. SMITH
DUKE		and		SNEDIKER		VA. bk. 2A pg. 043
Shepherd	11	Mar	1826	Lavina		off. C. MURRAY
DUNCAN		and		MC KOWN		VA. bk. 2A pg. 083
James	29	Apr	1841	Mary		off. R. WHITE
DUNCAN		and		FLEMING		WV. bk. 4A pg. 108
John A.	28	Feb	1872	Miriam		off. W. LATIMER
DUNGAN		and		CAMERON		VA. bk. 1A pg. 061
Levi	02	Apr	1811	Margret		off. E. MACURDY
DUNLAP		and		LYONS		VA. bk. 3A pg. 046
Hugh	08	Dec	1857	Mary		off. J. NAYLOR
DUNLAP		and		COX		VA. bk. 1A pg. 009
Josiah	12	Aug	1800	Sarah		off. UNKNOWN

BROOKE CO., VA./WV. LICENSES & MARRIAGES, 1797-1874 37

Groom				Bride	Reference
DUNLAP		and		KIRKWOOD	VA. bk. 3A pg. 004
Mary Ann	06	Oct	1852	Joseph	off. J. NAYLOR
DUNLAP		and		BOUNDS	VA. bk. 1A pg. 009
Rebekah	04	Jul	1799	John	off. UNKNOWN
DUNLAP		and		HEDGES	VA. bk. 1A pg. 008
Sarah	15	Aug	1802	William	off. J. HUGHES
DUNLAP		and		ZINCK	VA. bk. 2A pg. 074
William	17	Aug	1842	Sarah	off. C. WEIRICK
DUNN		and		CARDEHAM	WV. bk. 4A pg. 134
Hugh	21	Jan	1874	Bridget	off. W. LATIMER
DUNN		and		HARPER	VA. bk. 2A pg. 004
Robert	27	Feb	1817	Sarah	off. G. SCOTT
DUNN		and		MC INTIRE	WV. bk. 4A pg. 029
Sarah E. (Mrs.)	02	Sep	1867	Robert (Sr.)	off. C. MELVIN
DUNWELL		and		COATES	WV. bk. 4A pg. 081
Mary Ann	26	Dec	1870	William B.	off. W. WHITE
DURANT		and		QUEST	WV. bk. 3A pg. 138
William L.	25	Feb	1864	Elizabeth C.	off. H. SHEPHERD
DURBIN		and		PROSSER	VA. bk. 2A pg. 083
Ephraim	16	Sep	1841	Mary	off. R. WHITE
DURBIN		and		THARL	VA. bk. 2A pg. 049
Frances	17	Dec	1827	James	off. S. REED
DURBIN		and		REED	VA. bk. 2A pg. 082
Hester	06	Dec	1838	Elijah	off. R. WHITE
DURBIN		and		COCHRAN	VA. bk. 2A pg. 082
John	10	Apr	1838	Nancy	off. R. WHITE
DURRETT		and		MENDEL	VA. bk. 01 pg. 006
Henry C.	01	Sep	1857	Sarah H.	off. A. CAMPBELL
DUVALL		and		CROTHERS	VA. bk. 2A pg. 090
Ann Hooper	12	Aug	1847	Hugh W.	off. T. NEWELL
DUVALL		and		MILLER	VA. bk. 01 pg. 005
Isaac	09	Jul	1856	Sarah	off. A. ENDSLEY
DUVALL		and		KUHN	VA. bk. 2A pg. *14
Isaac H.	22	Jun	1853	Mary D.	off. E. QUILLEN
DUVALL		and		MURPHY	VA. bk. 2A pg. 090
James M.	31	Oct	1847	Catharine	off. J. MONROE
DUVALL		and		JEFFERS	VA. bk. 2A pg. 085
Julia	03	Aug	1845	Henry	off. W. LEMON
DUVALL		and		DECAMPS	VA. bk. 2A pg. 072
Julia A.	02	Nov	1841	T.J.	off. S. FULTON
DUVALL		and		WILCOXON	VA. bk. 2A pg. 031
Matilda	14	Oct	1824	Thomas	off. G. SCOTT
DUVALL		and		LEMMON	VA. bk. 2A pg. 067
William	06	Jan	1839	Charity	off. A. YOUNG
DUVALL		and		STEWART	VA. bk. 3A pg. 051
William	06	Mar	1858	Henrietta	off. J. NAYLOR
EASTERDAY		and		SCHALK	VA. bk. 3A pg. 055
Lusetta	18	Aug	1858	Conrad	off. J. NAYLOR
EASTERDAY		and		WALTERS	WV. bk. 4A pg. 063
Magdaline	22	Jul	1869	Lucas	off. W. WHITE
EASTERDAY		and		BENTZ	VA. bk. 3A pg. 119
Martin	10	Nov	1862	Josephine	off. J. NAYLOR

38 BROOKE CO., VA./WV. LICENSES & MARRIAGES, 1797-1874

EASTINGHOUSEN		and		CHENOTH		VA. bk. 1A pg. 023
Lewis	16	Apr	1807	Sophia		off. J. PRITCHARD
EBBERT		and		HALL		WV. bk. 4A pg. 019
William B.	24	Dec	1866	Cornelia B.		off. R. NICHOLLS
EBERLINE		and		DAWSON		VA. bk. 3A pg. 071
John	24	Jun	1859	Mary A.		off. J. NAYLOR
EBERLINE		and		ELLIOTT		VA. bk. 3A pg. 071
John	24	Jun	1859	Mary A.		off. J. NAYLOR
EBIATH		and		MOREHEAD		VA. bk. 2A pg. 060
Thomas	19	Feb	1829	Margaret		off. S. REED
EDER		and		MOORE		VA. bk. 2A pg. 037
Thomas	21	Dec	1825	Sarah		off. G. SCOTT
EDERSON		and		PRITCHARD		VA. bk. 1A pg. 077
John	16	Nov	1812	Sarah		off. J. PRITCHARD
EDGINGTON		and		MARSHALL		VA. bk. 1A pg. 028
Aaron	15	Aug	1807	Rachel		off. UNKNOWN
EDGINGTON		and		MEEK		VA. bk. 1A pg. 053
John	07	Jun	1810	Susanah		off. J. PRITCHARD
EDGINGTON		and		MC CADDEN		VA. bk. 1A pg. 054
Mary	--	--	1810	John		off. J. DODDRIDGE
EDGINGTON		and		BRICELAND		VA. bk. 1A pg 060
Rachel	20	May	1810	James		off. E. MACURDY
EDGINGTON		and		EDWARD		VA. bk. 1A pg. 038
Rebeccah	07	Nov	1799	David		off. J. DODDRIDGE
EDGINGTON		and		HARTFORD		VA. bk. 1A pg. 044
Sally	--	--	1802	George		off. UNKNOWN
EDIE		and		FLOWERS		VA. bk. 2A pg. 083
Catharine	15	Jul	1841	Isaac		off. R. WHITE
EDIE		and		SCOTT		VA. bk. 2A pg. 026
Elizabeth	04	Mar	1823	Robert		off. G. SCOTT
EDIE		and		ANDREWS		VA. bk. 2A pg. 073
John	24	Mar	1842	Rebecca		off. J. HERBERT
EDIE		and		NEWELL		VA. bk. 2A pg. 049
Lydia	28	Nov	1826	John		off. S. REED
EDIE		and		WYLIE		VA. bk. 1A pg. 069
Mary	25	Apr	1814	David		off. UNKNOWN
EDIE		and		PUGH		VA. bk. 2A pg. 083
Samuel	29	Dec	1841	Elizabeth		off. R. WHITE
EDWARD		and		EDGINGTON		VA. bk. 1A pg. 038
David	07	Nov	1799	Rebeccah		off. J. DODDRIDGE
ELLIOT		and		STEVENSON		VA. bk. 1A pg. 013
Andrew	16	Aug	1803	Lurea		off. E. MACURDY
ELLIOT		and		MORROW		VA. bk. 1A pg. 076
Nancy	29	Dec	1812	James		off. UNKNOWN
ELLIOTT		and		FINLEY		VA. bk. 1A pg. 069
Alivia	16	Apr	1814	David		off. UNKNOWN
ELLIOTT		and		ELLIOTT		VA. bk. 2A pg. 015
Ann (...)	25	Mar	1820	Thomas		off. L. BROWNING
ELLIOTT		and		CHRISTIAN		VA. bk. 3A pg. 043
Jemima	13	Oct	1857	Edmund		off. J. NAYLOR
ELLIOTT		and		GORSUCH		VA. bk. 2A pg. *16
Mary	13	Nov	1853	John B.		off. S. TOMPKINS

BROOKE CO., VA./WV. LICENSES & MARRIAGES, 1797-1874   39

Name		Day	Month	Year	Spouse		Reference
ELLIOTT			and		EBERLINE		VA. bk. 3A pg. 071
Mary A.		24	Jun	1859	John		off. J. NAYLOR
ELLIOTT			and		ELLIOTT		VA. bk. 2A pg. 015
Thomas		25	Mar	1820	Ann (...)		off. L. BROWNING
ELLIOTT			and		TAYLOR		VA. bk. 3A pg. 019
Thomas		25	Apr	1853	Elizabeth		off. J. NAYLOR
ELSESSER			and		EMIG		WV. bk. 4A pg. 011
Julia		10	Oct	1866	Peter		off. R. NICHOLLS
ELSON			and		NICHOLLS		VA. bk. 2A pg. 069
Alexander M.		30	Jan	1840	Charlotte		off. M. TELCHENELL
ELSON			and		EVERET		VA. bk. 1A pg. 068
Edward		05	Sep	1814	Blanch		off. J. PRITCHARD
ELSON			and		CARIENS		WV. bk. 3A pg. 154
John Randolph		08	Mar	1865	Amanda		off. H. SHEPHERD
EMIG			and		ELSESSER		WV. bk. 4A pg. 011
Peter		10	Oct	1866	Julia		off. R. NICHOLLS
ENCIL			and		GIST		VA. bk. 2A pg. 048
John		18	Oct	1827	Helen		off. A. CAMPBELL
ENGLE			and		WILLIAMS		VA. bk. 1A pg. 043
Margaret		25	Feb	1802	John		off. J. DODDRIDGE
ERVIN			and		DAVIS		WV. bk. 4A pg. 132
James		26	Nov	1873	Susan		off. W. LATIMER
EVANS			and		JOHNSON		VA. bk. 2A pg. 074
Margaretta V.		04	Jun	1842	William		off. C. WEIRICK
EVANS			and		SWEARINGEN		VA. bk. 2A pg. 084
Mary		02	Jun	1842	George		off. R. WHITE
EVANS			and		FORD		VA. bk. 1A pg. 040
Mary		07	Dec	1802	Robert		off. J. DODDRIDGE
EVERET			and		ELSON		VA. bk. 1A pg. 068
Blanch		05	Sep	1814	Edward		off. J. PRITCHARD
EVERET			and		BURT		VA. bk. 1A pg. 030
James		20	Oct	1807	Elisabeth		off. J. HUGHES
EVERET			and		MC CAULY		VA. bk. 1A pg. 030
Sally		09	Jul	1807	John		off. J. HUGHES
EVERETT			and		CAMPBELL		VA. bk. 2A pg. 052
Elisabeth		24	Jan	1828	John		off. G. BUCHANAN
EVERETT			and		HALLY		VA. bk. 2A pg. *14
Elizabeth		31	Mar	1853	John		off. E. QUILLEN
EVERETT			and		BRACKEN		WV. bk. 4A pg. 061
Maggie V.		03	May	1869	Caleb H.		off. W. WHITE
FACKSBERRY			and		SMITH		VA. bk. 2A pg. 003
Lavina		19	Feb	1818	Stephen		off. E. MACURDY
FARNSWORTH			and		MC DOWELL		VA. bk. 2A pg. 083
Henry		21	Apr	1842	Eleanor		off. R. WHITE
FARNSWORTH			and		LOWERY		VA. bk. 2A pg. 060
Sylvia		26	Mar	1829	William		off. S. REED
FARQUER			and		BOYD		VA. bk. 2A pg. 059
Elisabeth		06	May	1828	Mathew		off. E. SMITH
FARQUER			and		STEWART		VA. bk. 01 pg. 004
John (Jr.)		28	Feb	1856	Mary Ann		off. A. ENDSLEY
FARQUER			and		LUCAS		VA. bk. 3A pg. 058
Keziah		11	Nov	1858	John		off. J. NAYLOR

40 BROOKE CO., VA./WV. LICENSES & MARRIAGES, 1797-1874

Name		Day	Month	Year	Spouse	Reference
FARQUER	and				WEAR	VA. bk. 3A pg. 041
Susan		12	Sep	1857	James	off. J. NAYLOR
FENWICK	and				MURPHY	VA. bk. 2A pg. 090
Edith		26	Oct	1847	Joseph	off. J. MONROE
FENWICK	and				SWINER	VA. bk. 01 pg. 004
Edward		28	Mar	1856	Bell	off. S. NESBITT
FERREL	and				ARBAUGH	VA. bk. 2A pg. 067
William		07	Feb	1839	Catharine	off. A. YOUNG
FETRAR	and				PHEISTER	WV. bk. 4A pg. 015
Frederick		10	Nov	1866	Isabella	off. R. NICHOLLS
FIELDING	and				WILLIAMS	VA. bk. 2A pg. 050
Joseph		02	Mar	1827	Rebecca	off. L. BROWNING
FILLY	and				MC DUGAN	WV. bk. 4A pg. 128
Mary		04	Oct	1873	James	off. W. LATIMER
FILSON	and				COULTER	VA. bk. 2A pg. 029
Joseph		27	Jan	1824	Hannah	off. G. BUCHANAN
FINK	and				MAY	VA. bk. 01 pg. 004
Elizabeth		11	May	1856	Jacob	off. A. ENDSLEY
FINLEY	and				MERRYMAN	VA. bk. 3A pg. 128
Alexander		28	Apr	1863	Mary	off. W. NAYLOR
FINLEY	and				ELLIOTT	VA. bk. 1A pg. 069
David		16	Apr	1814	Alivia	off. UNKNOWN
FINLEY	and				HENNES	VA. bk. 2A pg. 058
John		17	Feb	1830	Elizabeth	off. T. BEEKS
FISHER	and				CARTER	VA. bk. 01 pg. 004
Catharine		06	Sep	1855	Stephen	off. J. MEANS
FISHER	and				BUCKEY	WV. bk. 4A pg. 057
Mary		14	Jan	1869	John	off. W. WHITE
FITCH	and				WITMORE	VA. bk. 2A pg. 009
Dyer		22	Sep	1819	Amelia	off. O. JENNINGS
FITCH	and				NELSON	PA. bk. 01 pg. 054
K.A.		10	Aug	1858	Nathaniel	off. J. MC CONAUGHY
FITZ-PATRICK	and				HINES	WV. bk. 4A pg. 041
Anne		29	Jan	1868	Bartley	off. H. MELVIN
FITZ-RANDOLPH	and				CONGLETON	VA. bk. 2A pg. 010
Cornelius		13	Mar	1819	Julianna	off. A. CAMPBELL
FLANEGAN	and				CRISWELL	VA. bk. 2A pg. 082
Margaret		23	Aug	1838	Thomas	off. R. WHITE
FLEMING	and				ATWELL	WV. bk. 3A pg. 132
Amelia Francis		13	Oct	1863	Mervin R.	off. H. SHEPHERD
FLEMING	and				AMICK	VA. bk. 2A pg. 061
James		29	Sep	1832	Catherine	off. G. MC CASHEY
FLEMING	and				WORSTELL	WV. bk. 4A pg. 091
Leander B.		01	Jun	1871	Mary L.	off. W. WHITE
FLEMING	and				DUNCAN	WV. bk. 4A pg. 108
Miriam		28	Feb	1872	John A.	off. W. LATIMER
FLEMING	and				SIMPSON	VA. bk. 3A pg. 084
Nannie E.		26	Apr	1860	Charles L.	off. J. NAYLOR
FLETCHER	and				ROBINSON	VA. bk. 3A pg. 071
Isaac		07	Jul	1859	Ellen	off. J. NAYLOR
FLOWERS	and				EDIE	VA. bk. 2A pg. 083
Isaac		15	Jul	1841	Catharine	off. R. WHITE

BROOKE CO., VA./WV. LICENSES & MARRIAGES, 1797-1874   41

Surname	Given	Day	Month	Year	and	Spouse Surname	Spouse Given	Source
FLOWERS	J.W.	03	Sep	1874	and	MC CONKEY	Mary	WV. bk. 4A pg. 141 off. J. LATIMER
FOGG	Thomas P.	07	Nov	1843	and	CONNELL	Sarah	VA. bk. 2A pg. 078 off. J. HARRISON
FORBES	James C.	03	Jul	1868	and	HARCUM	Ella	WV. bk. 4A pg. 048 off. C. MELVIN
FORBES	Mary	07	May	1861	and	CARMICHAEL	James W. M.	VA. bk. 3A pg. 101 off. J. NAYLOR
FORBES	Thomas	08	Aug	1866	and	CARMICHAEL	Nancy E.	WV. bk. 3A pg. 167 off. R. NICHOLLS
FORBES	William	18	Mar	1871	and	GELSTHORPE	Alice	WV. bk. 4A pg. 085 off. W. WHITE
FORBES	William	18	Mar	1871	and	WILLOUGHBY	Alice	WV. bk. 4A pg. 085 off. W. WHITE
FORBS	James	22	Oct	1857	and	JAMES	Nancy Ann	VA. bk. 3A pg. 043 off. J. NAYLOR
FORD	Hugh	18	Dec	1800	and	KIRK	Nancy	VA. bk. 1A pg. 007 off. UNKNOWN
FORD	Robert	07	Dec	1802	and	EVANS	Mary	VA. bk. 1A pg. 040 off. J. DODDRIDGE
FORMAN	Charles D.	03	Apr	1817	and	PARKS	Ann	VA. bk. 2A pg. 001 off. E. MACURDY
FORSE	John H.	05	Jul	1871	and	MC LAUGHLIN	Elizabeth	WV. bk. 4A pg. 093 off. W. WHITE
FORSYTHE	Oliver C.	24	May	1872	and	GRIMES	Sarah A.	WV. bk. 4A pg. 112 off. W. LATIMER
FOSTER	Elisabeth	29	Sep	1825	and	DORSEY	Owen	VA. bk. 2A pg. 036 off. N. HEADINGTON
FOSTER	G.B.	17	Oct	1837	and	HANNAH	Elizabeth G.	VA. bk. 2A pg. 064 off. A. YOUNG
FOSTER	James Jacob	27	Mar	1860	and	BENCE	Cidonia	VA. bk. 3A pg. 082 off. J. NAYLOR
FOSTER	Margaret	19	Dec	1811	and	TAYLOR	Ebenezer	VA. bk. 1A pg. 056 off. J. PRITCHARD
FOULK	Elizabeth	15	Mar	1829	and	JONES	Isaac	VA. bk. 2A pg. 061 off. A. COLEMAN
FOULK	Henry	05	Jul	1838	and	SILSON	Juliana	VA. bk. 2A pg. 064 off. A. YOUNG
FOUTS	Absalom	12	Oct	1819	and	HEDGES	Nancy	VA. bk. 2A pg. 017 off. S. LAUCK
FOUTS	Andrew	24	Dec	1829	and	STECALES	Sophia	VA. bk. 2A pg. 058 off. T. BEEKS
FOUTS	Jacob	24	Mar	1818	and	HEDGES	Margaret	VA. bk. 2A pg. 018 off. S. LAUCK
FOUTS	Mary	--	Sep	1809	and	HEDGES	Isaac	VA. bk. 1A pg. 035 off. UNKNOWN
FOUTS	Nancy	04	Dec	1825	and	WELLS	Isaiah	VA. bk. 2A pg. 038 off. T. BEEKS
FOUTS	William	09	May	1816	and	HEDGES	Johanna	VA. bk. 2A pg. 007 off. S. LAUCK
FOWLER	Amy	09	Jun	1826	and	MAGEE	John	VA. bk. 2A pg. 050 off. N. HEADINGTON

42 BROOKE CO., VA./WV. LICENSES & MARRIAGES, 1797-1874

Name				Spouse	Reference
FOWLER Hiram	27	Nov	1856	and SMITH Francis	VA. bk. 01 pg. 005 off. G. CRANAGE
FOWLER John	--	--	1826	and MACLARY Sarah	VA. bk. 2A pg. 053 off. N. HEADINGTON
FOWLER Mary	05	Jan	1844	and ALLISON James	VA. bk. 2A pg. 084 off. R. WHITE
FOWLER Mary Jane	29	Dec	1848	and DOUGLASS Robert N.	VA. bk. 2A pg. 094 off. T. MC CLEARY
FOWLER Mr.	--	--	1809	and ATKINSON Miss.	VA. bk. 1A pg. 048 off. J. DODDRIDGE
FOWLER Nancy	07	Sep	1856	and HEDGES Otho	VA. bk. 01 pg. 004 off. E. QUILLEN
FOWLER Richard	29	Jan	1807	and PARKY Mary	VA. bk. 1A pg. 026 off. E. MACURDY
FOWLER Richard	21	Apr	1814	and BAKER Elizabeth	VA. bk. 1A pg. 073 off. J. PRITCHARD
FOWLER Verlinda	16	Aug	1838	and ARBUCKEL Isaac	VA. bk. 2A pg. 082 off. R. WHITE
FOWLER William	29	Apr	1802	and CALLENDINE Elizabeth	VA. bk. 1A pg. 040 off. J. DODDRIDGE
FOWLER William B.	14	Nov	1839	and PUGH Ann	VA. bk. 2A pg. 083 off. R. WHITE
FOWLER William M.	15	Mar	1853	and WIGGINS Domatrius	VA. bk. 2A pg. *16 off. S. TOMPKINS
FOWLER Zadok	19	Dec	1850	and HUNTER Francis	VA. bk. 2A pg. *07 off. J. MC GAN
FRANCIS Joseph S.	09	Dec	1824	and PELLY Rachel	VA. bk. 2A pg. 031 off. J. CAZAD
FRANK Amanda E.	03	Aug	1861	and BOWMAN John (Jr.)	VA. bk. 3A pg. 105 off. S. NAYLOR
FRANK William	25	Dec	1856	and PATTERSON Mary Eliza.	VA. bk. 01 pg. 005 off. E. QUILLEN
FRATER Robert F.	07	May	1869	and HAGGERTY Rossa A.	WV. bk. 4A pg. 062 off. W. WHITE
FRAZIER George A.	22	Mar	1864	and MC LAUGHLIN Carrie	WV. bk. 3A pg. 140 off. H. SHEPHERD
FRAZIER Hiram	30	Aug	1871	and GREEN Amelia J.	WV. bk. 4A pg. 095 off. W. WHITE
FRAZIER John	24	Apr	1860	and KEITH Margaret	VA. bk. 3A pg. 084 off. J. NAYLOR
FRAZIER John	24	Apr	1860	and MARTIN Margaret	VA. bk. 3A pg. 084 off. J. NAYLOR
FRAZIER John B.	23	May	1852	and SOMERVILLE Mary	VA. bk. 2A pg. *11 off. H. SNYDER
* FRAZIER John Wesley	07	Dec	1864	and BRIAN Elizabeth	WV. bk. 3A pg. 148 off. H. SHEPHERD
FRAZIER Laura A.	04	Apr	1872	and CALDERWOOD D.W. (Rev.)	WV. bk. 4A pg. 111 off. W. LATIMER
FREEMAN James L.	02	Oct	1838	and GAMBLE Priscilla	VA. bk. 2A pg. 065 off. J. BEATTY
FREEMAN Patty	04	Sep	1804	and DAVIS David	VA. bk. 1A pg. 015 off. J. PRITCHARD

BROOKE CO., VA./WV. LICENSES & MARRIAGES, 1797-1874   43

Groom Surname	Groom Given	Day	Month	Year	Bride Surname	Bride Given	Reference
FRESHWATER	Frances	02	Aug	1838	JONES	Josiah	VA. bk. 2A pg. 065 off. A. YOUNG
FRESHWATER	John	25	Jan	1867	CALDWELL	Martha	WV. bk. 4A pg. 021 off. H. MELVIN
FRESHWATER	Melissa A.	27	Nov	1868	SANDERS	Fredus A.	WV. bk. 4A pg. 053 off. S. QUEST
FRESHWATER	Milton R.	26	Jun	1871	PATTERSON	Melissa	WV. bk. 4A pg. 093 off. W. WHITE
FRESHWATER	Philip	21	Sep	1830	ARCHER	Eleanor	VA. bk. 2A pg. 057 off. G. BUCHANAN
FRESHWATER	Reuben	28	Apr	1842	RIDGLEY	Lydia	VA. bk. 2A pg. 084 off. R. WHITE
FRESHWATER	Sarah Jane	28	Nov	1862	ROBINSON	Elijah	VA. bk. 3A pg. 120 off. J. NAYLOR
FRESHWATER	Sarah Jane	24	Apr	1871	JONES	Robert T.	WV. bk. 4A pg. 086 off. W. WHITE
FRIKE	Johanna	16	May	1864	JOHNS	Gustav	WV. bk. 3A pg. 141 off. H. SHEPHERD
FRITZ	Andrew D.	12	Mar	1860	RUSSELL	Caroline E.	VA. bk. 3A pg. 083 off. J. NAYLOR
FULLER	Samuel	02	Jan	1838	WEAVER	Matilda	VA. bk. 2A pg. 064 off. A. YOUNG
FULLERTON	Henry	25	Jan	1859	OWINGS	Verlinda	VA. bk. 3A pg. 062 off. J. NAYLOR
FULLUM	Catharine	26	Oct	1861	GARRISON	Johnson L.	VA. bk. 3A pg. 106 off. S. NAYLOR
FULTON	William P.	07	Aug	1872	WHITE	Mattie J.	WV. bk. 4A pg. 115 off. W. LATIMER
GAFFNEY	Michael	02	Jan	1861	HOW	Mary	VA. bk. 3A pg. 099 off. J. NAYLOR
GALLAHER	Mary	25	Mar	1841	HOOVER	William	VA. bk. 2A pg. 071 off. L. BURTON
GALLAHER	Nancy M.	08	Nov	1841	KING	Robert R.	VA. bk. 2A pg. 074 off. J. SPENCER
GALLOWAY	Nancy (...)	--	--	1809	GALLOWAY	Samuel	VA. bk. 1A pg. 049 off. J. DODDRIDGE
GALLOWAY	Samuel	--	--	1809	GALLOWAY	Nancy (...)	VA. bk. 1A pg. 049 off. J. DODDRIDGE
GAMBLE	Allen	01	Feb	1821	BAKER	Mary	VA. bk. 2A pg. 016 off. J. PRITCHARD
GAMBLE	Henry	26	Jan	1841	LOVE	Elizabeth	VA. bk. 2A pg. 070 off. J. HERBERT
GAMBLE	Lucinda	19	Jan	1843	WELCH	William	VA. bk. 2A pg. 084 off. R. WHITE
GAMBLE	Priscilla	02	Oct	1838	FREEMAN	James L.	VA. bk. 2A pg. 065 off. J. BEATTY
GAMBLE	Prudence	22	Aug	1808	SANDERS	Lewis	VA. bk. 1A pg. 032 off. J. PRITCHARD
GANT	John	25	Apr	1801	DODDRIDGE	Eleanor R.	VA. bk. 1A pg. 043 off. J. DODDRIDGE
GANT	Juliana P.	02	Feb	1854	KUHN	Adam	VA. bk. 01 pg. 002 off. S. TOMPKINS

44 BROOKE CO., VA./WV. LICENSES & MARRIAGES, 1797-1874

Surname	Given	Day	Month	Year	Spouse Surname	Spouse Given	Reference
GARDNER	David	10	Feb	1820	DONOVAN	Ann	VA. bk. 2A pg. 011 off. J. PRITCHARD
GARDNER	James C.	21	Jul	1857	SANDERS	Mary E.	VA. bk. 01 pg. 006 off. S. TEAGARDEN
GARDNER	James M.	11	Nov	1863	MC GUIRE	Mary Agnes	WV. bk. 3A pg. 133 off. H. SHEPHERD
GARDNER	Levi	28	Oct	1847	VANORDSTRAND	Hannah	VA. bk. 2A pg. 091 off. J. GALLOWAY
GARDNER	Rachel	29	May	1844	PUSEY	William C.	VA. bk. 2A pg. 084 off. R. WHITE
GARDNER	William	09	Mar	1854	HENDRICKS	Charity	VA. bk. 01 pg. 002 off. S. TOMPKINS
GARRETT	Robert W.	27	Apr	1870	TARR	Mary F.	WV. bk. 4A pg. 071 off. W. WHITE
GARRISON	Johnson L.	26	Oct	1861	FULLUM	Catharine	VA. bk. 3A pg. 106 off. S. NAYLOR
GASS	Margaret	13	Nov	1800	SHEPHARD	Enoch	VA. bk. 1A pg. 007 off. UNKNOWN
GASS	Mary	09	Aug	1803	MITCHELL	Francis	VA. bk. 1A pg. 037 off. J. DODDRIDGE
GASSAGE	Benjamin	16	Nov	1797	MC GUIRE	Nancy	VA. bk. 1A pg. 003 off. J DODDRIDGE
GASSAGE	Mary Ann	13	Sep	1849	CHESTER	John	VA. bk. 2A pg. *02 off. J. IRWIN
GASSAGE	Samuel	02	Mar	1848	LEE	Margaret	VA. bk. 2A pg. 092 off. J. MONROE
GATWOOD	Susanna	14	Feb	1828	LEE	Samuel	VA. bk. 2A pg. 059 off. E. SMITH
GAUSE	Caroline	13	Jul	1868	LETZKUS	George	WV. bk. 4A pg. 049 off. C. MELVIN
GAUSE	Diana	10	Dec	1868	HALL	Charles	WV. bk. 4A pg. 053 off. S. QUEST
GAUSE	Mary	21	Apr	1870	SCHUEY	Peter	WV. bk. 4A pg. 071 off. W. WHITE
GEER	Hannah	05	Sep	1844	CARRIER	John	VA. bk. 2A pg. 084 off. R. WHITE
GELSTHORPE	Alice	18	Mar	1871	FORBES	William	WV. bk. 4A pg. 085 off. W. WHITE
GELSTHORPE	John	07	Sep	1852	RODGERS	Marg't Jane	VA. bk. 3A pg. 003 off. J. NAYLOR
GEORGE	Frances	24	Sep	1853	JONES	Patrick H.	VA. bk. 3A pg. 025 off. J. NAYLOR
GEORGE	James	18	Jan	1869	BUCKEY	Mary L.	WV. bk. 4A pg. 057 off. W. WHITE
GEORGE	Samuel	09	Nov	1854	MILLER	Elenora	VA. bk. 01 pg. 003 off. E. QUILLEN
GEORGE	Samuel	12	Jul	1858	KIMBERLAND	Elizabeth	VA. bk. 3A pg. 054 off. J. NAYLOR
GIBSON	Joseph	14	Jun	1821	GIBSON	Mary (...)	VA. bk. 2A pg. 019 off. G. BUCHANAN
GIBSON	Mary (...)	14	Jun	1821	GIBSON	Joseph	VA. bk. 2A pg. 019 off. G. BUCHANAN

BROOKE CO., VA./WV. LICENSES & MARRIAGES, 1797-1874   45

Surname	Given	Day	Month	Year	Spouse Surname	Spouse Given	Location
GIBSON			and		MARSHALL		VA. bk. 1A pg. 070
	Nancy	25	May	1815		Alexander	off. UNKNOWN
GIFFORD			and		HUPP		WV. bk. 4A pg. 055
	James E.	29	Dec	1868		Mary E.	off. S. QUEST
GILBERT			and		BALLETT		WV. bk. 3A pg. 160
	Bridget	11	Sep	1865		Edward	off. H. SHEPHERD
GILCRIST			and		HAGAN		VA. bk. 2A pg. 089
	Ruenmia	22	Jul	1847		John B.	off. J. MONROE
GILES			and		RICHARDS		VA. bk. 2A pg. 079
	Mary Ann	01	Feb	1844		Samuel (Jr.)	off. S. WORTHINGTON
GILES			and		BECK		VA. bk. 2A pg. 017
	Samuel	22	Jun	1820		Lenore	off. S. LAUCK
GILLESPIE			and		GREEN		VA. bk. 2A pg. 069
	William	22	Aug	1839		Hester Ann	off. M. TELCHENELL
GILMORE			and		DUFFY		WV. bk. 4A pg. 133
	F.H.	02	Dec	1873		Anne	off. W. LATIMER
GILSTON			and		STEVENSON		VA. bk. 1A pg. 013
	Moses	24	Apr	1804		Nancy	off. E. MACURDY
GIST			and		DAUMONT		VA. bk. 01 pg. 005
	Clara A.	03	Sep	1856		Alfred A.	off. G. CRANAGE
GIST			and		BROWN		VA. bk. 3A pg. 107
	Clara A.	11	Nov	1861		Leondas	off. S. NAYLOR
GIST			and		JONES		VA. bk. 2A pg. 016
	Elizabeth	24	Aug	1820		Lewis	off. T. BEEKS
GIST			and		HOWARD		VA. bk. 2A pg. 069
	Elizabeth	17	Oct	1839		Abraham	off. M. TELCHENELL
GIST			and		ENCIL		VA. bk. 2A pg. 048
	Helen	18	Oct	1827		John	off. A. CAMPBELL
GIST			and		HAMMOND		VA. bk. 1A pg. 038
	James	24	Nov	1799		Rachel	off. J. DODDRIDGE
GIST			and		BEALL		VA. bk. 2A pg. 059
	Louisana	14	Feb	1828		Bazel	off. E. SMITH
GIST			and		HANEY		VA. bk. 1A pg. 029
	Nancy	25	Nov	1807		Thomas	off. J. PRITCHARD
GIST			and		BAXTER		VA. bk. 1A pg. 014
	Samuel	01	Jul	1804		Ann	off. J. PRITCHARD
GIST			and		REEVES		VA. bk. 3A pg. 122
	Sarah B.	24	Nov	1862		John C.	off. J. NAYLOR
GIST			and		BURNS		WV. bk. 4A pg. 063
	William H.	08	Sep	1869		Callie	off. W. WHITE
GIVEN			and		HUNTER		VA. bk. 1A pg. 060
	Rachel	06	Mar	1810		James	off. E. MACURDY
GLASS			and		BROWN		VA. bk. 1A pg. 004
	Ann	12	Sep	1797		John	off. J. HUGHES
GLASS			and		MARTIN		VA. bk. 1A pg. 021
	Ann	--	--	1806		Robert	off. UNKNOWN
GLASS			and		WRIGHTMAN		WV. bk. 4A pg. 116
	Francis C.	28	Aug	1872		Ella V.	off. W. LATIMER
GLASS			and		WILLIAMSON		VA. bk. 3A pg. 100
	James	01	Mar	1861		Anne G.	off. J. NAYLOR
GLASS			and		MC DUGAN		WV. bk. 3A pg. 164
	John J.	10	May	1866		Wealthy E.	off. R. NICHOLLS

Name		Day	Month	Year	Spouse	Reference
GLASS			and		LAZEAR	WV. bk. 4A pg. 043
Margaret		19	Feb	1868	Robert M.	off. H. MELVIN
GLASS			and		VANSICKLE	WV. bk. 4A pg. 135
Robert		20	Feb	1874	Ellie	off. J. LATIMER
GLASS			and		WALKER	VA. bk. 2A pg. *14
Robert P.		30	May	1853	Anne	off. E. QUILLEN
GLASS			and		SWORDS	WV. bk. 4A pg. 036
Terrissa		01	Feb	1868	Robert M.	off. H. MELVIN
GLENN			and		JEFFERS	WV. bk. 3A pg. 135
Robert S.		22	Dec	1863	Emily	off. H. SHEPHERD
GOADING			and		TIPTON	VA. bk. 1A pg. 018
Abednigo		08	Mar	1805	Hannah	off. J. PRITCHARD
GODDARD			and		NISWANGER	VA. bk. 2A pg. 069
Mary		06	Apr	1840	George	off. M. TELCHENELL
GOOD			and		DEFFENBACH	WV. bk. 4A pg. 131
Elizabeth I.		12	Nov	1873	N. Lee	off. W. LATIMER
GOOD			and		CONGLETON	VA. bk. 2A pg. 019
Thomas		12	Oct	1820	Maria	off. A. CAMPBELL
GOOD			and		PRATHER	VA. bk. 2A pg. *14
Thomas C.		08	Feb	1853	Mary	off. S. NESBITT
GOODING			and		TIPTON	VA. bk. 1A pg. 018
Abednigo		08	Mar	1805	Hannah	off. J. PRITCHARD
GOODWIN			and		CROWLEY	VA. bk. 2A pg. 022
John		17	Feb	1820	Elizabeth	off. J. LAWS
GORDON			and		CAIN	WV. bk. 3A pg. 159
Anthony		05	Sep	1865	Catherine	off. H. SHEPHERD
GORDON			and		MOORE	VA. bk. 2A pg. 064
Jane		27	Sep	1838	James W.	off. D. HERVEY
GORDON			and		MARSH	WV. bk. 4A pg. 100
John E.		21	Nov	1871	Mary J.	off. W. LATIMER
GORDON			and		HALL	WV. bk. 3A pg. 137
Samuel		22	Feb	1864	Cynthia Ann	off. H. SHEPHERD
GORELY			and		SMITH	VA. bk. 2A pg. 094
Harriet		17	May	1848	James	off. J. GALLOWAY
GORELY			and		STRAIN	VA. bk. 1A pg. 064
John		15	Aug	1815	Hannah	off. G. SCOTT
GORRELL			and		ARCHER	VA. bk. 1A pg. 030
Margaret		09	Apr	1807	William	off. J. HUGHES
GORRELL			and		BUNTING	VA. bk. 2A pg. 082
Mary		21	Mar	1838	Samuel	off. R. WHITE
GORRELL			and		BONER	VA. bk. 1A pg. 078
Sarah		29	Dec	1814	William	off. W. WILLSON
GORSUCH			and		ELLIOTT	VA. bk. 2A pg. *16
John B.		13	Nov	1853	Mary	off. S. TOMPKINS
GORSUCH			and		LAZIER	VA. bk. 1A pg. 051
Miss.		--	--	1809	Mr.	off. J. DODDRIDGE
GOSHORN			and		HOLLEY	VA. bk. 2A pg. *14
Isabella		25	Oct	1852	Thomas	off. S. NESBITT
GOUDY			and		BLANKENSOP	WV. bk. 4A pg. 033
Mary R.		24	Oct	1867	John	off. C. MELVIN
GOULD			and		HEDGES	VA. bk. 2A pg. 088
Lewis B.		05	Mar	1846	Mary A.	off. H. CREE,JR.

GOULDING		and		WYNN	VA. bk. 2A pg. 060
William	18	Dec	1828	Lydia	off. E. SMITH
GOURLEY		and		WALKER	VA. bk. 3A pg. 054
James M.	06	Jul	1858	Catharine T.	off. J. NAYLOR
GOURLEY		and		ARCHER	VA. bk. 2A pg. 021
William	12	Feb	1822	Nancy	off. G. BUCHANAN
GOVER		and		RUSSELL	VA. bk. 01 pg. 005
Clara	25	Jan	1857	Samuel	off. E. QUILLEN
GRAFTON		and		BONSALL	VA. bk. 2A pg. 066
Christiana	04	Jul	1839	Thomas	off. W. SCULL
GRAFTON		and		CHAPMAN	VA. bk. 2A pg. 091
Nathan B.	20	Jan	1848	Rachel	off. E. REGAL
GRAFTON		and		BAKER	VA. bk. 1A pg. 054
William	04	Dec	1807	Nancy	off. J. PRITCHARD
GRAHAM		and		RALSTON	VA. bk. 2A pg. 055
Robert	16	Jun	1830	Kesiah	off. J. MC KENNAR
GRANDFIELD		and		CASNER	VA. bk. 3A pg. 070
Dennis M.	24	Jun	1859	Scintha M.	off. J. NAYLOR
GRANT		and		BROWN	VA. bk. 1A pg. 045
Eleanor	--	--	1802	John	off. UNKNOWN
GRATIGNY		and		CUMMINS	VA. bk. 2A pg. 076
Cyrus	01	Feb	1843	Mary E.	off. C. BEST
GREEN		and		SPAHR	VA. bk. 2A pg. 066
Abigal	28	Jul	1839	Jesse	off. J. BOYLE
GREEN		and		FRAZIER	WV. bk. 4A pg. 095
Amelia J.	30	Aug	1871	Hiram	off. W. WHITE
GREEN		and		SCAMAHORN	WV. bk. 4A pg. 141
Arabella V.	22	Sep	1874	George W.	off. J. LATIMER
GREEN		and		HALL	VA. bk. 3A pg. 117
Callie S.	27	Aug	1862	Leonard C.	off. J. NAYLOR
GREEN		and		SHRINER	WV. bk. 4A pg. 003
Caroline	02	Nov	1865	William	off. H. SHEPHERD
GREEN		and		RICHARDSON	WV. bk. 4A pg. 034
Drusilla	30	Oct	1867	I.L.	off. H. MELVIN
GREEN		and		ADAMS	VA. bk. 2A pg. 060
Elisabeth	06	Oct	1828	Samuel	off. E. SMITH
GREEN		and		HERVEY	VA. bk. 2A pg. *12
Elisabeth	30	Jun	1852	Adam Faris	off. D. HERVEY
GREEN		and		GILLESPIE	VA. bk. 2A pg. 069
Hester Ann	22	Aug	1839	William	off. M. TELCHENELL
GREEN		and		CARTER	VA. bk. 2A pg. 046
Hugh	30	May	1827	Mary Anne	off. J. CAZAD
GREEN		and		SMITH	VA. bk. 2A pg. 052
Jane	01	Jul	1827	Andrew	off. L. BROWNING
GREEN		and		PARK	WV. bk. 4A pg. 131
Jennie May	19	Nov	1873	Madison W.	off. W. LATIMER
GREEN		and		BACHELL	WV. bk. 4A pg. 095
Marshall S.	19	Sep	1871	Jennie	off. W. WHITE
GREEN		and		HEDGES	VA. bk. 2A pg. *01
Mary C.	13	Jul	1848	G.W.	off. J. MOFFITT
GREEN		and		DAVIS	VA. bk. 01 pg. 006
Miriam	11	Aug	1857	Thomas M.	off. E. QUILLEN

GREEN			and		RUSSELL	VA.	bk. 2A	pg. *02
Obediah		07	Dec	1848	Maria	off. I.	DALLAS	
GREEN			and		SMITH	VA.	bk. 3A	pg. 127
Permelia		04	Mar	1863	John E.	off. J.	NAYLOR	
GREEN			and		LINTON	WV.	bk. 4A	pg. 012
Sarah		09	Oct	1866	William D.	off. R.	NICHOLLS	
GREEN			and		BOWMAN	WV.	bk. 4A	pg. 069
Thomas Hood		23	Feb	1870	Sarah	off. W.	WHITE	
GREEN			and		LUCAS	VA.	bk. 2A	pg. 038
William		25	Aug	1825	Elizabeth	off. T.	BEEKS	
GREEN			and		ANTILL	VA.	bk. 3A	pg. 053
William L.		19	May	1858	Sarah E.	off. J.	NAYLOR	
GREGORY			and		CHAPMAN	VA.	bk. 2A	pg. 056
William		22	Apr	1830	Elisabeth	off. L.	BROWNING	
GRIFFIN			and		ROBERTS	VA.	bk. 2A	pg. 076
Thomas		26	Feb	1843	Nancy	off. C.	BEST	
GRIFFITH			and		HAMILTON	VA.	bk. 1A	pg. 061
Elizabeth		10	Jul	1811	William	off. J.	DODDRIDGE	
GRIFFITH			and		COLE	VA.	bk. 3A	pg. 104
Jacob B.		26	Sep	1862	Rebecca M.	off. J.	NAYLOR	
GRIFFITH			and		ATKINSON	VA.	bk. 2A	pg. 072
Jane		22	Oct	1841	James	off. S.	FULTON	
GRIFFITH			and		OWENS	VA.	bk. 01	pg. 010
John A.		15	Feb	1860	Helen	off. J.	CALHOUN	
GRIFFITH			and		ATKINSON	VA.	bk. 2A	pg. 065
Margaret Ann		14	Feb	1839	Joseph	off. G.	BUCHANAN	
GRIFFITH			and		TRINE	VA.	bk. 1A	pg. 045
Mary		- -	- -	1802	Jacob	off.	UNKNOWN	
GRIFFITH			and		BAKER	VA.	bk. 2A	pg. 003
Rebecca		12	Nov	1818	William	off. G.	SCOTT	
GRIFFITH			and		WELLS	VA.	bk. 1A	pg. 001
Sarah		23	Jun	1797	Bezeleel	off. J.	DODDRIDGE	
GRIMES			and		MC CAUSLAND	VA.	bk. 2A	pg. 027
Elizabeth		08	Jan	1823	William	off. J.	CAZAD	
GRIMES			and		LAUGHEAD	VA.	bk. 2A	pg. 055
Jane		12	Jan	1831	Robert	off. J.	MC KENNAR	
GRIMES			and		WILLIAMS	WV.	bk. 4A	pg. 144
Lucy		24	Jun	1874	Frank	off. J.	LATIMER	
GRIMES			and		FORSYTHE	WV.	bk. 4A	pg. 112
Sarah A.		24	May	1872	Oliver C.	off. W.	LATIMER	
GRIMES			and		LOGAN	VA.	bk. 1A	pg. 040
Thomas		06	Apr	1802	Nancy	off. J.	DODDRIDGE	
GROVES			and		DUKE	VA.	bk. 2A	pg. 060
Andrew		29	Jan	1829	Catharine	off. E.	SMITH	
GUNION			and		WHITE	WV.	bk. 4A	pg. 105
James		17	Jan	1872	Mary	off. W.	LATIMER	
GUNION			and		ADAMS	WV.	bk. 4A	pg. 037
Margaret		08	Jan	1868	John A.	off. H.	MELVIN	
GUNION			and		BRANNON	VA.	bk. 3A	pg. 094
Wilson		20	Sep	1860	Rebecca	off. J.	NAYLOR	
GUY			and		MILLER	VA.	bk. 3A	pg. 126
Shepherd L.		20	Feb	1863	Agnes A.	off. J.	NAYLOR	

Name		Date		Spouse	Reference
HACKETT		and		MC CAMANT	VA. bk. 2A pg. *15
Peter	15	Aug	1853	Elizabeth	off. E. QUILLEN
HAGAN		and		GILCRIST	VA. bk. 2A pg. 089
John B.	22	Jul	1847	Ruenmia	off. J. MONROE
HAGAN		and		PILLINGS	VA. bk. 2A pg. *14
John B.	11	Nov	1852	Margaret	off. S. NESBITT
HAGAN		and		PERRY	VA. bk. 2A pg. 058
Sarah	24	Jan	1830	John	off. D. MERRYMAN
HAGEMAN		and		JOHNSTON	VA. bk. 2A pg. *01
Isaac	01	Feb	1849	Margaret	off. J. MOFFITT
HAGGERTY		and		FRATER	WV. bk. 4A pg. 062
Rossa A.	07	May	1869	Robert F.	off. W. WHITE
HAGIN		and		SMITH	VA. bk. 2A pg. 009
Jane	05	Oct	1819	Joseph	off. G. BUCHANAN
HAINES		and		WALKER	VA. bk. 2A pg. 035
David	28	Dec	1825	Sarah	off. N. HEADINGTON
HAINES		and		DAVIS	WV. bk. 4A pg. 120
Thomas J.	28	Nov	1872	Rachel	off. W. LATIMER
HALE		and		JONES	VA. bk. 3A pg. 037
Balinda	05	Jan	1854	Jackson	off. J. NAYLOR
HALE		and		CULLIN	VA. bk. 2A pg. *15
Emma S.	07	Nov	1853	Alexander H.	off. G. LOWMAN
HALE		and		WILCOXON	VA. bk. 2A pg. 041
Margaret	20	Apr	1826	Anthony	off. J. BROWNING, JR.
HALES		and		ADAMS	VA. bk. 2A pg. *02
Amity	08	Apr	1849	Benjamin F.	off. I. DALLAS
HALL		and		SHRINER	WV. bk. 4A pg. 003
Caroline (Mrs.)	02	Nov	1865	William	off. H. SHEPHERD
HALL		and		GAUSE	WV. bk. 4A pg. 053
Charles	10	Dec	1868	Diana	off. S. QUEST
HALL		and		EBBERT	WV. bk. 4A pg. 019
Cornelia B.	24	Dec	1866	William B.	off. R. NICHOLLS
HALL		and		GORDON	WV. bk. 3A pg. 137
Cynthia Ann	22	Feb	1864	Samuel	off. H. SHEPHERD
HALL		and		DOWLER	VA. bk. 01 pg. 003
David	09	Nov	1854	Mahala	off. C. HOLMES
HALL		and		MILLER	WV. bk. 4A pg. 092
Elizabeth	02	Jun	1871	James L.	off. W. WHITE
HALL		and		GREEN	VA. bk. 3A pg. 117
Leonard C.	27	Aug	1862	Callie S.	off. J. NAYLOR
HALL		and		PADEN	WV. bk. 4A pg. 034
Lewis C.	23	Nov	1867	Ella	off. H. MELVIN
HALL		and		SPEIDEL	VA. bk. 3A pg. 013
Margaret	29	Jan	1853	Clemens	off. J. NAYLOR
HALL		and		MC KEE	WV. bk. 4A pg. 102
Mary E.	14	Feb	1872	James A.	off. W. LATIMER
HALL		and		PORTER	VA. bk. 1A pg. 049
Sally	--	--	1808	Thomas	off. UNKNOWN
HALLIE		and		PRIEST	WV. bk. 4A pg. 077
Micha	26	Sep	1870	William	off. W. WHITE
HALLY		and		EVERETT	VA. bk. 2A pg. *14
John	31	Mar	1853	Elizabeth	off. E. QUILLEN

Name		Date		Spouse	Reference
HALSTEAD	and			STEVENS	VA. bk. 1A pg. 053
Catherine	24	Apr	1809	Ezra	off. J. PRITCHARD
HALSTED	and			WILLIAMSON	WV. bk. 4A pg. 143
Mary A.	10	Oct	1874	Mathew H.	off. J. LATIMER
HAMBLETON	and			BOYCE	VA. bk. 1A pg. 062
Mary	06	Feb	1812	Timothy	off. J. PRITCHARD
HAMILTON	and			CLINTON	VA. bk. 1A pg. 083
Daniel	02	Nov	1815	Sarah Ann	off. UNKNOWN
HAMILTON	and			SPENCER	VA. bk. 2A pg. 084
Daniel	15	Nov	1843	Lydia L.	off. R. WHITE
HAMILTON	and			HOBBS	VA. bk. 2A pg. 031
Elizabeth	01	Dec	1824	Nathaniel	off. G. SCOTT
HAMILTON	and			PLATTENBURGH	VA. bk. 2A pg. 049
Isabella	04	Oct	1827	Levi	off. S. REED
HAMILTON	and			MAHON	VA. bk. 3A pg. 100
James S.	05	Mar	1861	Anne E.	off. J. NAYLOR
HAMILTON	and			MORROW	VA. bk. 2A pg. 017
John	07	Mar	1820	Elizabeth	off. S. LAUCK
HAMILTON	and			WELLS	VA. bk. 2A pg. 023
John	11	Apr	1822	Nancy	off. L. BROWNING
HAMILTON	and			JESTER	VA. bk. 2A pg. *16
Rachel	08	Dec	1853	David	off. G. LOWMAN
HAMILTON	and			BROWNLEE	VA. bk. 2A pg. *06
Sophia	28	Aug	1850	Joseph	off. R. WHITE
HAMILTON	and			WELLS	VA. bk. 2A pg. 070
Susannah	09	Jan	1840	George	off. J. SWAYZE
HAMILTON	and			MC CORMACK	VA. bk. 1A pg. 072
Thomas	12	Feb	1812	Sarah	off. J. PRITCHARD
HAMILTON	and			RAY	VA. bk. 2A pg. 024
Thomas	14	Nov	1822	Rebecca	off. G. BUCHANAN
HAMILTON	and			GRIFFITH	VA. bk. 1A pg. 061
William	10	Jul	1811	Elizabeth	off. J. DODDRIDGE
HAMMOND	and			TILLINGHART	VA. bk. 1A pg. 046
Charles	--	--	1803	Sally	off. UNKNOWN
HAMMOND	and			WAUGH	VA. bk. 3A pg. 096
Elizabeth	07	Dec	1860	James	off. J. NAYLOR
HAMMOND	and			BELL	VA. bk. 1A pg. 047
Henry	--	--	1803	Miss.	off. J. DODDRIDGE
HAMMOND	and			TARR	VA. bk. 2A pg. 091
Mary	13	Jan	1848	Campbell (Jr.)	off. T. NEWELL
HAMMOND	and			GIST	VA. bk. 1A pg. 038
Rachel	24	Nov	1799	James	off. J. DODDRIDGE
HAMMOND	and			BUCHANAN	VA. bk. 2A pg. 094
Sarah	05	Oct	1848	Thomas	off. T. NEWELL
HAMMOND	and			BELL	VA. bk. 1A pg. 047
Suky	--	--	1809	Mr.	off. J. DODDRIDGE
HANCOCK	and			MORGAN	VA. bk. 2A pg. 079
John	14	Mar	1844	Emily	off. S. WORTHINGTON
HANEY	and			BRIGGS	WV. bk. 4A pg. 027
Henry	19	Jun	1867	Clara E.	off. H. MELVIN
HANEY	and			PARSONS	WV. bk. 3A pg. 166
James M.	11	Jun	1866	Olivia	off. R. NICHOLLS

BROOKE CO., VA./WV. LICENSES & MARRIAGES, 1797-1874   51

HANEY		and		DAILY		WV. bk. 3A pg. 156
John	28	Jun	1865	Elizabeth		off. H. SHEPHERD
HANEY		and		THOMPSON		WV. bk. 4A pg. 070
Margaret	24	Mar	1870	Robert		off. W. WHITE
HANEY		and		GIST		VA. bk. 1A pg. 029
Thomas	25	Nov	1807	Nancy		off. J. PRITCHARD
HANNA		and		SCOTT		WV. bk. 4A pg. 045
J.G.	09	Mar	1868	Jane A.		off. H. MELVIN
HANNAH		and		FOSTER		VA. bk. 2A pg. 064
Elizabeth G.	17	Oct	1837	G.B.		off. A. YOUNG
HANNAH		and		SHIRLY		VA. bk. 2A pg. 002
Polly	08	Feb	1816	William		off. E. MACURDY
HANSON		and		CRAWFORD		VA. bk. 1A pg. 021
James	02	Jul	1806	Ann		off. UNKNOWN
HANSON		and		BANE		VA. bk. 2A pg. 058
Louisa	09	Feb	1829	Hugh		off. T. BEEKS
HAPNER		and		DEIGHTON		VA. bk. 3A pg. 112
Charles Wm.	13	Feb	1862	Ophelia		off. J. NAYLOR
HARCUM		and		FORBES		WV. bk. 4A pg. 048
Ella	03	Jul	1868	James C.		off. C. MELVIN
HARDIN		and		RAINSFORTH		VA. bk. 2A pg. *08
Mary	12	Sep	1851	Job		off. C. JACKSON
HARDING		and		QUEST		WV. bk. 4A pg. 039
Joseph E.	24	Dec	1867	Minerva J.		off. H. MELVIN
HARDING		and		KIMBERLAND		VA. bk. 3A pg. 075
Margaret Ann	18	Oct	1859	Campbell		off. J. NAYLOR
HARKNESS		and		KINKAID		VA. bk. 2A pg. *02
John	24	Aug	1848	Maria		off. I. DALLAS
HARPER		and		MUNTY		VA. bk. 2A pg. 088
Jane	08	Oct	1848	Hugh		off. J. MONROE
HARPER		and		SANDERS		VA. bk. 2A pg. 071
John	01	Jul	1841	Catharine		off. J. GALLOWAY
HARPER		and		SMITH		VA. bk. 1A pg. 004
Sally	14	Dec	1797	John		off. J. DODDRIDGE
HARPER		and		DUNN		VA. bk. 2A pg. 004
Sarah	27	Feb	1817	Robert		off. G. SCOTT
HARPER		and		STEWART		VA. bk. 2A pg. 083
William	03	Jun	1841	Jane		off. R. WHITE
HARRIS		and		CORRIEGYS		VA. bk. 2A pg. 074
Benjamin F.	18	Aug	1841	Sarah		off. W. STEVENS
HARRIS		and		ARMSTRONG		VA. bk. 2A pg. 060
Jacob	26	Mar	1829	Nancy		off. S. REED
HARRIS		and		COLE		VA. bk. 1A pg. 071
James	06	Jun	1815	Sarah		off. W. WILLSON
HARRIS		and		COX		VA. bk. 2A pg. 059
Mathias	06	May	1828	Susannah		off. E. SMITH
HARRIS		and		THOMPSON		VA. bk. 2A pg. 074
Sarah	11	Nov	1841	James		off. W. STEVENS
HARRIS		and		BROWNING		VA. bk. 3A pg. 066
Sarah J.	24	Mar	1859	Jasper		off. J. NAYLOR
HART		and		MERCER		VA. bk. 2A pg. 049
Betsy	07	Jun	1827	William		off. S. REED

Surname	Given	Day	Month	Year	Spouse Surname	Spouse Given	Reference
HART	Sarah	20	May	1819	ATEN	John	VA. bk. 2A pg. 008 off. G. SCOTT
HARTFORD	George	--	--	1802	EDGINGTON	Sally	VA. bk. 1A pg. 044 off. UNKNOWN
HARTFORD	Rachel	22	Jan	1850	AGNEW	James M.	VA. bk. 2A pg. *03 off. T. NEWELL
HARVEY	Amos D.	29	Oct	1868	KIRKER	Narcissa	WV. bk. 4A pg. 052 off. S. QUEST
HARVEY	Wm. Hamilton	13	Sep	1870	LEWIS	Virginia	WV. bk. 4A pg. 076 off. W. WHITE
HASEN	Mary	15	Sep	1815	PETERSON	Peter	VA. bk. 1A pg. 064 off. G. SCOTT
HASLETT	William K.	02	Dec	1874	CARUTH	Rachel B.	WV. bk. 4A pg. 146 off. J. LATIMER
HAUTE	Elizabeth	08	Mar	1813	HUNTER	Richard	VA. bk. 1A pg. 082 off. UNKNOWN
HAVELIN	John	20	Apr	1848	BOND	Elizabeth	VA. bk. 2A pg. 093 off. J. MONROE
HAWKINS	Margaret	17	Dec	1825	WHITE	Aubey?	VA. bk. 2A pg. 040 off. J. CAZAD
HAWKINS	Sarah	14	Oct	1812	DAVISON	William	VA. bk. 1A pg. 072 off. J. PRITCHARD
HAWKINS	William S.	09	Jul	1859	TURNER	Georgeanna	VA. bk. 3A pg. 072 off. J. NAYLOR
HAWLEY	Andrew	27	Mar	1842	BAKER	Elizabeth	VA. bk. 2A pg. 078 off. J. HARRISON
HAYDEN	Thomas W.	17	Mar	1842	LOVE	Sarah	VA. bk. 2A pg. 075 off. J. GALLOWAY
HAYS	David	08	Sep	1825	SIMPSON	Rebecca	VA. bk. 2A pg. 038 off. G. BUCHANAN
HAYS	Elizabeth	09	Aug	1854	JACK	James	VA. bk. 01 pg. 002 off. D. HERVEY
HAYS	Jane	19	Dec	1822	MOSS	William	VA. bk. 2A pg. 025 off. G. BUCHANAN
HAYS	John N.	29	Aug	1866	MATTHEWS	Lavinia S.	WV. bk. 4A pg. 008 off. R. NICHOLLS
HAYS	Julia Ann	01	Jan	1856	PUGH	John	VA. bk. 01 pg. 004 off. D. HERVEY
HAYS	Lettice	20	Nov	1832	WILLIAMS	George	VA. bk. 2A pg. 063 off. R. BROWN
HAYS	Mary A.	26	Apr	1869	NICHOLLS	Alexander C.	WV. bk. 4A pg. 061 off. W. WHITE
HAYS	Samuel	21	Aug	1810	MEEK	Elizabeth	VA. bk. 1A pg. 072 off. J. PRITCHARD
HAYS	William	21	Apr	1842	WOODROW	Lydia	VA. bk. 2A pg. 084 off. R. WHITE
HEADINGTON	Greenberry	10	Feb	1820	MEEK	Mary	VA. bk. 2A pg. 010 off. O. JENNINGS
HEADINGTON	Isabel	19	Sep	1849	WIGGINS	John	VA. bk. 2A pg. *03 off. J. GOODWIN
HEADINGTON	John	11	Sep	1828	MURCHLAND	Jane	VA. bk. 2A pg. 059 off. E. SMITH

BROOKE CO., VA./WV. LICENSES & MARRIAGES, 1797-1874   53

HEADINGTON John	10	Jan	1870	and CARTER Martha L.	WV. bk. 4A pg. 067 off. W. WHITE
HEADINGTON Maggie E.	23	Oct	1871	and CASSIDY Joseph N.	WV. bk. 4A pg. 097 off. W. LATIMER
HEADINGTON Margaret	17	Oct	1848	and HINDMAN Samuel	VA. bk. 2A pg. 094 off. G. BUCHANAN
HEADINGTON Mary E.	17	Jan	1854	and SUTHERLAND William	VA. bk. 3A pg. 039 off. J. NAYLOR
HEADINGTON Nicholas	03	Feb	1859	and BUCHANAN Rebecca	VA. bk. 3A pg. 063 off. J. NAYLOR
HEADINGTON Rachel D.	27	Feb	1868	and SCOTT William	WV. bk. 4A pg. 044 off. H. MELVIN
HEADLEY Amanda	28	Oct	1873	and HUKILL Jesse	PA. bk. 4A pg. 129 off. W. LATIMER
HEALY Catharine	21	Jun	1859	and WELSH Edward	VA. bk. 3A pg. 070 off. J. NAYLOR
HEDGELY George	15	Oct	1852	and LETZKUS Ablon	VA. bk. 3A pg. 005 off. J. NAYLOR
HEDGES Aaron	05	Dec	1850	and LINDSAY Catharine A.	VA. bk. 2A pg. *07 off. J. MC GAN
HEDGES Amanda J.	09	Dec	1867	and WELLS William B.	WV. bk. 4A pg. 035 off. H. MELVIN
HEDGES Ann Elizabeth	18	Nov	1852	and MORGAN John M.	VA. bk. 2A pg. *14 off. S. NESBITT
HEDGES Catharine	11	Jul	1815	and STONE William	VA. bk. 1A pg. 070 off. UNKNOWN
HEDGES Charles B.	30	Jun	1852	and WALKER Hessy	VA. bk. 2A pg. *12 off. S. TOMPKINS
HEDGES Elijah	--	--	1799	and BAXTER Mary	VA. bk. 1A pg. 037 off. J. DODDRIDGE
HEDGES Elizabeth	02	Nov	1797	and MEEK Joshua	VA. bk. 1A pg. 002 off. J. DODDRIDGE
HEDGES Elizabeth	13	Jan	1820	and MORGAN Edward	VA. bk. 2A pg. 022 off. J. LAWS
HEDGES Ephraim	03	Mar	1814	and CARTER Edith	VA. bk. 1A pg. 078 off. W. WILLSON
HEDGES G.W.	13	Jul	1848	and GREEN Mary C.	VA. bk. 2A pg. *01 off. J. MOFFITT
HEDGES Isaac	--	Sep	1809	and FOUTS Mary	VA. bk. 1A pg. 035 off. UNKNOWN
HEDGES Johanna	09	May	1816	and FOUTS William	VA. bk. 2A pg. 007 off. S. LAUCK
HEDGES John M.	19	Oct	1837	and COLEMAN Sarah	VA. bk. 2A pg. 064 off. A. YOUNG
HEDGES Margaret	24	Mar	1818	and FOUTS Jacob	VA. bk. 2A pg. 018 off. S. LAUCK
HEDGES Mary	02	May	1832	and WORTHINGTON Samuel	VA. bk. 2A pg. 061 off. G. MC CASHEY
HEDGES Mary A.	05	Mar	1846	and GOULD Lewis B.	VA. bk. 2A pg. 088 off. H. CREE,JR.
HEDGES Moses	22	Jun	1826	and JONES Nancy	VA. bk. 2A pg. 042 off. C. MURRAY

HEDGES		and		FOUTS	VA.	bk. 2A	pg. 017	
Nancy	12	Oct	1819	Absalom	off. S. LAUCK			
HEDGES		and		BONAR	VA.	bk. 2A	pg. 075	
Nancy	12	Jan	1843	George	off. C. WEIRICK			
HEDGES		and		CLAYTON	VA.	bk. 01	pg. 004	
Otho	07	Sep	1856	Nancy	off. E. QUILLEN			
HEDGES		and		FOWLER	VA.	bk. 01	pg. 004	
Otho	07	Sep	1856	Nancy	off. E. QUILLEN			
HEDGES		and		CRIDER	VA.	bk. 3A	pg. 048	
Permelia	20	Jan	1858	William	off. J. NAYLOR			
HEDGES		and		VIERS	VA.	bk. 2A	pg. 064	
Rebecca Ann	13	Nov	1833	A.E.	off. G. ROBINSON			
HEDGES		and		NOLAND	VA.	bk. 1A	pg. 034	
Ruth	--	Sep	1809	James	off. UNKNOWN			
HEDGES		and		COOPER	VA.	bk. 3A	pg. 093	
Sallie B.	19	Sep	1860	John M.	off. J. NAYLOR			
HEDGES		and		MILLER	VA.	bk. 2A	pg. 007	
Sarah	11	Feb	1817	David	off. S. LAUCK			
HEDGES		and		COX	VA.	bk. 2A	pg. 038	
Sarah	25	May	1825	Joseph	off. T. BEEKS			
HEDGES		and		WARD	VA.	bk. 2A	pg. *17	
Sarah Eliza.	15	Dec	1853	William B.	off. W. LONG			
HEDGES		and		SNEDIKER	VA.	bk. 2A	pg. 080	
Susan	25	Oct	1821	George	off. S. LAUCK			
HEDGES		and		BLANKENSOP	VA.	bk. 2A	pg. 064	
Thomas	04	Mar	1838	Rosett	off. A. YOUNG			
HEDGES		and		DUNLAP	VA.	bk. 1A	pg. 008	
William	15	Aug	1802	Sarah	off. J. HUGHES			
HEDGES		and		WILSON	WV.	bk. 4A	pg. 036	
William B.	01	Jan	1868	Mary/Rebecca	off. H. MELVIN			
HELM		and		ANDERSON	VA.	bk. 2A	pg. 086	
George K.	31	Dec	1845	Catharine	off. W. LEMON			
HELMICK		and		BURGOYNE	PA.	bk. 4A	pg. 080	
Andrew S.	09	Nov	1870	Rebecca J.	off. W. WHITE			
HELMS		and		BRINDLEY	VA.	bk. 01	pg. 003	
Luisa	--	Nov	1854	Zachariah	off. E. QUILLEN			
HELSTINE		and		SICKLER	WV.	bk. 4A	pg. 148	
Mary	26	Dec	1874	John Francis	off. C. TURNER			
HEMPHILL		and		JONES	WV.	bk. 4A	pg. 139	
George T.	08	Jun	1874	Lena E.	off. J. LATIMER			
HENDERSON		and		CAMPBELL	VA.	bk. 2A	pg. 067	
Andrew	17	Sep	1839	Isabella J. E.	off. J. GALLOWAY			
HENDERSON		and		WILLSON	VA.	bk. 1A	pg. 009	
Elisabeth	04	Jul	1799	James	off. UNKNOWN			
HENDERSON		and		LYONS	VA.	bk. 2A	pg. 063	
Emeline	27	Dec	1832	William	off. R. BROWN			
HENDERSON		and		MC CASKEY	VA.	bk. 1A	pg. 067	
Jane	25	Jan	1814	William	off. UNKNOWN			
HENDRICKS		and		MILLER	WV.	bk. 4A	pg. 020	
Catharine M.	29	Dec	1866	Robert L.	off. R. NICHOLLS			
HENDRICKS		and		GARDNER	VA.	bk. 01	pg. 002	
Charity	09	Mar	1854	William	off. S. TOMPKINS			

BROOKE CO., VA./WV. LICENSES & MARRIAGES, 1797-1874   55

Surname	Given	Day	Month	Year	Surname	Given	Reference
HENDRICKS	Edward	08	Dec	1842	SNYDER	Rebecca	VA. bk. 2A pg. 076 off. G. BUCHANAN
HENDRICKS	Mary E.	30	Oct	1872	CAMPBELL	Barclay	WV. bk. 4A pg. 118 off. W. LATIMER
HENDRIX	Rebecca	02	Aug	1827	HINDMAN	James	VA. bk. 2A pg. 049 off. S. REED
HENNES	Elizabeth	17	Feb	1830	FINLEY	John	VA. bk. 2A pg. 058 off. T. BEEKS
HENNES	Mary Jane	15	Mar	1855	SOULES	Washington	VA. bk. 01 pg. 003 off. W. LONG
HENRY	Mary	23	Jan	1812	SMITH	Joseph	VA. bk. 1A pg. 072 off. J. PRITCHARD
HENRY	Sarah	22	Jun	1824	MALHOLEN	Thomas	VA. bk. 2A pg. 032 off. J. CAZAD
HERFORD	Ann	05	Apr	1833	BLAIR	Robert	VA. bk. 2A pg. 063 off. G. ROBINSON
HERON	Joseph	11	Jan	1869	HUMBLE	Ann	WV. bk. 4A pg. 056 off. W. WHITE
HERRON	Nancy	08	Oct	1850	MAGEE	John	VA. bk. 2A pg. *05 off. D. HERVEY
HERVEY	Adam Faris	30	Jun	1852	GREEN	Elisabeth	VA. bk. 2A pg. *12 off. D. HERVEY
HERVEY	Mary	19	Aug	1863	MORGAN	Wm. Finley	WV. bk. 3A pg. 131 off. H. SHEPHERD
HESSEY	Caroline	26	Mar	1865	CRISS	Jacob P.	WV. bk. 3A pg. 154 off. H. SHEPHERD
HESSEY	James	23	Dec	1838	MILLER	Mary Ann	VA. bk. 2A pg. 067 off. A. YOUNG
HESSEY	Jennie	30	Apr	1872	PARK	George M.	WV. bk. 4A pg. 111 off. W. LATIMER
HESSEY	Kate	01	Mar	1871	BLANKENSOP	George	WV. bk. 4A pg. 084 off. W. WHITE
HESSEY	Mary Ann	31	May	1855	SIMPSON	Isaac G.	VA. bk. 01 pg. 003 off. E. QUILLEN
HESTON	John	23	Apr	1842	RACE	Tamar	VA. bk. 2A pg. 074 off. W. STEVENS
HEWIT	Nancy	14	Feb	1816	DOWNING	James	VA. bk. 1A pg. 073 off. G. SCOTT
HEWIT	Thomas	04	Jan	1827	BRENNEMAN	Nancy	VA. bk. 2A pg. 044 off. J. BROWNING, JR.
HIATE	Elizabeth	08	Mar	1813	HUNTER	Richard	VA. bk. 1A pg. 082 off. UNKNOWN
HIBBIT	Nancy	09	Jun	1800	COOK	Thomas	VA. bk. 1A pg. 041 off. J. DODDRIDGE
HIBBITTS	Daniel	14	Apr	1843	WYLIE	Isabel	VA. bk. 2A pg. 077 off. J. SCOTT
HIBBITTS	Jane A.	05	May	1841	HUSTON	James	VA. bk. 2A pg. 083 off. R. WHITE
HIBBITTS	Margaret B.	24	Dec	1838	KING	M. Simpson	VA. bk. 2A pg. 082 off. R. WHITE
HIBBITTS	Sarah	19	Nov	1839	LOWRY	John	VA. bk. 2A pg. 083 off. R. WHITE

56 BROOKE CO., VA./WV. LICENSES & MARRIAGES, 1797-1874

Surname	Given	Day	Mo	Year	Spouse	Reference
HICKMAN	Bayard	27	Jun	1860	JOHNSON Eleanor Jane	VA. bk. 3A pg. 086 off. J. NAYLOR
HILL	Salathiel	24	Oct	1863	BUKER Mary	WV. bk. 3A pg. 132 off. H. SHEPHERD
HILL	Salathiel	24	Oct	1863	MYERS Mary (Mrs.)	WV. bk. 3A pg. 132 off. H. SHEPHERD
HILL	Thomas	13	Apr	1848	MARSH Mary Ann	VA. bk. 2A pg. 093 off. T. NEWELL
HINDMAN	Anna L.	20	Aug	1870	HOOKER Richard	WV. bk. 4A pg. 073 off. W. WHITE
HINDMAN	Charity	30	Nov	1854	PARKS Robert	VA. bk. 01 pg. 003 off. W. LEMON
HINDMAN	Elisabeth	11	Oct	1839	CLELAND Robert	VA. bk. 2A pg. 068 off. J. GALLOWAY
HINDMAN	Elizabeth	14	May	1867	MC CLURG John I.	WV. bk. 4A pg. 024 off. H. MELVIN
HINDMAN	Elizabeth Jane	27	Sep	1842	CAMPBELL George W.	VA. bk. 2A pg. 077 off. J. SCOTT
HINDMAN	Francis	06	Sep	1841	PEOPLES Eleanor	VA. bk. 2A pg. *06 off. E. SMITH
HINDMAN	Harriet	04	Mar	1848	DEFFENBAUGH William H.	VA. bk. 2A pg. 093 off. G. BUCHANAN
HINDMAN	Harriet	25	Nov	1849	MURCHLAND Robert	VA. bk. 2A pg. *04 off. J. GALLOWAY
HINDMAN	James	02	Aug	1827	HENDRIX Rebecca	VA. bk. 2A pg. 049 off. S. REED
HINDMAN	John (Jr.)	09	Mar	1866	WRIGHT Nancy Jane	WV. bk. 3A pg. 123 off. H. SHEPHERD
HINDMAN	Kate E.	11	Dec	1873	SANDERS Jonathan D.	WV. bk. 4A pg. 133 off. W. LATIMER
HINDMAN	Maggie M.	06	Oct	1874	MEEK Thomas V.	WV. bk. 4A pg. 142 off. J. LATIMER
HINDMAN	Margaret	08	Feb	1849	BARBER Abraham	VA. bk. 2A pg. *05 off. J. STOCKTON
HINDMAN	Margaret Jane	16	Mar	1867	VIRTUE William	WV. bk. 4A pg. 025 off. H. MELVIN
HINDMAN	Mary	08	Nov	1827	DONOVAN Cornelius	VA. bk. 2A pg. 048 off. G. BUCHANAN
HINDMAN	Mathew	22	Feb	1871	ORAM Addie	WV. bk. 4A pg. 083 off. W. WHITE
HINDMAN	Samuel	23	Jun	1808	DAVIS Catherine	VA. bk. 1A pg. 031 off. J. PRITCHARD
HINDMAN	Samuel	17	Oct	1848	HEADINGTON Margaret	VA. bk. 2A pg. 094 off. G. BUCHANAN
HINDMAN	Samuel	20	Mar	1868	MURCHLAND Nancy	WV. bk. 4A pg. 046 off. H. MELVIN
HINDMAN	Samuel	02	Oct	1872	MARSH Narcissa	WV. bk. 01 pg. 021 off. J. GRAHAM
HINDMAN	Samuel B.	15	Nov	1866	CARTER Mary	WV. bk. 4A pg. 014 off. R. NICHOLLS
HINDMAN	Samuel L.	23	Nov	1851	SIMERAL Elizabeth	VA. bk. 2A pg. *09 off. L. AULD

BROOKE CO., VA./WV. LICENSES & MARRIAGES, 1797-1874   57

Groom	First	Day	Month	Year		Bride	Location
HINES					and	FITZ-PATRICK	WV. bk. 4A pg. 041
	Bartley	29	Jan	1868		Anne	off. H. MELVIN
HINES					and	PATTERSON	VA. bk. 1A pg. 065
	Isaac	27	Jan	1815		Sarah	off. E. MACURDY
HINKSTON					and	THORP	VA. bk. 1A pg. 036
	William	13	Apr	1808		Charlotte	off. J. HUGHES
HIRP					and	SMITH	VA. bk. 2A pg. *14
	Joseph	10	Mar	1853		Sarah	off. S. NESBITT
HITCHCOCK					and	CLOSEN	VA. bk. 2A pg. 075
	Josiah	03	May	1843		Sophia	off. C. WEIRICK
HOBBS					and	RAY	VA. bk. 2A pg. 060
	Hanson	02	Dec	1828		Elisabeth	off. S. REED
HOBBS					and	SMITH	VA. bk. 2A pg. 069
	John	17	Oct	1839		Rachel	off. M. TELCHENELL
HOBBS					and	RAY	VA. bk. 2A pg. 032
	Leonard	15	Jul	1824		Margaret	off. L. BROWNING
HOBBS					and	HUTSON	VA. bk. 2A pg. 070
	Margaret	31	Jan	1841		John	off. J. HERBERT
HOBBS					and	HAMILTON	VA. bk. 2A pg. 031
	Nathaniel	01	Dec	1824		Elizabeth	off. G. SCOTT
HOFFMAN					and	UHLRICH	WV. bk. 4A pg. 140
	Frederick	20	Jun	1874		Emma F.	off. J. LATIMER
HOGG					and	BROWNING	VA. bk. 2A pg. *12
	Hannah	16	Jun	1852		Clinton	off. W. SUMMERS
HOGG					and	WELLS	WV. bk. 3A pg. 137
	Harriet	01	Feb	1864		Bazil (Jr.)	off. H. SHEPHERD
HOGG					and	MC CORD	VA. bk. 2A pg. *12
	Sarah Ann	07	Sep	1852		George W.	off. H. SNYDER
HOGG					and	PUMPHREY	VA. bk. 2A pg. 027
	Thomas	03	Apr	1823		Elizabeth	off. T. BEEKS
HOLLEY					and	KIMBERLAND	VA. bk. 3A pg. 114
	Samuel G.	15	May	1862		Sallie	off. J. NAYLOR
HOLLEY					and	GOSHORN	VA. bk. 2A pg. *14
	Thomas	25	Oct	1852		Isabella	off. S. NESBITT
HOLLINGSWORTH					and	ADAMS	VA. bk. 1A pg. 039
	Joshua	22	Nov	1802		Mary	off. J. DODDRIDGE
HOLLY					and	WARTENBEE	VA. bk. 1A pg. 017
	Edward	23	May	1805		Mary	off. J. PRITCHARD
HOLMES					and	RUSSELL	VA. bk. 1A pg. 059
	Isabella	23	May	1811		Arthur	off. E. MACURDY
HOLMES					and	RALSTON	VA. bk. 2A pg. 006
	Priscilla	13	Nov	1817		Joseph	off. E. MACURDY
HOLTON					and	CAMPBELL	VA. bk. 3A pg. 121
	Thomas F.	17	Nov	1862		Ellen M.	off. J. NAYLOR
HOOD					and	PUMPHREY	VA. bk. 2A pg. 016
	James	25	May	1820		Credilla	off. T. BEEKS
HOOD					and	BROWN	VA. bk. 2A pg. 017
	Rachel	23	Dec	1819		Joseph	off. S. LAUCK
HOOD					and	BOWMAN	VA. bk. 2A pg. 048
	Sarah	08	Aug	1827		Jacob	off. S. BROCKUNIER
HOOKER					and	SANDERS	WV. bk. 4A pg. 092
	Cornelia Hull	13	Jun	1871		Frank A.	off. W. WHITE

58   BROOKE CO., VA./WV. LICENSES & MARRIAGES, 1797-1874

HOOKER		and		KUHN		WV. bk. 3A pg. 134
Cynanthia	16	Dec	1863	Albert W.		off. H. SHEPHERD
HOOKER		and		HINDMAN		WV. bk. 4A pg. 073
Richard	20	Aug	1870	Anna L.		off. W. WHITE
HOOKER		and		SWEARINGEN		PA., bk. 01 pg. 023
Sallie J.	09	Jul	1874	George		off. J. SHIELDS
HOOKER		and		TUCKER		WV. bk. 4A pg. 139
Sarah P.	25	May	1874	William		off. J. LATIMER
HOOVER		and		PERRY		VA. bk. 2A pg. *16
Sarah Jane	22	Dec	1853	Andrew J.		off. G. LOWMAN
HOOVER		and		GALLAHER		VA. bk. 2A pg. 071
William	25	Mar	1841	Mary		off. L. BURTON
HORN		and		SCHUEY		WV. bk. 4A pg. 016
George	26	Nov	1866	Barbara		off. R. NICHOLLS
HOUGH		and		PELLY		WV. bk. 4A pg. 087
John W.	24	Apr	1871	Francine R.		off. W. WHITE
HOUSEHOLDER		and		RODGERS		VA. bk. 2A pg. 084
John	20	Feb	1844	Margaret		off. R. WHITE
HOUSTON		and		MC DONALD		WV. bk. 4A pg. 107
James F.	19	Feb	1872	Angeline		off. W. LATIMER
HOW		and		GAFFNEY		VA. bk. 3A pg. 099
Mary	02	Jan	1861	Michael		off. J. NAYLOR
HOWARD		and		GIST		VA. bk. 2A pg. 069
Abraham	17	Oct	1839	Elizabeth		off. M. TELCHENELL
HOWARD		and		MC CONKEY		VA. bk. 01 pg. 003
W.W.	23	Nov	1854	Maria		off. C. HOLMES
HOWE		and		SMITH		VA. bk. 2A pg. 075
Sarah Ann	21	Aug	1842	Jesse S.		off. S. GRAFTON
HOWLET		and		BRIERLY		VA. bk. 1A pg. 026
Elizabeth	04	Mar	1807	Thomas		off. UNKNOWN
HOWLETT		and		STRAIN		VA. bk. 2A pg. 074
Drusilla	14	Jul	1842	John D.		off. C. WEIRICK
HUBBARD		and		TALBOTT		VA. bk. 2A pg. 074
John	23	Nov	1841	Michael		off. W. STEVENS
HUDSON		and		MORGAN		VA. bk. 3A pg. 102
Cynthia A.	08	Jun	1861	Henry C.		off. J. NAYLOR
HUDSON		and		SCOTT		VA. bk. 2A pg. *04
George B. (Rev.	12	Feb	1850	Rachel A.		off. R. HOPKINS
HUDSON		and		MORGAN		WV. bk. 3A pg. 129
M. Belle	17	Jul	1863	John (Jr.)		off. H. SHEPHERD
HUFF		and		LEE		VA. bk. 3A pg. 016
Hannah	29	Mar	1853	Duncan		off. J. NAYLOR
HUFFMAN		and		STRONG		VA. bk. 1A pg. 034
Elizabeth	--	Aug	1809	Samuel		off. UNKNOWN
HUGGINS		and		SHAW		VA. bk. 1A pg. 063
Mary	24	Aug	1815	Charles		off. L. BROWNING
HUGHES		and		MC GEE		VA. bk. 2A pg. 072
Elizabeth	14	Apr	1841	W.T.		off. T. MAGILL
HUGHES		and		WEYMAN		VA. bk. 1A pg. 042
John	18	Sep	1800	Mary		off. J. DODDRIDGE
HUKILL		and		ORAM		VA. bk. 3A pg. 121
Elizabeth	17	Nov	1862	Philip C.		off. J. NAYLOR

BROOKE CO., VA./WV. LICENSES & MARRIAGES, 1797-1874   59

Name		Day	Month	Year		Spouse	Reference
HUKILL	Ethelinda	02	Sep	1867	and	WAUGH David	WV. bk. 4A pg. 029 off. C. MELVIN
HUKILL	James	23	Jan	1858	and	ROBINSON Providence	VA. bk. 3A pg. 049 off. J. NAYLOR
HUKILL	Jesse	28	Oct	1873	and	HEADLEY Amanda	PA. bk. 4A pg. 129 off. W. LATIMER
HUKILL	Joseph	03	Feb	1863	and	ORAM Matilda	VA. bk. 3A pg. 125 off. J. NAYLOR
HUKILL	Martin	17	Jan	1861	and	COX Sally W.	VA. bk. 3A pg. 098 off. J. NAYLOR
HUKILL	Mary	16	Jan	1865	and	MILLER David B.	WV. bk. 3A pg. 150 off. H. SHEPHERD
HUKILL	Matilda	14	Sep	1870	and	ADAMS Richard	WV. bk. 4A pg. 076 off. W. WHITE
HUKILL	William	06	May	1827	and	BANE Mary	VA. bk. 2A pg. 046 off. C. MURRAY
HULFORD	John	--	--	1809	and	COXTON Miss.	VA. bk. 1A pg. 048 off. J. DODDRIDGE
HULLIHAN	Hannah	05	May	1865	and	KELLY William	WV. bk. 3A pg. 155 off. H. SHEPHERD
HUMBLE	Ann	11	Jan	1869	and	HERON Joseph	WV. bk. 4A pg. 056 off. W. WHITE
HUNT	George C.	27	May	1841	and	PENIX Emily	VA. bk. 2A pg. 080 off. S. LAUCK
HUNTER	Catharine	13	May	1861	and	MAGEE William	VA. bk. 3A pg. 102 off. J. NAYLOR
HUNTER	Frances	21	Feb	1828	and	TARR Campbell	VA. bk. 2A pg. 059 off. E. SMITH
HUNTER	Francis	19	Dec	1850	and	FOWLER Zadok	VA. bk. 2A pg. *07 off. J. MC GAN
HUNTER	George C.	25	Mar	1852	and	WELLS Elizabeth	VA. bk. 2A pg. *11 off. C. JACKSON
HUNTER	James	06	Mar	1810	and	GIVEN Rachel	VA. bk. 1A pg. 060 off. E. MACURDY
HUNTER	John	19	Oct	1848	and	WYLIE Harriet A.	VA. bk. 2A pg. *01 off. J. MOFFITT
HUNTER	John H.	01	Dec	1853	and	SMITH Marianna L.	VA. bk. 2A pg. *17 off. W. LONG
HUNTER	John V.	12	Sep	1839	and	CREAL Ann	VA. bk. 2A pg. 067 off. G. BUCHANAN
HUNTER	Nathaniel	25	Mar	1824	and	SMITH Katharine	VA. bk. 2A pg. 038 off. T. BEEKS
HUNTER	Nathaniel	03	Oct	1850	and	SMITH Sarah E.	VA. bk. 2A pg. *06 off. J. MC GAN
HUNTER	Rebecca E.	23	Aug	1860	and	WHITE William	VA. bk. 3A pg. 090 off. J. NAYLOR
HUNTER	Richard	08	Mar	1813	and	HAUTE Elizabeth	VA. bk. 1A pg. 082 off. UNKNOWN
HUNTER	Susan B.	27	Oct	1853	and	SMITH William	VA. bk. 2A pg. *17 off. W. LONG
HUNTER	William S.	26	May	1853	and	SMITH Nancy J.	VA. bk. 2A pg. *14 off. S. NESBITT

60 BROOKE CO., VA./WV. LICENSES & MARRIAGES, 1797-1874

HUPP			and		NEELEY	VA. bk. 3A pg. 117
Emma		08	Oct	1862	Hugh N.	off. J. NAYLOR
HUPP			and		ATKINSON	VA. bk. 2A pg. 075
Isaac		26	Apr	1842	Mary Ann	off. G. BUCHANAN
HUPP			and		GIFFORD	WV. bk. 4A pg. 055
Mary E.		29	Dec	1868	James E.	off. S. QUEST
HURFORD			and		PUMPHREY	VA. bk. 2A pg. 081
Joseph E.		18	Apr	1844	Susanna	off. T. BAKER
HURFORD			and		WILCOXON	VA. bk. 1A pg. 033
Thomas		28	Sep	1809	Mary	off. J. DODDRIDGE
HUSTON			and		HIBBITTS	VA. bk. 2A pg. 083
James		05	May	1841	Jane A.	off. R. WHITE
HUSTON			and		RIDGLEY	WV. bk. 4A pg. 048
Mary V.		23	Jun	1868	William C.	off. C. MELVIN
HUTSON			and		HOBBS	VA. bk. 2A pg. 070
John		31	Jan	1841	Margaret	off. J. HERBERT
HUTSON			and		BROWN	VA. bk. 1A pg. 008
Sarah		05	Jun	1802	James	off. J. HUGHES
HUTTON			and		TONER	VA. bk. 2A pg. 022
Joseph		28	Jun	1821	Mary	off. J. LAWS
HYATE			and		BUNN	VA. bk. 1A pg. 016
Marjerit		16	Aug	1804	Benjamin	off W. WILLSON
HYATE			and		PICKET	VA. bk. 1A pg. 068
William		11	Feb	1814	Susannah	off. J. PRITCHARD
HYATT			and		BROWN	VA. bk. 1A pg. 016
Margaret		16	Aug	1804	Benjamin	off. W. WILLSON
HYDE			and		RUSH	WV. bk. 4A pg. 001
Mary		21	Oct	1865	William	off. H. SHEPHERD
INGLEBRIGHT			and		CLARK	VA. bk. 3A pg. 089
Elizabeth J.		21	Aug	1860	William A.	off. J. NAYLOR
INGLEBRIGHT			and		O'NEAL	WV. bk. 4A pg. 004
Harriet		01	Dec	1865	William J.	off. H. SHEPHERD
INGLEBRIGHT			and		ORR	WV. bk. 4A pg. 017
Levi W.		20	Dec	1866	Mary	off. R. NICHOLLS
INGLEBRIGHT			and		SMITH	VA. bk. 3A pg. 090
Lina E.		21	Aug	1860	John P.	off. J. NAYLOR
INGRAM			and		DEVORE	OH. bk. 3A pg. 164
Charles W.		03	May	1866	Ruth Ann	off. R. NICHOLLS
IRWIN			and		NELSON	VA. bk. 1A pg. 058
James		03	Aug	1810	Mary	off. J. PRITCHARD
IRWIN			and		MENDEL	VA. bk. 2A pg. *08
John L.		17	Jun	1851	Ellen	off. R. WHITE
IRWIN			and		CUMMINS	VA. bk. 2A pg. 014
Joseph		06	Sep	1820	Martha	off. J. CAZAD
JACK			and		HAYS	VA. bk. 01 pg. 002
James		09	Aug	1854	Elizabeth	off. D. HERVEY
JACKSON			and		MERCER	VA. bk. 2A pg. 060
Andrew		04	Sep	1828	Ellen	off. S. REED
JACKSON			and		KELLY	WV. bk. 4A pg. 079
Florence		08	Oct	1870	Andrew	off. W. WHITE
JACKSON			and		SANFORD	VA. bk. 2A pg. 074
John		05	Oct	1841	Sarah	off. W. STEVENS

BROOKE CO., VA./WV. LICENSES & MARRIAGES, 1797-1874   61

Surname	Given	Day	Month	Year	Spouse Surname	Spouse Given	Reference
JACKSON	Matilda	27	Dec	1827	ABRAHAMS	Robert	VA. bk. 2A pg. 049 off. S. REED
JACKSON	Philip	14	Mar	1816	TELAND	Betsy	VA. bk. 2A pg. 002 off. E. MACURDY
JACKSON	William	15	Jan	1840	MERCER	Mary	VA. bk. 2A pg. 083 off. R. WHITE
JACOB	Alice W.	08	Jun	1867	BAXTER	George A.	WV. bk. 4A pg. 026 off. H. MELVIN
JACOB	Benjamin	23	Dec	1841	ST. LEDGER	Jane	VA. bk. 2A pg. 074 off. W. STEVENS
JACOB	Charles	22	Feb	1873	MEYERS	Sallie	WV. bk. 4A pg. 123 off. W. LATIMER
JACOB	Cornelia E.	17	Nov	1874	ROBINSON	Walter A.	WV. bk. 4A pg. 146 off. J. LATIMER
JACOB	John G.	20	Dec	1859	TARR	Isabella	VA. bk. 3A pg. 078 off. J. NAYLOR
JACOBS	Samuel	21	Jan	1847	KLEIN	Margarette	VA. bk. 2A pg. 089 off. J. MONROE
JAMES	Matilda	08	Jul	1831	COULTER	James	VA. bk. 2A pg. 055 off. G. SCOTT
JAMES	Nancy Ann	22	Oct	1857	FORBS	James	VA. bk. 3A pg. 043 off. J. NAYLOR
JAMES	Surrilla	13	Nov	1856	KEMP	Adam	VA. bk. 01 pg. 005 off. E. CHRISTIAN
JAMISON	Easter	08	May	1806	CAMBLE	Alexander	VA. bk. 1A pg. 022 off. UNKNOWN
JAMISON	Mary	20	May	1856	JAMISON	Richard	VA. bk. 01 pg. 004 off. E. QUILLEN
JAMISON	Richard	20	May	1856	JAMISON	Mary	VA. bk. 01 pg. 004 off. E. QUILLEN
JARRETT	Nancy	26	Dec	1816	BAILEY	Robert	VA. bk. 2A pg. 004 off. G. SCOTT
JEFFERS	Elen	12	Feb	1826	PLATTENBURGH	John	VA. bk. 2A pg. 041 off. J. BROWNING, JR.
JEFFERS	Emily	22	Dec	1863	GLENN	Robert S.	WV. bk. 3A pg. 135 off. H. SHEPHERD
JEFFERS	Harvey	10	Jul	1873	CHESTER	Callie	WV. bk. 4A pg. 126 off. W. LATIMER
JEFFERS	Henry	03	Aug	1845	DUVALL	Julia	VA. bk. 2A pg. 085 off. W. LEMON
JEFFERS	John	03	Dec	1818	DONOVAN	Henrietta	VA. bk. 2A pg. 012 off. J. PRITCHARD
JEFFERS	Ruth Ann	11	Apr	1854	SWEARINGEN	John C.	VA. bk. 01 pg. 002 off. E. QUILLEN
JEFFERS	William	16	Mar	1848	TORREYSON	Vetessy Ann	VA. bk. 2A pg. 092 off. J. MONROE
JEFFREY	William	29	Mar	1842	SCOTT	Mary	VA. bk. 2A pg. 083 off. R. WHITE
JEFFRIES	Henry	15	Apr	1819	STEEL	Emily	VA. bk. 2A pg. 010 off. A. CAMPBELL
JENKINS	Benjamin	--	--	1802	LUTZ	Kitty	VA. bk. 1A pg. 045 off. UNKNOWN

62   BROOKE CO., VA./WV. LICENSES & MARRIAGES, 1797-1874

JENKINS		and		ANDREWS		VA. bk. 2A pg. 071
David	03	Jun	1841	Elizabeth		off. J. GALLOWAY
JENKINS		and		JONES		WV. bk. 4A pg. 099
Sylvester B.	09	Nov	1871	Mary		off. W. LATIMER
JENNINGS		and		BROWNING		WV. bk. 4A pg. 127
John	04	Sep	1873	Margaret A.		off. W. LATIMER
JEROME		and		MILLER		VA. bk. 1A pg. 078
John	16	Jun	1814	Emily		off. W. WILLSON
JESTER		and		BEAL		VA. bk. 2A pg. 059
A.O.	25	Aug	1828	Elizabeth		off. E. SMITH
JESTER		and		HAMILTON		VA. bk. 2A pg. *16
David	08	Dec	1853	Rachel		off. G. LOWMAN
JESTER		and		BUCKEY		VA. bk. 3A pg. 081
David E.	03	Jan	1860	Kate C.		off. J. NAYLOR
JESTER		and		MC KEE		VA. bk. 3A pg. 076
Mary E.	07	Nov	1859	William H.		off. J. NAYLOR
JESTY		and		MOURLAND		WV. bk. 01 pg. 014
Hugh	13	Nov	1864	Margaret		off. S. HUBER
JOHNS		and		FRIKE		WV. bk. 3A pg. 141
Gustav	16	May	1864	Johanna		off. H. SHEPHERD
JOHNSON		and		SCOTT		VA. bk. 2A pg. 073
David P.	12	May	1842	Mary Ann		off. J. HERBERT
JOHNSON		and		HICKMAN		VA. bk. 3A pg. 086
Eleanor Jane	27	Jun	1860	Bayard		off. J. NAYLOR
JOHNSON		and		WINESBURG		WV. bk. 4A pg. 114
Eli	22	Jun	1872	Elizabeth		off. W. LATIMER
JOHNSON		and		RIEN		WV. bk. 4A pg. 012
Elizabeth	29	Sep	1866	George W.		off. R. NICHOLLS
JOHNSON		and		ALEXANDER		VA. bk. 2A pg. 060
Isabella	18	Sep	1828	John		off. S. REED
JOHNSON		and		RIPLEY		WV. bk. 4A pg. 106
James	30	Apr	1872	Lena		off. W. LATIMER
JOHNSON		and		TUCKER		VA. bk. 2A pg. 072
Jane	14	Oct	1841	Martin		off. S. FULTON
JOHNSON		and		CORNELIUS		VA. bk. 1A pg. 059
Joal/Jacob	21	Aug	1810	Elizabeth		off. J. PRITCHARD
JOHNSON		and		BLACK		VA. bk. 2A pg. 060
Mary	18	Sep	1828	James		off. S. REED
JOHNSON		and		JOHNSTON		VA. bk. 2A pg. 089
Mary	05	May	1847	Nimrod		off. D. SHAMPSON
JOHNSON		and		THRASHER		VA. bk. 2A pg. *16
Sarah Ann	12	Mar	1853	Frederick A.		off. S. DUNLAP
JOHNSON		and		EVANS		VA. bk. 2A pg. 074
William	04	Jun	1842	Margaretta V.		off. C. WEIRICK
JOHNSTON		and		WHEELER		VA. bk. 1A pg. 058
Isaac	24	Mar	1811	Martha		off. J. PRITCHARD
JOHNSTON		and		BAUER		VA. bk. 1A pg. 072
James	03	May	1812	Nancy		off. J. PRITCHARD
JOHNSTON		and		MURCHLAND		VA. bk. 2A pg. 093
James	15	Jun	1848	Isabella		off. J. MONROE
JOHNSTON		and		MICK		VA. bk. 2A pg. 083
John	05	Nov	1840	Mary		off. R. WHITE

Surname	First	Day	Mo	Year	Spouse	Location
JOHNSTON	Margaret	01	Feb	1849	and HAGEMAN Isaac	VA. bk. 2A pg. *01 off. J. MOFFITT
JOHNSTON	Nimrod	05	May	1847	and JOHNSON Mary	VA. bk. 2A pg. 089 off. D. SHAMPSON
JOHNSTON	Sarah	02	May	1844	and MC ATTEE Jeremiah B.	VA. bk. 2A pg. 079 off. S. WORTHINGTON
JOHNSTON	Susan	18	Feb	1860	and O'SHANDER Jacob Charles	VA. bk. 01 pg. 009 off. G. CHESTER
JOHNSTON	William	01	Sep	1825	and COCHRAN Mary J.	VA. bk. 2A pg. 034 off. G. SCOTT
JONES	Amy H.	22	Dec	1870	and MOSS William Rose	WV. bk. 4A pg. 078 off. W. WHITE
JONES	Catherine	09	Oct	1832	and COLE William	VA. bk. 2A pg. 061 off. G. ROBINSON
JONES	Edward	26	Feb	1852	and WRIGHT Susanna	VA. bk. 2A pg. *11 off. J. STOCKTON
JONES	Ellis	09	Feb	1815	and CRAWFORD Ann	VA. bk. 1A pg. 078 off. W. WILLSON
JONES	Hannah	04	Nov	1873	and ARMSTRONG Robert	WV. bk. 4A pg. 129 off. W. LATIMER
JONES	Hattie	31	Jan	1874	and SNEDIKER Ellis M.	WV. bk. 4A pg. 135 off. W. LATIMER
JONES	Isaac	15	Mar	1829	and FOULK Elizabeth	VA. bk. 2A pg. 061 off. A. COLEMAN
JONES	Jackson	05	Jan	1854	and HALE Balinda	VA. bk. 3A pg. 037 off. J. NAYLOR
JONES	James M.	12	Oct	1867	and MILLER Elizabeth A.	WV. bk. 4A pg. 032 off. H. MELVIN
JONES	Jane	03	Apr	1830	and PERSELL William	VA. bk. 2A pg. 058 off. D. MERRYMAN
JONES	Joseph	14	Aug	1805	and CONOWAY Elisabeth	VA. bk. 1A pg. 019 off. J. PRITCHARD
JONES	Josiah	02	Aug	1838	and FRESHWATER Frances	VA. bk. 2A pg. 065 off. A. YOUNG
JONES	Josiah	08	Sep	1860	and TRUAXE Ann	VA. bk. 3A pg. 093 off. J. NAYLOR
JONES	Lena E.	08	Jun	1874	and HEMPHILL George T.	WV. bk. 4A pg. 139 off. J. LATIMER
JONES	Lewis	24	Aug	1820	and GIST Elizabeth	VA. bk. 2A pg. 016 off. T. BEEKS
JONES	Lewis	13	Apr	1826	and CRAWFORD Ann	VA. bk. 2A pg. 043 off. C. MURRAY
JONES	Margaret	06	May	1813	and PELLY James	VA. bk. 1A pg. 082 off. UNKNOWN
JONES	Mary	09	Nov	1871	and JENKINS Sylvester B.	WV. bk. 4A pg. 099 off. W. LATIMER
JONES	Nancy	22	Jun	1826	and HEDGES Moses	VA. bk. 2A pg. 042 off. C. MURRAY
JONES	Pamelia	12	Apr	1849	and PLUMMER Franklin	VA. bk. 2A pg. *01 off. J. MOFFITT
JONES	Patrick H.	24	Sep	1853	and GEORGE Frances	VA. bk. 3A pg. 025 off. J. NAYLOR

BROOKE CO., VA./WV. LICENSES & MARRIAGES, 1797-1874

Surname	Given	Day	Month	Year	Spouse Surname	Spouse Given	Location
JONES	Rebecca	13	Jan	1815	MILLER	Charles	VA. bk. 1A pg. 078 off. W. WILLSON
JONES	Robert T.	24	Apr	1871	FRESHWATER	Sarah Jane	WV. bk. 4A pg. 086 off. W. WHITE
JONES	Robert T.	24	Apr	1871	ROBINSON	Sarah Jane	WV. bk. 4A pg. 086 off. W. WHITE
JONES	Sarah Elizabeth	16	Jan	1840	DOUGHERTY	John	VA. bk. 2A pg. 069 off. M. TELCHENELL
JUSTICE	James	25	Sep	1804	MC CLOUD	Christiana	VA. bk. 1A pg. 024 off. E. MACURDY
KAY	John	28	Oct	1821	BORING	Elizabeth	VA. bk. 2A pg. 019 off. J. PRITCHARD
KEACH	James	04	Jul	1815	BONER	Jane	VA. bk. 1A pg. 070 off. UNKNOWN
KEARNS	George	01	Mar	1838	PORTERFIELD	Rachael	VA. bk. 2A pg. 064 off. G. ROBINSON
KEEN	Rosetta E.	06	Jul	1848	LOOS	Charles Louis	VA. bk. 01 pg. 012 off. A. CAMPBELL
KEENAN	Ann	01	Sep	1825	BAMBRICK	Thomas	VA. bk. 2A pg. 034 off. G. SCOTT
KEESEY	Kate	01	Mar	1871	BLANKENSOP	George	WV. bk. 4A pg. 084 off. W. WHITE
KEESEY	Nancy	23	Jul	1868	MORROW	William	WV. bk. 01 pg. 019 off. R. PRICE
KEITH	Clara Jane	21	Oct	1873	ADAMS	James A.	WV. bk. 4A pg. 128 off. W. LATIMER
KEITH	Margaret	24	Apr	1860	FRAZIER	John	VA. bk. 3A pg. 084 off. J. NAYLOR
KEITH	Margaret Ellen	10	Sep	1848	MARTIN	Isaac	VA. bk. 2A pg. 094 off. S. WORTHINGTON
KEITH	Mary	18	Oct	1849	STARR	John	VA. bk. 2A pg. *03 off. J. IRWIN
KEITH	Sallie	04	Dec	1871	BROWNLEE	James	WV. bk. 4A pg. 101 off. W. LATIMER
KEITH	Samuel	13	Nov	1858	REED	Marg't Jane	VA. bk. 3A pg. 059 off. J. NAYLOR
KELLY	Andrew	21	Sep	1867	MC MANIS	Sarah	WV. bk. 4A pg. 030 off. C. MELVIN
KELLY	Andrew	08	Oct	1870	JACKSON	Florence	WV. bk. 4A pg. 079 off. W. WHITE
KELLY	Elizabeth	02	Apr	1859	DARRAH	Thomas J.	VA. bk. 3A pg. 067 off. J. NAYLOR
KELLY	Elizabeth	17	Aug	1811	THOMPSON	Robert	VA. bk. 1A pg. 056 off. UNKNOWN
KELLY	John	--	--	1809	WILLSON	Elisabeth	VA. bk. 1A pg. 049 off. UNKNOWN
KELLY	Margaret	10	Apr	1870	KELLY	Robert	WV. bk. 01 pg. 020 off. E. BRINDLEY
KELLY	Robert	10	Apr	1870	KELLY	Margaret	WV. bk. 01 pg. 020 off. E. BRINDLEY
KELLY	Samuel	15	Jun	1813	CHAMBERS	Sarah	VA. bk. 1A pg. 067 off. UNKNOWN

BROOKE CO., VA./WV. LICENSES & MARRIAGES, 1797-1874   65

Surname	Given				and	Spouse Surname	Spouse Given	Source
KELLY	Susan Ann	20	Mar	1873	and	DAUGHERTY	George	WV. bk. 4A pg. 124 off. W. LATIMER
KELLY	Timothy	06	Nov	1817	and	RALSTON	Henrietta	VA. bk. 2A pg. 005 off. J. PRITCHARD
KELLY	William	05	May	1865	and	HULLIHAN	Hannah	WV. bk. 3A pg. 155 off. H. SHEPHERD
KELLY	William	05	May	1865	and	MORENTZ	Hannah	WV. bk. 3A pg. 155 off. H. SHEPHERD
KELLY	William F.	08	Jan	1873	and	DEGARMO	Amanda	WV. bk. 4A pg. 120 off. W. LATIMER
KEMP	Adam	13	Nov	1856	and	BURK	Surrilla (Mrs.)	VA. bk. 01 pg. 005 off. E. CHRISTIAN
KEMP	Adam	13	Nov	1856	and	JAMES	Surrilla	VA. bk. 01 pg. 005 off. E. CHRISTIAN
KEMP	Ann Elizabeth	12	Aug	1863	and	ABRAHAMS	Mort. Benton	WV. bk. 3A pg. 130 off. H. SHEPHERD
KEMP	Jesse	06	Feb	1848	and	LODGE	Amanda	VA. bk. 2A pg. 091 off. J. MONROE
KEMP	Rachel	05	Sep	1859	and	LEWIS	Edward L.	VA. bk. 3A pg. 074 off. J. NAYLOR
KEMP	William H.	29	Jul	1858	and	MC CONVILLE	Bridget	VA. bk. 3A pg. 055 off. J. NAYLOR
KENEDY	Garlan B.	14	Nov	1838	and	BRASHEARS	Mary	VA. bk. 2A pg. 067 off. A. YOUNG
KENEDY	Patrick	07	Oct	1868	and	MALOY	Ann	WV. bk. 4A pg. 050 off. S. QUEST
KENNAR	Frederica	16	Aug	1849	and	SPAIGHT	Adam	VA. bk. 2A pg. *01 off. H. KOCH
KERNS	Ann Rebecca	04	Jan	1859	and	PERRY	John	VA. bk. 3A pg. 062 off. J. NAYLOR
KERNS	Ann Rebecca J.	24	Feb	1865	and	ALEXANDER	Samuel H.	WV. bk. 3A pg. 152 off. H. SHEPHERD
KERR	Alexander	19	Aug	1817	and	BLAIR	Mary	VA. bk. 2A pg. 018 off. S. LAUCK
KERR	James L.	22	Oct	1860	and	LAUCK	Mollie L.	VA. bk. 3A pg. 095 off. J. NAYLOR
KERR	John C.	19	Feb	1850	and	NEWELL	Sarah	VA. bk. 2A pg. *05 off. J. STOCKTON
KIMBERLAND	Angeline	16	Mar	1854	and	PATTON	Thomas	VA. bk. 01 pg. 002 off. E. QUILLEN
KIMBERLAND	Campbell	18	Oct	1859	and	HARDING	Margaret Ann	VA. bk. 3A pg. 075 off. J. NAYLOR
KIMBERLAND	Cornelius H.	13	Sep	1870	and	LEWIS	Melissa	WV. bk. 4A pg. 075 off. W. WHITE
KIMBERLAND	Elizabeth	12	Jul	1858	and	GEORGE	Samuel	VA. bk. 3A pg. 054 off. J. NAYLOR
KIMBERLAND	Harriet	08	Nov	1870	and	BAILEY	William T.	WV. bk. 4A pg. 079 off. W. WHITE
KIMBERLAND	Jane	01	Mar	1865	and	LEMMON	William	WV. bk. 3A pg. 153 off. H. SHEPHERD
KIMBERLAND	Prudence	30	Oct	1838	and	ABRAHAMS	James	VA. bk. 2A pg. 067 off. A. YOUNG

Surname	Given	Day	Mon	Year		Surname	Given	Location
KIMBERLAND	Sallie	15	May	1862	and	HOLLEY	Samuel G.	VA. bk. 3A pg. 114 off. J. NAYLOR
KINDRICKS	James	05	Sep	1860	and	DONNELLY	Catherine	VA. bk. 3A pg. 091 off. J. NAYLOR
KINDRICKS	James	05	Sep	1860	and	MC FADDEN	Catherine	VA. bk. 3A pg. 091 off. J. NAYLOR
KING	Jacob	23	Aug	1853	and	DERBYSHIRE	Emily T.	VA. bk. 2A pg. *15 off. E. QUILLEN
KING	M. Simpson	24	Dec	1838	and	HIBBITTS	Margaret B.	VA. bk. 2A pg. 082 off. R. WHITE
KING	Robert R.	08	Nov	1841	and	GALLAHER	Nancy M.	VA. bk. 2A pg. 074 off. J. SPENCER
KINKAID	Jane	17	Dec	1818	and	STEEN	James	VA. bk. 2A pg. 003 off. G. BUCHANAN
KINKAID	Maria	24	Aug	1848	and	HARKNESS	John	VA. bk. 2A pg. *02 off. I. DALLAS
KINKAID	Mary A.	01	Feb	1821	and	LEE	Hugh	VA. bk. 2A pg. 020 off. E. MACURDY
KINKAID	Robert	08	Mar	1827	and	STANSBERRY	Sarah	VA. bk. 2A pg. 054 off. L. BROWNING
KIRK	Isabella	19	May	1839	and	PARK	Robert	VA. bk. 2A pg. 066 off. W. SCULL
KIRK	Martha	02	Dec	1800	and	RUSH	Enoch	VA. bk. 1A pg. 007 off. UNKNOWN
KIRK	Nancy	18	Dec	1800	and	FORD	Hugh	VA. bk. 1A pg. 007 off. UNKNOWN
KIRKER	Narcissa	29	Oct	1868	and	HARVEY	Amos D.	WV. bk. 4A pg. 052 off. S. QUEST
KIRKPATRICK	Samuel	05	Aug	1838	and	VIERS	Sarah Marg't	VA. bk. 2A pg. 065 off. A. YOUNG
KIRKWOOD	Francis	04	Mar	1852	and	ROBERTS	Jemima	VA. bk. 2A pg. *10 off. H. SNYDER
KIRKWOOD	Joseph	06	Oct	1852	and	DUNLAP	Mary Ann	VA. bk. 3A pg. 004 off. J. NAYLOR
KISSINGER	John A.	01	Nov	1853	and	BONSALL	Mary Jane	VA. bk. 3A pg. 029 off. J. NAYLOR
KLEIN	Catharine	20	Nov	1828	and	DODDRIDGE	John	VA. bk. 2A pg. 060 off. E. SMITH
KLEIN	Christopher	19	Oct	1848	and	CASNER	Elizabeth	VA. bk. 2A pg. *02 off. I. DALLAS
KLEIN	Margarette	21	Jan	1847	and	JACOBS	Samuel	VA. bk. 2A pg. 089 off. J. MONROE
KLEIN	Pamela T.	11	Mar	1852	and	SCOTT	Washington	VA. bk. 2A pg. *10 off. H. SNYDER
KLINE	Charles	27	Apr	1872	and	BENTZ	Barbara	WV. bk. 4A pg. 106 off. W. LATIMER
KLINE	Joseph	26	Jan	1826	and	BURKE	Sarah	VA. bk. 2A pg. 036 off. G. BUCHANAN
KLINE	William	03	Feb	1870	and	STEWART	Harriet	WV. bk. 4A pg. 068 off. W. WHITE
KLINEFELTER	Frances	19	Jan	1870	and	POTTER	James M.	WV. bk. 4A pg. 066 off. W. WHITE

Surname	Given	Day	Mo	Year		Spouse Surname	Spouse Given	Reference
KNEFF	John	08	Jul	1802	and	WELLS	Temperance	VA. bk. 1A pg. 041 off. J. DODDRIDGE
KNIGHT	Wilson L.	05	Oct	1868	and	STEWART Ruemma E.		WV. bk. 4A pg. 050 off. S. QUEST
KNOX	Andrew	11	Mar	1824	and	LOWRY	Margaret	VA. bk. 2A pg. 030 off. G. BUCHANAN
KNOX	James Newton	07	Sep	1865	and	UTZ	Rachel M.	WV. bk. 3A pg. 159 off. H. SHEPHERD
KNOX	John	21	Aug	1845	and	PURDY	Elizabeth	VA. bk. 2A pg. 085 off. W. LEMON
KUHN	Adam	02	Feb	1854	and	GANT	Juliana P.	VA. bk. 01 pg. 002 off. S. TOMPKINS
KUHN	Albert Wheeler	16	Dec	1863	and	HOOKER	Cynanthia	WV. bk. 3A pg. 134 off. H. SHEPHERD
KUHN	Anne H.	03	Mar	1862	and	LE MOYNE	Julius	VA. bk. 3A pg. 113 off. J. NAYLOR
KUHN	Emily M.	02	Dec	1852	and	BARCLAY	W.C.	VA. bk. 2A pg. *13 off. E. QUILLEN
KUHN	John	02	Jun	1856	and	BULLOCK	Ann	VA. bk. 01 pg. 004 off. A. ENDSLEY
KUHN	Mary D.	22	Jun	1853	and	DUVALL	Isaac H.	VA. bk. 2A pg. *14 off. E. QUILLEN
LAKE	Elisabeth	13	Feb	1873	and	MORTON	J.C.	WV. bk. 4A pg. 122 off. W. LATIMER
LALLANCE	Charles N.	02	Jun	1864	and	PARKER	Martha E.	WV. bk. 3A pg. 141 off. H. SHEPHERD
LANDIS	Evan Fairchild	04	Feb	1865	and	RUSSELL	Anna M.	WV. bk. 3A pg. 152 off. H. SHEPHERD
LANDIS	Martha A.	08	Aug	1860	and	DORLAND	George S.	VA. bk. 3A pg. 088 off. J. NAYLOR
LANE	Dutton	04	Jan	1810	and	BAXTER	Martha	VA. bk. 1A pg. 055 off. J. PRITCHARD
LANE	Elisabeth	23	Oct	1828	and	MAXWELL	Samuel S.	VA. bk. 2A pg. 060 off. S. REED
LANE	William	04	Jan	1816	and	COCHRAN	Margaret	VA. bk. 1A pg. 067 off. E. MACURDY
LANGFITT	Martha	20	Sep	1838	and	MC MILLAN	Samuel	VA. bk. 2A pg. 082 off. R. WHITE
LANGFITT	Mary	08	Apr	1842	and	MARSHALL	Aaron	VA. bk. 2A pg. 083 off. R. WHITE
LANGFITT	Obediah W.	20	Nov	1855	and	TARR	Virginia	VA. bk. 01 pg. 004 off. W. BEARD
LANNUM	Aaron	05	Feb	1873	and	LUCAS	Susan	WV. bk. 4A pg. 121 off. W. LATIMER
LANNUM	Milton	06	Mar	1871	and	LEWIS	Martha A.	WV. bk. 4A pg. 084 off. W. WHITE
LANNUM	Samuel	02	Dec	1871	and	LUCAS	Elizabeth	WV. bk. 4A pg. 101 off. W. LATIMER
LARGE	Robert E.	25	Jan	1862	and	WILKINSON	Anne	VA. bk. 3A pg. 112 off. J. NAYLOR
LATHAM	William	19	Jun	1828	and	THAYER	Ann	VA. bk. 2A pg. 060 off. S. REED

68   BROOKE CO., VA./WV. LICENSES & MARRIAGES, 1797-1874

Name		Date		Spouse	Reference
LATIMER	and			CARIENS	WV. bk. 4A pg. 006
John H.	23	Jan	1866	Narcissa	off. H. SHEPHERD
LATIMER	and			LEWIS	WV. bk. 4A pg. 088
William P.	15	May	1871	Clara	off. W. WHITE
LATTIMORE	and			PATTON	VA. bk. 2A pg. 078
David	22	Mar	1843	Nancy	off. J. HARRISON
LAUCK	and			MAGEE	VA. bk. 2A pg. 092
Catharine S.	28	Sep	1847	Jesse B.	off. J. MOFFITT
LAUCK	and			KERR	VA. bk. 3A pg. 095
Mollie L.	22	Oct	1860	James L.	off. J. NAYLOR
LAUCK	and			MC CULLIE	VA. bk. 2A pg. 074
Rebecca C.	27	Jan	1842	Samuel	off. C. WEIRICK
LAUGHEAD	and			GRIMES	VA. bk. 2A pg. 055
Robert	12	Jan	1831	Jane	off. J. MC KENNAR
LAUGHEAD	and			SERVIS	VA. bk. 01 pg. 003
Sarah	12	Jul	1855	Charles M.	off. D. HERVEY
LAUGHEAD	and			PILLINGS	VA. bk. 3A pg. 094
Sophia	30	Sep	1860	Charles	off. J. NAYLOR
LAUGHEAD	and			MONTGOMERY	WV. bk. 4A pg. 007
Sophia	03	Oct	1867	Joseph	off. H. MELVIN
LAWRENCE	and			STRAIN	VA. bk. 2A pg. 086
Benjamin	25	Feb	1846	Nancy	off. D. THOMPSON
LAWTON	and			QUEST	VA. bk. 01 pg. 004
Joseph K.	12	Aug	1856	Mary L.	off. E. QUILLEN
LAYPORT	and			MC CONKEY	VA. bk. 3A pg. 011
John	24	Nov	1852	Isabella	off. J. NAYLOR
LAZEAR	and			SHRIMPLIN	WV. bk. 4A pg. 103
Hugh	20	Dec	1871	Amanda	off. W. LATIMER
LAZEAR	and			PARSONS	VA. bk. 3A pg. 125
James	11	Feb	1863	Sebrina J.	off. J. NAYLOR
LAZEAR	and			REEVES	WV. bk. 4A pg. 030
Jane	23	Sep	1867	Wheeler	off. C. MELVIN
LAZEAR	and			LEWIS	VA. bk. 2A pg. 067
Leah	17	Feb	1839	John	off. A. YOUNG
LAZEAR	and			MOORE	WV. bk. 3A pg. 150
Lorinda	17	Jan	1865	Asbury S.	off. H. SHEPHERD
LAZEAR	and			BANE	VA. bk. 3A pg. 005
Maria W.	18	Oct	1852	William	off. J. NAYLOR
LAZEAR	and			SELBY	PA. bk. 4A pg. 104
Milton	10	Jan	1872	Sarah C.	off. W. LATIMER
LAZEAR	and			GLASS	WV. bk. 4A pg. 043
Robert M.	19	Feb	1868	Margaret	off. H. MELVIN
LAZEAR	and			PITTMAN	WV. bk. 4A pg. 031
Thomas B.	28	Sep	1867	Hannah	off. C. MELVIN
LAZIER	and			MC INTIRE	VA. bk. 2A pg. 010
Charlotte	05	May	1819	John	off. A. CAMPBELL
LAZIER	and			GORSUCH	VA. bk. 1A pg. 051
Mr.	--	--	1809	Miss.	off. J. DODDRIDGE
LE MOYNE	and			KUHN	VA. bk. 3A pg. 113
Julius	03	Mar	1862	Anne H.	off. J. NAYLOR
LEADLIE	and			CRAWFORD	VA. bk. 2A pg. 019
Nancy	03	Jul	1821	John	off. G. BUCHANAN

BROOKE CO., VA./WV. LICENSES & MARRIAGES, 1797-1874

Name		Day	Mo	Year	Spouse	Reference
LEADLIE	and				BROWN	VA. bk. 2A pg. 004
Sarah		10	Apr	1817	Robert	off. G. BUCHANAN
LEE	and				WOODS	VA. bk. 2A pg. *02
Catharine		30	Nov	1848	John	off. I. DALLAS
LEE	and				POWELL	VA. bk. 2A pg. 087
Dorcus Jane		26	Mar	1846	O.R.	off. S. LAUCK
LEE	and				HUFF	VA. bk. 3A pg. 016
Duncan		29	Mar	1853	Hannah	off. J. NAYLOR
LEE	and				DONNAL	VA. bk. 2A pg. *13
Elias M.		14	Apr	1853	Eleanor	off. H. SNYDER
LEE	and				ORR	VA. bk. 1A pg. 014
Hugh		14	Aug	1804	Hannah	off. E. MACURDY
LEE	and				KINKAID	VA. bk. 2A pg. 020
Hugh		01	Feb	1821	Mary A.	off. E. MACURDY
LEE	and				NUNEMAKER	VA. bk. 01 pg. 005
Julia Ann		19	Feb	1857	William	off. G. CRANAGE
LEE	and				GASSAGE	VA. bk. 2A pg. 092
Margaret		02	Mar	1848	Samuel	off. J. MONROE
LEE	and				ARCHER	VA. bk. 2A pg. 020
Mary		08	Mar	1821	Samuel	off. E. MACURDY
LEE	and				GATWOOD	VA. bk. 2A pg. 059
Samuel		14	Feb	1828	Susanna	off. E. SMITH
LEE	and				BEATTY	VA. bk. 2A pg. *04
William D.		14	Mar	1850	Nancy M.	off. E. NICHOLSON
LEHEKS	and				WENNINGCOUGH	VA. bk. 3A pg. 045
Ursula		21	Nov	1857	Ferdinard	off. J. NAYLOR
LEMMON	and				DUVALL	VA. bk. 2A pg. 067
Charity		06	Jan	1839	William	off. A. YOUNG
LEMMON	and				LITTON	VA. bk. 2A pg. 071
Jane		18	Oct	1840	John	off. T. STEIRSHCOMB
LEMMON	and				KIMBERLAND	WV. bk. 3A pg. 153
William		01	Mar	1865	Jane	off. H. SHEPHERD
LEMON	and				MC INTYRE	VA. bk. 2A pg. 059
Rebecca		22	Nov	1827	Joseph	off. E. SMITH
LETZKUS	and				HEDGELY	VA. bk. 3A pg. 005
Ablon		15	Oct	1852	George	off. J. NAYLOR
LETZKUS	and				MC MAHON	WV. bk. 4A pg. 134
Adam		22	Jan	1874	Anne E.	off. W. LATIMER
LETZKUS	and				BEITER	WV. bk. 3A pg. 151
Ambrose		20	Jan	1865	Mary Ann	off. H. SHEPHERD
LETZKUS	and				BARTH	VA. bk. 01 pg. 009
Frances		26	Nov	1860	Hugh	off. S. HUBER
LETZKUS	and				POTTS	WV. bk. 4A pg. 110
Francis		02	Apr	1872	Jasper	off. W. LATIMER
LETZKUS	and				GAUSE	WV. bk. 4A pg. 049
George		13	Jul	1868	Caroline	off. C. MELVIN
LETZKUS	and				MILELECH	WV. bk. 4A pg. 022
John		31	Jan	1867	Eva	off. H. MELVIN
LETZKUS	and				ROBINETT	WV. bk. 3A pg. 166
Joseph		23	May	1866	Emma	off. R. NICHOLLS
LETZKUS	and				PATTERSON	WV. bk. 4A pg. 075
Lena		31	Aug	1870	James	off. W. WHITE

70   BROOKE CO., VA./WV. LICENSES & MARRIAGES, 1797-1874

LETZKUS		and		SPRINGBORN	WV. bk. 4A	pg. 009
Mary	10	Oct	1866	Frederick	off. R. NICHOLLS	
LETZKUS		and		LIAS	WV. bk. 01	pg. 015
Nancy	03	Apr	1866	George	off. J. PIERCE	
LETZKUS		and		CUNNINGHAM	WV. bk. 4A	pg. 090
Pierce	26	May	1871	Rebecca J.	off. W. WHITE	
LEWIS		and		LATIMER	WV. bk. 4A	pg. 088
Clara	15	May	1871	William P.	off. W. WHITE	
LEWIS		and		KEMP	VA. bk. 3A	pg. 074
Edward L.	05	Sep	1859	Rachel	off. J. NAYLOR	
LEWIS		and		COLEMAN	VA. bk. 3A	pg. 107
Elizabeth	13	Nov	1861	De Witt C.	off. S. NAYLOR	
LEWIS		and		CARTER	VA. bk. 1A	pg. 078
Ephraim	11	Sep	1814	Juliana	off. W. WILLSON	
LEWIS		and		BELL	VA. bk. 3A	pg. 060
Hezekiah	16	Dec	1858	Sarah Adaline	off. J. NAYLOR	
LEWIS		and		LAZEAR	VA. bk. 2A	pg. 067
John	17	Feb	1839	Leah	off. A. YOUNG	
LEWIS		and		MC ELROY	VA. bk. 01	pg. 004
Kezeah	22	Apr	1856	John R.	off. E. QUILLEN	
LEWIS		and		RALSTON	VA. bk. 2A	pg. 087
Kezia	05	Feb	1846	John	off. S. WORTHINGTON	
LEWIS		and		WILSON	WV. bk. 4A	pg. 059
Leah	11	Feb	1869	John M.	off. W. WHITE	
LEWIS		and		WILSON	WV. bk. 4A	pg. 145
Marg't Jennie	03	Nov	1874	Robert Bane	off. J. LATIMER	
LEWIS		and		LANNUM	WV. bk. 4A	pg. 084
Martha A.	06	Mar	1871	Milton	off. W. WHITE	
LEWIS		and		MAHAN	WV. bk. 3A	pg. 146
Melissa	25	Oct	1864	Robert M.	off. H. SHEPHERD	
LEWIS		and		KIMBERLAND	WV. bk. 4A	pg. 075
Melissa	13	Sep	1870	Cornelius H.	off. W. WHITE	
LEWIS		and		BUCHANAN	WV. bk. 4A	pg. 065
Micha	29	Nov	1869	Richard W.	off. W. WHITE	
LEWIS		and		CARTER	VA. bk. 2A	pg. 018
Samuel	23	Sep	1817	Rebecca Ann	off. S. LAUCK	
LEWIS		and		NOBLE	WV. bk. 4A	pg. 006
Sarah J.	12	Feb	1866	Tarlton	off. R. NICHOLLS	
LEWIS		and		ROBERTS	VA. bk. 2A	pg. *08
Susan	08	Dec	1850	Ortho	off. R. WHITE	
LEWIS		and		HARVEY	WV. bk. 4A	pg. 076
Virginia	13	Sep	1870	William H.	off. W. WHITE	
LIAS		and		LETZKUS	WV. bk. 01	pg. 015
George	03	Apr	1866	Nancy	off. J. PIERCE	
LINDSAY		and		HEDGES	VA. bk. 2A	pg. *07
Catharine A.	05	Dec	1850	Aaron	off. J. MC GAN	
LINDSAY		and		BROWN	VA. bk. 2A	pg. *12
Elizabeth	03	Jun	1852	C.T.	off. W. SUMMERS	
LINDSAY		and		AMOLA	VA. bk. 2A	pg. 051
John	17	Oct	1827	Elisabeth	off. J. CAZAD	
LINDSAY		and		COUNSELMAN	VA. bk. 2A	pg. 060
Joshua	05	Mar	1829	Elisabeth	off. E. SMITH	

LINDSAY			and	ZINK	VA. bk. 2A pg. *07
Lemuel B.	21	Dec	1850	Elizabeth	off. J. MC GAN
LINDSAY			and	WORTHINGTON	VA. bk. 2A pg. 055
Samuel	17	Mar	1823	Rebecca	off. A. COLEMAN
LINDSAY			and	TWEED	VA. bk. 3A pg. 097
Samuel	07	Jan	1861	Mary	off. J. NAYLOR
LINTON			and	MAYHALL	VA. bk. 2A pg. *17
Joseph	17	Nov	1853	Marg't Jane	off. E. QUILLEN
LINTON			and	PATTON	WV. bk. 01 pg. 019
Mahala	25	Aug	1868	James C.	off. M. WELLS
LINTON			and	COLLINS	VA. bk. 2A pg. *10
Susanna	25	Dec	1851	Augustus	off. H. SNYDER
LINTON			and	THOMPSON	VA. bk. 01 pg. 005
William	15	Nov	1856	S. Elizabeth	off. A. ENDSLEY
LINTON			and	GREEN	WV. bk. 4A pg. 012
William D.	09	Oct	1866	Sarah	off. R. NICHOLLS
LITTLE			and	SCOTT	WV. bk. 3A pg. 145
Mary Jane	05	Jul	1864	John S.	off. H. SHEPHERD
LITTON			and	LEMMON	VA. bk. 2A pg. 071
John	18	Oct	1840	Jane	off. T. STEIRSHCOMB
LLEWELLYN			and	BROWN	VA. bk. 3A pg. 057
Jane L.	06	Nov	1858	S. Turner	off. J. NAYLOR
LLEWELLYN			and	LOCKHEART	VA. bk. 3A pg. 072
Julia R.	11	Jul	1859	Josiah B.	off. J. NAYLOR
LLOYD			and	MERRYMAN	WV. bk. 3A pg. 145
James H.	20	Oct	1864	Ella	off. H. SHEPHERD
LOCKHART			and	APPLEGATE	VA. bk. 2A pg. 082
Jeptha	05	Apr	1838	Eda	off. R. WHITE
LOCKHEART			and	LLEWELLYN	VA. bk. 3A pg. 072
Josiah B.	11	Jul	1859	Julia R.	off. J. NAYLOR
LODGE			and	KEMP	VA. bk. 2A pg. 091
Amanda	06	Feb	1848	Jesse	off. J. MONROE
LOFFER			and	SCHALK	VA. bk. 3A pg. 055
Lusetta/Lucy	18	Aug	1858	Conrad	off. J. NAYLOR
LOGAN			and	GRIMES	VA. bk. 1A pg. 040
Nancy	06	Apr	1802	Thomas	off. J. DODDRIDGE
LOGAN			and	BRICE	VA. bk. 2A pg. 063
William	25	Apr	1833	Margaret	off. R. BROWN
LOGUE			and	MAHON	VA. bk. 2A pg. 064
John	08	Mar	1838	Elizabeth	off. A. YOUNG
LOGUE			and	MORROW	VA. bk. 1A pg. 025
Samuel	06	Aug	1805	Nancy	off. E. MACURDY
LONG			and	PATTERSON	WV. bk. 4A pg. 028
David W.	27	Jul	1867	Sarah A.	off. H. MELVIN
LONG			and	BARNES	WV. bk. 4A pg. 014
James	03	Nov	1866	Mary E.	off. R. NICHOLLS
LONG			and	WELLS	WV. bk. 4A pg. 067
Rebecca J.	27	Dec	1869	Richard T.	off. W. WHITE
LOOS			and	KEEN	VA. bk. 01 pg. 012
Charles Louis	06	Jul	1848	Rosetta E.	off. A. CAMPBELL
LOVE			and	GAMBLE	VA. bk. 2A pg. 070
Elizabeth	26	Jan	1841	Henry	off. J. HERBERT

72   BROOKE CO., VA./WV. LICENSES & MARRIAGES, 1797-1874

Name				Spouse	Reference
LOVE		and		HAYDEN	VA. bk. 2A pg. 075
Sarah	17	Mar	1842	Thomas W.	off. J. GALLOWAY
LOWERY		and		FARNSWORTH	VA. bk. 2A pg. 060
William	26	Mar	1829	Sylvia	off. S. REED
LOWRY		and		SIMPSON	VA. bk. 2A pg. 015
Ann J.	02	Nov	1820	James	off. G. BUCHANAN
LOWRY		and		RUSSELL	VA. bk. 2A pg. 092
Elizabeth	08	Apr	1848	Edward	off. J. MONROE
LOWRY		and		HIBBITTS	VA. bk. 2A pg. 083
John	19	Nov	1839	Sarah	off. R. WHITE
LOWRY		and		KNOX	VA. bk. 2A pg. 030
Margaret	11	Mar	1824	Andrew	off. G. BUCHANAN
LUCAS		and		GREEN	VA. bk. 2A pg. 038
Elisabeth	25	Aug	1825	William	off. T. BEEKS
LUCAS		and		DOWNEY	VA. bk. 2A pg. 038
Elisabeth	01	Dec	1825	John	off. T. BEEKS
LUCAS		and		LANNUM	WV. bk. 4A pg. 101
Elizabeth	02	Dec	1871	Samuel	off. W. LATIMER
LUCAS		and		MC BURNEY	WV. bk. 4A pg. 077
Elizabeth A.	21	Sep	1870	James	off. W. WHITE
LUCAS		and		LUCAS	VA. bk. 2A pg. 059
James	14	Aug	1828	Margaret (...)	off. E. SMITH
LUCAS		and		FARQUER	VA. bk. 3A pg. 058
John	11	Nov	1858	Keziah	off. J. NAYLOR
LUCAS		and		LUCAS	VA. bk. 2A pg. 059
Margaret (...)	14	Aug	1828	James	off. E. SMITH
LUCAS		and		CHURCHMAN	WV. bk. 4A pg. 089
Nancy	17	May	1871	Joseph	off. W. WHITE
LUCAS		and		LANNUM	WV. bk. 4A pg. 121
Susan	05	Feb	1873	Aaron	off. W. LATIMER
LUTZ		and		JENKINS	VA. bk. 1A pg. 045
Kitty	--	--	1802	Benjamin	off. UNKNOWN
LYON		and		BARNET	VA. bk. 1A pg. 033
Andrew	26	Sep	1809	Susannah	off. J. DODDRIDGE
LYON		and		MOORE	VA. bk. 2A pg. 006
Andrew	31	Oct	1816	Elizabeth	off. G. SCOTT
LYON		and		WILEY	VA. bk. 1A pg. 058
John	03	Aug	1811	Nancy	off. E. MACURDY
LYONS		and		DOUGHERTY	VA. bk. 01 pg. 004
David	15	Sep	1855	Matilda	off. J. BRAZILL
LYONS		and		DUNLAP	VA. bk. 3A pg. 046
Mary	08	Dec	1857	Hugh	off. J. NAYLOR
LYONS		and		CALGORE	VA. bk. 1A pg. 012
Mathew	12	May	1803	Nancy	off. E. MACURDY
LYONS		and		HENDERSON	VA. bk. 2A pg. 063
William	27	Dec	1832	Emeline	off. R. BROWN
LYTLE		and		RICHARDSON	VA. bk. 1A pg. 081
George	10	Dec	1812	Ruth	off. UNKNOWN
MACKDANIEL		and		CONN	VA. bk. 1A pg. 071
Ester	21	Jan	1814	George	off. W. WILLSON
MACKEY		and		APPLEGATE	VA. bk. 2A pg. *14
Elizabeth	16	Jun	1853	Moses	off. S. NESBITT

MACKEY		and		SISSON	VA. bk. 2A pg. 073
Joseph	16	Feb	1842	Martha A. M.	off. J. HERBERT
MACKEY		and		RAMSEY	VA. bk. 2A pg. 027
Robert	21	Feb	1823	Margaret	off. J. CAZAD
MACKEY		and		DEIGHTON	WV. bk. 3A pg. 143
Robert	30	Aug	1864	Millie	off. H. SHEPHERD
MACLARY		and		FOWLER	VA. bk. 2A pg. 053
Sarah	--	--	1826	John	off. N. HEADINGTON
MACURDY		and		COLWELL	VA. bk. 2A pg. 008
Elisha (Rev.)	30	Mar	1819	Sarah (Mrs.)	off. O. JENNINGS
MAGEE		and		MULLANY	WV. bk. 3A pg. 144
Ellen	11	Sep	1864	Thomas	off. H. SHEPHERD
MAGEE		and		LAUCK	VA. bk. 2A pg. 092
Jesse B.	28	Sep	1847	Catharine S.	off. J. MOFFITT
MAGEE		and		FOWLER	VA. bk. 2A pg. 050
John	09	Jun	1826	Amy	off. N. HEADINGTON
MAGEE		and		HERRON	VA. bk. 2A pg. *05
John	08	Oct	1850	Nancy	off. D. HERVEY
MAGEE		and		MENDEL	VA. bk. 2A pg. *02
John J.	22	Feb	1849	Elizabeth J.	off. I. DALLAS
MAGEE		and		POOL	VA. bk. 3A pg. 128
Martha Ann	06	Apr	1863	William	off. W. NAYLOR
MAGEE		and		POOL	VA. bk. 2A pg. *05
Nancy	10	Feb	1850	William	off. C. LOOS
MAGEE		and		WIGGINS	VA. bk. 01 pg. 002
Silas	26	Oct	1854	Margaret	off. S. TOMPKINS
MAGEE		and		HUNTER	VA. bk. 3A pg. 102
William	13	May	1861	Catharine	off. J. NAYLOR
MAGERS		and		BOSMAN	VA. bk. 1A pg. 057
Elias	31	Oct	1811	Sarah	off. J. PRITCHARD
MAGERS		and		MORRISON	VA. bk. 2A pg. 035
Nancy	28	Oct	1824	John B.	off. N. HEADINGTON
MAGOINGAN		and		RIDOUT	VA. bk. 3A pg. 091
Martha	30	Aug	1860	John	off. J. NAYLOR
MAGRUDER		and		WILLIAMS	VA. bk. 1A pg. 050
Charlotte	07	Feb	1808	William	off. J. DODDRIDGE
MAGRUDER		and		CONNELL	VA. bk. 1A pg. 050
Sally	31	Jan	1808	Solomon	off. UNKNOWN
MAHAN		and		TEAFF	VA. bk. 2A pg. 020
Eleanor	14	Jun	1821	James	off. L. BROWNING
MAHAN		and		OWINGS	VA. bk. 2A pg. 093
James	02	Dec	1847	Michel	off. G. HOLMES
MAHAN		and		WHITE	WV. bk. 4A pg. 055
Jennie M.	26	Dec	1868	Samuel K.	off. S. QUEST
MAHAN		and		LEWIS	WV. bk. 3A pg. 146
Robert M.	25	Oct	1864	Melissa	off. H. SHEPHERD
MAHAN		and		BURGOIN	VA. bk. 2A pg. 069
Sarah	04	Jun	1840	Joshua	off. S. BABCOCK
MAHON		and		HAMILTON	VA. bk. 3A pg. 100
Anne E.	05	Mar	1861	James S.	off. J. NAYLOR
MAHON		and		LOGUE	VA. bk. 2A pg. 064
Elizabeth	08	Mar	1838	John	off. A. YOUNG

Surname	Given	Day	Mo	Yr	Surname	Given	Location
MAHON	John L.	07	Dec	1837	BRENNEMAN	Barbara	OH. bk. 2A pg. 065 off. G. HOLMES
MAHON	Richard	13	May	1868	WELLS	Mary	WV. bk. 4A pg. 047 off. H. MELVIN
MAHON	William B.	01	Oct	1857	BROWNING	Margaret C.	VA. bk. 3A pg. 042 off. J. NAYLOR
MAJORS	John (Jr.)	08	Jun	1820	MODERWELL	Isabel	VA. bk. 2A pg. 015 off. L. BROWNING
MALHOLEN	Thomas	22	Jun	1824	HENRY	Sarah	VA. bk. 2A pg. 032 off. J. CAZAD
MALONE	Elmira	24	Apr	1838	CAUGHEY	Josiah	VA. bk. 2A pg. 082 off. R. WHITE
MALONEY	John M.	20	Oct	1852	MC COY	Nancy Jane	VA. bk. 3A pg. 006 off. J. NAYLOR
MALOY	Ann	07	Oct	1868	KENEDY	Patrick	WV. bk. 4A pg. 050 off. S. QUEST
MARION	Morse	11	May	1871	MARSH	Ruth E.	WV. bk. 4A pg. 088 off. W. WHITE
MARKLY	Susanna	21	Jan	1830	BLANKENSOP	Peter	VA. bk. 2A pg. 058 off. D. MERRYMAN
MARKS	Amanda	11	Apr	1833	BOUGHER	John M.	VA. bk. 2A pg. 063 off. G. SCOTT
MARKS	Elizabeth	30	Mar	1848	BROWN	John	VA. bk. 2A pg. 092 off. T. NEWELL
MARKS	T.H.	17	Feb	1874	WHEELER	Sallie	WV. bk. 4A pg. 136 off. J. LATIMER
MARQUIS	Samuel F.	02	Apr	1840	RALSTON	Sarah L.	VA. bk. 2A pg. 083 off. R. WHITE
MARS	Hiram	13	May	1872	SMITH	Elizabeth H.	WV. bk. 4A pg. 112 off. W. LATIMER
MARSH	Harriet	18	Mar	1859	MORTON	John (Jr.)	VA. bk. 3A pg. 065 off. J. NAYLOR
MARSH	James	25	Oct	1827	ATKINSON	Sarah Ann	VA. bk. 2A pg. 048 off. G. BUCHANAN
MARSH	Jemima E.	27	Jun	1866	WAY	Francis E.	WV. bk. 3A pg. 165 off. R. NICHOLLS
MARSH	Mary Ann	13	Apr	1848	HILL	Thomas	VA. bk. 2A pg. 093 off. T. NEWELL
MARSH	Mary J.	21	Nov	1871	GORDON	John E.	WV. bk. 4A pg. 100 off. W. LATIMER
MARSH	Narcissa	02	Oct	1872	HINDMAN	Samuel	WV. bk. 01 pg. 021 off. J. GRAHAM
MARSH	Ruth E.	11	May	1871	MARION	Morse	WV. bk. 4A pg. 088 off. W. WHITE
MARSHALL	Aaron	08	Apr	1842	LANGFITT	Mary	VA. bk. 2A pg. 083 off. R. WHITE
MARSHALL	Alexander	25	May	1815	GIBSON	Nancy	VA. bk. 1A pg. 070 off. UNKNOWN
MARSHALL	Elizabeth	29	Mar	1832	DONAHUE	James	VA. bk. 2A pg. 061 off. G. MC CASHEY
MARSHALL	Elizabeth	15	Feb	1838	CULLIN	Isaac	VA. bk. 2A pg. 082 off. R. WHITE

BROOKE CO., VA./WV. LICENSES & MARRIAGES, 1797-1874   75

MARSHALL		and		MC CLUNEY		
Jane	23	Dec	1800	William	off. J. DODDRIDGE	VA. bk. 1A pg. 042
MARSHALL		and		DAWSON		VA. bk. 2A pg. 018
Mary	07	Sep	1820	Robert	off. A. CAMPBELL	
MARSHALL		and		EDGINGTON		VA. bk. 1A pg. 028
Rachel	15	Aug	1807	Aaron	off. UNKNOWN	
MARSHALL		and		AGNEW		VA. bk. 01 pg. 005
Rebecca C.	25	Mar	1857	James M.	off. E. QUILLEN	
MARSHALL		and		CONNELL		VA. bk. 1A pg. 044
Samuel A.	--	--	1802	Polly	off. UNKNOWN	
MARSHALL		and		MOORE		VA. bk. 1A pg. 072
William	12	Mar	1812	Jane	off. J. PRITCHARD	
MARTIN		and		ALLISON		VA. bk. 2A pg. 086
Allison	25	Sep	1845	Lucinda	off. G. SCOTT	
MARTIN		and		KEITH		VA. bk. 2A pg. 094
Isaac	10	Sep	1848	Marg't Ellen	off. S. WORTHINGTON	
MARTIN		and		MARTIN		VA. bk. 2A pg. 002
James	16	May	1816	Velinda (...)	off. E. MACURDY	
MARTIN		and		FRAZIER		VA. bk. 3A pg. 084
Margaret	24	Apr	1860	John	off. J. NAYLOR	
MARTIN		and		SAUNDERS		VA. bk. 2A pg. 004
Nathaniel	07	Jan	1817	Elizabeth	off. G. BUCHANAN	
MARTIN		and		GLASS		VA. bk. 1A pg. 021
Robert	--	--	1806	Ann	off. UNKNOWN	
MARTIN		and		MARTIN		VA. bk. 2A pg. 002
Velinda (...)	16	May	1816	James	off. E. MACURDY	
MATHEWSON		and		PITTINGER		VA. bk. 2A pg. 006
Elizabeth	01	Oct	1818	Nicholas	off. G. SCOTT	
MATTHEWS		and		HAYS		WV. bk. 4A pg. 008
Lavinia S.	29	Aug	1866	John N.	off. R. NICHOLLS	
MATTHEWS		and		BLACK		VA. bk. 3A pg. 001
Oscar L.	--	--	1852	Catherine	off. J. NAYLOR	
MAXWELL		and		WALSH		VA. bk. 2A pg. 063
Betsey	01	Nov	1832	Robert	off. R. BROWN	
MAXWELL		and		REYNOLDS		VA. bk. 2A pg. 045
Elisabeth	07	Nov	1826	Joseph	off. J. CAZAD	
MAXWELL		and		WILLSON		VA. bk. 1A pg. 011
Elizabeth	07	Jul	1802	David	off. J. HUGHES	
MAXWELL		and		BROWNLEE		VA. bk. 2A pg. 060
Henry	01	Jan	1829	Nancy	off. E. SMITH	
MAXWELL		and		BEALL		VA. bk. 2A pg. 067
Robert	28	May	1839	Elizabeth	off. J. GALLOWAY	
MAXWELL		and		LANE		VA. bk. 2A pg. 060
Samuel S.	23	Oct	1828	Elisabeth	off. S. REED	
MAY		and		PORTERFIELD		VA. bk. 2A pg. 051
Isaac	01	Apr	1825	Assenith	off. L. BROWNING	
MAY		and		DAVIS		VA. bk. 2A pg. 064
Jacob	05	Dec	1837	Margaret	off. A. YOUNG	
MAY		and		FINK		VA. bk. 01 pg. 004
Jacob	11	May	1856	Elizabeth	off. A. ENDSLEY	
MAYHALL		and		ANTILL		VA. bk. 2A pg. *02
John	24	Jul	1848	Elizabeth	off. I. DALLAS	

76   BROOKE CO., VA./WV. LICENSES & MARRIAGES, 1797-1874

MAYHALL			and	LINTON	VA. bk. 2A pg. *17
Margaret Jane	17	Nov	1853	Joseph	off. E. QUILLEN
MAYHALL			and	DEIGHTON	WV. bk. 4A pg. 082
William A.	11	Jan	1871	Isabella	off. W. WHITE
MC ARRAH			and	MC NELLY	VA. bk. 3A pg. 020
Mary	02	May	1853	Peter	off. J. NAYLOR
MC ATTEE			and	SMALL	VA. bk. 2A pg. 005
Abraham	28	Aug	1817	Tamer	off. L. BROWNING
MC ATTEE			and	JOHNSTON	VA. bk. 2A pg. 079
Jeremiah B.	02	May	1844	Sarah	off. S. WORTHINGTON
MC BURNEY			and	LUCAS	WV. bk. 4A pg. 077
James	21	Sep	1870	Elizabeth A.	off. W. WHITE
MC CADDEN			and	EDGINGTON	VA. bk. 1A pg. 054
John	--	--	1810	Mary	off. J. DODDRIDGE
MC CAMANT			and	HACKETT	VA. bk. 2A pg. *15
Elizabeth	15	Aug	1853	Peter	off. E. QUILLEN
MC CAMICK			and	MC CAMICK	PA. bk. 01 pg. 017
Francis H.	05	Jul	1867	Mary A. (...)	off. D. BOYD
MC CAMICK			and	MC CAMICK	PA. bk. 01 pg. 017
Mary A. (...)	05	Jul	1867	Francis H.	off. D. BOYD
MC CAMICK			and	DOWDEN	WV. bk. 4A pg. 133
Nathan	16	Jan	1874	Frances P.	off. W. LATIMER
MC CAMMON			and	CRISWELL	VA. bk. 1A pg. 079
Samuel	10	Oct	1815	Patty	off. J. PRITCHARD
MC CASKEY			and	HENDERSON	VA. bk. 1A pg. 067
William	25	Jan	1814	Jane	off. UNKNOWN
MC CAULY			and	EVERET	VA. bk. 1A pg. 030
John	09	Jul	1807	Sally	off. J. HUGHES
MC CAUSLAND			and	STANSBERRY	VA. bk. 2A pg. *14
Francis Mary	17	Apr	1853	Daniel B.	off. J. BAINBRIDGE
MC CAUSLAND			and	GRIMES	VA. bk. 2A pg. 027
William	08	Jan	1823	Elizabeth	off. J. CAZAD
MC CHRISTAL			and	O'WESNEY	VA. bk. 3A pg. 083
Rose Ann	10	Apr	1860	James	off. J. NAYLOR
MC CLEARY			and	BRADY	WV. bk. 4A pg. 098
Sallie	07	Nov	1871	John D.	off. W. LATIMER
MC CLELLAND			and	DEGARMO	WV. bk. 4A pg. 132
George	28	Nov	1873	Anne	off. W. LATIMER
MC CLELLAND			and	WRIGHT	VA. bk. 2A pg. *11
John K.	24	Nov	1851	Jemima	off. J. STOCKTON
MC CLOUD			and	JUSTICE	VA. bk. 1A pg. 024
Christiana	25	Sep	1804	James	off. E. MACURDY
MC CLUNEY			and	MARSHALL	VA. bk. 1A pg. 042
William	23	Dec	1800	Jane	off. J. DODDRIDGE
MC CLURE			and	RUSSELL	WV. bk. 4A pg. 032
Anne (AIKEN)	12	Oct	1867	George W.	off. H. MELVIN
MC CLURE			and	CAMPBELL	VA. bk. 2A pg. 032
Robert	30	Dec	1824	Catherine	off. G. BUCHANAN
MC CLURG			and	SODIKE	PA. bk. 01 pg. 016
Harriet E.	13	Oct	1867	William	off. J. WILLIAMS
MC CLURG			and	HINDMAN	WV. bk. 4A pg. 024
John I.	14	May	1867	Elizabeth	off. H. MELVIN

BROOKE CO., VA./WV. LICENSES & MARRIAGES, 1797-1874   77

MC COLLOCH		and		WALKER		WV. bk. 4A pg. 068	
Ebenezer Z.	16	Feb	1870	Ella J.		off. W. WHITE	
MC CONKEY		and		REED		VA. bk. 3A pg. 006	
Cobane	20	Oct	1852	Sarah Jane		off. J. NAYLOR	
MC CONKEY		and		LAYPORT		VA. bk. 3A pg. 011	
Isabella	24	Nov	1852	John		off. J. NAYLOR	
MC CONKEY		and		WETHERELL		VA. bk. 3A pg. 076	
Joseph Grafton	03	Nov	1859	Mary Ann		off. J. NAYLOR	
MC CONKEY		and		REED		VA. bk. 3A pg. 010	
Kennedy	24	Nov	1852	Mary		off. J. NAYLOR	
MC CONKEY		and		HOWARD		VA. bk. 01 pg. 003	
Maria	23	Nov	1854	W.W.		off. C. HOLMES	
MC CONKEY		and		FLOWERS		WV. bk. 4A pg. 141	
Mary	03	Sep	1874	J.W.		off. J. LATIMER	
MC CONNEL		and		CRUTH		VA. bk. 01 pg. 005	
Mary Jane	17	Feb	1857	Alexander		off. E. QUILLEN	
MC CONNELL		and		CRISS		VA. bk. 3A pg. 101	
George	04	May	1861	Rebecca W.		off. J. NAYLOR	
MC CONNELL		and		WILCOXON		VA. bk. 2A pg. 078	
James	23	Oct	1843	Ruth Ann		off. J. HARRISON	
MC CONNELL		and		O'HARA		VA. bk. 01 pg. 005	
James	01	Sep	1857	Anne		off. J. BRAZILL	
MC CONNELL		and		BAUSMAN		VA. bk. 2A pg. 044	
Jane	25	Jan	1827	James		off. J. CAZAD	
MC CONNELL		and		ROBERTS		VA. bk. 2A pg. 037	
John	--	--	1826	Margaret A.		off. N. HEADINGTON	
MC CONNELL		and		MC KAHEN		VA. bk. 2A pg. 001	
Margaret	02	Jul	1818	Daniel		off. J. PRITCHARD	
MC CONNELL		and		SHRIMPLIN		VA. bk. 2A pg. 039	
Richard	26	Oct	1825	Frances		off. J. CAZAD	
MC CONNELL		and		BROTHERS		VA. bk. 2A pg. 058	
William	25	Feb	1829	Susanna		off. T. BEEKS	
MC CONVILLE		and		KEMP		VA. bk. 3A pg. 055	
Bridget	29	Jul	1858	William H.		off. J. NAYLOR	
MC CORD		and		HOGG		VA. bk. 2A pg. *12	
George W.	07	Sep	1852	Sarah Ann		off. H. SNYDER	
MC CORMACK		and		BOND		VA. bk. 1A pg. 029	
Catherine	07	Dec	1807	Richard		off. J. PRITCHARD	
MC CORMACK		and		CLENDENING		VA. bk. 1A pg. 083	
George	24	Jun	1813	Polly		off. UNKNOWN	
MC CORMACK		and		COLEMAN		VA. bk. 1A pg. 021	
John	--	--	1806	Sarah		off. UNKNOWN	
MC CORMACK		and		HAMILTON		VA. bk. 1A pg. 072	
Sarah	12	Feb	1812	Thomas		off. J. PRITCHARD	
MC CORMICK		and		CRAWFORD		VA. bk. 1A pg. 022	
Sarah	20	Aug	1806	William		off. UNKNOWN	
MC COWAN		and		ORR		VA. bk. 2A pg. 063	
James	15	Jun	1833	Mary		off. R. BROWN	
MC COWN		and		SPROWL		VA. bk. 2A pg. 049	
John	05	Jul	1827	Elizabeth		off. S. REED	
MC COY		and		WELLS		VA. bk. 3A pg. 080	
Abraham	28	Dec	1859	Ann		off. J. NAYLOR	

78 BROOKE CO., VA./WV. LICENSES & MARRIAGES, 1797-1874

MC	COY			and		RUTH		WV. bk. 3A pg. 140
	Agnes A.	22	Mar	1864		John		off. H. SHEPHERD
MC	COY			and	/	MEEKER		WV. bk. 3A pg. 161
	Lydia	21	Apr	1866		Daniel		off. H. SHEPHERD
MC	COY			and		MALONEY		VA. bk. 3A pg. 006
	Nancy Jane	20	Oct	1852		John M.		off. J. NAYLOR
MC	CRACKEN			and		SIMPSON		VA. bk. 2A pg. *10
	Alexander	26	Jun	1851		Margaret		off. G. BUCHANAN
MC	CRACKEN			and		ROBERTS		VA. bk. 2A pg. 059
	Rachael	03	Apr	1828		Henry		off. E. SMITH
MC	CREA			and		WRIGHT		VA. bk. 2A pg. *03
	John	23	Sep	1846		Martha		off. J. GOODWIN
MC	CREA			and		MC GUIRE		VA. bk. 3A pg. 065
	William	07	Mar	1859		Elizabeth		off. J. NAYLOR
MC	CREARY			and		SMITH		WV. bk. 4A pg. 040
	Almira	31	Dec	1867		Clarence A.		off. C. MELVIN
MC	CREARY			and		SMITH		VA. bk. 3A pg. 081
	Elizabeth	27	Feb	1860		George W.		off. J. NAYLOR
MC	CREARY			and		BUCKEY		WV. bk. 01 pg. 019
	George W.	05	Sep	1868		Sarah E.		off. W. BROWN
MC	CREARY			and		SMITH		WV. bk. 4A pg. 002
	Virginia	01	Nov	1865		George W.		off. H. SHEPHERD
MC	CREARY			and		ROBERTS		VA. bk. 01 pg. 002
	William	27	Apr	1854		Nancy		off. D. HERVEY
MC	CULLIE			and		LAUCK		VA. bk. 2A pg. 074
	Samuel	27	Jan	1842		Rebecca C.		off. C. WEIRICK
MC	CURDY			and		ANDREWS		VA. bk. 2A pg. 056
	William	11	Mar	1830		Nancy		off. G. SCOTT
MC	DONALD			and		WALKER		VA. bk. 2A pg. 038
	Angelena	29	Dec	1825		Benjamin		off. T. BEEKS
MC	DONALD			and		HOUSTON		WV. bk. 4A pg. 107
	Angeline	19	Feb	1872		James F.		off. W. LATIMER
MC	DOWELL			and		FARNSWORTH		VA. bk. 2A pg. 083
	Eleanor	21	Apr	1842		Henry		off. R. WHITE
MC	DOWELL			and		DONALD		VA. bk. 2A pg. 046
	Nancy	08	Feb	1827		Daniel		off. J. CAZAD
MC	DOWELL			and		RICHARDSON		VA. bk. 2A pg. 059
	Sarah	25	Mar	1828		Thomas		off. E. SMITH
MC	DUGAN			and		BAXTER		VA. bk. 01 pg. 002
	James	26	Oct	1854		Sarah		off. F. GUTHRIE
MC	DUGAN			and		STEDMAN		VA. bk. 3A pg. 049
	James	28	Jan	1858		Melvina		off. J. NAYLOR
MC	DUGAN			and		FILLY		WV. bk. 4A pg. 128
	James	04	Oct	1873		Mary		off. W. LATIMER
MC	DUGAN			and		GLASS		WV. bk. 3A pg. 164
	Wealthy E.	10	May	1866		John J.		off. R. NICHOLLS
MC	EA- - -			and		STEENROD		VA. bk. 2A pg. 041
	Nancy	29	Mar	1825		Daniel		off. W. WYLIE
MC	ELFRESH			and		CUPPLES		VA. bk. 3A pg. 114
	Mary A.	11	Mar	1862		James		off. J. NAYLOR
MC	ELHANY			and		ANDERSON		VA. bk. 1A pg. 021
	Martha	01	May	1806		James		off. UNKNOWN

BROOKE CO., VA./WV. LICENSES & MARRIAGES, 1797-1874   79

MC	ELROY		and		CRUSON	VA.	bk. 2A	pg. 074	
	Elizabeth	05	Jan	1842	Coleman	off. W. STEVENS			
MC	ELROY		and		LEWIS	VA.	bk. 01	pg. 004	
	John R.	22	Apr	1856	Kezeah	off. E. QUILLEN			
MC	EWING		and		PARK	VA.	bk. 2A	pg. 026	
	John	09	Jan	1823	Joanna	off. G. SCOTT			
MC	FADDEN		and		KINDRICKS	VA.	bk. 3A	pg. 091	
	Catherine	05	Sep	1860	James	off. J. NAYLOR			
MC	FADDEN		and		DONNELLY	VA.	bk. 3A	pg. 036	
	Charles	03	Jan	1854	Catherine	off. J. NAYLOR			
MC	FADDEN		and		DINSMORE	VA.	bk. 3A	pg. 008	
	John	09	Nov	1852	Elenor	off. J. NAYLOR			
MC	FADDEN		and		WAUGH	WV.	bk. 4A	pg. 074	
	Leonard D.	31	Aug	1870	Amanda	off. W. WHITE			
MC	FARLAND		and		WYCOFF	VA.	bk. 2A	pg. 084	
	Andrew	14	Sep	1842	Mary	off. R. WHITE			
MC	FERRAN		and		COLWELL	VA.	bk. 2A	pg. 005	
	William	04	Nov	1816	Abigale	off. E. MACURDY			
MC	GEE		and		BANNON	VA.	bk. 3A	pg. 061	
	Charles	01	Jan	1859	Catharine	off. J. NAYLOR			
MC	GEE		and		BEHIN	VA.	bk. 01	pg. 003	
	Felix	19	Feb	1855	Margaret	off. J. BRAZILL			
MC	GEE		and		NOLAND	VA.	bk. 3A	pg. 104	
	Margaret	14	Sep	1861	Richard	off. J. NAYLOR			
MC	GEE		and		HUGHES	VA.	bk. 2A	pg. 072	
	W.T.	14	Apr	1841	Elizabeth	off. T. MAGILL			
MC	GLAUGHLIN		and		FORSE	WV.	bk. 4A	pg. 093	
	Elizabeth	05	Jul	1871	John H.	off. W. WHITE			
MC	GLAUGHLIN		and		CRANE	VA.	bk. 2A	pg. 043	
	William	30	Sep	1826	Sarah	off. C. MURRAY			
MC	GREGOR		and		TAYLOR	VA.	bk. 2A	pg. 080	
	Alexander	22	Feb	1825	Nancy	off. S. LAUCK			
MC	GREW		and		STEWART	WV.	bk. 4A	pg. 082	
	John	17	Feb	1871	Mary	off. W. WHITE			
MC	GROUERTY		and		DOUGHERTY	VA.	bk. 3A	pg. 068	
	Martha	30	Apr	1859	Patrick	off. J. NAYLOR			
MC	GUIRE		and		MC CREA	VA.	bk. 3A	pg. 065	
	Elizabeth	07	Mar	1859	William	off. J. NAYLOR			
MC	GUIRE		and		SMITH	VA.	bk. 1A	pg. 003	
	James	14	Dec	1797	Margaret	off. J. DODDRIDGE			
MC	GUIRE		and		GARDNER	WV.	bk. 3A	pg. 133	
	Mary Agnes	11	Nov	1863	James M.	off. H. SHEPHERD			
MC	GUIRE		and		GASSAGE	VA.	bk. 1A	pg. 003	
	Nancy	16	Nov	1797	Benjamin	off. J. DODDRIDGE			
MC	HENRY		and		PARISH	VA.	bk. 2A	pg. *15	
	Benjamin	03	Jul	1853	Mary	off. E. QUILLEN			
MC	HENRY		and		SOMERVILLE	VA.	bk. 2A	pg. 083	
	Jane	01	Jul	1841	William	off. R. WHITE			
MC	HENRY		and		CURRAN	VA.	bk. 01	pg. 004	
	Joseph	30	Mar	1856	Joanna	off. A. ENDSLEY			
MC	HENRY		and		RALSTON	WV.	bk. 3A	pg. 153	
	Lucy	01	Mar	1865	Joseph	off. H. SHEPHERD			

MC	HENRY		and		PARK		WV.	bk. 4A	pg. 142
	Mary	02	Sep	1874	Thomas C.		off. J.	LATIMER	
MC	HUGH		and		CRUTH		VA.	bk. 3A	pg. 109
	Mary Ann	11	Nov	1861	Andrew		off. J.	NAYLOR	
MC	HUGH		and		STOCK		VA.	bk. 01	pg. 004
	Rosanna	01	May	1856	Benjamin		off. J.	MEANS	
MC	INTIRE		and		LAZIER		VA.	bk. 2A	pg. 010
	John	05	May	1819	Charlotte		off. A.	CAMPBELL	
MC	INTIRE		and		BAIR		WV.	bk. 4A	pg. 029
	Robert (Sr.)	02	Sep	1867	Sarah E.		off. C.	MELVIN	
MC	INTIRE		and		DUNN		WV.	bk. 4A	pg. 029
	Robert (Sr.)	02	Sep	1867	Sarah (Mrs.)		off. C.	MELVIN	
MC	INTYRE		and		LEMON		VA.	bk. 2A	pg. 059
	Joseph	22	Nov	1827	Rebecca		off. E.	SMITH	
MC	INTYRE		and		WELLS		VA.	bk. 2A	pg. 059
	Margaret	28	Sep	1828	Ephraim		off. E.	SMITH	
MC	INTYRE		and		PETERS		VA.	bk. 01	pg. 005
	Margarett	26	Feb	1857	William		off. E.	QUILLEN	
MC	KAHEN		and		MC CONNELL		VA.	bk. 2A	pg. 001
	Daniel	02	Jul	1818	Margaret		off. J.	PRITCHARD	
MC	KEE		and		AKERS		VA.	bk. 2A	pg. 080
	Harriet	15	Feb	1828	Alexander		off. S.	LAUCK	
MC	KEE		and		HALL		WV.	bk. 4A	pg. 102
	James A.	14	Feb	1872	Mary E.		off. W.	LATIMER	
MC	KEE		and		JESTER		VA.	bk. 3A	pg. 076
	William H.	07	Nov	1859	Mary E.		off. J.	NAYLOR	
MC	KEEHAN		and		BLAIR		VA.	bk. 1A	pg. 008
	Samuel	14	Apr	1803	Elizabeth		off. J.	HUGHES	
MC	KEEVEN		and		ROGERS		VA.	bk. 2A	pg. 032
	John	07	Jul	1824	Elizabeth		off. J.	CAZAD	
MC	KIM		and		STRAIN		VA.	bk. 01	pg. 002
	Elizabeth	24	Aug	1854	Eleazer G.		off. S.	TOMPKINS	
MC	KIM		and		BEATTY		VA.	bk. 2A	pg. *09
	John	25	Sep	1851	Martina A.		off. C.	JACKSON	
MC	KIM		and		BENCE		VA.	bk. 3A	pg. 095
	Mary Jane	05	Oct	1860	Casper		off. J.	NAYLOR	
MC	KIM		and		ATKINSON		VA.	bk. 2A	pg. 040
	Thomas	16	Mar	1826	Nancy		off. G.	BUCHANAN	
MC	KINLEY		and		WAUGH		WV.	bk. 4A	pg. 002
	John W.	25	Oct	1865	Sarah		off. H.	SHEPHERD	
MC	KINLEY		and		POTTS		VA.	bk. 2A	pg. 069
	Sophia	20	Dec	1837	Stephen		off. J.	HERVEY	
MC	KINLEY		and		WAUGH		WV.	bk. 4A	pg. 046
	William L.	25	Mar	1868	Michael J.		off. H.	MELVIN	
MC	KINZIE		and		O'BRIEN		VA.	bk. 01	pg. 005
	Catharine	30	Sep	1856	Simpson		off. A.	ENDSLEY	
MC	KOWN		and		DUNCAN		VA.	bk. 2A	pg. 083
	Mary	29	Apr	1841	James		off. R.	WHITE	
MC	LAUGHLIN		and		FRAZIER		WV.	bk. 3A	pg. 140
	Carrie	22	Mar	1864	George A.		off. H.	SHEPHERD	
MC	LAUGHLIN		and		FORSE		WV.	bk. 4A	pg. 093
	Elizabeth	05	Jul	1871	John H.		off. W.	WHITE	

BROOKE CO., VA./WV. LICENSES & MARRIAGES, 1797-1874   81

Groom				Bride	Reference
MC LAUGHLIN Emily	15	Aug	1865	NIXON James	WV. bk. 3A pg. 157 off. H. SHEPHERD
MC LAUGHLIN Martha J.	13	Mar	1864	SHEARER Andrew J.	WV. bk. 3A pg. 139 off. H. SHEPHERD
MC LEASH James/John	06	Oct	1858	RODGERS Sarah	VA. bk. 3A pg. 057 off. J. NAYLOR
MC MAHAN Ann	15	Oct	1797	WORRELL Edward	VA. bk. 1A pg. 005 off. J. DODDRIDGE
MC MAHAN John	--	--	1803	COX Nancy	VA. bk. 1A pg. 047 off. UNKNOWN
MC MAHON Anne E.	22	Jan	1874	LETZKUS Adam	WV. bk. 4A pg. 134 off. W. LATIMER
MC MANIS Sarah	21	Sep	1867	KELLY Andrew	WV. bk. 4A pg. 030 off. C. MELVIN
MC MILLAN Catharine	03	May	1838	RABBITT Thomas	VA. bk. 2A pg. 082 off. R. WHITE
MC MILLAN Samuel	20	Sep	1838	LANGFITT Martha	VA. bk. 2A pg. 082 off. R. WHITE
MC MILLAN William	18	Feb	1841	ALLISON Jane	VA. bk. 2A pg. 083 off. R. WHITE
MC MILLEN Joseph	03	Sep	1828	CAMPBELL Susanna	VA. bk. 2A pg. 060 off. S. REED
MC MILLEN Melissa	24	Feb	1857	WABLE Samuel	VA. bk. 01 pg. 005 off. W. GAMBLE, JR.
MC NAIR Catherine	31	Dec	1853	WHETZELL Everett	VA. bk. 3A pg. 036 off. J. NAYLOR
MC NALLY Arthur F.	--	--	1867	CONNELL Ellen E.	WV. bk. 4A pg. 028 off. C. MELVIN
MC NALLY John B.	26	Oct	1867	DONNELLY Margaret	WV. bk. 4A pg. 033 off. H. MELVIN
MC NARY Robert	16	Nov	1827	MEEK Sarah	VA. bk. 2A pg. 048 off. J. CAZAD
MC NELLY Peter	02	May	1853	MC ARRAH Mary	VA. bk. 3A pg. 020 off. J. NAYLOR
MC WHA Mary E.	13	Oct	1864	STURGEON J.R.	WV. bk. 3A pg. 144 off. H. SHEPHERD
MEEK Elizabeth	21	Aug	1810	HAYS Samuel	VA. bk. 1A pg. 072 off. J. PRITCHARD
MEEK Joshua	02	Nov	1797	HEDGES Elizabeth	VA. bk. 1A pg. 002 off. J. DODDRIDGE
MEEK Mary	10	Feb	1820	HEADINGTON Greenberry	VA. bk. 2A pg. 010 off. O. JENNINGS
MEEK Matilda	21	Mar	1825	THORLEY John	VA. bk. 2A pg. 039 off. J. CAZAD
MEEK Sarah	16	Nov	1827	MC NARY Robert	VA. bk. 2A pg. 048 off. J. CAZAD
MEEK Susanah	07	Jun	1810	EDGINGTON John	VA. bk. 1A pg. 053 off. J. PRITCHARD
MEEK Thomas V.	06	Oct	1874	HINDMAN Maggie M.	WV. bk. 4A pg. 142 off. J. LATIMER
MEEKER Daniel	21	Apr	1866	MC COY Lydia	WV. bk. 3A pg. 161 off. H. SHEPHERD

82   BROOKE CO., VA./WV. LICENSES & MARRIAGES, 1797-1874

MELCHS			and	SEARS		WV. bk. 4A pg. 044
Margaret	27	Feb	1868	James		off. H. MELVIN
MELVIN			and	NAYLOR		VA. bk. 3A pg. 113
Addie	13	Feb	1862	Samuel G.		off. J. NAYLOR
MELVIN			and	SNOWDEN		VA. bk. 2A pg. 084
Alexander	20	Jun	1844	Jane		off. R. WHITE
MELVIN			and	THAYER		VA. bk. 2A pg. 041
Henry	22	Dec	1825	Elzina		off. J. BROWNING, JR.
MELVIN			and	MOORE		VA. bk. 2A pg. 084
Margaret	02	Jan	1843	Jackson		off. R. WHITE
MELVIN			and	ARMSTRONG		VA. bk. 2A pg. 068
Sarah	07	May	1840	Ebenezer		off. G. SCOTT
MELVIN			and	QUEST		WV. bk. 4A pg. 027
William H.	19	Jun	1867	Melissa E.		off. H. MELVIN
MENDEL			and	CHALLENCE		VA. bk. 01 pg. 004
Clarinda E.	11	Aug	1856	Elijah B.		off. A. CAMPBELL
MENDEL			and	CONNELL		VA. bk. 2A pg. 044
Elizabeth	22	Oct	1826	James S.		off. J. BROWNING, JR.
MENDEL			and	PRATHER		VA. bk. 2A pg. 044
Elizabeth	22	Oct	1826	John		off. J. BROWNING, JR.
MENDEL			and	MAGEE		VA. bk. 2A pg. *02
Elizabeth J.	22	Feb	1849	John J.		off. I. DALLAS
MENDEL			and	IRWIN		VA. bk. 2A pg. *08
Ellen	17	Jun	1851	John L.		off. R. WHITE
MENDEL			and	REEVES		VA. bk. 2A pg. 059
Henry	30	Mar	1828	Sarah		off. E. SMITH
MENDEL			and	MYERS		VA. bk. 2A pg. 075
Henry	21	Nov	1841	Rebecca		off. S. GRAFTON
MENDEL			and	MILLER		VA. bk. 3A pg. 047
Henry I.	05	Jan	1858	Martha S.		off. J. NAYLOR
MENDEL			and	DAWSON		VA. bk. 2A pg. *01
Mary	24	Jul	1849	Augustus M.		off. J. IRWIN
MENDEL			and	CONNELL		VA. bk. 2A pg. 090
Sarah	14	Dec	1847	Charles H.		off. J. MONROE
MENDEL			and	DURRETT		VA. bk. 01 pg. 006
Sarah H.	01	Sep	1857	Henry C.		off. A. CAMPBELL
MENDEL			and	OBNEY		VA. bk. 01 pg. 005
Tabitha	03	Mar	1857	James		off. A. ENDSLEY
MERCER			and	JACKSON		VA. bk. 2A pg. 060
Ellen	04	Sep	1828	Andrew		off. S. REED
MERCER			and	JACKSON		VA. bk. 2A pg. 083
Mary	15	Jan	1840	William		off. R. WHITE
MERCER			and	HART		VA. bk. 2A pg. 049
William	07	Jun	1827	Betsy		off. S. REED
MERRYMAN			and	BLANKENSOP		VA. bk. 3A pg. 085
Angeline	16	Jun	1860	George		off. J. NAYLOR
MERRYMAN			and	LLOYD		WV. bk. 3A pg. 145
Ella	20	Oct	1864	James H.		off. H. SHEPHERD
MERRYMAN			and	SHUPE		WV. bk. 4A pg. 097
Emma J.	11	Oct	1871	David D.		off. W. WHITE
MERRYMAN			and	MOORE		VA. bk. 2A pg. 012
John	04	Mar	1819	Malinda		off. L. BROWNING

BROOKE CO., VA./WV. LICENSES & MARRIAGES, 1797-1874   83

MERRYMAN		and		FINLEY	VA. bk. 3A pg. 128	
Mary	28	Apr	1863	Alexander	off. W. NAYLOR	
MERRYMAN		and		ROBERTS	VA. bk. 2A pg. *10	
William	18	Dec	1851	Elizabeth M.	off. H. SNYDER	
MEYERS		and		JACOB	WV. bk. 4A pg. 123	
Sallie	22	Feb	1873	Charles	off. W. LATIMER	
MICK		and		JOHNSTON	VA. bk. 2A pg. 083	
Mary	05	Nov	1840	John	off. R. WHITE	
MICK		and		SISSON	VA. bk. 2A pg. 083	
Peter	08	Oct	1840	Elizabeth	off. R. WHITE	
MILELECH		and		LETZKUS	WV. bk. 4A pg. 022	
Eva	31	Jan	1867	John	off. H. MELVIN	
MILLER		and		GUY	VA. bk. 3A pg. 126	
Agnes A.	20	Feb	1863	Shepherd L.	off. J. NAYLOR	
MILLER		and		PITTINGER	VA. bk. 2A pg. 040	
Benjamin	29	Jun	1826	Margaret	off. G. SCOTT	
MILLER		and		JONES	VA. bk. 1A pg. 078	
Charles	13	Jan	1815	Rebecca	off. W. WILLSON	
MILLER		and		THOMPSON	WV. bk. 3A pg. 138	
Cyrus	25	Feb	1864	Elizabeth	off. H. SHEPHERD	
MILLER		and		HEDGES	VA. bk. 2A pg. 007	
David	11	Feb	1817	Sarah	off. S. LAUCK	
MILLER		and		BOWMAN	VA. bk. 3A pg. 108	
David B.	05	Nov	1861	Cecelia M.	off. S. NAYLOR	
MILLER		and		HUKILL	WV. bk. 3A pg. 150	
David B.	16	Jan	1865	Mary	off. H. SHEPHERD	
MILLER		and		GEORGE	VA. bk. 01 pg. 003	
Elenora	09	Nov	1854	Samuel	off. E. QUILLEN	
MILLER		and		JONES	WV. bk. 4A pg. 032	
Elizabeth A.	12	Oct	1867	James M.	off. H. MELVIN	
MILLER		and		JEROME	VA. bk. 1A pg. 078	
Emily	16	Jun	1814	John	off. W. WILLSON	
MILLER		and		BLANKENSOP	WV. bk. 4A pg. 122	
Frank	10	Feb	1873	Sallie	off. W. LATIMER	
MILLER		and		CASNER	WV. bk. 4A pg. 074	
George	27	Aug	1870	Cora	off. W. WHITE	
MILLER		and		STEWART	WV. bk. 4A pg. 054	
Jacob	21	Dec	1868	Elizabeth C.	off. S. QUEST	
MILLER		and		HALL	WV. bk. 4A pg. 092	
James L.	02	Jun	1871	Elizabeth	off. W. WHITE	
MILLER		and		CUNNINGHAM	VA. bk. 3A pg. 038	
Jane	11	Jan	1854	Cyrus H.	off. J. NAYLOR	
MILLER		and		WYLIE	VA. bk. 2A pg. 007	
John	13	Apr	1818	Mary	off. E. MACURDY	
MILLER		and		CALENDINE	VA. bk. 2A pg. 060	
John	17	Mar	1829	Catharine	off. E. SMITH	
MILLER		and		RICHARDSON	VA. bk. 2A pg. *10	
John	07	Mar	1852	Nancy	off. H. SNYDER	
MILLER		and		SANDERS	WV. bk. 4A pg. 065	
John H.	29	Nov	1869	Letitia J.	off. W. WHITE	
MILLER		and		BECK	VA. bk. 2A pg. 007	
Joseph	31	Oct	1816	Sarah	off. S. LAUCK	

Name		Date		Spouse	Location
MILLER Joseph	15	and Aug	1824	MUNCY Unity	VA. bk. 2A pg. 033 off. A. CAMPBELL
MILLER Martha S.	05	and Jan	1858	MENDEL Henry I.	VA. bk. 3A pg. 047 off. J. NAYLOR
MILLER Mary	03	and Jun	1826	SNEDIKER Garret	VA. bk. 2A pg. 042 off. C. MURRAY
MILLER Mary Ann	23	and Dec	1838	HESSEY James	VA. bk. 2A pg. 067 off. A. YOUNG
MILLER Robert	14	and Mar	1868	NAYLOR Sallie	WV. bk. 4A pg. 045 off. H. MELVIN
MILLER Robert L.	29	and Dec	1866	HENDRICKS Catharine M.	WV. bk. 4A pg. 020 off. R. NICHOLLS
MILLER Rosann	21	and Jul	1870	DOW Isaac	WV. bk. 4A pg. 072 off. W. WHITE
MILLER Samuel	18	and Dec	1866	BICKERSTAFF Nancy	WV. bk. 4A pg. 017 off. R. NICHOLLS
MILLER Sarah	09	and Jul	1856	DUVALL Isaac	VA. bk. 01 pg. 005 off. A. ENDSLEY
MILLER Sarah	13	and Nov	1814	TALBOTT James	VA. bk. 1A pg. 078 off. W. WILLSON
MILLER Sarah J.	06	and Jun	1848	WALKER Nathan U.	VA. bk. 2A pg. 093 off. S. WORTHINGTON
MILLER Unity (Mrs.)	26	and Dec	1859	COX George	VA. bk. 3A pg. 080 off. J. NAYLOR
MILLIGAN Mary Ann	22	and Nov	1859	CONAWAY Evan	VA. bk. 3A pg. 077 off. J. NAYLOR
MILLIGAN Sarah	20	and Nov	1865	RIDDLE David	WV. bk. 4A pg. 003 off. H. SHEPHERD
MILLS Elizabeth Jane	--	and --	1844	BAXTER John	VA. bk. 2A pg. 080 off. R. SIMONTAIS
MILLS Jonathan	05	and Aug	1829	PENTECOST Lucinda	VA. bk. 2A pg. 058 off. D. MERRYMAN
MINGUS Luthada	19	and Aug	1848	VANHORN John	VA. bk. 2A pg. *02 off. I. DALLAS
MITCHELL Elizabeth	16	and Nov	1864	MURPHY George Wash.	WV. bk. 3A pg. 147 off. H. SHEPHERD
MITCHELL Francis	09	and Aug	1803	GASS Mary	VA. bk. 1A pg. 037 off. J. DODDRIDGE
MITCHELL Mary	15	and Oct	1868	WILLQUES Lewis	WV. bk. 4A pg. 051 off. S. QUEST
MITCHELL William H.	09	and Feb	1859	BARNES Lydia M.	VA. bk. 3A pg. 064 off. J. NAYLOR
MODERWELL Isabel	08	and Jun	1820	MAJORS John (Jr.)	VA. bk. 2A pg. 015 off. L. BROWNING
MONTGOMERY Joseph	03	and Oct	1867	LAUGHEAD Sophia	WV. bk. 4A pg. 007 off. R. NICHOLLS
MONTGOMERY Joseph	03	and Oct	1867	PILLINGS Sophia (Mrs.)	WV. bk. 4A pg. 007 off. H. MELVIN
MONTGOMERY Joseph E.	21	and Dec	1861	PILLINGS Sarah E.	VA. bk. 3A pg. 110 off. S. NAYLOR
MONTGOMERY Mary E.	23	and Jan	1868	CARTER Ewing T.	WV. bk. 4A pg. 058 off. W. WHITE

BROOKE CO., VA./WV. LICENSES & MARRIAGES, 1797-1874   85

Groom		Date		Bride	Reference
MONTGOMERY Robert	and 29	Nov	1832	CAMERON Lucinda	VA. bk. 2A pg. 062 off. G. BUCHANAN
MOOKLAR James Phillips	and 22	Dec	1865	PENDLETON Alexandria C.	WV. bk. 4A pg. 004 off. H. SHEPHERD
MOORE Asbury S.	and 17	Jan	1865	LAZEAR Lorinda	WV. bk. 3A pg. 150 off. H. SHEPHERD
MOORE Eli H.	and 11	Oct	1853	WILSON Narcissa	VA. bk. 2A pg. *16 off. S. TOMPKINS
MOORE Elizabeth	and 31	Oct	1816	LYON Andrew	VA. bk. 2A pg. 006 off. G. SCOTT
MOORE Elizabeth	and 10	Nov	1857	PALMER James	VA. bk. 3A pg. 044 off. J. NAYLOR
MOORE Jackson	and 02	Jan	1843	MELVIN Margaret	VA. bk. 2A pg. 084 off. R. WHITE
MOORE James W.	and 27	Sep	1838	GORDON Jane	VA. bk. 2A pg. 064 off. D. HERVEY
MOORE Jane	and 12	Mar	1812	MARSHALL William	VA. bk. 1A pg. 072 off. J. PRITCHARD
MOORE Jane	and 15	Jul	1852	SCOTT James	VA. bk. 2A pg. *12 off. D. HERVEY
MOORE John	and 01	Feb	1806	WILLIAMSON Jane	VA. bk. 1A pg. 022 off. UNKNOWN
MOORE John	and 07	May	1806	WILLIAMSON Jane	VA. bk. 1A pg. 030 off. J. HUGHES
MOORE Malinda	and 04	Mar	1819	MERRYMAN John	VA. bk. 2A pg. 012 off. L. BROWNING
MOORE Maria	and 18	Feb	1830	WAUGH David	VA. bk. 2A pg. 055 off. J. MC KENNAR
MOORE Robert	and 06	May	1840	WELLS Eliza. Jane	VA. bk. 2A pg. 069 off. M. TELCHENELL
MOORE Sarah	and 21	Dec	1825	EDER Thomas	VA. bk. 2A pg. 037 off. G. SCOTT
MOORE William	and 30	Aug	1832	WILLIAMS Jane	VA. bk. 2A pg. 062 off. G. BUCHANAN
MORAN James A.	and 07	Mar	1849	ROBINSON Sarah J.	VA. bk. 2A pg. *02 off. I. DALLAS
MOREHEAD Abraham	and 28	Jun	1841	RALSTON Martha	VA. bk. 2A pg. 071 off. J. GALLOWAY
MOREHEAD Margaret	and 19	Feb	1829	EBIATH Thomas	VA. bk. 2A pg. 060 off. S. REED
MOREHEAD Martha Jane	and 17	Nov	1842	RALSTON George	VA. bk. 2A pg. 077 off. J. GALLOWAY
MOREHEAD Mary	and 02	Aug	1813	RALSTON Joseph	VA. bk. 1A pg. 065 off. UNKNOWN
MOREN Harriet	and 21	Jul	1841	CRAWFORD George	VA. bk. 2A pg. 072 off. D. HERVEY
MOREN John T.	and 13	Jan	1848	ADAMS Agnes	VA. bk. 2A pg. 090 off. J. MONROE
MORENTZ Hannah	and 05	May	1865	KELLY William	WV. bk. 3A pg. 155 off. H. SHEPHERD
MORGAN Edward	and 13	Jan	1820	HEDGES Elizabeth	VA. bk. 2A pg. 022 off. J. LAWS

Groom		Date		Bride	Reference
MORGAN Emily	14	and Mar	1844	HANCOCK John	VA. bk. 2A pg. 079 off. S. WORTHINGTON
MORGAN Henry C.	08	and Jun	1861	HUDSON Cynthia A.	VA. bk. 3A pg. 102 off. J. NAYLOR
MORGAN John (Jr.)	17	and Jul	1863	HUDSON M. Belle	WV. bk. 3A pg. 129 off. H. SHEPHERD
MORGAN John M.	18	and Nov	1852	HEDGES Ann Eliza.	VA. bk. 2A pg. *14 off. S. NESBITT
MORGAN McCullough	31	and Dec	1866	COLEMAN Clara B.	WV. bk. 4A pg. 021 off. H. SHEPHERD
MORGAN William Finley	19	and Aug	1863	HERVEY Mary	WV. bk. 3A pg. 131 off. H. SHEPHERD
MORLEY Evander	16	and Sep	1872	BRIGGS Alice U.	WV. bk. 4A pg. 117 off. W. LATIMER
MORRIS Micheal	04	and Nov	1853	DINSMORE Mary	VA. bk. 3A pg. 029 off. J. NAYLOR
MORRISON John	27	and Jan	1825	SNEDIKER Aliche	VA. bk. 2A pg. 080 off. S. LAUCK
MORRISON John B.	28	and Oct	1824	MAGERS Nancy	VA. bk. 2A pg. 035 off. N. HEADINGTON
MORROW Aaron	03	and Mar	1842	CLARK Jane	VA. bk. 2A pg. 083 off. R. WHITE
MORROW Alexander	26	and Sep	1820	WELCH Susanna	VA. bk. 2A pg. 019 off. E. MACURDY
MORROW Elizabeth	07	and Mar	1820	HAMILTON John	VA. bk. 2A pg. 017 off. S. LAUCK
MORROW James	28	and Dec	1802	DAVIS Ruth	VA. bk. 1A pg. 037 off. J. DODDRIDGE
MORROW James	29	and Dec	1812	ELLIOT Nancy	VA. bk. 1A pg. 076 off. UNKNOWN
MORROW James	20	and Feb	1839	ALLISON Eleanor	VA. bk. 2A pg. 082 off. R. WHITE
MORROW James	12	and May	1846	CUNNINGHAM Nancy	VA. bk. 2A pg. 088 off. J. GALLOWAY
MORROW Margaret	25	and Jun	1839	SWEARINGEN Benjamin	VA. bk. 2A pg. 066 off. W. SCULL
MORROW Nancy	06	and Aug	1805	LOGUE Samuel	VA. bk. 1A pg. 025 off. E. MACURDY
MORROW Nancy	04	and Mar	1841	YOUNG Andrew	VA. bk. 2A pg. 083 off. R. WHITE
MORROW Robert	19	and Jan	1847	WARWICK Margaret	VA. bk. 2A pg. 089 off. J. GALLOWAY
MORROW William	23	and Jul	1868	KEESEY Nancy	WV. bk. 01 pg. 019 off. R. PRICE
MORTON Amanda J.	16	and May	1871	BROWN George W.	WV. bk. 4A pg. 089 off. W. WHITE
MORTON Elizabeth	16	and Mar	1864	CAMPBELL Greer M.	WV. bk. 3A pg. 139 off. H. SHEPHERD
MORTON J.C.	13	and Feb	1873	LAKE Elisabeth	WV. bk. 4A pg. 122 off. W. LATIMER
MORTON John (Jr.)	18	and Mar	1859	MARSH Harriet	VA. bk. 3A pg. 065 off. J. NAYLOR

BROOKE CO., VA./WV. LICENSES & MARRIAGES, 1797-1874   87

Name 1				Name 2	Reference
MORTON	and			CORNELIUS	VA. bk. 3A pg. 037
Mary	07	Jan	1854	John	off. J. NAYLOR
MOSS	and			HAYS	VA. bk. 2A pg. 025
William	19	Dec	1822	Jane	off. G. BUCHANAN
MOSS	and			JONES	WV. bk. 4A pg. 078
William Rose	22	Dec	1870	Amy H.	off. W. WHITE
MOUNTAIN	and			TERLY	WV. bk. 3A pg. 147
Margaret	12	Nov	1864	Hugh	off. H. SHEPHERD
MOUNTS	and			DARLING	VA. bk. 1A pg. 081
Providence	29	Aug	1811	Sarah	off. UNKNOWN
MOURLAND	and			JESTY	WV. bk. 01 pg. 014
Margaret	13	Nov	1864	Hugh	off. S. HUBER
MULLANY	and			MAGEE	WV. bk. 3A pg. 144
Thomas	11	Sep	1864	Ellen	off. H. SHEPHERD
MUNCY	and			PLATTENBURGH	VA. bk. 2A pg. 053
Sarah	04	May	1826	Joshua	off. L. BROWNING
MUNCY	and			MILLER	VA. bk. 2A pg. 033
Unity	15	Aug	1824	Joseph	off. A. CAMPBELL
MUNCY	and			COX	VA. bk. 3A pg. 080
Unity	26	Dec	1859	George	off. J. NAYLOR
MUNTY	and			HARPER	VA. bk. 2A pg. 088
Hugh	08	Oct	1848	Jane	off. J. MONROE
MURCHLAND	and			BUCKALEW	VA. bk. 3A pg. 116
David H.	31	May	1862	Josephine	off. J. NAYLOR
MURCHLAND	and			BOWLES	WV. bk. 4A pg. 054
Elizabeth	16	Dec	1868	John W.	off. S. QUEST
MURCHLAND	and			JOHNSTON	VA. bk. 2A pg. 093
Isabella	15	Jun	1848	James	off. J. MONROE
MURCHLAND	and			HEADINGTON	VA. bk. 2A pg. 059
Jane	11	Sep	1828	John	off. E. SMITH
MURCHLAND	and			NEAL	VA. bk. 2A pg. 060
Mary	11	Dec	1828	James	off. E. SMITH
MURCHLAND	and			BOYD	VA. bk. 2A pg. *05
Nancy	15	Aug	1850	Robert	off. J. STOCKTON
MURCHLAND	and			HINDMAN	WV. bk. 4A pg. 046
Nancy	20	Mar	1868	Samuel	off. H. MELVIN
MURCHLAND	and			HINDMAN	VA. bk. 2A pg. *04
Robert	25	Nov	1849	Harriet	off. J. GALLOWAY
MURCHLAND	and			WHEELER	VA. bk. 2A pg. 088
Sarah	12	Mar	1846	Thomas	off. G. BUCHANAN
MURCHLAND	and			WRIGHT	VA. bk. 3A pg. 066
Sarah E.	25	Apr	1859	Nathaniel W.	off. J. NAYLOR
MURDOCK	and			MURDOCK	VA. bk. 2A pg. 068
Eliza. (...ROW)	07	May	1840	Ezekiel	off. G. SCOTT
MURDOCK	and			MURDOCK	VA. bk. 2A pg. 068
Ezekiel	07	May	1840	Eliza. (...)	off. G. SCOTT
MURPHY	and			CARR	VA. bk. 3A pg. 038
Benjamin	14	Jan	1854	Rebecca	off. J. NAYLOR
MURPHY	and			COLLINS	WV. bk. 4A pg. 130
Bridget	04	Nov	1873	Timothy	off. W. LATIMER
MURPHY	and			DUVALL	VA. bk. 2A pg. 090
Catharine	31	Oct	1847	James M.	off. J. MONROE

88   BROOKE CO., VA./WV. LICENSES & MARRIAGES, 1797-1874

Groom surname	Groom given		Date		Bride surname	Bride given	Reference
MURPHY	Elizabeth	02 Jan	1863	STARR	Joseph		VA. bk. 3A pg. 124 off. J. NAYLOR
MURPHY	George Wash.	20 Jul	1863	STARR	Nancy J.		WV. bk. 3A pg. 129 off. H. SHEPHERD
MURPHY	George Wash.	16 Nov	1864	MITCHELL	Elizabeth		WV. bk. 3A pg. 147 off. H. SHEPHERD
MURPHY	Hannah	31 May	1838	PROSSER	Daniel		VA. bk. 2A pg. 064 off. L. BROWNING
MURPHY	James F.	04 May	1868	REEVES	Sallie E.		WV. bk. 4A pg. 047 off. C. MELVIN
MURPHY	Joseph	26 Oct	1847	FENWICK	Edith		VA. bk. 2A pg. 090 off. J. MONROE
MURPHY	Matilda	01 Jun	1855	RIDDLE	David		VA. bk. 01 pg. 003 off. E. QUILLEN
MURRAY	Eleanor J.	04 Dec	1867	NEDENGARDEN	Henry		WV. bk. 4A pg. 035 off. H. MELVIN
MURRAY	James A.	08 Jul	1870	CAMPBELL	Anna B.		WV. bk. 01 pg. 020 off. A. CAMPBELL
MURRAY	James A.	08 Jul	1870	POSTON	Anna B. (Mrs.)		WV. bk. 01 pg. 020 off. A. CAMPBELL
MURRY	Nicholas	26 Jul	1802	ADAMS	Nancy		VA. bk. 1A pg. 039 off. J. DODDRIDGE
MUSSER	Sarah	-- --	1809	WILLIAMSON	James C.		VA. bk. 1A pg. 048 off. UNKNOWN
MUSSER	Sophia	-- --	1802	DODDRIDGE	Benjamin		VA. bk. 1A pg. 045 off. UNKNOWN
MUSTARD	John	12 Mar	1812	RUSSELL	Elizabeth		VA. bk. 1A pg. 066 off. E. MACURDY
MYERS	Betsy	30 Jun	1817	NATCHY	Thomas		VA. bk. 2A pg. 001 off. E. MACURDY
MYERS	Mary (Mrs.)	24 Oct	1863	HILL	Salathiel		WV. bk. 3A pg. 132 off. H. SHEPHERD
MYERS	Rebecca	21 Nov	1841	MENDEL	Henry		VA. bk. 2A pg. 075 off. S. GRAFTON
MYLAR	Mary	22 Jun	1822	ATEN	John		VA. bk. 2A pg. 023 off. G. SCOTT
NALLINGER	Rosena	24 Jul	1873	PERKINS	Asbury		WV. bk. 4A pg. 126 off. W. LATIMER
NAMRY	Sarah	05 May	1807	STEVENSON	Thomas		VA. bk. 1A pg. 030 off. J. HUGHES
NANGLE	Elizabeth	08 Feb	1859	D'FOSSIT	John A.		VA. bk. 3A pg. 063 off. J. NAYLOR
NANGLE	Mary	25 Aug	1859	WILLIAMS	Valentine		VA. bk. 3A pg. 073 off. J. NAYLOR
NANGLE	Samuel G.	02 Jan	1864	BRASHEARS	Mary		WV. bk. 3A pg. 136 off. H. SHEPHERD
NASMITH	Mary	02 Jan	1866	DEIGHTON	Ralph		WV. bk. 4A pg. 005 off. H. SHEPHERD
NATCHY	Thomas	30 Jun	1817	MYERS	Betsy		VA. bk. 2A pg. 001 off. E. MACURDY
NAYLOR	Elizabeth T.	24 Feb	1872	SCARBOROUGH	J.A.		WV. bk. 4A pg. 107 off. W. LATIMER

BROOKE CO., VA./WV. LICENSES & MARRIAGES, 1797-1874   89

Name					Spouse	Location
NAYLOR			and		MILLER	WV. bk. 4A pg. 045
Sallie	14	Mar	1868		Robert	off. H. MELVIN
NAYLOR			and		MELVIN	VA. bk. 3A pg. 113
Samuel G.	13	Feb	1862		Addie	off. J. NAYLOR
NEAL			and		MURCHLAND	VA. bk. 2A pg. 060
James	11	Dec	1828		Mary	off. E. SMITH
NEAUGIN			and		STEWART	VA. bk. 2A pg. 082
Mary	20	Sep	1838		Robert	off. R. WHITE
NEDENGARDEN			and		MURRAY	WV. bk. 4A pg. 035
Henry	04	Dec	1867		Eleanor J.	off. H. MELVIN
NEELEY			and		HUPP	VA. bk. 3A pg. 117
Hugh N.	08	Oct	1862		Emma	off. J. NAYLOR
NELSON			and		ANTILL	WV. bk. 3A pg. 149
John M.	28	Dec	1864		Rebecca V.	off. H. SHEPHERD
NELSON			and		COLEMAN	VA. bk. 1A pg. 005
Joseph	18	Sep	1798		Ann	off. J. HUGHES
NELSON			and		IRWIN	VA. bk. 1A pg. 058
Mary	03	Aug	1810		James	off. J. PRITCHARD
NELSON			and		FITCH	PA. bk. 01 pg. 054
Nathaniel	10	Aug	1858		K.A.	off. J. MC CONAUGHY
NEWELL			and		EDIE	VA. bk. 2A pg. 049
John	28	Nov	1826		Lydia	off. S. REED
NEWELL			and		KERR	VA. bk. 2A pg. *05
Sarah	19	Feb	1850		John C.	off. J. STOCKTON
NEWLAND			and		CRAFT	VA. bk. 2A pg. 080
Rebecca	16	May	1821		Charles H.	off. S. LAUCK
NICHOLLS			and		HAYS	WV. bk. 4A pg. 061
Alexander C.	26	Apr	1869		Mary A.	off. W. WHITE
NICHOLLS			and		ELSON	VA. bk. 2A pg. 069
Charlotte	30	Jan	1840		Alexander M.	off. M. TELCHENELL
NICHOLLS			and		DONOVAN	VA. bk. 2A pg. 059
Elizabeth	28	Feb	1828		Absalom	off. E. SMITH
NICHOLLS			and		BARNES	WV. bk. 4A pg. 039
Mary Elizabeth	28	Dec	1867		Shepley	off. C. MELVIN
NISWANGER			and		GODDARD	VA. bk. 2A pg. 069
George	06	Apr	1840		Mary	off. M. TELCHENELL
NIXON			and		MC LAUGHLIN	WV. bk. 3A pg. 157
James	15	Aug	1865		Emily	off. H. SHEPHERD
NOAH			and		BUXTON	VA. bk. 3A pg. 111
Marg't Ellenor	03	Dec	1862		James	off. S. NAYLOR
NOBLE			and		LEWIS	WV. bk. 4A pg. 006
Tarlton	12	Feb	1866		Sarah J.	off. R. NICHOLLS
NOBLE			and		BEERBOWER	WV. bk. 4A pg. 104
Westley	09	Jan	1872		Elizabeth	off. W. LATIMER
NOLAN			and		CARTER	VA. bk. 1A pg. 081
Sampson	08	Jun	1812		Elisabeth	off. UNKNOWN
NOLAND			and		HEDGES	VA. bk. 1A pg. 034
James	--	Sep	1809		Ruth	off. UNKNOWN
NOLAND			and		PADEN	VA. bk. 2A pg. *02
Rebecca A.	11	Jan	1849		William	off. I. DALLAS
NOLAND			and		MC GEE	VA. bk. 3A pg. 104
Richard	14	Sep	1861		Margaret	off. J. NAYLOR

NORMAN		and		PERRY	VA.	bk. 2A	pg.	058
Nathaniel	29	Oct	1829	Tabitha	off. D. MERRYMAN			
NUNEMAKER		and		ADAMS	VA.	bk. 2A	pg.	*09
Catharine	09	Oct	1851	Richard	off. H. SNYDER			
NUNEMAKER		and		WELLS	VA.	bk. 2A	pg.	076
George	06	Apr	1843	Ruth	off. C. BEST			
NUNEMAKER		and		STOCKS	VA.	bk. 2A	pg.	*13
Jacob	02	Dec	1852	Mary	off. H. SNYDER			
NUNEMAKER		and		LEE	VA.	bk. 01	pg.	005
William	19	Feb	1857	Julia Ann	off. G. CRANAGE			
O'BRIEN		and		MC KINZIE	VA.	bk. 01	pg.	005
Simpson	30	Sep	1856	Catharine	off. A. ENDSLEY			
O'HARA		and		MC CONNELL	VA.	bk. 01	pg.	005
Anne	01	Sep	1857	James	off. J. BRAZILL			
O'HARA		and		CONNERS	WV.	bk. 4A	pg.	087
Bernard	09	May	1871	Margery	off. W. LATIMER			
O'HARA		and		DEVINNEY	VA.	bk. 01	pg.	005
Margaret	15	Oct	1856	Charles	off. J. BRAZILL			
O'HARE		and		DOWNEY	VA.	bk. 3A	pg.	096
John	04	Dec	1860	Rosanna	off. J. NAYLOR			
O'NEAL		and		INGLEBRIGHT	WV.	bk. 4A	pg.	004
William J.	01	Dec	1865	Harriet	off. H. SHEPHERD			
O'SHANDER		and		JOHNSTON	VA.	bk. 01	pg.	009
Jacob Charles	18	Feb	1860	Susan	off. G. CHESTER			
O'WESNEY		and		MC CHRISTAL	VA.	bk. 3A	pg.	083
James	10	Apr	1860	Rose Ann	off. J. NAYLOR			
OBNEY		and		MENDEL	VA.	bk. 01	pg.	005
James	03	Mar	1857	Tabitha	off. A. ENDSLEY			
OGDEN		and		SWEARINGEN	VA.	bk. 2A	pg.	060
John	27	May	1828	Martha	off. S. REED			
OGDEN		and		SCOTT	VA.	bk. 2A	pg.	049
Rachael	22	Feb	1827	Josiah	off. S. REED			
ORAM		and		HINDMAN	WV.	bk. 4A	pg.	083
Addie	22	Feb	1871	Mathew	off. W. WHITE			
ORAM		and		PARKINSON	VA.	bk. 3A	pg.	052
Margaret E.	31	Mar	1858	George A.	off. J. NAYLOR			
ORAM		and		HUKILL	VA.	bk. 3A	pg.	125
Matilda	03	Feb	1863	Joseph	off. J. NAYLOR			
ORAM		and		BOWERS	VA.	bk. 01	pg.	005
Nancy	30	Oct	1856	Adam	off. E. QUILLEN			
ORAM		and		HUKILL	VA.	bk. 3A	pg.	121
Philip C.	17	Nov	1862	Elizabeth	off. J. NAYLOR			
ORAM		and		CAIN	VA.	bk. 1A	pg.	040
Smallwood	06	May	1802	Nancy	off. J. DODDRIDGE			
ORAM		and		BUNN	VA.	bk. 1A	pg.	039
Thomas	05	Sep	1802	Elizabeth	off. J. DODDRIDGE			
ORANGE		and		TAYLOR	WV.	bk. 4A	pg.	125
Sarah	14	Jun	1873	Robert	off. W. LATIMER			
ORR		and		CURRAN	VA.	bk. 3A	pg.	068
Edward	09	May	1859	Margaret	off. J. NAYLOR			
ORR		and		ARCHER	VA.	bk. 2A	pg.	083
George G.	09	Nov	1841	Elizabeth	off. R. WHITE			

ORR			and	LEE	VA. bk. 1A pg. 014
Hannah	14	Aug	1804	Hugh	off. E. MACURDY
ORR			and	RIDGELEY	VA. bk. 1A pg. 065
Jane	21	Mar	1816	William	off. J. CONNELL
ORR			and	ANDERSON	WV. bk. 4A pg. 031
Maggy B.	21	Oct	1867	T.F.	off. H. MELVIN
ORR			and	BROWN	VA. bk. 3A pg. 015
Margaret	14	Mar	1853	William	off. J. NAYLOR
ORR			and	ARMSTRONG	VA. bk. 2A pg. 020
Margaret	29	Apr	1821	Martin	off. E. MACURDY
ORR			and	MC COWAN	VA. bk. 2A pg. 063
Mary	15	Jun	1833	James	off. R. BROWN
ORR			and	INGLEBRIGHT	WV. bk. 4A pg. 017
Mary	20	Dec	1866	Levi W.	off. R. NICHOLLS
ORSPBODY?			and	SENSHODY	VA. bk. 3A pg. 079
Jane C.	15	Dec	1859	John	off. UNKNOWN
OWEN			and	BRANDON	WV. bk. 3A pg. 134
George	09	Dec	1863	Margaret C.	off. H. SHEPHERD
OWEN			and	WELLS	VA. bk. 1A pg. 055
Henry	19	Jan	1809	Elizabeth	off. W. WILLSON
OWEN			and	BUTLER	VA. bk. 1A pg. 022
Phebe	20	Nov	1806	Nicholas	off. J. PRITCHARD
OWENS			and	ACKINSON	VA. bk. 1A pg. 079
Amelia	22	May	1813	William	off. J. PRITCHARD
OWENS			and	RALSTON	WV. bk. 3A pg. 149
Elizabeth	26	Dec	1864	William	off. H. SHEPHERD
OWENS			and	GRIFFITH	VA. bk. 01 pg. 010
Helen	15	Feb	1860	John A.	off. J. CALHOUN
OWENS			and	SWEARINGEN	VA. bk. 2A pg. 026
Micha	03	Jul	1823	Nicholas	off. G. BUCHANAN
OWINGS			and	SWEARINGEN	VA. bk. 2A pg. 029
Absalom	29	Jan	1824	Sarah	off. G. BUCHANAN
OWINGS			and	DONOVAN	VA. bk. 2A pg. 057
Asa	04	Feb	1830	Ruth	off. G. BUCHANAN
OWINGS			and	DONOVAN	VA. bk. 2A pg. 053
Catherine	19	Oct	1826	Thomas	off. G. BUCHANAN
OWINGS			and	SWEARINGEN	VA. bk. 2A pg. 036
Ephraim	12	Jan	1826	Blanche	off. G. BUCHANAN
OWINGS			and	COULTER	VA. bk. 2A pg. 018
John	02	May	1821	Olivia	off. G. BUCHANAN
OWINGS			and	MAHAN	VA. bk. 2A pg. 093
Michel	02	Dec	1847	James	off. G. HOLMES
OWINGS			and	WELLS	VA. bk. 2A pg. 073
Rebecca	30	Jun	1842	Nathaniel	off. G. BUCHANAN
OWINGS			and	FULLERTON	VA. bk. 3A pg. 062
Verlinda	25	Jan	1859	Henry	off. J. NAYLOR
OWINGS			and	WHEELER	VA. bk. 2A pg. 072
Wells	11	Mar	1841	Honor	off. G. BUCHANAN
PADEN			and	HALL	WV. bk. 4A pg. 034
Ella	23	Nov	1867	Lewis C.	off. H. MELVIN
PADEN			and	NOLAND	VA. bk. 2A pg. *02
William	11	Jan	1849	Rebecca A.	off. I. DALLAS

Surname	Given	Day	Mo	Year	Spouse Surname	Spouse Given	Location	Book	Page
PALMER	Arthur Stone	01	Aug	1863	WRIGHTMAN	Sallie C.	off. H. SHEPHERD	WV. bk. 3A	pg. 130
PALMER	Caroline A.	07	Feb	1856	WAUGH	James	off. E. QUILLEN	VA. bk. 01	pg. 004
PALMER	Francis	05	Oct	1854	BROWNLEE	Nancy	off. S. NESBITT	VA. bk. 01	pg. 002
PALMER	James	10	Nov	1857	WAUGH	Elizabeth	off. J. NAYLOR	VA. bk. 3A	pg. 044
PALMER	John C.	16	Aug	1859	WAUGH	Fannie T.	off. J. NAYLOR	VA. bk. 3A	pg. 073
PALMER	Samuel	14	Dec	1851	DOWDEN	Mary	off. H. SNYDER	VA. bk. 2A	pg. *10
PARISH	Ellen	09	Dec	1852	APPLEGATE	Andrew	off. E. QUILLEN	VA. bk. 2A	pg. *13
PARISH	John D.	30	Mar	1872	BEALL	Lillie	off. W. LATIMER	WV. bk. 4A	pg. 109
PARISH	Mary	03	Jul	1853	MC HENRY	Benjamin	off. E. QUILLEN	VA. bk. 2A	pg. *15
PARISH	Thomas B.	19	Feb	1873	DORSEY	Drusilla	off. W. LATIMER	WV. bk. 4A	pg. 123
PARK	George M.	30	Apr	1872	HESSEY	Jennie	off. W. LATIMER	WV. bk. 4A	pg. 111
PARK	Joanna	09	Jan	1823	MC EWING	John	off. G. SCOTT	VA. bk. 2A	pg. 026
PARK	Julia A.E.	27	Jun	1841	THORN	Zadoc S.	off. T. STEIRSHCOMB	VA. bk. 2A	pg. 071
PARK	Madison W.	19	Nov	1873	GREEN	Jennie May	off. W. LATIMER	WV. bk. 4A	pg. 131
PARK	Mathew C.	19	Mar	1872	WRIGHT	Louisa	off. W. LATIMER	WV. bk. 4A	pg. 109
PARK	Robert	19	May	1839	KIRK	Isabella	off. W. SCULL	VA. bk. 2A	pg. 066
PARK	Robert (Jr.)	21	Aug	1823	SWEARINGEN	Velinda	off. G. BUCHANAN	VA. bk. 2A	pg. 027
PARK	Thomas C.	02	Sep	1874	MC HENRY	Mary	off. J. LATIMER	WV. bk. 4A	pg. 142
PARK	William	07	Nov	1829	ADAMS	Jane	off. T. BEEKS	VA. bk. 2A	pg. 058
PARKER	Martha E.	02	Jun	1864	LALLANCE	Charles N.	off. H. SHEPHERD	WV. bk. 3A	pg. 141
PARKINSON	David	17	Nov	1825	TALBOTT	Antionette	off. A. CAMPBELL	VA. bk. 2A	pg. 038
PARKINSON	George A.	31	Mar	1858	ORAM	Margaret E.	off. J. NAYLOR	VA. bk. 3A	pg. 052
PARKINSON	Martha	19	Dec	1808	COULTROUGH	Benjamin	off. J. HUGHES	VA. bk. 1A	pg. 036
PARKS	Ann	03	Apr	1817	FORMAN	Charles D.	off. E. MACURDY	VA. bk. 2A	pg. 001
PARKS	Robert	30	Nov	1854	HINDMAN	Charity	off. W. LEMON	VA. bk. 01	pg. 003
PARKY	Mary	29	Jan	1807	FOWLER	Richard	off. E. MACURDY	VA. bk. 1A	pg. 026

BROOKE CO., VA./WV. LICENSES & MARRIAGES, 1797-1874   93

Name		Day	Month	Year	Spouse	Officiant/Ref
PARROTT	and				TRIMBLE	VA. bk. 2A pg. 061
William	07	Mar	1832		Martha	off. G. MC CASHEY
PARSONS	and				RUSSELL	WV. bk. 4A pg. 022
Electa M.	28	Jan	1867		James A.	off. H. MELVIN
PARSONS	and				HANEY	WV. bk. 3A pg. 166
Olivia	11	Jun	1866		James M.	off. R. NICHOLLS
PARSONS	and				LAZEAR	VA. bk. 3A pg. 125
Sebrina J.	11	Feb	1863		James	off. J. NAYLOR
PARSONS	and				DOWLER	VA. bk. 3A pg. 041
Sue G.	23	Sep	1857		John F.	off. J. NAYLOR
PATTERSON	and				CHAMBERS	VA. bk. 1A pg. 051
Andrew	--	--	1809		Margaret	off. J. DODDRIDGE
PATTERSON	and				POOL	VA. bk. 3A pg. 046
Elizabeth	23	Dec	1857		Reason Bell	off. J. NAYLOR
PATTERSON	and				RAMSEY	VA. bk. 2A pg. 030
Euphenia	06	Apr	1824		Alexander	off. G. BUCHANAN
PATTERSON	and				LETZKUS	WV. bk. 4A pg. 075
James	31	Aug	1870		Lena	off. W. WHITE
PATTERSON	and				WILLSON	VA. bk. 1A pg. 047
John	--	--	1803		Massa	off. UNKNOWN
PATTERSON	and				FRANK	VA. bk. 01 pg. 005
Mary Elizabeth	25	Dec	1856		William	off. E. QUILLEN
PATTERSON	and				FRESHWATER	WV. bk. 4A pg. 093
Melissa	26	Jun	1871		Milton R.	off. W. WHITE
PATTERSON	and				DODGE	VA. bk. 2A pg. 028
Nancy	18	Sep	1823		John	off. J. CAZAD
PATTERSON	and				HINES	VA. bk. 1A pg. 065
Sarah	27	Jan	1815		Isaac	off. E. MACURDY
PATTERSON	and				LONG	WV. bk. 4A pg. 028
Sarah A.	27	Jul	1867		David W.	off. H. MELVIN
PATTON	and				CHURCHMAN	VA. bk. 2A pg. 087
Elizabeth Jane	14	Nov	1845		William	off. S. WORTHINGTON
PATTON	and				LINTON	WV. bk. 01 pg. 019
James C.	25	Aug	1868		Mahala	off. M. WELLS
PATTON	and				WADDLE	WV. bk. 4A pg. 096
Maria	21	Sep	1871		Thomas	off. W. WHITE
PATTON	and				LATTIMORE	VA. bk. 2A pg. 078
Nancy	22	Mar	1843		David	off. J. HARRISON
PATTON	and				VASBINDER	VA. bk. 2A pg. 060
Robert	12	Oct	1828		Mary	off. E. SMITH
PATTON	and				KIMBERLAND	VA. bk. 01 pg. 002
Thomas	16	Mar	1854		Angeline	off. E. QUILLEN
PATTON	and				ROMINE	VA. bk. 01 pg. 002
Thomas	16	Mar	1854		Angeline	off. E. QUILLEN
PATTON	and				RAMSEY	VA. bk. 2A pg. 014
William	20	Apr	1820		Susannah	off. J. CAZAD
PEARCE	and				BURTON	VA. bk. 2A pg. *08
Matilda	06	Feb	1851		John	off. R. WHITE
PELLY	and				HOUGH	WV. bk. 4A pg. 087
Francine R.	24	Apr	1871		John W.	off. W. WHITE
PELLY	and				JONES	VA. bk. 1A pg. 082
James	06	May	1813		Margaret	off. UNKNOWN

Name		Day	Month	Year	Spouse	Reference
PELLY	and				FRANCIS	VA. bk. 2A pg. 031
Rachel		09	Dec	1824	Joseph S.	off. J. CAZAD
PENDEGRASS	and				SWEENEY	WV. bk. 4A pg. 059
Patrick		15	Mar	1869	Hannah	off. W. WHITE
PENDLETON	and				MOOKLAR	WV. bk. 4A pg. 004
Alexandria C.		22	Dec	1865	James P.	off. H. SHEPHERD
PENIX	and				HUNT	VA. bk. 2A pg. 080
Emily		27	May	1841	George C.	off. S. LAUCK
PENNINGTON	and				WILLSON	VA. bk. 2A pg. 023
Elisabeth Ann		29	Aug	1822	William D.	off. L. BROWNING
PENTECOST	and				CHAMBERS	VA. bk. 2A pg. 066
George W.		14	Mar	1839	Nancy	off. G. BUCHANAN
PENTECOST	and				MILLS	VA. bk. 2A pg. 058
Lucinda		05	Aug	1829	Jonathan	off. D. MERRYMAN
PEOPLES	and				HINDMAN	VA. bk. 2A pg. *06
Eleanor		06	Sep	1841	Francis	off. E. SMITH
PERINE	and				ROBINSON	WV. bk. 3A pg. 165
Mary Elizabeth		22	May	1866	John D.	off. R. NICHOLLS
PERKINS	and				NALLINGER	WV. bk. 4A pg. 126
Asbury		24	Jul	1873	Rosena	off. W. LATIMER
PERKINS	and				COOK	VA. bk. 2A pg. *01
James		02	Nov	1848	Elizabeth	off. T. NEWELL
PERKINS	and				DAVIDSON	WV. bk. 4A pg. 143
Minnie		08	Oct	1874	Samuel M.	off. J. LATIMER
PERRIN	and				WILLIAMSON	VA. bk. 1A pg. 030
Edward		22	Oct	1807	Sarah	off. J. HUGHES
PERRY	and				HOOVER	VA. bk. 2A pg. *16
Andrew Jackson		22	Dec	1853	Sarah Jane	off. G. LOWMAN
PERRY	and				ALEXANDER	WV. bk. 3A pg. 152
Ann Rebecca J.		24	Feb	1865	Samuel H.	off. H. SHEPHERD
PERRY	and				CHURCHMAN	VA. bk. 2A pg. *17
Elizabeth		08	Nov	1853	Joseph	off. S. NESBITT
PERRY	and				WILCOXON	VA. bk. 2A pg. 047
Jemima		23	Dec	1827	Thomas	off. A. COLEMAN
PERRY	and				HAGAN	VA. bk. 2A pg. 058
John		24	Jan	1830	Sarah	off. D. MERRYMAN
PERRY	and				CHAPMAN	VA. bk. 2A pg. 086
John		03	Dec	1845	Margaret	off. W. LEMON
PERRY	and				KERNS	VA. bk. 3A pg. 062
John		04	Jan	1859	Ann Rebecca	off. J. NAYLOR
PERRY	and				BOWMAN	VA. bk. 2A pg. 086
Oliver		11	Feb	1846	Susan	off. W. LEMON
PERRY	and				NORMAN	VA. bk. 2A pg. 058
Tabitha		29	Oct	1829	Nathaniel	off. D. MERRYMAN
PERSELL	and				JONES	VA. bk. 2A pg. 058
William		03	Apr	1830	Jane	off. D. MERRYMAN
PETERS	and				MC INTYRE	VA. bk. 01 pg. 005
William		26	Feb	1857	Margarett	off. E. QUILLEN
PETERSON	and				ATEN	VA. bk. 2A pg. 083
Ann		09	Apr	1840	Richard	off. R. WHITE
PETERSON	and				YOUNG	VA. bk. 2A pg. 084
Lucinda		06	Jul	1843	William	off. R. WHITE

BROOKE CO., VA./WV. LICENSES & MARRIAGES, 1797-1874

Name				Spouse	Reference
PETERSON	and			PITTINGER	VA. bk. 2A pg. 083
Peter	03	Mar	1842	Nancy	off. R. WHITE
PETERSON	and			HASEN	VA. bk. 1A pg. 064
Peter	15	Sep	1815	Mary	off. G. SCOTT
PETERSON	and			CULLIN	VA. bk. 2A pg. 084
Rebecca	25	Oct	1842	Israel	off. R. WHITE
PETERSON	and			SCOTT	VA. bk. 2A pg. 084
Sarah	15	Sep	1842	Alexander W.	off. R. WHITE
PHEISTER	and			FETRAR	WV. bk. 4A pg. 015
Isabella	10	Nov	1866	Frederick	off. R. NICHOLLS
PICKET	and			HYATE	VA. bk. 1A pg. 068
Susannah	11	Feb	1814	William	off. J. PRITCHARD
PICKLEMAN	and			BLOTTAN	WV. bk. 4A pg. 086
Julia A.	10	Apr	1871	John A.	off. W. WHITE
PIKIRRA	and			SEILA	WV. bk. 3A pg. 155
Adrian	10	Apr	1865	Therisia	off. H. SHEPHERD
PILLINGS	and			LAUGHEAD	VA. bk. 3A pg. 094
Charles	30	Sep	1860	Sophia	off. J. NAYLOR
PILLINGS	and			HAGAN	VA. bk. 2A pg. *14
Margaret	11	Nov	1852	John B.	off. S. NESBITT
PILLINGS	and			MONTGOMERY	VA. bk. 3A pg. 110
Sarah E.	21	Dec	1861	Joseph E.	off. S. NAYLOR
PILLINGS	and			MONTGOMERY	WV. bk. 4A pg. 007
Sophia (Mrs.)	03	Oct	1867	Joseph	off. H. MELVIN
PIQUAWAY	and			PLUMMER	VA. bk. 1A pg. 020
Henry	15	May	1806	Elisabeth	off. J. PRITCHARD
PITTINGER	and			PUGH	VA. bk. 2A pg. 083
Ahynias	15	Feb	1842	Sulynia	off. R. WHITE
PITTINGER	and			PITTINGER	VA. bk. 2A pg. 030
Catherine (...)	22	Mar	1824	John	off. G. SCOTT
PITTINGER	and			ATEN	VA. bk. 2A pg. 087
Elizabeth	14	May	1846	William (Jr.)	off. G. SCOTT
PITTINGER	and			PITTINGER	VA. bk. 2A pg. 030
John	22	Mar	1824	Catherine (...)	off. G. SCOTT
PITTINGER	and			MILLER	VA. bk. 2A pg. 040
Margaret	29	Jun	1826	Benjamin	off. G. SCOTT
PITTINGER	and			PETERSON	VA. bk. 2A pg. 083
Nancy	03	Mar	1842	Peter	off. R. WHITE
PITTINGER	and			MATHEWSON	VA. bk. 2A pg. 006
Nicholas	01	Oct	1818	Elizabeth	off. G. SCOTT
PITTMAN	and			LAZEAR	WV. bk. 4A pg. 031
Hannah	28	Sep	1867	Thomas B.	off. C. MELVIN
PLANTS	and			CARMICHAEL	WV. bk. 4A pg. 108
David	12	Mar	1872	Catherine A.	off. W. LATIMER
PLATTENBURG	and			STEPHENS	VA. bk. 2A pg. 091
Mary	25	Jan	1848	Lewis W.	off. J. MONROE
PLATTENBURGH	and			JEFFERS	VA. bk. 2A pg. 041
John	12	Feb	1826	Elen	off. J. BROWNING, JR.
PLATTENBURGH	and			MUNCY	VA. bk. 2A pg. 053
Joshua	04	May	1826	Sarah	off. L. BROWNING
PLATTENBURGH	and			HAMILTON	VA. bk. 2A pg. 049
Levi	04	Oct	1827	Isabella	off. S. REED

96   BROOKE CO., VA./WV. LICENSES & MARRIAGES, 1797-1874

Name				Spouse	Reference
PLUMMER		and		PIQUAWAY	VA. bk. 1A pg. 020
Elisabeth	15	May	1806	Henry	off. J. PRITCHARD
PLUMMER		and		JONES	VA. bk. 2A pg. *01
Franklin	12	Apr	1849	Pamelia	off. J. MOFFITT
POLSLY		and		BROWN	VA. bk. 2A pg. 047
Daniel	16	Aug	1827	Elizabeth	off. L. BROWNING
POOL		and		WHITE	VA. bk. 2A pg. 054
Melinda	27	Mar	1828	John	off. G. BUCHANAN
POOL		and		PATTERSON	VA. bk. 3A pg. 046
Reason Bell	23	Dec	1857	Elizabeth	off. J. NAYLOR
POOL		and		MAGEE	VA. bk. 2A pg. *05
William	10	Feb	1850	Nancy	off. C. LOOS
POOL		and		MAGEE	VA. bk. 3A pg. 128
William	06	Apr	1863	Martha Ann	off. W. NAYLOR
PORTER		and		BURNS	VA. bk. 1A pg. 031
Thomas	17	Mar	1807	Catherine	off. W. WILLSON
PORTER		and		HALL	VA. bk. 1A pg. 049
Thomas	--	--	1808	Sally	off. UNKNOWN
PORTERFIELD		and		MAY	VA. bk. 2A pg. 051
Assenith	01	Apr	1825	Isaac	off. L. BROWNING
PORTERFIELD		and		KEARNS	VA. bk. 2A pg. 064
Rachael	01	Mar	1838	George	off. G. ROBINSON
POSTON		and		MURRAY	WV. bk. 01 pg. 020
Anna B. (Mrs.)	08	Jul	1870	James A.	off. A. CAMPBELL
POTTER		and		KLINEFELTER	WV. bk. 4A pg. 066
James M.	19	Jan	1870	Frances	off. W. WHITE
POTTS		and		LETZKUS	WV. bk. 4A pg. 110
Jasper	02	Apr	1872	Francis	off. W. LATIMER
POTTS		and		MC KINLEY	VA. bk. 2A pg. 069
Stephen	20	Dec	1837	Sophia	off. J. HERVEY
POWELL		and		LEE	VA. bk. 2A pg. 087
O.R.	26	Mar	1846	Dorcus Jane	off. S. LAUCK
POWER		and		BRADY	VA. bk. 3A pg. 017
Joseph C.	06	Apr	1853	Mary A.	off. J. NAYLOR
PRATHER		and		COCHRANE	VA. bk. 01 pg. 002
Elbert	24	Aug	1854	Mary	off. E. QUILLEN
PRATHER		and		TAYLOR	VA. bk. 3A pg. 089
George M.	11	Aug	1860	Amelia C.	off. J. NAYLOR
PRATHER		and		MENDEL	VA. bk. 2A pg. 044
John	22	Oct	1826	Elizabeth	off. J. BROWNING, JR.
PRATHER		and		GOOD	VA. bk. 2A pg. *14
Mary	08	Feb	1853	Thomas C.	off. S. NESBITT
PRICE		and		WALKER	VA. bk. 2A pg. 003
Hiram	19	Nov	1818	Sarah	off. G. BUCHANAN
PRICE		and		ARMSTRONG	VA. bk. 2A pg. 001
John	20	Aug	1815	Betsy	off. E. MACURDY
PRIEST		and		HALLIE	WV. bk. 4A pg. 077
William	26	Sep	1870	Micha	off. W. WHITE
PRITCHARD		and		TIPTON	VA. bk. 1A pg. 016
Elizabeth	07	Mar	1805	Solomon	off. J. PRITCHARD
PRITCHARD		and		ADRIAN	VA. bk. 2A pg. 013
Mary	31	Aug	1820	Mordicai	off. J. PRITCHARD

BROOKE CO., VA./WV. LICENSES & MARRIAGES, 1797-1874

Name		Day	Month	Year	Spouse	Reference
PRITCHARD	and				EDERSON	VA. bk. 1A pg. 077
Sarah		16	Nov	1812	John	off. J. PRITCHARD
PROSSER	and				ATEN	VA. bk. 1A pg. 063
Abraham		16	Mar	1815	Elizabeth	off. G. SCOTT
PROSSER	and				STEWART	VA. bk. 2A pg. 014
Benjamin		05	Apr	1820	Sarah Jane	off. G. SCOTT
PROSSER	and				MURPHY	VA. bk. 2A pg. 064
Daniel		31	May	1838	Hannah	off. L. BROWNING
PROSSER	and				SILVERTHORN	VA. bk. 2A pg. 082
Elizabeth		05	Sep	1839	Joseph	off. R. WHITE
PROSSER	and				DAVIS	VA. bk. 2A pg. 083
Elizabeth		23	Feb	1841	John S.	off. R. WHITE
PROSSER	and				SCOTT	VA. bk. 2A pg. 083
Jane		06	Jan	1842	Joseph	off. R. WHITE
PROSSER	and				CARIENS	VA. bk. 2A pg. *03
John A.		04	Jan	1849	Elizabeth	off. J. GOODWIN
PROSSER	and				DURBIN	VA. bk. 2A pg. 083
Mary		16	Sep	1841	Ephraim	off. R. WHITE
PROSSER	and				DAVIS	VA. bk. 2A pg. 083
Rachel		07	Sep	1841	Samuel L.	off. R. WHITE
PROSSER	and				TROUP	VA. bk. 2A pg. 084
Susan		20	Mar	1845	David	off. R. WHITE
PUGH	and				FOWLER	VA. bk. 2A pg. 083
Ann		14	Nov	1839	William B.	off. R. WHITE
PUGH	and				SNOWDEN	VA. bk. 1A pg. 063
David		21	Mar	1815	Mary	off. G. SCOTT
PUGH	and				EDIE	VA. bk. 2A pg. 083
Elizabeth		29	Dec	1841	Samuel	off. R. WHITE
PUGH	and				ALISON	VA. bk. 2A pg. 057
Fanny		14	Jan	1830	Samuel	off. G. SCOTT
PUGH	and				STEWART	VA. bk. 2A pg. 084
James		31	Aug	1843	Mary Ann	off. R. WHITE
PUGH	and				HAYS	VA. bk. 01 pg. 004
John		01	Jan	1856	Julia Ann	off. D. HERVEY
PUGH	and				SCOTT	VA. bk. 2A pg. 047
John P.		26	Sep	1826	Sarah F.	off. G. SCOTT
PUGH	and				ALISON	VA. bk. 2A pg. 060
Lena		28	Sep	1828	Jonathan	off. S. REED
PUGH	and				ALLISON	VA. bk. 2A pg. 084
Moses		15	Nov	1843	Christina	off. R. WHITE
PUGH	and				SNOWDEN	VA. bk. 2A pg. 034
Polly		01	Sep	1825	William	off. G. SCOTT
PUGH	and				ALLISON	VA. bk. 2A pg. 056
Sarah		25	Nov	1830	James	off. G. SCOTT
PUGH	and				STEWART	VA. bk. 2A pg. 083
Sarah Ann		03	Apr	1841	James	off. R. WHITE
PUGH	and				PITTINGER	VA. bk. 2A pg. 083
Sulynia		15	Feb	1842	Ahynias	off. R. WHITE
PUMPHREY	and				VIERS	VA. bk. 2A pg. 078
Beal		10	Mar	1842	Maria M. D.	off. J. HARRISON
PUMPHREY	and				PUMPHREY	VA. bk. 1A pg. 075
Casandra (...)		14	Apr	1814	Nimrod	off. J. MEEK

98   BROOKE CO., VA./WV. LICENSES & MARRIAGES, 1797-1874

PUMPHREY			and	HOOD		VA. bk. 2A pg. 016
Credilla	25	May	1820	James		off. T. BEEKS
PUMPHREY			and	COOK		VA. bk. 2A pg. 058
Drusilla	02	Feb	1830	William J.		off. T. BEEKS
PUMPHREY			and	HOGG		VA. bk. 2A pg. 027
Elizabeth	03	Apr	1823	Thomas		off. T. BEEKS
PUMPHREY			and	PUMPHREY		VA. bk. 2A pg. 081
Elizabeth (...)	30	May	1844	William R.		off. T. BAKER
PUMPHREY			and	BOON		VA. bk. 1A pg. 021
John	02	Jul	1805	Nelly		off. W. WILLSON
PUMPHREY			and	STALEY		VA. bk. 2A pg. 027
Lovey	14	Nov	1822	Eli		off. T. BEEKS
PUMPHREY			and	PUMPHREY		VA. bk. 1A pg. 075
Nimrod	14	Apr	1814	Casandra (...)		off. J. MEEK
PUMPHREY			and	HURFORD		VA. bk. 2A pg. 081
Susanna	18	Apr	1844	Joseph E.		off. T. BAKER
PUMPHREY			and	TALBOTT		VA. bk. 1A pg. 083
Susannah	04	Mar	1813	George		off. UNKNOWN
PUMPHREY			and	PUMPHREY		VA. bk. 2A pg. 081
William R.	30	May	1844	Elizabeth (...)		off. T. BAKER
PUNTNEY			and	CLAYTON		VA. bk. 2A pg. 058
Elizabeth	--	--	1830	William		off. N. HEADINGTON
PUNTNEY			and	CARTER		WV. bk. 3A pg. 131
Isabelle	13	Oct	1863	Lewis Wash.		off. H. SHEPHERD
PUNTNEY			and	CLAYTON		VA. bk. 2A pg. 050
John	29	Jun	1826	Charlotte		off. N. HEADINGTON
PURDAY			and	CAMPBELL		VA. bk. 2A pg. 057
Margaret	06	May	1830	Robert		off. G. BUCHANAN
PURDY			and	KNOX		VA. bk. 2A pg. 085
Elizabeth	21	Aug	1845	John		off. W. LEMON
PUSEY			and	GARDNER		VA. bk. 2A pg. 084
William C.	29	May	1844	Rachel		off. R. WHITE
QUEST			and	DURANT		WV. bk. 3A pg. 138
Elizabeth C.	25	Feb	1864	William L.		off. H. SHEPHERD
QUEST			and	LAWTON		VA. bk. 01 pg. 004
Mary L.	12	Aug	1856	Joseph K.		off. E. QUILLEN
QUEST			and	MELVIN		WV. bk. 4A pg. 027
Melissa E.	19	Jun	1867	William H.		off. H. MELVIN
QUEST			and	HARDING		WV. bk. 4A pg. 039
Minerva J.	24	Dec	1867	Joseph E.		off. H. MELVIN
QUINN			and	CAMERON?		VA. bk. 2A pg. 004
William	27	Mar	1817	Peggy		off. G. SCOTT
RABBITT			and	MC MILLAN		VA. bk. 2A pg. 082
Thomas	03	May	1838	Catharine		off. R. WHITE
RACE			and	HESTON		VA. bk. 2A pg. 074
Tamar	23	Apr	1842	John		off. W. STEVENS
RAINSFORTH			and	HARDIN		VA. bk. 2A pg. *08
Job	12	Sep	1851	Mary		off. C. JACKSON
RALSTON			and	ATKINSON		VA. bk. 2A pg. 033
Alexander	25	Aug	1825	Ann		off. G. BUCHANAN
RALSTON			and	CURTIS		VA. bk. 2A pg. 060
Catharine	23	Apr	1829	Alexander		off. S. REED

BROOKE CO., VA./WV. LICENSES & MARRIAGES, 1797-1874   99

Groom Surname	Groom Given		Date		Bride Surname	Bride Given	Source
RALSTON	Elizabeth	26	Jul	1873	WILKEY	Joseph J.	WV. bk. 4A pg. 127 off. W. LATIMER
RALSTON	George	17	Nov	1842	MOREHEAD	Martha Jane	VA. bk. 2A pg. 077 off. J. GALLOWAY
RALSTON	Henrietta	06	Nov	1817	KELLY	Timothy	VA. bk. 2A pg. 005 off. J. PRITCHARD
RALSTON	John	05	Feb	1846	LEWIS	Kezia	VA. bk. 2A pg. 087 off. S. WORTHINGTON
RALSTON	Joseph	02	Aug	1813	MOREHEAD	Mary	VA. bk. 1A pg. 065 off. UNKNOWN
RALSTON	Joseph	13	Nov	1817	HOLMES	Priscilla	VA. bk. 2A pg. 006 off. E. MACURDY
RALSTON	Joseph	01	Mar	1865	MC HENRY	Lucy	WV. bk. 3A pg. 153 off. H. SHEPHERD
RALSTON	Kesiah	16	Jun	1830	GRAHAM	Robert	VA. bk. 2A pg. 055 off. J. MC KENNAR
RALSTON	Martha	28	Jun	1841	MOREHEAD	Abraham	VA. bk. 2A pg. 071 off. J. GALLOWAY
RALSTON	Mary	02	Nov	1815	COCHRAN	James	VA. bk. 1A pg. 080 off. J. PRITCHARD
RALSTON	Rezin	29	May	1845	BAILE	Ellen	VA. bk. 2A pg. 087 off. J. GALLOWAY
RALSTON	Robert	11	Apr	1816	WILLSON	Nancy	VA. bk. 2A pg. 002 off. E. MACURDY
RALSTON	Robert	14	Dec	1824	CHAPMAN	Mary	VA. bk. 2A pg. 031 off. G. SCOTT
RALSTON	Sarah L.	02	Apr	1840	MARQUIS	Samuel F.	VA. bk. 2A pg. 083 off. R. WHITE
RALSTON	William	26	Dec	1864	OWENS	Elizabeth	WV. bk. 3A pg. 149 off. H. SHEPHERD
RAMSAY	Basil	24	Oct	1849	BELL	Adeline	VA. bk. 2A pg. *03 off. J. IRWIN
RAMSAY	Benjamin	02	Oct	1838	DODDRIDGE	Julia Adeline	VA. bk. 2A pg. 067 off. A. YOUNG
RAMSEY	Alexander	06	Apr	1824	PATTERSON	Euphenia	VA. bk. 2A pg. 030 off. G. BUCHANAN
RAMSEY	Jane E.	11	Mar	1852	BRICK	Robinson	VA. bk. 3A pg. 002 off. J. NAYLOR
RAMSEY	Macky	06	Aug	1854	SWINER	Peter	VA. bk. 01 pg. 002 off. C. HOLMES
RAMSEY	Margaret	21	Feb	1823	MACKEY	Robert	VA. bk. 2A pg. 027 off. J. CAZAD
RAMSEY	Rachael	14	May	1825	CLELAND	William	VA. bk. 2A pg. 039 off. J. CAZAD
RAMSEY	Robert	05	Jun	1828	CLELAND	Jane	VA. bk. 2A pg. 059 off. E. SMITH
RAMSEY	Susannah	20	Apr	1820	PATTON	William	VA. bk. 2A pg. 014 off. J. CAZAD
RAY	Elisabeth	02	Dec	1828	HOBBS	Hanson	VA. bk. 2A pg. 060 off. S. REED
RAY	Joseph	03	Apr	1828	STRONG	Rebecca	VA. bk. 2A pg. 059 off. E. SMITH

RAY		and		BRADY	VA. bk. 2A pg. 085
Joseph	03	Oct	1844	Permelia	off. S. WORTHINGTON
RAY		and		CORY	VA. bk. 2A pg. 016
Lydia	30	Nov	1820	Elijah D.	off. G. BUCHANAN
RAY		and		HOBBS	VA. bk. 2A pg. 032
Margaret	15	Jul	1824	Leonard	off. L. BROWNING
RAY		and		HAMILTON	VA. bk. 2A pg. 024
Rebecca	14	Nov	1822	Thomas	off. G. BUCHANAN
RAY		and		VINCENT	VA. bk. 2A pg. 045
Thomas	20	Sep	1826	Anne	off. J. CAZAD
RAY		and		RUSSELL	VA. bk. 2A pg. 072
William	03	Mar	1841	Julia A.	off. S. FULTON
REDICK		and		DONOVAN	VA. bk. 1A pg. 074
David	13	Jun	1815	Eleanor	off. J. PRITCHARD
REED		and		DURBIN	VA. bk. 2A pg. 082
Elijah	06	Dec	1838	Hester	off. R. WHITE
REED		and		SMITH	VA. bk. 1A pg. 041
Elizabeth	06	Jul	1802	Jacob	off. J. DODDRIDGE
REED		and		WHEELER	WV. bk. 3A pg. 142
George F.	17	Aug	1864	Anne E.	off. H. SHEPHERD
REED		and		ROBERTS	VA. bk. 3A pg. 087
John	01	Aug	1861	Susan	off. J. NAYLOR
REED		and		KEITH	VA. bk. 3A pg. 059
Margaret Jane	13	Nov	1858	Samuel	off. J. NAYLOR
REED		and		MC CONKEY	VA. bk. 3A pg. 010
Mary	24	Nov	1852	Kennedy	off. J. NAYLOR
REED		and		MC CONKEY	VA. bk. 3A pg. 006
Sarah Jane	20	Oct	1852	Cobane	off. J. NAYLOR
REEVES		and		COX	VA. bk. 01 pg. 004
Cornelia K.	29	Nov	1855	James W.	off. A. ENDSLEY
REEVES		and		GIST	VA. bk. 3A pg. 122
John C.	24	Nov	1862	Sarah B.	off. J. NAYLOR
REEVES		and		BICKERSTAFF	WV. bk. 4A pg. 098
Julia C.	25	Oct	1871	Isaac	off. W. LATIMER
REEVES		and		MURPHY	WV. bk. 4A pg. 047
Sallie E.	04	May	1868	James F.	off. C. MELVIN
REEVES		and		MENDEL	VA. bk. 2A pg. 059
Sarah	30	Mar	1828	Henry	off. E. SMITH
REEVES		and		LAZEAR	WV. bk. 4A pg. 030
Wheeler	23	Sep	1867	Jane	off. C. MELVIN
REYNOLDS		and		WHITE	VA. bk. 2A pg. 061
Elizabeth	09	Feb	1832	Thomas	off. G. MC CASHEY
REYNOLDS		and		MAXWELL	VA. bk. 2A pg. 045
Joseph	07	Nov	1826	Elisabeth	off. J. CAZAD
RHODES		and		WILLSON	VA. bk. 1A pg. 021
Nancy	--	--	1806	William	off. UNKNOWN
RICE		and		BOWMAN	VA. bk. 2A pg. *08
Edward W.	15	May	1851	Marietta	off. J. MC GAN
RICE		and		COOK	VA. bk. 2A pg. 093
Mary Catharine	29	Apr	1847	William H.	off. G. JONES
RICHARDS		and		GILES	VA. bk. 2A pg. 079
Samuel (Jr.)	01	Feb	1844	Mary Ann	off. S. WORTHINGTON

BROOKE CO., VA./WV. LICENSES & MARRIAGES, 1797-1874   101

Name				Spouse	Reference
RICHARDSON		and		ADAMS	VA. bk. 1A pg. 074
Catharine	13	Jan	1815	James	off. L. BROWNING
RICHARDSON		and		GREEN	WV. bk. 4A pg. 034
I.L.	30	Oct	1867	Drusilla	off. H. MELVIN
RICHARDSON		and		CHAPLINE	WV. bk. 3A pg. 160
Mary B.	26	Sep	1865	Albert W.	off. H. SHEPHERD
RICHARDSON		and		MILLER	VA. bk. 2A pg. *10
Nancy	07	Mar	1852	John	off. H. SNYDER
RICHARDSON		and		LYTLE	VA. bk. 1A pg. 081
Ruth	10	Dec	1812	George	off. UNKNOWN
RICHARDSON		and		MC DOWELL	VA. bk. 2A pg. 059
Thomas	25	Mar	1828	Sarah	off. E. SMITH
RIDDLE		and		MURPHY	VA. bk. 01 pg. 003
David	01	Jun	1855	Matilda	off. E. QUILLEN
RIDDLE		and		MILLIGAN	WV. bk. 4A pg. 003
David	20	Nov	1865	Sarah	off. H. SHEPHERD
RIDGELEY		and		ORR	VA. bk. 1A pg. 065
William	21	Mar	1816	Jane	off. J. CONNELL
RIDGLEY		and		SMITH	WV. bk. 4A pg. 009
Horace	10	Sep	1866	Nancy M.	off. R. NICHOLLS
RIDGLEY		and		FRESHWATER	VA. bk. 2A pg. 084
Lydia	28	Apr	1842	Reuben	off. R. WHITE
RIDGLEY		and		DAVIS	VA. bk. 3A pg. 042
Rebecca E.	12	Oct	1857	John	off. J. NAYLOR
RIDGLEY		and		HUSTON	WV. bk. 4A pg. 048
William C.	23	Jun	1868	Mary V.	off. C. MELVIN
RIDOUT		and		MAGOINGAN	VA. bk. 3A pg. 091
John	30	Aug	1860	Martha	off. J. NAYLOR
RIEN		and		JOHNSON	WV. bk. 4A pg. 012
George W.	29	Sep	1866	Elizabeth	off. R. NICHOLLS
RINEHART		and		SILVERS	WV. bk. 4A pg. 026
William S.	23	Mar	1867	Sally	off. H. MELVIN
RIPLEY		and		JOHNSON	WV. bk. 4A pg. 106
Lena	30	Apr	1872	James	off. W. LATIMER
RISHER		and		BEATTY	VA. bk. 2A pg. *07
Asa	07	Nov	1850	Elizabeth	off. C. JACKSON
RIZER		and		ARMSTRONG	VA. bk. 2A pg. 007
Catharine	19	Feb	1819	George	off. E. MACURDY
ROBERTS		and		SHARP	VA. bk. 2A pg. 074
Alexander	12	Oct	1841	Mary	off. W. STEVENS
ROBERTS		and		DEIGHTON	VA. bk. 01 pg. 003
Andrew J.	01	May	1855	Rosetta	off. E. QUILLEN
ROBERTS		and		MERRYMAN	VA. bk. 2A pg. *10
Elizabeth M.	18	Dec	1851	William	off. H. SNYDER
ROBERTS		and		MC CRACKEN	VA. bk. 2A pg. 059
Henry	03	Apr	1828	Rachael	off. E. SMITH
ROBERTS		and		KIRKWOOD	VA. bk. 2A pg. *10
Jemima	04	Mar	1852	Francis	off. H. SNYDER
ROBERTS		and		BUCKALEW	VA. bk. 01 pg. 005
Marcellus	30	Oct	1856	Ann Eliza.	off. W. GAMBLE, JR.
ROBERTS		and		MC CONNELL	VA. bk. 2A pg. 037
Margaret A.	--	--	1826	John	off. N. HEADINGTON

ROBERTS		and		ALEXANDER	VA. bk. 2A pg. 022	
Nancy	30	May	1822	Joseph	off. G. BUCHANAN	
ROBERTS		and		GRIFFIN	VA. bk. 2A pg. 076	
Nancy	26	Feb	1843	Thomas	off. C. BEST	
ROBERTS		and		MC CREARY	VA. bk. 01 pg. 002	
Nancy	27	Apr	1854	William	off. D. HERVEY	
ROBERTS		and		LEWIS	VA. bk. 2A pg. *08	
Ortho	08	Dec	1850	Susan	off. R. WHITE	
ROBERTS		and		TURNER	VA. bk. 2A pg. 049	
Polly	14	Dec	1826	Thompson	off. S. REED	
ROBERTS		and		SAUNDERS	VA. bk. 1A pg. 027	
Richard	13	Jun	1807	Ann	off. UNKNOWN	
ROBERTS		and		DEIGHTON	VA. bk. 3A pg. 047	
Richard T.	26	Dec	1857	Margaret V.	off. J. NAYLOR	
ROBERTS		and		VANDOVERT	VA. bk. 1A pg. 030	
Samuel	05	Mar	1807	Polly	off. J. HUGHES	
ROBERTS		and		BRANNON	VA. bk. 2A pg. 056	
Samuel	20	Oct	1829	Margaret	off. G. BUCHANAN	
ROBERTS		and		DOUBLE	VA. bk. 2A pg. 067	
Samuel	29	Oct	1838	Susanna	off. A. YOUNG	
ROBERTS		and		REED	VA. bk. 3A pg. 087	
Susan	01	Aug	1861	John	off. J. NAYLOR	
ROBERTS		and		COLEMAN	WV. bk. 4A pg. 020	
William	31	Dec	1866	Emma D.	off. R. NICHOLLS	
ROBERTSON		and		TALLENLINE	VA. bk. 2A pg. 066	
Eleanor	30	Aug	1838	John R.	off. J. HUNTSMAN	
ROBINETT		and		BRASHEARS	WV. bk. 4A pg. 078	
Catharine M.	28	Sep	1870	Calvin B.	off. W. WHITE	
ROBINETT		and		LETZKUS	WV. bk. 3A pg. 166	
Emma	23	May	1866	Joseph	off. R. NICHOLLS	
ROBINETT		and		STEWART	VA. bk. 01 pg. 004	
James	01	Jun	1856	Elmira	off. A. ENDSLEY	
ROBINETT		and		WETHERELL	WV. bk. 4A pg. 011	
Mary A.	22	Sep	1866	Christopher	off. R. NICHOLLS	
ROBINSON		and		BACHELL	WV. bk. 4A pg. 103	
A.W.	30	Dec	1871	Mary Eliza.	off. W. LATIMER	
ROBINSON		and		WELLS	VA. bk. 2A pg. 038	
Amanda	09	Feb	1826	Jesse	off. T. BEEKS	
ROBINSON		and		FRESHWATER	VA. bk. 3A pg. 120	
Elijah	28	Nov	1862	Sarah Jane	off. J. NAYLOR	
ROBINSON		and		YOUNG	VA. bk. 3A pg. 116	
Elizabeth E.	10	Jun	1862	Octavis	off. J. NAYLOR	
ROBINSON		and		SILVER	WV. bk. 3A pg. 136	
Elizabeth E.	11	Jan	1864	James M.	off. H. SHEPHERD	
ROBINSON		and		DAVIS	VA. bk. 3A pg. 077	
Elizabeth Jane	17	Dec	1859	Isaac L.	off. J. NAYLOR	
ROBINSON		and		FLETCHER	VA. bk. 3A pg. 071	
Ellen	07	Jul	1859	Isaac	off. J. NAYLOR	
ROBINSON		and		BOWMAN	WV. bk. 4A pg. 137	
Gilbert E.	05	Mar	1874	Dora	off. J. LATIMER	
ROBINSON		and		CLEARY	VA. bk. 2A pg. 071	
Israel	02	May	1841	Margaret E.	off. T. STEIRSHCOMB	

ROBINSON		and	DAVIS	VA. bk. 3A pg. 099	
Jesse	20	Feb 1861	Mary Jane	off. J. NAYLOR	
ROBINSON		and	PERINE	WV. bk. 3A pg. 165	
John D.	22	May 1866	Mary Eliza.	off. R. NICHOLLS	
ROBINSON		and	WILCOXON	VA. bk. 2A pg. 082	
Martin	15	Nov 1838	Margaret	off. R. WHITE	
ROBINSON		and	WALKER	VA. bk. 2A pg. 026	
Mary	10	Jun 1823	James	off. G. BUCHANAN	
ROBINSON		and	CHAPMAN	VA. bk. 3A pg. 109	
Mary	25	Nov 1861	Jacob	off. J. NAYLOR	
ROBINSON		and	HUKILL	VA. bk. 3A pg. 049	
Providence	23	Jan 1858	James	off. J. NAYLOR	
ROBINSON		and	ROUSE	WV. bk. 4A pg. 062	
Sally A.	08	May 1869	Alexander	off. W. WHITE	
ROBINSON		and	SWEARINGEN	VA. bk. 2A pg. 049	
Sarah	27	Dec 1827	Bennett	off. S. REED	
ROBINSON		and	MORAN	VA. bk. 2A pg. *02	
Sarah J.	07	Mar 1849	James A.	off. I. DALLAS	
ROBINSON		and	JONES	WV. bk. 4A pg. 086	
Sarah Jane	24	Apr 1871	Robert T.	off. W. WHITE	
ROBINSON		and	JACOB	WV. bk. 4A pg. 146	
Walter A.	17	Nov 1874	Cornelia E.	off. J. LATIMER	
ROBISON		and	SELLERS	VA. bk. 1A pg. 008	
Elisabeth	--	Sep 1802	James	off. J. HUGHES	
ROBISON		and	WELLS	VA. bk. 1A pg. 046	
James	--	-- 1802	Sally	off. UNKNOWN	
ROBSON		and	CHARLTON	VA. bk. 3A pg. 059	
Margaret	08	Dec 1858	Edward	off. J. NAYLOR	
RODGERS		and	WYLIE	VA. bk. 2A pg. 077	
Elizabeth	31	Aug 1843	David	off. J. SCOTT	
RODGERS		and	SERGEANT	VA. bk. 2A pg. 092	
Ezekiel	26	Oct 1847	Jane Ann	off. S. LAUCK	
RODGERS		and	HOUSEHOLDER	VA. bk. 2A pg. 084	
Margaret	20	Feb 1844	John	off. R. WHITE	
RODGERS		and	GELSTHORPE	VA. bk. 3A pg. 003	
Margaret Jane	07	Sep 1852	John	off. J. NAYLOR	
RODGERS		and	CURTIS	WV. bk. 4A pg. 125	
Mary	10	Apr 1873	George C.	off. W. LATIMER	
RODGERS		and	SHRIVER	WV. bk. 4A pg. 115	
Rebecca E.	07	Aug 1872	C.	off. W. LATIMER	
RODGERS		and	MC LEASH	VA. bk. 3A pg. 057	
Sarah	06	Oct 1858	James/John	off. J. NAYLOR	
ROGERS		and	MC KEEVEN	VA. bk. 2A pg. 032	
Elizabeth	07	Jul 1824	John	off. J. CAZAD	
ROGERS		and	BEATY	VA. bk. 1A pg. 005	
Hugh	01	Nov 1798	Catherine	off. J. HUGHES	
ROGERS		and	BLACK	VA. bk. 2A pg. 048	
Hugh	22	May 1828	Elizabeth	off. A. CAMPBELL	
ROGERS		and	SNEDIKER	VA. bk. 1A pg. 072	
Margaret	08	Jul 1813	Isaac	off. J. PRITCHARD	
ROLAND		and	WAUGH	WV. bk. 4A pg. 007	
Ann M.	15	Feb 1866	E.R.	off. R. NICHOLLS	

ROMINE			and		PATTON	VA.	bk. 01	pg. 002
Angeline	16	Mar	1854		Thomas	off. E. QUILLEN		
ROSE			and		BARCLAY	VA.	bk. 2A	pg. 078
Mary Hooper	05	Dec	1843		John Rowan	off. S. WORTHINGTON		
ROSE			and		BARNES	VA.	bk. 3A	pg. 103
William Henry	18	Jul	1861		Rebecca	off. S. NAYLOR		
ROSS			and		TALBOTT	VA.	bk. 2A	pg. *06
John	05	Sep	1850		Nancy	off. R. WHITE		
ROSS			and		BROWNLEE	VA.	bk. 2A	pg. *14
Susan	15	May	1853		James	off. S. NESBITT		
ROUSE			and		ROBINSON	WV.	bk. 4A	pg. 062
Alexander	08	May	1869		Sally A.	off. W. WHITE		
RUNNELLS			and		CONAWAY	VA.	bk. 2A	pg. *17
Jemima	14	Nov	1853		Evan	off. S. NESBITT		
RUSH			and		KIRK	VA.	bk. 1A	pg. 007
Enoch	02	Dec	1800		Martha	off. UNKNOWN		
RUSH			and		HYDE	WV.	bk. 4A	pg. 001
William	21	Oct	1865		Mary	off. H. SHEPHERD		
RUSSELL			and		LANDIS	WV.	bk. 3A	pg. 152
Anna M.	04	Feb	1865		Evan F.	off. H. SHEPHERD		
RUSSELL			and		HOLMES	VA.	bk. 1A	pg. 059
Arthur	23	May	1811		Isabella	off. E. MACURDY		
RUSSELL			and		FRITZ	VA.	bk. 3A	pg. 083
Caroline E.	12	Mar	1860		Andrew D.	off. J. NAYLOR		
RUSSELL			and		STRAIN	VA.	bk. 1A	pg. 076
Catherine	21	Mar	1816		Ebenezer	off. W. WILLSON		
RUSSELL			and		DONOVAN	VA.	bk. 3A	pg. 067
Charles P.	12	Apr	1859		Ruth C.	off. J. NAYLOR		
RUSSELL			and		LOWRY	VA.	bk. 2A	pg. 092
Edward	08	Apr	1848		Elizabeth	off. J. MONROE		
RUSSELL			and		CONNELL	VA.	bk. 2A	pg. 065
Elizabeth	11	Sep	1838		Harrison	off. A. YOUNG		
RUSSELL			and		MUSTARD	VA.	bk. 1A	pg. 066
Elizabeth	12	Mar	1812		John	off. E. MACURDY		
RUSSELL			and		WRIGHTMAN	VA.	bk. 3A	pg. 045
George W.	21	Nov	1857		Ann Jane	off. J. NAYLOR		
RUSSELL			and		MC CLURE	WV.	bk. 4A	pg. 032
George W.	12	Oct	1867		Anne (Mrs.)	off. H. MELVIN		
RUSSELL			and		ATKINS	VA.	bk. 2A	pg. 055
James	28	Sep	1830		Sarah	off. R. HATTEN		
RUSSELL			and		PARSONS	WV.	bk. 4A	pg. 022
James A.	28	Jan	1867		Electa M.	off. H. MELVIN		
RUSSELL			and		RAY	VA.	bk. 2A	pg. 072
Julia A.	03	Mar	1841		William	off. S. FULTON		
RUSSELL			and		YOUNG	WV.	bk. 4A	pg. 072
Lucy A.S.	23	Jun	1870		William F.	off. W. WHITE		
RUSSELL			and		GREEN	VA.	bk. 2A	pg. *02
Maria	07	Dec	1848		Obediah	off. I. DALLAS		
RUSSELL			and		BORING	VA.	bk. 2A	pg. *09
Oliver G.	17	Sep	1851		Elizabeth	off. C. JACKSON		
RUSSELL			and		GOVER	VA.	bk. 01	pg. 005
Samuel	25	Jan	1857		Clara	off. E. QUILLEN		

Name		Day	Month	Year	Spouse	Reference
RUSSELL	and				CHESTER	WV. bk. 3A pg. 142
Travilla A.		30	Jun	1864	Mary E.	off. H. SHEPHERD
RUTH	and				MC COY	WV. bk. 3A pg. 140
John		22	Mar	1864	Agnes A.	off. H. SHEPHERD
RUTH	and				TALBOTT	VA. bk. 3A pg. 035
Mary		26	Dec	1853	John	off. J. NAYLOR
RUTHERFORD	and				BURGESS	VA. bk. 2A pg. *08
Marian		23	Apr	1851	John	off. R. WHITE
RYLEY	and				SMITH	VA. bk. 2A pg. 007
Margaret		06	Mar	1817	Henry	off. S. LAUCK
SALMON	and				SWEARINGEN	WV. bk. 4A pg. 140
Cornelius B.		10	Jun	1874	Mattie L.	off. J. LATIMER
SALMON	and				BURKE	VA. bk. 2A pg. 033
Cutler		28	Apr	1825	Ann	off. G. BUCHANAN
SANDERS	and				HARPER	VA. bk. 2A pg. 071
Catharine		01	Jul	1841	John	off. J. GALLOWAY
SANDERS	and				WILSON	VA. bk. 3A pg. 122
Fanny		31	Dec	1862	John M.	off. J. NAYLOR
SANDERS	and				HOOKER	WV. bk. 4A pg. 092
Frank A.		13	Jun	1871	Cornelia Hull	off. W. WHITE
SANDERS	and				FRESHWATER	WV. bk. 4A pg. 053
Fredus A.		27	Nov	1868	Melissa A.	off. S. QUEST
SANDERS	and				HINDMAN	WV. bk. 4A pg. 133
Jonathan D.		11	Dec	1873	Kate E.	off. W. LATIMER
SANDERS	and				MILLER	WV. bk. 4A pg. 065
Letitia J.		29	Nov	1869	John H.	off. W. WHITE
SANDERS	and				GAMBLE	VA. bk. 1A pg. 032
Lewis		22	Aug	1808	Prudence	off. J. PRITCHARD
SANDERS	and				CONN	VA. bk. 1A pg. 069
Linney		28	Jan	1815	Samuel	off. UNKNOWN
SANDERS	and				GARDNER	VA. bk. 01 pg. 006
Mary E.		21	Jul	1857	James C.	off. S. TEAGARDEN
SANDERSON	and				STRONG	VA. bk. 3A pg. 078
James Y.		12	Dec	1859	Elizabeth A.	off. J. NAYLOR
SANFORD	and				JACKSON	VA. bk. 2A pg. 074
Sarah		05	Oct	1841	John	off. W. STEVENS
SAUNDERS	and				ROBERTS	VA. bk. 1A pg. 027
Ann		13	Jun	1807	Richard	off. UNKNOWN
SAUNDERS	and				MARTIN	VA. bk. 2A pg. 004
Elizabeth		07	Jan	1817	Nathaniel	off. G. BUCHANAN
SAUNER	and				DEIGHTON	WV. bk. 4A pg. 083
Hannah		23	Feb	1871	John M.	off. W. WHITE
SCAMAHORN	and				GREEN	WV. bk. 4A pg. 141
George W.		22	Sep	1874	Arabella V.	off. J. LATIMER
SCARBOROUGH	and				NAYLOR	WV. bk. 4A pg. 107
J.A.		24	Feb	1872	Elizabeth T.	off. W. LATIMER
SCHALK	and				EASTERDAY	VA. bk. 3A pg. 055
Conrad		18	Aug	1858	Lusetta (Mrs.)	off. J. NAYLOR
SCHALK	and				LOFFER	VA. bk. 3A pg. 055
Conrad		18	Aug	1858	Lusetta	off. J. NAYLOR
SCHELL	and				CRAFT	WV. bk. 01 pg. 019
William H.		20	Aug	1868	Clara C.	off. J. DARSIE

Groom Surname	Groom Given	Day	Month	Year	Bride Surname	Bride Given	Reference
SCHEVENKLE	Christian	16	Dec	1874	WALTON	Alice	WV. bk. 4A pg. 147 off. C. TURNER
SCHUEY	Barbara	26	Nov	1866	HORN	George	WV. bk. 4A pg. 016 off. R. NICHOLLS
SCHUEY	Peter	21	Apr	1870	GAUSE	Mary	WV. bk. 4A pg. 071 off. W. WHITE
SCOTT	Alexander W.	15	Sep	1842	PETERSON	Sarah	VA. bk. 2A pg. 084 off. R. WHITE
SCOTT	Catharine	07	Oct	1846	CREE	Hamilton	VA. bk. 2A pg. 088 off. R. HOPKINS
SCOTT	Charles	12	Dec	1816	CULLEY	Hannah	VA. bk. 2A pg. 007 off. S. LAUCK
SCOTT	James	15	Jul	1852	MOORE	Jane	VA. bk. 2A pg. *12 off. D. HERVEY
SCOTT	James B.	17	Dec	1826	TOMLINSON	Ellen	VA. bk. 2A pg. 044 off. J. BROWNING, JR.
SCOTT	Jane	16	Jan	1822	CAMERON	James	VA. bk. 2A pg. 021 off. G. SCOTT
SCOTT	Jane A.	09	Mar	1868	HANNA	J.G.	WV. bk. 4A pg. 045 off. H. MELVIN
SCOTT	John	01	Dec	1814	STEWART	Sarah	VA. bk. 1A pg. 083 off. UNKNOWN
SCOTT	John S.	05	Jul	1864	LITTLE	Mary Jane	WV. bk. 3A pg. 145 off. H. SHEPHERD
SCOTT	Joseph	06	Jan	1842	PROSSER	Jane	VA. bk. 2A pg. 083 off. R. WHITE
SCOTT	Josiah	22	Feb	1827	OGDEN	Rachael	VA. bk. 2A pg. 049 off. S. REED
SCOTT	Mary	29	Mar	1842	JEFFREY	William	VA. bk. 2A pg. 083 off. R. WHITE
SCOTT	Mary Ann	12	May	1842	JOHNSON	David P.	VA. bk. 2A pg. 073 off. J. HERBERT
SCOTT	Rachel A.	12	Feb	1850	HUDSON	Geo. B. (Rev.)	VA. bk. 2A pg. *04 off. R. HOPKINS
SCOTT	Robert	04	Mar	1823	EDIE	Elizabeth	VA. bk. 2A pg. 026 off. G. SCOTT
SCOTT	Robert	03	Mar	1831	COOK	Nancy	VA. bk. 2A pg. 057 off. G. SCOTT
SCOTT	Sarah F.	26	Sep	1826	PUGH	John P.	VA. bk. 2A pg. 047 off. G. SCOTT
SCOTT	Washington S.	11	Mar	1852	KLEIN	Pamela T.	VA. bk. 2A pg. *10 off. H. SNYDER
SCOTT	William	27	Feb	1868	HEADINGTON	Rachel D.	WV. bk. 4A pg. 044 off. H. MELVIN
SEARS	James	27	Feb	1868	MELCHS	Margaret	WV. bk. 4A pg. 044 off. H. MELVIN
SEILA	Therisia	10	Apr	1865	PIKIRRA	Adrian	WV. bk. 3A pg. 155 off. H. SHEPHERD
SELBY	Sarah C.	10	Jan	1872	LAZEAR	Milton	PA. bk. 4A pg. 104 off. W. LATIMER
SELLERS	James	0?	Sep	1802	ROBISON	Elisabeth	VA. bk. 1A pg. 008 off. J. HUGHES

BROOKE CO., VA./WV. LICENSES & MARRIAGES, 1797-1874   107

SENS		and		WENNINGCOUGH		VA. bk. 3A pg. 045
Ursula	21	Nov	1857	Ferdinand		off. J. NAYLOR
SENSHODY		and		ORSPBODY?		VA. bk. 3A pg. 079
John	15	Dec	1859	Jane C.		off. UNKNOWN
SERGEANT		and		RODGERS		VA. bk. 2A pg. 092
Jane Ann	26	Oct	1847	Ezekiel		off. S. LAUCK
SERVIS		and		LAUGHEAD		VA. bk. 01 pg. 003
Charles M.	12	Jul	1855	Sarah		off. D. HERVEY
SHADE		and		CLOSE		VA. bk. 2A pg. 075
Margaret	16	Feb	1843	Peter		off. S. GRAFTON
SHARP		and		WOLCOTT		WV. bk. 4A pg. 133
Elizabeth K.	23	Dec	1873	Francis L.		off. W. LATIMER
SHARP		and		ROBERTS		VA. bk. 2A pg. 074
Mary	12	Oct	1841	Alexander		off. W. STEVENS
SHARPE		and		ATKINSON		VA. bk. 2A pg. 051
John F.	29	Mar	1827	Narcissa		off. G. BUCHANAN
SHARRON		and		CLENDENEN		VA. bk. 1A pg. 009
Anna	15	Apr	1799	John		off. UNKNOWN
SHAW		and		HUGGINS		VA. bk. 1A pg. 063
Charles	24	Aug	1815	Mary		off. L. BROWNING
SHEARER		and		MC LAUGHLIN		WV. bk. 3A pg. 139
Andrew J.	13	Mar	1864	Martha J.		off. H. SHEPHERD
SHEARER		and		WILLIAMS		VA. bk. 2A pg. 092
Robert	11	Apr	1848	Elizabeth		off. J. MONROE
SHELL		and		WELLS		VA. bk. 2A pg. *15
Charles T.	18	Oct	1853	Charlotte		off. A. MYERS
SHEPARD		and		CLARK		VA. bk. 1A pg. 007
Ruhanna	05	Apr	1801	Samuel		off. UNKNOWN
SHEPHARD		and		GASS		VA. bk. 1A pg. 007
Enoch	13	Nov	1800	Margaret		off. UNKNOWN
SHIELDS		and		DOW		VA. bk. 3A pg. 124
Henry T.	12	Jan	1863	Samantha		off. J. NAYLOR
SHIRLY		and		HANNAH		VA. bk. 2A pg. 002
William	08	Feb	1816	Polly		off. E. MACURDY
SHIVELY		and		WAUGH		WV. bk. 4A pg. 013
S. Elizabeth	27	Oct	1866	Robert		off. R. NICHOLLS
SHOUP		and		THOMPSON		WV. bk. 4A pg. 100
Mary J.	19	Nov	1871	William		off. W. LATIMER
SHRIMPLIN		and		LAZEAR		WV. bk. 4A pg. 103
Amanda	20	Dec	1871	Hugh		off. W. LATIMER
SHRIMPLIN		and		BARTHOLOMEW		WV. bk. 4A pg. 042
Ella	18	Feb	1868	Samuel D.		off. H. MELVIN
SHRIMPLIN		and		MC CONNELL		VA. bk. 2A pg. 039
Frances	26	Oct	1825	Richard		off. J. CAZAD
SHRINER		and		GREEN		WV. bk. 4A pg. 003
William	02	Nov	1865	Caroline		off. H. SHEPHERD
SHRINER		and		HALL		WV. bk. 4A pg. 003
William	02	Nov	1865	Caroline		off. H. SHEPHERD
SHRIVER		and		RODGERS		WV. bk. 4A pg. 115
C.	07	Aug	1872	Rebecca E.		off. W. LATIMER
SHUPE		and		MERRYMAN		WV. bk. 4A pg. 097
David D.	11	Oct	1871	Emma J.		off. W. WHITE

SICKLER		and		HELSTINE		WV. bk. 4A pg. 148
John Francis	26	Dec	1874	Mary		off. C. TURNER
SILSON		and		FOULK		VA. bk. 2A pg. 064
Juliana	05	Jul	1838	Henry		off. A. YOUNG
SILVER		and		ROBINSON		WV. bk. 3A pg. 136
James M.	11	Jan	1864	Elizabeth E.		off. H. SHEPHERD
SILVERS		and		CRAIG		VA. bk. 2A pg. 045
Matilda	25	Oct	1826	Absalom		off. J. CAZAD
SILVERS		and		RINEHART		WV. bk. 4A pg. 026
Sally	23	Mar	1867	William S.		off. H. MELVIN
SILVERTHORN		and		COULTER		VA. bk. 2A pg. 029
Jane	24	Jun	1823	John (Jr.)		off. G. SCOTT
SILVERTHORN		and		PROSSER		VA. bk. 2A pg. 082
Joseph	05	Sep	1839	Elizabeth		off. R. WHITE
SILVERTHORN		and		SPROWL		VA. bk. 2A pg. 055
Samuel	11	May	1830	Isabella		off. G. SCOTT
SIMERAL		and		HINDMAN		VA. bk. 2A pg. *09
Elizabeth	23	Nov	1851	Samuel L.		off. L. AULD
SIMPSON		and		FLEMING		VA. bk. 3A pg. 084
Charles L.	26	Apr	1860	Nannie E.		off. J. NAYLOR
SIMPSON		and		HESSEY		VA. bk. 01 pg. 003
Isaac G.	31	May	1855	Mary Ann		off. E. QUILLEN
SIMPSON		and		WHITE		VA. bk. 01 pg. 003
Isaac G.	31	May	1855	Mary Ann		off. E. QUILLEN
SIMPSON		and		LOWRY		VA. bk. 2A pg. 015
James	02	Nov	1820	Ann J.		off. G. BUCHANAN
SIMPSON		and		MC CRACKEN		VA. bk. 2A pg. *10
Margaret	26	Jun	1851	Alexander		off. G. BUCHANAN
SIMPSON		and		HAYS		VA. bk. 2A pg. 038
Rebecca	08	Sep	1825	David		off. G. BUCHANAN
SIMPSON		and		WYLIE		VA. bk. 01 pg. 004
Rebecca Ann	04	Mar	1856	Oliver		off. E. QUILLEN
SIMPSON		and		BEALL		VA. bk. 2A pg. 051
William	22	Mar	1827	Nancy		off. G. BUCHANAN
SISSON		and		MICK		VA. bk. 2A pg. 083
Elizabeth	08	Oct	1840	Peter		off. R. WHITE
SISSON		and		MACKEY		VA. bk. 2A pg. 073
Martha A.M.	16	Feb	1842	Joseph		off. J. HERBERT
SLY		and		BRAFFORD		VA. bk. 2A pg. 065
Lucinda	12	Sep	1838	Noah		off. A. YOUNG
SMALL		and		MC ATTEE		VA. bk. 2A pg. 005
Tamer	28	Aug	1817	Abraham		off. L. BROWNING
SMITH		and		SMITH		VA. bk. 1A pg. 060
Abraham	12	Apr	1810	Ester (...)		off. E. MACURDY
SMITH		and		GREEN		VA. bk. 2A pg. 052
Andrew	01	Jul	1827	Jane		off. L. BROWNING
SMITH		and		MC CREARY		WV. bk. 4A pg. 040
Clarence A.C.	31	Dec	1867	Almira		off. C. MELVIN
SMITH		and		MARS		WV. bk. 4A pg. 112
Elizabeth H.	13	May	1872	Hiram		off. W. LATIMER
SMITH		and		WRIGHT		VA. bk. 2A pg. *10
Emma R.	10	Mar	1852	E.N.		off. H. SNYDER

BROOKE CO., VA./WV. LICENSES & MARRIAGES, 1797-1874   109

Surname	Given	Day	Month	Year	Surname	Given	Officiant
SMITH	Ester (...)	12	Apr	1810	SMITH and FOWLER	Abraham	VA. bk. 1A pg. 060 off. E. MACURDY
SMITH	Francis	27	Nov	1856	and	Hiram ?	VA. bk. 01 pg. 005 off. G. CRANAGE
SMITH	George F.	09	Nov	1861	and CORNELIUS	Sarah	VA. bk. 3A pg. 108 off. S. NAYLOR
SMITH	George W.	27	Feb	1860	and MC CREARY	Elizabeth	VA. bk. 3A pg. 081 off. J. NAYLOR
SMITH	George W.	01	Nov	1865	and MC CREARY	Virginia	WV. bk. 4A pg. 002 off. H. SHEPHERD
SMITH	Henry	06	Mar	1817	and RYLEY	Margaret	VA. bk. 2A pg. 007 off. S. LAUCK
SMITH	Isaac Y.	--	Sep	1866	and ADAMS	Ruth A.	WV. bk. 4A pg. 010 off. R. NICHOLLS
SMITH	Jacob	06	Jul	1802	and REED	Elizabeth	VA. bk. 1A pg. 041 off. J. DODDRIDGE
SMITH	James	17	May	1848	and GORELY	Harriet	VA. bk. 2A pg. 094 off. J. GALLOWAY
SMITH	James Pursel	02	Sep	1865	and BONAR	Sallie/Sarah	WV. bk. 3A pg. 158 off. H. SHEPHERD
SMITH	Jesse S.	21	Aug	1842	and HOWE	Sarah Ann	VA. bk. 2A pg. 075 off. S. GRAFTON
SMITH	Job	29	Oct	1811	and CAMPBELL	Jane	VA. bk. 1A pg. 057 off. J. PRITCHARD
SMITH	John	14	Dec	1797	and HARPER	Sally	VA. bk. 1A pg. 004 off. J. DODDRIDGE
SMITH	John E.	04	Mar	1863	and GREEN	Permelia	VA. bk. 3A pg. 127 off. J. NAYLOR
SMITH	John P.	21	Aug	1860	and INGLEBRIGHT	Lina E.	VA. bk. 3A pg. 090 off. J. NAYLOR
SMITH	Joseph	05	Oct	1819	and HAGIN	Jane	VA. bk. 2A pg. 009 off. G. BUCHANAN
SMITH	Joseph	23	Jan	1812	and HENRY	Mary	VA. bk. 1A pg. 072 off. J. PRITCHARD
SMITH	Juliana	15	Apr	1849	and DAVIDSON	James	VA. bk. 2A pg. *01 off. J. MOFFITT
SMITH	Kate P.	03	Sep	1861	and BURSLEY	Gilbert E.	VA. bk. 3A pg. 105 off. S. NAYLOR
SMITH	Katharine	25	Mar	1824	and HUNTER	Nathaniel	VA. bk. 2A pg. 038 off. T. BEEKS
SMITH	Margaret	14	Dec	1797	and MC GUIRE	James	VA. bk. 1A pg. 003 off. J. DODDRIDGE
SMITH	Marianna L.	01	Dec	1853	and HUNTER	John H.	VA. bk. 2A pg. *17 off. W. LONG
SMITH	Mary	03	Apr	1813	and DOTY	Peter	VA. bk. 1A pg. 076 off. E. MACURDY
SMITH	Matilda	07	Jan	1841	and DAWSON	John	VA. bk. 2A pg. 071 off. T. STEIRSHCOMB
SMITH	Nancy Jane	26	May	1853	and HUNTER	William S.	VA. bk. 2A pg. *14 off. S. NESBITT
SMITH	Nancy M.	10	Sep	1866	and RIDGLEY	Horace	WV. bk. 4A pg. 009 off. R. NICHOLLS

110 BROOKE CO., VA./WV. LICENSES & MARRIAGES, 1797-1874

Name		Day	Month	Year	Spouse	Reference
SMITH	and				HOBBS	VA. bk. 2A pg. 069
Rachel		17	Oct	1839	John	off. M. TELCHENELL
SMITH	and				WELLS	WV. bk. 3A pg. 135
Robert		17	Dec	1863	Elizabeth	off. H. SHEPHERD
SMITH	and				BRADY	VA. bk. 3A pg. 119
Robert N.		14	Oct	1862	Anne	off. J. NAYLOR
SMITH	and				CASNER	VA. bk. 3A pg. 058
Rose V.		06	Nov	1858	John C.	off. J. NAYLOR
SMITH	and				DAVIS	VA. bk. 1A pg. 062
Sally		11	May	1815	Jacob	off. L. BROWNING
SMITH	and				HIRP	VA. bk. 2A pg. *14
Sarah		10	Mar	1853	Joseph	off. S. NESBITT
SMITH	and				HUNTER	VA. bk. 2A pg. *06
Sarah E.		03	Oct	1850	Nathaniel	off. J. MC GAN
SMITH	and				FACKSBERRY	VA. bk. 2A pg. 003
Stephen		19	Feb	1818	Lavina	off. E. MACURDY
SMITH	and				HUNTER	VA. bk. 2A pg. *17
William		27	Oct	1853	Susan B.	off. W. LONG
SMITH	and				BANE	VA. bk. 1A pg. 036
William		17	Mar	1808	Margaret	off. J. HUGHES
SMOTE	and				BROWNLEE	VA. bk. 01 pg. 002
Elizabeth Jane		26	Feb	1854	William E.	off. S. NESBITT
SNEARY	and				CAMPBELL	WV. bk. 4A pg. 049
Stewart		11	Aug	1868	Elizabeth	off. S. QUEST
SNEDIKER	and				MORRISON	VA. bk. 2A pg. 080
Aliche		27	Jan	1825	John	off. S. LAUCK
SNEDIKER	and				BRYCOFF	VA. bk. 1A pg. 018
Anne		21	Feb	1805	Arthur	off. W. WILLSON
SNEDIKER	and				ATKINSON	WV. bk. 4A pg. 052
Clarinda L.		29	Oct	1868	Samuel W.	off. S. QUEST
SNEDIKER	and				COOK	WV. bk. 4A pg. 058
Clay		01	Feb	1869	Samuel	off. W. WHITE
SNEDIKER	and				JONES	WV. bk. 4A pg. 135
Ellis M.		31	Jan	1874	Hattie	off. W. LATIMER
SNEDIKER	and				BOTHWELL	VA. bk. 3A pg. 056
Elvira Virginia		02	Oct	1858	John H.	off. J. NAYLOR
SNEDIKER	and				MILLER	VA. bk. 2A pg. 042
Garret		03	Jun	1826	Mary	off. C. MURRAY
SNEDIKER	and				HEDGES	VA. bk. 2A pg. 080
George		25	Oct	1821	Susan	off. S. LAUCK
SNEDIKER	and				ROGERS	VA. bk. 1A pg. 072
Isaac		08	Jul	1813	Margaret	off. J. PRITCHARD
SNEDIKER	and				COULTER	VA. bk. 1A pg. 021
John		--	--	1806	Mary	off. UNKNOWN
SNEDIKER	and				DUKE	VA. bk. 2A pg. 043
Lavina		11	Mar	1826	Shepherd	off. C. MURRAY
SNOWDEN	and				WELCH	VA. bk. 2A pg. 076
David		21	Feb	1843	Mary Ann	off. R. SIMONTAIS
SNOWDEN	and				WILCOXON	VA. bk. 2A pg. 001
Isaac		31	Dec	1818	Rebecca	off. G. SCOTT
SNOWDEN	and				MELVIN	VA. bk. 2A pg. 084
Jane		20	Jun	1844	Alexander	off. R. WHITE

SNOWDEN			and	WILKINSON	VA. bk. 2A pg. 021	
Martha	20	Dec	1821	Samuel	off. G. SCOTT	
SNOWDEN			and	PUGH	VA. bk. 1A pg. 063	
Mary	21	Mar	1815	David	off. G. SCOTT	
SNOWDEN			and	STEWART	WV. bk. 4A pg. 138	
Sarah Ann	20	May	1874	Ellson	off. J. LATIMER	
SNOWDEN			and	PUGH	VA. bk. 2A pg. 034	
William	01	Sep	1825	Polly	off. G. SCOTT	
SNYDER			and	COCHRAN	VA. bk. 2A pg. 065	
Huldah	10	Jan	1839	Jabez H.	off. G. BUCHANAN	
SNYDER			and	SPEAKER	VA. bk. 3A pg. 053	
Mary C.	03	Jul	1858	Benja. Frank.	off. J. NAYLOR	
SNYDER			and	HENDRICKS	VA. bk. 2A pg. 076	
Rebecca	08	Dec	1842	Edward	off. G. BUCHANAN	
SODIKE			and	MC CLURG	PA. bk. 01 pg. 016	
William	13	Oct	1867	Harriet E.	off. J. WILLIAMS	
SOMERVILLE			and	FRAZIER	VA. bk. 2A pg. *11	
Mary	23	May	1852	John B.	off. H. SNYDER	
SOMERVILLE			and	MC HENRY	VA. bk. 2A pg. 083	
William	01	Jul	1841	Jane	off. R. WHITE	
SOULES			and	HENNES	VA. bk. 01 pg. 003	
Washington	15	Mar	1855	Mary Jane	off. W. LONG	
SPAHR			and	GREEN	VA. bk. 2A pg. 066	
Jesse	28	Jul	1839	Abigal	off. J. BOYLE	
SPAIGHT			and	KENNAR	VA. bk. 2A pg. *01	
Adam	16	Aug	1849	Frederica	off. H. KOCH	
SPEAKER			and	SNYDER	VA. bk. 3A pg. 053	
Benja. Frank.	03	Jul	1858	Mary C.	off. J. NAYLOR	
SPEER			and	DECAMP	VA. bk. 1A pg. 022	
Sarah	27	May	1806	Jacob	off. UNKNOWN	
SPEIDEL			and	HALL	VA. bk. 3A pg. 013	
Clemens	29	Jan	1853	Margaret	off. J. NAYLOR	
SPENCER			and	HAMILTON	VA. bk. 2A pg. 084	
Lydia L.	15	Nov	1843	Daniel	off. R. WHITE	
SPENCER			and	DOWDEN	VA. bk. 2A pg. 071	
Priscilla	08	Jun	1841	Thomas	off. J. GALLOWAY	
SPIVY			and	WILCOXON	VA. bk. 2A pg. 011	
Rebecca	24	Apr	1810	Fulsia	off. G. SCOTT	
SPRAGUE			and	THOMPSON	WV. bk. 4A pg. 116	
Cora	03	Sep	1872	W.H.	off. W. LATIMER	
SPRINGBORN			and	LETZKUS	WV. bk. 4A pg. 009	
Frederick	10	Oct	1866	Mary	off. R. NICHOLLS	
SPROWL			and	MC COWN	VA. bk. 2A pg. 049	
Elizabeth	05	Jul	1827	John	off. S. REED	
SPROWL			and	SILVERTHORN	VA. bk. 2A pg. 055	
Isabella	11	May	1830	Samuel	off. G. SCOTT	
SPROWL			and	VANIMAN	VA. bk. 2A pg. 084	
Margaret	26	Mar	1844	Garret	off. R. WHITE	
SPURVIER			and	ANDREWS	VA. bk. 2A pg. 059	
Owen	24	Jun	1830	Elizabeth	off. G. BUCHANAN	
SRIMPLIN			and	CARR	VA. bk. 1A pg. 037	
Mary	09	Dec	1808	Joshua	off. J. DODDRIDGE	

Name		Date		Spouse	Reference
ST. CLAIR James	and 25	Feb	1850	WILLIAMS Eliza. (Mrs.)	VA. bk. 2A pg. *04 off. E. NICHOLSON
ST. CLAIR John D.	and 11	Jun	1843	APPLEGATE Elizabeth	VA. bk. 2A pg. 076 off. C. BEST
ST. LEDGER Jane	and 23	Dec	1841	JACOB Benjamin	VA. bk. 2A pg. 074 off. W. STEVENS
ST. LEDGER Mary Ann	and 05	Oct	1854	UHLRICH Robert	VA. bk. 01 pg. 002 off. W. LEMON
STALEY Eli	and 14	Nov	1822	PUMPHREY Lovey	VA. bk. 2A pg. 027 off. T. BEEKS
STANSBERRY Daniel B.	and 17	Apr	1853	MC CAUSLAND Francis Mary	VA. bk. 2A pg. *14 off. J. BAINBRIDGE
STANSBERRY Daniel Bosley	and 04	Feb	1865	CAMPBELL Jane	WV. bk. 3A pg. 151 off. H. SHEPHERD
STANSBERRY Dorcus	and 08	Jun	1827	TRUAXE William	VA. bk. 2A pg. 050 off. L. BROWNING
STANSBERRY Hudson R.	and 22	Feb	1868	CRISS Hanna	WV. bk. 4A pg. 043 off. H. MELVIN
STANSBERRY Sarah	and 08	Mar	1827	KINKAID Robert	VA. bk. 2A pg. 054 off. L. BROWNING
STARK James	and 07	Jan	1840	TODD Margaret	VA. bk. 2A pg. 069 off. M. TELCHENELL
STARKEY Mary	and 01	May	1858	BORING George W.	VA. bk. 3A pg. 052 off. J. NAYLOR
STARR John	and 18	Oct	1849	KEITH Mary	VA. bk. 2A pg. *03 off. J. IRWIN
STARR Joseph	and 02	Jan	1863	MURPHY Elizabeth	VA. bk. 3A pg. 124 off. J. NAYLOR
STARR Nancy J.	and 20	Jul	1863	MURPHY George Wash.	WV. bk. 3A pg. 129 off. H. SHEPHERD
STECALES Sophia	and 24	Dec	1829	FOUTS Andrew	VA. bk. 2A pg. 058 off. T. BEEKS
STEDMAN Melvina	and 28	Jan	1858	MC DUGAN James	VA. bk. 3A pg. 049 off. J. NAYLOR
STEEL Emily	and 15	Apr	1819	JEFFRIES Henry	VA. bk. 2A pg. 010 off. A. CAMPBELL
STEEN Elizabeth	and 01	Jul	1841	CUNNINGHAM George	VA. bk. 2A pg. 071 off. D. HERVEY
STEEN James	and 17	Dec	1818	KINKAID Jane	VA. bk. 2A pg. 003 off. G. BUCHANAN
STEENROD Daniel	and 29	Mar	1825	MC EA- - - Nancy	VA. bk. 2A pg. 041 off. W. WYLIE
STEPHENS Lewis W.	and 25	Jan	1848	PLATTENBURG Mary	VA. bk. 2A pg. 091 off. J. MONROE
STEPHENSON Hans	and 20	Nov	1852	TAYLOR Ann	VA. bk. 3A pg. 010 off. J. NAYLOR
STEPHENSON John	and 20	Apr	1815	DONOVAN Sarah	VA. bk. 1A pg. 066 off. UNKNOWN
STEPHENSON Thomas	and 01	Jun	1847	STEWART Isabel	VA. bk. 2A pg. *05 off. D. ROBINSON
STEVENS Ezra	and 24	Apr	1809	HALSTEAD Catherine	VA. bk. 1A pg. 053 off. J. PRITCHARD

STEVENSON		and		ELLIOT	VA. bk. 1A pg. 013
Lurea	16	Aug	1803	Andrew	off. E. MACURDY
STEVENSON		and		COLWELL	VA. bk. 1A pg. 036
Mary	15	Sep	1808	William	off. J. HUGHES
STEVENSON		and		GILSTON	VA. bk. 1A pg. 013
Nancy	24	Apr	1804	Moses	off. E. MACURDY
STEVENSON		and		NAMRY	VA. bk. 1A pg. 030
Thomas	05	May	1807	Sarah	off. J. HUGHES
STEWART		and		MILLER	WV. bk. 4A pg. 054
Elizabeth C.	21	Dec	1868	Jacob	off. S. QUEST
STEWART		and		SNOWDEN	WV. bk. 4A pg. 138
Ellson	20	May	1874	Sarah Ann	off. J. LATIMER
STEWART		and		ROBINETT	VA. bk. 01 pg. 004
Elmira J.	01	Jun	1856	James	off. A. ENDSLEY
STEWART		and		STIER	VA. bk. 2A pg. 089
George	24	Mar	1847	Delina	off. J. MONROE
STEWART		and		KLINE	WV. bk. 4A pg. 068
Harriet	03	Feb	1870	William	off. W. WHITE
STEWART		and		DUVALL	VA. bk. 3A pg. 051
Henrietta	06	Mar	1858	William	off. J. NAYLOR
STEWART		and		STEPHENSON	VA. bk. 2A pg. *05
Isabel	01	Jun	1847	Thomas	off. D. ROBINSON
STEWART		and		PUGH	VA. bk. 2A pg. 083
James	03	Apr	1841	Sarah Ann	off. R. WHITE
STEWART		and		CHESTER	WV. bk. 4A pg. 070
James Clinton	29	Mar	1870	Georgianna	off. W. WHITE
STEWART		and		HARPER	VA. bk. 2A pg. 083
Jane	03	Jun	1841	William	off. R. WHITE
STEWART		and		CUNNINGHAM	VA. bk. 2A pg. 084
John	20	Jun	1844	Nancy Ann	off. R. WHITE
STEWART		and		CHAMBERLAIN	WV. bk. 4A pg. 001
John Gibson	21	Oct	1865	Ellen	off. H. SHEPHERD
STEWART		and		CAMPBELL	VA. bk. 2A pg. 014
Joseph	26	Jun	1820	Elizabeth	off. G. SCOTT
STEWART		and		CATHCART	VA. bk. 2A pg. 083
Joseph	17	Jun	1841	Sarah	off. R. WHITE
STEWART		and		STOCKER	WV. bk. 4A pg. 010
L.D. Jesse	19	Sep	1866	Hattie E.	off. R. NICHOLLS
STEWART		and		BELL	VA. bk. 2A pg. 063
Mary	05	Dec	1832	John	off. G. SCOTT
STEWART		and		MC GREW	WV. bk. 4A pg. 082
Mary	17	Feb	1871	John	off. W. WHITE
STEWART		and		PUGH	VA. bk. 2A pg. 084
Mary Ann	31	Aug	1843	James	off. R. WHITE
STEWART		and		FARQUER	VA. bk. 01 pg. 004
Mary Ann	28	Feb	1856	John (Jr.)	off. A. ENDSLEY
STEWART		and		NEAUGIN	VA. bk. 2A pg. 082
Robert	20	Sep	1838	Mary	off. R. WHITE
STEWART		and		KNIGHT	WV. bk. 4A pg. 050
Ruemma Elen	05	Oct	1868	Wilson L.	off. S. QUEST
STEWART		and		SCOTT	VA. bk. 1A pg. 083
Sarah	01	Dec	1814	John	off. UNKNOWN

Surname	Given	Day	Month	Year	Spouse Surname	Spouse Given	Reference
STEWART	Sarah Jane	05	Apr	1820	PROSSER	Benjamin	VA. bk. 2A pg. 014 off. G. SCOTT
STEWART	William	20	Aug	1823	CUMMINS	Mary	VA. bk. 2A pg. 028 off. J. CAZAD
STIER	Delina	24	Mar	1847	STEWART	George	VA. bk. 2A pg. 089 off. J. MONROE
STIETZE	Wellhemine	08	Sep	1856	BERTRAM	Henry	VA. bk. 01 pg. 004 off. E. QUILLEN
STILES	Hannah	26	Nov	1840	TEASDALE	William	VA. bk. 2A pg. 083 off. R. WHITE
STILL	Samuel	05	Apr	1816	BEAL	Ruth	VA. bk. 1A pg. 066 off. UNKNOWN
STOCK	Benjamin	01	May	1856	MC HUGH	Rosanna	VA. bk. 01 pg. 004 off. J. MEANS
STOCKER	Hattie E.	19	Sep	1866	STEWART	L.D. Jesse	WV. bk. 4A pg. 010 off. R. NICHOLLS
STOCKS	Mary	02	Dec	1852	NUNEMAKER	Jacob	VA. bk. 2A pg. *13 off. H. SNYDER
STONE	William	11	Jul	1815	HEDGES	Catharine	VA. bk. 1A pg. 070 off. UNKNOWN
STRAIN	Ebenezer	21	Mar	1816	RUSSELL	Catherine	VA. bk. 1A pg. 076 off. W. WILLSON
STRAIN	Eleazer G.	24	Aug	1854	MC KIM	Elizabeth	VA. bk. 01 pg. 002 off. S. TOMPKINS
STRAIN	Hannah	15	Aug	1815	GORELY	John	VA. bk. 1A pg. 064 off. G. SCOTT
STRAIN	John	13	Mar	1845	ANDREWS	Mary	VA. bk. 2A pg. 081 off. D. THOMPSON
STRAIN	John D.	14	Jul	1842	HOWLETT	Drusilla	VA. bk. 2A pg. 074 off. C. WEIRICK
STRAIN	Nancy	25	Feb	1846	LAWRENCE	Benjamin	VA. bk. 2A pg. 086 off. D. THOMPSON
STRAIN	William P.	20	May	1845	WALLACE	Margaret	VA. bk. 2A pg. 082 off. D. THOMPSON
STRATE	Christian	31	Oct	1805	YOUNG	Lydia	VA. bk. 1A pg. 024 off. E. MACURDY
STRINGER	Ruth Jane	08	Nov	1853	DARE	Edmund	VA. bk. 01 pg. 004 off. G. CRANAGE
STRONG	Elizabeth A.	12	Dec	1859	SANDERSON	James Y.	VA. bk. 3A pg. 078 off. J. NAYLOR
STRONG	Rebecca	03	Apr	1828	RAY	Joseph	VA. bk. 2A pg. 059 off. E. SMITH
STRONG	Samuel	--	Aug	1809	HUFFMAN	Elizabeth	VA. bk. 1A pg. 034 off. UNKNOWN
STURGEON	J.R.	13	Oct	1864	MC WHA	Mary E.	WV. bk. 3A pg. 144 off. H. SHEPHERD
SUNDERLAND	Francis	18	Nov	1800	CUPPY	Anne	VA. bk. 1A pg. 042 off. J. DODDRIDGE
SUTER	Clarinda	02	Nov	1864	BIER	Henry A.	WV. bk. 3A pg. 146 off. H. SHEPHERD
SUTER	Mary C.	14	Jul	1860	ANDERSON	George	VA. bk. 2A pg. 080 off. J. NAYLOR

Name		Day	Month	Year	Name	Officiant / Location
SUTER	and				TONI	WV. bk. 3A pg. 156
Sarah Elizabeth	--	Jun	1865		William M.	off. H. SHEPHERD
SUTHERLAND	and				HEADINGTON	VA. bk. 3A pg. 039
William	17	Jan	1854		Mary E.	off. J. NAYLOR
SWEARINGEN	and				CHAMBERS	VA. bk. 2A pg. 013
Ann	29	Aug	1820		John	off. J. PRITCHARD
SWEARINGEN	and				MORROW	VA. bk. 2A pg. 066
Benjamin	25	Jun	1839		Margaret	off. W. SCULL
SWEARINGEN	and				ROBINSON	VA. bk. 2A pg. 049
Bennett	27	Dec	1827		Sarah	off. S. REED
SWEARINGEN	and				OWINGS	VA. bk. 2A pg. 036
Blanche	12	Jan	1826		Ephraim	off. G. BUCHANAN
SWEARINGEN	and				CONNELL	VA. bk. 1A pg. 044
Eleanor	14	Mar	1802		John	off. J. DODDRIDGE
SWEARINGEN	and				ATKINSON	VA. bk. 2A pg. 029
Elenor	22	Jan	1824		Richard	off. G. BUCHANAN
SWEARINGEN	and				SWEARINGEN	VA. bk. 2A pg. 009
Elizabeth (...)	27	Oct	1819		George	off. E. MACURDY
SWEARINGEN	and				WILCOXON	VA. bk. 1A pg. 054
Emauel	--	--	1810		Miss.	off. J. DODDRIDGE
SWEARINGEN	and				SWEARINGEN	VA. bk. 2A pg. 009
George	27	Oct	1819		Elizabeth (...)	off. E. MACURDY
SWEARINGEN	and				EVANS	VA. bk. 2A pg. 084
George	02	Jun	1842		Mary	off. R. WHITE
SWEARINGEN	and				HOOKER	PA., bk. 01 pg. 023
George	09	Jul	1874		Sallie J.	off. J. SHIELDS
SWEARINGEN	and				JEFFERS	VA. bk. 01 pg. 002
John C.	11	Apr	1854		Ruth Ann	off. E. QUILLEN
SWEARINGEN	and				OGDEN	VA. bk. 2A pg. 060
Martha	27	May	1828		John	off. S. REED
SWEARINGEN	and				CHAMBERS	VA. bk. 2A pg. 047
Mary	31	May	1827		James	off. G. BUCHANAN
SWEARINGEN	and				ATKINSON	VA. bk. 2A pg. 025
Matilda	06	Feb	1823		James	off. G. BUCHANAN
SWEARINGEN	and				SALMON	WV. bk. 4A pg. 140
Mattie L.	10	Jun	1874		Cornelius B.	off. J. LATIMER
SWEARINGEN	and				SWEARINGEN	VA. bk. 2A pg. 060
N.D.	18	Sep	1828		Ruth (...)	off. S. REED
SWEARINGEN	and				OWENS	VA. bk. 2A pg. 026
Nicholas	03	Jul	1823		Micha	off. G. BUCHANAN
SWEARINGEN	and				CAMERON	VA. bk. 2A pg. 036
Rebecca	05	Jan	1826		John	off. G. BUCHANAN
SWEARINGEN	and				SWEARINGEN	VA. bk. 2A pg. 033
Ruth (...)	17	Mar	1825		William	off. G. BUCHANAN
SWEARINGEN	and				SWEARINGEN	VA. bk. 2A pg. 060
Ruth (...)	18	Sep	1828		N.D.	off. S. REED
SWEARINGEN	and				OWINGS	VA. bk. 2A pg. 029
Sarah	29	Jan	1824		Absalom	off. G. BUCHANAN
SWEARINGEN	and				PARK	VA. bk. 2A pg. 027
Velinda	21	Aug	1823		Robert (Jr.)	off. G. BUCHANAN
SWEARINGEN	and				SWEARINGEN	VA. bk. 2A pg. 033
William	17	Mar	1825		Ruth (...)	off. G. BUCHANAN

SWEENEY		and		PENDEGRASS	WV.	bk. 4A	pg. 059
Hannah	15	Mar	1869	Patrick	off. W. WHITE		
SWINER		and		FENWICK	VA.	bk. 01	pg. 004
Bell	28	Mar	1856	Edward	off. S. NESBITT		
SWINER		and		BROWNLEE	VA.	bk. 01	pg. 003
Mary Ann	27	Dec	1854	William J.	off. S. NESBITT		
SWINER		and		RAMSEY	VA.	bk. 01	pg. 002
Peter	06	Aug	1854	Macky	off. C. HOLMES		
SWINER		and		WOOD	VA.	bk. 01	pg. 002
Peter	06	Aug	1854	Macky	off. C. HOLMES		
SWORDS		and		GLASS	WV.	bk. 4A	pg. 036
Robert M.	01	Feb	1868	Terrissa	off. H. MELVIN		
TALBOTT		and		PARKINSON	VA.	bk. 2A	pg. 038
Antionette	17	Nov	1825	David	off. A. CAMPBELL		
TALBOTT		and		TALBOTT	VA.	bk. 2A	pg. 042
Emily (...)	13	Jan	1826	Lloyd	off. C. MURRAY		
TALBOTT		and		PUMPHREY	VA.	bk. 1A	pg. 083
George	04	Mar	1813	Susannah	off. UNKNOWN		
TALBOTT		and		MILLER	VA.	bk. 1A	pg. 078
James	13	Nov	1814	Sarah	off. W. WILLSON		
TALBOTT		and		RUTH	VA.	bk. 3A	pg. 035
John	26	Dec	1853	Mary	off. J. NAYLOR		
TALBOTT		and		TALBOTT	VA.	bk. 2A	pg. 042
Lloyd	13	Jan	1826	Emily (...)	off. C. MURRAY		
TALBOTT		and		HUBBARD	VA.	bk. 2A	pg. 074
Michael	23	Nov	1841	John	off. W. STEVENS		
TALBOTT		and		ROSS	VA.	bk. 2A	pg. *06
Nancy	05	Sep	1850	John	off. R. WHITE		
TALBOTT		and		AGNEW	VA.	bk. 2A	pg. 069
Richard	29	Oct	1839	Ann	off. M. TELCHENELL		
TALLENLINE		and		ROBERTSON	VA.	bk. 2A	pg. 066
John R.	30	Aug	1838	Eleanor	off. J. HUNTSMAN		
TALLMAN		and		WELLS	VA.	bk. 1A	pg. 043
Samuel	26	Mar	1801	Sarah	off. UNKNOWN		
TARR		and		WYLIE	VA.	bk. 2A	pg. 062
Amanda	08	Jan	1833	Unknown	off. G. BUCHANAN		
TARR		and		HUNTER	VA.	bk. 2A	pg. 059
Campbell	21	Feb	1828	Frances	off. E. SMITH		
TARR		and		HAMMOND	VA.	bk. 2A	pg. 091
Campbell (Jr.)	13	Jan	1848	Mary	off. T. NEWELL		
TARR		and		JACOB	VA.	bk. 3A	pg. 078
Isabella	20	Dec	1859	John G.	off. J. NAYLOR		
TARR		and		CRAWFORD	VA.	bk. 2A	pg. 081
Jackson	18	Apr	1844	Mary Ann	off. J. GALLOWAY		
TARR		and		WEIR	VA.	bk. 2A	pg. 059
Mary	28	Aug	1828	Thomas	off. E. SMITH		
TARR		and		ALLEN	WV.	bk. 4A	pg. 113
Mary Belle	04	Jun	1872	Edwin T.	off. W. LATIMER		
TARR		and		GARRETT	WV.	bk. 4A	pg. 071
Mary F.	27	Apr	1870	Robert W.	off. W. WHITE		
TARR		and		LANGFITT	VA.	bk. 01	pg. 004
Virginia	20	Nov	1855	Obediah W.	off. W. BEARD		

TARRISON		and		CAMPBELL	VA. bk. 2A pg. 059
Joseph	16	Jan	1828	Isabella	off. J. CAZAD
TAYLOR		and		BAIL	WV. bk. 3A pg. 161
Alice	27	Mar	1866	Thomas W.	off. H. SHEPHERD
TAYLOR		and		PRATHER	VA. bk. 3A pg. 089
Amelia C.	11	Aug	1860	George M.	off. J. NAYLOR
TAYLOR		and		STEPHENSON	VA. bk. 3A pg. 010
Ann	20	Nov	1852	Hans	off. J. NAYLOR
TAYLOR		and		BURGESS	VA. bk. 3A pg. 120
Anne	10	Dec	1862	John S.	off. J. NAYLOR
TAYLOR		and		FOSTER	VA. bk. 1A pg. 056
Ebenezer	19	Dec	1811	Margaret	off. J. PRITCHARD
TAYLOR		and		ELLIOTT	VA. bk. 3A pg. 019
Elizabeth	25	Apr	1853	Thomas	off. J. NAYLOR
TAYLOR		and		WILLIAMS	VA. bk. 2A pg. 085
James	25	Mar	1845	Mary Jane	off. S. WORTHINGTON
TAYLOR		and		WINDSOR	VA. bk. 2A pg. *02
Mary J.	05	Apr	1849	Joshua R.	off. I. DALLAS
TAYLOR		and		MC GREGOR	VA. bk. 2A pg. 080
Nancy	22	Feb	1825	Alexander	off. S. LAUCK
TAYLOR		and		ORANGE	WV. bk. 4A pg. 125
Robert	14	Jun	1873	Sarah	off. W. LATIMER
TEAFF		and		MAHAN	VA. bk. 2A pg. 020
James	14	Jun	1821	Eleanor	off. L. BROWNING
TEAL		and		COX	VA. bk. 1A pg. 038
Nicholas	02	Jun	1803	Elizabeth	off. J. DODDRIDGE
TEALIN		and		COBB	VA. bk. 2A pg. 049
Jane	04	Jan	1827	Samuel	off. S. REED
TEASDALE		and		STILES	VA. bk. 2A pg. 083
William	26	Nov	1840	Hannah	off. R. WHITE
TELAND		and		JACKSON	VA. bk. 2A pg. 002
Betsy	14	Mar	1816	Philip	off. E. MACURDY
TENCK		and		BEATY	VA. bk. 2A pg. 067
William	03	Mar	1839	Lucinda	off. A. YOUNG
TERLY		and		MOUNTAIN	WV. bk. 3A pg. 147
Hugh	12	Nov	1864	Margaret	off. H. SHEPHERD
THARL		and		DURBIN	VA. bk. 2A pg. 049
James	17	Dec	1827	Frances	off. S. REED
THAYER		and		LATHAM	VA. bk. 2A pg. 060
Ann	19	Jun	1828	William	off. S. REED
THAYER		and		MELVIN	VA. bk. 2A pg. 041
Elzina	22	Dec	1825	Henry	off. J. BROWNING, JR.
THAYER		and		WALSH	VA. bk. 2A pg. 065
Nathan	30	Aug	1838	Elizabeth	off. J. BEATTY
THOMAS		and		DAVIS	VA. bk. 2A pg. 041
Jane	27	Dec	1825	Irvin	off. J. BROWNING, JR.
THOMAS		and		DILL	VA. bk. 2A pg. 078
Mary	03	Nov	1842	John	off. J. HARRISON
THOMAS		and		WYCOFF	VA. bk. 2A pg. 084
Mary Ann	17	May	1842	James	off. R. WHITE
THOMPSON		and		MILLER	WV. bk. 3A pg. 138
Elizabeth	25	Feb	1864	Cyrus	off. H. SHEPHERD

118   BROOKE CO., VA./WV. LICENSES & MARRIAGES, 1797-1874

THOMPSON		and		CHAPMAN	VA. bk. 2A pg. 021
Giles S.	21	Jan	1822	Joana	off. G. SCOTT
THOMPSON		and		HARRIS	VA. bk. 2A pg. 074
James	11	Nov	1841	Sarah	off. W. STEVENS
THOMPSON		and		BOWMAN	VA. bk. 01 pg. 003
Joseph	04	Oct	1855	Sarah E.	off. J. MEANS
THOMPSON		and		HANEY	WV. bk. 4A pg. 070
Robert	24	Mar	1870	Margaret	off. W. WHITE
THOMPSON		and		KELLY	VA. bk. 1A pg. 056
Robert	17	Aug	1811	Elizabeth	off. UNKNOWN
THOMPSON		and		LINTON	VA. bk. 01 pg. 005
S. Elizabeth	15	Nov	1856	William	off. A. ENDSLEY
THOMPSON		and		SPRAGUE	WV. bk. 4A pg. 116
W.H.	03	Sep	1872	Cora	off. W. LATIMER
THOMPSON		and		SHOUP	WV. bk. 4A pg. 100
William	19	Nov	1871	Mary J.	off. W. LATIMER
THOMPSON		and		CAMPBELL	WV. bk. 3A pg. 133
William R.	26	Oct	1863	Virginia A.	off. H. SHEPHERD
THOMSON		and		WILLIAMS	VA. bk. 2A pg. 047
Hugh	29	Nov	1827	Margaret	off. G. BUCHANAN
THORLEY		and		WILLIAMSON	VA. bk. 2A pg. *13
James	28	Oct	1852	Margaret H.	off. J. GALLOWAY
THORLEY		and		MEEK	VA. bk. 2A pg. 039
John	21	Mar	1825	Matilda	off. J. CAZAD
THORLEY		and		WILLIAMSON	VA. bk. 2A pg. *02
Thomas	21	Jun	1849	Esther	off. J. GALLOWAY
THORN		and		PARK	VA. bk. 2A pg. 071
Zadok S.	27	Jun	1841	Julia A.E.	off. T. STEIRSHCOMB
THORP		and		HINKSTON	VA. bk. 1A pg. 036
Charlotte	13	Apr	1808	William	off. J. HUGHES
THORP		and		COGAN	VA. bk. 01 pg. 004
Mary	12	Sep	1856	John	off. W. GAMBLE, JR.
THRASHER		and		JOHNSON	VA. bk. 2A pg. *16
Frederick Aug.	12	Mar	1853	Sarah Ann	off. S. DUNLAP
TIERMAN		and		DEMPSEY	VA. bk. 01 pg. 005
Thomas	02	Oct	1856	Margarett	off. J. BRAZILL
TILLINGHART		and		HAMMOND	VA. bk. 1A pg. 046
Sally	--	--	1803	Charles	off. UNKNOWN
TILTON		and		COOPER	WV. bk. 4A pg. 085
Joseph	07	Mar	1871	Valinda J.	off. W. WHITE
TIPTON		and		GOADING	VA. bk. 1A pg. 018
Hannah	08	Mar	1805	Abednigo	off. J. PRITCHARD
TIPTON		and		PRITCHARD	VA. bk. 1A pg. 016
Solomon	07	Mar	1805	Elizabeth	off. J. PRITCHARD
TODD		and		STARK	VA. bk. 2A pg. 069
Margaret	07	Jan	1840	James	off. M. TELCHENELL
TOLAND		and		CAMPBELL	VA. bk. 2A pg. 082
James	13	Sep	1838	Elizabeth	off. R. WHITE
TOMLINSON		and		SCOTT	VA. bk. 2A pg. 044
Ellen	17	Dec	1826	James B.	off. J. BROWNING, JR.
TONER		and		HUTTON	VA. bk. 2A pg. 022
Mary	28	Jun	1821	Joseph	off. J. LAWS

BROOKE CO., VA./WV. LICENSES & MARRIAGES, 1797-1874

Surname/Name		Day	Month	Year	Spouse	Location
TONI		and			SUTER	WV. bk. 3A pg. 156
William M.	--	Jun		1865	Sarah Eliza.	off. H. SHEPHERD
TORREYSON		and			JEFFERS	VA. bk. 2A pg. 092
Vetessy Ann	16	Mar		1848	William	off. J. MONROE
TOSTEN		and			DORSEY	VA. bk. 2A pg. 019
Hannah	04	Apr		1820	Joseph	off. A. CAMPBELL
TOWN		and			BROWNLEE	VA. bk. 2A pg. *02
Eli C.	07	Mar		1849	Mary J.	off. I. DALLAS
TRIMBLE		and			PARROTT	VA. bk. 2A pg. 061
Martha	07	Mar		1832	William	off. G. MC CASHEY
TRINE		and			GRIFFITH	VA. bk. 1A pg. 045
Jacob	--	--		1802	Mary	off. UNKNOWN
TROUP		and			PROSSER	VA. bk. 2A pg. 084
David	20	Mar		1845	Susan	off. R. WHITE
TRUAXE		and			JONES	VA. bk. 3A pg. 093
Ann	08	Sep		1860	Josiah	off. J. NAYLOR
TRUAXE		and			STANSBERRY	VA. bk. 2A pg. 050
William	08	Jun		1827	Dorcus	off. L. BROWNING
TUCKER		and			JOHNSON	VA. bk. 2A pg. 072
Martin	14	Oct		1841	Jane	off. S. FULTON
TUCKER		and			HOOKER	WV. bk. 4A pg. 139
William	25	May		1874	Sarah P.	off. J. LATIMER
TURNER		and			HAWKINS	VA. bk. 3A pg. 072
Georgeanna	09	Jul		1859	William S.	off. J. NAYLOR
TURNER		and			DOWNEY	VA. bk. 2A pg. 091
Matthew	05	Dec		1847	Louisa	off. T. NEWELL
TURNER		and			ROBERTS	VA. bk. 2A pg. 049
Thompson	14	Dec		1826	Polly	off. S. REED
TWEED		and			WYLIE	VA. bk. 3A pg. 056
John	30	Sep		1858	Ann	off. J. NAYLOR
TWEED		and			LINDSAY	VA. bk. 3A pg. 097
Mary	07	Jan		1861	Samuel	off. J. NAYLOR
UBY		and			ABEY	VA. bk. 3A pg. 110
Alexander C.	25	Dec		1861	Mary P.	off. J. OXFORD
UHLRICH		and			HOFFMAN	WV. bk. 4A pg. 140
Emma F.	20	Jun		1874	Frederick	off. J. LATIMER
UHLRICH		and			ST. LEDGER	VA. bk. 01 pg. 002
Robert	05	Oct		1854	Mary Ann	off. W. LEMON
UTZ		and			KNOX	WV. bk. 3A pg. 159
Rachel Marg't	07	Sep		1865	Jas. Newton	off. H. SHEPHERD
VANDOVERT		and			ROBERTS	VA. bk. 1A pg. 030
Polly	05	Mar		1807	Samuel	off. J. HUGHES
VANDYKE		and			WALKER	VA. bk. 2A pg. 055
John	17	Apr		1828	Elisabeth	off. G. BUCHANAN
VANHORN		and			MINGUS	VA. bk. 2A pg. *02
John	19	Aug		1848	Luthada	off. I. DALLAS
VANIMAN		and			SPROWL	VA. bk. 2A pg. 084
Garret	26	Mar		1844	Margaret	off. R. WHITE
VANMATRE		and			BARCUS	VA. bk. 1A pg. 035
Elizabeth	14	Apr		1808	Ebenezer	off. W. WILLSON
VANMETER		and			CROUCH	VA. bk. 1A pg. 081
John	27	Aug		1812	Anna	off. UNKNOWN

120   BROOKE CO., VA./WV. LICENSES & MARRIAGES, 1797-1874

Name					Spouse	Reference
VANORDSTRAND			and		GARDNER	VA. bk. 2A pg. 091
Hannah		28	Oct	1847	Levi	off. J. GALLOWAY
VANSICKLE			and		GLASS	WV. bk. 4A pg. 135
Ellie		20	Feb	1874	Robert	off. J. LATIMER
VASBINDER			and		PATTON	VA. bk. 2A pg. 060
Mary		12	Oct	1828	Robert	off. E. SMITH
VAUGHN			and		ALLISON	VA. bk. 2A pg. 084
Jacob		19	Sep	1844	Elizabeth	off. R. WHITE
VAUSE			and		WOODS	VA. bk. 2A pg. 023
Rebcca		19	Feb	1822	Robert	off. J. CAZAD
VERMILLION			and		CUNNINGHAM	WV. bk. 4A pg. 023
C.A.		30	Jan	1867	Ella I.	off. H. MELVIN
VESY			and		CUNNINGHAM	VA. bk. 2A pg. 068
Susan (Mrs.)		19	Dec	1839	James	off. W. SCULL
VIERS			and		HEDGES	VA. bk. 2A pg. 064
A.E.		13	Nov	1833	Rebecca Ann	off. G. ROBINSON
VIERS			and		PUMPHREY	VA. bk. 2A pg. 078
Maria M.D.		10	Mar	1842	Beal	off. J. HARRISON
VIERS			and		BUKEY	VA. bk. 2A pg. *10
Rebecca Ann		18	Sep	1851	Robert	off. W. SUMMERS
VIERS			and		KIRKPATRICK	VA. bk. 2A pg. 065
Sarah Margaret		05	Aug	1838	Samuel	off. A. YOUNG
VINCENT			and		RAY	VA. bk. 2A pg. 045
Anne		20	Sep	1826	Thomas	off. J. CAZAD
VIRTUE			and		HINDMAN	WV. bk. 4A pg. 025
William		16	Mar	1867	Marg't Jane	off. H. MELVIN
WABLE			and		BARCUS	VA. bk. 2A pg. 067
George		30	Dec	1838	Nancy	off. A. YOUNG
WABLE			and		MC MILLEN	VA. bk. 01 pg. 005
Samuel		24	Feb	1857	Melissa	off. W. GAMBLE, JR.
WADDLE			and		PATTON	WV. bk. 4A pg. 096
Thomas		21	Sep	1871	Maria	off. W. WHITE
WALDRON			and		CHESTER	WV. bk. 3A pg. 157
Joseph		14	Aug	1865	Sarah Eliza.	off. H. SHEPHERD
WALKER			and		GLASS	VA. bk. 2A pg. *14
Anne		30	May	1853	Robert P.	off. E. QUILLEN
WALKER			and		WALLACE	WV. bk. 4A pg. 137
Anne M.		16	Mar	1874	John C.	off. J. LATIMER
WALKER			and		MC DONALD	VA. bk. 2A pg. 038
Benjamin		29	Dec	1825	Angelena	off. T. BEEKS
WALKER			and		GOURLEY	VA. bk. 3A pg. 054
Catharine T.		06	Jul	1858	James M.	off. J. NAYLOR
WALKER			and		VANDYKE	VA. bk. 2A pg. 055
Elisabeth		17	Apr	1828	John	off. G. BUCHANAN
WALKER			and		MC COLLOCH	WV. bk. 4A pg. 068
Ella J.		16	Feb	1870	Ebenezer Z.	off. W. WHITE
WALKER			and		HEDGES	VA. bk. 2A pg. *12
Hessy		30	Jun	1852	Charles B.	off. S. TOMPKINS
WALKER			and		ROBINSON	VA. bk. 2A pg. 026
James		10	Jun	1823	Mary	off. G. BUCHANAN
WALKER			and		WELLS	VA. bk. 2A pg. *01
Mary		08	Mar	1849	Milton	off. T. NEWELL

WALKER				WILSON	VA. bk. 2A pg. 076
Minerva E.	13	Sep	1842	Jonathan W.	off. C. BEST
WALKER		and		MILLER	VA. bk. 2A pg. 093
Nathan U.	06	Jun	1848	Sarah J.	off. S. WORTHINGTON
WALKER		and		PRICE	VA. bk. 2A pg. 003
Sarah	19	Nov	1818	Hiram	off. G. BUCHANAN
WALKER		and		HAINES	VA. bk. 2A pg. 035
Sarah	28	Dec	1825	David	off. N. HEADINGTON
WALLACE		and		WALKER	WV. bk. 4A pg. 137
John C.	16	Mar	1874	Anne M.	off. J. LATIMER
WALLACE		and		STRAIN	VA. bk. 2A pg. 082
Margaret	20	May	1845	William P.	off. D. THOMPSON
WALSH		and		THAYER	VA. bk. 2A pg. 065
Elizabeth	30	Aug	1838	Nathan	off. J. BEATTY
WALSH		and		MAXWELL	VA. bk. 2A pg. 063
Robert	01	Nov	1832	Betsey	off. R. BROWN
WALTERS		and		BAXTER	VA. bk. 2A pg. *03
Louisa	17	Dec	1846	George	off. J. GOODWIN
WALTERS		and		EASTERDAY	WV. bk. 4A pg. 063
Lucas	22	Jul	1869	Magdaline	off. W. WHITE
WALTERS		and		CORBIN	VA. bk. 2A pg. 078
Mary Ann	26	Aug	1841	Joseph	off. J. HARRISON
WALTON		and		SCHEVENKLE	WV. bk. 4A pg. 147
Alice	16	Dec	1874	Christian	off. C. TURNER
WARD		and		ADAMS	WV. bk. 4A pg. 080
Mary A.	14	Dec	1870	James M.	off. W. WHITE
WARD		and		HEDGES	VA. bk. 2A pg. *17
William B.	15	Dec	1853	Sarah Eliza.	off. W. LONG
WARTENBEE		and		BAKER	VA. bk. 1A pg. 043
Margaret	11	Mar	1802	Otho	off. J. DODDRIDGE
WARTENBEE		and		HOLLY	VA. bk. 1A pg. 017
Mary	23	May	1805	Edward	off. J. PRITCHARD
WARTENBY		and		CALENDINE	VA. bk. 1A pg. 028
Francis	29	Sep	1807	Catherine	off. UNKNOWN
WARWICK		and		MORROW	VA. bk. 2A pg. 089
Margaret	19	Jan	1847	Robert	off. J. GALLOWAY
WATKINS		and		BAILEY	WV. bk. 4A pg. 079
Harriet	08	Nov	1870	William T.	off. W. WHITE
WATKINS		and		BAILEY	VA. bk. 2A pg. 090
Mary	21	Nov	1847	William T.	off. J. MONROE
WATSON		and		BEALL	WV. bk. 4A pg. 113
Green	19	Jun	1872	Leanna	off. W. LATIMER
WATT		and		ANDREWS	VA. bk. 1A pg. 010
William	29	Apr	1802	Ester	off. J. HUGHES
WAUGH		and		MC FADDEN	WV. bk. 4A pg. 074
Amanda	31	Aug	1870	Leonard D.	off. W. WHITE
WAUGH		and		MOORE	VA. bk. 2A pg. 055
David	18	Feb	1830	Maria	off. J. MC KENNAR
WAUGH		and		HUKILL	WV. bk. 4A pg. 029
David	02	Sep	1867	Ethelinda	off. C. MELVIN
WAUGH		and		ROLAND	WV. bk. 4A pg. 007
E.R.	15	Feb	1866	Ann M.	off. R. NICHOLLS

WAUGH Elizabeth	and 10	Nov	1857	PALMER James	VA. bk. 3A off. J. NAYLOR	pg. 044
WAUGH Fannie T.	and 16	Aug	1859	PALMER John C.	VA. bk. 3A off. J. NAYLOR	pg. 073
WAUGH James	and 07	Feb	1856	PALMER Caroline A.	VA. bk. 01 off. E. QUILLEN	pg. 004
WAUGH James	and 07	Dec	1860	HAMMOND Elizabeth	VA. bk. 3A off. J. NAYLOR	pg. 096
WAUGH Jane	and 15	Sep	1857	DODDS Thomas	VA. bk. 3A off. J. NAYLOR	pg. 040
WAUGH Michael J.	and 25	Mar	1868	MC KINLEY William L.	WV. bk. 4A off. H. MELVIN	pg. 046
WAUGH Robert	and 27	Oct	1866	SHIVELY S. Elizabeth	WV. bk. 4A off. R. NICHOLLS	pg. 013
WAUGH Sarah	and 25	Oct	1865	MC KINLEY John W.	WV. bk. 4A off. H. SHEPHERD	pg. 002
WAUGH Sarah Ann	and 24	Oct	1859	CRAFT Charles H.	VA. bk. 3A off. J. NAYLOR	pg. 075
WAY Francis E.	and 27	Jun	1866	MARSH Jemima E.	WV. bk. 3A off. R. NICHOLLS	pg. 165
WAY William	and 30	Aug	1871	DEULEY Mary E.	WV. bk. 4A off. W. WHITE	pg. 094
WEAR James	and 12	Sep	1857	FARQUER Susan	VA. bk. 3A off. J. NAYLOR	pg. 041
WEAVER Matilda	and 02	Jan	1838	FULLER Samuel	VA. bk. 2A off. A. YOUNG	pg. 064
WEAVER Robert	and 20	Apr	1853	CHAPMAN Elsa	VA. bk. 3A off. J. NAYLOR	pg. 019
WEIR Thomas	and 28	Aug	1828	TARR Mary	VA. bk. 2A off. E. SMITH	pg. 059
WELCH Mary Ann	and 21	Feb	1843	SNOWDEN David	VA. bk. 2A off. R. SIMONTAIS	pg. 076
WELCH Rebekah	and 08	Apr	1800	BURNS John	VA. bk. 1A off. UNKNOWN	pg. 009
WELCH Susanna	and 26	Sep	1820	MORROW Alexander	VA. bk. 2A off. E. MACURDY	pg. 019
WELCH William	and 19	Jan	1843	GAMBLE Lucinda	VA. bk. 2A off. R. WHITE	pg. 084
WELLS Ann	and 28	Dec	1859	MC COY Abraham	VA. bk. 3A off. J. NAYLOR	pg. 080
WELLS Bazil (Jr.)	and 01	Feb	1864	HOGG Harriet	WV. bk. 3A off. H. SHEPHERD	pg. 137
WELLS Bazil (Jr.)	and 14	Nov	1871	COOPER Nancy	WV. bk. 4A off. W. LATIMER	pg. 099
WELLS Bezeleel	and 23	Jun	1797	GRIFFITH Sarah	VA. bk. 1A off. J. DODDRIDGE	pg. 001
WELLS Charlotte	and 18	Oct	1853	SHELL Charles T.	VA. bk. 2A off. A. MYERS	pg. *15
WELLS Elizabeth	and 19	Jan	1809	OWEN Henry	VA. bk. 1A off. W. WILLSON	pg. 055
WELLS Elizabeth	and 07	Jun	1826	DUKE Alexander	VA. bk. 2A off. C. MURRAY	pg. 043

BROOKE CO., VA./WV. LICENSES & MARRIAGES, 1797-1874   123

WELLS		and		HUNTER	VA. bk. 2A pg. *11
Elizabeth	25	Mar	1852	George C.	off. C. JACKSON
WELLS		and		SMITH	WV. bk. 3A pg. 135
Elizabeth	17	Dec	1863	Robert	off. H. SHEPHERD
WELLS		and		MOORE	VA. bk. 2A pg. 069
Elizabeth J.	06	May	1840	Robert	off. M. TELCHENELL
WELLS		and		BONE	WV. bk. 4A pg. 016
Emma B.	19	Nov	1866	Russell	off. R. NICHOLLS
WELLS		and		MC INTYRE	VA. bk. 2A pg. 059
Ephraim	28	Sep	1828	Margaret	off. E. SMITH
WELLS		and		HAMILTON	VA. bk. 2A pg. 070
George	09	Jan	1840	Susannah	off. J. SWAYZE
WELLS		and		FOUTS	VA. bk. 2A pg. 038
Isaiah	04	Dec	1825	Nancy	off. T. BEEKS
WELLS		and		BAXTER	VA. bk. 2A pg. *03
James	15	Jul	1849	Nancy	off. J. GOODWIN
WELLS		and		DAVIS	VA. bk. 1A pg. 042
Jesse	04	Sep	1800	Miss.	off. J. DODDRIDGE
WELLS		and		ROBINSON	VA. bk. 2A pg. 038
Jesse	09	Feb	1826	Amanda	off. T. BEEKS
WELLS		and		ANDERSON	VA. bk. 3A pg. 126
John Dusty	21	Feb	1863	Rebecca E.	off. J. NAYLOR
WELLS		and		BECKWITH	WV. bk. 4A pg. 060
Josephine	15	Mar	1869	Oscar J.	off. W. WHITE
WELLS		and		CONNELL	VA. bk. 2A pg. 085
Martha Ann	08	Oct	1844	James	off. S. WORTHINGTON
WELLS		and		MAHON	WV. bk. 4A pg. 047
Mary	13	May	1868	Richard	off. H. MELVIN
WELLS		and		BERRY	VA. bk. 2A pg. *15
Michael	18	Oct	1853	Thomas V.	off. A. MYERS
WELLS		and		CARTER	VA. bk. 2A pg. 079
Michel	21	Jan	1844	Samuel	off. S. WORTHINGTON
WELLS		and		WALKER	VA. bk. 2A pg. *01
Milton	08	Mar	1849	Mary	off. T. NEWELL
WELLS		and		WILLSON	VA. bk. 1A pg. 050
N.	--	--	1808	Alexander	off. UNKNOWN
WELLS		and		HAMILTON	VA. bk. 2A pg. 023
Nancy	11	Apr	1822	John	off. L. BROWNING
WELLS		and		OWINGS	VA. bk. 2A pg. 073
Nathaniel	30	Jun	1842	Rebecca	off. G. BUCHANAN
WELLS		and		LONG	WV. bk. 4A pg. 067
Richard T.	27	Dec	1869	Rebecca J.	off. W. WHITE
WELLS		and		NUNEMAKER	VA. bk. 2A pg. 076
Ruth	06	Apr	1843	George	off. C. BEST
WELLS		and		ROBISON	VA. bk. 1A pg. 046
Sally	--	--	1802	James	off. UNKNOWN
WELLS		and		TALLMAN	VA. bk. 1A pg. 043
Sarah	26	Mar	1801	Samuel	off. UNKNOWN
WELLS		and		DENER	VA. bk. 3A pg. 097
Susan A.	25	Dec	1860	Franklin	off. J. NAYLOR
WELLS		and		KNEFF	VA. bk. 1A pg. 041
Temperance	08	Jul	1802	John	off. J. DODDRIDGE

BROOKE CO., VA./WV. LICENSES & MARRIAGES, 1797-1874

Groom		Date		Bride	Reference
WELLS	and			HEDGES	WV. bk. 4A pg. 035
William B.	09	Dec	1867	Amanda J.	off. H. MELVIN
WELLS	and			BUCHANAN	VA. bk. 2A pg. *12
William C.	18	Sep	1852	Sarah Jane	off. H. SNYDER
WELSH	and			HEALY	VA. bk. 3A pg. 070
Edward	21	Jun	1859	Catherine	off. J. NAYLOR
WELSH	and			ADAMS	VA. bk. 2A pg. 085
Elizabeth	25	Sep	1844	Josiah	off. J. SCOTT
WENNINGCOUGH	and			LEHEKS	VA. bk. 3A pg. 045
Ferdinand	21	Nov	1857	Ursula	off. J. NAYLOR
WENNINGCOUGH	and			SENS	VA. bk. 3A pg. 045
Ferdinand	21	Nov	1857	Ursula	off. J. NAYLOR
WEST	and			BROWNLEE	WV. bk. 4A pg. 118
Elisha	21	Sep	1872	Elizabeth	off. W. LATIMER
WESTBROOK	and			DAWSON	VA. bk. 2A pg. 074
Alexander	14	Oct	1841	Sarah	off. W. STEVENS
WETHERELL	and			ROBINETT	WV. bk. 4A pg. 011
Christopher	22	Sep	1866	Mary A.	off. R. NICHOLLS
WETHERELL	and			MC CONKEY	VA. bk. 3A pg. 076
Mary Ann	03	Nov	1859	Jos. Grafton	off. J. NAYLOR
WEYMAN	and			HUGHES	VA. bk. 1A pg. 042
Mary	18	Sep	1800	John	off. J. DODDRIDGE
WHARTON	and			BOWMAN	VA. bk. 3A pg. 044
Gipson	09	Nov	1857	Caroline	off. J. NAYLOR
WHEELER	and			REED	WV. bk. 3A pg. 142
Anne E.	17	Aug	1864	George F.	off. H. SHEPHERD
WHEELER	and			BOSMAN	VA. bk. 2A pg. 059
Elisabeth	04	Sep	1828	William	off. E. SMITH
WHEELER	and			BUCKEY	VA. bk. 2A pg. 060
Henrietta	08	Jan	1829	George	off. E. SMITH
WHEELER	and			OWINGS	VA. bk. 2A pg. 072
Honor	11	Mar	1841	Wells	off. G. BUCHANAN
WHEELER	and			BOSMAN	VA. bk. 2A pg. 059
Ignatius	29	Dec	1827	Happuck	off. E. SMITH
WHEELER	and			JOHNSTON	VA. bk. 1A pg. 058
Martha	24	Mar	1811	Isaac	off. J. PRITCHARD
WHEELER	and			MARKS	WV. bk. 4A pg. 136
Sallie	17	Feb	1874	T.H.	off. J. LATIMER
WHEELER	and			MURCHLAND	VA. bk. 2A pg. 088
Thomas	12	Mar	1846	Sarah	off. G. BUCHANAN
WHEELER	and			AMSPOKER	VA. bk. 01 pg. 003
Zachariah C.	15	Feb	1855	Eliza. Ann	off. J. THOMAS
WHELAN	and			COTINGHAM	WV. bk. 4A pg. 091
Michael	29	May	1871	Mary	off. W. WHITE
WHETZELL	and			MC NAIR	VA. bk. 3A pg. 036
Everett	31	Dec	1853	Catherine	off. J. NAYLOR
WHICKERLY	and			DAUGHERTY	WV. bk. 4A pg. 117
Mary	10	Sep	1872	Charles	off. W. LATIMER
WHINN	and			CUPPY	VA. bk. 2A pg. 052
Joshua	29	Mar	1827	Jane	off. G. SCOTT
WHITE	and			HAWKINS	VA. bk. 2A pg. 040
Aubey?	17	Dec	1825	Margaret	off. J. CAZAD

BROOKE CO., VA./WV. LICENSES & MARRIAGES, 1797-1874   125

Surname 1	Given 1	D	M	Y	Surname 2	Given 2	Ref
WHITE	Caroline	05	May	1853	DOUGHERTY	George	VA. bk. 2A pg. *16 off. J. DAWSON
WHITE	Isaac	22	Jan	1849	DOUGHERTY	Grace	VA. bk. 2A pg. *02 off. I. DALLAS
WHITE	James	27	Sep	1869	BOWMAN	Sarah	WV. bk. 4A pg. 064 off. W. WHITE
WHITE	James M.	02	Jan	1871	BAKER	Mary	WV. bk. 4A pg. 081 off. W. WHITE
WHITE	John	27	Mar	1828	POOL	Melinda	VA. bk. 2A pg. 054 off. G. BUCHANAN
WHITE	Mary	17	Jan	1872	GUNION	James	WV. bk. 4A pg. 105 off. W. LATIMER
WHITE	Mary Ann	31	May	1855	SIMPSON	Isaac G.	VA. bk. 01 pg. 003 off. E. QUILLEN
WHITE	Mattie J.	07	Aug	1872	FULTON	William P.	WV. bk. 4A pg. 115 off. W. LATIMER
WHITE	Samuel Archer	26	Aug	1865	WILLIAMSON	Maggie M.	WV. bk. 3A pg. 158 off. H. SHEPHERD
WHITE	Samuel K.	26	Dec	1868	MAHAN	Jennie M.	WV. bk. 4A pg. 055 off. S. QUEST
WHITE	Sarah	30	Aug	1827	ALISON	Charles	VA. bk. 2A pg. 052 off. G. SCOTT
WHITE	Thomas	09	Feb	1832	REYNOLDS	Elizabeth	VA. bk. 2A pg. 061 off. G. MC CASHEY
WHITE	William	23	Aug	1860	HUNTER	Rebecca E.	VA. bk. 3A pg. 090 off. J. NAYLOR
WIGGINS	Domatrius	15	Mar	1853	FOWLER	William M.	VA. bk. 2A pg. *16 off. S. TOMPKINS
WIGGINS	John	19	Sep	1849	HEADINGTON	Isabel	VA. bk. 2A pg. *03 off. J. GOODWIN
WIGGINS	Margaret	26	Oct	1854	MAGEE	Silas	VA. bk. 01 pg. 002 off. S. TOMPKINS
WILCOXON	Anthony	20	Apr	1826	HALE	Margaret	VA. bk. 2A pg. 041 off. J. BROWNING, JR.
WILCOXON	Blanche	18	Jul	1838	ALLISON	Robert	VA. bk. 2A pg. 082 off. R. WHITE
WILCOXON	Elizabeth	21	Jan	1830	DOAK	Robert	VA. bk. 2A pg. 057 off. G. SCOTT
WILCOXON	Fulsia	24	Apr	1810	SPIVY	Rebecca	VA. bk. 2A pg. 011 off. G. SCOTT
WILCOXON	John	17	Oct	1820	BAKER	Fanny	VA. bk. 2A pg. 016 off. G. BUCHANAN
WILCOXON	Margaret	15	Nov	1838	ROBINSON	Martin	VA. bk. 2A pg. 082 off. R. WHITE
WILCOXON	Mary	28	Sep	1809	HURFORD	Thomas	VA. bk. 1A pg. 033 off. J. DODDRIDGE
WILCOXON	Miss.	--	--	1810	SWEARINGEN	Emanuel	VA. bk. 1A pg. 054 off. J. DODDRIDGE
WILCOXON	Rebecca	31	Dec	1818	SNOWDEN	Isaac	VA. bk. 2A pg. 001 off. G. SCOTT
WILCOXON	Ruth Ann	23	Oct	1843	MC CONNELL	James	VA. bk. 2A pg. 078 off. J. HARRISON

WILCOXON		and		BAKER		VA. bk. 1A pg. 023
Samuel	25	Mar	1806	Christiana		off. J. PRITCHARD
WILCOXON		and		DUVALL		VA. bk. 2A pg. 031
Thomas	14	Oct	1824	Matilda		off. G. SCOTT
WILCOXON		and		PERRY		VA. bk. 2A pg. 047
Thomas	23	Dec	1827	Jemima		off. A. COLEMAN
WILEY		and		LYON		VA. bk. 1A pg. 058
Nancy	03	Aug	1811	John		off. E. MACURDY
WILHELM		and		BOYCE		VA. bk. 2A pg. 015
Christiana	28	Nov	1819	Robert		off. G. SCOTT
WILHELM		and		CRITZER		VA. bk. 2A pg. 001
George	31	Dec	1818	Nancy		off. G. SCOTT
WILHELM		and		BROWN		VA. bk. 2A pg. 056
Hannah	19	Nov	1829	James		off. L. BROWNING
WILKEY		and		RALSTON		WV. bk. 4A pg. 127
Joseph J.	26	Jul	1873	Elizabeth		off. W. LATIMER
WILKINSON		and		LARGE		VA. bk. 3A pg. 112
Anne	25	Jan	1862	Robert E.		off. J. NAYLOR
WILKINSON		and		DEIGHTON		VA. bk. 3A pg. 050
James	16	Feb	1858	Sarah		off. J. NAYLOR
WILKINSON		and		SNOWDEN		VA. bk. 2A pg. 021
Samuel	20	Dec	1821	Martha		off. G. SCOTT
WILLIAMS		and		SHEARER		VA. bk. 2A pg. 092
Elizabeth	11	Apr	1848	Robert		off. J. MONROE
WILLIAMS		and		ST. CLAIR		VA. bk. 2A pg. *04
Elizabeth (Mrs.)	25	Feb	1850	James		off. E. NICHOLSON
WILLIAMS		and		GRIMES		WV. bk. 4A pg. 144
Frank	24	Jun	1874	Lucy		off. J. LATIMER
WILLIAMS		and		HAYS		VA. bk. 2A pg. 063
George	20	Nov	1832	Lettice		off. R. BROWN
WILLIAMS		and		BAXTER		VA. bk. 2A pg. 083
Henry	25	Nov	1841	Elizabeth		off. R. WHITE
WILLIAMS		and		MOORE		VA. bk. 2A pg. 062
Jane	30	Aug	1832	William		off. G. BUCHANAN
WILLIAMS		and		BROWN		VA. bk. 2A pg. 063
John	09	Sep	1833	Elizabeth		off. R. BROWN
WILLIAMS		and		ENGLE		VA. bk. 1A pg. 043
John	25	Feb	1802	Margaret		off. J. DODDRIDGE
WILLIAMS		and		THOMSON		VA. bk. 2A pg. 047
Margaret	29	Nov	1827	Hugh		off. G. BUCHANAN
WILLIAMS		and		TAYLOR		VA. bk. 2A pg. 085
Mary Jane	25	Mar	1845	James		off. S. WORTHINGTON
WILLIAMS		and		FIELDING		VA. bk. 2A pg. 050
Rebecca	02	Mar	1827	Joseph		off. L. BROWNING
WILLIAMS		and		NANGLE		VA. bk. 3A pg. 073
Valentine	25	Aug	1859	Mary		off. J. NAYLOR
WILLIAMS		and		MAGRUDER		VA. bk. 1A pg. 050
William	07	Feb	1808	Charlotte		off. J. DODDRIDGE
WILLIAMSON		and		GLASS		VA. bk. 3A pg. 100
Anne G.	01	Mar	1861	James		off. J. NAYLOR
WILLIAMSON		and		BOYD		WV. bk. 4A pg. 025
E.A.	25	Mar	1867	Robert		off. H. MELVIN

Surname	Given	Day	Month	Year	Spouse	Location
WILLIAMSON	Esther	21	Jun	1849	THORLEY Thomas	VA. bk. 2A pg. *02 off. J. GALLOWAY
WILLIAMSON	James	31	Dec	1861	BAXTER Mary Ann	VA. bk. 3A pg. 111 off. S. NAYLOR
WILLIAMSON	James C.	--	--	1809	MUSSER Sarah	VA. bk. 1A pg. 048 off. UNKNOWN
WILLIAMSON	Jane	01	Feb	1806	MOORE John	VA. bk. 1A pg. 022 off. UNKNOWN
WILLIAMSON	Mackwright	12	May	1852	BAIL Elizabeth	VA. bk. 2A pg. *11 off. D. HERVEY
WILLIAMSON	Maggie M.	26	Aug	1865	WHITE Samuel A.	WV. bk. 3A pg. 158 off. H. SHEPHERD
WILLIAMSON	Margaret H.	28	Oct	1852	THORLEY James	VA. bk. 2A pg. *13 off. J. GALLOWAY
WILLIAMSON	Mary	26	Apr	1855	BOSLEY Samuel	VA. bk. 01 pg. 003 off. E. QUILLEN
WILLIAMSON	Mathew H.	10	Oct	1874	HALSTED Mary A.	WV. bk. 4A pg. 143 off. J. LATIMER
WILLIAMSON	Rachel	13	Sep	1814	CRAWFORD Lewis	VA. bk. 1A pg. 077 off. J. PRITCHARD
WILLIAMSON	Sarah	22	Oct	1807	PERRIN Edward	VA. bk. 1A pg. 030 off. J. HUGHES
WILLOUGHBY	Alice	18	Mar	1871	FORBES William	WV. bk. 4A pg. 085 off. W. WHITE
WILLQUES	Lewis	15	Oct	1868	MITCHELL Mary	WV. bk. 4A pg. 051 off. S. QUEST
WILLSON	Aaron	22	Dec	1812	BAIRD Esther	VA. bk. 1A pg. 072 off. J. PRITCHARD
WILLSON	Alexander	--	--	1808	WELLS N.	VA. bk. 1A pg. 050 off. UNKNOWN
WILLSON	David	07	Jul	1802	MAXWELL Elizabeth	VA. bk. 1A pg. 011 off. J. HUGHES
WILLSON	Elisabeth	--	--	1809	KELLY John	VA. bk. 1A pg. 049 off. UNKNOWN
WILLSON	James	04	Jul	1799	HENDERSON Elisabeth	VA. bk. 1A pg. 009 off. UNKNOWN
WILLSON	Massa	--	--	1803	PATTERSON John	VA. bk. 1A pg. 047 off. UNKNOWN
WILLSON	Nancy	11	Apr	1816	RALSTON Robert	VA. bk. 2A pg. 002 off. E. MACURDY
WILLSON	William	--	--	1806	RHODES Nancy	VA. bk. 1A pg. 021 off. UNKNOWN
WILLSON	William D.	29	Aug	1822	PENNINGTON Elisa. Ann	VA. bk. 2A pg. 023 off. L. BROWNING
WILSON	Adam	19	Apr	1854	BANE Amanda	VA. bk. 01 pg. 003 off. E. QUILLEN
WILSON	Andrew J.	28	Mar	1854	BANE Margaret	VA. bk. 01 pg. 002 off. E. QUILLEN
WILSON	Florence K.	22	Dec	1867	WILSON Winfield M.	WV. bk. 4A pg. 038 off. H. MELVIN
WILSON	George A.	28	Dec	1866	CRUSON Mary E.	WV. bk. 4A pg. 019 off. R. NICHOLLS

WILSON		and		BELL	VA. bk. 1A pg. 012	
Jean	27	Jun	1803	William	off. E. MACURDY	
WILSON		and		BRADY	WV. bk. 4A pg. 119	
John	25	Nov	1872	Hannah J.	off. W. LATIMER	
WILSON		and		SANDERS	VA. bk. 3A pg. 122	
John M.	31	Dec	1862	Fanny	off. J. NAYLOR	
WILSON		and		LEWIS	WV. bk. 4A pg. 059	
John M.	11	Feb	1869	Leah	off. W. WHITE	
WILSON		and		WALKER	VA. bk. 2A pg. 076	
Jonathan W.	13	Sep	1842	Minerva E.	off. C. BEST	
WILSON		and		BANE	WV. bk. 4A pg. 124	
Joseph B.	17	Mar	1873	Sarah Jane	off. W. LATIMER	
WILSON		and		HEDGES	WV. bk. 4A pg. 036	
Mary/Rebecca	01	Jan	1868	William B.	off. H. MELVIN	
WILSON		and		MOORE	VA. bk. 2A pg. *16	
Narcissa	11	Oct	1853	Eli H.	off. S. TOMPKINS	
WILSON		and		WORTHINGTON	VA. bk. 2A pg. 075	
Peter	24	May	1843	Elizabeth	off. C. WEIRICK	
WILSON		and		LEWIS	WV. bk. 4A pg. 145	
Robert Bane	03	Nov	1874	Marg't Jennie	off. J. LATIMER	
WILSON		and		WILSON	WV. bk. 4A pg. 038	
Winfield M.	22	Dec	1867	Florence K.	off. H. MELVIN	
WINDSOR		and		TAYLOR	VA. bk. 2A pg. *02	
Joshua R.	05	Apr	1849	Mary J.	off. I. DALLAS	
WINESBURG		and		JOHNSON	WV. bk. 4A pg. 114	
Elizabeth	22	Jun	1872	Eli	off. W. LATIMER	
WITHERS		and		ATEN	VA. bk. 2A pg. 049	
James	17	Apr	1827	Mary	off. S. REED	
WITHERS		and		BROWN	VA. bk. 1A pg. 001	
Robert	18	Jun	1797	Nabby	off. J. DODDRIDGE	
WITMORE		and		FITCH	VA. bk. 2A pg. 009	
Amelia	22	Sep	1819	Dyer	off. O. JENNINGS	
WOLCOTT		and		SHARP	WV. bk. 4A pg. 133	
Francis L.	23	Dec	1873	Elizabeth K.	off. W. LATIMER	
WOLCOTT		and		CROTHERS	WV. bk. 4A pg. 114	
William M.	24	Jun	1872	Sallie H.	off. W. LATIMER	
WOOD		and		SWINER	VA. bk. 01 pg. 002	
Macky	06	Aug	1854	Peter	off. C. HOLMES	
WOODROW		and		WYCOFF	VA. bk. 2A pg. 024	
Elizabeth	25	Apr	1822	Peter	off. G. SCOTT	
WOODROW		and		HAYS	VA. bk. 2A pg. 084	
Lydia	21	Apr	1842	William	off. R. WHITE	
WOODS		and		LEE	VA. bk. 2A pg. *02	
John	30	Nov	1848	Catharine	off. I. DALLAS	
WOODS		and		VAUSE	VA. bk. 2A pg. 023	
Robert	19	Feb	1822	Rebecca	off. J. CAZAD	
WOODY		and		DAVIS	VA. bk. 01 pg. 004	
Tarlton	04	Oct	1856	Rachel	off. UNKNOWN	
WORK		and		ALLISON	VA. bk. 2A pg. 082	
Amos	24	Jan	1839	Elizabeth	off. R. WHITE	
WORRELL		and		MC MAHAN	VA. bk. 1A pg. 005	
Edward	15	Oct	1797	Ann	off. J. DODDRIDGE	

WORSTELL		and		BARNES	VA. bk. 2A pg. 080
Mary	20	Mar	1822	Alexander	off. S. LAUCK
WORSTELL		and		FLEMING	WV. bk. 4A pg. 091
Mary L.	01	Jun	1871	Leander B.	off. W. WHITE
WORTHINGTON		and		WILSON	VA. bk. 2A pg. 075
Elizabeth	24	May	1843	Peter	off. C. WEIRICK
WORTHINGTON		and		LINDSAY	VA. bk. 2A pg. 055
Rebecca	17	Mar	1823	Samuel	off. A. COLEMAN
WORTHINGTON		and		HEDGES	VA. bk. 2A pg. 061
Samuel	02	May	1832	Mary	off. G. MC CASHEY
WRAY		and		CORY	VA. bk. 2A pg. 016
Lydia	30	Nov	1820	Elijah D.	off. G. BUCHANAN
WRIGHT		and		BOLES	WV. bk. 4A pg. 094
Amelia	17	Aug	1871	S.P.	off. W. WHITE
WRIGHT		and		SMITH	VA. bk. 2A pg. *10
E.N.	10	Mar	1852	Emma R.	off. H. SNYDER
WRIGHT		and		DAVIS	VA. bk. 2A pg. 059
Jacob	24	Jun	1830	Peggy	off. G. BUCHANAN
WRIGHT		and		CRAFT	VA. bk. 2A pg. 078
Jane	14	Dec	1843	Alexander	off. S. WORTHINGTON
WRIGHT		and		MC CLELLAND	VA. bk. 2A pg. *11
Jemima	24	Nov	1851	John K.	off. J. STOCKTON
WRIGHT		and		WRIGHT	VA. bk. 2A pg. *05
John	01	Mar	1849	Sophia (...)	off. J. STOCKTON
WRIGHT		and		COX	VA. bk. 2A pg. 075
Jonathan	29	Dec	1842	Serina	off. C. WEIRICK
WRIGHT		and		PARK	WV. bk. 4A pg. 109
Louisa	19	Mar	1872	Mathew C.	off. W. LATIMER
WRIGHT		and		MC CREA	VA. bk. 2A pg. *03
Martha	23	Sep	1846	John	off. J. GOODWIN
WRIGHT		and		COX	WV. bk. 4A pg. 018
Nancy J.	16	Jan	1867	Jonathan	off. H. MELVIN
WRIGHT		and		HINDMAN	WV. bk. 3A pg. 123
Nancy Jane	09	Mar	1866	John (Jr.)	off. H. SHEPHERD
WRIGHT		and		MURCHLAND	VA. bk. 3A pg. 066
Nathaniel W.	25	Apr	1859	Sarah E.	off. J. NAYLOR
WRIGHT		and		WRIGHT	VA. bk. 2A pg. *05
Sophia (...)	01	Mar	1849	John	off. J. STOCKTON
WRIGHT		and		JONES	VA. bk. 2A pg. *11
Susanna	26	Feb	1852	Edward	off. J. STOCKTON
WRIGHTMAN		and		RUSSELL	VA. bk. 3A pg. 045
Ann Jane	21	Nov	1857	George	off. J. NAYLOR
WRIGHTMAN		and		GLASS	WV. bk. 4A pg. 116
Ella V.	28	Aug	1872	Francis C.	off. W. LATIMER
WRIGHTMAN		and		PALMER	WV. bk. 3A pg. 130
Sallie C.	01	Aug	1863	Arthur Stone	off. H. SHEPHERD
WYCOFF		and		SNEDIKER	VA. bk. 1A pg. 018
Asher	21	Feb	1805	Anne	off. W. WILLSON
WYCOFF		and		ANDERSON	VA. bk. 2A pg. 026
Hannah	13	Jan	1823	Andrew	off. G. SCOTT
WYCOFF		and		THOMAS	VA. bk. 2A pg. 084
James	17	May	1842	Mary Ann	off. R. WHITE

WYCOFF			and	MC FARLAND		VA. bk. 2A pg. 084
	Mary	14	Sep 1842		Andrew	off. R. WHITE
WYCOFF			and	WOODROW		VA. bk. 2A pg. 024
	Peter	25	Apr 1822		Elizabeth	off. G. SCOTT
WYLIE			and	TWEED		VA. bk. 3A pg. 056
	Ann	30	Sep 1858		John	off. J. NAYLOR
WYLIE			and	EDIE		VA. bk. 1A pg. 069
	David	25	Apr 1814		Mary	off. UNKNOWN
WYLIE			and	RODGERS		VA. bk. 2A pg. 077
	David	31	Aug 1843		Elizabeth	off. J. SCOTT
WYLIE			and	ALLISON		VA. bk. 2A pg. 077
	Elizabeth	31	May 1842		Samuel	off. J. SCOTT
WYLIE			and	CHAMBERS		VA. bk. 2A pg. 083
	Emeline	21	Jun 1841		James	off. R. WHITE
WYLIE			and	HUNTER		VA. bk. 2A pg. *01
	Harriet A.	19	Oct 1848		John	off. J. MOFFITT
WYLIE			and	HIBBITTS		VA. bk. 2A pg. 077
	Isabel	14	Apr 1843		Daniel	off. J. SCOTT
WYLIE			and	CAMPBELL		VA. bk. 2A pg. *10
	James	09	Sep 1851		Mary	off. J. GALLOWAY
WYLIE			and	ADAMS		VA. bk. 2A pg. 060
	John	24	Mar 1829		Elisabeth	off. S. REED
WYLIE			and	BEALL		VA. bk. 2A pg. 062
	Martha	22	Mar 1832		William (Jr.)	off. C. BEATTY
WYLIE			and	MILLER		VA. bk. 2A pg. 007
	Mary	13	Apr 1818		John	off. E. MACURDY
WYLIE			and	LYON		VA. bk. 1A pg. 058
	Nancy	03	Aug 1811		John	off. E. MACURDY
WYLIE			and	SIMPSON		VA. bk. 01 pg. 004
	Oliver	04	Mar 1856		Rebecca Ann	off. E. QUILLEN
WYLIE			and	BROWN		VA. bk. 2A pg. 020
	Robert	26	Mar 1821		Elizabeth	off. E. MACURDY
WYLIE			and	TARR		VA. bk. 2A pg. 062
	Unknown	08	Jan 1833		Amanda	off. G. BUCHANAN
WYNN			and	GOULDING		VA. bk. 2A pg. 060
	Lydia	18	Dec 1828		William	off. E. SMITH
YATES			and	COLEMAN		WV. bk. 4A pg. 013
	Elijah M.	10	Oct 1866		Mary	off. R. NICHOLLS
YOUNG			and	MORROW		VA. bk. 2A pg. 083
	Andrew	04	Mar 1841		Nancy	off. R. WHITE
YOUNG			and	BROWN		WV. bk. 4A pg. 090
	Caroline	19	May 1871		Jacob	off. W. WHITE
YOUNG			and	CAMPBELL		VA. bk. 2A pg. 060
	Elenor	19	Mar 1829		Robert	off. S. REED
YOUNG			and	DAUGHERTY		WV. bk. 4A pg. 138
	Lucy A.	23	May 1874		Abram M.	off. J. LATIMER
YOUNG			and	STRATE		VA. bk. 1A pg. 024
	Lydia	31	Oct 1805		Christian	off. E. MACURDY
YOUNG			and	ROBINSON		VA. bk. 3A pg. 116
	Octavis	10	Jun 1862		Elizabeth E.	off. J. NAYLOR
YOUNG			and	PETERSON		VA. bk. 2A pg. 084
	William	06	Jul 1843		Lucinda	off. R. WHITE

YOUNG		and		CLENDENEN	VA. bk. 1A pg. 081
William	15	May	1814	Margaret	off. UNKNOWN
YOUNG		and		RUSSELL	WV. bk. 4A pg. 072
William F.	23	Jun	1870	Lucy A.S.	off. W. WHITE
ZINCK		and		DUNLAP	VA. bk. 2A pg. 074
Sarah	17	Aug	1842	William	off. C. WEIRICK
ZINK		and		LINDSAY	VA. bk. 2A pg. *07
Elizabeth	21	Dec	1850	Lemuel B.	off. J. MC GAN
ZINK		and		COUNSELMAN	VA. bk. 2A pg. 043
Emma	22	Mar	1826	George	off. C. MURRAY
ZINK		and		COUNSELMAN	VA. bk. 2A pg. 042
John	04	Apr	1826	Phrania	off. C. MURRAY
ZINK		and		DORSEY	VA. bk. 2A pg. *17
John F.	29	Dec	1853	Rebecca Ann	off. W. LONG
ZINK		and		DORSEY	WV. bk. 4A pg. 015
William	10	Nov	1866	Rebecca Ann	off. R. NICHOLLS
ZINK		and		ZINK	WV. bk. 4A pg. 015
William	10	Nov	1866	Rebecca (Mrs.)	off. R. NICHOLLS

BROOKE COUNTY
VIRGINIA / WEST VIRGINIA
MARRIAGE RECORDS
1853 - 1874

BOOK 1

ABRAHAMS, Mortimore B.　　　book 01 page 13 line 04
born Hancock Co., VA., resides Hancock Co., WV. boatman,
age 22 yrs. single, child of Robert & Matilda ABRAHAMS,
married 12 Aug 1863 Bethany, WV. to Ann Elizabeth KEMP,
born Brooke Co., Virginia, resides Brooke Co., West Virginia,
age 18 yrs. single, child of Adam & Elizabeth KEMP,
married by William K. PENDLETON. remarks : none.

ACKERMAN, Eliza. Jane　　　book 01 page 03 line 37
born Washington Co., PA., resides Brooke Co., Virginia,
age 33 yrs. single, child of Abraham & Marg't ACKERMAN,
married 08 Nov 1855 VA. to Peter CLOSE,
born Washington Co., PA., resides Brooke Co., VA.
age 45 yrs. widow, child of John & Nancy CLOSE,
married by Ezekiel QUILLEN. remarks : none.

ADAMS, Eli　　　book 01 page 19 line 33
born Wellsburg, VA., resides Wellsburg, WV. laborer,
age 23 yrs. single, child of Thomas & Ann ADAMS,
married 25 Mar 1869 WV. to Lydia Jane BUCKALEW,
born Wellsburg, Virginia, resides Wellsburg, West Virginia,
age 21 yrs. single, child of Garrett & Lydia BUCKALEW,
married by A.R. CHAPMAN. remarks : married Wellsburg.

ADAMS, James A.　　　book 01 page 22 line 19
born Brooke Co., VA., resides Brooke Co., West Virginia,
age 21 yrs. unknown, child of unknown & unk. ADAMS,
married 23 Oct 1873 Wellsburg, WV. to Clara Jane KEITH,
born Brooke Co., Virginia, resides Brooke Co., West Virginia,
age 17 yrs. unknown, child of unknown & unk. KEITH,
married by James A. ADAMS. remarks : none.

ADAMS, James M.　　　book 01 page 20 line 23
born Bethany, Virginia, resides Bethany, WV. carpenter,
age -- yrs. single, child of Richard & unknown ADAMS,
married 15 Dec 1870 Bethany, WV. to Mary A. WARD,
born unknown, resides Bethany, West Virginia,
age -- yrs. widow, child of unk. & unk. WARD,
married by A.W. CAMPBELL. remarks : none.

ADAMS, John A.　　　book 01 page 18 line 10
born Brooke Co., VA., resides Brooke Co., WV.
age 25 yrs. single, child of John & Maria ADAMS,
married 09 Jan 1868 WV. to Margaret GUNION,
born Jefferson Co., Ohio, resides Brooke Co., WV.
age 21 yrs. single, child of Henry & Eliza. GUNION,
married by J.A. PIERCE. remarks : none.

AGNEW, James M.　　　book 01 page 05 line 20
born Brooke Co., VA., resides Brooke Co., VA. farmer,
age 46 yrs. widow, child of John & Mary AGNEW,
married 25 Mar 1857 VA. to Rebecca C. MARSHALL,
born Brooke Co., Virginia, resides Brooke Co., Virginia,
age 33 yrs. single, child of Thomas & Sarah MARSHALL,
married by Ezekiel QUILLEN. remarks : married Wellsburg.

AIKEN, Anne A.   book 01 page 17 line 08
born Erie, Pennsylvania, resides West Middletown, PA.
age 33 yrs. widow, child of Denison & Mary AIKEN,
married 15 Oct 1867 WV. to George W. RUSSELL,
born Wellsburg, Virginia, resides Brooke Co., West Virginia,
age 33 yrs. widow, child of Jas. & Sarah (ATKINS) RUSSELL,
married by E. BRINDLEY. remarks : Anne (AIKEN) MC CLURE.

ALEXANDER, Samuel H.   book 01 page 14 line 48
born Musk. Co., Ohio, resides Musk. Co., Ohio, cabinets,
age 24 yrs. single, child of Mathew & unk. ALEXANDER,
married 26 Feb 1865 WV. to Ann Rebecca J. PERRY,
born Brooke Co., Virginia, resides Wellsburg, West Virginia,
age 20 yrs. widow, child of David & Rebecca KERNS,
married by J. PIERCE. remarks : married house of KERNS.

ALLEN, Edwin T.   book 01 page 21 line 37
born Brunswick, Missouri, resides Brunswick, MO. farmer,
age 27 yrs. single, child of Thomas & Mariah ALLEN,
married 05 Jun 1872 Wellsburg, WV. to Mary Belle TARR,
born Brooke Co., Virginia, resides Brooke Co., West Virginia,
age 23 yrs. single, child of Campbell & Mary TARR,
married by Robert R. MOORE. remarks : none.

ALLEN, Elizabeth   book 01 page 20 line 01
born Washington Co., PA., resides Brooke Co., WV.
age 24 yrs. single, child of Amos & Elizabeth ALLEN,
married 10 Mar 1870 WV. to George CALENDINE,
born Brooke Co., VA., resides Brooke Co., West Virginia,
age 26 yrs. single, child of Sam'l & Maria CALENDINE,
married by Milton WELLS. remarks : none.

ALLISON, John   book 01 page 16 line 07
born Brooke Co., VA., resides Hancock Co., WV.
age 38 yrs. single, child of John & Mary ALLISON,
married 08 Jan 1867 WV. to Mary CARIENS,
born Brooke Co., Virginia, resides Brooke Co., WV.
age 30 yrs. single, child of James & Mary CARIENS,
married by Thomas M. HUDSON. remarks : none.

AMSPOKER, Elizabeth Ann   book 01 page 03 line 29
born Brooke Co., Virginia, resides Brooke Co., Virginia,
age 21 yrs. single, child of George & Rebecca AMSPOKER,
married 15 Feb 1855 VA. to Zachariah C. WHEELER,
born Brooke Co., Virginia, resides Brooke Co., Virginia,
age 27 yrs. single, child of Thomas H. & Honor WHEELER,
married by John THOMAS. remarks : none.

AMSPOKER, Mary Ann   book 01 page 08 line 07
born Brooke Co., Virginia, resides Brooke Co., Virginia,
age 22 yrs. single, child of George & Rebecca AMSPOKER,
married 23 Dec 1858 VA. to Asa O. DONOVAN,
born Brooke Co., Virginia, resides Brooke Co., Virginia,
age 23 yrs. single, child of Thomas & Catherine DONOVAN,
married by J. DAVIS. remarks : married house of AMSPOKER.

ANDERSON, Rebecca Eliza. book 01 page 11 line 35
 born Brooke Co., Virginia, resides Brooke Co., VA.
 age 17 yrs. single, child of Wm. & unk. ANDERSON,
 married 21 Feb 1863 VA. to John Dusty WELLS,
 born Brooke Co., Virginia, resides Brooke Co., VA.
 age 23 yrs. single, child of Bazil & Nancy WELLS,
 married by C. LOOS. remarks : married S. LINDSAY house.

ANDERSON, T.F. book 01 page 18 line 04
 born Hancock Co., VA., resides Han. Co., WV. brickmaker,
 age 23 yrs. single, child of Thomas & Martha ANDERSON,
 married 21 Oct 1867 WV. to Maggy B. ORR,
 born Brooke Co., VA., resides Brooke Co., West Virginia,
 age 21 yrs. single, child of George G. & Elisabeth ORR,
 married by John B. GRAHAM. remarks : none.

ANTILL, Rebecca V. book 01 page 14 line 42
 born Wellsburg, Virginia, resides Wellsburg, West Virginia,
 age 21 yrs. single, child of unknown & unknown ANTILL,
 married 28 Dec 1864 Wellsburg, WV. to John M. NELSON,
 born Wellsburg, Virginia, resides Wellsburg, West Virginia,
 age 23 yrs. single, child of Andrew & Rachel NELSON,
 married by J.A. PIERCE. remarks : none.

ANTILL, Sarah E. book 01 page 07 line 14
 born Johnson Co.?, Illinois resides Brooke Co., Virginia,
 age 16 yrs. single, child of Thomas & Mary ANTILL,
 married 25 May 1858 Wellsburg, VA. to Wm. L. GREEN,
 born Frederick Co., Virginia, resides Brooke Co., Virginia,
 age 24 yrs. single, child of William & Elizabeth GREEN,
 married by Ezekiel QUILLEN. remarks : none.

ARMSTRONG, Robert book 01 page 22 line 21
 born Ohio Co., Virginia, resides Brooke Co., WV.
 age 36 yrs. unk., child of unk. & unk. ARMSTRONG,
 married 04 Nov 1873 WV. to Hannah JONES,
 born unknown, resides Brooke Co., West Virginia,
 age 26 yrs. unknown, child of unk. & unk. JONES,
 married by George B. HUDSON. remarks : none.

ATKINSON, Flora A. book 01 page 19 line 43
 born Brooke Co., Virginia, resides Brooke Co., WV.
 age 22 yrs. single, child of John & Marg't ATKINSON,
 married 27 Jan 1870 WV. to Robert CALDWELL,
 born Belmont Co., Ohio, resides Harrison Co., Ohio,
 age 26 yrs. single, child of John & Eliza. CALDWELL,
 married by Josias STEVENSON. remarks : none.

ATKINSON, Margaret book 01 page 08 line 08
 born Brooke Co., Virginia, resides Brooke Co., Virginia,
 age 23 yrs. single, child of John & Marg't ATKINSON,
 married 26 Dec 1858 VA. to James F. BLAYNEY,
 born Ohio Co., Virginia, resides Ohio Co., Virginia,
 age 27 yrs. single, child of Charles & Nancy BLAYNEY,
 married by Robert BURGESS. remarks : none.

ATKINSON, Samuel W. book 01 page 19 line 16
born Brooke Co., VA., resides Brooke Co., WV. farmer,
age 29 yrs. single, child of John & Mary ATKINSON,
married 04 Nov 1868 WV. to Clarinda L. SNEDIKER,
born Brooke Co., Virginia, resides Brooke Co., WV.
age 23 yrs. single, child of Wm. & Mary A. SNEDIKER,
married by J.W. KESLER. remarks : none.

ATWELL, Mervin Richard book 01 page 12 line 54
born Ireland, resides Brooke Co., West Virginia, farmer,
age 30 yrs. widow, child of John & Elizabeth ATWELL,
married 15 Oct 1863 WV. to Amelia Francis FLEMING,
born Brooke Co., Virginia, resides Brooke Co., West Virginia,
age 20 yrs. single, child of Coleman & Elizabeth FLEMING,
married by T. HUDSON. remarks : married FLEMING house.

BACHELL, Jennie book 01 page 21 line 05
born Brooke Co., Virginia, resides Brooke Co., WV.
age 21 yrs. single, child of John & Jane BACHELL,
married 21 Sep 1871 WV. to Marshall S. GREEN,
born Brooke Co., Virginia, resides Brooke Co., WV.
age 26 yrs. single, child of Wm. E. & Eliza. GREEN,
married by J.C. CASTLE. remarks : none.

BACHELL, Mary Eliza. book 01 page 21 line 19
born Brooke Co., Virginia, resides Brooke Co., WV.
age 21 yrs. single, child of John & Jane BACHELL,
married 31 Dec 1871 WV. to A.W. ROBINSON,
born Brooke Co., VA., resides Brooke Co., West Virginia,
age 22 yrs. single, child of Joseph & Eliza. ROBINSON,
married by A. Ealion WARD. remarks : none.

BAIL, Thomas W. book 01 page 15 line 73
born Pennsylvania, resides Cincinnati, Ohio, solicitor,
age 34 yrs. single, child of James & Elizabeth BAIL,
married 27 Mar 1866 WV. to Alice TAYLOR,
born Pennsylvania, resides Wellsburg, West Virginia,
age 21 yrs. single, child of unknown & unknown TAYLOR,
married by J. BROWN. remarks : married THOMPSON house.

BAILEY, William T. book 01 page 20 line 20
born Belmont Co., Ohio, resides Brooke Co., WV. farmer,
age 46 yrs. widow, child of John & Margaret BAILEY,
married 08 Nov 1870 WV. to Harriet KIMBERLAND,
born Jefferson Co., Ohio, resides Brooke Co., West Virginia,
age 40 yrs. widow, child of Benjamin & Mary WATKINS,
married by R.R. MOORE. remarks : married Wellsburg.

BAILEY, William T. book 01 page 03 line 21
born Belmont Co., Ohio, resides Brooke Co., VA. laborer,
age 29 yrs. widow, child of John & Margaret BAILEY,
married 26 Oct 1854 Wellsburg, VA. to Evaline BLAIR,
born Brooke Co., Virginia, resides Brooke Co., Virginia.
age 20 yrs. single, child of Walter & Rachael BLAIR,
married by Charles A. HOLMES. remarks : none.

BAIR, Sarah E. book 01 page 17 line 03
born Allegheny Co., PA., resides Brooke Co., WV.
age 62 yrs. widow, child of James & Sarah BAIR,
married 04 Sep 1867 WV. to Robert MC INTIRE,
born Brooke Co., Virginia, resides Jefferson Co., Ohio,
age 42 yrs. widow, child of Robert & Ann MC INTIRE,
married by R.T. PRICE. remarks: Sarah (BAIR) DUNN.

BAKER, Mary book 01 page 20 line 27
born Virginia, resides Wellsburg, West Virginia,
age 21 yrs. single, child of unknown & unknown BAKER,
married 02 Jan 1871 Wellsburg, WV. to James M. WHITE,
born Brooke Co., Virginia, resides Wellsburg, West Virginia,
age 21 yrs. single, child of Isaac & Grace WHITE,
married by J. COUPLAND. remarks: both listed as colored.

BAKEWELL, Emma C. book 01 page 16 line 17
born Wellsburg, Virginia, resides West Virginia,
age 23 yrs. single, child of unk. & unk. BAKEWELL,
married 07 Mar 1867 WV. to Robert J. BARCLAY,
born Albemarle Co., Virginia, resides Virginia,
age 34 yrs. widow, child of James T. & unk. BARCLAY,
married by Archibald W. CAMPBELL. remarks: none.

BALLENTINE, James book 01 page 07 line 12
born Ireland, resides Washington Co., PA. farmer,
age 23 yrs. single, child of Joseph & Rosa BALLENTINE,
married 24 Feb 1858 VA. to Jane CRUTH,
born Ireland, resides Washington Co., Pennsylvania,
age 23 yrs. single, child of unknown & unknown CRUTH,
married by D. HERVEY. remarks: mother Rosa (MC BRIDE).

BALLETT, Edward book 01 page 15 line 61
born Ireland, resides Ireland, laborer,
age 20 yrs. single, child of P. & C. BALLETT,
married 11 Sep 1865 WV. to Bridget GILBERT,
born Ireland, resides Ireland,
age 22 yrs. single, child of Charles & H. GILBERT,
married by S. HUBER. remarks: married Wellsburg.

BANE, Amanda book 01 page 03 line 25
born Brooke Co., VA., resides Brooke Co., VA.
age 20 yrs. single, child of John & Mary BANE,
married 19 Apr 1854 VA. to Adam WILSON,
born Brooke Co., Virginia, resides Brooke Co., VA.
age 26 yrs. single, child of Sam'l & Nancy WILSON,
married by Ezekiel QUILLEN. remarks: none.

BANE, Margaret book 01 page 02 line 05
born Brooke Co., Virginia, resides Wellsburg, VA.
age 21 yrs. single, child of Robert & Maria BANE,
married 28 Mar 1854 VA. to Andrew J. WILSON,
born Ohio Co., Virginia, resides Wellsburg, Virginia,
age 23 yrs. single, child of Joseph & Rebecca WILSON,
married by E. QUILLEN. remarks: married BANE house.

BANE, Sarah Jane   book 01 page 22 line 11
born Brooke Co., Virginia, resides Brooke Co., WV.
age 30 yrs. single, child of Robert & Maria BANE,
married 19 Mar 1873   WV. to Joseph B. WILSON,
born Ohio Co., Virginia, resides Ohio Co., WV.
age 39 yrs. single, child of Jos. & Rebecca WILSON,
married by J.A. BROWN. remarks : none.

BANNON, Bridget   book 01 page 19 line 24
born Ireland, resides Wellsburg, West Virginia,
age 28 yrs. single, child of Thomas & Anne BANNON,
married 08 Jan 1869 Wellsburg, WV. to Patrick DOWNEY,
born Ireland, resides Brooke Co., West Virginia,
age 35 yrs. single, child of Thomas & unk. DOWNEY,
married by Stephen HUBER. remarks : none.

BANNON, Catherine   book 01 page 08 line 05
born Co. West Mayo, Ireland, resides Wellsburg, Virginia,
age 20 yrs. single, child of Thomas & Anne BANNON,
married 06 Jan 1859 Wellsburg, VA. to Charles MC GEE,
born County Down, Ireland, resides Wellsburg, Virginia,
age 24 yrs. single, child of Bernard & Nancy MC GEE,
married by S. HUBER. remarks : mother Anne (O'BRIEN)

BARBER, Mary   book 01 page 04 line 61
born Westmoreland Co., PA., resides Wellsburg, Virginia,
age 32 yrs. widow, child of Aaron & Catherine THORP,
married 12 Sep 1856 Wellsburg, VA. to John COGAN,
born Cumberland Co., PA., resides Wellsburg, Virginia,
age 30 yrs. single, child of John & Martha ? COGAN,
married by W. GAMBLE. remarks : Mrs. Mary BARBER.

BARCLAY, John J.   book 01 page 12 line 48
born Virginia, resides Cyprus, Turkey, U.S. Counsel,
age 26 yrs. single, child of James T. & Jillian BARCLAY,
married 07 Apr 1863   VA. to Decima H. CAMPBELL,
born Virginia, resides Brooke Co., Virginia,
age 22 yrs. single, child of Alex. & Selina H. CAMPBELL,
married by W.K. PENDLETON. remarks : married Bethany.

BARCLAY, Robert J.   book 01 page 16 line 17
born Albemarle Co., Virginia, resides Virginia, physician,
age 34 yrs. widow, child of James T. & unk. BARCLAY,
married 07 Mar 1867   WV. to Emma C. BAKEWELL,
born Wellsburg, Virginia, resides West Virginia,
age 23 yrs. single, child of unk. & unk. BAKEWELL,
married by Archibald W. CAMPBELL. remarks : none.

BARNES, Lydia M.   book 01 page 08 line 12
born Brooke Co., Virginia, resides Brooke Co., Virginia,
age 27 yrs. single, child of Ephraim & Elizabeth BARNES,
married 10 Feb 1859   VA. to William H. MITCHELL,
born Belmont Co., Ohio, resides Madison Co., Illinois,
age 41 yrs. widow, child of James & Elizabeth MITCHELL,
married by I. BEACOM. remarks : married BARNES house.

BARNES, Mary E. book 01 page 17 line 18
born Brooke Co., Virginia, resides Brooke Co., WV.
age 20 yrs. single, child of John & Eliza. BARNES,
married 04 Nov 1866 WV. to James LONG,
born Wash. Co., PA., resides Christian Co., Illinois,
age 25 yrs. single, child of Lorenze & Margaret LONG,
married by J.A. PIERCE. remarks: none.

BARNES, Shepley book 01 page 18 line 08
born Wash. Co., PA., resides Wellsburg, WV. laborer,
age 23 yrs. single, child of Thomas & Mary BARNES,
married 28 Dec 1867 WV. to Mary Elizabeth NICHOLLS,
born Brooke Co., Virginia, resides Wellsburg, West Virginia,
age 16 yrs. single, child of Robert & Mary Ann NICHOLLS,
married by Edward A. BRINDLEY. remarks: none.

BARNES, Walter D. book 01 page 03 line 38
born Ohio, resides Ohio, farmer,
age 27 yrs. single, child of John & Rachel BARNES,
married -- -- 1855 VA. to Sarah BLAYNEY,
born Pittsburgh, PA., resides Brooke Co., Virginia,
age 21 yrs. single, child of Richard & Eliza. BLAYNEY,
married by A.J. ENDSLEY. remarks: none.

BARTH, Hugh book 01 page 09 line 19
born Germany, resides Wellsburg, Virginia, carpenter,
age 23 yrs. single, child of Fidel & Martha BARTH,
married 26 Nov 1860 VA. to Frances LETZKUS,
born Wellsburg, Virginia, resides Brooke Co., Virginia,
age 18 yrs. single, child of Geo. & Michelia LETZKUS,
married by S. HUBER. remarks: mother Martha (PFIFFER).

BARTHOLOMEW, George K. book 01 page 09 line 21
born Hartford, Vermont, resides Cincinnati, Ohio, teacher,
age 25 yrs. single, child of Noah & Mary BARTHOLOMEW,
married 09 Aug 1860 VA. to Elvyn Jane BRIGGS,
born Saugus, Essex Co., MA., resides Brooke Co., VA.
age 28 yrs. single, child of James & Nancy BRIGGS,
married by J.M. SMITH. remarks: none.

BARTHOLOMEW, Samuel D. book 01 page 18 line 16
born Jefferson Co., Ohio, resides Brooke Co., WV. railroad,
age 28 yrs. single, child of Samuel & Mary BARTHOLOMEW,
married 19 Feb 1868 WV. to Ella SHRIMPLIN,
born Brooke Co., Virginia, resides Brooke Co., West Virginia,
age 25 yrs. single, child of John & Elizabeth SHRIMPLIN,
married by J.A. PIERCE. remarks: none.

BAXTER, Ellen V. book 01 page 18 line 18
born Brooke Co., Virginia, resides Brooke Co., West Virginia,
age 17 yrs. single, child of William E. & Ellen M. BAXTER,
married 20 Feb 1868 WV. to John L. BROWN,
born Brooke Co., Virginia, resides Jefferson Co., Ohio,
age 33 yrs. single, child of James W. & Hanna BROWN,
married by Thomas M. HUDSON. remarks: none.

BAXTER, George A. book 01 page 16 line 23
born Brooke Co., VA., resides Brooke Co., WV. merchant,
age 25 yrs. single, child of William & Ellen BAXTER,
married 12 Jun 1867 WV. to Alice W. JACOB,
born Brooke Co., Virginia, resides Brooke Co., WV.
age 20 yrs. single, child of Benjamin & Jane JACOB,
married by J.L. HARRISON. remarks : none.

BAXTER, Mary Ann book 01 page 12 line 44
born Brooke Co., Virginia, resides Brooke Co., Virginia,
age 27 yrs. single, child of William & Ellen BAXTER,
married 01 Jan 1862 VA. to James WILLIAMSON,
born Washington Co., PA., resides Brooke Co., Virginia,
age 26 yrs. single, child of James & Sarah WILLIAMSON,
married by I. MORSE. remarks : married BAXTER house.

BAXTER, Sarah book 01 page 02 line 17
born Washington Co., PA., resides Wellsburg, VA.
age 19 yrs. single, child of Daniel & Mary BAXTER,
married 26 Oct 1854 VA. to James MC DUGAN,
born Hampshire Co., Virginia, resides Wellsburg, Virginia,
age 32 yrs. widow, child of Wm. & Mary MC DUGAN,
married by Francis GUTHRIE. remarks : none.

BEALL, Ellen book 01 page 20 line 09
born Brooke Co., VA., resides Brooke Co., WV.
age 17 yrs. single, child of Aaron & Jane BEALL,
married 01 Aug 1870 WV. to Augustus DAVIS,
born Uniontown, PA., resides Wellsburg, West Virginia,
age 26 yrs. single, child of Jacob & Sarah Ann DAVIS,
married by J. CASTLE. remarks : both listed as colored.

BEALL, Leanna book 01 page 21 line 38
born Culpeper Co., Virginia, resides Brooke Co., WV.
age 24 yrs. widow, child of unknown & unknown BEALL,
married 19 Jun 1872 Wellsburg, WV. to Green WATSON,
born Monroe Co., Virginia, resides Brooke Co., WV.
age 29 yrs. widow, child of Samuel & Nancy WATSON,
married by J. COUPLAND. remarks : listed as colored.

BEALL, Lillie book 01 page 21 line 28
born Jefferson Co., Ohio, resides Brooke Co., WV.
age 18 yrs. single, child of Conrad & unk. BEALL,
married 02 Apr 1872 WV. to John D. PARISH,
born Steubenville, Ohio, resides Brooke Co., WV.
age 23 yrs. single, child of Richard & Nancy PARISH,
married by J.M. BERRY. remarks : married Wellsburg.

BEATER, Agnes (...) book 01 page 13 line 30
born Germany, resides Wellsburg, West Virginia,
age 38 yrs. widow, child of unknown & unk. (...),
married 31 Aug 1864 WV. to Casper BEATER,
born Germany, resides Wellsburg, West Virginia,
age 38 yrs. single, child of Mingus & Ann BEATER,
married by S. HUBER. remarks : married Wellsburg.

BEATER, Casper book 01 page 13 line 30
born Germany, resides Wellsburg, WV. soldier,
age 38 yrs. single, child of Mingus & Ann BEATER,
married 31 Aug 1864 WV. to Agnes (...) BEATER,
born Germany, resides Wellsburg, West Virginia,
age 38 yrs. widow, child of unknown & unk. (...),
married by S. HUBER. remarks : married Wellsburg.

BEATTY, Sarah Amelia book 01 page 05 line 04
born Brooke Co., Virginia, resides Brooke Co., Virginia,
age 18 yrs. single, child of Thos. H. & Rachel BEATTY,
married 02 Oct 1856 VA. to David O. COLEMAN,
born Jefferson Co., Ohio, resides Wayne Twp.,
age 24 yrs. single, child of Richard & Mary COLEMAN,
married by J.D. CARVER. remarks : none.

BECKWITH, Oscar J. book 01 page 19 line 31
born Jackson Co., VA., resides Jackson Co., WV. farmer,
age 26 yrs. single, child of Louis & Esther BECKWITH,
married 16 Mar 1869 WV. to Josephine WELLS,
born Brooke Co., Virginia, resides Brooke Co., WV.
age 19 yrs. single, child of Milton & Mary WELLS,
married by C.L. LOOS. remarks : married Wellsburg.

BEDILLION, Joseph book 01 page 07 line 09
born Wash. Co., VA., resides Marshall Co., VA. miller,
age 29 yrs. widow, child of Abraham & Marg't BEDILLION,
married 23 Feb 1858 VA. to Abigail CONANT,
born Worcester Co., MA., resides Brooke Co., Virginia,
age 30 yrs. single, child of Lot & Mary CONANT,
married by E. QUILLEN. remarks : married CONANT house.

BEERBOWER, Elizabeth book 01 page 21 line 20
born Jefferson Co., Ohio, resides Brooke Co., WV.
age 21 yrs. single, child of Reed & Anna BEERBOWER,
married 09 Jan 1872 Wellsburg, WV. to Westley NOBLE,
born Jefferson Co., Ohio, resides Jefferson Co., Ohio,
age 24 yrs. single, child of William & Narcissa NOBLE,
married by Robert R. MOORE. remarks : none.

BEHIN, Margaret book 01 page 03 line 28
born Tackles, Co. Carlow, Ireland, resides Brooke Co., VA.
age 18 yrs. single, child of unknown & unknown BEHIN,
married 19 Feb 1855 VA. to Felix MC GEE,
born Clonablan, Co. Down, Ireland, resides Brooke Co., VA.
age 28 yrs. single, child of unknown & unknown MC GEE,
married by John F. BRAZILL. remarks : none.

BEITER, Mary Ann book 01 page 14 line 45
born Germany, resides Wellsburg, West Virginia,
age 19 yrs. single, child of Francis & unknown BEITER,
married 23 Jan 1865 Wellsburg, WV. to Ambrose LETZKUS,
born Germany, resides Wellsburg, West Virginia,
age 26 yrs. single, child of Richard & Millie LETZKUS,
married by Stephen HUBER. remarks : none.

BELL, Sarah Adaline   book 01 page 08 line 04
born Brooke Co., Virginia, resides Brooke Co., VA.
age 16 yrs. single, child of Aaron & Jane BELL,
married 19 Dec 1858 VA. to Hezekiah LEWIS,
born Jefferson Co., Ohio, resides Brooke Co., Virginia,
age 24 yrs. single, child of Douglass & Mary LEWIS,
married by J. BEACOM. remarks : married BELL house.

BENCE, Casper   book 01 page 10 line 05A
born Germany, resides Bethany, Virginia, shoemaker,
age 23 yrs. single, child of Richus & Justina BENCE,
married 14 Oct 1860 Bethany, VA. to Mary Jane MC KIM,
born Ireland, resides Bethany, Virginia,
age 19 yrs. single, child of Felix & Mary (O'HEIR) MC KIM,
married by S. HUBER. remarks : mother Justina (LETZKUS).

BENCE, Cidonia   book 01 page 09 line 12
born Bobingen?, Germany, resides Wellsburg, Virginia,
age 20 yrs. single, child of Richus & Justina BENCE,
married 09 Apr 1860 Wellsburg, VA. to Jacob FOSTER,
born Waldenberg, Germany, resides Wellsburg, Virginia,
age 24 yrs. single, child of Jacob & Elisabeth FOSTER,
married by Stephen HUBER. remarks. none.

BENTZ, Barbara   book 01 page 21 line 32
born Germany, resides Brooke Co., West Virginia,
age 24 yrs. single, child of unknown & unk. BENTZ,
married 30 Apr 1872 Wellsburg, WV. to Charles KLINE,
born Germany, resides Wheeling, West Virginia,
age 23 yrs. single, child of Christian & Francis KLINE,
married by Stephen HUBER. remarks : none.

BENTZ, Josephine   book 01 page 12 line 47
born Germany, resides Brooke Co., West Virginia,
age 22 yrs. single, child of Richus & Justina BENTZ,
married 11 Nov 1862 VA. to Martin EASTERDAY,
born Germany, resides Wellsburg, West Virginia,
age 22 yrs. single, child of Christian & Agnes EASTERDAY,
married by Stephen HUBER. remarks : married Wellsburg.

BERTRAM, Henry   book 01 page 04 line 60
born Brunswick, Saxony, GER. resides Brooke Co., VA. farmer,
age 27 yrs. single, child of Christian & Isabell BERTRAM,
married 08 Sep 1856 Wellsburg, VA. to Wellhemine STIETZE,
born Curscean, Germany, resides Brooke Co., Virginia,
age 23 yrs. single, child of John & Catherine STIETZE,
married by Ezekiel QUILLEN. remarks : none.

BICKERSTAFF, Isaac C.   book 01 page 21 line 09
born Beaver Co., PA., resides Brooke Co., WV. mechanic,
age 24 yrs. single, child of unk. & unk. BICKERSTAFF,
married 26 Oct 1871 Wellsburg, WV. to Julia C. COX,
born Brooke Co., Virginia, resides Brooke Co., WV.
age 24 yrs. widow, child of Reason & Elizabeth REEVES,
married by J. CASTLE. remarks : Julia (REEVES) COX.

BIER, Henry A.   book 01 page 14 line 36
born Wheeling, VA., resides Wheeling, WV. soldier,
age 21 yrs. single, child of Jacob & Mary BIER,
married 03 Nov 1864 WV. to Clarinda SUTER,
born Bethany, Virginia, resides Bethany, WV.
age 19 yrs. single, child of unk. & unk. SUTER,
married by Wm. K. PENDLETON. remarks: none.

BLAIR, Evaline   book 01 page 03 line 21
born Brooke Co., VA. resides Brooke Co., Virginia,
age 20 yrs. single, child of Walter & Rachael BLAIR,
married 26 Oct 1854 VA. to William T. BAILEY,
born Belmont Co., Ohio, resides Brooke Co. Virginia,
age 29 yrs. widow, child of John & Margaret BAILEY,
married by C. HOLMES. remarks: married Wellsburg.

BLANKENSOP, George   book 01 page 20 line 31
born Brooke Co., VA., resides Brooke Co., WV. moulder,
age 30 yrs. divorced, child of Jos. & Ellen BLANKENSOP,
married 01 Mar 1871 Wellsburg, WV. to Kate HESSEY,
born Steubenville, Ohio, resides Brooke Co., West Virginia,
age 22 yrs. single, child of unknown & unk. HESSEY,
married by J.C. CASTLE. remarks: Kate KEESEY?

BLANKENSOP, George   book 01 page 09 line 24
born Wellsburg, Virginia, resides unknown,
age 21 yrs. single, child of unk. & unk. BLANKENSOP,
married 16 Jun 1860 VA. to Angeline MERRYMAN,
born Tuscarawas Co., Ohio, resides unknown,
age 20 yrs. single, child of unk. & unk. MERRYMAN,
married by UNKNOWN. remarks: married Wellsburg.

BLANKENSOP, James   book 01 page 21 line 22
born Brooke Co., VA., resides Brooke Co., WV. foundry,
age 24 yrs. single, child of Peter & Susan BLANKENSOP,
married 18 Jan 1872 WV. to Anna CAMPBELL,
born Brooke Co., Virginia, resides Brooke Co., West Virginia,
age 21 yrs. single, child of Archibald & Lousia CAMPBELL,
married by E.H. JONES. remarks: married Hollidays Cove.

BLANKENSOP, John   book 01 page 17 line 25
born Brooke Co., VA., resides Wellsburg, VA. painter,
age 34 yrs. single, child of Peter & Susan BLANKENSOP,
married 24 Oct 1867 WV. to Mary R. GOUDY,
born Brooke Co., Virginia, resides Brooke Co., WV.
age 23 yrs. single, child of Robert & Nancy GOUDY,
married by Alexander E. ANDERSON. remarks: none.

BLANKENSOP, Sallie   book 01 page 22 line 07
born Brooke Co., Virginia, resides Wellsburg, West Virginia,
age 23 yrs. single, child of Peter & Susan BLANKENSOP,
married 10 Feb 1873 Wellsburg, WV. to Frank MILLER,
born Beaver Co., Pennsylvania, resides Allegheny Co., PA.
age 23 yrs. single, child of George & Rebecca MILLER,
married by Joshua COUPLAND. remarks: none.

BLAYNEY, James F. book 01 page 08 line 08
born Ohio Co., Virginia, resides Ohio Co., VA. farmer,
age 27 yrs. single, child of Charles & Nancy BLAYNEY,
married 26 Dec 1858 VA. to Margaret ATKINSON,
born Brooke Co., Virginia, resides Brooke Co., Virginia,
age 23 yrs. single, child of John & Margaret ATKINSON,
married by Robert BURGESS. remarks : none.

BLAYNEY, Sarah book 01 page 03 line 38
born Pittsburgh, Pennsylvania, resides Brooke Co., VA.
age 21 yrs. single, child of Richard & Eliza. BLAYNEY,
married - - - - 1855 VA. to Walter D. BARNES,
born Ohio, resides Ohio,
age 27 yrs. single, child of John & Rachel BARNES,
married by A.J. ENDSLEY. remarks : none.

BLOTTAN, John A. book 01 page 20 line 34
born Maryland, resides Baltimore, Maryland, teacher,
age 23 yrs. single, child of Anton & Margaret BLOTTAN,
married 11 Apr 1871 WV. to Julia A. PICKLEMAN,
born Wellsburg, VA., resides Brooke Co., West Virginia,
age 21 yrs. single, child of John & Mary A. PICKLEMAN,
married by S. HUBER. remarks : married Wellsburg.

BOLES, S.P. book 01 page 21 line 02
born Wash. Co., PA., resides Wash. Co., PA. farmer,
age 23 yrs. single, child of Jacob & Rachael BOLES,
married 17 Aug 1871 WV. to Amelia WRIGHT,
born Brooke Co., Virginia, resides Brooke Co., WV.
age 21 yrs. single, child of John & Sofiah WRIGHT,
married by J.B. LUCAS. remarks : none.

BONAR, Mary Jane book 01 page 14 line 39
born Brooke Co., Virginia, resides Brooke Co., WV.
age 21 yrs. single, child of unknown & unk. BONAR,
married 24 Nov 1864 WV. to Edward W. CLENDENEN,
born Brooke Co., VA., resides Brooke Co., West Virginia,
age 23 yrs. widow, child of Wm. & Rachel CLENDENEN,
married by E.C. WAYMAN. remarks : none.

BONAR, Sallie/Sarah book 01 page 15 line 58
born Brooke Co., Virginia, resides Brooke Co., WV.
age 21 yrs. single, child of George & Ellen BONAR,
married 15 Sep 1865 WV. to James Pursel SMITH,
born Brooke Co., Virginia, resides Brooke Co., WV.
age 27 yrs. single, child of Fergus & Nancy SMITH,
married by J. BROWN. remarks : married BONAR house.

BORING, George W. book 01 page 07 line 13
born Ohio Co., Virginia, resides Ohio Co., VA. bricklayer,
age 34 yrs. widow, child of Ephraim & Margaret BORING,
married 01 May 1858 Wellsburg, VA. to Mary STARKEY,
born Ohio Co., Virginia, resides Ohio Co., Virginia,
age 16 yrs. single, child of William & Isabelle STARKEY,
married by Ezekiel QUILLEN. remarks : none.

BOSLEY, James book 01 page 08 line 10
born Brooke Co., VA., resides Virginia, cooper-carpenter,
age 38 yrs. single, child of William & Jane BOSLEY,
married 14 Feb 1859 VA. to Ruth E. CAIRNES,
born Brooke Co., Virginia, resides Brooke Co., VA.
age 37 yrs. single, child of James & Nancy CAIRNES,
married by M. BETISE. remarks: Fulton Co., Ohio.

BOSLEY, Samuel book 01 page 03 line 32
born Brooke Co., VA., resides Brooke Co., VA. carpenter,
age 24 yrs. single, child of William & Susannah BOSLEY,
married 26 Apr 1855 VA. to Mary WILLIAMSON,
born Washington Co., PA., resides Brooke Co., Virginia,
age 22 yrs. single, child of James & Sarah WILLIAMSON,
married by Ezekiel QUILLEN. remarks: none.

BOTHWELL, John H. book 01 page 08 line 03
born Baltimore Co., MD., resides Ohio Co., VA. tailor,
age 38 yrs. widow, child of Charles & Phoebe BOTHWELL,
married 14 Oct 1858 VA. to Elvira Virginia SNEDIKER,
born Brooke Co., Virginia, resides Brooke Co., Virginia,
age 20 yrs. single, child of William & Mary A. SNEDIKER,
married by Thomas M. HUDSON. remarks: none.

BOWERS, Adam book 01 page 05 line 08
born Wash. Co., MD., resides Brooke Co., VA. miller,
age 21 yrs. single, child of Jacob & Mary BOWERS,
married 30 Oct 1856 VA. to Nancy ORAM,
born Brooke Co., Virginia, resides Brooke Co., VA.
age 20 yrs. single, child of George & Cath. ORAM,
married by Ezekiel QUILLEN. remarks: none.

BOWLES, John W. book 01 page 19 line 19
born Washington Co., PA., resides Wash. Co., PA. farmer,
age 21 yrs. single, child of James & Isabella BOWLES,
married 24 Dec 1868 WV. to Elizabeth MURCHLAND,
born Brooke Co., Virginia, resides Brooke Co., West Virginia,
age 19 yrs. single, child of Andrew & Eliza. MURCHLAND,
married by David HERVEY. remarks: none.

BOWMAN, Cecelia M.L.S. book 01 page 11 line 14
born Brooke Co., Virginia, resides Brooke Co., Virginia,
age 26 yrs. single, child of Abraham & Henrietta BOWMAN,
married 08 Nov 1861 VA. to David B. MILLER,
born Ohio Co., Virginia, resides Brooke Co., Virginia,
age 21 yrs. single, child of Nicholas & Rebecca MILLER,
married by Thomas M. HUDSON. remarks: none.

BOWMAN, Dora book 01 page 22 line 35
born Brooke Co., Virginia, resides Brooke Co., WV.
age 21 yrs. unknown, child of unk. & unk. BOWMAN,
married 05 Mar 1874 WV. to Gilbert E. ROBINSON,
born Brooke Co., Virginia, resides Brooke Co., WV.
age 20 yrs. unknown, child of unk. & unk. ROBINSON,
married by J. COUPLAND. remarks: married Wellsburg.

BOWMAN, Jane book 01 page 22 line 06
born Brooke Co., Virginia, resides Brooke Co., WV.
age 22 yrs. single, child of John & Sarah BOWMAN,
married 14 Nov 1872 WV. to Darwin E.R. BUCY,
born Jefferson Co., Ohio, resides Brooke Co., WV.
age 24 yrs. single, child of Joshua & Margarett BUCY,
married by Robert MOORE. remarks : married Wellsburg.

BOWMAN, John book 01 page 03 line 22
born Pennsylvania, resides Brooke Co., Virginia, miller,
age 64 yrs. widow, child of John & Elizabeth BOWMAN,
married 28 Dec 1854 VA. to Mary CARSON,
born Maryland, resides Brooke Co., Virginia,
age 31 yrs. single, child of unk. & Elizabeth CARSON,
married by Francis GUTHRIE. remarks : none.

BOWMAN, John book 01 page 11 line 12
born Brooke Co., VA., resides Brooke Co., VA. farmer,
age 25 yrs. single, child of John & Sarah A. BOWMAN,
married 11 Aug 1861 VA. to Amanda E. FRANK,
born Brooke Co., Virginia, resides Brooke Co., Virginia,
age 21 yrs. single, child of Hogan & Fredirick FRANK,
married by Charles Louis LOOS. remarks : none.

BOWMAN, Sarah book 01 page 19 line 40
born Brooke Co., VA., resides Wellsburg, West Virginia,
age 40 yrs. single, child of unknown & unk. BOWMAN,
married 27 Sep 1869 Wellsburg, WV. to James WHITE,
born Petersburgh, VA., resides Brooke Co., West Virginia,
age 45 yrs. widow, child of John & Tempe WHITE,
married by A. CHAPMAN. remarks : both listed as colored.

BOWMAN, Sarah book 01 page 19 line 48
born Brooke Co., Virginia, resides Brooke Co., WV.
age 22 yrs. single, child of John & Sarah A. BOWMAN,
married 24 Feb 1870 WV. to Thomas Hood GREEN,
born Jefferson Co., Ohio, resides Jefferson Co., Ohio,
age 21 yrs. single, child of Henry & Nancy GREEN,
married by Robert R. MOORE. remarks : none.

BOWMAN, Sarah E. book 01 page 03 line 36
born Brooke Co., Virginia, resides Brooke Co., Virginia,
age 22 yrs. single, child of Abraham & Henrietta BOWMAN,
married 04 Oct 1855 VA. to Joseph THOMPSON,
born Ohio Co., Virginia, resides Brooke Co., Virginia,
age 22 yrs. single, child of George S. & Mary THOMPSON,
married by J.R. MEANS. remarks : none.

BOYD, Robert book 01 page 16 line 20
born Wash. Co., PA., resides Brooke Co., WV. farmer,
age 46 yrs. widow, child of James & Mary BOYD,
married 10 Apr 1867 WV. to E. A. WILLIAMSON,
born Brooke Co., VA., resides Brooke Co., West Virginia,
age 30 yrs. single, child of Wm. & Sarah WILLIAMSON,
married by James C. CAMPBELL. remarks : none.

BRACKEN, Caleb H. book 01 page 19 line 35
born Fayette Co., PA. resides Lagrange, Ohio, merchant,
age 39 yrs. widow, child of Solomon & Sarah BRACKEN,
married 04 May 1869 Wellsburg, WV. to Maggie EVERETT,
born Brooke Co., Virginia, resides Brooke Co., West Virginia,
age 20 yrs. single, child of Thomas & Martha EVERETT,
married by T.A. CRENSHAW. remarks : none.

BRADLEY, Thomas book 01 page 05 line 19
born England, resides Brooke Co., Virginia, miner,
age 29 yrs. single, child of John & Frances BRADLEY,
married 07 Mar 1857 VA. to Sarah CHAMBERLAIN,
born Beaver Co., Pennsylvania, resides Brooke Co., VA.
age 22 yrs. single, child of Daniel & Jane CHAMBERLAIN,
married by Ezekiel QUILLEN. remarks : married Wellsburg.

BRADY, Anne book 01 page 11 line 24
born New Jersey, resides Brooke Co., Virginia,
age 25 yrs. single, child of Bernard & Bridget BRADY,
married 16 Oct 1862 VA. to Robert N. SMITH,
born Washington Co., PA., resides Jefferson Co., Ohio,
age 35 yrs. single, child of William & Rebecca SMITH,
married by Stephen HUBER. remarks : none.

BRADY, Hannah J. book 01 page 22 line 03
born Brooke Co., Virginia, resides Brooke Co., WV.
age 21 yrs. single, child of Bernard & Bridget BRADY,
married 28 Nov 1872 Wellsburg, WV. to John WILSON,
born Brooke Co., Virginia, resides Brooke Co., WV.
age 22 yrs. single, child of Jonathan & Eliza. WILSON,
married by Stephen HUBER. remarks : none.

BRADY, John D. book 01 page 21 line 10
born Brooke Co., VA., resides Brooke Co., WV. farmer,
age 25 yrs. single, child of William & Hannah BRADY,
married 09 Nov 1871 WV. to Sallie MC CLEARY,
born Brooke Co., Virginia, resides Brooke Co., WV.
age 23 yrs. single, child of Ewing & unk. MC CLEARY,
married by Robert R. MOORE. remarks : none.

BRANDON, Marg't Cecelia book 01 page 12 line 56
born Brooke Co., Virginia, resides Wellsburg, WV.
age 21 yrs. single, child of William & Jane BRANDON,
married 16 Dec 1863 WV. to George OWEN,
born Jefferson Co., Ohio, resides Jefferson Co., Ohio,
age 23 yrs. single, child of Joshua & Rachel OWEN,
married by G. CHESTER. remarks : married BRANDON house.

BRANNON, Rebecca book 01 page 09 line 20
born Washington Co., PA., resides Wellsburg, Virginia,
age 24 yrs. single, child of William & Jane BRANNON,
married 26 Sep 1860 Wellsburg, VA. to Wilson GUNION,
born Jefferson Co., Ohio, resides Wellsburg, Virginia,
age 26 yrs. single, child of Henry & Elizabeth GUNION,
married by George W. CHESTER. remarks : none.

BRASHEARS, Calvin B. book 01 page 20 line 18
born Paris, Pennsylvania, resides Wellsburg, WV. dentist,
age 26 yrs. single, child of Bazle & Jane BRASHEARS,
married 29 Sep 1870 WV. to Catharine M. ROBINETT,
born Wellsburg, VA., resides Wellsburg, West Virginia,
age 21 yrs. single, child of Allen & Marg't ROBINETT,
married by William K. PENDLETON. remarks : none.

BRASHEARS, Mary book 01 page 13 line 15
born Brooke Co., VA., resides Brooke Co., West Virginia,
age 21 yrs. single, child of George & Eliza. BRASHEARS,
married 02 Jan 1864 Wellsburg, WV. to Sam'l G. NANGLE,
born Wellsburg, Virginia, resides Wellsburg, West Virginia,
age 23 yrs. single, child of Thomas & Susan NANGLE,
married by William ROBINSON. remarks : none.

BRIAN, Elizabeth book 01 page 14 line 40
born Wellsburg, Virginia, resides Wellsburg, WV.
age 19 yrs. single, child of Farnum & unk. BRIAN,
married 07 Dec 1864 WV. to John Wesley FRAZIER,
born Wellsburg, Virginia, resides Wellsburg, WV.
age 19 yrs. single, child of John & unk. FRAZIER,
married by George W. CHESTER. remarks : none.

BRIGGS, Alice U. book 01 page 21 line 46
born New Hampshire, resides Brooke Co., WV.
age 26 yrs. single, child of James & Nancy BRIGGS,
married 17 Sep 1872 WV. to Evander MORLEY,
born New York, resides Sioux City, Iowa,
age 36 yrs. single, child of Russell & Betsey MORLEY,
married by Robert R. MOORE. remarks : none.

BRIGGS, Caroline A. book 01 page 09 line 18
born Hallam, Pennsylvania, resides Brooke Co., VA.
age 23 yrs. single, child of James & Nancy BRIGGS,
married 01 Aug 1860 VA. to Thomas L. COULBURN,
born Somerset Co., Maryland, resides Somerset Co., MD.
age 33 yrs. widow, child of Jas. & Zepporah COULBURN,
married by J.M. SMITH. remarks : none.

BRIGGS, Clara E. book 01 page 16 line 22
born Washington Co., PA., resides Brooke Co., WV.
age 26 yrs. single, child of James & Nancy BRIGGS,
married 20 Jun 1867 WV. to Henry HANEY,
born Washington Co., PA., resides Wellsburg, WV.
age 34 yrs. single, child of John & Jane HANEY,
married by Edward A. BRINDLEY. remarks : none.

BRIGGS, Elvyn Jane book 01 page 09 line 21
born Saugus, Essex Co., MA., resides Brooke Co., VA.
age 28 yrs. single, child of James & Nancy BRIGGS,
married 09 Aug 1860 VA. to George K. BARTHOLOMEW,
born Hartford, Vermont, resides Cincinnati, Ohio,
age 25 yrs. single, child of Noah & Mary BARTHOLOMEW,
married by J.M. SMITH. remarks : none.

BRINDLEY, Zachariah book 01 page 03 line 23
born Harford Co., MD., resides Brooke Co., VA. farmer,
age 26 yrs. single, child of Benja. & Eleanor BRINDLEY,
married Nov 1854 VA. to Luisa HELMS,
born Green Co., Pennsylvania, resides Brooke Co., VA.
age 14 yrs. single, child of Samuel & Mary HELMS,
married by E. QUILLEN. remarks : married HELMS house.

BROWN, Elizabeth P. book 01 page 04 line 51
born Washington Co., Pennsylvania, resides unknown,
age 22 yrs. single, child of Robert & Leanetta BROWN,
married 10 Apr 1856 Wellsburg, VA. to Samuel W. BURT,
born Brooke Co., Virginia, resides unknown,
age 37 yrs. widow, child of William & Martha BURT,
married by Ezekiel QUILLEN. remarks : none.

BROWN, George W. book 01 page 20 line 39
born Jeff. Co., Ohio, resides Mont. Co., IL. livery keeper,
age 52 yrs. widow, child of Nichodemus & Eliza. BROWN,
married 16 May 1871 Wellsburg, WV. to Amanda MORTON,
born Brooke Co., Virginia, resides Brooke Co., West Virginia,
age 30 yrs. single, child of Thomas & Elizabeth MORTON,
married by J.C. CASTLE. remarks : none.

BROWN, Jacob book 01 page 20 line 40
born Germany, resides Wellsburg, WV. butcher,
age 23 yrs. single, child of Jacob & Phoebe BROWN,
married 22 May 1871 WV. to Caroline YOUNG,
born Germany, resides Wellsburg, West Virginia,
age 21 yrs. single, child of Peter & Elizabeth YOUNG,
married by Robert MOORE. remarks : married Wellsburg.

BROWN, John L. book 01 page 18 line 18
born Brooke Co., Virginia, resides Jeff. Co., Ohio, farmer,
age 33 yrs. single, child of James W. & Hanna BROWN,
married 20 Feb 1868 WV. to Ellen V. BAXTER,
born Brooke Co., Virginia, resides Brooke Co., WV.
age 17 yrs. single, child of Wm. E. & Ellen M. BAXTER,
married by Thomas M. HUDSON. remarks : none.

BROWN, Leondas book 01 page 11 line 16
born Knox Co., Ohio, resides Brooke Co., VA. farmer,
age 23 yrs. single, child of Joseph & Rachel BROWN,
married 15 Nov 1861 VA. to Clara A. DAUMONT,
born Brooke Co., Virginia, resides Brooke Co., Virginia,
age 25 yrs. widow, child of Cornelius H. & Isabel GIST,
married by Thomas M. HUDSON. remarks : none.

BROWNING, Jasper book 01 page 08 line 15
born Brooke Co., VA., resides Jefferson Co., Ohio, machinist,
age 26 yrs. single, child of Arnold & Catherine BROWNING,
married 24 Mar 1859 VA. to Sarah J. HARRIS,
born Jefferson Co., Virginia, resides Brooke Co., Virginia,
age 23 yrs. single, child of unknown & unknown HARRIS,
married by H. LUCAS. remarks : HARRIS parents deceased.

BROWNING, Margaret A. book 01 page 22 line 18
born Brooke Co., Virginia, resides Brooke Co., WV.
age 18 yrs. unk., child of unk. & unk. BROWNING,
married 04 Sep 1873 WV. to John JENNINGS,
born Meigs Co., Ohio, resides Brooke Co., WV.
age 25 yrs. unk., child of unk. & unk. JENNINGS,
married by S.H. CRAVENS. remarks : none.

BROWNING, Margaret C. book 01 page 06 line 07
born Brooke Co., Virginia, resides Brooke Co., Virginia,
age 21 yrs. single, child of Lewis & Marg't BROWNING,
married 06 Oct 1857 VA. to William B. MAHON,
born Hancock Co., Virginia, resides Brooke Co., VA.
age 24 yrs. single, child of Thomas & Judith MAHON,
married by Intrepid MORSE. remarks : none.

BROWNLEE, Elizabeth book 01 page 21 line 47
born Brooke Co., Virginia, resides Brooke Co., WV.
age 35 yrs. single, child of Thos. & Juliane BROWNLEE,
married 21 Sep 1872 Wellsburg, WV. to Elisha WEST,
born New Jersey, resides Belmont Co., Ohio,
age 39 yrs. single, child of Thomas & Charity WEST,
married by Robert R. MOORE. remarks : none.

BROWNLEE, James book 01 page 21 line 16
born Jefferson Co., Ohio, resides Brooke Co., WV. miner,
age 49 yrs. widow, child of Thos. & Juliane BROWNLEE,
married 04 Dec 1871 Wellsburg, WV. to Sallie KEITH,
born Brooke Co., Virginia, resides Brooke Co., WV.
age 40 yrs. widow, child of unknown & Susan KEITH,
married by R. MOORE. remarks : Sallie CEATH.

BROWNLEE, Martin V. book 01 page 21 line 17
born Jeff. Co., Ohio, resides Brooke Co., WV. moulder,
age 32 yrs. single, child of Thos. & Juliane BROWNLEE
married 16 Dec 1871 Wellsburg, WV. to Daisy DOWDLE,
born unknown, resides Brooke Co., West Virginia,
age 20 yrs. single, child of Jonas & Charlotte DOWDLE,
married by J.M. BERRY. remarks : none.

BROWNLEE, Nancy book 01 page 02 line 16
born Ohio, resides Wellsburg, Virginia,
age 33 yrs. single, child of James & Mary BROWNLEE,
married 05 Oct 1854 Wellsburg, VA. to Francis PALMER,
born Ohio, resides Wellsburg, Virginia,
age 24 yrs. single, child of John & Elba PALMER,
married by Samuel H. NESBITT. remarks : none.

BROWNLEE, William E. book 01 page 02 line 10
born Brooke Co., Virginia, resides Wellsburg, VA. farmer,
age 25 yrs. single, child of Walter B. & Unity BROWNLEE,
married 26 Feb 1854 Wellsburg, VA. to Elizabeth SMOTE,
born Noble Co., Ohio, resides Wellsburg, Virginia,
age 24 yrs. single, child of John & Sarah SMOTE,
married by Samuel H. NESBITT. remarks : none.

BROWNLEE, William J. book 01 page 03 line 27
born Wellsburg, Virginia, resides Brooke Co., Virginia,
age 20 yrs. single, child of Thos. & Juliane BROWNLEE,
married 27 Dec 1854 Wellsburg, VA. to Mary A. SWINER,
born Jacksonville, Ohio, resides Brooke Co., Virginia,
age 20 yrs. single, child of Peter & Mary SWINER,
married by Samuel H. NESBITT. remarks : none.

BUCHANAN, Rebecca book 01 page 08 line 11
born Brooke Co., Virginia, resides Brooke Co., Virginia,
age 20 yrs. single, child of John & unk BUCHANAN,
married 03 Feb 1859 VA. to Nicholas HEADINGTON,
born Brooke Co., Virginia, resides Brooke Co., Virginia,
age 24 yrs. single, child of John & Jane HEADINGTON,
married by John F. BRAZILL. remarks : none.

BUCHANAN, Richard W. book 01 page 19 line 41
born Brooke Co., VA., resides Wellsburg, WV. merchant,
age 23 yrs. single, child of Wm. & Sarah J. BUCHANAN,
married 30 Nov 1869 WV. to Micha LEWIS,
born Brooke Co., Virginia, resides Brooke Co., WV.
age 21 yrs. single, child of John & Leah LEWIS,
married by Robert R. MOORE. remarks : none.

BUCKALEW, Ann Eliza. book 01 page 05 line 07
born Wellsburg, Virginia, resides Wellsburg, Virginia,
age 19 yrs. single, child of Garrett & Lydia BUCKALEW,
married 30 Oct 1856 VA. to Marcellus ROBERTS,
born Wellsburg, Virginia, resides Wellsburg, Virginia,
age 22 yrs. single, child of Isaiah & Margaret ROBERTS,
married by William GAMBLE, JR. remarks : none.

BUCKALEW, Josephine book 01 page 12 line 37
born Wellsburg, Virginia, resides Brooke Co., Virginia,
age 19 yrs. single, child of Garrett & unk. BUCKALEW,
married 01 Jun 1862 VA. to David H. MURCHLAND,
born Brooke Co., Virginia, resides Brooke Co., Virginia,
age 37 yrs. widow, child of Rob't & Sallie MURCHLAND,
married by Edward A. BRINDLEY. remarks : none.

BUCKALEW, Lydia Jane book 01 page 19 line 33
born Wellsburg, Virginia, resides Wellsburg, West Virginia,
age 21 yrs. single, child of Garrett & Lydia BUCKALEW,
married 25 Mar 1869 Wellsburg, WV. to Eli ADAMS,
born Wellsburg, Virginia, resides Wellsburg, WV.
age 23 yrs. single, child of Thomas & Ann ADAMS,
married by A.R. CHAPMAN. remarks : none.

BUCKEY, John book 01 page 19 line 25
born Brooke Co., Virginia, resides Brooke Co., WV. farmer,
age 55 yrs. widow, child of Volentia & Elizabeth BUCKEY,
married 21 Jan 1869 WV. to Mary FISHER,
born Brooke Co., Virginia, resides Brooke Co., WV.
age 45 yrs. single, child of Henry & Beth Ann FISHER,
married by Walter BROWN. remarks : none.

BUCKEY, Kate C. book 01 page 09 line 02
born Brooke Co., Virginia, resides Brooke Co., Virginia,
age 23 yrs. single, child of John & Elizabeth BUCKEY,
married 04 Jan 1860 VA. to David E. JESTER,
born Brooke Co., Virginia, resides Brooke Co., Virginia,
age 30 yrs. single, child of Andrew & Eliza. A. JESTER,
married by George G. WALTERS. remarks : none.

BUCKEY, Mary L. book 01 page 19 line 26
born Brooke Co., Virginia, resides Brooke Co., WV.
age 25 yrs. single, child of John & Elizabeth BUCKEY,
married 19 Jan 1869 WV. to James GEORGE,
born Washington Co., PA., resides Fulton Co., IL.
age 38 yrs. single, child of Thomas & Sarah GEORGE,
married by H. CREE. remarks : none.

BUCKEY, Sarah E. book 01 page 19 line 11
born Brooke Co., Virginia, resides Brooke Co., WV.
age 20 yrs. single, child of John & Elizabeth BUCKEY,
married 05 Sep 1868 WV. to George W. MC CREARY,
born Brooke Co., Virginia, resides Brooke Co., WV.
age 24 yrs. single, child of William & A. MC CREARY,
married by Walter BROWN, remarks : none.

BUCY, Darwin E. Rasmus book 01 page 22 line 06
born Jefferson Co., Ohio, resides Brooke Co., WV. miner,
age 24 yrs. single, child of Joshua & Margarett BUCY,
married 14 Nov 1872 Wellsburg, WV. to Jane BOWMAN,
born Brooke Co., Virginia, resides Brooke Co., WV.
age 22 yrs. single, child of John & Sarah BOWMAN,
married by R. MOORE remarks : pg. 22 line 1, date 30 Oct.

BUKER, Mary book 01 page 12 line 53
born Pennsylvania, resides Brooke Co., West Virginia,
age 36 yrs. widow, child of Henry & Jane BUKER,
married 28 Oct 1863 WV. to Salathiel HILL,
born Pennsylvania, resides Brooke Co., West Virginia,
age 45 yrs. widow, child of George & Alice Ann HILL,
married by J. CAMPBELL. remarks : Mrs. Mary MYERS.

BULLOCK, Ann book 01 page 04 line 55
born St. Clairsville, Ohio, resides Brooke Co., Virginia,
age 18 yrs. single, child of Charles & Harriet BULLOCK,
married 02 Jun 1856 Wellsburg, VA. to John KUHN,
born Allegheny Co., PA., resides Wellsburg, Virginia,
age 22 yrs. single, child of Peter & Barbara Ann KUHN,
married by A.J. ENDSLEY. remarks : none.

BURGESS, John S. book 01 page 11 line 28
born New Jersey, resides Wheeling, VA. pumpmaker,
age 26 yrs. single, child of Francis & Pheby BURGESS,
married 14 Dec 1862 Wellsburg, VA. to Anne TAYLOR,
born Brooke Co., Virginia, resides Wellsburg, Virginia,
age 18 yrs. single, child of Thomas & Ann TAYLOR,
married by Edward A. BRINDLEY. remarks : none.

BURGOYNE, Rebecca J.　　　book 01 page 20 line 22
born unknown, resides Brooke Co., West Virginia,
age 30 yrs. single, child of Joshua R. & unk. BURGOYNE,
married 10 Nov 1870 Paris, PA. to Andrew S. HELMICK,
born Jefferson Co., Ohio, resides Tuscarawas Co., Ohio,
age 37 yrs. widow, child of Joseph & Mary HELMICK,
married by James C. CAMPBELL. remarks: none.

BURK, Surrilla　　　book 01 page 05 line 10
born Ohio, resides Ohio,
age 28 yrs. widow, child of John & Eliza. JAMES,
married 13 Nov 1856 VA. to Adam KEMP,
born Washington Co., PA., resides Brooke Co., VA.
age 30 yrs. widow, child of Adam & Rachel KEMP,
married by E. CHRISTIAN. remarks: none.

BURNS, Callie　　　book 01 page 19 line 39
born Jefferson Co., Ohio, resides Brooke Co., WV.
age 25 yrs. single, child of unknown & unk. BURNS,
married 09 Sep 1869 WV. to William H. GIST,
born Brooke Co., Virginia, resides St. Louis, Missouri,
age 26 yrs. single, child of Thomas & Mary GIST,
married by A.R. CHAPMAN. remarks: none.

BURT, Mary Jane　　　book 01 page 11 line 13
born Ohio, resides Brooke Co., Virginia,
age 24 yrs. single, child of unk. & unk. BURT,
married 26 Sep 1861 VA. to Berhart DANNER,
born Germany, resides Brooke Co., Virginia,
age 23 yrs. single, child of Lewis & Sabrina DANNER,
married by Stephen HUBER. remarks: married Wellsburg.

BURT, Samuel Wm.　　　book 01 page 04 line 51
born Brooke Co., VA., resides unk., steamboat pilot,
age 37 yrs. widow, child of William & Martha BURT,
married 10 Apr 1856 VA. to Elizabeth P. BROWN,
born Washington Co., Pennsylvania, resides unknown,
age 22 yrs. single, child of Robert & Leanetta BROWN,
married by Ezekiel QUILLEN. remarks: married Wellsburg.

BUXTON, James　　　book 01 page 12 line 41
born Brooke Co., VA., resides Wash. Co., PA. farmer,
age 21 yrs. single, child of Amos & Mary A. BUXTON,
married 02 Jan 1863 VA. to Margaret Ellenor NOAH,
born Pennsylvania, resides Brooke Co., Virginia,
age 18 yrs. single, child of James & unknown NOAH,
married by T. HUDSON. remarks: married KLEIN house.

CAIN, Catharine　　　book 01 page 15 line 59
born Ireland, resides Pittsburgh, Pennsylvania,
age 20 yrs. single, child of James & Ellen CAIN,
married 05 Sep 1865 WV. to Anthony GORDON,
born Ireland, resides Pittsburgh, Pennsylvania,
age 23 yrs. single, child of Anthony & Mary GORDON,
married by Stephen HUBER. remarks: married Wellsburg.

CAIRNES, Margaret E. book 01 page 10 line 01B
born Brooke Co., Virginia, resides Brooke Co., VA.
age 19 yrs. single, child of James & Anne CAIRNES,
married 10 Jan 1861   VA. to Joseph J. CARTER,
born Brooke Co., Virginia, resides Brooke Co., VA.
age 26 yrs. single, child of Lewis & Martha CARTER,
married by Thomas M. HUDSON. remarks : none.

CAIRNES, Ruth E. book 01 page 08 line 10
born Brooke Co., Virginia, resides Brooke Co., VA.
age 37 yrs. single, child of James & Nancy CAIRNES,
married 14 Feb 1859 VA. to James BOSLEY,
born Brooke Co., Virginia, resides Brooke Co., VA.
age 38 yrs. single, child of William & Jane BOSLEY,
married by Morse BETISE. remarks : none.

CALDERWOOD, D.W. book 01 page 21 line 30
born Salona, Pennsylvania, resides Plymouth, PA. minister,
age 35 yrs. single, child of Samuel & Sarah CALDERWOOD,
married 04 Apr 1872 Wellsburg, WV. to Laura A. FRAZIER,
born Brooke Co., Virginia, resides Brooke Co., West Virginia,
age 20 yrs. single, child of John & Nancy FRAZIER,
married by E.Y. PINKERTON. remarks : none.

CALDWELL, Martha book 01 page 16 line 15
born Wash. Co., Pennsylvania, resides Brooke Co., WV.
age 20 yrs. single, child of Andrew & Isabel CALDWELL,
married 29 Feb 1867   WV. to John FRESHWATER,
born Brooke Co., Virginia, resides Brooke Co., West Virginia,
age 23 yrs. single, child of Reuben & Lydia FRESHWATER,
married by James C. CAMPBELL. remarks : none.

CALDWELL, Robert book 01 page 19 line 43
born Belmont Co., Ohio, resides Harrison Co., Ohio, farmer,
age 26 yrs. single, child of John & Elizabeth CALDWELL,
married 27 Jan 1870   WV. to Flora A. ATKINSON,
born Brooke Co., Virginia, resides Brooke Co., WV.
age 22 yrs. single, child of John & Marg't ATKINSON,
married by Josias STEVENSON. remarks : none.

CALENDINE, Edward book 01 page 02 line 18
born Brooke Co., Virginia, resides Wellsburg, Virginia,
age 23 yrs. single, child of Henry & unk. CALENDINE,
married 02 Nov 1854 VA. to Susan DOUBLAZIER,
born Brooke Co., Virginia, resides Wellsburg, Virginia,
age 18 yrs. single, child of Henry & Nancy DOUBLAZIER,
married by W.A. DAVIDSON. remarks : married Wellsburg.

CALENDINE, George book 01 page 20 line 01
born Brooke Co., Virginia, resides Brooke Co., WV. farmer,
age 26 yrs. single, child of Sam'l & Maria J. CALENDINE,
married 10 Mar 1870   WV. to Elizabeth ALLEN,
born Washington Co., PA., resides Brooke Co., WV.
age 24 yrs. single, child of Amos & Elizabeth ALLEN,
married by Milton WELLS. remarks : none.

BROOKE CO., VA./WV. MARRIAGE BOOK 1, 1853-1874   157

CAMPBELL, Anna   book 01 page 21 line 22
born Brooke Co., Virginia, resides Brooke Co., WV.
age 21 yrs. single, child of Arch. & Lousia CAMPBELL,
married 18 Jan 1872 WV. to James BLANKENSOP,
born Brooke Co., Virginia, resides Brooke Co., West Virginia,
age 24 yrs. single, child of Peter & Susan BLANKENSOP,
married by E.H. JONES. remarks : married Hollidays Cove.

CAMPBELL, Anna B.   book 01 page 20 line 07
born Newry, Ireland, resides Bethany, West Virginia,
age 27 yrs. widow, child of Archibald & Anne CAMPBELL,
married 08 Jul 1870 Bethany, WV. to James A. MURRAY,
born Simpson Co., Kentucky, resides Palmyra, Missouri,
age 27 yrs. single, child of William & Nancy MURRAY,
married by A. CAMPBELL. remarks : Anna B. POSTON.

CAMPBELL, Decima H.   book 01 page 12 line 48
born Virginia, resides Brooke Co., Virginia,
age 22 yrs. single, child of Alex. & Selina H. CAMPBELL,
married 07 Apr 1863 Bethany, VA. to John J. BARCLAY,
born Virginia, resides Cyprus, Turkey,
age 26 yrs. single, child of James T. & Jillian BARCLAY,
married by William PENDLETON. remarks : none.

CAMPBELL, Elizabeth   book 01 page 19 line 08
born Carroll Co., Ohio, resides Carroll Co., Ohio,
age 23 yrs. single, child of unk. & unk. CAMPBELL,
married 11 Aug 1868 WV. to Stewart SNEARY,
born Carroll Co., Ohio, resides Carroll Co., Ohio,
age 21 yrs. single, child of H.S. & Susan SNEARY,
married by A. CHAPMAN. remarks : married Wellsburg.

CAMPBELL, Ellen M.   book 01 page 11 line 33
born Ireland, resides Brooke Co., Virginia,
age 27 yrs. single, child of Arch. & Anne CAMPBELL,
married 23 Nov 1862 VA. to Thomas F. HOLTON,
born Brown Co., Ohio, resides Jefferson Co., Kentucky,
age 23 yrs. single, child of Wm. B. & Sally P. HOLTON,
married by A. CAMPBELL. remarks : married Bethany.

CAMPBELL, Greer M.   book 01 page 13 line 22
born unknown, resides unknown,
age -- yrs. unknown, child of unk. & unk. CAMPBELL,
married 16 Mar 1864 WV. to Elizabeth MORTON,
born unknown, resides Brooke Co., West Virginia,
age -- yrs. unknown, child of unk. & unk. MORTON,
married by UNKNOWN. remarks : none.

CAMPBELL, Jane   book 01 page 14 line 46
born Brooke Co., Virginia, resides Brooke Co., WV.
age 30 yrs. single, child of R. & Marg't CAMPBELL,
married 07 Feb 1865 WV. to Daniel B. STANSBERRY,
born Brooke Co., Virginia, resides Brooke Co., WV.
age 37 yrs. widow, child of N. & K. STANSBERRY,
married by T. HUDSON. remarks : married Hollidays Cove.

CAMPBELL, Virginia A.   book 01 page 13 line 09
born unknown, resides Brooke Co., West Virginia,
age -- yrs. single, child of Alex. & Selina H. CAMPBELL,
married 26 Oct 1863 WV. to William R. THOMPSON,
born unknown, resides Louisville, Kentucky,
age -- yrs. single, child of unk. & unk. THOMPSON,
married by W. PENDLETON. remarks : married Bethany.

CARDEHAM, Bridget   book 01 page 22 line 32
born Belmont Co., Ohio, resides Brooke Co., West Virginia,
age 18 yrs. unknown, child of unk. & unk. CARDEHAM,
married 21 Jan 1874 Wellsburg, WV. to Hugh DUNN,
born Ohio, resides Steubenville, Ohio,
age 23 yrs. unknown, child of unk. & unk. DUNN,
married by Stephen HUBER. remarks : none.

CARIENS, Amanda   book 01 page 14 line 51
born Brooke Co., Virginia, resides Brooke Co., WV.
age 22 yrs. single, child of Elliott & Sarah CARIENS,
married 09 Mar 1865 WV. to John Randolph ELSON,
born Brooke Co., Virginia, resides Brooke Co., WV.
age 24 yrs. single, child of Alex. M. & Charlotte ELSON,
married by I. MORSE. remarks : married CARIENS house.

CARIENS, Mary   book 01 page 16 line 07
born Brooke Co., Virginia, resides Brooke Co., WV.
age 30 yrs. single, child of James & Mary CARIENS,
married 08 Jan 1867 WV. to John ALLISON,
born Brooke Co., VA., resides Hancock Co., WV.
age 38 yrs. single, child of John & Mary ALLISON,
married by Thomas M. HUDSON. remarks : none.

CARIENS, Narcissa   book 01 page 15 line 72
born Brooke Co., Virginia, resides Brooke Co., WV.
age 21 yrs. single, child of Elliott & Sarah CARIENS,
married 18 Jan 1866 WV. to John H. LATIMER,
born Brooke Co., Virginia, resides Brooke Co., WV.
age 26 yrs. single, child of unk. & unk. LATIMER,
married by T. HUDSON. remarks : married house of mother.

CARMICHAEL, Catherine A.   book 01 page 21 line 29
born Brooke Co., Virginia, resides Brooke Co., West Virginia,
age 24 yrs. single, child of Geo. & Nancy CARMICHAEL,
married 12 Mar 1872 Wellsburg, WV. to David PLANTS,
born Beaver Co., Pennsylvania, resides Steubenville, Ohio,
age 24 yrs. single, child of Joseph & Rosana PLANTS,
married by Robert R. MOORE. remarks : none.

CARMICHAEL, James W.M.   book 01 page 10 line 8 B
born Washington Co. PA., resides Brooke Co., VA. miner,
age 21 yrs. single, child of Geo. W. & Nancy CARMICHAEL,
married 07 May 1861 Wellsburg, VA. to Mary FORBES,
born Ireland, resides Wellsburg, Virginia,
age 18 yrs. single, child of Thomas & Nancy FORBES,
married by David HERVEY. remarks : none.

CARMICHAEL, Nancy E.　　　　book 01 page 17 line 09
born Brooke Co., Virginia, resides Brooke Co., West Virginia,
age 19 yrs. single, child of Geo. W. & Nancy CARMICHAEL,
married 09 Aug 1866 Wellsburg, WV. to Thomas FORBES,
born Ireland, resides Wellsburg, West Virginia,
age 25 yrs. single, child of Thomas & Nancy FORBES,
married by R.T. PRICE. remarks: none.

CARSON, Mary　　　　book 01 page 03 line 22
born Maryland, resides Brooke Co., Virginia,
age 31 yrs. single, child of unk. & Eliza. CARSON,
married 28 Dec 1854 VA. to John BOWMAN,
born Pennsylvania, resides Brooke Co., Virginia,
age 64 yrs. widow, child of John & Eliza. BOWMAN,
married by Francis GUTHRIE. remarks: none.

CARTER, Ewing T.　　　　book 01 page 19 line 27
born Brooke Co., VA., resides Brooke Co., WV. farmer,
age 28 yrs. single, child of L.W. & Martha A. CARTER,
married 28 Jan 1868 WV. to Mary E. MONTGOMERY,
born Brooke Co., Virginia, resides Brooke Co., West Virginia,
age 27 yrs. single, child of Daniel & Julia MONTGOMERY,
married by L. SOUTHMAY. remarks: none.

CARTER, Joseph J.　　　　book 01 page 10 line 01B
born Brooke Co., VA., resides Brooke Co., VA. farmer,
age 26 yrs. single, child of Lewis & Martha CARTER,
married 10 Jan 1861 VA. to Margaret E. CAIRNES,
born Brooke Co., Virginia, resides Brooke Co., VA.
age 19 yrs. single, child of James & Anne CAIRNES,
married by Thomas M. HUDSON. remarks: none.

CARTER, Lewis Washington　　　　book 01 page 13 line 60
born Brooke Co., Virginia, resides Brooke Co., WV. farmer,
age 23 yrs. single, child of Lewis W. & Martha A. CARTER,
married 15 Oct 1863 WV. to Isabelle PUNTNEY,
born Jefferson Co., Ohio, resides Brooke Co., West Virginia,
age 24 yrs. single, child of James & Polly PUNTNEY,
married by G. WHARTON. remarks: married PUNTNEY house.

CARTER, Martha Louisa　　　　book 01 page 19 line 44
born Brooke Co., Virginia, resides Brooke Co., WV.
age 24 yrs. single, child of Lewis & Martha A. CARTER,
married 13 Jan 1870 WV. to John HEADINGTON,
born Brooke Co., Virginia, resides Brooke Co., WV.
age 27 yrs. single, child of John & Jane HEADINGTON,
married by William B. MAYBERRY. remarks: none.

CARTER, Stephen　　　　book 01 page 04 line 43
born Brooke Co., Virginia, resides unknown, farmer,
age 34 yrs. single, child of Joseph & Catharine CARTER,
married 06 Sep 1855 VA. to Catharine FISHER,
born Brooke Co., Virginia, resides unknown,
age 26 yrs. single, child of Henry & Beth Ann FISHER,
married by J.R. MEANS. remarks: none.

CARUTH, Rachel B. book 01 page 23 line 05
born Brooke Co., Virginia, resides Brooke Co., WV.
age 19 yrs. unknown, child of unk. & unk. CARUTH,
married 03 Dec 1874 WV. to William K. HASLETT,
born Brooke Co., Virginia, resides Brooke Co., WV.
age 24 yrs. unknown, child of unk. & unk. HASLETT,
married by David HERVEY. remarks : none.

CASNER, Cora book 01 page 20 line 21
born Brooke Co., Virginia, resides Brooke Co., WV.
age 22 yrs. single, child of William & Mary CASNER,
married 01 Sep 1870 WV. to George MILLER,
born Washington Co., PA., resides Brooke Co., WV.
age 48 yrs. widow, child of George & Susan MILLER,
married by J. WARDEN. remarks : married West Liberty.

CASNER, John C. book 01 page 08 line 02
born Brooke Co., VA., resides Brooke Co., VA. carpenter,
age 30 yrs. single, child of James & Elizabeth CASNER,
married 09 Nov 1858 VA. to Rose V. SMITH,
born Brooke Co., Virginia, resides Brooke Co., VA.
age 28 yrs. single, child of Andrew & Jane SMITH,
married by Thomas M. HUDSON. remarks : none.

CASSIDY, Joseph N. book 01 page 21 line 08
born Wash. Co., PA., resides Brooke Co., WV. farmer,
age 29 yrs. single, child of Robert & Isabel CASSIDY
married 24 Oct 1871 WV. to Maggie E. HEADINGTON
born Brooke Co., Virginia, resides Brooke Co., WV.
age 26 yrs. single, child of John & Jane HEADINGTON,
married by J.B. LUCAS. remarks : none.

CAVANAUGH, John book 01 page 10 line 10 B
born Ireland, resides Bethany, Virginia,
age 52 yrs. single, child of Thos. & Eliza. CAVANAUGH,
married 23 Jun 1861 Bethany, VA. to Susan DOWNEY,
born Ireland, resides Bethany, Virginia,
age 35 yrs. single, child of Turns & unk. DOWNEY,
married by Stephen HUBER. remarks : none.

CEATH, Sallie book 01 page 21 line 16
born Brooke Co., Virginia, resides Brooke Co., West Virginia,
age 40 yrs. widow, child of unknown & Susan CEATH,
married 04 Dec 1871 Wellsburg, WV. to James BROWNLEE,
born Jefferson Co., Ohio, resides Brooke Co., West Virginia,
age 49 yrs. widow, child of Thomas & Juliane BROWNLEE,
married by R. MOORE. remarks : Sallie KEITH?

CHALLENCE, Elijah B. book 01 page 04 line 58
born Chas. City Co., VA., resides James City Co., VA.
age 22 yrs. single, child of B.D. & M.A. CHALLENCE,
married 11 Aug 1856 VA. to Clarinda E. MENDEL,
born Brooke Co., Virginia, resides Bethany, Virginia,
age 17 yrs. single, child of John & Ann MENDEL,
married by A. CAMPBELL. remarks : married Bethany.

CHAMBERLAIN, Ellen book 01 page 15 line 64
born Brooke Co., Virginia, resides Brooke Co., West Virginia,
age 21 yrs. single, child of Daniel & Jane CHAMBERLAIN,
married 26 Oct 1865 WV. to John G. STEWART,
born Ohio Co., Virginia, resides Brooke Co., West Virginia,
age 26 yrs. single, child of William & M. STEWART,
married by G. CHESTER. remarks : married E. GIVENS house.

CHAMBERLAIN, Sarah book 01 page 05 line 19
born Beaver Co., Pennsylvania, resides Brooke Co., Virginia,
age 22 yrs. single, child of Daniel & Jane CHAMBERLAIN,
married 07 Mar 1857 Wellsburg, VA. to Thomas BRADLEY,
born England, resides Brooke Co., Virginia,
age 29 yrs. single, child of John & Frances BRADLEY,
married by Ezekiel QUILLEN. remarks : none.

CHAPLINE, Albert W. book 01 page 15 line 62
born Wheeling, VA., resides Brooke Co., WV. farmer,
age 30 yrs. single, child of Wm. & Ann CHAPLINE,
married 27 Sep 1865 WV. to Mary B. RICHARDSON,
born Brooke Co., Virginia, resides Brooke Co., WV.
age 26 yrs. single, child of R. & K. RICHARDSON,
married by W. PENDLETON. remarks : married Bethany.

CHAPMAN, Jacob book 01 page 11 line 17
born Pennsylvania, resides Brooke Co., VA. blacksmith,
age 25 yrs. single, child of Harry & Nancy CHAPMAN,
married 28 Nov 1861 VA. to Mary ROBINSON,
born Pennsylvania, resides Brooke Co., Virginia,
age 25 yrs. single, child of Samuel & Mary ROBINSON,
married by J.B. PATTERSON. remarks : none.

CHEEK, James book 01 page 17 line 11
born Rappa. Co., VA., resides Brooke Co., WV. farmer,
age 22 yrs. single, child of Oscar & Amanda CHEEK,
married 06 Sep 1866 WV. to Rebecca COX,
born Brooke Co., Virginia, resides Brooke Co., VA.
age 30 yrs. single, child of William & Nancy COX,
married by Thomas M. HUDSON. remarks : none.

CHESTER, Callie book 01 page 22 line 15
born Brooke Co., Virginia, resides Steubenville, Ohio,
age 21 yrs. unknown, child of unknown & unk. CHESTER,
married 11 Jul 1873 Wellsburg, WV. to Harvey JEFFERS,
born Brooke Co., Virginia, resides Wellsburg, West Virginia,
age 25 yrs. unknown, child of unknown & unk. JEFFERS,
married by S.H. CRAVENS. remarks : none.

CHESTER, Georgianna book 01 page 20 line 02
born Wellsburg, VA., resides Wellsburg, West Virginia,
age 19 yrs. single, child of Geo. W. & Eliza. CHESTER,
married 30 Mar 1870 WV. to James C. STEWART,
born Ohio Co., Virginia, resides Venango Co., PA.
age 23 yrs. single, child of Jackson & Mary STEWART,
married by E.A. BRINDLEY. remarks : married Wellsburg.

CHESTER, Mary E. book 01 page 13 line 27
born Wellsburg, VA., resides Wellsburg, West Virginia,
age 21 yrs. single, child of Geo. W. & Eliza. CHESTER,
married 30 Jun 1864 WV. to Travilla A. RUSSELL,
born Wellsburg, VA., resides Wellsburg, West Virginia,
age 21 yrs. single, child of James & Sarah RUSSELL,
married by E.A. BRINDLEY. remarks : married Wellsburg.

CHESTER, Sarah Eliza. book 01 page 15 line 56
born Wellsburg, Virginia, resides Wellsburg, WV.
age 26 yrs. single, child of Geo. W. & Eliza. CHESTER,
married 14 Aug 1865 WV. to Joseph WALDRON,
born Hardy Co., ? Virginia, resides Wellsburg, WV.
age 28 yrs. single, child of Elias & Elizabeth WALDRON,
married by G. CHESTER. remarks : married CHESTER house.

CHRISTIAN, Edmund book 01 page 06 line 09
born Whitehaven, ENG., resides Brooke Co., VA. minister,
age 46 yrs. widow, child of William & Ruth CHRISTIAN,
married 15 Oct 1857 VA. to Jemima ELLIOTT,
born Brooke Co., Virginia, resides Brooke Co., Virginia,
age 26 yrs. single, child of James & Elizabeth ELLIOTT,
married by Intrepid MORSE. remarks : none.

CHURCHMAN, Joseph book 01 page 20 line 41
born Brooke Co., VA., resides Brooke Co., WV. farmer,
age 48 yrs. widow, child of Jacob & Mary CHURCHMAN,
married 25 May 1871 WV. to Nancy LUCAS,
born Brooke Co., Virginia, resides Brooke Co., WV.
age 32 yrs. single, child of Samuel & Rebecca LUCAS,
married by A.E. WARD. remarks : none.

CLARK, William A. book 01 page 10 line 11A
born New Lisbon, Ohio, resides Steuben., OH. carriage trim.,
age 24 yrs. single, child of Samuel & Ruhanna CLARK,
married 30 Aug 1860 VA. to Elizabeth J. INGLEBRIGHT,
born Brooke Co., Virginia, resides Brooke Co., Virginia,
age 24 yrs. single, child of Wm. & Sarah INGLEBRIGHT,
married by C. BEATTY. remarks : married Half Moon Farm.

CLAYTON, Nancy book 01 page 04 line 62
born Brooke Co., Virginia, resides Brooke Co., Virginia,
age 46 yrs. widow, child of Wm. & Susannah FOWLER,
married 07 Sep 1856 VA. to Otho HEDGES,
born Brooke Co., Virginia, resides Brooke Co., Virginia,
age 55 yrs. widow, child of Joseph & Nancy HEDGES,
married by Ezekiel QUILLEN. remarks : none.

CLEMENS, Sarah book 01 page 22 line 23
born Brooke Co., Virginia, resides Brooke Co., WV.
age 16 yrs. unknown, child of unk. & unk. CLEMENS,
married 06 Nov 1873 WV. to Hugh DENINGEN,
born Ireland, resides Brooke Co., West Virginia,
age 25 yrs. unk., child of unk. & unk. DENINGEN,
married by Joshua COUPLAND. remarks : none.

CLENDENEN, Edward W.   book 01 page 14 line 39
born Brooke Co., VA., resides Brooke Co., WV. farmer,
age 23 yrs. widow, child of Wm. & Rachel CLENDENEN,
married 24 Nov 1864   WV. to Mary Jane BONAR,
born Brooke Co., Virginia, resides Brooke Co., WV.
age 21 yrs. single, child of unk. & unk. BONAR,
married by E.C. WAYMAN. remarks : none.

CLERKIN, Bridget   book 01 page 09 line 15
born Co. Coleraine, Ireland, resides Wheeling, VA.
age 24 yrs. single, child of Peter & Julia CLERKIN,
married 25 May 1860 Wellsburg, VA. to John DORSEY,
born Pennsylvania, resides Wheeling, Virginia,
age 21 yrs. single, child of Edward & Eliza. DORSEY,
married by Thomas M. HUDSON. remarks : none.

CLOSE, Peter   book 01 page 03 line 37
born Wash. Co., PA., resides Brooke Co., VA. farmer,
age 45 yrs. widow, child of John & Nancy CLOSE,
married 08 Nov 1855 VA. to Elizabeth Jane ACKERMAN,
born Washington Co., PA., resides Brooke Co., Virginia,
age 33 yrs. single, child of Abraham & Marg't ACKERMAN,
married by Ezekiel QUILLEN. remarks : none.

CLOW, William   book 01 page 06 line 02
born Brooke Co., Virginia, resides unknown, boat pilot,
age 38 yrs. widow, child of Thomas & Susannah CLOW,
married 30 Jul 1857   VA. to Jane CONANT,
born Ohio Co., Virginia, resides unknown,
age 23 yrs. single, child of Lot & Mary CONANT,
married by Ezekiel QUILLEN. remarks : none.

COATES, William B.   book 01 page 20 line 25
born Philadelphia, PA., resides Wellsburg, West Virginia,
age 34 yrs. divorced, child of John & Esther COATES,
married 26 Dec 1870   WV. to Mary Ann DUNWELL,
born Smithfield, Ohio, resides Wellsburg, West Virginia,
age 29 yrs. single, child of Wm. & Margaret DUNWELL,
married by E.A. BRINDLEY. remarks : married Wellsburg.

COCHRANE, Mary   book 01 page 02 line 11
born New York City, NY., resides Wellsburg, Virginia,
age 23 yrs. single, child of John & Agnes COCHRANE,
married 24 Aug 1854 Wellsburg, VA. to Elbert PRATHER,
born Wellsburg, Virginia, resides Wellsburg, Virginia,
age 23 yrs. widow, child of John & Elizabeth PRATHER,
married by Ezekiel QUILLEN. remarks : none.

COGAN, John   book 01 page 04 line 61
born Cumberland Co., PA., resides Wellsburg, VA. laborer,
age 30 yrs. single, child of John & Martha ? COGAN,
married 12 Sep 1856 Wellsburg, VA. to Mary BARBER,
born Westmoreland Co., PA., resides Wellsburg, Virginia,
age 32 yrs. widow, child of Aaron & Catherine THORP,
married by William GAMBLE,JR. remarks : none.

COLE, Rebecca M. book 01 page 11 line 27
born Virginia, resides Brooke Co., Virginia,
age 23 yrs. single, child of Wm. & Cath. COLE,
married 02 Oct 1862 VA. to Jacob B. GRIFFITH,
born Ohio, resides Brooke Co., Virginia,
age 28 yrs. single, child of M.E. & F. GRIFFITH,
married by William M. ROBINSON. remarks: none.

COLEMAN, Clara B. book 01 page 16 line 08
born Brooke Co., Virginia, resides Brooke Co., WV.
age 20 yrs. single, child of David & Mary J. COLEMAN,
married 01 Jan 1867 WV. to McCullough MORGAN,
born Brooke Co., Virginia, resides Ohio Co., West Virginia,
age 20 yrs. single, child of Edward & Margaret MORGAN,
married by W. HOWE. remarks: married house of brides father.

COLEMAN, David O. book 01 page 05 line 04
born Jefferson Co., Ohio, resides Wayne Twp., farmer,
age 24 yrs. single, child of Richard & Mary COLEMAN,
married 02 Oct 1856 VA. to Sarah Amelia BEATTY,
born Brooke Co., Virginia, resides Brooke Co., Virginia,
age 18 yrs. single, child of Thos. H. & Rachel BEATTY,
married by J.D. CARVER. remarks: none.

COLEMAN, DeWitt C. book 01 page 11 line 21
born Brooke Co., Virginia, resides Brooke Co., VA.
age 32 yrs. single, child of David & Mary COLEMAN,
married 14 Nov 1861 VA. to Elizabeth LEWIS,
born Brooke Co., Virginia, resides Brooke Co., VA.
age 22 yrs. single, child of Job & Margaret LEWIS,
married by Thomas M. HUDSON. remarks: none.

COLEMAN, Emma D. book 01 page 17 line 22
born Ohio Co., Virginia, resides Brooke Co., WV.
age 23 yrs. single, child of David & Mary COLEMAN,
married 01 Jan 1867 WV. to William ROBERTS,
born Harrison Co., Ohio, resides Christian Co., IL.
age 26 yrs. single, child of James & Eliza. ROBERTS,
married by William R. HOWE. remarks: none.

COLLINS, Timothy book 01 page 22 line 22
born Ireland, resides Brooke Co., West Virginia,
age 32 yrs. unknown, child of unk. & unk. COLLINS,
married 04 Nov 1873 WV. to Bridget MURPHY,
born Ireland, resides Brooke Co., West Virginia,
age 30 yrs. unknown, child of unk. & unk. MURPHY,
married by Stephen HUBER. remarks: none.

CONANT, Abigail book 01 page 07 line 09
born Worcester Co., MA., resides Brooke Co., VA.
age 30 yrs. single, child of Lot & Mary CONANT,
married 23 Feb 1858 VA. to Joseph BEDILLION,
born Washington Co., Virginia, resides Marshall Co., VA.
age 29 yrs. widow, child of Abraham & Marg't BEDILLION,
married by E. QUILLEN. remarks: married CONANT house.

CONANT, Jane book 01 page 06 line 02
born Ohio Co., Virginia, resides unknown,
age 23 yrs. single, child of Lot & Mary CONANT,
married 30 Jul 1857 VA. to William CLOW,
born Brooke Co., Virginia, resides unknown,
age 38 yrs. widow, child of Thomas & Susannah CLOW,
married by Ezekiel QUILLEN. remarks: none.

CONAWAY, Evan book 01 page 09 line 09
born Monongalia Co., VA., resides Brooke Co., VA.
age 31 yrs. widow, child of Eli & Mary CONAWAY,
married 23 Nov 1859 VA. to Mary Ann MILLIGAN,
born Jefferson Co., Ohio, resides Brooke Co., Virginia,
age 33 yrs. single, child of George & Mary MILLIGAN,
married by J.M. SMITH. remarks: none.

CONE, Michael book 01 page 18 line 12
born Ireland, resides Brooke Co., West Virginia, farmer,
age 24 yrs. single, child of Patrick & Elizabeth CONE,
married 25 Dec 1867 WV. to Anne CUNNINGHAM,
born Ireland, resides Brooke Co., West Virginia,
age 19 yrs. single, child of Jas. & Susan CUNNINGHAM,
married by Stephen HUBER. remarks: none.

CONNELL, Ellen E. book 01 page 16 line 25
born Wellsburg, Virginia, resides Wellsburg, West Virginia,
age 21 yrs. single, child of Harrison & Eliza. CONNELL,
married -- -- 1867 WV. to Arthur F. MC NALLY,
born Brownsville, Pennsylvania, resides Wellsburg, WV.
age 23 yrs. single, child of Bernard & Mary MC NALLY,
married by G.W. CHESTER. remarks: Jun/Jul/Aug 1867.

CONNELLY, Bridget book 01 page 18 line 13
born Ireland, resides Brooke Co., West Virginia,
age 22 yrs. single, child of Wm. & Ellen CONNELLY,
married 22 Jan 1868 WV. to Dusty DAVIN,
born Ireland, resides Brooke Co., West Virginia,
age 30 yrs. single, child of John & Mary DAVIN,
married by Stephen HUBER. remarks: none.

CONNERS, Margery book 01 page 20 line 37
born unknown, resides Brooke Co., West Virginia,
age 30 yrs. widow, child of unk. & unk. CONNERS,
married 09 May 1871 WV. to Bernard O'HARA,
born Ireland, resides Steubenville, Ohio,
age 25 yrs. single, child of Andrew & Rose O'HARA,
married by R.R. MOORE. remarks: married Wellsburg.

COOK, Samuel book 01 page 19 line 28
born Wash. Co., PA., resides Wash. Co., PA. farmer,
age 24 yrs. single, child of Godfrey & Martha COOK,
married 02 Feb 1869 WV. to Clay SNEDIKER,
born Brooke Co., Virginia, resides Brooke Co., WV.
age 21 yrs. single, child of Wm. & Mary SNEDIKER,
married by J.W. KESLER. remarks: none.

166   BROOKE CO., VA./WV. MARRIAGE BOOK 1, 1853-1874

COOPER, John M.   book 01 page 10 line 12A
born Bel. Co., Ohio, resides West Liberty, VA. physician,
age 28 yrs. single, child of Francis & Elizabeth COOPER,
married 20 Sep 1860 VA. to Sallie B. HEDGES,
born Brooke Co., Virginia, resides Brooke Co., Virginia,
age 26 yrs. single, child of Joseph & Marg't HEDGES,
married by David HERVEY. remarks : none.

COOPER, Nancy   book 01 page 21 line 12
born Belmont Co., Ohio, resides Brooke Co., WV.
age 31 yrs. single, child of Francis & Eliza. COOPER,
married 14 Nov 1871 WV. to Bazil WELLS,
born Brooke Co., Virginia, resides Brooke Co., WV.
age 37 yrs. widow, child of Bazil & Nancy WELLS,
married by Robert R. MOORE. remarks : none.

COOPER, Valinda J.   book 01 page 20 line 32
born Belmont Co., Ohio, resides Brooke Co., West Virginia,
age 23 yrs. single, child of Francis & Elizabeth COOPER,
married 07 Mar 1871 Wellsburg, WV. to Joseph TILTON,
born Belmont Co., Ohio, resides Belmont Co., Ohio,
age 27 yrs. single, child of Joel & Cynthiann TILTON,
married by Robert R. MOORE. remarks : none.

CORNELIUS, Sarah   book 01 page 11 line 15
born Brooke Co., Virginia, resides Brooke Co., Virginia,
age 36 yrs. single, child of Elijah & Lettice CORNELIUS,
married 10 Nov 1861 VA. to George F. SMITH,
born Tuscarawas Co., Ohio, resides Brooke Co., VA.
age 28 yrs. single, child of William & Mary SMITH,
married by George W. WHARTON. remarks : none.

COTINGHAM, Mary   book 01 page 20 line 43
born Belmont Co., Ohio, resides Brooke Co., West Virginia,
age 17 yrs. single, child of Geo. & Winford COTINGHAM,
married 29 May 1871 Wellsburg, WV. to Michael WHELAN,
born Ireland, resides Brooke Co., West Virginia,
age 25 yrs. single, child of Michael & Mary WHELAN,
married by Stephen HUBER. remarks : none.

COULBURN, Thomas L.   book 01 page 09 line 18
born Somerset Co., MD., resides Somerset Co., MD. planter,
age 33 yrs. widow, child of Jas. C. & Zepporah COULBURN,
married 01 Aug 1860 VA. to Caroline A. BRIGGS,
born Hallam, Pennsylvania, resides Brooke Co., VA.
age 23 yrs. single, child of James & Nancy BRIGGS,
married by J.M. SMITH. remarks : none.

COWAN, Patrick   book 01 page 07 line 06
born Co. Galway?, Ireland, resides Wellsburg, VA. laborer,
age 43 yrs. single, child of Micheal & Mary COWAN,
married 24 Jan 1858 Wellsburg, VA. to Gracy DINSMORE,
born County Donegal?, Ireland, resides Wellsburg, Virginia,
age 32 yrs. single, child of Patrick & Nancy DINSMORE,
married by J. ROBERTS. remarks : mother Mary (LYONS).

COX, George   book 01 page 08 line 21
born Brooke Co., VA., resides Brooke Co., VA. farmer,
age 68 yrs. widow, child of George & Susannah COX,
married 29 Dec 1859 Wellsburg, VA. to Unity MILLER,
born Brooke Co., Virginia, resides Brooke Co., Virginia,
age 57 yrs. widow, child of John & Martha MUNCY,
married by Thomas M. HUDSON. remarks : none.

COX, James W.   book 01 page 04 line 47
born Brooke Co., VA., resides Brooke Co., VA. farmer,
age 28 yrs. single, child of George & unknown COX,
married 29 Nov 1855 VA. to Cornelia K. REEVES,
born Brooke Co., Virginia, resides Brooke Co., VA.
age 18 yrs. single, child of Reason & Eliza. REEVES,
married by A. ENDSLEY. remarks : married Wellsburg.

COX, Jonathan   book 01 page 16 line 10
born Brooke Co., VA. resides Brooke Co., WV.
age 32 yrs. single, child of Isreal & Ruth COX,
married 16 Jan 1867 WV. to Nancy J. WRIGHT,
born Brooke Co., VA., resides Brooke Co., VA.
age 30 yrs. single, child of John & Edie WRIGHT,
married by James FLEMING. remarks : none.

COX, Julia C.   book 01 page 21 line 09
born Brooke Co., Virginia, resides Brooke Co., WV.
age 24 yrs. widow, child of Reason & Eliza. REEVES,
married 26 Oct 1871 WV. to Isaac BICKERSTAFF,
born Beaver Co., Pennsylvania, resides Brooke Co., WV.
age 24 yrs. single, child of unk. & unk. BICKERSTAFF,
married by J.C. CASTLE. remarks : married Wellsburg.

COX, Rebecca   book 01 page 17 line 11
born Brooke Co., Virginia, resides Brooke Co., WV.
age 30 yrs. single, child of William & Nancy COX,
married 06 Sep 1866 WV. to James CHEEK,
born Rappa. Co., Virginia, resides Brooke Co., WV.
age 22 yrs. single, child of Oscar & Amanda CHEEK,
married by Thomas M. HUDSON. remarks : none.

COX, Sally W.   book 01 page 10 line 2 B
born Brooke Co., Virginia, resides Brooke Co., VA.
age 23 yrs. single, child of James & Ruth COX,
married 24 Jan 1861 VA. to Martin HUKILL,
born Brooke Co., Virginia, resides Brooke Co., VA.
age 24 yrs. single, child of Wm. & Mary HUKILL,
married by Thomas M. HUDSON. remarks : none.

COX, Wylie   book 01 page 19 line 14
born Ohio Co., VA., resides Ohio Co., WV. farmer,
age 21 yrs. single, child of Abraham & Eliza. COX,
married 15 Oct 1868 WV. to Mary DOW,
born unknown, resides Brooke Co., West Virginia,
age 25 yrs. single, child of unk. & unk. DOW,
married by James M. WARDEN. remarks : none.

CRAFT, Charles H. book 01 page 09 line 04
born Wash. Co., PA., resides Brooke Co., VA. farmer,
age 64 yrs. widow, child of George M. & Sarah CRAFT,
married 26 Oct 1859 VA. to Sarah Ann WAUGH,
born Washington Co., PA., resides Brooke Co., Virginia,
age 47 yrs. single, child of Wm. & Sarah Ann WAUGH,
married by J.M. SMITH. remarks : none.

CRAFT, Clara C. book 01 page 19 line 09
born Wellsburg, Virginia, resides near Bethany, WV.
age 22 yrs. single, child of Alexander & Jane CRAFT,
married 20 Aug 1868 WV. to William H. SCHELL,
born Bedford Co., Pennsylvania, resides Ebensburg, PA.
age 28 yrs. single, child of Henry & Maria L. SCHELL,
married by James DARSIE. remarks : married Bethany.

CRIDER, William book 01 page 07 line 11
born Brooke Co., VA., resides Brooke Co., VA. laborer,
age 29 yrs. single, child of Obediah & Jane CRIDER,
married 21 Jan 1858 VA. to Permelia HEDGES,
born Brooke Co., Virginia, resides Brooke Co., VA.
age 20 yrs. single, child of Samuel & Mary HEDGES,
married by Thomas M. HUDSON. remarks : none.

CRISS, Hanna book 01 page 18 line 22
born Brooke Co., Virginia, resides Brooke Co., WV.
age 24 yrs. single, child of Nicholas & Nancy CRISS,
married 13 Mar 1868 WV. to Hudson R. STANSBERRY,
born Brooke Co., Virginia, resides Brooke Co., West Virginia,
age 26 yrs. single, child of John & Matilda STANSBERRY,
married by H. LUCAS. remarks : none.

CRISS, Jacob P. book 01 page 14 line 52
born Washington Co., PA., resides Wash. Co., PA. farmer,
age 40 yrs. widow, child of William & Polly CRISS,
married 02 Apr 1865 Wellsburg, WV. to Caroline HESSEY,
born Brooke Co., Virginia, resides Brooke Co., West Virginia,
age 28 yrs. single, child of James & Mary Ann HESSEY,
married by George W. CHESTER. remarks : none.

CRISS, Rebecca W. book 01 page 10 line 9 B
born unknown, resides Brooke Co., Virginia,
age - - yrs. single, child of unknown & unk. CRISS,
married 07 May 1861 VA. to George MC CONNELL,
born Washington Co., PA., resides Washington Co., PA.
age - - yrs. single, child of unk. & unk. MC CONNELL,
married by James C. CAMPBELL. remarks : none.

CROTHERS, Sallie H. book 01 page 21 line 40
born Brooke Co., VA., resides Brooke Co., West Virginia,
age 23 yrs. single, child of Hugh & Ann CROTHERS,
married 25 Jun 1872 WV. to William M. WOLCOTT,
born Akron, Ohio, resides New Brighton, Pennsylvania,
age 24 yrs. single, child of Christ. R. & Philis WOLCOTT,
married by J. COUPLAND. remarks : married Wellsburg.

CRUSON, Mary E.　　　　book 01 page 17 line 23
born Jefferson Co., Ohio, resides Brooke Co., WV.
age 18 yrs. single, child of Coleman & Eliza. CRUSON,
married 01 Jan 1867　WV. to George A. WILSON,
born Ohio Co., VA., resides Ohio Co., West Virginia,
age 21 yrs. single, child of John & Sarah WILSON,
married by J. PIERCE. remarks : George W. WILSON?

CRUTH, Alexander　　　　book 01 page 05 line 14
born Ireland, resides Brooke Co., Virginia, farmer,
age 27 yrs. single, child of Andrew & Lou CRUTH,
married 17 Feb 1857　VA. to Mary Jane MC CONNELL,
born Ireland, resides Washington Co., Pennsylvania,
age 22 yrs. single, child of William & Eliza. MC CONNELL,
married by E. QUILLEN. remarks : married CRUTH house.

CRUTH, Andrew　　　　book 01 page 11 line 18
born Ireland, resides Ohio, farmer,
age 27 yrs. single, child of Andrew & Jane CRUTH,
married 12 Nov 1861　VA. to Mary Ann MC HUGH,
born Brooke Co., Virginia, resides Brooke Co., Virginia,
age 24 yrs. single, child of Alex. & Susannah MC HUGH,
married by David HERVEY. remarks : none.

CRUTH, Jane　　　　book 01 page 07 line 12
born Ireland, resides Washington Co., Pennsylvania,
age 23 yrs. single, child of unknown & unknown CRUTH,
married 24 Feb 1858　VA. to James BALLENTINE,
born Ireland, resides Washington Co., Pennsylvania,
age 23 yrs. single, child of Joseph & Rosa BALLENTINE,
married by D. HERVEY. remarks : mother Rosa (MC BRIDE).

CUNNINGHAM, Anne　　　　book 01 page 18 line 12
born Ireland, resides Brooke Co., West Virginia,
age 19 yrs. single, child of James & Susan CUNNINGHAM,
married 25 Dec 1867　WV. to Michael CONE,
born Ireland, resides Brooke Co., West Virginia,
age 24 yrs. single, child of Patrick & Elizabeth CONE,
married by Stephen HUBER. remarks : none.

CUNNINGHAM, Cyrus H.　　　　book 01 page 02 line 08
born Washington Co., PA., resides Wellsburg, VA. farmer,
age 43 yrs. widow, child of Hugh & Christine CUNNINGHAM,
married 12 Jan 1854 Wellsburg, VA. to Jane MILLER,
born Brooke Co., Virginia, resides Wellsburg, Virginia,
age 37 yrs. single, child of Nicholas & Sarah MILLER,
married by E. QUILLEN. remarks : married S. REIDLER house.

CUNNINGHAM, Ella I.　　　　book 01 page 16 line 16
born Brooke Co., Virginia, resides Brooke Co., WV.
age 21 yrs. single, child of Cyrus & Jane CUNNINGHAM,
married 31 Jan 1867　WV. to C.A. VERMILLION,
born Jefferson Co., Ohio, resides Jefferson Co., Ohio,
age 26 yrs. single, child of C. & E. VERMILLION,
married by R.T. PRICE. remarks : none.

CUNNINGHAM, Rebecca J. book 01 page 20 line 42
born Pennsylvania, resides Brooke Co., West Virginia,
age 21 yrs. single, child of unk. & unk. CUNNINGHAM,
married 28 May 1871 Wellsburg, WV. to Pierce LETZKUS,
born Wellsburg, Virginia, resides Brooke Co., West Virginia,
age 23 yrs. single, child of Richard & Apolonia LETZKUS,
married by Stephen HUBER. remarks : none.

CUPPLES, James book 01 page 12 line 40
born Allegheny Co., PA., resides Brooke Co., VA. saddler,
age 32 yrs. single, child of Joseph & Esther CUPPLES,
married 21 Apr 1862 VA. to Mary MC ELFRESH,
born Brooke Co., Virginia, resides Brooke Co., Virginia,
age 26 yrs. single, child of Zacharia & unk. MC ELFRESH,
married by E. BRINDLEY. remarks : married Wellsburg.

CURRAN, Joanna book 01 page 04 line 40
born Ireland, resides Wellsburg, Virginia,
age 21 yrs. single, child of Stephen & unknown CURRAN,
married 30 Mar 1856 Wellsburg, VA. to Joseph MC HENRY,
born Ohio, resides Wellsburg, Virginia,
age 20 yrs. single, child of William & Rachel MC HENRY,
married by A.J. ENDSLEY. remarks : none.

CURTIS, George C. book 01 page 22 line 13
born Bethany, Virginia, resides Bethany, WV. merchant,
age 22 yrs. single, child of Jacob E. & Sarah B. CURTIS,
married 15 Apr 1873 WV. to Mary RODGERS,
born Brooke Co., Virginia, resides Brooke Co., WV.
age 22 yrs. single, child of Wm. & Margaret RODGERS,
married by Robert R. MOORE. remarks : none.

D'FOSSIT, John A. book 01 page 08 line 13
born France, resides Wellsburg, Virginia,
age 32 yrs. widow, child of David & Marg't D'FOSSIT,
married 13 Feb 1859 Wellsburg, VA. to Eliza. NANGLE,
born Wellsburg, Virginia, resides Wellsburg, Virginia,
age 23 yrs. single, child of Thomas & Eliza. NANGLE,
married by S. HUBER. remarks : mother Marg't (KUNTZES).

DAILY, Elizabeth book 01 page 15 line 55
born Ireland, resides Steubenville, Ohio,
age 21 yrs. single, child of Martin & Mary DAILY,
married 29 Jun 1865 Wellsburg, WV. to John HANEY,
born Ireland, resides Hollidays Cove, West Virginia,
age 26 yrs. single, child of Michael & Mary HANEY,
married by Stephen HUBER. remarks : none.

DANNER, Berhart book 01 page 11 line 13
born Germany, resides Brooke Co., Virginia, farmer,
age 23 yrs. single, child of Lewis & Sabrina DANNER,
married 26 Sep 1861 VA. to Mary Jane BURT,
born Ohio, resides Brooke Co., Virginia,
age 24 yrs. single, child of unknown & unk. BURT,
married by S. HUBER. remarks : married Wellsburg.

DARE, Edmund book 01 page 04 line 44
born New Jersey, resides unknown, blacksmith,
age 26 yrs. single, child of Edmund & Hannah DARE,
married 08 Nov 1853 VA. to Ruth Jane STRINGER,
born Pennsylvania, resides unknown,
age 24 yrs. single, child of Robert & Ruth STRINGER,
married by G. CRANAGE. remarks: married Fowlersville.

DARRAH, Thomas J. book 01 page 08 line 16
born Allegheny Co., PA., resides Wellsburg, VA. farmer,
age 26 yrs. single, child of James & unknown DARRAH,
married 07 Apr 1859 VA. to Elizabeth KELLY,
born Mercer Co., PA., resides Wellsburg, Virginia,
age 23 yrs. single, child of Andrew & unknown KELLY,
married by George W. CHESTER. remarks: none.

DAUGHERTY, Abram M. book 01 page 22 line 40
born Monroe Co., New York, resides Barry Co., Michigan,
age 31 yrs. unknown, child of unk. & unk. DAUGHERTY,
married 24 May 1874 Wellsburg, WV. to Lucy A. YOUNG,
born Brooke Co., Virginia, resides Brooke Co., West Virginia,
age 23 yrs. unknown, child of unk. & unk. YOUNG,
married by C.K. STILLWAGON. remarks: none.

DAUGHERTY, Charles W. book 01 page 21 line 45
born Germany, resides Wellsburg, West Virginia, laborer,
age 22 yrs. single, child of Charles & Ethel DAUGHERTY,
married 12 Sep 1872 Wellsburg, WV. to Mary WHICKERLY,
born Marshall Co., Virginia, resides Wellsburg, West Virginia,
age 20 yrs. single, child of Michael & Francis WHICKERLY,
married by Stephen HUBER. remarks: none.

DAUGHERTY, George book 01 page 22 line 12
born Brooke Co., VA., resides Brooke Co., WV. laborer,
age 46 yrs. widow, child of Geo. & Dolly DAUGHERTY,
married 20 Mar 1873 WV. to Susan Ann KELLY,
born Washington Co., PA., resides Brooke Co., WV.
age 22 yrs. single, child of Whit & unknown KELLY,
married by S.H. CRAVENS. remarks: married Wellsburg.

DAUMONT, Alfred A. book 01 page 05 line 02
born N.Y.C., NY., resides Louisana, KY. hatchmaker,
age 27 yrs. single, child of P. & Z. DAUMONT,
married 03 Sep 1856 VA. to Clara A. GIST,
born Wellsburg, Virginia, resides Brooke Co., Virginia,
age 21 yrs. single, child of Cornelius H. & Isabel GIST,
married by George W. CRANAGE. remarks: none.

DAUMONT, Clara A. book 01 page 11 line 16
born Brooke Co., Virginia, resides Brooke Co., Virginia,
age 25 yrs. widow, child of Cornelius H. & Isabel GIST,
married 15 Nov 1861 VA. to Leondas BROWN,
born Knox Co., Ohio, resides Brooke Co., Virginia,
age 23 yrs. single, child of Joseph & Rachel BROWN,
married by Thomas M. HUDSON. remarks: none.

DAVIDSON, Samuel M. book 01 page 22 line 49
born Jefferson Co., Ohio, resides Steubenville, Ohio,
age 30 yrs. unknown, child of unk. & unk. DAVIDSON,
married 09 Oct 1874 Wellsburg, WV. to Minnie PERKINS,
born Brooke Co., Virginia, resides Brooke Co., WV.
age 19 yrs. unknown, child of unk. & unk. PERKINS,
married by D.W. CALDERWOOD. remarks : none.

DAVIN, Dusty book 01 page 18 line 13
born Ireland, resides Brooke Co., WV. laborer,
age 30 yrs. single, child of John & Mary DAVIN,
married 22 Jan 1868 WV. to Bridget CONNELLY,
born Ireland, resides Brooke Co., West Virginia,
age 22 yrs. single, child of Wm. & Ellen CONNELLY,
married by Stephen HUBER. remarks : none.

DAVIS, Augustus book 01 page 20 line 09
born Uniontown, PA., resides Wellsburg, WV. barber,
age 26 yrs. single, child of Jacob & Sarah Ann DAVIS,
married 01 Aug 1870 WV. to Ellen BEALL,
born Brooke Co., Virginia, resides Brooke Co., WV.
age 17 yrs. single, child of Aaron & Jane BEALL,
married by J. CASTLE. remarks : both listed as colored.

DAVIS, Isaac L. book 01 page 09 line 01
born Belmont Co., Ohio, resides Brooke Co., VA. laborer,
age 24 yrs. single, child of James & Susannah DAVIS,
married 22 Dec 1859 VA. to Elizabeth Jane ROBINSON,
born Brooke Co., Virginia, resides Brooke Co., Virginia,
age 16 yrs. single, child of Joseph S. & Eliza. ROBINSON,
married by Thomas M. HUDSON. remarks : none.

DAVIS, John book 01 page 06 line 08
born Brooke Co., VA., resides Pomeroy, Ohio, carpenter,
age -- yrs. widow, child of unknown & unk. DAVIS,
married 15 Oct 1857 VA. to Rebecca E. RIDGLEY,
born Brooke Co., Virginia, resides Brooke Co., Virginia,
age -- yrs. single, child of unknown & unk. RIDGLEY,
married by J. CAMPBELL. remarks : none.

DAVIS, Rachel book 01 page 04 line 49
born Ohio Co., Virginia, resides Castlemen's Run, VA.
age 28 yrs. single, child of Alexander & Sarah DAVIS,
married 04 Oct 1856 VA. to Tarlton WOODY,
born Winchester, Virginia, resides unknown,
age 27 yrs. single, child of Tarlton & Eliena WOODY,
married by UNKNOWN. remarks : none.

DAVIS, Rachel book 01 page 22 line 02
born unknown, resides Brooke Co., West Virginia,
age 25 yrs. single, child of unknown & unk. DAVIS,
married 28 Nov 1872 WV. to Thomas J. HAINES,
born Newark, Ohio, resides Newark, Ohio,
age 30 yrs. single, child of unk. & unk. HAINES,
married by J. CRAVENS. remarks : married Wellsburg.

DAVIS, Susan   book 01 page 22 line 26
born Jefferson Co., Ohio, resides Brooke Co., WV.
age 58 yrs. unknown, child of unk. & unk. DAVIS,
married 27 Nov 1873 WV. to James ERVIN,
born Ohio Co., Virginia, resides Jeff. Co., Ohio,
age 58 yrs. unknown, child of unk. & unk. ERVIN,
married by C.K. STILLWAGON. remarks : none.

DAVIS, Thomas M.   book 01 page 06 line 03
born Philadelphia, PA., resides Phila., PA., merchant,
age 39 yrs. widow, child of Morgan & Mary V. DAVIS,
married 11 Aug 1857 VA. to Miriam GREEN,
born Brooke Co., Virginia, resides Brooke Co., VA.
age 29 yrs. single, child of Eli & Priscilla GREEN,
married by Ezekiel QUILLEN. remarks : none.

DAWSON, Mary A.   book 01 page 08 line 19
born Jefferson Co., Ohio, resides New Alexandria, Ohio,
age 26 yrs. widow, child of Nath'l & Amelia DAWSON,
married 24 Jun 1859 VA. to John EBERLINE,
born Amsterdam, Holland, resides Steubenville, Ohio,
age 36 yrs. single, child of Johanes & Cath. EBERLINE,
married by W. MARTIN. remarks : Mrs. Mary ELLIOTT.

DEFFENBACH, N. Lee   book 01 page 22 line 24
born Montour Co., Pennsylvania, resides Williamsport, PA.
age 30 yrs. unknown, child of unk. & unk. DEFFENBACH,
married 13 Nov 1873 Wellsburg, WV. to Elizabeth GOOD,
born Brooke Co., Virginia, resides Wellsburg, West Virginia,
age 19 yrs. unknown, child of unk. & unk. GOOD,
married by Robert R. MOORE. remarks : none.

DEGARMO, Amanda   book 01 page 22 line 04
born Ohio Co., VA., resides Brooke Co., West Virginia,
age 23 yrs. single, child of John & Parthenia DEGARMO,
married 09 Jan 1873 WV. to William F. KELLY,
born Canada, resides Brooke Co., West Virginia,
age 24 yrs. single, child of John & Ellen KELLY,
married by C.P. GOODRICH. remarks : none.

DEGARMO, Anne   book 01 page 22 line 27
born Brooke Co., Virginia, resides Brooke Co., WV.
age 27 yrs. unknown, child of unk. & unk. DEGARMO,
married 28 Nov 1873 WV. to George MC CLELLAND,
born Harrison Co., Ohio, resides Brooke Co., West Virginia,
age 24 yrs. unk., child of unk. & unk. MC CLELLAND,
married by C. STILLWAGON. remarks : married Wellsburg.

DEGARMO, Margaret   book 01 page 22 line 05
born Ohio Co., Virginia, resides Brooke Co., West Virginia,
age 20 yrs. single, child of John & Parthenia DEGARMO,
married 09 Jan 1873 WV. to George DEULEY,
born Ohio Co., Virginia, resides Brooke Co., West Virginia,
age 20 yrs. single, child of Wm. W. & Marg't J. DEULEY,
married by C.P. GOODRICH. remarks : none.

DEIGHTON, Isabella book 01 page 20 line 26
born Brooke Co., Virginia, resides Wellsburg, WV.
age 31 yrs. single, child of Wm. & Sarah DEIGHTON,
married 12 Jan 1871 WV. to William A. MAYHALL,
born Brooke Co., Virginia, resides Wellsburg, West Virginia,
age 32 yrs. single, child of William H. & Jane MAYHALL,
married by D. CALDERWOOD. remarks : married Wellsburg.

DEIGHTON, John M. book 01 page 20 line 30
born Brooke Co., VA., resides Brooke Co., WV. miner,
age 26 yrs. single, child of William & Sarah DEIGHTON,
married 23 Feb 1871 Wellsburg, WV. to Hannah SAUNER,
born Germany, resides Brooke Co., West Virginia,
age 24 yrs. single, child of unknown & unknown SAUNER,
married by D.W. CALDERWOOD. remarks : none.

DEIGHTON, Margaret V. book 01 page 07 line 03
born Brooke Co., Virginia, resides Brooke Co., Virginia,
age 21 yrs. single, child of Wm. & Sarah DEIGHTON,
married 27 Dec 1857 VA. to Richard T. ROBERTS,
born Brooke Co., Virginia, resides Brooke Co., Virginia,
age 25 yrs. single, child of Wm. & Rebecca ROBERTS,
married by E. QUILLEN. remarks : married Wellsburg.

DEIGHTON, Millie book 01 page 13 line 29
born Wellsburg, VA., resides Wellsburg, West Virginia,
age 23 yrs. single, child of William & Sarah DEIGHTON,
married 30 Aug 1864 Wellsburg, WV. to Robert MACKEY,
born Ayreshire, Scotland, resides Pittsburgh, Pennsylvania,
age 22 yrs. single, child of Alexander & Rosa MACKEY,
married by Edward A. BRINDLEY. remarks : none.

DEIGHTON, Ophelia book 01 page 12 line 46
born Brooke Co., Virginia, resides Wellsburg, Virginia,
age 20 yrs. single, child of Wm. & Sarah DEIGHTON
married 13 Feb 1862 VA. to Charles Wm. HAPNER
born Wheeling, Virginia, resides Wellsburg, Virginia,
age 22 yrs. single, child of Fred. & Caroline HAPNER,
married by Edward A. BRINDLEY. remarks : none.

DEIGHTON, Ralph book 01 page 15 line 71
born Massillon, Ohio, resides Massillon, Ohio, miner,
age 39 yrs. widow, child of unk. & unk. DEIGHTON,
married 02 Jan 1866 WV. to Mary NASMITH,
born Massillon, Ohio, resides Massillon, Ohio,
age 26 yrs. single, child of Henry & Mary NASMITH,
married by G. CHESTER. remarks : married Wellsburg.

DEIGHTON, Rosetta book 01 page 03 line 33
born Brooke Co., Virginia, resides Brooke Co., VA.
age 17 yrs. single, child of Wm. & Sarah DEIGHTON,
married 01 May 1855 VA. to Andrew J. ROBERTS,
born Brooke Co., Virginia, resides Brooke Co., Virginia,
age 25 yrs. single, child of Wm. & Rebecca ROBERTS,
married by E. QUILLEN. remarks : married Wellsburg.

DEIGHTON, Sarah book 01 page 07 line 08
born Brooke Co., Virginia, resides Brooke Co., VA.
age 23 yrs. single, child of Wm. & Sarah DEIGHTON,
married 16 Feb 1858 VA. to James WILKINSON,
born Ireland, resides Brooke Co., Virginia,
age 23 yrs. single, child of Wm. & Mary WILKINSON,
married by E. QUILLEN. remarks : married Bethany.

DEMPSEY, Margarett book 01 page 05 line 05
born Co. Tipperary, Ireland, resides Wellsburg, VA.
age 21 yrs. single, child of John & Mary DEMPSEY,
married 02 Oct 1856 VA. to Thomas TIERMAN,
born Co. Dublin, Ireland, resides Wellsburg, Virginia,
age 27 yrs. single, child of Michael & Rosa TIERMAN,
married by John BRAZILL. remarks : married Wellsburg.

DENINGEN, Hugh book 01 page 22 line 23
born Ireland, resides Brooke Co., West Virginia,
age 25 yrs. unk., child of unk. & unk. DENINGEN,
married 06 Nov 1873 WV. to Sarah CLEMENS,
born Brooke Co., Virginia, resides Brooke Co., WV.
age 16 yrs. unk., child of unk. & unk. CLEMENS,
married by Joshua COUPLAND, JR. remarks : none.

DEULEY, George book 01 page 22 line 05
born Ohio Co., Virginia, resides Brooke Co., WV. farmer,
age 20 yrs. single, child of Wm. W. & Marg't J. DEULEY,
married 09 Jan 1873 WV. to Margaret DEGARMO,
born Ohio Co., Virginia, resides Brooke Co., West Virginia,
age 20 yrs. single, child of John & Parthenia DEGARMO,
married by C.P. GOODRICH. remarks : none.

DEULEY, Mary E. book 01 page 21 line 03
born Ohio Co., VA., resides Brooke Co., West Virginia,
age 23 yrs. single, child of Wm. W. & Marg't J. DEULEY,
married 30 Aug 1871 WV. to William WAY,
born Brooke Co., Virginia, resides Brooke Co., WV.
age 27 yrs. single, child of Abel & Elizabeth WAY,
married by J.C. CASTLE. remarks : none.

DEVINNEY, Charles book 01 page 05 line 06
born County Kerry, Ireland, resides unknown, laborer,
age 28 yrs. single, child of Charles & Sarah DEVINNEY,
married 15 Oct 1856 Wellsburg, VA. to Margaret O'HARA,
born Wellsburg, Virginia, resides unknown,
age 18 yrs. single, child of Samuel & Mary O'HARA,
married by John F. BRAZILL. remarks : none.

DEVORE, Ruth Ann book 01 page 16 line 02
born Brooke Co., Virginia, resides Brooke Co., WV.
age 22 yrs. single, child of John & Sarah DEVORE,
married 03 May 1866 OH. to Charles W. INGRAM,
born Beaver Co., PA., resides Brooke Co., WV.
age 26 yrs. single, child of unk. & unk. INGRAM,
married by H. PARKER. remarks : married Steubenville.

DINSMORE, Gracy book 01 page 07 line 06
born Co. Donegal?, Ireland, resides Wellsburg, Virginia,
age 32 yrs. single, child of Pat. & Nancy DINSMORE,
married 24 Jan 1858 Wellsburg, VA. to Patrick COWAN,
born Co. Galway?, Ireland, resides Wellsburg, Virginia,
age 43 yrs. single, child of Micheal & Mary COWAN,
married by J. ROBERTS. remarks : Nancy (MCKINLEY).

DODDS, Thomas book 01 page 06 line 06
born Hopewell Twp., VA., resides Brooke Co., VA.
age 37 yrs. single, child of John & Sally DODDS,
married 15 Sep 1857 VA. to Jane WAUGH,
born Hopewell Twp., VA., resides Brooke Co., VA.
age 26 yrs. single, child of David & Mariah WAUGH,
married by David HERVEY. remarks : none.

DONNELLY, Catherine book 01 page 10 line 08A
born Ireland, resides Bethany, Virginia,
age 29 yrs. widow, child of Owen & Marg't DONNELLY,
married 10 Sep 1860 Bethany, VA. to James KINDRICKS,
born Ireland, resides Bethany, Virginia,
age 34 yrs. single, child of Edw. & Marg't KINDRICKS,
married by 3. HUBER. remarks : Mrs. Cath. MC FADDEN.

DONNELLY, Margaret book 01 page 18 line 01
born Ireland, resides Wellsburg, West Virginia,
age 23 yrs. single, child of unk. & unk. DONNELLY,
married 28 Oct 1867 WV. to John B. MC NALLY,
born Pittsburgh, Pennsylvania, resides Wellsburg, WV.
age 27 yrs. single, child of Bernard & Mary MC NALLY,
married by Stephen HUBER. remarks : none.

DONOVAN, Asa O. book 01 page 08 line 07
born Brooke Co., Virginia, resides Brooke Co., VA. farmer,
age 23 yrs. single, child of Thomas & Cath. DONOVAN,
married 23 Dec 1858 VA. to Mary Ann AMSPOKER,
born Brooke Co., Virginia, resides Brooke Co., Virginia,
age 22 yrs. single, child of George & Rebecca AMSPOKER,
married by J. DAVIS. remarks : married AMSPOKER house.

DONOVAN, Ruth C. book 01 page 08 line 17
born Brooke Co., Virginia, resides Brooke Co., Virginia,
age 27 yrs. single, child of Thomas & Cath. DONOVAN,
married 13 Apr 1859 VA. to Charles P. RUSSELL,
born Tyler Co., Virginia, resides Tyler Co., Virginia,
age 35 yrs. single, child of William & Betsy RUSSELL,
married by A. MYERS. remarks : marriage record reversed.

DORLAND, George S. book 01 page 10 line 09A
born Ohio, resides Rousbury, Ohio, farmer,
age 24 yrs. single, child of Garrett & Elizabeth DORLAND,
married 09 Aug 1860 Wellsburg, VA. to Martha A. LANDIS,
born Ohio, resides Wellsburg, Virginia,
age 24 yrs. single, child of David & Charlotte LANDIS,
married by Thomas M. HUDSON. remarks : none.

DORSEY, Drusilla book 01 page 22 line 09
born Brooke Co., Virginia, resides Wellsburg, WV.
age 19 yrs. single, child of Joshua & Ann DORSEY,
married 19 Feb 1873 WV. to Thomas B. PARISH,
born Jefferson Co., Ohio, resides Wellsburg, WV.
age 27 yrs. single, child of Richard & Nancy PARISH,
married by C. GOODRICH. remarks: married Wellsburg.

DORSEY, John book 01 page 09 line 15
born Pennsylvania, resides Wheeling, Virginia, laborer,
age 21 yrs. single, child of Edward & Elizabeth DORSEY,
married 25 May 1860 Wellsburg, VA. to Bridget CLERKIN,
born Co. Coleraine, Ireland, resides Wheeling, Virginia,
age 24 yrs. single, child of Peter & Julia CLERKIN,
married by Thomas M. HUDSON. remarks: none.

DOUBLAZIER, Susan Eliza. book 01 page 02 line 18
born Brooke Co., Virginia, resides Wellsburg, Virginia,
age 18 yrs. single, child of Henry & Nancy DOUBLAZIER,
married 02 Nov 1854 Wellsburg, VA. to Edward CALENDINE,
born Brooke Co., Virginia, resides Wellsburg, Virginia,
age 23 yrs. single, child of Henry & unknown CALENDINE,
married by W.A. DAVIDSON. remarks: none.

DOUGHERTY, Matilda book 01 page 04 line 45
born Brooke Co., Virginia, resides unknown,
age 22 yrs. single, child of George & unk. DOUGHERTY,
married 15 Sep 1855 Wellsburg, VA. to David LYONS,
born Washington Co., Pennsylvania, resides unknown,
age 28 yrs. single, child of Benjamin & unknown LYONS,
married by John F. BRAZILL. remarks: none.

DOUGHERTY, Patrick book 01 page 08 line 18
born Ireland, resides Brooke Co., Virginia, laborer,
age 37 yrs. widow, child of And. & Ann DOUGHERTY,
married 26 May 1859 VA. to Martha MC GROUERTY,
born Ireland, resides Wellsburg, Virginia,
age 28 yrs. single, child of Jas. & Martha MC GROUERTY,
married by S. HUBER. remarks: mother Ann (CAGLAND).

DOW, Isaac book 01 page 20 line 08
born Morgan Co., Ohio, resides Bethany, WV. laborer,
age 45 yrs. widow, child of Isaac & Rebecca DOW,
married 21 Jul 1870 Bethany, WV. to Rosann MILLER,
born Belmont Co., Ohio, resides Bethany, West Virginia,
age 30 yrs. single, child of William & Mary MILLER,
married by William K. PENDLETON. remarks: none.

DOW, Mary book 01 page 19 line 14
born unknown, resides Brooke Co., West Virginia,
age 24 yrs. single, child of unknown & unk. DOW,
married 15 Oct 1868 WV. to Wylie COX,
born Ohio Co., Virginia, resides Ohio Co., WV.
age 21 yrs. single, child of Abraham & Eliza. COX,
married by James M. WARDEN. remarks: none.

DOW, Samantha book 01 page 11 line 31
born Ohio, resides Brooke Co., Virginia,
age 17 yrs. single, child of T. H. & Jane DOW,
married 13 Jan 1863 VA. to Henry T. SHIELDS,
born Belmont Co., Ohio, resides Brooke Co., VA.
age 21 yrs. single, child of Wm. & Anne SHIELDS,
married by W. WILLIAMSON. remarks : married Glen Higher.

DOWDEN, Frances P. book 01 page 22 line 31
born unknown, resides Brooke Co., West Virginia,
age 22 yrs. unknown, child of unk. & unk. DOWDEN,
married 18 Jan 1874 WV. to Nathan MC CAMICK,
born Monroe Co., Ohio, resides Brooke Co., WV.
age 22 yrs. unk., child of unk. & unk. MC CAMICK,
married by C. STILLWAGON. remarks : married Wellsburg.

DOWDLE, Daisy book 01 page 21 line 17
born unknown, resides Brooke Co., West Virginia,
age 20 yrs. single, child of Jonas & Charlotte DOWDLE,
married 16 Dec 1871 WV. to Martin V. BROWNLEE,
born Jefferson Co., Ohio, resides Brooke Co., West Virginia,
age 32 yrs. single, child of Thomas & Juliane BROWNLEE,
married by Joseph M. BERRY. remarks : married Wellsburg.

DOWLER, John F. book 01 page 06 line 10
born Ohio Co., Virginia, resides unknown, farmer,
age 22 yrs. single, child of Joseph & Hannah DOWLER,
married 25 Sep 1857 Wellsburg, VA. to Sue G. PARSONS,
born Jefferson Co., Ohio, resides unknown,
age 25 yrs. single, child of John & Sarah PARSONS,
married by Ezekiel QUILLEN. remarks : none.

DOWLER, Mahala book 01 page 03 line 20
born Ohio Co., Virginia, resides Brooke Co., Virginia,
age 21 yrs. single, child of Joseph & Hannah DOWLER,
married 09 Nov 1854 Wellsburg, VA. to David HALL,
born Washington Co., PA., resides Brooke Co., VA.
age 23 yrs. single, child of John & Abba HALL,
married by Charles A. HOLMES. remarks : none.

DOWNEY, Patrick book 01 page 19 line 24
born Ireland, resides Brooke Co., West Virginia, laborer,
age 35 yrs. single, child of Thomas & unknown DOWNEY,
married 08 Jan 1869 Wellsburg, WV. to Bridget BANNON,
born Ireland, resides Wellsburg, West Virginia,
age 28 yrs. single, child of Thomas & Anne BANNON,
married by Stephen HUBER. remarks : none.

DOWNEY, Rosanna book 01 page 10 line 03A
born Ireland, resides near Bethany, Virginia,
age 23 yrs. single, child of Terrance & Mary DOWNEY,
married 09 Dec 1860 Bethany, VA. to John O'HARE,
born Ireland, resides Bethany, Virginia,
age 24 yrs. single, child of Denis & Mary (HENRY) O'HARE,
married by S. HUBER. remarks : mother Mary (MC CONNELL).

DOWNEY, Susan book 01 page 10 line 10 B
   born Ireland, resides Bethany, Virginia,
   age 35 yrs. single, child of Turns & unknown DOWNEY,
   married 23 Jun 1861 Bethany, VA. to John CAVANAUGH,
   born Ireland, resides Bethany, Virginia,
   age 52 yrs. single, child of Thomas & Eliza. CAVANAUGH,
   married by Stephen HUBER. remarks : none.

DUFFY, Anne book 01 page 22 line 28
   born Jefferson Co., Ohio, resides Steubenville, Ohio,
   age 21 yrs. unknown, child of unk. & unk. DUFFY,
   married 02 Dec 1873 Wellsburg, WV. to F.H. GILMORE,
   born Jefferson Co, Ohio, resides Steubenville, Ohio,
   age 22 yrs. unknown, child of unk. & unk. GILMORE,
   married by Joshua COUPLAND, JR. remarks : none.

DUNCAN, John A. book 01 page 21 line 26
   born Wash. Co., PA., resides Brooke Co., WV. photographer,
   age 25 yrs. single, child of Norris M. & Ellen DUNCAN,
   married 29 Feb 1872 Wellsburg, WV. to Miriam FLEMING,
   born Brooke Co., Virginia, resides Brooke Co., West Virginia,
   age 21 yrs. single, child of Joseph & Naomi FLEMING,
   married by Robert R. MOORE. remarks : none.

DUNLAP, Hugh book 01 page 07 line 02
   born Ireland, resides Brooke Co., Virginia, miner,
   age 21 yrs. single, child of Hugh & Ann DUNLAP,
   married 08 Dec 1857 Wellsburg, VA. to Mary LYONS,
   born Ireland, resides Brooke Co., Virginia,
   age 24 yrs. widow, child of Jermy & Mary LYONS,
   married by Ezekiel QUILLEN. remarks : none.

DUNN, Hugh book 01 page 22 line 32
   born Ohio, resides Steubenville, Ohio,
   age 23 yrs. unknown, child of unk. & unk. DUNN,
   married 21 Jan 1874 WV. to Bridget CARDEHAM,
   born Belmont Co., Ohio, resides Brooke Co., WV.
   age 18 yrs. unk., child of unk. & unk. CARDEHAM,
   married by S. HUBER. remarks : married Wellsburg.

DUNN, Sarah E. book 01 page 17 line 03
   born Allegheny Co., PA., resides Brooke Co., WV.
   age 62 yrs. widow, child of James & Sarah BAIR,
   married 04 Sep 1867 WV. to Robert MC INTIRE,
   born Brooke Co., Virginia, resides Jeff. Co., Ohio,
   age 42 yrs. widow, child of Rob't & Ann MC INTIRE,
   married by R.T. PRICE. remarks : none.

DUNWELL, Mary Ann book 01 page 20 line 25
   born Smithfield, Ohio, resides Wellsburg, West Virginia,
   age 29 yrs. single, child of Wm. & Marg't DUNWELL,
   married 26 Dec 1870 WV. to William B. COATES,
   born Philadelphia, PA., resides Wellsburg, West Virginia,
   age 34 yrs. divorced, child of John & Esther COATES,
   married by E. BRINDLEY. remarks : married Wellsburg.

DURANT, William L. book 01 page 13 line 19
born Wash. Co., PA., resides Wash. Co., PA. teacher,
age 26 yrs. single, child of Henry & Mary DURANT,
married 25 Feb 1864 WV. to Elizabeth C. QUEST,
born Washington Co., PA., resides Wellsburg, WV.
age 25 yrs. single, child of E.C. & unknown QUEST,
married by J.A. PIERCE. remarks : married Wellsburg.

DURRETT, Henry C. book 01 page 06 line 04
born Hopkinsville, KY., resides Christ. Co., KY. professor,
age 20 yrs. single, child of Richard & Nancie DURRETT,
married 01 Sep 1857 Bethany, VA. to Sarah H. MENDEL,
born Wellsburg, Virginia, resides Bethany, Virginia,
age 20 yrs. single, child of John & Ann MENDEL,
married by A. CAMPBELL. remarks : none.

DUVALL, Isaac book 01 page 05 line 01
born Wellsburg, VA., resides Peoria, Illinois, engineer,
age 24 yrs. single, child of Gabriel & Nancy DUVALL,
married 09 Jul 1856 Wellsburg, VA. to Sarah MILLER,
born Ohio Co., Virginia, resides Wellsburg, Virginia,
age 20 yrs. single, child of Nicholas & Rebecca MILLER,
married by A.J. ENDSLEY. remarks : none.

DUVALL, William book 01 page 07 line 10
born Wellsburg, VA., resides Wellsburg, VA. machinist,
age 20 yrs. single, child of Gabriel & Nancy DUVALL,
married 07 Mar 1858 VA. to Henrietta STEWART,
born Cadiz, Ohio, resides Wellsburg, Virginia,
age 19 yrs. single, child of Jackson & Mary STEWART,
married by E.L. FLETCHER. remarks : married Wellsburg.

EASTERDAY, Lusetta book 01 page 07 line 19
born Sillinger, Germany, resides Wellsburg, Virginia,
age 35 yrs. widow, child of Andrew & Catherine LOFFER,
married 23 Aug 1858 VA. to Conrad SCHALK,
born Limbach, Germany, resides Wellsburg, Virginia,
age 32 yrs. single, child of John & Mary SCHALK,
married by S. HUBER. remarks : mother Cath. (LETZKUS).

EASTERDAY, Magdaline book 01 page 19 line 38
born Prussia, resides Wellsburg, West Virginia,
age 21 yrs. single, child of Christian & Agnes EASTERDAY,
married 25 Jul 1869 Wellsburg, WV. to Lucas WALTERS,
born Wittenberg, Germany, resides Brooke Co., West Virginia,
age 21 yrs. single, child of Marcus & Rheann WALTERS,
married by Stephen HUBER. remarks : none.

EASTERDAY, Martin book 01 page 12 line 47
born Germany, resides Wellsburg, West Virginia, shoemaker,
age 22 yrs. single, child of Christian & Agnes EASTERDAY,
married 11 Nov 1862 Wellsburg, VA. to Josephine BENTZ,
born Germany, resides Brooke Co., West Virginia,
age 22 yrs. single, child of Richus & Justina BENTZ,
married by Stephen HUBER. remarks : none.

EBBERT, William B. book 01 page 17 line 20
born Ohio Co., VA., resides Pittsburgh, PA. book keeper,
age 21 yrs. single, child of John & Charlotte EBBERT,
married 25 Dec 1866 WV. to Cornelia B. HALL,
born Brooke Co., Virginia, resides Brooke Co., WV.
age 20 yrs. single, child of Lewis & Sarah HALL,
married by Charles Louis LOOS. remarks : none.

EBERLINE, John book 01 page 08 line 19
born Amsterdam, Holland, resides Jeff. Co., Ohio, horticulture,
age 36 yrs. single, child of Johanes & Cath. S. EBERLINE,
married 24 Jun 1859 Wellsburg, VA. to Mary A. ELLIOTT,
born Jefferson Co., Ohio, resides New Alexandria, Ohio,
age 40 yrs. widow, child of Nath'l & Amelia DAWSON,
married by W.H. MARTIN. remarks : none.

ELLIOTT, Jemima book 01 page 06 line 09
born Brooke Co., Virginia, resides Brooke Co., Virginia,
age 26 yrs. single, child of James & Elizabeth ELLIOTT,
married 15 Oct 1857 VA. to Edmund CHRISTIAN,
born Whitehaven, England, resides Brooke Co., Virginia,
age 46 yrs. widow, child of Wm. & Ruth CHRISTIAN,
married by Intrepid MORSE. remarks : none.

ELLIOTT, Mary A. book 01 page 08 line 19
born Jefferson Co., Ohio, resides New Alexandria, Ohio,
age 26 yrs. widow, child of Nathaniel & Amelia DAWSON,
married 24 Jun 1859 Wellsburg, VA. to John EBERLINE,
born Amsterdam, Holland, resides Jefferson Co., Ohio,
age 36 yrs. single, child of Johanes & Cath. EBERLINE,
married by W.H. MARTIN. remarks : none.

ELSESSER, Julia book 01 page 17 line 15
born Brooke Co., Virginia, resides Brooke Co., WV.
age 17 yrs. single, child of John & Cath. ELSESSER,
married 11 Oct 1866 WV. to Peter EMIG,
born Prussia, resides Brooke Co., West Virginia,
age 30 yrs. single, child of Christopher & Mary EMIG,
married by Stephen HUBER. remarks : none.

ELSON, John Randolph book 01 page 14 line 51
born Brooke Co., VA., resides Brooke Co., WV. farmer,
age 24 yrs. single, child of Alex. M. & Charlotte ELSON,
married 09 Mar 1865 WV. to Amanda CARIENS,
born Brooke Co., Virginia, resides Brooke Co., WV.
age 22 yrs. single, child of Elliott & Sarah CARIENS,
married by I. MORSE. remarks : married CARIENS house.

EMIG, Peter book 01 page 17 line 15
born Prussia, resides Brooke Co., WV. coal miner,
age 30 yrs. single, child of Christopher & Mary EMIG,
married 11 Oct 1866 WV. to Julia ELSESSER,
born Brooke Co., Virginia, resides Brooke Co., WV.
age 17 yrs. single, child of John & Cath. ELSESSER,
married by Stephen HUBER. remarks : none.

ERVIN, James book 01 page 22 line 26
born Ohio Co., Virginia, resides Jefferson Co., Ohio,
age 58 yrs. unknown, child of unk. & unk. ERVIN,
married 27 Nov 1873 WV. to Susan DAVIS,
born Jefferson Co., Ohio, resides Brooke Co., WV.
age 58 yrs. unknown, child of unk. & unk. DAVIS,
married by C.K. STILLWAGON. remarks: none.

EVERETT, Maggie V. book 01 page 19 line 35
born Brooke Co., Virginia, resides Brooke Co., WV.
age 20 yrs. single, child of Thomas & Martha EVERETT,
married 04 May 1869 WV. to Caleb H. BRACKEN,
born Fayette Co., Pennsylvania, resides Lagrange, Ohio,
age 39 yrs. widow, child of Solomon & Sarah BRACKEN,
married by T. CRENSHAW. remarks: married Wellsburg.

FARQUER, John, Jr. book 01 page 04 line 41
born Brooke Co., VA., resides Brooke Co., VA. farmer,
age 21 yrs. single, child of John & Nancy FARQUER,
married 28 Feb 1856 VA. to Mary Ann STEWART,
born Maine, resides Wellsburg, Virginia,
age 17 yrs. single, child of Joseph & Dianna STEWART,
married by A T ENDSLEY. remarks: none.

FARQUER, Keziah book 01 page 07 line 21
born Brooke Co., Virginia, resides Brooke Co., Virginia,
age 22 yrs. single, child of Thomas & Eliza. FARQUER,
married 11 Nov 1858 Wellsburg, VA. to John LUCAS,
born Brooke Co., Virginia, resides Brooke Co., Virginia,
age 22 yrs. single, child of Samuel & Rebecca LUCAS,
married by Ezekiel QUILLEN. remarks: none.

FARQUER, Susan book 01 page 06 line 05
born Wellsburg, Virginia, resides Wellsburg, Virginia,
age 18 yrs. single, child of Thomas & Eliza. FARQUER,
married 13 Sep 1857 Wellsburg, VA. to James WEAR,
born St. Clairsville, Ohio, resides Wheeling, Virginia,
age 21 yrs. single, child of William & Comfort WEAR,
married by E.L. FLETCHER. remarks: none.

FENWICK, Edward book 01 page 04 line 54
born Jeff. Co., Ohio, resides unknown, brick layer,
age 21 yrs. single, child of James & Ann FENWICK,
married 28 Mar 1856 Wellsburg, VA. to Bell SWINER,
born Jefferson Co., Ohio, resides unknown,
age 19 yrs. single, child of Peter & Mary SWINER,
married by S.H. NESBITT. remarks: none.

FINK, Elizabeth book 01 page 04 line 56
born Germany, resides unknown,
age 40 yrs. single, child of Henry & Catherine FINK,
married 11 May 1856 Wellsburg, VA. to Jacob MAY,
born Germany, resides Wellsburg, Virginia,
age 45 yrs. widow, child of Jacob & Catherine MAY,
married by A.J. ENDSLEY. remarks: none.

FINLEY, Alexander book 01 page 12 line 50
born Co. Cavan, Ireland, resides Wellsburg, VA. laborer,
age 27 yrs. single, child of Alexander & Ann FINLEY,
married 28 Apr 1863 VA. to Mary MERRYMAN,
born Brooke Co., Virginia, resides Brooke Co., Virginia,
age 26 yrs. single, child of John & Cath. MERRYMAN,
married by J. PIERCE. remarks : married M.E. Parsonage.

FISHER, Catharine book 01 page 04 line 43
born Brooke Co., Virginia, resides unknown,
age 26 yrs. single, child of Henry & Beth Ann FISHER,
married 06 Sep 1855 VA. to Stephen CARTER,
born Brooke Co., Virginia, resides unknown,
age 34 yrs. single, child of Joseph & Catharine CARTER,
married by J.R. MEANS. remarks : none.

FISHER, Mary book 01 page 19 line 25
born Brooke Co., Virginia, resides Brooke Co., WV.
age 45 yrs. single, child of Henry & Beth Ann FISHER,
married 21 Jan 1869 WV. to John BUCKEY,
born Brooke Co., Virginia, resides Brooke Co., WV.
age 55 yrs. widow, child of Volentia & Eliza. BUCKEY,
married by Walter BROWN. remarks : none.

FITCH, K.A. book 01 page 54 line 77
born unknown, resides Wellsburg, Virginia,
age - - yrs. unknown, child of unknown & unk. FITCH,
married 10 Aug 1858 Independence, PA. to Nath'l NELSON,
born unknown, resides Wellsburg, Virginia,
age - - yrs. unknown, child of unknown & unk. NELSON,
married by J. MC CONAUGHY. remarks : none.

FITZ-PATRICK, Anne book 01 page 18 line 14
born Ireland, resides Brooke Co., West Virginia,
age 21 yrs. single, child of James & Mary FITZ-PATRICK,
married 02 Feb 1868 WV. to Bartley HINES,
born Ireland, resides Brooke Co., West Virginia,
age 30 yrs. single, child of Patrick & Ellen HINES,
married by Stephen HUBER. remarks : none.

FLEMING, Amelia Francis book 01 page 12 line 54
born Brooke Co., Virginia, resides Brooke Co., WV.
age 20 yrs. single, child of Coleman & Eliza. FLEMING,
married 15 Oct 1863 WV. to Mervin Richard ATWELL,
born Ireland, resides Brooke Co., West Virginia,
age 30 yrs. widow, child of John & Elizabeth ATWELL,
married by T. HUDSON. remarks : married FLEMING house.

FLEMING, Leander B. book 01 page 21 line 01
born Brooke Co., VA., resides Brooke Co., WV. farmer,
age 24 yrs. single, child of Coleman & Eliza. FLEMING,
married 04 Jun 1871 WV. to Mary L. WORSTELL,
born Washington Co., PA., resides Brooke Co., WV.
age 24 yrs. single, child of Isaac & Eliza. WORSTELL,
married by A.E. WARD. remarks : none.

FLEMING, Miriam book 01 page 21 line 26
born Brooke Co., Virginia, resides Brooke Co., WV.
age 21 yrs. single, child of Joseph & Naomi FLEMING,
married 29 Feb 1872 Wellsburg, WV. to John DUNCAN,
born Washington Co., PA., resides Brooke Co., WV.
age 25 yrs. single, child of Norris M. & Ellen DUNCAN,
married by Robert R. MOORE. remarks : none.

FLEMING, Nannie E. book 01 page 09 line 14
born Ohio Co., Virginia, resides Brooke Co., Virginia,
age 20 yrs. single, child of Coleman & Eliza. FLEMING,
married 26 Apr 1860 VA. to Charles L. SIMPSON,
born Brooke Co., Virginia, resides Brooke Co., Virginia,
age 30 yrs. single, child of James & Ann T. SIMPSON,
married by G. WALTERS. remarks : married mothers house.

FLOWERS, J.W. book 01 page 22 line 45
born Hancock Co. Virginia, resides Hancock Co. WV.
age 32 yrs. unknown, child of unk. & unk. FLOWERS,
married 03 Sep 1874 WV. to Mary MC CONKEY,
born Brooke Co., Virginia, resides Wellsburg, WV.
age 30 yrs. unk., child of unk. & unk. MC CONKEY,
married by George SLADE. remarks : married Wellsburg.

FORBES, James C. book 01 page 19 line 04
born Wheeling, VA., resides Wheeling, WV. merchant,
age 21 yrs. single, child of Donald & Christina FORBES,
married 03 Jul 1868 Wellsburg, WV. to Ella HARCUM,
born Wellsburg, Virginia, resides Brooke Co., WV.
age 18 yrs. single, child of Denis & Isabella HARCUM,
married by A.R. CHAPMAN. remarks : none.

FORBES, Mary book 01 page 10 line 8 B
born Ireland, resides Wellsburg, Virginia,
age 18 yrs. single, child of Thomas & Nancy FORBES,
married 07 May 1861 VA. to James W.M. CARMICHAEL,
born Washington Co., PA., resides Brooke Co., Virginia,
age 21 yrs. single, child of Geo. W. & Nancy CARMICHAEL,
married by David HERVEY. remarks : married Wellsburg.

FORBES, Thomas book 01 page 17 line 09
born Ireland, resides Wellsburg, WV. coal miner,
age 25 yrs. single, child of Thomas & Nancy FORBES,
married 09 Aug 1866 WV. to Nancy E. CARMICHAEL,
born Brooke Co., Virginia, resides Brooke Co., West Virginia,
age 19 yrs. single, child of Geo. W. & Nancy CARMICHAEL,
married by R.T. PRICE. remarks : married Wellsburg.

FORBES, William book 01 page 20 line 33
born Ireland, resides Brooke Co., WV. coal merchant,
age 35 yrs. single, child of Thomas & Nancy FORBES,
married 19 Mar 1871 WV. to Alice WILLOUGHBY.
born England, resides Brooke Co., West Virginia,
age 25 yrs. widow, child of John & unk. GELSTHORPE,
married by D. CALDERWOOD. remarks : married Wellsburg.

FORBS, James   book 01 page 06 line 11
born Ireland, resides unknown, laborer,
age 25 yrs. single, child of Thomas & Ann Beth FORBS,
married 24 Oct 1857 Wellsburg, VA. to Nancy A. JAMES,
born Tyler Co., Virginia, resides unknown,
age 25 yrs. single, child of John A. & Elizabeth JAMES,
married by Ezekiel QUILLEN. remarks : none.

FORSE, John H.   book 01 page 20 line 48
born Bernseyham, PA., resides Allegh. Co., PA. patternmaker,
age 23 yrs. single, child of David & Margaret FORSE,
married 05 Jul 1871 WV. to Elizabeth MC LAUGHLIN,
born Washington Co., PA., resides Wellsburg, West Virginia,
age 17 yrs. single, child of Andrew & Mary MC LAUGHLIN,
married by D. CALDERWOOD. remarks : married Wellsburg.

FORSYTHE, Oliver C.   book 01 page 21 line 36
born Washington Co., PA., resides Bethany, WV. tailor,
age 34 yrs. divorced, child of Thomas & Marg't FORSYTHE,
married 27 May 1872 Bethany, WV. to Sarah A. GRIMES,
born Washington Co., PA., resides Bethany, West Virginia,
age 21 yrs. single, child of Darius & Catharine GRIMES,
married by William K. PENDLETON. remarks : none.

FOSTER, Jacob   book 01 page 09 line 12
born Waldenberg, GER. resides Wellsburg, VA. schoolmaster,
age 24 yrs. single, child of Jacob & Elisabeth FOSTER,
married 09 Apr 1860 Wellsburg, VA. to Cidonia BENCE,
born Bobingen?, Germany, resides Wellsburg, Virginia,
age 20 yrs. single, child of Richus & Justina BENCE,
married by S. HUBER. remarks : mother Elisa. (KUNTZES).

FOWLER, Hiram?   book 01 page 05 line 11
born Brooke Co., VA., resides Brooke Co., VA. yeoman,
age 22 yrs. single, child of John & Sarah FOWLER,
married 27 Nov 1856 VA. to Francis SMITH,
born Brooke Co., Virginia, resides Brooke Co., Virginia,
age 18 yrs. single, child of T. Edward & unknown SMITH,
married by G. CRANAGE. remarks : T.E. SMITH deceased.

FOWLER, Nancy   book 01 page 04 line 62
born Brooke Co., Virginia, resides Brooke Co., Virginia,
age 46 yrs. widow, child of Wm. & Susannah FOWLER,
married 07 Sep 1856 VA. to Otho HEDGES,
born Brooke Co., Virginia, resides Brooke Co., Virginia,
age 55 yrs. widow, child of Joseph & Nancy HEDGES,
married by E. QUILLEN. remarks : Nancy CLAYTON.

FRANK, Amanda E.   book 01 page 11 line 12
born Brooke Co., Virginia, resides Brooke Co., Virginia,
age 21 yrs. single, child of Hogan & Fredirick FRANK,
married 11 Aug 1861 VA. to John BOWMAN,
born Brooke Co., Virginia, resides Brooke Co., Virginia,
age 25 yrs. single, child of John & Sarah A. BOWMAN,
married by Charles Louis LOOS. remarks : none.

FRANK, William book 01 page 05 line 12
born Brooke Co., Virginia, resides unknown, butcher,
age 22 yrs. single, child of Hogan & Fredirick FRANK,
married 25 Dec 1856 VA. to Mary Eliza. PATTERSON,
born Jefferson Co., Ohio, resides unknown,
age 17 yrs. single, child of Reuben & M.A. PATTERSON,
married by E. QUILLEN. remarks : married Wellsburg.

FRATER, Robert F. book 01 page 19 line 36
born Harrison Co., Ohio, resides Bel. Co., Ohio, farmer,
age 35 yrs. single, child of George & Susan FRATER,
married 11 May 1869 WV. to Rossa A. HAGGERTY,
born Brooke Co., Virginia, resides Brooke Co., WV.
age 27 yrs. single, child of Wm. & Sarah HAGGERTY,
married by J. MC CLURE. remarks : married Wheeling.

FRAZIER, George A. book 01 page 13 line 23
born Wellsburg, VA., resides Wellsburg, WV. moulder,
age 22 yrs. single, child of John & Mary FRAZIER,
married 21 Mar 1864 WV. to Carrie MC LAUGHLIN,
born Washington Co., PA., resides Wellsburg, West Virginia,
age 18 yrs. single, child of Andrew & unk. MC LAUGHLIN,
married by W.M. ROBINSON. remarks : married Wellsburg.

FRAZIER, Hiram book 01 page 21 line 04
born Belmont Co., Ohio, resides Brooke Co., WV.
age 24 yrs. single, child of Hiram & Lucinda FRAZIER,
married 31 Aug 1871 WV. to Amelia J. GREEN,
born Brooke Co., Virginia, resides Brooke Co., WV.
age 24 yrs. single, child of John F. & Nancy E. GREEN,
married by Robert R. MOORE. remarks : none.

FRAZIER, John book 01 page 09 line 17
born Winchester, VA., resides Brooke Co., VA. foundryman,
age 47 yrs. widow, child of Alexander & Mary FRAZIER,
married 24 Apr 1860 Wellsburg, VA. to Margaret MARTIN,
born Westmoreland Co., PA., resides Brooke Co., Virginia,
age 31 yrs. widow, child of Aquilla & Sarah KEITH,
married by George W. CHESTER. remarks : none.

FRAZIER, John Wesley book 01 page 14 line 40
born Wellsburg, VA., resides Wellsburg, WV. soldier,
age 19 yrs. single, child of John & unknown FRAZIER,
married 07 Dec 1864 WV. to Elizabeth BRIAN,
born Wellsburg, VA., resides Wellsburg, West Virginia,
age 19 yrs. single, child of Farnum & unknown BRIAN,
married by George W. CHESTER. remarks : none.

FRAZIER, Laura A. book 01 page 21 line 30
born Brooke Co., Virginia, resides Brooke Co., WV.
age 20 yrs. single, child of John & Nancy FRAZIER,
married 04 Apr 1872 WV. to D.W. CALDERWOOD,
born Salona, Pennsylvania, resides Plymouth, Pennsylvania,
age 35 yrs. single, child of Sam'l & Sarah CALDERWOOD,
married by E.Y. PINKERTON. remarks : married Wellsburg.

FRESHWATER, John book 01 page 16 line 15
born Brooke Co., Virginia, resides Brooke Co., WV. farmer,
age 23 yrs. single, child of Reuben & Lydia FRESHWATER,
married 29 Feb 1867 WV. to Martha CALDWELL,
born Washington Co., PA., resides Brooke Co., WV.
age 20 yrs. single, child of Andrew & Isabel CALDWELL,
married by James C. CAMPBELL. remarks : none.

FRESHWATER, Melissa A. book 01 page 19 line 17
born Carroll Co., Ohio, resides Brooke Co., West Virginia,
age 21 yrs. single, child of Geo. & Marg't FRESHWATER,
married 01 Dec 1868 WV. to Fredus A. SANDERS,
born Washington Co., PA., resides Wellsburg, WV.
age 29 yrs. single, child of B.D. & M.A. SANDERS,
married by T.A. CRENSHAW. remarks : none.

FRESHWATER, Milton R. book 01 page 20 line 47
born Brooke Co., VA., resides Brooke Co., WV. lawyer,
age 26 yrs. single, child of Geo. & Marg't FRESHWATER,
married 29 Jun 1871 WV. to Melissa PATTERSON,
born Jefferson Co., Ohio, resides Brooke Co., West Virginia,
age 26 yrs. single, child of Reuben & Martha PATTERSON,
married by Henry MATWOOD. remarks : married Wheeling.

FRESHWATER, Sarah Jane book 01 page 20 line 35
born Carroll Co., Ohio, resides Brooke Co., West Virginia,
age 26 yrs. widow, child of Reuben & Lydia FRESHWATER,
married 25 Apr 1871 Wellsburg, WV. to Robert T. JONES,
born Allegheny Co., PA., resides Brooke Co., West Virginia,
age 25 yrs. single, child of Jackson & Rebecca JONES,
married by J. CASTLE. remarks : Sarah Jane ROBINSON.

FRESHWATER, Sarah Jane book 01 page 11 line 26
born Brooke Co., Virginia, resides Brooke Co., Virginia,
age 15 yrs. single, child of Reuben & Lydia FRESHWATER,
married 30 Nov 1862 VA. to Elijah ROBINSON,
born Brooke Co., Virginia, resides Brooke Co., Virginia,
age 31 yrs. single, child of John & Nancy ROBINSON,
married by Thomas M. HUDSON. remarks : none.

FRIKE, Johanna book 01 page 13 line 25
born Prussia, resides Wellsburg, West Virginia,
age 17 yrs. single, child of unk. & Mary FRIKE,
married 16 May 1864 WV. to Gustav JOHNS,
born Bavaria, Germany, resides Steubenville, Ohio,
age 22 yrs. single, child of Mark & Mary JOHNS,
married by G. CHESTER. remarks : married Wellsburg.

FRITZ, Andrew D. book 01 page 09 line 13
born Grand Blanc, MI., resides Tiffin, Ohio, physician,
age 24 yrs. single, child of John & Sarah FRITZ,
married 13 Mar 1860 VA. to Caroline E. RUSSELL,
born Wellsburg, Virginia, resides Wellsburg, Virginia,
age 25 yrs. single, child of James & Sarah RUSSELL,
married by James ROBISON. remarks : married Wellsburg.

FULLERTON, Henry book 01 page 08 line 06
born unknown, resides unknown,
age -- yrs. unknown, child of unk. & unk. FULLERTON,
married 27 Jan 1859 VA. to Verlinda OWINGS,
born unknown, resides unknown,
age -- yrs. unknown, child of unknown & unknown OWINGS,
married by J. CAMPBELL. remarks : married E. OWINGS house.

FULTON, William P. book 01 page 21 line 43
born Licking Co., Ohio, resides Pittsburgh, PA. merchant,
age 24 yrs. single, child of Robert & Elizabeth FULTON,
married 08 Aug 1872 Wellsburg, WV. to Mattie J. WHITE,
born Brooke Co., Virginia, resides Brooke Co., West Virginia,
age 23 yrs. single, child of Thomas & Sarah WHITE,
married by Henry FULTON. remarks : none.

GAFFNEY, Michael book 01 page 10 line 4 B
born Ireland, resides Bethany, Virginia, laborer,
age 35 yrs. single, child of Matthew & Mary GAFFNEY,
married 10 Feb 1861 Bethany, VA. to Mary HOW,
born Ireland, resides Bethany, Virginia,
age 35 yrs. widow, child of Michael & Mary HOW,
married by Stephen HUBER. remarks : none.

GANT, Juliana P. book 01 page 02 line 03
born unknown, resides Wellsburg, Virginia,
age -- yrs. single, child of unknown & unk. GANT,
married 02 Feb 1854 Wellsburg, VA. to Adam KUHN,
born unknown, resides Wellsburg, Virginia,
age -- yrs. widow, child of unknown & unk. KUHN,
married by S. TOMPKINS. remarks : unsatisfactory report.

GARDNER, James C. book 01 page 06 line 01
born Eldersville, PA., resides Indianola, Iowa, farmer,
age 28 yrs. single, child of David & Nancy GARDNER,
married 21 Jul 1857 VA. to Mary E. SANDERS,
born Hollidays Cove, Virginia, resides Hollidays Cove, VA.
age 21 yrs. single, child of Benjamin & Martha SANDERS,
married by S. TEAGARDEN. remarks : married Hollidays Cove.

GARDNER, James M. book 01 page 12 line 55
born Brooke Co., VA., resides Hancock Co., WV. farmer,
age 31 yrs. single, child of James & Mary GARDNER,
married 15 Nov 1863 WV. to Mary A. MC GUIRE,
born Brooke Co., Virginia, resides Brooke Co., WV.
age 25 yrs. single, child of Luke & Jane MC GUIRE,
married by S. HUBER. remarks : married MC GUIRE house.

GARDNER, William book 01 page 02 line 04
born Wash. Co., PA. resides Wellsburg, Virginia, farmer,
age 21 yrs. single, child of David & Nancy GARDNER,
married 09 Mar 1854 VA. to Charity HENDRICKS,
born Brooke Co., Virginia, resides Wellsburg, Virginia,
age 19 yrs. single, child of John & Mary HENDRICKS,
married by Samuel D. TOMPKINS. remarks : none.

GARRETT, Robert W. book 01 page 20 line 06
born Co. Down, IRE., resides Leavenworth, KS. merchant,
age 24 yrs. single, child of Alexander & Eliza. GARRETT,
married 27 Apr 1870 WV. to Mary F. TARR,
born Brooke Co., Virginia, resides Brooke Co., WV.
age 22 yrs. single, child of Campbell & Frances TARR,
married by Robert R. MOORE. remarks : none.

GAUSE, Caroline book 01 page 19 line 06
born Germany, resides Brooke Co., West Virginia,
age 22 yrs. single, child of Lorence & Magdaline GAUSE,
married 18 Jul 1868 WV. to George LETZKUS,
born Brooke Co., Virginia, resides Brooke Co., WV.
age 23 yrs. single, child of George & Mary LETZKUS,
married by Stephen HUBER. remarks : none.

GAUSE, Diana book 01 page 19 line 20
born Germany, resides Wellsburg, West Virginia,
age 18 yrs. single, child of Joseph & Eve GAUSE,
married 29 Dec 1868 Wellsburg, WV. to Charles HALL,
born England, resides Brooke Co., West Virginia,
age 21 yrs. single, child of Matthew & Grace HALL,
married by Stephen HUBER. remarks : none.

GAUSE, Mary book 01 page 20 line 05
born Whitenberg, Germany, resides Brooke Co., WV.
age 22 yrs. single, child of Lorence & Magdaline GAUSE,
married 25 Apr 1870 Wellsburg, WV. to Peter SCHUEY,
born Nausan, Germany, resides Brooke Co., West Virginia,
age 24 yrs. single, child of Wm. & Frances SCHUEY,
married by Stephen HUBER. remarks : none.

GELSTHORPE, Alice book 01 page 20 line 33
born England, resides Brooke Co., West Virginia,
age 25 yrs. widow, child of John & unk. GELSTHORPE,
married 19 Mar 1871 WV. to William FORBES,
born Ireland, resides Brooke Co., West Virginia,
age 35 yrs. single, child of Thomas & Nancy FORBES,
married by D. CALDERWOOD. remarks : Alice WILLOUGHBY.

GEORGE, James book 01 page 19 line 26
born Washington Co., PA., resides Fulton Co., IL. farmer,
age 38 yrs. single, child of Thomas & Sarah GEORGE,
married 19 Jan 1869 WV. to Mary L. BUCKEY,
born Brooke Co., Virginia, resides Brooke Co., WV.
age 25 yrs. single, child of John & Elizabeth BUCKEY,
married by H. CREE. remarks : none.

GEORGE, Samuel book 01 page 03 line 24
born Wash. Co., PA., resides Brooke Co., VA. merchant,
age 27 yrs. single, child of Thomas & Sarah GEORGE,
married 09 Nov 1854 Wellsburg, VA. to Elenora MILLER,
born Brooke Co., Virginia, resides Brooke Co., Virginia,
age 20 yrs. single, child of James W. & Ellen MILLER,
married by Ezekiel QUILLEN. remarks : none.

GEORGE, Samuel   book 01 page 07 line 17
born Wash. Co., PA., resides Wellsburg, VA. grocer,
age 31 yrs. widow, child of Thomas & Sarah GEORGE,
married 15 Jul 1858 VA. to Elizabeth KIMBERLAND,
born Wellsburg, Virginia, resides Wellsburg, Virginia,
age 20 yrs. single, child of Henry & Mary KIMBERLAND,
married by Ezekiel QUILLEN. remarks : married Wellsburg.

GIFFORD, James E.   book 01 page 19 line 30
born Albany Co., NY., resides Brooke Co., WV. farmer,
age 22 yrs. single, child of Philip & Hannah GIFFORD,
married 31 Dec 1868 WV. to Mary E. HUPP,
born Brooke Co., Virginia, resides Brooke Co., WV.
age 16 yrs. single, child of Isaac & Mary A. HUPP,
married by James M. WARDEN. remarks : none.

GILBERT, Bridget   book 01 page 15 line 61
born Ireland, resides Ireland,
age 22 yrs. single, child of Charles & H. GILBERT,
married 11 Sep 1865 WV. to Edward BALLETT,
born Ireland, resides Ireland,
age 20 yrs. single, child of P. & C. BALLETT,
married by S. HUBER. remarks . married Wellsburg.

GILMORE, F.H.   book 01 page 22 line 28
born Jefferson Co., Ohio, resides Steubenville, Ohio,
age 22 yrs. unknown, child of unk. & unk. GILMORE,
married 02 Dec 1873 Wellsburg, WV. to Anne DUFFY,
born Jefferson Co., Ohio, resides Steubenville, Ohio,
age 21 yrs. unknown, child of unk. & unk. DUFFY,
married by Joshua COUPLAND, JR. remarks : none.

GIST, Clara A.   book 01 page 05 line 02
born Wellsburg, Virginia, resides Brooke Co., Virginia,
age 21 yrs. single, child of Cornelius H. & Isabel GIST,
married 03 Sep 1856 VA. to Alfred A. DAUMONT,
born New York City, New York, resides Louisana, KY.
age 27 yrs. single, child of P. & Z. DAUMONT,
married by George W. CRANAGE. remarks : none.

GIST, Clara A.   book 01 page 11 line 16
born Brooke Co., Virginia, resides Brooke Co., Virginia,
age 25 yrs. widow, child of Cornelius H. & Isabel GIST,
married 15 Nov 1861 VA. to Leondas BROWN,
born Knox Co., Ohio, resides Brooke Co., Virginia,
age 23 yrs. single, child of Joseph & Rachel BROWN,
married by T. HUDSON. remarks : Clara A. DAUMONT.

GIST, Sarah B.   book 01 page 11 line 32
born Brooke Co., Virginia, resides Brooke Co., Virginia,
age 25 yrs. single, child of Cornelius H. & Isabel GIST,
married 26 Nov 1862 VA. to John C. REEVES,
born Brooke Co., Virginia, resides Brooke Co., Virginia,
age 28 yrs. single, child of Reason & Elizabeth REEVES,
married by T. HUDSON. remarks : married B. BEALL'S house.

BROOKE CO., VA./WV. MARRIAGE BOOK 1, 1853-1874   191

GIST, William H.   book 01 page 19 line 39
born Brooke Co., VA., resides St. Louis, MO. farmer,
age 26 yrs. single, child of Thomas & Mary GIST,
married 09 Sep 1869 WV. to Callie BURNS,
born Jefferson Co., Ohio, resides Brooke Co., WV.
age 25 yrs. single, child of unk. & unk. BURNS,
married by A.R. CHAPMAN. remarks : none.

GLASS, Francis C.   book 01 page 21 line 41
born Armstrong Co., PA. resides Wellsburg, WV.
age 24 yrs. single, child of Alfred & Eleanor GLASS,
married 05 Sep 1872 WV. to Ella V. WRIGHTMAN,
born Allegheny Co., PA., resides Wellsburg, WV.
age 23 yrs. single, child of unk. & unk. WRIGHTMAN,
married by E. MATHEWS. remarks : married Wellsburg.

GLASS, James   book 01 page 10 line 5 B
born unknown, resides unknown,
age - - yrs. unknown, child of unk. & unk. GLASS,
married 07 Mar 1861 VA. to Anne G. WILLIAMSON,
born unknown, resides unknown,
age - - yrs. unk., child of unk. & unk. WILLIAMSON,
married by James C. CAMPBELL. remarks : none.

GLASS, John J.   book 01 page 16 line 05
born Pennsylvania, resides Pennsylvania, farmer,
age 28 yrs. single, child of James & Sidney GLASS,
married 16 May 1866 WV. to Wealthy E. MC DUGAN,
born Brooke Co., Virginia, resides Brooke Co., WV.
age 20 yrs. single, child of unk. & unk. MC DUGAN,
married by Charles Louis LOOS. remarks : none.

GLASS, Margaret   book 01 page 18 line 17
born Brooke Co., Virginia, resides Brooke Co., WV.
age 22 yrs. single, child of James & Sidney GLASS,
married 20 Feb 1868 WV. to Robert M. LAZEAR,
born Brooke Co., Virginia, resides Brooke Co., WV.
age 25 yrs. single, child of Jerome & Susan LAZEAR,
married by William F. POOR. remarks : none.

GLASS, Robert   book 01 page 22 line 37
born Brooke Co., Virginia, resides Wellsburg, WV.
age 23 yrs. unknown, child of unk. & unk. GLASS,
married 20 Feb 1874 WV. to Ellie VANSICKLE,
born Brooke Co., Virginia, resides Wellsburg, WV.
age 18 yrs. unk., child of unk. & unk. VANSICKLE,
married by C. STILLWAGON. remarks : married Wellsburg.

GLASS, Terrissa   book 01 page 18 line 15
born Jefferson Co., Ohio, resides Brooke Co., WV.
age 19 yrs. single, child of Henry & unk. GLASS,
married 18 Feb 1868 WV. to Robert M. SWORDS,
born Jefferson Co., Ohio, resides Brooke Co., WV.
age 38 yrs. single, child of Finey & Sally SWORDS,
married by Stephen HUBER. remarks : none.

GLENN, Robert S. book 01 page 13 line 14
born Wash. Co., PA., resides Wash. Co., PA. dentist,
age 38 yrs. single, child of William & Sarah GLENN,
married 22 Dec 1863 Wellsburg, WV. to Emily JEFFERS,
born Brooke Co., Virginia, resides Wellsburg, West Virginia,
age 26 yrs. single, child of John & Harriet JEFFERS,
married by William K. PENDLETON. remarks: none.

GOOD, Elizabeth I. book 01 page 22 line 24
born Brooke Co., VA., resides Wellsburg, West Virginia,
age 19 yrs. unknown, child of unknown & unk. GOOD,
married 13 Nov 1873 WV. to N. Lee DEFFENBACH,
born Montour Co., PA., resides Williamsport, PA.
age 30 yrs. unk., child of unk. & unk. DEFFENBACH,
married by R.R. MOORE. remarks: married Wellsburg.

GORDON, Anthony book 01 page 15 line 59
born Ireland, resides Pittsburgh, Pennsylvania, laborer,
age 23 yrs. single, child of Anthony & Mary GORDON,
married 05 Sep 1865 Wellsburg, WV. to Catharine CAIN,
born Ireland, resides Pittsburgh, Pennsylvania,
age 20 yrs. single, child of James & Ellen CAIN,
married by Stephen HUBER. remarks: none.

GORDON, John E. book 01 page 21 line 14
born Wash. Co., PA., resides Brooke Co., WV. farmer,
age 24 yrs. single, child of William & Eliza. GORDON,
married 26 Nov 1871 Wellsburg, WV. to Mary J. MARSH,
born Brooke Co., Virginia, resides Brooke Co., West Virginia,
age 23 yrs. single, child of Thomas & Elizabeth MARSH,
married by J.C. CASTLE. remarks: none.

GORDON, Samuel book 01 page 13 line 18
born Belmont Co., Ohio, resides Jeff. Co., Ohio, teacher,
age 22 yrs. single, child of David & Elizabeth GORDON,
married 22 Feb 1864 WV. to Cynthia Ann HALL,
born Jefferson Co., Ohio, resides Belmont Co., Ohio,
age 18 yrs. single, child of Clarkson & Mary HALL,
married by J.A. PIERCE. remarks: married Wellsburg.

GOUDY, Mary R. book 01 page 17 line 25
born Brooke Co., Virginia, resides Brooke Co., WV.
age 23 yrs. single, child of Robert & Nancy GOUDY,
married 24 Oct 1867 WV. to John BLANKENSOP,
born Brooke Co., Virginia, resides Wellsburg, West Virginia,
age 34 yrs. single, child of Peter & Susan BLANKENSOP,
married by Alexander E. ANDERSON. remarks: none.

GOURLEY, James M. book 01 page 07 line 16
born unknown, resides Brooke Co., Virginia, farmer,
age 28 yrs. single, child of John & unk. GOURLEY,
married 06 Jul 1858 VA. to Catherine T. WALKER,
born unknown, resides Brooke Co., Virginia,
age 20 yrs. single, child of unknown & unknown WALKER,
married by J. CAMPBELL. remarks: married CAMPBELL house.

GOVER, Clara book 01 page 05 line 13
born Virginia, resides Brooke Co., Virginia,
age 26 yrs. single, child of Jacob & Sarah GOVER,
married 25 Jan 1857 VA. to Samuel RUSSELL,
born Brooke Co., Virginia, resides Brooke Co., VA.
age 40 yrs. single, child of John & Eliza. RUSSELL,
married by E. QUILLEN. remarks : married Wellsburg.

GREEN, Amelia J. book 01 page 21 line 04
born Brooke Co., Virginia, resides Brooke Co., WV.
age 24 yrs. single, child of John F. & Nancy E. GREEN,
married 31 Aug 1871 WV. to Hiram FRAZIER,
born Belmont Co., Ohio, resides Brooke Co., WV.
age 24 yrs. single, child of Hiram & Lucinda FRAZIER,
married by Robert R. MOORE. remarks : none.

GREEN, Arabella V. book 01 page 23 line 03
born Brooke Co., Virginia, resides Brooke Co., WV.
age 19 yrs. unknown, child of unk. & unk. GREEN,
married 23 Sep 1874 WV. to George W. SCAMAHORN,
born Jefferson Co., Ohio, resides Jefferson Co., Ohio,
age 24 yrs. unknown, child of unk. & unk. SCAMAHORN,
married by James F. HUDDLESTON. remarks : none.

GREEN, Callie S. book 01 page 11 line 23
born Brooke Co., Virginia, resides Brooke Co., VA.
age 25 yrs. single, child of Wm. E. & Eliza. GREEN,
married 28 Aug 1862 VA. to Leonard C. HALL,
born Hamilton Co., Ohio, resides Wellsburg, VA.
age 20 yrs. single, child of F.P. & Barbara HALL,
married by William M. ROBINSON. remarks : none.

GREEN, Caroline book 01 page 15 line 67
born Wellsburg, Virginia, resides Wellsburg, WV.
age 25 yrs. widow, child of Wm. & Elizabeth GREEN,
married 02 Nov 1865 Wellsburg, WV. to Wm. SHRINER,
born Jefferson Co., Ohio, resides Wellsburg, West Virginia,
age 23 yrs. single, child of unknown & unk. SHRINER,
married by J. BROWN. remarks : Mrs. Caroline HALL.

GREEN, Drusilla book 01 page 17 line 26
born Brooke Co., Virginia, resides Brooke Co., WV.
age 20 yrs. single, child of Wm. E. & Eliza. GREEN,
married 05 Nov 1867 WV. to I.L. RICHARDSON,
born Washington Co., PA., resides Marietta, Ohio,
age 25 yrs. single, child of Isaac & Nancy RICHARDSON,
married by J.A. PIERCE. remarks : none.

GREEN, Jennie May book 01 page 22 line 25
born Brooke Co., Virginia, resides Brooke Co., WV.
age 22 yrs. unknown, child of unk. & unk. GREEN,
married 20 Nov 1873 WV. to Madison W. PARK,
born Jackson Co., VA., resides Jackson Co., WV.
age 23 yrs. unknown, child of unk. & unk. PARK,
married by Jonathan CROSS. remarks : none.

GREEN, Marshall S. book 01 page 21 line 05
born Brooke Co., VA., resides Brooke Co., WV. farmer,
age 26 yrs. single, child of William E. & Eliza. GREEN,
married 21 Sep 1871 WV. to Jennie BACHELL,
born Brooke Co., Virginia, resides Brooke Co., WV.
age 21 yrs. single, child of John & Jane BACHELL,
married by J.C. CASTLE. remarks: none.

GREEN, Miriam book 01 page 06 line 03
born Brooke Co., Virginia, resides Brooke Co., VA.
age 29 yrs. single, child of Eli & Priscilla GREEN,
married 11 Aug 1857 VA. to Thomas M. DAVIS,
born Philadelphia, PA., resides Philadelphia, PA.
age 39 yrs. widow, child of Morgan & Mary V. DAVIS,
married by Ezekiel QUILLEN. remarks: none.

GREEN, Sarah book 01 page 17 line 16
born Brooke Co., Virginia, resides Brooke Co., WV.
age 23 yrs. single, child of William & unk. GREEN,
married 11 Oct 1866 WV. to William D. LINTON,
born Jefferson Co., Ohio, resides Jefferson Co., Ohio,
age 26 yrs. single, child of Benjamin & Ann LINTON,
married by J.A. PIERCE. remarks: married Wellsburg.

GREEN, Thomas Hood book 01 page 19 line 48
born Jeff. Co., Ohio, resides Jeff. Co., Ohio, farmer,
age 21 yrs. single, child of Henry & Nancy GREEN,
married 24 Feb 1870 WV. to Sarah BOWMAN,
born Brooke Co., Virginia, resides Brooke Co., WV.
age 22 yrs. single, child of John & Sarah BOWMAN,
married by Robert R. MOORE. remarks: none.

GREEN, William L. book 01 page 07 line 14
born Frederick Co., Virginia, resides Brooke Co., VA.
age 24 yrs. single, child of William & Eliza. GREEN,
married 25 May 1858 VA. to Sarah E. ANTILL,
born Johnson Co.?, Illinois, resides Brooke Co., VA.
age 16 yrs. single, child of Thomas & Mary ANTILL,
married by E. QUILLEN. remarks: married Wellsburg.

GRIFFITH, Jacob B. book 01 page 11 line 27
born Ohio, resides Brooke Co., VA. shoemaker,
age 28 yrs. single, child of M.E. & F. GRIFFITH,
married 02 Oct 1862 VA. to Rebecca M. COLE,
born Virginia, resides Brooke Co., Virginia,
age 23 yrs. single, child of William & Catherine COLE,
married by William M. ROBINSON. remarks: none.

GRIFFITH, John A. book 01 page 10 line 07A
born Hollidays Cove, VA., resides H. Cove VA. farmer,
age 30 yrs. single, child of A.W. & Nancy A. GRIFFITH,
married 15 Feb 1860 VA. to Helen OWENS,
born Brooke Co., Virginia, resides Brooke Co., Virginia,
age 23 yrs. single, child of Ephraim & Blanche OWENS,
married by J.Y. CALHOUN. remarks: none.

GRIMES, Lucy book 01 page 22 line 44
born Brooke Co., VA., resides Wellsburg, West Virginia,
age 22 yrs. unknown, child of unknown & unk. GRIMES,
married 26 Jun 1874 Wellsburg, WV. to Frank WILLIAMS,
born Brooke Co., Virginia, resides Wellsburg, West Virginia,
age 24 yrs. unknown, child of unk. & unk. WILLIAMS,
married by Thomas M. HUDSON. remarks : none.

GRIMES, Sarah A. book 01 page 21 line 36
born Washington Co., PA., resides Bethany, WV.
age 21 yrs. single, child of Darius & Cath. GRIMES,
married 27 May 1872 WV. to Oliver C. FORSYTHE,
born Washington Co., PA., resides Bethany, West Virginia,
age 34 yrs. divorced, child of Thos. & Marg't FORSYTHE,
married by W. PENDLETON. remarks : married Bethany.

GUNION, James book 01 page 21 line 23
born Jeff. Co., Ohio, resides Brooke Co., WV. farmer,
age 23 yrs. single, child of Henry & Eliza. GUNION,
married 18 Jan 1872 WV. to Mary WHITE,
born unknown, resides Brooke Co., West Virginia,
age 19 yrs. single, child of unk. & unk. WHITE,
married by J.W. KESLER. remarks : none.

GUNION, Margaret book 01 page 18 line 10
born Jefferson Co., Ohio, resides Brooke Co., WV.
age 21 yrs. single, child of Henry & Eliza. GUNION,
married 09 Jan 1868 WV. to John A. ADAMS,
born Brooke Co., Virginia, resides Brooke Co., WV.
age 25 yrs. single, child of John & Maria ADAMS,
married by J.A. PIERCE. remarks : none.

GUNION, Wilson book 01 page 09 line 20
born Jeff. Co., Ohio, resides Wellsburg, VA. miner,
age 26 yrs. single, child of Henry & Eliza. GUNION,
married 26 Sep 1860 VA. to Rebecca BRANNON,
born Washington Co., PA., resides Wellsburg, Virginia,
age 24 yrs. single, child of William & Jane BRANNON,
married by G. CHESTER. remarks : married Wellsburg.

HAGGERTY, Rossa A. book 01 page 19 line 36
born Brooke Co., Virginia, resides Brooke Co., WV.
age 27 yrs. single, child of Wm. & Sarah HAGGERTY,
married 11 May 1869 WV. to Robert F. FRATER,
born Harrison Co., Ohio, resides Belmont Co., Ohio,
age 35 yrs. single, child of George & Susan FRATER,
married by J. MC CLURE. remarks : married Wheeling.

HAINES, Thomas J. book 01 page 22 line 02
born Newark, Ohio, resides Newark, Ohio, laborer,
age 30 yrs. single, child of unk. & unk. HAINES,
married 28 Nov 1872 WV. to Rachel DAVIS,
born unknown, resides Brooke Co., West Virginia,
age 25 yrs. single, child of unk. & unk. DAVIS,
married by S. CRAVENS. remarks : married Wellsburg.

HALL, Caroline book 01 page 15 line 67
born Wellsburg, Virginia, resides Wellsburg, WV.
age 25 yrs. widow, child of Wm. & Eliza. GREEN,
married 02 Nov 1865 WV. to William SHRINER,
born Jefferson Co., Ohio, resides Wellsburg, WV.
age 23 yrs. single, child of unk. & unk. SHRINER,
married by J. BROWN. remarks: married Wellsburg.

HALL, Charles book 01 page 19 line 20
born England, resides Brooke Co., WV. miner,
age 21 yrs. single, child of Matthew & Grace HALL,
married 29 Dec 1868 Wellsburg, WV. to Diana GAUSE,
born Germany, resides Wellsburg, West Virginia,
age 18 yrs. single, child of Joseph & Eve GAUSE,
married by Stephen HUBER. remarks: none.

HALL, Cornelia B. book 01 page 17 line 20
born Brooke Co., Virginia, resides Brooke Co., WV.
age 20 yrs. single, child of Lewis & Sarah HALL,
married 25 Dec 1866 WV. to William B. EBBERT,
born Ohio Co., VA., resides Pittsburgh, Pennsylvania,
age 21 yrs. single, child of John & Charlotte EBBERT,
married by Charles L. LOOS. remarks: none

HALL, Cynthia Ann book 01 page 13 line 18
born Jefferson Co., Ohio, resides Belmont Co., Ohio,
age 18 yrs. single, child of Clarkson & Mary HALL,
married 22 Feb 1864 WV. to Samuel GORDON,
born Belmont Co., Ohio, resides Jefferson Co., Ohio,
age 22 yrs. single, child of David & Eliza. GORDON,
married by J. PIERCE. remarks: married Wellsburg.

HALL, David book 01 page 03 line 20
born Wash. Co., PA., resides Brooke Co., VA. farmer,
age 23 yrs. single, child of John & Abba HALL,
married 09 Nov 1854 VA. to Mahala DOWLER,
born Ohio Co., Virginia, resides Brooke Co., Virginia,
age 21 yrs. single, child of Joseph & Hannah DOWLER,
married by C. HOLMES. remarks: married Wellsburg.

HALL, Elizabeth book 01 page 20 line 45
born Brooke Co., Virginia, resides Wellsburg, WV.
age 21 yrs. single, child of F.P. & unknown HALL,
married 04 Jun 1871 WV. to James L. MILLER,
born Wheeling, Virginia, resides Brooke Co., WV.
age 22 yrs. single, child of Robert & Eliza. MILLER,
married by Robert R. MOORE. remarks: none.

HALL, Leonard C. book 01 page 11 line 23
born Hamilton Co., Ohio, resides Wellsburg, VA. grocer,
age 20 yrs. single, child of F.P. & Barbara HALL,
married 28 Aug 1862 VA. to Callie S. GREEN,
born Brooke Co., Virginia, resides Brooke Co., Virginia,
age 25 yrs. single, child of Wm. E. & Elizabeth GREEN,
married by William M. ROBINSON. remarks: none.

HALL, Lewis C. book 01 page 18 line 02
born Lagrange, Ohio, resides Wellsburg, WV. farmer,
age 27 yrs. single, child of Sewell & Susan HALL,
married 24 Nov 1867 WV. to Ella PADEN,
born Wellsburg, Virginia, resides Wellsburg, WV.
age 23 yrs. single, child of Wm. & Rebecca PADEN,
married by Edward A. BRINDLEY. remarks: none.

HALL, Mary E. book 01 page 21 line 24
born Brooke Co., Virginia, resides Brooke Co., WV.
age 23 yrs. single, child of Lewis & Sallie HALL,
married 15 Feb 1872 WV. to James A. MC KEE,
born Putnam Co., Indiana, resides Cincinnati, Ohio,
age 24 yrs. single, child of Melvin & Matilda MC KEE,
married by E.Y. PINKERTON. remarks: none.

HALLIE, Micha book 01 page 20 line 17
born Brooke Co., Virginia, resides Brooke Co., WV.
age 35 yrs. single, child of William & unk. HALLIE,
married 26 Sep 1870 Bethany, WV. to William PRIEST,
born Brooke Co., Virginia, resides Christian Co., IL.
age 60 yrs. widow, child of William & Eliza. PRIEST,
married by William K. PENDLETON. remarks: none.

HALSTED, Mary A. book 01 page 22 line 48
born Washington Co., PA., resides Brooke Co., WV.
age 20 yrs. unknown, child of unk. & unk. HALSTED,
married 14 Oct 1874 WV. to Mathew WILLIAMSON,
born Brooke Co., Virginia, resides Brooke Co., WV.
age 33 yrs. unk., child of unk. & unk. WILLIAMSON,
married by W.T. WILSON. remarks: none.

HAMILTON, James S. book 01 page 10 line 6 B
born Columbiana Co., Ohio, resides Han. Co., VA. miller,
age 30 yrs. single, child of William & unk. HAMILTON,
married 05 Mar 1861 VA. to Anne E. MAHON,
born Brooke Co., Virginia, resides Brooke Co., Virginia,
age 25 yrs. single, child of Thomas & Judith MAHON,
married by George G. WALTERS. remarks: none.

HAMMOND, Elizabeth book 01 page 10 line 10A
born Brooke Co., Virginia, resides Brooke Co., Virginia,
age 22 yrs. single, child of Talbott & Hannah HAMMOND,
married 18 Dec 1860 VA. to James WAUGH,
born Brooke Co., Virginia, resides Brooke Co., Virginia,
age 27 yrs. widow, child of Richard & Eliza. WAUGH,
married by David HERVEY. remarks: none.

HANEY, Henry book 01 page 16 line 22
born Washington Co., PA., resides Wellsburg, WV.
age 34 yrs. single, child of John & Jane HANEY,
married 20 Jun 1867 WV. to Clara E. BRIGGS,
born Washington Co., PA., resides Brooke Co., WV.
age 26 yrs. single, child of James & Nancy BRIGGS,
married by Edward A. BRINDLEY. remarks: none.

HANEY, James M. book 01 page 16 line 06
born Wellsburg, Virginia, resides Brooke Co., WV.
age 26 yrs. single, child of John & Sarah HANEY,
married 12 Jun 1866 WV. to Olivia PARSONS,
born Wellsburg, Virginia, resides Wellsburg, WV.
age 22 yrs. single, child of unk. & unk. PARSONS,
married by Charles Louis LOOS. remarks: none.

HANEY, John book 01 page 15 line 55
born Ireland, resides Hollidays Cove, WV. laborer,
age 26 yrs. single, child of Michael & Mary HANEY,
married 29 Jun 1865 WV. to Elizabeth DAILY,
born Ireland, resides Steubenville, Ohio,
age 21 yrs. single, child of Martin & Mary DAILY,
married by S. HUBER. remarks: married Wellsburg.

HANEY, Margaret book 01 page 20 line 03
born Ohio, resides Wellsburg, West Virginia,
age 41 yrs. single, child of unk. & unk. HANEY,
married 26 Mar 1870 WV. to Robert THOMPSON,
born Washington Co., PA., resides Wellsburg, West Virginia,
age 55 yrs. widow, child of Rob't & Phoebe THOMPSON,
married by Charles L. LOOS. remarks: married Wellsburg.

HANNA, J.G. book 01 page 18 line 20
born Wash. Co., PA., resides Brooke Co., WV. farmer,
age 30 yrs. widow, child of Richard & Mary HANNA,
married 12 Mar 1868 WV. to Jane A. SCOTT,
born Brooke Co., Virginia, resides Brooke Co., WV.
age 21 yrs. single, child of John & Jane SCOTT,
married by A.J. LANE. remarks: none.

HAPNER, Charles W. book 01 page 12 line 46
born Wheeling, VA., resides Wellsburg, VA. saloon keeper,
age 22 yrs. single, child of Fred. W. & Caroline HAPNER,
married 13 Feb 1862 VA. to Ophelia DEIGHTON,
born Brooke Co., Virginia, resides Wellsburg, Virginia,
age 20 yrs. single, child of William & Sarah DEIGHTON,
married by Edward A. BRINDLEY. remarks: none.

HARCUM, Ella book 01 page 19 line 04
born Wellsburg, Virginia, resides Brooke Co., WV.
age 18 yrs. single, child of Denis & Isabella HARCUM,
married 03 Jul 1868 WV. to James C. FORBES,
born Wheeling, Virginia, resides Wheeling, West Virginia,
age 21 yrs. single, child of Donald & Christina FORBES,
married by A.R. CHAPMAN. remarks: married Wellsburg.

HARDING, Joseph E. book 01 page 18 line 05
born Lewiston, Maine, resides Brooke Co., WV. city hall,
age 25 yrs. single, child of J.B. & Mary Ann HARDING,
married 25 Dec 1867 WV. to Minerva J. QUEST,
born Middletown, Pennsylvania, resides Brooke Co., WV.
age 21 yrs. single, child of Sam'l S. & Martha C. QUEST,
married by Edward A. BRINDLEY. remarks: none.

HARDING, Margaret Ann book 01 page 09 line 06
born So. Brunswick, NH., resides Wellsburg, Virginia,
age 24 yrs. single, child of J.B. & Mary HARDING,
married 18 Oct 1859 VA. to Campbell KIMBERLAND,
born Wellsburg, Virginia, resides Wellsburg, Virginia,
age 27 yrs. single, child of Henry & Mary KIMBERLAND,
married by J.M. SMITH. remarks : married Wellsburg.

HARRIS, Sarah J. book 01 page 08 line 15
born Jefferson Co., Ohio, resides Brooke Co., Virginia,
age 23 yrs. single, child of unknown & unk. HARRIS,
married 24 Mar 1859 VA. to Jasper BROWNING,
born Brooke Co., Virginia, resides Brooke Co., VA.
age 26 yrs. single, child of Arnold & Cath. BROWNING,
married by H. LUCAS. remarks : HARRIS parents deceased.

HARVEY, Amos D. book 01 page 19 line 15
born Pennsylvania, resides West Virginia, papermaker,
age 25 yrs. single, child of W.H. & Alina HARVEY,
married 29 Oct 1868 WV. to Narcissa KIRKER,
born Ohio, resides West Virginia,
age 25 yrs. single, child of W.C. & Mary C. KIRKER,
married by R. PRICE. remarks : married Wellsburg.

HARVEY, Wm. Hamilton book 01 page 20 line 13
born Beaver Co., PA., resides Brooke Co., WV. papermaker,
age 23 yrs. single, child of William H. & Jane E. HARVEY,
married 15 Sep 1870 Wellsburg, WV. to Virginia LEWIS,
born Ohio, resides Wellsburg, West Virginia,
age 20 yrs. single, child of Henry & unknown LEWIS,
married by Edward A. BRINDLEY. remarks : none.

HASLETT, William K. book 01 page 23 line 05
born Brooke Co., Virginia, resides Brooke Co., WV.
age 24 yrs. unknown, child of unk. & unk. HASLETT,
married 03 Dec 1874 WV. to Rachel B. CARUTH,
born Brooke Co., Virginia, resides Brooke Co., WV.
age 19 yrs. unknown, child of unk. & unk. CARUTH,
married by David HERVEY. remarks : none.

HAYS, Elizabeth book 01 page 02 line 01
born Brooke Co., Virginia, resides Brooke Co., VA.
age 21 yrs. single, child of Enoch & Nancy HAYS,
married 09 Aug 1854 VA. to James JACK,
born Washington Co., PA., resides Brooke Co., VA.
age 21 yrs. single, child of David & Jane JACK,
married by David HERVEY. remarks : none.

HAYS, John N. book 01 page 17 line 10
born Franklin Co., Ohio, resides Ohio Co., WV.
age 25 yrs. single, child of Abraham & Sarah HAYS,
married 04 Sep 1866 WV. to Lavinia S. MATTHEWS,
born Virginia, resides Brooke Co., West Virginia,
age 22 yrs. single, child of James & Lavinia MATTHEWS,
married by William K. PENDLETON. remarks : none.

HAYS, Julia Ann　　　book 01 page 04 line 48
born Brooke Co., Virginia, resides Brooke Co., VA.
age 21 yrs. single, child of Enoch & Nancy HAYS,
married 01 Jan 1856 VA. to John PUGH,
born Hancock Co., VA., resides Hancock Co., VA.
age 22 yrs. single, child of Hugh & Nancy PUGH,
married by David HERVEY. remarks: none.

HAYS, Mary A.　　　book 01 page 19 line 34
born unknown, resides Wellsburg, West Virginia,
age 27 yrs. single, child of unknown & unknown HAYS,
married 27 Apr 1869 WV. to Alexander C. NICHOLLS,
born Wellsburg, VA., resides Wellsburg, West Virginia,
age 32 yrs. single, child of Robert & Ellen NICHOLLS,
married by A.R. CHAPMAN. remarks: married Wellsburg.

HEADINGTON, John　　　book 01 page 19 line 44
born Brooke Co., VA., resides Brooke Co., WV. farmer,
age 27 yrs. single, child of John & Jane HEADINGTON,
married 13 Jan 1870 WV. to Martha Louisa CARTER,
born Brooke Co., VA., resides Brooke Co., West Virginia,
age 24 yrs. single, child of Lewis & Martha A. CARTER,
married by William D. MAYBERRY. remarks: none.

HEADINGTON, Maggie E.　　　book 01 page 21 line 08
born Brooke Co., Virginia, resides Brooke Co., WV.
age 26 yrs. single, child of John & Jane HEADINGTON,
married 24 Oct 1871 WV. to Joseph N. CASSIDY,
born Washington Co., PA., resides Brooke Co., WV.
age 29 yrs. single, child of Robert & Isabel CASSIDY,
married by J.B. LUCAS. remarks: none.

HEADINGTON, Nicholas　　　book 01 page 08 line 11
born Brooke Co., VA., resides Brooke Co., VA. farmer,
age 24 yrs. single, child of John & Jane HEADINGTON,
married 03 Feb 1859 VA. to Rebecca BUCHANAN,
born Brooke Co., Virginia, resides Brooke Co., Virginia,
age 20 yrs. single, child of John & unk. BUCHANAN,
married by John F. BRAZILL. remarks: none.

HEADINGTON, Rachel D.　　　book 01 page 18 line 21
born Brooke Co., Virginia, resides Brooke Co., WV.
age 21 yrs. single, child of John & Jane HEADINGTON,
married 04 Mar 1868 WV. to William SCOTT,
born Washington Co., PA., resides Wash. Co., PA.
age 28 yrs. single, child of Charles & Marg't SCOTT,
married by H. LUCAS. remarks: none.

HEADLEY, Amanda　　　book 01 page 22 line 20
born Brooke Co., Virginia, resides Brooke Co., WV.
age 26 yrs. unknown, child of unk. & unk. HEADLEY,
married 29 Oct 1873 Independence, PA. to Jesse HUKILL,
born Brooke Co., Virginia, resides Ohio Co., West Virginia,
age 26 yrs. unknown, child of unk. & unk. HUKILL,
married by N.B. STEWART. remarks: none.

HEALY, Catharine book 01 page 08 line 20
 born Ireland, resides Bethany, Virginia,
 age 26 yrs. single, child of Patrick & Ellen HEALY,
 married 17 Jul 1859 Wellsburg, VA. to Edward WELSH,
 born Ireland, resides Bethany, Virginia,
 age 39 yrs. widow, child of Thomas & Bridget WELSH,
 married by S. HUBER. remarks: Ellen (CARBINTUR).

HEDGES, Amanda J. book 01 page 18 line 03
 born Brooke Co., Virginia, resides Brooke Co., WV.
 age 18 yrs. single, child of James & Louisa HEDGES,
 married 10 Dec 1867 WV. to William B. WELLS,
 born Brooke Co., Virginia, resides Brooke Co., WV.
 age 23 yrs. single, child of Bazil & Nancy WELLS,
 married by Charles Louis LOOS. remarks: none.

HEDGES, Otho book 01 page 04 line 62
 born Brooke Co., VA., resides Brooke Co., VA. farmer,
 age 55 yrs. widow, child of Joseph & Nancy HEDGES,
 married 07 Sep 1856 VA. to Nancy CLAYTON,
 born Brooke Co., Virginia, resides Brooke Co., Virginia,
 age 46 yrs. widow, child of Wm. & Susannah FOWLER,
 married by Ezekiel QUILLEN. remarks: none.

HEDGES, Permelia book 01 page 07 line 11
 born Brooke Co., Virginia, resides Brooke Co., VA.
 age 20 yrs. single, child of Samuel & Mary HEDGES,
 married 21 Jan 1858 VA. to William CRIDER,
 born Brooke Co., Virginia, resides Brooke Co., VA.
 age 29 yrs. single, child of Obediah & Jane CRIDER,
 married by Thomas M. HUDSON. remarks: none.

HEDGES, Sallie B. book 01 page 10 line 12A
 born Brooke Co., Virginia, resides Brooke Co., Virginia,
 age 26 yrs. single, child of Joseph & Margaret HEDGES,
 married 20 Sep 1860 VA. to John M. COOPER,
 born Belmont Co., Ohio, resides West Liberty, Virginia,
 age 28 yrs. single, child of Francis & Eliza. COOPER,
 married by David HERVEY. remarks: none.

HEDGES, William B. book 01 page 18 line 11
 born Brooke Co., VA., resides Polk Co., Iowa, farmer,
 age 22 yrs. single, child of James & Louisa HEDGES,
 married 01 Jan 1868 WV. to Mary/Rebecca WILSON,
 born Brooke Co., Virginia, resides Brooke Co., WV.
 age 17 yrs. single, child of Abraham & Eliza. WILSON,
 married by William F. POOR. remarks: none.

HELMICK, Andrew S. book 01 page 20 line 22
 born Jeff. Co., Ohio, resides Tuscarawas Co., Ohio, farmer,
 age 37 yrs. widow, child of Joseph & Mary HELMICK,
 married 10 Nov 1870 Paris, PA. to Rebecca BURGOYNE,
 born unknown, resides Brooke Co., West Virginia,
 age 30 yrs. single, child of Joshua R. & unk. BURGOYNE,
 married by James C. CAMPBELL. remarks: none.

HELMS, Luisa book 01 page 03 line 23
born Green Co., Pennsylvania, resides Brooke Co., VA.
age 14 yrs. single, child of Samuel & Mary HELMS,
married Nov 1854 VA. to Zachariah BRINDLEY,
born Harford Co., Maryland, resides Brooke Co., Virginia,
age 26 yrs. single, child of Benja. & Eleanor BRINDLEY,
married by E. QUILLEN. remarks: married HELMS house.

HELSTINE, Mary book 01 page 23 line 07
born Brooke Co., Virginia, resides Brooke Co., WV.
age 18 yrs. single, child of unk. & unk. HELSTINE,
married 29 Dec 1874 WV. to John Francis SICKLER,
born Jefferson Co., Ohio, resides Steubenville, Ohio,
age 24 yrs. unknown, child of unk. & unk. SICKLER,
married by Stephen HUBER. remarks: none.

HENDRICKS, Catharine book 01 page 16 line 12
born Brooke Co., Virginia, resides Brooke Co., WV.
age 20 yrs. single, child of Edw. & Rebecca HENDRICKS,
married 01 Jan 1867 WV. to Robert L. MILLER,
born Washington Co., PA., resides Brooke Co., WV.
age 24 yrs. single, child of George & Jane MILLER,
married by James C. CAMPBELL. remarks: none.

HENDRICKS, Charity book 01 page 02 line 04
born Brooke Co., Virginia, resides Wellsburg, Virginia,
age 19 yrs. single, child of John & Mary HENDRICKS,
married 09 Mar 1854 VA. to William GARDNER,
born Washington Co., PA., resides Wellsburg, Virginia,
age 21 yrs. single, child of David & Nancy GARDNER,
married by Samuel D. TOMPKINS. remarks: none.

HENNES, Mary Jane book 01 page 03 line 30
born Brooke Co., Virginia, resides Brooke Co., Virginia,
age 24 yrs. single, child of Samuel & Lucinda HENNES,
married 15 Mar 1855 VA. to Washington SOULES,
born Pennsylvania, resides Brooke Co., Virginia,
age 46 yrs. widow, child of Jacob & Sarah SOULES,
married by Warner LONG. remarks: none.

HERON, Joseph book 01 page 19 line 22
born England, resides Brooke Co., WV. miner,
age 37 yrs. widow, child of John & unknown HERON,
married 11 Jan 1869 Wellsburg, WV. to Ann HUMBLE,
born England, resides Wheeling, West Virginia,
age 32 yrs. single, child of Benjamin & unk. HUMBLE,
married by A.R. CHAPMAN. remarks: none.

HERVEY, Mary book 01 page 12 line 52
born Washington Co., PA., resides Brooke Co., WV.
age 30 yrs. single, child of David & Dora HERVEY,
married 25 Aug 1863 WV. to Wm. Finley MORGAN,
born Lancaster Co., PA., resides Rural Valley, PA.
age 40 yrs. widow, child of Isaac & Margaret MORGAN,
married by D. HERVEY. remarks: married HERVEY house.

HESSEY, Caroline   book 01 page 14 line 52
   born Brooke Co., Virginia, resides Brooke Co., WV.
   age 28 yrs. single, child of James & Mary Ann HESSEY,
   married 02 Apr 1865 Wellsburg, WV. to Jacob P. CRISS,
   born Washington Co., PA., resides Washington Co., PA.
   age 40 yrs. widow, child of William & Polly CRISS,
   married by George W. CHESTER. remarks : none.

HESSEY, Jennie   book 01 page 21 line 33
   born Brooke Co., Virginia, resides Brooke Co., WV.
   age 18 yrs. single, child of Thos. & Eliza. HESSEY,
   married 02 May 1872 WV. to George M. PARK,
   born Brooke Co., Virginia, resides Brooke Co., WV.
   age 18 yrs. single, child of Robert & Anne PARK,
   married by Robert R. MOORE. remarks : none.

HESSEY, Kate   book 01 page 20 line 31
   born Steubenville, Ohio, resides Brooke Co., WV.
   age 22 yrs. single, child of unk. & unk. HESSEY,
   married 01 Mar 1871 WV. to George BLANKENSOP,
   born Brooke Co., VA., resides Brooke Co., West Virginia,
   age 30 yrs. divorced, child of Jos. & Ellen BLANKENSOP,
   married by J.C. CASTLE. remarks : married Wellsburg.

HESSEY, Mary Ann   book 01 page 03 line 34
   born Jefferson Co., Ohio, resides Brooke Co., Virginia,
   age 30 yrs. widow, child of Robert & Jane WHITE,
   married 31 May 1855 Wellsburg, VA. to Isaac SIMPSON,
   born Jefferson Co., Ohio, resides Brooke Co., Virginia,
   age 48 yrs. widow, child of Robert & Eliza. SIMPSON,
   married by E. QUILLEN. remarks : married WHITE house.

HICKMAN, Bayard   book 01 page 10 line 04A
   born Wetzel Co., VA., resides Brooke Co., VA. farmer,
   age 19 yrs. single, child of Jacob & Nancy HICKMAN,
   married 28 Jun 1860 VA. to Eleanor Jane JOHNSON,
   born Washington Co., PA., resides Brooke Co., Virginia,
   age 16 yrs. single, child of Wm. & Margaretta JOHNSON,
   married by Thomas M. HUDSON. remarks : none.

HILL, Salathiel   book 01 page 12 line 53
   born Pennsylvania, resides Brooke Co., WV. carpenter,
   age 45 yrs. widow, child of George & Alice Ann HILL,
   married 28 Oct 1863 WV. to Mary MYERS,
   born Pennsylvania, resides Brooke Co., WV.
   age 36 yrs. widow, child of Henry & Jane BUKER,
   married by J. CAMPBELL. remarks : married BUKER house.

HINDMAN, Anna L.   book 01 page 20 line 10
   born Brooke Co., Virginia, resides Brooke Co., WV.
   age 28 yrs. single, child of John & Amelia HINDMAN,
   married 22 Aug 1870 WV. to Richard HOOKER,
   born Hancock Co., Virginia, resides Hancock Co., WV.
   age 27 yrs. single, child of Tallman & Sarah J. HOOKER,
   married by P.H. JONES. remarks : married Hollidays Cove.

HINDMAN, Charity book 01 page 03 line 19
born Brooke Co., Virginia, resides Brooke Co., Virginia,
age 22 yrs. single, child of James & Rebecca HINDMAN,
married 30 Nov 1854 Wellsburg, VA. to Robert PARKS,
born Hancock Co., Virginia, resides Brooke Co., Virginia,
age 27 yrs. single, child of John & Jane PARKS,
married by William D. LEMON. remarks: none.

HINDMAN, Elizabeth book 01 page 16 line 21
born Brooke Co., VA., resides Brooke Co., West Virginia,
age 25 yrs. single, child of James & Rebecca HINDMAN,
married 16 May 1867 WV. to John I. MC CLURG,
born Washington Co., PA., resides Wash. Co., PA.
age 35 yrs. single, child of John & Nancy MC CLURG,
married by James C. CAMPBELL. remarks: none.

HINDMAN, John, Jr. book 01 page 15 line 74
born Brooke Co., VA., resides Brooke Co., WV. farmer,
age 33 yrs. single, child of John & unk. HINDMAN,
married 15 Mar 1866 WV. to Nancy Jane WRIGHT,
born Brooke Co., Virginia, resides Brooke Co., WV.
age 23 yrs. single, child of unk. & Nancy J. WRIGHT,
married by A. CAMPBELL. remarks: none.

HINDMAN, Kate E. book 01 page 22 line 30
born Brooke Co., Virginia, resides Brooke Co., WV.
age 21 yrs. unknown, child of unk. & unk. HINDMAN,
married 16 Dec 1873 WV. to Jonathan D. SANDERS,
born Brooke Co., Virginia, resides Brooke Co., WV.
age 25 yrs. unknown, child of unk. & unk. SANDERS,
married by George B. HUDSON. remarks: none.

HINDMAN, Maggie M. book 01 page 22 line 47
born Brooke Co., Virginia, resides Brooke Co., WV.
age 18 yrs. unk., child of unk. & unk. HINDMAN,
married 07 Oct 1874 WV. to Thomas V. MEEK,
born Brooke Co., Virginia, resides Brooke Co., WV.
age 21 yrs. unknown, child of unk. & unk. MEEK,
married by Joshua COUPLAND, JR. remarks: none.

HINDMAN, Marg't Jane book 01 page 16 line 18
born Brooke Co., Virginia, resides Brooke Co., WV.
age 22 yrs. single, child of Wm. & unk. HINDMAN,
married 28 Mar 1867 WV. to William VIRTUE,
born Washington Co., PA., resides Wash. Co., PA.
age 19 yrs. single, child of James & unk. VIRTUE,
married by James C. CAMPBELL. remarks: none.

HINDMAN, Mathew book 01 page 20 line 29
born Wetzel Co., VA., resides Brooke Co., WV. carpenter,
age 23 yrs. single, child of James & Hester HINDMAN,
married 23 Feb 1871 WV. to Addie ORAM,
born Brooke Co., Virginia, resides Brooke Co., WV.
age 19 yrs. single, child of George & Catherine ORAM,
married by D.W. CALDERWOOD. remarks: none.

HINDMAN, Samuel   book 01 page 21 line 48
   born Brooke Co., VA., resides Brooke Co., WV. farmer,
   age 36 yrs. widow, child of Wm. & Elizabeth HINDMAN,
   married 02 Oct 1872 WV. to Narcissa MARSH,
   born Brooke Co., Virginia, resides Brooke Co., WV.
   age 32 yrs. single, child of James & Sarah Ann MARSH,
   married by John B. GRAHAM. remarks : none.

HINDMAN, Samuel   book 01 page 18 line 24
   born Brooke Co., VA., resides Brooke Co., WV. farmer,
   age 30 yrs. single, child of Wm. & Betsy HINDMAN,
   married 24 Mar 1868 WV. to Nancy MURCHLAND,
   born Brooke Co., Virginia, resides Brooke Co., WV.
   age 20 yrs. single, child of And. & Eliza. MURCHLAND,
   married by James C. CAMPBELL. remarks : none.

HINES, Bartley   book 01 page 18 line 14
   born Ireland, resides Brooke Co., WV. laborer,
   age 30 yrs. single, child of Patrick & Ellen HINES,
   married 02 Feb 1868 WV. to Anne FITZ-PATRICK,
   born Ireland, resides Brooke Co., West Virginia,
   age 21 yrs. single, child of James & Mary FITZ-PATRICK,
   married by Stephen HUBER. remarks : none.

HOFFMAN, Frederick   book 01 page 22 line 43
   born Germany, resides Wayne Co., Ohio,
   age 26 yrs. unknown, child of unk. & unk. HOFFMAN,
   married 23 Jun 1874 WV. to Emma F. UHLRICH,
   born Germany, resides Brooke Co., West Virginia,
   age 39 yrs. unknown, child of unk. & unk. UHLRICH,
   married by C.L. LOOS. remarks : married Bethany.

HOGG, Harriet   book 01 page 13 line 17
   born Brooke Co., VA., resides Brooke Co., WV.
   age 21 yrs. single, child of George & Sarah HOGG,
   married 01 Feb 1864 WV. to Bazil WELLS,
   born Brooke Co., VA., resides Brooke Co., WV.
   age 30 yrs. single, child of Bazil & Nancy WELLS,
   married by R.S. HOGUE. remarks : none.

HOLLEY, Samuel G.   book 01 page 12 line 38
   born Brooke Co., VA., resides Brooke Co., VA. farmer,
   age 21 yrs. single, child of Wm. & Isabel HOLLEY,
   married 16 May 1862 VA. to Sallie KIMBERLAND,
   born Brooke Co., Virginia, resides Brooke Co., Virginia,
   age 21 yrs. single, child of Wm. & Mary KIMBERLAND,
   married by George W. CHESTER. remarks : none.

HOLTON, Thomas F.   book 01 page 11 line 33
   born Brown Co., Ohio, resides Jefferson Co., KY. teacher,
   age 23 yrs. single, child of Wm. B. & Sally P. HOLTON,
   married 23 Nov 1862 Bethany, VA. to Ellen CAMPBELL,
   born Ireland, resides Brooke Co., Virginia,
   age 27 yrs. single, child of Archibald & Anne CAMPBELL,
   married by A. CAMPBELL. remarks : none.

HOOKER, Cornelia Hull book 01 page 20 line 46
born Brooke Co., Virginia, resides Brooke Co., West Virginia,
age 23 yrs. single, child of George & Margaret HOOKER,
married 13 Jun 1871 Wellsburg, WV. to Frank A. SANDERS,
born Brooke Co., Virginia, resides Brooke Co., West Virginia,
age 21 yrs. single, child of Benjamin & Martha SANDERS,
married by Joshua COUPLAND, JR. remarks : none.

HOOKER, Cynanthia book 01 page 13 line 12
born Brooke Co., Virginia, resides Brooke Co., WV.
age 21 yrs. single, child of George & Mary HOOKER,
married 14 Dec 1863 WV. to Albert Wheeler KUHN,
born Wellsburg, Virginia, resides Brooke Co., WV.
age 27 yrs. single, child of Adam & Priscilla KUHN,
married by Charles C. BEATTY. remarks : none.

HOOKER, Richard book 01 page 20 line 10
born Hancock Co., VA., resides Hancock Co., WV. farmer,
age 27 yrs. single, child of Tallman & Sarah J. HOOKER,
married 22 Aug 1870 WV. to Anna HINDMAN,
born Brooke Co., Virginia, resides Brooke Co., WV.
age 28 yrs. single, child of John & Amelia HINDMAN,
married by P. JONES. remarks : married Hollidays Cove.

HOOKER, Sallie J. book 01 page 23 line 04
born Hancock Co., Virginia, resides Hancock Co., WV.
age 30 yrs. unknown, child of unk. & unk. HOOKER,
married 09 Jul 1874 PA., to George SWEARINGEN,
born Brooke Co., Virginia, resides Brooke Co., WV.
age 27 yrs. unk., child of unk. & unk. SWEARINGEN,
married by J. SHIELDS. remarks : married Bridgewater, PA.

HOOKER, Sarah P. book 01 page 22 line 41
born Brooke Co., Virginia, resides Brooke Co., WV.
age 33 yrs. unknown, child of unk. & unk. HOOKER,
married 26 May 1874 WV. to William TUCKER,
born Monongalia Co., VA., resides Martins Hill, WV.
age 34 yrs. unk., child of unk. & unk. TUCKER,
married by Robert R. MOORE. remarks : none.

HORN, George book 01 page 17 line 19
born Germany, resides Brooke Co., WV. laborer,
age 33 yrs. single, child of George & Elizabeth HORN,
married 29 Nov 1866 WV. to Barbara SCHUEY,
born Germany, resides Wellsburg, West Virginia,
age 19 yrs. single, child of William & Frances SCHUEY,
married by Stephen HUBER. remarks : married Wellsburg.

HOUGH, John W. book 01 page 20 line 36
born Ohio Co., VA., resides Brooke Co., WV. teacher,
age 28 yrs. single, child of James & Tabitha HOUGH,
married 27 Apr 1871 WV. to Francine R. PELLY,
born Brooke Co., Virginia, resides Brooke Co., WV.
age 18 yrs. single, child of James & Margaret PELLY,
married by J.B. WALLACE. remarks : none.

HOUSTON, James F. book 01 page 23 line 06
born Wheeling, Virginia, resides Brooke Co., WV.
age 23 yrs. unk., child of unk. & unk. HOUSTON,
married 20 Feb 1872 WV. to Angeline MC DONALD,
born Jefferson Co., Ohio, resides Brooke Co., WV.
age 19 yrs. unk., child of unk. & unk. MC DONALD,
married by L.H. JORDON. remarks : none.

HOW, Mary book 01 page 10 line 4 B
born Ireland, resides Bethany, Virginia,
age 35 yrs. widow, child of Michael & Mary HOW,
married 10 Feb 1861 VA. to Michael GAFFNEY,
born Ireland, resides Bethany, Virginia,
age 35 yrs. single, child of Matthew & Mary GAFFNEY,
married by Stephen HUBER. remarks : married Bethany.

HOWARD, W.W. book 01 page 03 line 26
born Philadelphia, PA., resides Brooke Co., VA. panemaker,
age 24 yrs. single, child of Daniel & Catherine HOWARD,
married 23 Nov 1854 Wellsburg, VA. to Maria MC CONKEY,
born Harrison Co., Ohio, resides Brooke Co., Virginia,
age 18 yrs. single, child of Joseph & Maria MC CONKEY,
married by Charles A. HOLMES. remarks : none.

HUDSON, Cynthia A. book 01 page 10 line 11 B
born Brooke Co., Virginia, resides Brooke Co., Virginia,
age 23 yrs. single, child of Thomas M. & S.E. HUDSON,
married 18 Jun 1861 VA. to Henry C. MORGAN,
born unknown, resides Wheeling, Virginia,
age 32 yrs. widow, child of John & Catherine MORGAN,
married by Thomas M. HUDSON. remarks : none.

HUDSON, M. Belle book 01 page 12 line 59
born Allegheny Co., PA., resides Brooke Co., WV.
age 19 yrs. single, child of Thomas M. & S.E. HUDSON,
married 21 Jul 1863 WV. to John MORGAN,
born Wheeling, Virginia, resides Wheeling, West Virginia,
age 22 yrs. single, child of John & Catherine MORGAN,
married by T. HUDSON. remarks : repeated pg. 13, line 57.

HUKILL, Elizabeth book 01 page 11 line 25
born Brooke Co., Virginia, resides Brooke Co., VA.
age 21 yrs. single, child of William & Mary HUKILL,
married 25 Nov 1862 VA. to Philip C. ORAM,
born Brooke Co., Virginia, resides Brooke Co., Virginia,
age 30 yrs. single, child of George & Catherine ORAM,
married by Charles Louis LOOS. remarks : none.

HUKILL, Ethelinda book 01 page 17 line 02
born Brooke Co., Virginia, resides Brooke Co., WV.
age 19 yrs. single, child of William & Sallie HUKILL,
married 03 Sep 1867 WV. to David WAUGH,
born Brooke Co., Virginia, resides Brooke Co., WV.
age 23 yrs. single, child of James & Mary WAUGH,
married by R.T. PRICE. remarks : none.

HUKILL, James book 01 page 07 line 07
born Brooke Co., VA., resides Brooke Co., VA. farmer,
age 23 yrs. single, child of William & Mary HUKILL,
married 28 Jan 1858 VA. to Providence ROBINSON,
born Brooke Co., Virginia, resides Brooke Co., Virginia,
age 20 yrs. single, child of Jos. S. & Eliza. Ann ROBINSON,
married by E. QUILLEN. remarks : married ROBINSON house.

HUKILL, Jesse book 01 page 22 line 20
born Brooke Co., Virginia, resides Ohio Co., WV.
age 26 yrs. unknown, child of unk. & unk. HUKILL,
married 29 Oct 1873 PA. to Amanda HEADLEY,
born Brooke Co., Virginia, resides Brooke Co., WV.
age 26 yrs. unknown, child of unk. & unk. HEADLEY,
married by N. STEWART. remarks : married Independence.

HUKILL, Martin book 01 page 10 line 2 B
born Brooke Co., VA., resides Brooke Co., VA. farmer,
age 24 yrs. single, child of William & Mary HUKILL,
married 24 Jan 1861 VA. to Sally W. COX,
born Brooke Co., VA., resides Brooke Co., VA.
age 23 yrs. single, child of James & Ruth COX,
married by Thomas M. HUDSON. remarks : none.

HUKILL, Mary book 01 page 14 line 43
born Brooke Co., Virginia, resides Brooke Co., WV.
age 21 yrs. single, child of William & Mary HUKILL,
married 17 Jan 1865 WV. to David B. MILLER,
born Ohio Co., Virginia, resides Brooke Co., West Virginia,
age 21 yrs. widow, child of Nicholas & Rebecca MILLER,
married by C. LOOS. remarks : married house of bride's father.

HULLIHAN, Hannah book 01 page 14 line 54
born Ireland, resides Brooke Co., West Virginia,
age 23 yrs. widow, child of John & Ann MORENTZ,
married 05 May 1865 WV. to William KELLY,
born Ireland, resides Brooke Co., West Virginia,
age 33 yrs. single, child of Wm. & Bridget KELLY,
married by S. HUBER. remarks : married Wellsburg.

HUMBLE, Ann book 01 page 19 line 22
born England, resides Wheeling, West Virginia,
age 32 yrs. single, child of Benjamin & unk. HUMBLE,
married 11 Jan 1869 Wellsburg, WV. to Joseph HERON,
born England, resides Brooke Co., West Virginia,
age 37 yrs. widow, child of John & unk. HERON,
married by A.R. CHAPMAN. remarks : none.

HUNTER, Catharine book 01 page 10 line 7 B
born Washington Co., PA., resides Brooke Co., Virginia,
age 24 yrs. single, child of Nath'l & Catharine HUNTER,
married 16 May 1861 VA. to William MAGEE,
born Washington Co., PA., resides Washington Co., PA.
age 33 yrs. single, child of William & Martha MAGEE,
married by Thomas M. HUDSON. remarks : none.

HUNTER, Rebecca L. book 01 page 09 line 22
born Baltimore Co., Maryland, resides unknown,
age 42 yrs. single, child of Nath'l & Racheal HUNTER,
married 26 Aug 1860 VA. to William WHITE,
born Delaware, resides unknown,
age 70 yrs. widow, child of James & Elizabeth WHITE,
married by Thomas M. HUDSON. remarks : none.

HUPP, Mary E. book 01 page 19 line 30
born Brooke Co., Virginia, resides Brooke Co., WV.
age 16 yrs. single, child of Isaac & Mary A. HUPP,
married 31 Dec 1868 WV. to James E. GIFFORD,
born Albany Co., New York, resides Brooke Co., WV.
age 22 yrs. single, child of Philip & Hannah GIFFORD,
married by James M. WARDEN. remarks : none.

HUSTON, Mary V. book 01 page 19 line 05
born Ohio Co., Virginia, resides Brooke Co., WV.
age 28 yrs. widow, child of Samuel & Mary HUSTON,
married 24 Jun 1868 WV. to William C. RIDGLEY,
born Brooke Co., Virginia, resides Brooke Co., WV.
age 22 yrs. widow, child of Franklin & Ann RIDGLEY,
married by William K. PENDLETON. remarks : none.

HYDE, Mary book 01 page 15 line 63
born Wheeling, Virginia, resides Brooke Co., WV.
age 26 yrs. single, child of John & A. HYDE,
married 26 Oct 1865 WV. to William RUSH,
born Brooke Co., Virginia, resides Brooke Co., WV.
age 26 yrs. single, child of Joseph & Mary RUSH,
married by E. WAYMAN. remarks : married RUSH house.

INGLEBRIGHT, Eliza. J. book 01 page 10 line 11A
born Brooke Co., Virginia, resides Brooke Co., Virginia,
age 24 yrs. single, child of Wm. & Sarah INGLEBRIGHT,
married 30 Aug 1860 VA. to William A. CLARK,
born New Lisbon, Ohio, resides Steubenville, Ohio,
age 24 yrs. single, child of Samuel L. & Ruhanna CLARK,
married by C. BEATTY. remarks : married Half Moon Farm.

INGLEBRIGHT, Harriet book 01 page 15 line 69
born Ohio, resides Ohio,
age 21 yrs. single, child of Wm. & Sarah INGLEBRIGHT,
married 05 Dec 1865 WV. to William J. O'NEAL,
born Ohio, resides Ohio,
age 23 yrs. single, child of George & Elizabeth O'NEAL,
married by Joseph WAUGH. remarks : none.

INGLEBRIGHT, Levi W. book 01 page 16 line 11
born Jeff. Co., Ohio, resides Belmont Co., Ohio, ferryman,
age 26 yrs. single, child of Wm. & Sarah INGLEBRIGHT,
married 05 Jan 1867 WV. to Mary ORR,
born Brooke Co., Virginia, resides Brooke Co., WV.
age 22 yrs. single, child of George G. & Elisabeth ORR,
married by J.B. GRAHAM. remarks : none.

INGLEBRIGHT, Lina E. book 01 page 10 line 06A
born Steubenville, Ohio, resides Brooke Co., Virginia,
age 22 yrs. single, child of Wm. & Sarah INGLEBRIGHT,
married 29 Aug 1860 VA. to John P. SMITH,
born Washington Co., PA., resides Pittsburgh, PA.
age 28 yrs. widow, child of Henry & Barbara SMITH,
married by C. BEATTY. remarks: married Half Moon Farm.

INGRAM, Charles W. book 01 page 16 line 02
born Beaver Co., PA., resides Brooke Co., WV. farmer,
age 26 yrs. single, child of unk. & unk. INGRAM,
married 03 May 1866 Ohio, to Ruth Ann DEVORE,
born Brooke Co., Virginia, resides Brooke Co., WV.
age 22 yrs. single, child of John & Sarah DEVORE,
married by H. PARKER. remarks: married Steubenville.

JACK, James book 01 page 02 line 01
born Wash. Co., PA., resides Brooke Co., VA. farmer,
age 21 yrs. single, child of David & Jane JACK,
married 09 Aug 1854 VA. to Elizabeth HAYS,
born Brooke Co., Virginia, resides Brooke Co., VA.
age 21 yrs. single, child of Enoch & Nancy HAYS,
married by David HERVEY. remarks: none.

JACKSON, Florence book 01 page 20 line 19
born Brooke Co., Virginia, resides Brooke Co., WV.
age 28 yrs. single, child of John & Mary JACKSON,
married 10 Oct 1870 Wellsburg, WV. to Andrew KELLY,
born Ireland, resides Brooke Co., West Virginia,
age 37 yrs. widow, child of Owen & Elizabeth KELLY,
married by Stephen HUBER. remarks: none.

JACOB, Alice W. book 01 page 16 line 23
born Brooke Co., Virginia, resides Brooke Co., WV.
age 20 yrs. single, child of Benjamin & Jane JACOB,
married 12 Jun 1867 WV. to George A. BAXTER,
born Brooke Co., Virginia, resides Brooke Co., WV.
age 25 yrs. single, child of Wm. & Ellen BAXTER,
married by J.L. HARRISON. remarks: none.

JACOB, Charles book 01 page 22 line 10
born Germany, resides Wellsburg, WV. butcher,
age 21 yrs. single, child of Jacob & Kate JACOB,
married 23 Feb 1873 Wellsburg, WV. to Sallie MEYERS,
born Steubenville, Ohio, resides Wellsburg, West Virginia,
age 22 yrs. single, child of Christian & Mary MEYERS,
married by Stephen HUBER. remarks: none.

JACOB, Cornelia E. book 01 page 23 line 02
born Brooke Co., Virginia, resides Brooke Co., WV.
age 28 yrs. unknown, child of unk. & unk. JACOB,
married 18 Nov 1874 WV. to Walter A. ROBINSON,
born Washtenaw Co., MI., resides Green Co., IN.
age 38 yrs. unk., child of unk. & unk. ROBINSON,
married by J.A. PIERCE. remarks: none.

JAMES, Nancy Ann book 01 page 06 line 11
born Tyler Co., Virginia, resides unknown,
age 25 yrs. single, child of John A. & Elizabeth JAMES,
married 24 Oct 1857 Wellsburg, VA. to James FORBS,
born Ireland, resides unknown,
age 25 yrs. single, child of Thomas & Ann Beth FORBS,
married by Ezekiel QUILLEN. remarks: none.

JAMES, Surrilla book 01 page 05 line 10
born Ohio, resides Ohio,
age 28 yrs. widow, child of John & Eliza. JAMES,
married 13 Nov 1856 VA. to Adam KEMP,
born Washington Co., PA., resides Brooke Co., VA.
age 30 yrs. widow, child of Adam & Rachel KEMP,
married by E. CHRISTIAN. remarks: Surrilla BURK.

JAMISON, Mary book 01 page 04 line 52
born Brooke Co., Virginia, resides Brooke Co., VA.
age 27 yrs. single, child of John & Nancy JAMISON,
married 20 May 1856 VA. to Richard JAMISON,
born Fayette Co., Pennsylvania, resides Fayette Co., PA.
age 35 yrs. single, child of Richard & Eliza. JAMISON,
married by Ezekiel QUILLEN. remarks: none.

JAMISON, Richard book 01 page 04 line 52
born Fayette Co., PA., resides Fayette Co., PA. farmer,
age 35 yrs. single, child of Richard & Eliza. JAMISON,
married 20 May 1856 VA. to Mary JAMISON,
born Brooke Co., Virginia, resides Brooke Co., VA.
age 27 yrs. single, child of John & Nancy JAMISON,
married by Ezekiel QUILLEN. remarks: none.

JEFFERS, Emily book 01 page 13 line 14
born Brooke Co., Virginia, resides Wellsburg, WV.
age 26 yrs. single, child of John & Harriet JEFFERS,
married 22 Dec 1863 WV. to Robert S. GLENN,
born Washington Co., PA., resides Washington Co., PA.
age 38 yrs. single, child of William & Sarah GLENN,
married by W. PENDLETON. remarks: married Wellsburg.

JEFFERS, Harvey book 01 page 22 line 15
born Brooke Co., Virginia, resides Wellsburg, WV.
age 25 yrs. unk., child of unk. & unk. JEFFERS,
married 11 Jul 1873 WV. to Callie CHESTER,
born Brooke Co., VA., resides Steubenville, Ohio,
age 21 yrs. unk., child of unk. & unk. CHESTER,
married by S. CRAVENS. remarks: married Wellsburg.

JEFFERS, Ruth Ann book 01 page 02 line 06
born Brooke Co., Virginia, resides Wellsburg, Virginia,
age 25 yrs. single, child of John & Harriet JEFFERS,
married 11 Apr 1854 VA. to John C. SWEARINGEN,
born Brooke Co., Virginia, resides Wellsburg, Virginia,
age 28 yrs. single, child of Geo. & Ruth SWEARINGEN,
married by E. QUILLEN. remarks: married JEFFERS house.

JENKINS, Sylvester B. book 01 page 21 line 11
born Hancock Co., VA., resides New Cumberland, WV.
age 25 yrs. single, child of David & Elizabeth JENKINS,
married 09 Nov 1871 Wellsburg, WV. to Mary JONES,
born Brooke Co., Virginia, resides Wellsburg, WV.
age 23 yrs. single, child of William & Emeline JONES,
married by Ebenezer MATHEWS. remarks : none.

JENNINGS, John book 01 page 22 line 18
born Meigs Co., Ohio, resides Brooke Co., West Virginia,
age 25 yrs. unknown, child of unk. & unk. JENNINGS,
married 04 Sep 1873 WV. to Margaret A. BROWNING,
born Brooke Co., Virginia, resides Brooke Co., WV.
age 18 yrs. unknown, child of unk. & unk. BROWNING,
married by S.H. CRAVENS. remarks : none.

JESTER, David E. book 01 page 09 line 02
born Brooke Co., Virginia, resides Brooke Co., VA. farmer,
age 30 yrs. single, child of Andrew & Eliza. Ann JESTER,
married 04 Jan 1860 VA. to Kate C. BUCKEY,
born Brooke Co., Virginia, resides Brooke Co., Virginia,
age 23 yrs. single, child of John & Elizabeth BUCKEY,
married by George G. WALTERS. remarks : none.

JESTER, Mary E. book 01 page 09 line 07
born Wellsburg, Virginia, resides Brooke Co., VA.
age 21 yrs. single, child of Andrew & Eliza. JESTER,
married 13 Nov 1859 VA. to William H. MC KEE,
born Independence, PA., resides Bethany, Virginia,
age 21 yrs. single, child of R.T. & Adaline MC KEE,
married by G. WALTERS. remarks : married mother's house.

JESTY, Hugh book 01 page 14 line 37
born Liverpool, ENG., resides Brooke Co., WV. laborer,
age 37 yrs. widow, child of Henry & Rose JESTY,
married 13 Nov 1864 WV. to Margaret MOURLAND,
born County Clare, Ireland, resides Brooke Co., WV.
age 35 yrs. single, child of unk. & unk. MOURLAND,
married by S. HUBER. remarks : married Wellsburg.

JOHNS, Gustav book 01 page 13 line 25
born Bavaria, Germany, resides Steuben., OH. cooper,
age 22 yrs. single, child of Mark & Mary JOHNS,
married 16 May 1864 WV. to Johanna FRIKE,
born Prussia, resides Wellsburg, West Virginia,
age 17 yrs. single, child of unknown & Mary FRIKE,
married by G. CHESTER. remarks : married Wellsburg.

JOHNSON, Eleanor Jane book 01 page 10 line 04A
born Washington Co., PA., resides Brooke Co., Virginia,
age 16 yrs. single, child of Wm. & Margaretta JOHNSON,
married 28 Jun 1860 VA. to Bayard HICKMAN,
born Wetzel Co., Virginia, resides Brooke Co., Virginia,
age 19 yrs. single, child of Jacob & Nancy HICKMAN,
married by Thomas M. HUDSON. remarks : none.

BROOKE CO., VA./WV. MARRIAGE BOOK 1, 1853-1874   213

JOHNSON, Eli   book 01 page 21 line 39
born Jefferson Co., Ohio, resides Jeff. Co., Ohio, farmer,
age 19 yrs. single, child of John & Nancy JOHNSON,
married 23 Jun 1872 WV. to Elizabeth WINESBURG,
born Brooke Co., Virginia, resides Brooke Co., WV.
age 20 yrs. single, child of George & Jane WINESBURG,
married by J. COUPLAND. remarks : married Wellsburg.

JOHNSON, Elizabeth   book 01 page 17 line 14
born Scotland, resides Jefferson Co., Ohio,
age 24 yrs. single, child of Peter & Eliza. JOHNSON,
married 30 Sep 1866 WV. to George W. RIEN,
born Jefferson Co., Ohio, resides Jeff. Co., Ohio,
age 22 yrs. single, child of Henry & Elizabeth RIEN,
married by J.A. PIERCE. remarks : none.

JOHNSON, James   book 01 page 21 line 34
born Ohio Co., VA., resides Brooke Co., WV. farmer,
age 24 yrs. single, child of John & Mary JOHNSON,
married 02 May 1872 Wellsburg, WV. to Lena RIPLEY,
born Pennsylvania, resides Brooke Co., West Virginia,
age 19 yrs. single, child of unk. & unk. RIPLEY,
married by Joshua COUPLAND,JR. remarks : none.

JOHNSTON, Susan   book 01 page 09 line 11
born Ohio Co., Virginia, resides Jefferson Co., Ohio,
age 18 yrs. single, child of John & Nancy JOHNSTON,
married 18 Feb 1860 VA. to Jacob Charles O'SHANDER,
born Amboy, New Jersey, resides Jefferson Co., Ohio,
age 30 yrs. single, child of Wm. & Henrietta O'SHANDER,
married by G. CHESTER. remarks : married Wellsburg.

JONES, Amy H.   book 01 page 20 line 24
born Brooke Co., Virginia, resides Brooke Co., WV.
age 17 yrs. single, child of Charles E. & A.A. JONES,
married 22 Dec 1870 WV. to William Rose MOSS,
born Guernsey Co., Ohio, resides Cambridge, Ohio,
age 25 yrs. single, child of James R. & Mary A. MOSS,
married by Robert R. MOORE. remarks : none.

JONES, Hannah   book 01 page 22 line 21
born unknown, resides Brooke Co., West Virginia,
age 26 yrs. unknown, child of unk. & unk. JONES,
married 04 Nov 1873 WV. to Robert ARMSTRONG,
born Ohio Co., Virginia, resides Brooke Co., WV.
age 36 yrs. unk., child of unk. & unk. ARMSTRONG.
married by George B. HUDSON. remarks : none.

JONES, Hattie   book 01 page 22 line 34
born Brooke Co., Virginia, resides Brooke Co., WV.
age 21 yrs. unknown, child of unk. & unk. JONES,
married 03 Feb 1874 WV. to Ellis M. SNEDIKER,
born Brooke Co., Virginia, resides Brooke Co., WV.
age 25 yrs. unk., child of unk. & unk. SNEDIKER,
married by N.B. STEWART. remarks : none.

JONES, James M.   book 01 page 17 line 24
born Brooke Co., VA., resides Wellsburg, WV. merchant,
age 23 yrs. single, child of Wm. & Emeline E. JONES,
married 14 Oct 1867   WV. to Elizabeth A. MILLER,
born Brownsville, PA., resides Brooke Co., WV.
age 21 yrs. single, child of James & Eliza. MILLER,
married by Edward A. BRINDLEY. remarks : none.

JONES, Josiah   book 01 page 09 line 23
born Wellsburg, VA., resides Wellsburg, VA. house joiner,
age 42 yrs. widow, child of Isaac & Ann Maria JONES,
married 09 Sep 1860 Wellsburg, VA. to Ann TRUAXE,
born Brooke Co., Virginia, resides Wellsburg, Virginia,
age 26 yrs. single, child of Wm. & Martha TRUAXE,
married by George W. CHESTER. remarks : none.

JONES, Mary   book 01 page 21 line 11
born Brooke Co., Virginia, resides Wellsburg, WV.
age 23 yrs. single, child of Wm. & Emeline JONES,
married 09 Nov 1871   WV. to Sylvester B. JENKINS,
born Hancock Co., VA., resides New Cumberland, WV.
age 25 yrs. single, child of David & Eliza. JENKINS,
married by E. MATHEWS. remarks : married Wellsburg.

JONES, Robert T.   book 01 page 20 line 35
born Allegh. Co., PA., resides Brooke Co., WV. laborer,
age 25 yrs. single, child of Jackson & Rebecca JONES,
married 25 Apr 1871   WV. to Sarah Jane FRESHWATER,
born Carroll Co., Ohio, resides Brooke Co., West Virginia,
age 26 yrs. widow, child of Reuben & Lydia FRESHWATER,
married by J.C. CASTLE. remarks : married Wellsburg.

KEEN, Rosetta E.   book 01 page 12 line 51
born Brooke Co., Virginia, resides Bethany Virginia,
age - - yrs. unknown, child of unknown & unk. KEEN,
married 06 Jul 1848   VA. to Charles Louis LOOS,
born France, resides Bethany, Virginia,
age - - yrs. unknown, child of unk. & unk. LOOS,
married by A. CAMPBELL. remarks : married Bethany.

KEESEY Kate   book 01 page 20 line 31
born Steubenville, Ohio, resides Brooke Co., WV.
age 22 yrs. single, child of unk. & unk. KEESEY
married 01 Mar 1871   WV. to George BLANKENSOP,
born Brooke Co., VA., resides Brooke Co., West Virginia,
age 30 yrs. divorced, child of Jos. & Ellen BLANKENSOP,
married by J.C. CASTLE. remarks : married Wellsburg.

KEESEY, Nancy   book 01 page 19 line 07
born Fayette Co., PA., resides Wellsburg, WV.
age 50 yrs. widow, child of unknown & unk. (...),
married 23 Jul 1868   WV. to William MORROW,
born Ohio Co., Virginia, resides Bethany, WV.
age 57 yrs. widow, child of John & May MORROW,
married by R. PRICE. remarks : married Wellsburg.

KEITH, Clara Jane book 01 page 22 line 19
born Brooke Co., Virginia, resides Brooke Co., WV.
age 17 yrs. unknown, child of unk. & unk. KEITH,
married 23 Oct 1873 WV. to James A. ADAMS,
born Brooke Co., Virginia, resides Brooke Co., WV.
age 21 yrs. unknown, child of unk. & unk. ADAMS,
married by J. ADAMS. remarks : married Wellsburg.

KEITH, Margaret book 01 page 09 line 17
born Westmoreland Co., PA., resides Brooke Co., VA.
age 31 yrs. widow, child of Aquilla & Sarah KEITH,
married 24 Apr 1860 Wellsburg, VA. to John FRAZIER,
born Winchester, Virginia, resides Brooke Co., Virginia,
age 47 yrs. widow, child of Alexander & Mary FRAZIER,
married by G. CHESTER. remarks : Marg't (KEITH) MARTIN.

KEITH, Sallie book 01 page 21 line 16
born Brooke Co., Virginia, resides Brooke Co., West Virginia,
age 40 yrs. widow, child of unknown & Susan KEITH,
married 04 Dec 1871 Wellsburg, WV. to James BROWNLEE,
born Jefferson Co., Ohio, resides Brooke Co., West Virginia,
age 49 yrs. widow, child of Thomas & Juliane BROWNLEE,
married by R. MOORE. remarks : Sallie CEATH.

KEITH, Samuel book 01 page 07 line 22
born Brooke Co., VA., resides Brooke Co., VA. miner,
age 19 yrs. single, child of Quillen & Jane KEITH,
married 17 Nov 1858 VA. to Margaret J. REED,
born Allegheny Co., PA., resides Brooke Co., VA.
age 30 yrs. single, child of John & Eliza. REED,
married by E. QUILLEN. remarks : married Wellsburg.

KELLY, Andrew book 01 page 17 line 04
born Ireland, resides Brooke Co., WV. laborer,
age 30 yrs. single, child of Owen & Elizabeth KELLY,
married 21 Sep 1867 WV. to Sarah MC MANIS,
born Ireland, resides Brooke Co., West Virginia,
age 22 yrs. single, child of John & Mary MC MANIS,
married by Stephen HUBER. remarks : none.

KELLY, Andrew book 01 page 20 line 19
born Ireland, resides Brooke Co., West Virginia, laborer,
age 37 yrs. widow, child of Owen & Elizabeth KELLY,
married 10 Oct 1870 WV. to Florence JACKSON,
born Brooke Co., Virginia, resides Brooke Co., WV.
age 28 yrs. single, child of John & Mary JACKSON,
married by Stephen HUBER. remarks : married Wellsburg.

KELLY, Elizabeth book 01 page 08 line 16
born Mercer Co., PA., resides Wellsburg, Virginia,
age 23 yrs. single, child of Andrew & unk. KELLY,
married 07 Apr 1859 VA. to Thomas J. DARRAH,
born Allegheny Co., PA., resides Wellsburg, Virginia,
age 26 yrs. single, child of James & unk. DARRAH,
married by George W. CHESTER. remarks : none.

KELLY, Margaret　　　　book 01 page 20 line 04
born Glasgow, Scotland, resides Wellsburg, WV.
age 28 yrs. single, child of John & Esther KELLY,
married 10 Apr 1870 WV. to Robert KELLY,
born Glasgow, Scotland, resides Hancock Co., WV.
age 30 yrs. single, child of John & Mary KELLY,
married by E. BRINDLEY. remarks : married Wellsburg.

KELLY, Robert　　　　book 01 page 20 line 04
born Glasgow, Scotland, resides Han. Co., WV. weaver,
age 30 yrs. single, child of John & Mary KELLY,
married 10 Apr 1870 Wellsburg, WV. to Marg't KELLY,
born Glasgow, Scotland, resides Wellsburg, West Virginia,
age 28 yrs. single, child of John & Esther KELLY,
married by Edward A. BRINDLEY. remarks : none.

KELLY, Susan Ann　　　　book 01 page 22 line 12
born Washington Co., PA., resides Brooke Co., WV.
age 22 yrs. single, child of Whit & unknown KELLY,
married 20 Mar 1873 WV. to George DAUGHERTY,
born Brooke Co., Virginia, resides Brooke Co., West Virginia,
age 46 yrs. widow, child of George & Dolly DAUGHERTY,
married by S.H. CRAVENS. remarks : married Wellsburg.

KELLY, William　　　　book 01 page 14 line 54
born Ireland, resides Brooke Co., West Virginia, laborer,
age 33 yrs. single, child of William & Bridget KELLY,
married 05 May 1865 WV. to Hannah HULLIHAN,
born Ireland, resides Brooke Co., West Virginia,
age 23 yrs. widow, child of John & Ann MORENTZ,
married by Stephen HUBER. remarks : married Wellsburg.

KELLY, William F.　　　　book 01 page 22 line 04
born Canada, resides Brooke Co., WV. farmer,
age 24 yrs. single, child of John & Ellen KELLY,
married 09 Jan 1873 WV. to Amanda DEGARMO,
born Ohio Co., Virginia, resides Brooke Co., West Virginia,
age 23 yrs. single, child of John & Parthenia DEGARMO,
married by C.P. GOODRICH. remarks : none.

KEMP, Adam　　　　book 01 page 05 line 10
born Wash. Co. PA., resides Brooke Co., VA. pumpmaker,
age 30 yrs. widow, child of Adam & Rachel KEMP,
married 13 Nov 1856 VA. to Surrilla BURK,
born Ohio, resides Ohio,
age 28 yrs. widow, child of John & Elizabeth JAMES,
married by Edmund CHRISTIAN. remarks : none.

KEMP, Ann Elizabeth　　　　book 01 page 13 line 04
born Brooke Co., Virginia, resides Brooke Co., WV.
age 18 yrs. single, child of Adam & Elizabeth KEMP,
married 12 Aug 1863 WV. to Mort. Benton ABRAHAMS,
born Hancock Co., Virginia, resides Hancock Co., WV.
age 22 yrs. single, child of Robert & Matilda ABRAHAMS,
married by W. PENDLETON. remarks : married Bethany.

BROOKE CO., VA./WV. MARRIAGE BOOK 1, 1853-1874 217

KEMP, William H. book 01 page 07 line 18
born Wheeling, VA., resides Bethany, VA., pumpmaker,
age 29 yrs. single, child of Adam & Elizabeth KEMP,
married 29 Jul 1858 VA. to Bridget MC CONVILLE,
born New Ireland, resides Bethany, Virginia,
age 18 yrs. single, child of Arthur & B. MC CONVILLE,
married by S. HUBER. remarks : mother Eliza.(HITCHCOCK).

KENEDY, Patrick book 01 page 19 line 12
born Ireland, resides Brooke Co., WV. laborer,
age 26 yrs. single, child of Phillip & Ann KENEDY,
married 07 Oct 1868 Wellsburg, WV. to Ann MALOY,
born unknown, resides Brooke Co., West Virginia,
age 17 yrs. single, child of unk. & unk. MALOY,
married by Stephen HUBER. remarks : none.

KERNS, Ann Rebecca book 01 page 08 line 09
born Brooke Co., Virginia, resides Brooke Co., VA.
age 14 yrs. single, child of David & Rebecca KERNS,
married 06 Jan 1859 VA. to John PERRY,
born Jefferson Co., Ohio, resides Brooke Co., Virginia,
age 29 yrs. widow, child of Henry & Elizabeth PERRY,
married by Thomas M. HUDSON. remarks : none.

KERNS, Ann Rebecca J. book 01 page 14 line 48
born Brooke Co., Virginia, resides Wellsburg, WV.
age 20 yrs. widow, child of David & Rebecca KERNS,
married 26 Feb 1865 WV. to Samuel H. ALEXANDER,
born Muskingum Co., Ohio, resides Muskingum Co., Ohio,
age 24 yrs. single, child of Mathew & unk. ALEXANDER,
married by J. PIERCE. remarks : married house of D. KERNS.

KIMBERLAND, Angeline book 01 page 02 line 07
born Monroe Co., Ohio, resides Wellsburg, Virginia,
age 23 yrs. widow, child of William & Naomi ROMINE,
married 16 Mar 1854 VA. to Thomas PATTON,
born Brooke Co., Virginia, resides Wellsburg, Virginia,
age 25 yrs. widow, child of John & Elizabeth PATTON,
married by E. QUILLEN. remarks : married FLEMING house.

KIMBERLAND, Campbell book 01 page 09 line 06
born Wellsburg, VA. resides Wellsburg, VA. merchant,
age 27 yrs. single, child of Henry & Mary KIMBERLAND,
married 18 Oct 1859 VA. to Margaret Ann HARDING,
born South Brunswick, NH., resides Wellsburg, Virginia,
age 24 yrs. single, child of J.B. & Mary Ann HARDING,
married by J.M. SMITH. remarks : married Wellsburg.

KIMBERLAND, Cornelius book 01 page 20 line 14
born Wellsburg, Virginia, resides Wellsburg, WV. carpenter,
age 31 yrs. single, child of Henry & Mary KIMBERLAND,
married 15 Sep 1870 Wellsburg, WV. to Melissa LEWIS,
born Ohio, resides Wellsburg, West Virginia,
age 23 yrs. single, child of Henry & unknown LEWIS,
married by Edward A. BRINDLEY. remarks : none.

KIMBERLAND, Elizabeth book 01 page 07 line 17
born Wellsburg, Virginia, resides Wellsburg, Virginia,
age 20 yrs. single, child of Henry & Mary KIMBERLAND,
married 15 Jul 1858 Wellsburg, VA. to Samuel GEORGE,
born Washington Co., PA., resides Wellsburg, Virginia,
age 31 yrs. widow, child of Thomas & Sarah GEORGE,
married by Ezekiel QUILLEN. remarks : none.

KIMBERLAND, Harriet book 01 page 20 line 20
born Jefferson Co., Ohio, resides Brooke Co., WV.
age 40 yrs. widow, child of Benja. & Mary WATKINS,
married 08 Nov 1870 WV. to William T. BAILEY,
born Belmont Co., Ohio, resides Brooke Co., WV.
age 46 yrs. widow, child of John & Margaret BAILEY,
married by R.R. MOORE. remarks : married Wellsburg.

KIMBERLAND, Jane book 01 page 14 line 49
born Brooke Co., Virginia, resides Brooke Co., WV.
age 24 yrs. single, child of Wm. & Mary KIMBERLAND,
married 02 Mar 1865 WV. to William LEMMON,
born Wash. Co., Pennsylvania, resides Brooke Co., WV.
age 27 yrs. single, child of S. & M. LEMMON,
married by T. HUDSON. remarks : married FLEMING house.

KIMBERLAND, Sallie book 01 page 12 line 38
born Brooke Co., Virginia, resides Brooke Co., Virginia,
age 21 yrs. single, child of Wm. & Mary KIMBERLAND,
married 16 May 1862 VA. to Samuel G. HOLLEY,
born Brooke Co., Virginia, resides Brooke Co., Virginia,
age 21 yrs. single, child of William & Isabel HOLLEY,
married by George W. CHESTER. remarks : none.

KINDRICKS, James book 01 page 10 line 08A
born Ireland, resides Bethany, Virginia, laborer,
age 34 yrs. single, child of E. & Marg't (MARKES) KINDRICKS,
married 10 Sep 1860 Bethany, VA. to Catherine MC FADDEN,
born Ireland, resides Bethany, Virginia,
age 29 yrs. widow, child of O. & Marg't (GRANT) DONNELLY,
married by Stephen HUBER. remarks : none.

KIRKER, Narcissa book 01 page 19 line 15
born Ohio, resides West Virginia,
age 25 yrs. single, child of W.C. & Mary C. KIRKER,
married 29 Oct 1868 WV. to Amos D. HARVEY,
born Pennsylvania, resides West Virginia,
age 25 yrs. single, child of W.H. & Alina HARVEY,
married by R. PRICE. remarks : married Wellsburg.

KLINE, Charles book 01 page 21 line 32
born Germany, resides Wheeling, WV. carpenter,
age 23 yrs. single, child of Christian & Francis KLINE,
married 30 Apr 1872 WV. to Barbara BENTZ,
born Germany, resides Brooke Co., West Virginia,
age 24 yrs. single, child of unk. & unk. BENTZ,
married by S. HUBER. remarks : married Wellsburg.

KLINE, William　　　　book 01 page 19 line 46
born Wellsburg, Virginia, resides Wash. Co., PA. farmer,
age 30 yrs. single, child of Frederick & Margaret KLINE,
married 08 Feb 1870　WV. to Harriet STEWART,
born Brooke Co., Virginia, resides Brooke Co., WV.
age 24 yrs. single, child of Robert & unk. STEWART,
married by Walter BROWN. remarks : none.

KLINEFELTER, Frances　　　　book 01 page 19 line 45
born Pittsburgh, Pennsylvania, resides Wellsburg, WV.
age 22 yrs. single, child of Mich'l & Keziah KLINEFELTER,
married 20 Jan 1870 Wellsburg, WV. to James M. POTTER,
born Clarion Co., Pennsylvania, resides Cincinnati, Ohio,
age 25 yrs. single, child of unk. & unk. POTTER,
married by Robert R. MOORE. remarks : none.

KNIGHT, Wilson L.　　　　book 01 page 19 line 21
born Allegh. Co., PA., resides Brooke Co., WV. laborer,
age 24 yrs. single, child of Phillip & Sarah KNIGHT,
married 06 Oct 1868　WV. to Ruemma Elen STEWART,
born　Ohio, resides Brooke Co., West Virginia,
age 17 yrs. single, child of William & Martha STEWART,
married by M. WELLS. remarks : Bapt. Church, Buff Twp.

KNOX, James Newton　　　　book 01 page 15 line 60
born Rappahannock Co., VA., resides Brooke Co., WV.
age 26 yrs. single, child of Wm. & Margaret KNOX,
married 07 Sep 1865　WV. to Rachel Margaret UTZ,
born Rappahannock Co., VA., resides Brooke Co., WV.
age 26 yrs. single, child of John & Margaret UTZ,
married by M. WELLS. remarks : married UTZ house.

KUHN, Adam　　　　book 01 page 02 line 03
born　unknown, resides Wellsburg, Virginia, bank officer,
age -- yrs. widow, child of unknown & unknown KUHN,
married 02 Feb 1854 Wellsburg, VA. to Juliana P. GANT,
born　unknown, resides Wellsburg, Virginia,
age -- yrs. single, child of unknown & unknown GANT,
married by Samuel D. TOMPKINS. remarks : none.

KUHN, Albert Wheeler　　　　book 01 page 13 line 12
born Wellsburg, Virginia, resides Brooke Co., WV.
age 27 yrs. single, child of Adam & Priscilla KUHN,
married 14 Dec 1863　WV. to Cynanthia HOOKER,
born Brooke Co., Virginia, resides Brooke Co., WV.
age 21 yrs. single, child of George & Mary HOOKER,
married by Charles C. BEATTY. remarks : none.

KUHN, Anne H.　　　　book 01 page 12 line 45
born Brooke Co., Virginia, resides Brooke Co., VA.
age 23 yrs. single, child of Adam & Priscilla KUHN,
married 04 Mar 1862　VA. to Julius LE MOYNE,
born Washington Co., PA., resides Washington Co., PA.
age 25 yrs. single, child of F.Julius & Madalene LE MOYNE,
married by Joseph WAUGH. remarks : none.

KUHN, John book 01 page 04 line 55
born Allegheny Co., PA., resides Wellsburg, VA. cooper,
age 22 yrs. single, child of Peter & Barbara Ann KUHN,
married 02 Jun 1856 Wellsburg, VA. to Ann BULLOCK,
born St. Clairsville, Ohio, resides Virginia,
age 18 yrs. single, child of Charles & Harriet BULLOCK,
married by A.J. ENDSLEY. remarks : none.

LAKE, Elisabeth book 01 page 22 line 08
born England, resides Wellsburg, West Virginia,
age 45 yrs. widow, child of unknown & unk. LAKE,
married 13 Feb 1873 Wellsburg, WV. to J.C. MORTON,
born Beaver Co., Pennsylvania, resides Wellsburg, WV.
age 46 yrs. widow, child of Wm. & Maryann MORTON,
married by S.H. CRAVENS. remarks : none.

LALLANCE, Charles N. book 01 page 13 line 26
born Racine, Ohio, resides Cincinnati, OH. photographer,
age 27 yrs. single, child of Peter & Mary LALLANCE,
married 02 Jun 1864 WV. to Martha E. PARKER,
born Long Bottoms, Ohio, resides Wellsburg, WV.
age 21 yrs. single, child of Adam & unk. PARKER,
married by J. PIERCE. remarks : married Wellsburg.

LANDIS, Evan Fairchild book 01 page 14 line 47
born Wellsburg, Virginia, resides CA. bricklayer,
age 35 yrs. single, child of S.A. & A.S. LANDIS,
married 05 Feb 1865 WV. to Anna M. RUSSELL,
born Wellsburg, Virginia, resides Wellsburg, WV.
age 28 yrs. single, child of James & Sarah RUSSELL,
married by G. CHESTER. remarks : married Wellsburg.

LANDIS, Martha A. book 01 page 10 line 09A
born Ohio, resides Wellsburg, Virginia,
age 24 yrs. single, child of David & Charlotte LANDIS,
married 09 Aug 1860 VA. to George S. DORLAND,
born Ohio, resides Rousbury, Ohio,
age 24 yrs. single, child of Garrett & Eliza. DORLAND,
married by T. HUDSON. remarks : married Wellsburg.

LANGFITT, Obediah Walford book 01 page 04 line 42
born Hancock Co., Virginia, resides unknown, lawyer,
age 35 yrs. widow, child of Wm. & Laodicy LANGFITT,
married 20 Nov 1855 Wellsburg, VA. to Virginia TARR,
born Brooke Co., Virginia, resides unknown,
age 20 yrs. single, child of Campbell & Mary TARR,
married by W.P. BEARD. remarks : none.

LANNUM, Samuel book 01 page 21 line 15
born Washington Co., PA., resides Brooke Co., WV. farmer,
age 29 yrs. single, child of Samuel & Margaret LANNUM,
married 06 Dec 1871 WV. to Elizabeth LUCAS,
born Brooke Co., Virginia, resides Brooke Co., Virginia,
age 26 yrs. single, child of Samuel & Rebecca LUCAS,
married by A.E. WARD. remarks : none.

LARGE, Robert E. book 01 page 12 line 36
born Jefferson Co., Ohio, resides Jeff. Co., Ohio, teacher,
age 28 yrs. single, child of Robert W. & Nancy LARGE,
married 06 Feb 1862 VA. to Anne WILKINSON,
born Canada, resides Brooke Co., Virginia,
age 26 yrs. single, child of Thos. & Eliza. WILKINSON,
married by Charles C. BEATTY. remarks : none.

LATIMER, John H. book 01 page 15 line 72
born Brooke Co., VA., resides Brooke Co., WV. carpenter,
age 26 yrs. single, child of unknown & unk. LATIMER,
married 18 Jan 1866 WV. to Narcissa CARIENS,
born Brooke Co., Virginia, resides Brooke Co., WV.
age 21 yrs. single, child of Elliott & Sarah CARIENS,
married by T. HUDSON. remarks : pg. 15 line 76.

LATIMER, William P. book 01 page 20 line 38
born Wellsburg, VA., resides Wellsburg, WV. saddler,
age 24 yrs. single, child of David & Nancy LATIMER,
married 16 May 1871 WV. to Clara LEWIS,
born Brooke Co., Virginia, resides Brooke Co., WV.
age 21 yrs. single, child of John & Leah LEWIS,
married by Robert R. MOORE. remarks : none.

LAUGHEAD, Sarah book 01 page 03 line 31
born Brooke Co., Virginia, resides Brooke Co., Virginia,
age 22 yrs. single, child of Robert & Jane LAUGHEAD,
married 12 Jul 1855 VA. to Charles M. SERVIS,
born Washington Co., PA., resides Brooke Co., VA.
age 25 yrs. single, child of John & Catherine SERVIS,
married by David HERVEY. remarks : none.

LAUGHEAD, Sophia book 01 page 10 line 13A
born Pennsylvania, resides Wellsburg, Virginia,
age 18 yrs. single, child of James & Rebecca LAUGHEAD,
married 30 Sep 1860 Wellsburg, VA. to Charles PILLINGS,
born Ohio, resides Wellsburg, Virginia,
age 21 yrs. single, child of Charles & Betty PILLINGS,
married by Thomas M. HUDSON. remarks : none.

LAUGHEAD, Sophia book 01 page 17 line 07
born Allegheny Co., PA., resides Brooke Co., West Virginia,
age 25 yrs. widow, child of James & Rebecca LAUGHEAD,
married 13 Oct 1867 WV. to Joseph MONTGOMERY,
born Ohio Co., Virginia, resides Brooke Co., West Virginia,
age 31 yrs. widow, child of Abram & Nancy MONTGOMERY,
married by A. ANDERSON. remarks : Mrs. Sophia PILLINGS.

LAWTON, Joseph K. book 01 page 04 line 59
born Wash. Co., PA., resides Wash. Co., PA. mechanic,
age 25 yrs. single, child of Pardon & Tabitha LAWTON,
married 12 Aug 1856 VA. to Mary L. QUEST,
born Jefferson Co., PA., resides Washington Co., PA.
age 20 yrs. single, child of Samuel & Martha QUEST,
married by E. QUILLEN. remarks : married Wellsburg.

LAZEAR, Hugh book 01 page 21 line 18
born Brooke Co., Virginia, resides Brooke Co., WV. farmer,
age 22 yrs. single, child of Jerome R. & Susan J. LAZEAR,
married 20 Dec 1871 WV. to Amanda SHRIMPLIN,
born Brooke Co., Virginia, resides Brooke Co., WV.
age 23 yrs. single, child of John & Eliza. SHRIMPLIN,
married by Robert R. MOORE. remarks : none.

LAZEAR, James book 01 page 11 line 34
born Wellsburg, VA., resides Wellsburg, VA. blacksmith,
age 23 yrs. single, child of John & Sarah LAZEAR,
married 12 Feb 1863 VA. to Sebrina J. PARSONS,
born Ohio, resides Wellsburg, Virginia,
age 22 yrs. single, child of John & Sarah PARSONS,
married by C. LOOS. remarks : married PARSONS house.

LAZEAR, Jane book 01 page 17 line 05
born Wellsburg, Virginia, resides Wellsburg, WV.
age 22 yrs. single, child of John & Sallie LAZEAR,
married 24 Sep 1867 WV. to Wheeler REEVES,
born Wellsburg, Virginia, resides Wellsburg, West Virginia,
age 30 yrs. single, child of Nathan & Rachel A. REEVES,
married by T M. HUDSON. remarks : married Wellsburg.

LAZEAR, Lorinda book 01 page 14 line 44
born Brooke Co., Virginia, resides Brooke Co., WV.
age 26 yrs. single, child of Asa & Mary LAZEAR,
married 18 Jan 1865 WV. to Asbury S. MOORE,
born Hancock Co., Virginia, resides Lee Co., Iowa,
age 27 yrs. single, child of John & K.T. MOORE,
married by William K. PENDLETON. remarks : none.

LAZEAR, Milton book 01 page 21 line 21
born Brooke Co., VA., resides Brooke Co., WV. farmer,
age 23 yrs. single, child of Joseph & Eliza. LAZEAR,
married 11 Jan 1872 PA. to Sarah C. SELBY,
born Jackson Co., Virginia, resides Brooke Co., WV.
age 21 yrs. single, child of Nathan & Marg't SELBY,
married by S. DAVIS. remarks : married Independence.

LAZEAR, Robert M. book 01 page 18 line 17
born Brooke Co., VA., resides Brooke Co., WV. farmer,
age 25 yrs. single, child of Jerome & Susan LAZEAR,
married 20 Feb 1868 WV. to Margaret GLASS,
born Brooke Co., Virginia, resides Brooke Co., WV.
age 22 yrs. single, child of James & Sidney GLASS,
married by William F. POOR. remarks : none.

LAZEAR, Thomas B. book 01 page 17 line 06
born Brooke Co., VA., resides Brooke Co., WV. farmer,
age 21 yrs. single, child of John & Matilda LAZEAR,
married 03 Oct 1867 WV. to Hannah PITTMAN,
born Monroe Co., Ohio, resides Brooke Co., WV.
age 20 yrs. single, child of Thomas & Ann PITTMAN,
married by Milton WELLS. remarks : married Wellsburg.

LE MOYNE, Julius　　　　book 01 page 12 line 45
born Washington Co., PA., resides Wash. Co., PA. farmer,
age 25 yrs. single, child of F. Julius & Madalene LE MOYNE,
married 04 Mar 1862 VA. to Anne H. KUHN,
born Brooke Co., Virginia, resides Brooke Co., VA.
age 23 yrs. single, child of Adam & Priscilla KUHN,
married by Joseph WAUGH. remarks : none.

LEE, Julia Ann　　　　book 01 page 05 line 15
born Brooke Co., Virginia, resides Brooke Co., VA.
age 25 yrs. single, child of Thomas & Rachel LEE,
married 19 Feb 1857 VA. to William NUNEMAKER,
born Washington Co., PA., resides Brooke Co., Virginia,
age 30 yrs. single, child of Daniel & Cath. NUNEMAKER,
married by G.W. CRANAGE. remarks : none.

LEHEKS, Ursula　　　　book 01 page 07 line 04
born Crisinger, Germany, resides Wellsburg, Virginia,
age 43 yrs. widow, child of Michael & Cecelia LEHEKS,
married 22 Dec 1857 VA. to Ferdinard WENNINGCOUGH,
born Germany, resides Wellsburg, Virginia,
age 42 yrs. single, child of unk. & unk. WENNINGCOUGH,
married by Stephen HUBER. remarks : Ursula (LEHEKS) SENS.

LEMMON, William　　　　book 01 page 14 line 49
born Washington Co., PA., resides Brooke Co., WV.
age 27 yrs. single, child of S. & M. LEMMON,
married 02 Mar 1865 WV. to Jane KIMBERLAND,
born Brooke Co., Virginia, resides Brooke Co., WV.
age 24 yrs. single, child of Wm. & Mary KIMBERLAND,
married by T. HUDSON. remarks : married FLEMING house.

LETZKUS, Adam　　　　book 01 page 22 line 33
born Brooke Co., Virginia, resides Wellsburg, WV.
age 21 yrs. unk., child of unk. & unk. LETZKUS,
married 22 Jan 1874 WV. to Anne E. MC MAHON,
born Allegheny Co., PA., resides Wellsburg, WV.
age 21 yrs. unk., child of unk. & unk. MC MAHON,
married by J. COUPLAND. remarks : married Wellsburg.

LETZKUS, Ambrose　　　　book 01 page 14 line 45
born Germany, resides Wellsburg, WV. shoemaker,
age 26 yrs. single, child of Richard & Millie LETZKUS,
married 23 Jan 1865 WV. to Mary Ann BEITER,
born Germany, resides Wellsburg, West Virginia,
age 19 yrs. single, child of Francis & unknown BEITER,
married by S. HUBER. remarks : married Wellsburg.

LETZKUS, Frances　　　　book 01 page 09 line 19
born Wellsburg, Virginia, resides Wellsburg, Virginia,
age 18 yrs. single, child of Geo. & Michelia LETZKUS,
married 26 Nov 1860 Wellsburg, VA. to Hugh BARTH,
born Germany, resides Wellsburg, Virginia,
age 23 yrs. single, child of Fidel & Martha BARTH,
married by S. HUBER. remarks : mother Michelia (PFIFFER).

LETZKUS, Francis　　　　book 01 page 21 line 31
born Brooke Co., Virginia, resides Brooke Co., West Virginia,
age 21 yrs. single, child of Richard & Apolonia LETZKUS,
married 04 Apr 1872 Wellsburg, WV. to Jasper POTTS,
born Beaver Co., Pennsylvania, resides Wellsburg, WV.
age 21 yrs. single, child of Nathan & Elizabeth POTTS,
married by Stephen HUBER. remarks : none.

LETZKUS, George　　　　book 01 page 19 line 06
born Brooke Co., VA., resides Brooke Co., WV. merchant,
age 23 yrs. single, child of George & Mary LETZKUS,
married 18 Jul 1868　WV. to Caroline GAUSE,
born　Germany, resides Brooke Co., West Virginia,
age 22 yrs. single, child of Lorence & Magdaline GAUSE,
married by Stephen HUBER. remarks : none.

LETZKUS, John　　　　book 01 page 16 line 14
born Wellsburg, VA., resides Wellsburg, WV. grocer,
age 22 yrs. single, child of John & unk. LETZKUS,
married 05 Feb 1867　WV. to Eva MILELECH,
born　Germany, resides Wellsburg, West Virginia,
age 19 yrs. single, child of unk. & Eva MILELECH,
married by Stephen HUBER. remarks : none.

LETZKUS, Joseph　　　　book 01 page 16 line 03
born Wellsburg, Virginia, resides Wellsburg, WV. butcher,
age 28 yrs. single, child of George & Michelia LETZKUS,
married 28 May 1866 Wellsburg, WV. to Emma ROBINETT,
born Brooke Co., Virginia, resides Brooke Co., West Virginia,
age 24 yrs. single, child of unknown & unk. ROBINETT,
married by Edward A. BRINDLEY. remarks : none.

LETZKUS, Lena　　　　book 01 page 20 line 12
born Brooke Co., Virginia, resides Wellsburg, West Virginia,
age 19 yrs. single, child of George & unknown LETZKUS,
married 01 Sep 1870　WV. to James PATTERSON,
born Jefferson Co., Ohio, resides Wellsburg, West Virginia,
age 24 yrs. single, child of Reuben & Martha PATTERSON,
married by Stephen HUBER. remarks : married Wellsburg.

LETZKUS, Mary　　　　book 01 page 17 line 17
born Brooke Co., Virginia, resides Wellsburg, West Virginia,
age 17 yrs. single, child of George & Michelia LETZKUS,
married 11 Oct 1866　WV. to Frederick SPRINGBORN,
born　Germany, resides Jefferson Co., Ohio,
age 25 yrs. single, child of Fred. & Mary SPRINGBORN,
married by Stephen HUBER. remarks : none.

LETZKUS, Nancy　　　　book 01 page 15 line 75
born Wellsburg, Virginia, resides Wellsburg, WV.
age -- yrs. single, child of unk. & unk. LETZKUS,
married 03 Apr 1866　WV. to George LIAS,
born　Pennsylvania, resides Wellsburg, WV.
age -- yrs. single, child of George & Mary LIAS,
married by J.A. PIERCE. remarks : none.

LETZKUS, Pierce book 01 page 20 line 42
born Wellsburg, VA., resides Brooke Co., WV. shoemaker,
age 23 yrs. single, child of Richard & Apolonia LETZKUS,
married 28 May 1871 WV. to Rebecca J. CUNNINGHAM,
born Pennsylvania, resides Brooke Co., West Virginia,
age 21 yrs. single, child of unk. & unk. CUNNINGHAM,
married by S. HUBER. remarks : married Wellsburg.

LEWIS, Clara book 01 page 20 line 38
born Brooke Co., VA., resides Brooke Co., WV.
age 21 yrs. single, child of John & Leah LEWIS,
married 16 May 1871 WV. to William P. LATIMER,
born Wellsburg, Virginia, resides Wellsburg, WV.
age 24 yrs. single, child of David & Nancy LATIMER,
married by Robert R. MOORE. remarks : none.

LEWIS, Elizabeth book 01 page 11 line 21
born Brooke Co., Virginia, resides Brooke Co., VA.
age 22 yrs. single, child of Job & Margaret LEWIS,
married 14 Nov 1861 VA. to De Witt C. COLEMAN,
born Brooke Co., Virginia, resides Brooke Co., Virginia,
age 32 yrs. single, child of David & Mary COLEMAN,
married by Thomas M. HUDSON. remarks : none.

LEWIS, Hezekiah book 01 page 08 line 04
born Jeff. Co., Ohio, resides Brooke Co., VA. laborer,
age 24 yrs. single, child of Douglass & Mary LEWIS,
married 19 Dec 1858 VA. to Sarah Adaline BELL,
born Brooke Co., Virginia, resides Brooke Co., VA.
age 16 yrs. single, child of Aaron & Jane BELL,
married by J. BEACOM. remarks : married BELL house.

LEWIS, Kezeah book 01 page 04 line 50
born Brooke Co., Virginia, resides Brooke Co., VA.
age 20 yrs. single, child of Job & Margaret LEWIS,
married 22 Apr 1856 VA. to John R. MC ELROY,
born Jefferson Co., Ohio, resides Jefferson Co., Ohio,
age 29 yrs. single, child of James & Mary MC ELROY,
married by Ezekiel QUILLEN. remarks : none.

LEWIS, Leah book 01 page 19 line 29
born Brooke Co., Virginia, resides Brooke Co., WV.
age 23 yrs. single, child of Job & unknown LEWIS,
married 11 Feb 1869 WV. to John M. WILSON,
born Brooke Co., Virginia, resides Brooke Co., WV.
age 28 yrs. single, child of James & Michael WILSON,
married by A. CHAPMAN. remarks : married Wellsburg.

LEWIS, Marg't Jennie book 01 page 23 line 01
born Brooke Co., Virginia, resides Brooke Co., WV.
age 21 yrs. single, child of unk. & unk. LEWIS,
married 04 Nov 1874 WV. to Robert Banc WILSON,
born Brooke Co., Virginia, resides Brooke Co., WV.
age 22 yrs. single, child of unk. & unk. WILSON,
married by Charles Louis LOOS. remarks : none.

LEWIS, Melissa　　　　book 01 page 20 line 14
　　born Ohio, resides Wellsburg, West Virginia,
　　age 23 yrs. single, child of Henry & unknown LEWIS,
　　married 15 Sep 1870 WV. to Cornelius KIMBERLAND,
　　born Wellsburg, Virginia, resides Wellsburg, West Virginia,
　　age 31 yrs. single, child of Henry & Mary KIMBERLAND,
　　married by E. BRINDLEY. remarks : married Wellsburg.

LEWIS, Melissa　　　　book 01 page 14 line 35
　　born Hampshire Co., VA., resides Brooke Co., WV.
　　age 23 yrs. single, child of Oliver & Ann LEWIS,
　　married 25 Oct 1864 WV. to Robert M. MAHAN,
　　born Washington Co., PA., resides Wash. Co., PA.
　　age 23 yrs. single, child of unk. & unk. MAHAN,
　　married by William PENDLETON. remarks : none.

LEWIS, Micha　　　　book 01 page 19 line 41
　　born Brooke Co., Virginia, resides Brooke Co., WV.
　　age 21 yrs. single, child of John & Leah LEWIS,
　　married 30 Nov 1869 WV. to Richard W. BUCHANAN,
　　born Brooke Co., Virginia, resides Wellsburg, West Virginia,
　　age 23 yrs. single, child of Wm. & Sarah J. BUCHANAN,
　　married by Robert R. MOORE. remarks : none.

LEWIS, Virginia　　　　book 01 page 20 line 13
　　born Ohio, resides Wellsburg, West Virginia,
　　age 20 yrs. single, child of Henry & unknown LEWIS,
　　married 15 Sep 1870 WV. to William H. HARVEY,
　　born Beaver Co., Pennsylvania, resides Brooke Co., WV.
　　age 23 yrs. single, child of Wm. H. & Jane E. HARVEY,
　　married by E. BRINDLEY. remarks : married Wellsburg.

LIAS, George　　　　book 01 page 15 line 75
　　born Pennsylvania, resides Wellsburg, WV. farmer,
　　age - - yrs. single, child of George & Mary LIAS,
　　married 03 Apr 1866 WV. to Nancy LETZKUS,
　　born Wellsburg, Virginia, resides Wellsburg, WV.
　　age - - yrs. single, child of unk. & unk. LETZKUS,
　　married by J.A. PIERCE. remarks : none.

LINDSAY, Samuel　　　　book 01 page 10 line 3 B
　　born Baltimore Co., MD., resides Brooke Co., VA. farmer,
　　age 54 yrs. widow, child of Joshua & Catharine LINDSAY,
　　married 10 Jan 1861 Wellsburg, VA. to Mary TWEED,
　　born Washington Co., PA., resides Brooke Co., Virginia,
　　age 45 yrs. single, child of Robert & Elizabeth TWEED,
　　married by Thomas M. HUDSON. remarks : none.

LINTON, Mahala　　　　book 01 page 19 line 10
　　born Brooke Co., Virginia, resides Brooke Co., WV.
　　age 29 yrs. single, child of William & Eliza. LINTON,
　　married 25 Aug 1868 WV. to James C. PATTON,
　　born Brooke Co., Virginia, resides Brooke Co., WV.
　　age 27 yrs. single, child of Thomas & Eliza PATTON,
　　married by Milton WELLS. remarks : none.

LINTON, William book 01 page 05 line 09
born Brooke Co., VA., resides Brooke Co., VA. laborer,
age 23 yrs. single, child of Wm. & Elizabeth LINTON,
married 15 Nov 1856 VA. to S. Elizabeth THOMPSON,
born Ohio Co., Virginia, resides Brooke Co., Virginia,
age 18 yrs. single, child of Geo. S. & Mary THOMPSON,
married by A.J. ENDSLEY. remarks : none.

LINTON, William D. book 01 page 17 line 16
born Jeff. Co., Ohio, resides Jeff. Co., Ohio, farmer,
age 26 yrs. single, child of Benjamin & Ann LINTON,
married 11 Oct 1866 Wellsburg, WV. to Sarah GREEN,
born Brooke Co., Virginia, resides Brooke Co., WV.
age 23 yrs. single, child of William & unk. GREEN,
married by J.A. PIERCE. remarks : none.

LITTLE, Mary Jane book 01 page 14 line 33
born Scotland, resides Brooke Co., West Virginia,
age 24 yrs. single, child of Jeremiah & unk. LITTLE,
married 05 Jul 1864 Wellsburg, WV. to John S. SCOTT,
born Hancock Co., Virginia, resides Harrison Co., Ohio,
age 38 yrs. single, child of John & Sarah SCOTT,
married by J.A. PIERCE. remarks : none.

LLOYD, James H. book 01 page 14 line 34
born Wash. Co., PA., resides Wellsburg, WV. salesman,
age 39 yrs. single, child of William & Susannah LLOYD,
married 20 Oct 1864 WV. to Ella MERRYMAN,
born Brooke Co., Virginia, resides Brooke Co., WV.
age 25 yrs. single, child of John & Cath. MERRYMAN,
married by Thomas M. HUDSON. remarks : none.

LOFFER, Lusetta/Lucy book 01 page 07 line 19
born Sillinger, Germany, resides Wellsburg, Virginia,
age 35 yrs. widow, child of A. & Cath. (LETZKUS) LOFFER,
married 23 Aug 1858 VA. to Conrad SCHALK,
born Limbach, Germany, resides Wellsburg, Virginia,
age 32 yrs. single, child of J. & Mary (GORNET) SCHALK,
married by S. HUBER. remarks : Lusetta EASTERDAY.

LONG, David W. book 01 page 17 line 01
born Jeff. Co., OH. resides Jeff. Co., OH. school teacher,
age 36 yrs. single, child of Charles & Mary J. LONG,
married 07 Aug 1867 WV. to Sarah A. PATTERSON,
born Brooke Co., Virginia, resides Brooke Co., WV.
age 30 yrs. single, child of Francis & Ann PATTERSON,
married by H. CREE. remarks : married Wellsburg.

LONG, James book 01 page 17 line 18
born Wash. Co., PA., resides Christian Co., IL. farmer,
age 25 yrs. single, child of Lorenze & Margaret LONG,
married 04 Nov 1866 WV. to Mary E. BARNES,
born Brooke Co., Virginia, resides Brooke Co., WV.
age 20 yrs. single, child of John & Eliza. BARNES,
married by J.A. PIERCE. remarks : none.

LONG, Rebecca J. book 01 page 19 line 42
born Brooke Co., Virginia, resides Brooke Co., WV.
age 18 yrs. single, child of Lorenze & Marg't LONG,
married 30 Dec 1869 WV. to Richard T. WELLS,
born Brooke Co., Virginia, resides Brooke Co., WV.
age 28 yrs. widow, child of Bazil & Nancy WELLS,
married by Walter BROWN. remarks : none.

LOOS, Charles Louis book 01 page 12 line 51
born France, resides Bethany, Virginia, Minister,
age - - yrs. unknown, child of unk. & unk. LOOS,
married 06 Jul 1848 VA. to Rosetta E. KEEN,
born Brooke Co., Virginia, resides Bethany, VA.
age - - yrs. unknown, child of unk. & unk. KEEN,
married by A. CAMPBELL. remarks : married Bethany.

LUCAS, Elizabeth book 01 page 21 line 15
born Brooke Co., Virginia, resides Brooke Co., WV.
age 26 yrs. single, child of Samuel & Rebecca LUCAS,
married 06 Dec 1871 WV. to Samuel LANNUM,
born Washington Co., PA., resides Brooke Co., WV.
age 29 yrs. single, child of Samuel & Marg't LANNUM,
married by A.E. WARD. remarks : none.

LUCAS, Elizabeth A. book 01 page 20 line 16
born Brooke Co., Virginia, resides Brooke Co., WV.
age 20 yrs. single, child of Samuel & Rebecca LUCAS,
married 22 Sep 1870 WV. to James MC BURNEY,
born Co. Antrim, Ireland, resides Brooke Co., WV.
age 21 yrs. single, child of John & Mary MC BURNEY,
married by George B. HUDSON. remarks : none.

LUCAS, John book 01 page 07 line 21
born Brooke Co., VA., resides Brooke Co., VA. farmer,
age 22 yrs. single, child of Samuel & Rebecca LUCAS,
married 11 Nov 1858 VA. to Keziah FARQUER,
born Brooke Co., Virginia, resides Brooke Co., Virginia,
age 22 yrs. single, child of Thomas & Eliza. FARQUER,
married by E. QUILLEN. remarks : married Wellsburg.

LUCAS, Nancy book 01 page 20 line 41
born Brooke Co., Virginia, resides Brooke Co., WV.
age 32 yrs. single, child of Samuel & Rebecca LUCAS,
married 25 May 1871 WV. to Joseph CHURCHMAN,
born Brooke Co., VA., resides Brooke Co., West Virginia,
age 48 yrs. widow, child of Jacob & Mary CHURCHMAN,
married by A.E. WARD. remarks : none.

LYONS, David book 01 page 04 line 45
born Washington Co., PA., resides unknown, farmer,
age 28 yrs. single, child of Benjamin & unk. LYONS,
married 15 Sep 1855 VA. to Matilda DOUGHERTY,
born Brooke Co., Virginia, resides unknown,
age 22 yrs. single, child of George & unk. DOUGHERTY,
married by J.T. BRAZILL. remarks : married Wellsburg.

LYONS, Mary book 01 page 07 line 02
born Ireland, resides Brooke Co., Virginia,
age 24 yrs. widow, child of Jerry & Mary LYONS,
married 08 Dec 1857 VA. to Hugh DUNLAP,
born Ireland, resides Brooke Co., Virginia,
age 21 yrs. single, child of Hugh & Ann DUNLAP,
married by E. QUILLEN. remarks : married Wellsburg.

MACKEY, Robert book 01 page 13 line 29
born Ayreshire, Scotland, resides Pittsburgh, PA. miner,
age 22 yrs. single, child of Alex. & Rosa MACKEY,
married 30 Aug 1864 WV. to Millie DEIGHTON,
born Wellsburg, Virginia, resides Wellsburg, WV.
age 23 yrs. single, child of Wm. & Sarah DEIGHTON,
married by E. BRINDLEY. remarks : married Wellsburg.

MAGEE, Ellen book 01 page 14 line 31
born Ireland, resides Brooke Co., West Virginia,
age 20 yrs. single, child of Bernard & Nancy MAGEE,
married 11 Sep 1864 WV. to Thomas MULLANY,
born Ireland, resides Benwood, West Virginia,
age 31 yrs. single, child of Thos. & Bridget MULLANY,
married by S. HUBER. remarks : married Wellsburg.

MAGEE, Martha Ann book 01 page 12 line 49
born Wash. Co., PA., resides Brooke Co., Virginia,
age 40 yrs. single, child of R.T. & Adaline MAGEE,
married 07 Apr 1863 VA. to William POOL,
born Brooke Co., Virginia, resides Brooke Co., VA.
age 36 yrs. widow, child of Benjamin & Eliza. POOL,
married by W. ROBINSON. remarks : see W.H. MC KEE.

MAGEE, Silas book 01 page 02 line 15
born Wash. Co., PA., resides Wellsburg, VA. farmer,
age 25 yrs. single, child of John & Amy MAGEE,
married 26 Oct 1854 VA. to Margaret WIGGINS,
born Brooke Co., Virginia, resides Wellsburg, Virginia,
age 21 yrs. single, child of John & Margaret WIGGINS,
married by S. TOMPKINS. remarks : married WIGGINS house.

MAGEE, William book 01 page 10 line 7 B
born Washington Co., PA., resides Wash. Co., PA. farmer,
age 33 yrs. single, child of William & Martha MAGEE,
married 16 May 1861 VA. to Catharine HUNTER,
born Washington Co., PA., resides Brooke Co., Virginia,
age 24 yrs. single, child of Nath'l & Catharine HUNTER,
married by Thomas M. HUDSON. remarks : none.

MAGOINGAN, Martha book 01 page 10 line 02A
born Washington Co., PA., resides Brooke Co., Virginia,
age 23 yrs. single, child of Jas. & Prudence MAGOINGAN,
married 04 Sep 1860 VA. to John RIDOUT,
born Allegheny Co., PA., resides Jefferson Co., Ohio,
age 23 yrs. single, child of Mark & unk. RIDOUT,
married by Watson RUSSELL. remarks : none.

MAHAN, Jennie M.　　　book 01 page 19 line 23
born Washington Co., PA., resides Brooke Co., WV.
age 24 yrs. single, child of John & Mary MAHAN,
married 31 Dec 1868　WV. to Samuel K. WHITE,
born Washington Co., PA., resides Wash. Co., PA.
age 34 yrs. single, child of William & Eliza. WHITE,
married by T. CRENSHAW. remarks: married Wellsburg.

MAHAN, Robert M.　　　book 01 page 14 line 35
born Wash. Co., PA., resides Wash. Co., PA. carpenter,
age 23 yrs. single, child of unknown & unk. MAHAN,
married 25 Oct 1864　WV. to Melissa LEWIS,
born Hampshire Co., VA., resides Brooke Co., WV.
age 23 yrs. single, child of Oliver & Ann LEWIS,
married by William K. PENDLETON. remarks: none.

MAHON, Anne E.　　　book 01 page 10 line 6 B
born Brooke Co., Virginia, resides Brooke Co., VA.
age 25 yrs. single, child of Thomas & Judith MAHON,
married 05 Mar 1861　VA. to James S. HAMILTON,
born Columbiana Co., Ohio, resides Hancock Co., VA.
age 30 yrs. single, child of Wm. & unk. HAMILTON,
married by George G. WALTERS. remarks: none.

MAHON, Richard　　　book 01 page 19 line 02
born Brooke Co., VA., resides Brooke Co., WV. farmer,
age 31 yrs. single, child of Thomas & Judith MAHON,
married 14 May 1868　WV. to Mary WELLS,
born Brooke Co., Virginia, resides Brooke Co., WV.
age 20 yrs. single, child of Nath'l & Rebecca WELLS,
married by L. SOUTHMAY. remarks: none.

MAHON, William B.　　　book 01 page 06 line 07
born Hancock Co., VA., resides Brooke Co., VA. farmer,
age 24 yrs. single, child of Thomas & Judith MAHON,
married 06 Oct 1857　VA. to Margaret C. BROWNING,
born Brooke Co., Virginia, resides Brooke Co., Virginia,
age 21 yrs. single, child of Lewis & Marg't BROWNING,
married by Intrepid MORSE. remarks: none.

MALOY, Ann　　　book 01 page 19 line 12
born unknown, resides Brooke Co., West Virginia,
age 17 yrs. single, child of unk. & unk. MALOY,
married 07 Oct 1868　WV. to Patrick KENEDY,
born Ireland, resides Brooke Co., West Virginia,
age 26 yrs. single, child of Phillip & Ann KENEDY,
married by S. HUBER. remarks: married Wellsburg.

MARION, Morse　　　book 01 page 20 line 44
born Steuben., Ohio, resides Brooke Co., WV. blacksmith,
age 26 yrs. single, child of Edward & Elizabeth MARION,
married 11 May 1871　WV. to Ruth E. MARSH,
born Brooke Co., Virginia, resides Brooke Co., WV.
age 30 yrs. widow, child of John & unk. MARSH,
married by M.M. SWEENEY. remarks: none.

MARKS, T.H. book 01 page 22 line 36
born Wellsburg, Virginia, resides Wellsburg, WV.
age 51 yrs. unk., child of unk. & unk. MARKS,
married 17 Feb 1874 WV. to Sallie WHEELER,
born Wellsburg, Virginia, resides Wellsburg, WV.
age 33 yrs. unk., child of unk. & unk. WHEELER,
married by J. CROSS. remarks : married Wellsburg.

MARS, Hiram book 01 page 21 line 35
born Oldham Co. KY. resides Galesburg, IL. lumber,
age 40 yrs. widow, child of Andrew & Eliza. MARS,
married 14 May 1872 WV. to Elizabeth H. SMITH,
born Brooke Co., Virginia, resides Brooke Co., WV.
age 32 yrs. single, child of Andrew & Jane SMITH,
married by Thomas M. HUDSON,SR. remarks : none.

MARSH, Mary J. book 01 page 21 line 14
born Brooke Co., Virginia, resides Brooke Co., WV.
age 23 yrs. single, child of Thomas & Eliza. MARSH,
married 26 Nov 1871 WV. to John E. GORDON,
born Washington Co., PA., resides Brooke Co., WV.
age 24 yrs. single, child of William & Eliza. GORDON,
married by J. CASTLE. remarks : married Wellsburg.

MARSH, Narcissa book 01 page 21 line 48
born Brooke Co., Virginia, resides Brooke Co., WV.
age 32 yrs. single, child of James & Sarah MARSH,
married 02 Oct 1872 WV. to Samuel HINDMAN,
born Brooke Co., Virginia, resides Brooke Co., WV.
age 36 yrs. widow, child of Wm. & Eliza. HINDMAN,
married by John B. GRAHAM. remarks : none.

MARSH, Ruth E. book 01 page 20 line 44
born Brooke Co., Virginia, resides Brooke Co., WV.
age 30 yrs. widow, child of John & unk. MARSH,
married 11 May 1871 WV. to Morse MARION,
born Steubenville, Ohio, resides Brooke Co., WV.
age 26 yrs. single, child of Edw. & Eliza. MARION,
married by M.M. SWEENEY. remarks : none.

MARSHALL, Rebecca C. book 01 page 05 line 20
born Brooke Co., Virginia, resides Brooke Co., Virginia,
age 33 yrs. single, child of Thos. & Sarah MARSHALL,
married 25 Mar 1857 VA. to James M. AGNEW,
born Brooke Co., Virginia, resides Brooke Co., VA.
age 46 yrs. widow, child of John & Mary AGNEW,
married by E. QUILLEN. remarks : married Wellsburg.

MARTIN, Margaret book 01 page 09 line 17
born Westmoreland Co., PA., resides Brooke Co., VA.
age 31 yrs. widow, child of Aquilla & Sarah KEITH,
married 24 Apr 1860 Wellsburg, VA. to John FRAZIER,
born Winchester, Virginia, resides Brooke Co., Virginia,
age 47 yrs. widow, child of Alexander & Mary FRAZIER,
married by George W. CHESTER. remarks : none.

BROOKE CO., VA./WV. MARRIAGE BOOK 1, 1853-1874

MATTHEWS, Lavinia S. book 01 page 17 line 10
born Virginia, resides Brooke Co., West Virginia,
age 22 yrs. single, child of Jas. & Lavinia MATTHEWS,
married 04 Sep 1866 WV. to John N. HAYS,
born Franklin Co., Ohio, resides Ohio Co., WV.
age 25 yrs. single, child of Abraham & Sarah HAYS,
married by William K. PENDLETON. remarks : none.

MAY, Jacob book 01 page 04 line 56
born Germany, resides Wellsburg, Virginia, laborer,
age 45 yrs. widow, child of Jacob & Catherine MAY,
married 11 May 1856 VA. to Elizabeth FINK,
born Germany, resides unknown,
age 40 yrs. single, child of Henry & Catherine FINK,
married by A.J. ENDSLEY. remarks : married Wellsburg.

MAYHALL, William A. book 01 page 20 line 26
born Brooke Co., VA. resides Wellsburg, WV. carpenter,
age 32 yrs. single, child of Wm. H. & Jane MAYHALL,
married 12 Jan 1871 WV. to Isabella DEIGHTON,
born Brooke Co., Virginia, resides Wellsburg, WV.
age 31 yrs. single, child of William & Sarah DEIGHTON,
married by D. CALDERWOOD. remarks : married Wellsburg.

MC BURNEY, James book 01 page 20 line 16
born Co. Antrim, Ireland, resides Brooke Co., WV. farmer,
age 21 yrs. single, child of John & Mary MC BURNEY,
married 22 Sep 1870 WV. to Elizabeth A. LUCAS,
born Brooke Co., VA., resides Brooke Co., West Virginia,
age 20 yrs. single, child of Samuel & Rebecca LUCAS,
married by George B. HUDSON. remarks : none.

MC CAMICK, Francis H. book 01 page 17 line 27
born unknown, resides Wellsburg, West Virginia,
age -- yrs. unknown, child of unk & unk MC CAMICK
married 05 Jul 1867 PA. to Mary A. (...) MC CAMICK
born unknown, resides Wellsburg, West Virginia,
age -- yrs. unknown, child of unknown & unk. (...),
married by D. BOYD. remarks : married Wash. Co., pg. 54.

MC CAMICK, Mary A. (...) book 01 page 17 line 27
born unknown, resides Wellsburg, West Virginia,
age -- yrs. unknown, child of unknown & unk. (...),
married 05 Jul 1867 PA. to Francis H. MC CAMICK,
born unknown, resides Wellsburg, West Virginia,
age -- yrs. unk., child of unk. & unk. MC CAMICK,
married by D. BOYD. remarks : affidavit pg 54.

MC CAMICK, Nathan book 01 page 22 line 31
born Monroe Co., Ohio, resides Brooke Co., West Virginia,
age 22 yrs. unknown, child of unk. & unk. MC CAMICK,
married 18 Jan 1874 WV. to Frances P. DOWDEN,
born unknown, resides Brooke Co., West Virginia,
age 22 yrs. unknown, child of unk. & unk. DOWDEN,
married by C. STILLWAGON. remarks : married Wellsburg.

MC CHRISTAL, Rose Ann book 01 page 09 line 10
born Beaver Co., Pennsylvania, resides Steubenville, Ohio,
age 21 yrs. single, child of Henry & Rose A. MC CHRISTAL,
married 16 Apr 1860 Wellsburg, VA. to James O'WESNEY,
born Steubenville, Ohio, resides Steubenville, Ohio,
age 21 yrs. single, child of Valentine & unk. O'WESNEY,
married by George W. CHESTER. remarks : none.

MC CLEARY, Sallie book 01 page 21 line 10
born Brooke Co., Virginia, resides Brooke Co., WV.
age 23 yrs. single, child of Ewing & unk. MC CLEARY,
married 09 Nov 1871 WV. to John D. BRADY,
born Brooke Co., Virginia, resides Brooke Co., WV.
age 25 yrs. single, child of William & Hannah BRADY,
married by Robert R. MOORE. remarks : none.

MC CLELLAND, George book 01 page 22 line 27
born Harrison Co., Ohio, resides Brooke Co., WV.
age 24 yrs. unk., child of unk. & unk. MC CLELLAND,
married 28 Nov 1873 WV. to Anne DEGARMO,
born Brooke Co., Virginia, resides Brooke Co., WV.
age 27 yrs. unk., child of unk. & unk. DEGARMO,
married by C. STILLWAGON. remarks : married Wellsburg.

MC CLURE, Anne A. book 01 page 17 line 08
born Erie, Pennsylvania, resides West Middletown, PA.
age 33 yrs. widow, child of Denison & Mary AIKEN,
married 15 Oct 1867 Wellsburg, WV. to Geo. W. RUSSELL,
born Wellsburg, Virginia, resides Wellsburg, West Virginia,
age 33 yrs. widow, child of Jas. & Sarah (ATKINS) RUSSELL,
married by E. BRINDLEY. remarks : married Union Chapel.

MC CLURG, Harriet E. book 01 page 16 line 26
born unknown, resides Bridgewater, Pennsylvania,
age -- yrs. unknown, child of unknown & unk. MC CLURG,
married 13 Oct 1867 Bridgewater, PA. to William SODIKE,
born unknown, resides Bridgewater, Pennsylvania,
age -- yrs. unknown, child of unk. & unk. SODIKE,
married by J. WILLIAMS. remarks : affidavit bk 01, pg. 55.

MC CLURG, John I. book 01 page 16 line 21
born Washington Co., PA., resides Wash. Co., PA. farmer,
age 35 yrs. single, child of John & Nancy MC CLURG,
married 16 May 1867 WV. to Elizabeth HINDMAN,
born Brooke Co., Virginia, resides Brooke Co., WV.
age 25 yrs. single, child of James & Rebecca HINDMAN,
married by James C. CAMPBELL. remarks : none.

MC COLLOCH, Ebenezer Z. book 01 page 19 line 47
born Ohio Co., Virginia, resides Ohio Co., WV. farmer,
age 24 yrs. single, child of Ebenezer Z. & Sarah MC COLLOCH,
married 17 Feb 1870 WV. to Ella J. WALKER,
born Brooke Co., Virginia, resides Brooke Co., West Virginia,
age 19 yrs. single, child of Montgomery & Jane WALKER,
married by Robert R. MOORE. remarks : none.

BROOKE CO., VA./WV. MARRIAGE BOOK 1, 1853-1874

MC CONKEY, Joseph Grafton book 01 page 09 line 08
born Wellsburg, VA., resides Wellsburg, VA. cotton spinner,
age 21 yrs. single, child of Joseph & Mariane MC CONKEY,
married 03 Nov 1859 VA. to Mary Ann WETHERELL,
born Pennsylvania, resides Wellsburg, Virginia,
age 18 yrs. single, child of William & Elisa. WETHERELL,
married by W.H. MARTIN. remarks : married Wellsburg.

MC CONKEY, Maria book 01 page 03 line 26
born Harrison Co., Pennsylvania, resides Brooke Co., VA.
age 18 yrs. single, child of Joseph & Maria MC CONKEY,
married 23 Nov 1854 Wellsburg, VA. to W.W. HOWARD,
born Philadelphia, Pennsylvania, resides Brooke Co., VA.
age 24 yrs. single, child of Daniel & Catherine HOWARD,
married by Charles A. HOLMES. remarks : none.

MC CONKEY, Mary book 01 page 22 line 45
born Brooke Co., Virginia, resides Wellsburg, WV.
age 30 yrs. unk., child of unk. & unk. MC CONKEY,
married 03 Sep 1874 WV. to J.W. FLOWERS,
born Hancock Co. VA., resides Hancock Co. WV.
age 32 yrs. unk., child of unk. & unk. FLOWERS,
married by Geo. SLADE. remarks : married Wellsburg.

MC CONNELL, George book 01 page 10 line 9 B
born Wash. Co., PA. resides Wash. Co., PA. machinist,
age -- yrs. single, child of unk. & unk. MC CONNELL,
married 07 May 1861 VA. to Rebecca W. CRISS,
born unknown, resides Brooke Co., Virginia,
age -- yrs. single, child of unk. & unk. CRISS,
married by James C. CAMPBELL. remarks : none.

MC CONNELL, James book 01 page 05 line 21
born Co. Down, Ireland, resides Brooke Co., VA. laborer,
age 23 yrs. single, child of Peter & Sendas? MC CONNELL,
married 01 Sep 1857 Wheeling, VA. to Anne O'HARA,
born Co. Down, Ireland, resides Brooke Co., Virginia,
age 23 yrs. single, child of Samuel & Mary O'HARA,
married by John F. BRAZILL. remarks : none.

MC CONNELL, Mary Jane book 01 page 05 line 14
born Ireland, resides Washington Co., Pennsylvania,
age 22 yrs. single, child of Wm. & Eliza. MC CONNELL,
married 17 Feb 1857 VA. to Alexander CRUTH,
born Ireland, resides Brooke Co., Virginia,
age 27 yrs. single, child of Andrew & Lou CRUTH,
married by E. QUILLEN. remarks : married CRUTH house.

MC CONVILLE, Bridget book 01 page 07 line 18
born New Ireland, resides Bethany, Virginia,
age 18 yrs. single, child of Arthur & Bridget MC CONVILLE,
married 29 Jul 1858 Wellsburg, VA. to William H. KEMP,
born Wheeling, Virginia, resides Bethany, Virginia,
age 29 yrs. single, child of A. & Eliza. (HITCHCOCK) KEMP,
married by S. HUBER. remarks : mother Bridget (MURPHY).

MC COY, Agnes A.   book 01 page 13 line 24
born Brooke Co., Virginia, resides Brooke Co., WV.
age 19 yrs. single, child of William & Mary MC COY,
married 23 Mar 1864 WV. to John RUTH,
born Monroe Co., Ohio, resides Brooke Co., WV.
age 25 yrs. single, child of Michael & Mary RUTH,
married by William M. ROBINSON. remarks : none.

MC COY, Lydia   book 01 page 16 line 01
born Brooke Co., Virginia, resides Brooke Co., WV.
age 23 yrs. single, child of unk. & unk. MC COY,
married 22 Apr 1866 WV. to Daniel MEEKER,
born Ohio, resides Ohio Co., West Virginia,
age 21 yrs. single, child of Isaac & Mary MEEKER,
married by J.A. PIERCE. remarks : married Wellsburg.

MC CREA, William   book 01 page 08 line 14
born Wash. Co., PA., resides Wash. Co., PA. farmer,
age 25 yrs. single, child of Robert & Mary MC CREA,
married 17 Mar 1859 VA. to Elizabeth MC GUIRE,
born Brooke Co., Virginia, resides Brooke Co., Virginia,
age 23 yrs. single, child of Thomas & Cath. MC GUIRE,
married by Thomas M. HUDSON. remarks : none.

MC CREARY, Almira   book 01 page 18 line 09
born Brooke Co., Virginia, resides Brooke Co., WV.
age 22 yrs. single, child of Wm. & unk. MC CREARY,
married 09 Jan 1868 WV. to Clarence A.C. SMITH,
born Brooke Co., Virginia, resides Brooke Co., WV.
age 22 yrs. single, child of Andrew & Jane SMITH,
married by A.J. LANE. remarks : none.

MC CREARY, Elizabeth   book 01 page 09 line 16
born Brooke Co., Virginia, resides Brooke Co., VA.
age 21 yrs. single, child of Wm. & A. MC CREARY,
married 01 Mar 1860 VA. to George W. SMITH,
born Brooke Co., Virginia, resides Brooke Co., VA.
age 24 yrs. single, child of Andrew & Jane SMITH,
married by Thomas M. HUDSON. remarks : none.

MC CREARY, George W.   book 01 page 19 line 11
born Brooke Co., VA. resides Brooke Co., WV. shoemaker,
age 24 yrs. single, child of William & A. MC CREARY,
married 05 Sep 1868 WV. to Sarah E. BUCKEY,
born Brooke Co., Virginia, resides Brooke Co., WV.
age 20 yrs. single, child of John & Elizabeth BUCKEY,
married by Walter BROWN. remarks : none.

MC CREARY, Virginia   book 01 page 15 line 66
born Brooke Co., Virginia, resides Brooke Co., WV.
age 25 yrs. single, child of Wm. & unk. MC CREARY,
married 02 Nov 1865 WV. to George W. SMITH,
born Brooke Co., Virginia, resides Brooke Co., VA.
age 29 yrs. widow, child of Andrew & Jane SMITH,
married by T. HUDSON. remarks : married GIST house.

MC CREARY, William book 01 page 02 line 02
born Wash. Co., PA. resides Brooke Co., VA. shoemaker,
age 50 yrs. widow, child of Thomas & Marg't MC CREARY,
married 27 Apr 1854 Wellsburg, VA. to Nancy ROBERTS,
born Ohio Co., Virginia, resides Brooke Co., Virginia,
age 36 yrs. widow, child of William & Rebecca ROBERTS,
married by David HERVEY. remarks: none.

MC DONALD, Angeline book 01 page 23 line 06
born Jefferson Co., Ohio, resides Brooke Co., WV.
age 19 yrs. unk., child of unk. & unk. MC DONALD,
married 20 Feb 1872 WV. to James F. HOUSTON,
born Wheeling, Virginia, resides Brooke Co., WV.
age 23 yrs. unk., child of unk. & unk. HOUSTON,
married by L.H. JORDON. remarks: none.

MC DUGAN, James book 01 page 02 line 17
born Hampshire Co., VA., resides Wellsburg, VA. farmer,
age 32 yrs. widow, child of William & Mary MC DUGAN,
married 26 Oct 1854 VA. to Sarah BAXTER,
born Washington Co., PA., resides Wellsburg, Virginia,
age 19 yrs. single, child of Daniel & Mary BAXTER,
married by Francis GUTHRIE. remarks: none.

MC DUGAN, Wealthy E. book 01 page 16 line 05
born Brooke Co., Virginia, resides Brooke Co., WV.
age 20 yrs. single, child of unk. & unk. MC DUGAN,
married 16 May 1866 WV. to John J. GLASS,
born Pennsylvania, resides Pennsylvania,
age 28 yrs. single, child of James & Sidney GLASS,
married by Charles Louis LOOS. remarks: none.

MC ELFRESH, Mary A. book 01 page 12 line 40
born Brooke Co., Virginia, resides Brooke Co., Virginia,
age 26 yrs. single, child of Zacharia & unk. MC ELFRESH,
married 21 Apr 1862 Wellsburg, VA. to James CUPPLES,
born Allegheny Co., PA., resides Brooke Co., Virginia,
age 32 yrs. single, child of Joseph & Esther CUPPLES,
married by Edward A. BRINDLEY. remarks: none.

MC ELROY, John R. book 01 page 04 line 50
born Jeff. Co., Ohio, resides Jeff. Co., Ohio, farmer,
age 29 yrs. single, child of James & Mary MC ELROY,
married 22 Apr 1856 VA. to Kezeah LEWIS,
born Brooke Co., Virginia, resides Brooke Co., VA.
age 20 yrs. single, child of Job & Margaret LEWIS,
married by Ezekiel QUILLEN. remarks: none.

MC FADDEN, Catherine book 01 page 10 line 08A
born Ireland, resides Bethany, Virginia,
age 29 yrs. widow, child of Owen & Marg't DONNELLY,
married 10 Sep 1860 Bethany, VA. to James KINDRICKS,
born Ireland, resides Bethany, Virginia,
age 34 yrs. single, child of Edw. & Marg't KINDRICKS,
married by S. HUBER. remarks: mother Marg't (GRANT).

MC FADDEN, Leonard D.   book 01 page 20 line 11
born Cadiz, Ohio, resides Bethany, WV. farmer,
age 22 yrs. single, child of David & Eliza. MC FADDEN,
married 01 Sep 1870 WV. to Amanda WAUGH,
born Washington Co., PA., resides Brooke Co., WV.
age 19 yrs. single, child of unk. & Sarah W. CRAFT,
married by William K. PENDLETON. remarks: none.

MC GEE, Charles   book 01 page 08 line 05
born County Down, Ireland, resides Wellsburg, VA. laborer,
age 24 yrs. single, child of Bernard & Nancy MC GEE,
married 06 Jan 1859 Wellsburg, VA. to Catherine BANNON,
born County West Mayo, Ireland, resides Wellsburg, VA.
age 20 yrs. single, child of Thomas & Anne BANNON,
married by S. HUBER. remarks: mother Nancy (MORAN).

MC GEE, Felix   book 01 page 03 line 28
born Clonablan, Co. Down, Ireland, resides VA. laborer,
age 28 yrs. single, child of unknown & unknown MC GEE,
married 19 Feb 1855 VA. to Margaret BEHIN,
born Tackles, Co. Carlow, Ireland, resides Brooke Co., VA.
age 18 yrs. single, child of unknown & unknown BEHIN,
married by John F. BRAZILL. remarks: none.

MC GEE, Margaret   book 01 page 11 line 20
born Ireland, resides Wellsburg, Virginia,
age 20 yrs. single, child of Bernard & Nancy MC GEE,
married 22 Sep 1861 VA. to Richard NOLAND,
born Ireland, resides Wheeling, Virginia,
age 22 yrs. single, child of John & Johanna NOLAND,
married by Stephen HUBER. remarks: married Wellsburg.

MC GREW, John   book 01 page 20 line 28
born Jeff. Co., Ohio, resides Mason Co., WV. millwright,
age 57 yrs. widow, child of James & Sarah MC GREW,
married 17 Feb 1871 WV. to Mary STEWART,
born Jefferson Co., Ohio, resides Brooke Co., WV.
age 56 yrs. widow, child of David & Mary STEWART,
married by Milton WELLS. remarks: none.

MC GROUERTY, Martha   book 01 page 08 line 18
born Ireland, resides Wellsburg, Virginia,
age 28 yrs. single, child of Jas. & Martha MC GROUERTY,
married 26 May 1859 Wellsburg, VA. to Pat. DOUGHERTY,
born Ireland, resides Brooke Co., Virginia,
age 37 yrs. widow, child of Aandrew & Ann DOUGHERTY,
married by S. HUBER. remarks: mother Martha (MC IVID).

MC GUIRE, Elizabeth   book 01 page 08 line 14
born Brooke Co., Virginia, resides Brooke Co., Virginia,
age 23 yrs. single, child of Thomas & Cath. MC GUIRE,
married 17 Mar 1859 VA. to William MC CREA,
born Washington Co., PA., resides Wash. Co., PA.
age 25 yrs. single, child of Robert & Mary MC CREA,
married by Thomas M. HUDSON. remarks: none.

MC GUIRE, Mary Agnes   book 01 page 12 line 55
born Brooke Co., Virginia, resides Brooke Co., WV.
age 25 yrs. single, child of Luke & Jane MC GUIRE,
married 15 Nov 1863   WV. to James M. GARDNER,
born Brooke Co., Virginia, resides Hancock Co., WV.
age 31 yrs. single, child of James & Mary GARDNER,
married by S. HUBER. remarks : married MC GUIRE house.

MC HENRY, Joseph   book 01 page 04 line 40
born Ohio, resides Wellsburg, Virginia, laborer,
age 20 yrs. single, child of Wm. & Rachel MC HENRY,
married 30 Mar 1856   VA. to Joanna CURRAN,
born Ireland, resides Wellsburg, Virginia,
age 21 yrs. single, child of Stephen & unk. CURRAN,
married by A.J. ENDSLEY. remarks : married Wellsburg.

MC HENRY, Lucy   book 01 page 14 line 50
born Brooke Co., Virginia, resides Brooke Co., WV.
age 22 yrs. single, child of unk. & Rachel MC HENRY,
married 02 Mar 1865   WV. to Joseph RALSTON,
born Brooke Co., Virginia, resides Brooke Co., WV.
age 22 yrs. single, child of Samuel & Eliza. RALSTON,
married by J. PIERCE. remarks : married MC HENRY house.

MC HENRY, Mary   book 01 page 22 line 46
born Jefferson Co., Ohio, resides Wellsburg, WV.
age 39 yrs. unk., child of unk. & unk. MC HENRY,
married 03 Sep 1874   WV. to Thomas C. PARK,
born Allegheny Co., PA., resides Wellsburg, WV.
age 50 yrs. unknown, child of unk. & unk. PARK,
married by C. STILLWAGON. remarks : married Wellsburg.

MC HUGH, Mary Ann   book 01 page 11 line 18
born Brooke Co., Virginia, resides Brooke Co., Virginia,
age 24 yrs. single, child of Alex. & Susannah MC HUGH,
married 12 Nov 1861   VA. to Andrew CRUTH,
born Ireland, resides Ohio,
age 27 yrs. single, child of Andrew & Jane CRUTH,
married by David HERVEY. remarks : none.

MC HUGH, Rosanna   book 01 page 04 line 53
born Brooke Co., Virginia, resides Brooke Co., Virginia,
age 22 yrs. single, child of Alex. & Susannah MC HUGH,
married 01 May 1856   VA. to Benjamin STOCK,
born Ohio, resides Brooke Co., Virginia,
age 22 yrs. single, child of Benjamin & Jane STOCK,
married by J.R. MEANS. remarks : none.

MC INTIRE, Robert   book 01 page 17 line 03
born Brooke Co., VA., resides Jeff. Co., Ohio, farmer,
age 42 yrs. widow, child of Robert & Ann MC INTIRE,
married 04 Sep 1867   WV. to Sarah E. DUNN,
born Allegheny Co., PA., resides Brooke Co., WV.
age 62 yrs. widow, child of James & Sarah BAIR,
married by R.T. PRICE. remarks : none.

MC INTYRE, Margarett book 01 page 05 line 17
born Jefferson Co., Ohio, resides Wellsburg, Virginia,
age 25 yrs. single, child of James & Marg't MC INTYRE,
married 26 Feb 1857 Wellsburg, VA. to William PETERS,
born Fayette Co., Pennsylvania, resides Wellsburg, Virginia,
age 31 yrs. single, child of David & Elizabeth PETERS,
married by Ezekiel QUILLEN. remarks : none.

MC KEE, James A. book 01 page 21 line 24
born Putnam Co., IN. resides Cincinnati, Ohio merchant,
age 24 yrs. single, child of Melvin & Matilda MC KEE,
married 15 Feb 1872 WV. to Mary E. HALL,
born Brooke Co., Virginia, resides Brooke Co., WV.
age 23 yrs. single, child of Lewis & Sallie HALL,
married by E.Y. PINKERTON. remarks : none.

MC KEE, William H. book 01 page 09 line 07
born Independence, PA., resides Bethany, VA. farmer,
age 21 yrs. single, child of R.T. & Adaline MC KEE,
married 13 Nov 1859 VA. to Mary E. JESTER,
born Wellsburg, Virginia, resides Brooke Co., Virginia,
age 21 yrs. single, child of Andrew & Eliza. JESTER,
married by G. WALTERS. remarks : married mother's house.

MC KIM, Elizabeth book 01 page 02 line 12
born Brooke Co., Virginia, resides Wellsburg, Virginia,
age 24 yrs. single, child of Thomas & Nancy MC KIM,
married 24 Aug 1854 VA. to Eleazer G. STRAIN,
born Brooke Co., Virginia, resides Wellsburg, Virginia,
age 33 yrs. single, child of Ebenezer & Cath. STRAIN,
married by Samuel D. TOMPKINS. remarks : none.

MC KIM, Mary Jane book 01 page 10 line 05A
born Ireland, resides Bethany, Virginia,
age 19 yrs. single, child of Felix & Mary MC KIM,
married 14 Oct 1860 Bethany, VA. to Casper BENCE,
born Germany, resides Bethany, Virginia,
age 23 yrs. single, child of Richus & Justina BENCE,
married by S. HUBER. remarks : mother Mary (O'HEIR).

MC KINLEY, John W. book 01 page 15 line 65
born Gallipolis, Ohio, resides Brooke Co., WV. farmer,
age 29 yrs. single, child of Wm. & Ellen MC KINLEY,
married 26 Oct 1865 WV. to Sarah WAUGH,
born Brooke Co., Virginia, resides Brooke Co., WV.
age 26 yrs. single, child of James & Mary WAUGH,
married by M. ATKINSON. remarks : married WAUGH house.

MC KINLEY, William L. book 01 page 18 line 23
born Gallipolis, Ohio, resides Brooke Co., WV. farmer,
age 27 yrs. single, child of Wm. & Ellen MC KINLEY,
married 26 Mar 1868 WV. to Michael J. WAUGH,
born Brooke Co., Virginia, resides Brooke Co., WV.
age 21 yrs. single, child of James & Mary WAUGH,
married by J.A. BROWN. remarks : none.

MC KINZIE, Catharine book 01 page 05 line 03
born Brooke Co., Virginia, resides Wellsburg, Virginia,
age 17 yrs. single, child of James & Teonas MC KINZIE,
married 30 Sep 1856 VA. to Simpson O'BRIEN,
born Wellsburg, Virginia, resides Cosmopolotan,
age 24 yrs. single, child of Thomas & Anne O'BRIEN,
married by A.J. ENDSLEY. remarks : married Wellsburg.

MC LAUGHLIN, Carrie book 01 page 13 line 23
born Washington Co., PA., resides Wellsburg, WV.
age 18 yrs. single, child of And. & unk. MC LAUGHLIN,
married 21 Mar 1864 WV. to George A. FRAZIER,
born Wellsburg, Virginia, resides Wellsburg, WV.
age 22 yrs. single, child of John & Mary FRAZIER,
married by W. ROBINSON. remarks : married Wellsburg.

MC LAUGHLIN, Elizabeth book 01 page 20 line 48
born Washington Co., PA., resides Wellsburg, West Virginia,
age 17 yrs. single, child of Andrew & Mary MC LAUGHLIN,
married 05 Jul 1871 WV. to John H. FORSE,
born Bernseyham, Pennsylvania, resides Allegheny Co., PA.
age 23 yrs. single, child of David & Margaret FORSE,
married by D. CALDERWOOD. remarks : MC GLAUGHLIN?

MC LAUGHLIN, Emily book 01 page 15 line 57
born Holmes Co., Ohio, resides Short Creek, West Virginia,
age 25 yrs. single, child of Peter & Eliza. MC LAUGHLIN,
married 15 Aug 1865 WV. to James NIXON,
born Belmont Co., Ohio, resides Short Creek, West Virginia,
age 22 yrs. single, child of Robert & Elizabeth NIXON,
married by E.C. WAYMAN. remarks : none.

MC LAUGHLIN, Martha J. book 01 page 13 line 21
born Washington Co., PA., resides Wellsburg, WV.
age 20 yrs. single, child of And. & unk. MC LAUGHLIN,
married 15 Mar 1864 WV. to Andrew J. SHEARER,
born Wellsburg, Virginia, resides Wellsburg, WV.
age 26 yrs. single, child of Robert & Mary SHEARER,
married by J.A. PIERCE. remarks : married Wellsburg.

MC LEASH, James/John book 01 page 08 line 01
born Scotland, resides Barnesville, Ohio, mechanic,
age 60 yrs. widow, child of John & Euphemia MC LEASH,
married 06 Oct 1858 VA. to Sarah RODGERS,
born Brooke Co., Virginia, resides Morristown, Ohio,
age 51 yrs. single, child of Abram & Sarah RODGERS,
married by W. AIKEN. remarks : married W. RODGERS house.

MC MAHON, Anne E. book 01 page 22 line 33
born Allegheny Co., PA., resides Wellsburg, West Virginia,
age 21 yrs. unknown, child of unk. & unk. MC MAHON,
married 22 Jan 1874 Wellsburg, WV. to Adam LETZKUS,
born Brooke Co., Virginia, resides Wellsburg, West Virginia,
age 21 yrs. unknown, child of unk. & unk. LETZKUS,
married by Joshua COUPLAND, JR. remarks : none.

MC MANIS, Sarah　　　　book 01 page 17 line 04
born Ireland, resides Brooke Co., West Virginia,
age 22 yrs. single, child of John & Mary MC MANIS,
married 21 Sep 1867 WV. to Andrew KELLY,
born Ireland, resides Brooke Co., West Virginia,
age 30 yrs. single, child of Owen & Elizabeth KELLY,
married by Stephen HUBER. remarks : none.

MC MILLEN, Melissa　　　　book 01 page 05 line 16
born Brooke Co., Virginia, resides Wellsburg, Virginia,
age 37 yrs. single, child of Hugh & Martha MC MILLEN,
married 24 Feb 1857 Wellsburg, VA. to Samuel WABLE,
born Westmoreland Co., PA., resides Harrison Co., Ohio,
age 41 yrs. widow, child of Samuel & Joanna WABLE,
married by William GAMBLE, JR. remarks : none.

MC NAIR, Catherine　　　　book 01 page 02 line 09
born Brooke Co., Virginia, resides Wellsburg, Virginia,
age 17 yrs. single, child of Samuel & Eliza. MC NAIR,
married 03 Jan 1853 VA. to Everett WHETZELL,
born Washington Co., PA., resides Wellsburg, Virginia,
age 23 yrs. single, child of John & Emma WHETZELL,
married by E. QUILLEN. remarks : married MOODY house.

MC NALLY, Arthur F.　　　　book 01 page 16 line 25
born Brownsville, PA., resides Wellsburg, WV. tradesman,
age 23 yrs. single, child of Bernard & Mary MC NALLY,
married -- -- 1867 WV. to Ellen E. CONNELL,
born Wellsburg, Virginia, resides Wellsburg, West Virginia,
age 21 yrs. single, child of Harrison & Eliza. CONNELL,
married by G.W. CHESTER. remarks : Jun/Jul/Aug 1867.

MC NALLY, John B.　　　　book 01 page 18 line 01
born Pittsburgh, PA., resides Wellsburg, WV. carpenter,
age 27 yrs. single, child of Bernard & Mary MC NALLY,
married 28 Oct 1867 WV. to Margaret DONNELLY,
born Ireland, resides Wellsburg, West Virginia,
age 23 yrs. single, child of unk. & unk. DONNELLY,
married by Stephen HUBER. remarks : none.

MEEK, Thomas V.　　　　book 01 page 22 line 47
born Brooke Co., Virginia, resides Brooke Co., WV.
age 21 yrs. unknown, child of unk. & unk. MEEK,
married 07 Oct 1874 WV. to Maggie M. HINDMAN,
born Brooke Co., Virginia, resides Brooke Co., WV.
age 18 yrs. unk., child of unk. & unk. HINDMAN,
married by Joshua COUPLAND, JR. remarks : none.

MEEKER, Daniel　　　　book 01 page 16 line 01
born Ohio, resides Ohio Co., West Virginia, miner,
age 21 yrs. single, child of Isaac & Mary MEEKER,
married 22 Apr 1866 WV. to Lydia MC COY,
born Brooke Co., VA., resides Brooke Co., WV.
age 23 yrs. single, child of unk. & unk. MC COY,
married by J. PIERCE. remarks : married Wellsburg.

BROOKE CO., VA./WV. MARRIAGE BOOK 1, 1853-1874

MELCHS, Margaret book 01 page 18 line 19
born Brooke Co., Virginia, resides Brooke Co., WV.
age 24 yrs. widow, child of George & Marg't MELCHS,
married 27 Feb 1868 WV. to James SEARS,
born Washington Co., PA., resides Jeff. Co., Ohio,
age 42 yrs. widow, child of Stephen & Eliza. SEARS,
married by Edward A. BRINDLEY. remarks : none.

MELVIN, Addie book 01 page 12 line 43
born Beaver Co., PA., resides Brooke Co., Virginia,
age 20 yrs. single, child of Henry & Alzina MELVIN,
married 13 Feb 1862 VA. to Samuel G. NAYLOR,
born Brooke Co., Virginia, resides Wellsburg, Virginia,
age 20 yrs. single, child of J.R. & Hester C. NAYLOR,
married by Charles L. LOOS. remarks : married Wellsburg.

MELVIN, William H. book 01 page 16 line 24
born Beaver Co., PA., resides Col. Co., Ohio, painter,
age 24 yrs. single, child of Henry & Alzina MELVIN,
married 23 Jun 1867 WV. to Melissa E. QUEST,
born Allegheny Co., PA. resides Brooke Co., WV.
age 23 yrs. single, child of Sam'l & Martha C. QUEST,
married by Edward A. BRINDLEY. remarks : none.

MENDEL, Clarinda E. book 01 page 04 line 58
born Brooke Co., Virginia, resides Bethany, Virginia,
age 17 yrs. single, child of John & Ann MENDEL,
married 11 Aug 1856 VA. to Elijah B. CHALLENCE,
born Charles City Co., VA., resides James City Co., VA.
age 22 yrs. single, child of B.D. & M.A. CHALLENCE,
married by A. CAMPBELL. remarks : married Bethany.

MENDEL, Sarah H. book 01 page 06 line 04
born Wellsburg, Virginia, resides Bethany, Virginia,
age 20 yrs. single, child of John & Ann MENDEL,
married 01 Sep 1857 VA. to Henry C. DURRETT,
born Hopkinsville, Kentucky, resides Christian Co., KY.
age 20 yrs. single, child of Rich'd & Nancie DURRETT,
married by A. CAMPBELL. remarks : married Bethany.

MENDEL, Tabitha book 01 page 05 line 18
born Jefferson Co., Ohio, resides Wellsburg, Virginia,
age - - yrs. single, child of Valentine & Roselane MENDEL,
married 03 Mar 1857 Wellsburg, VA. to James OBNEY,
born Jefferson Co., Ohio resides Jefferson Co., Ohio
age 21 yrs. single, child of James & Sarah OBNEY,
married by A.J. ENDSLEY. remarks : none.

MERRYMAN, Angeline book 01 page 09 line 24
born Tuscarawas Co., Ohio, resides unknown,
age 20 yrs. single, child of unk. & unk. MERRYMAN,
married 16 Jun 1860 VA. to George BLANKENSOP,
born Wellsburg, Virginia, resides unknown,
age 21 yrs. single, child of unk. & unk. BLANKENSOP,
married by UNKNOWN. remarks : 2 nd. page of record torn.

MERRYMAN, Ella book 01 page 14 line 34
born Brooke Co., Virginia, resides Brooke Co., WV.
age 25 yrs. single, child of John & Cath. MERRYMAN,
married 20 Oct 1864 WV. to James H. LLOYD,
born Washington Co., PA., resides Wellsburg, WV.
age 39 yrs. single, child of Wm. & Susannah LLOYD,
married by Thomas M. HUDSON. remarks: none.

MERRYMAN, Emma J. book 01 page 21 line 07
born Jefferson Co., Ohio, resides Brooke Co., WV.
age 21 yrs. single, child of Wm. & Joana MERRYMAN,
married 11 Oct 1871 Wellsburg, WV. to David D. SHUPE,
born Monroe Co., Ohio, resides Bellaire, Ohio,
age 27 yrs. single, child of Jonathan & Juliett SHUPE,
married by William K. PENDLETON. remarks: none.

MERRYMAN, Mary book 01 page 12 line 50
born Brooke Co., Virginia, resides Brooke Co., Virginia,
age 26 yrs. single, child of John & Cath. MERRYMAN,
married 28 Apr 1863 VA. to Alexander FINLEY,
born Co. Cavan, Ireland, resides Wellsburg, Virginia,
age 27 yrs. single, child of Alexander & Ann FINLEY,
married by J. PIERCE. remarks: married M.E. Parsonage.

MEYERS, Sallie book 01 page 22 line 10
born Steubenville, Ohio, resides Wellsburg, West Virginia,
age 22 yrs. single, child of Christian & Mary MEYERS,
married 23 Feb 1873 Wellsburg, WV. to Charles JACOB,
born Germany, resides Wellsburg, West Virginia,
age 21 yrs. single, child of Jacob & Kate JACOB,
married by Stephen HUBER. remarks: none.

MILELECH, Eva book 01 page 16 line 14
born Germany, resides Wellsburg, West Virginia,
age 19 yrs. single, child of unk. & Eva MILELECH,
married 05 Feb 1867 WV. to John LETZKUS,
born Wellsburg, Virginia, resides Wellsburg, WV.
age 22 yrs. single, child of John & unk. LETZKUS,
married by Stephen HUBER. remarks: none.

MILLER, Cyrus book 01 page 13 line 20
born Wash. Co., PA., resides Wash. Co., PA. coal merchant,
age 35 yrs. widow, child of unknown & unk. MILLER,
married 25 Feb 1864 WV. to Elizabeth THOMPSON,
born Washington Co., PA., resides Wellsburg, West Virginia,
age 21 yrs. single, child of Robert & Eleanor THOMPSON,
married by E.A. BRINDLEY. remarks: married Wellsburg.

MILLER, David B. book 01 page 14 line 43
born Ohio Co., VA., resides Brooke Co., WV. farmer,
age 21 yrs. widow, child of Nicholas & Rebecca MILLER,
married 17 Jan 1865 WV. to Mary HUKILL,
born Brooke Co., Virginia, resides Brooke Co., WV.
age 21 yrs. single, child of William & Mary HUKILL,
married by C. LOOS. remarks: married HUKILL house.

MILLER, David B. book 01 page 11 line 14
born Ohio Co., Virginia, resides Brooke Co., VA. farmer,
age 21 yrs. single, child of Nicholas & Rebecca MILLER,
married 08 Nov 1861 VA. to Cecelia M. BOWMAN
born Brooke Co., Virginia, resides Brooke Co., Virginia,
age 26 yrs. single, child of Abraham & Henrietta BOWMAN,
married by Thomas M. HUDSON. remarks : none.

MILLER, Elenora book 01 page 03 line 24
born Brooke Co., Virginia, resides Brooke Co., Virginia,
age 20 yrs. single, child of James W. & Ellen MILLER,
married 09 Nov 1854 VA. to Samuel GEORGE,
born Washington Co., PA., resides Brooke Co., Virginia,
age 27 yrs. single, child of Thomas & Sarah GEORGE,
married by E. QUILLEN. remarks : married Wellsburg.

MILLER, Elizabeth A. book 01 page 17 line 24
born Brownsville, PA., resides Brooke Co., WV.
age 21 yrs. single, child of James & Eliza. MILLER,
married 14 Oct 1867 WV. to James M. JONES,
born Brooke Co., Virginia, resides Wellsburg, WV.
age 23 yrs. single, child of Wm. & Emeline E. JONES,
married by Edward A. BRINDLEY. remarks : none.

MILLER, Frank book 01 page 22 line 07
born Beaver Co., PA., resides Allegh. Co., PA. machinist,
age 23 yrs. single, child of George & Rebecca MILLER,
married 10 Feb 1873 WV. to Sallie BLANKENSOP,
born Brooke Co., Virginia, resides Wellsburg, West Virginia,
age 23 yrs. single, child of Peter & Susan BLANKENSOP,
married by J. COUPLAND, JR. remarks : married Wellsburg.

MILLER, George book 01 page 20 line 21
born Wash. Co., PA., resides Brooke Co., WV. farmer,
age 48 yrs. widow, child of George & Susan MILLER,
married 01 Sep 1870 WV. to Cora CASNER,
born Brooke Co., Virginia, resides Brooke Co., WV.
age 22 yrs. single, child of Wm. & Mary CASNER,
married by J. WARDEN. remarks : married West Liberty.

MILLER, Jacob book 01 page 19 line 18
born Ohio Co., Virginia, resides Wellsburg, WV. laborer,
age 23 yrs. single, child of Joseph & Mary MILLER,
married 24 Dec 1868 WV. to Elizabeth C. STEWART,
born Wellsburg, Virginia, resides Wellsburg, West Virginia,
age 22 yrs. single, child of Jackson & Mary STEWART,
married by A.R. CHAPMAN. remarks : married Wellsburg.

MILLER, James L. book 01 page 20 line 45
born Wheeling, VA., resides Brooke Co., WV. farmer,
age 22 yrs. single, child of Robert & Eliza. MILLER,
married 04 Jun 1871 WV. to Elizabeth HALL,
born Brooke Co., Virginia, resides Wellsburg, WV.
age 21 yrs. single, child of F.P. & unknown HALL,
married by Robert R. MOORE. remarks : none.

BROOKE CO., VA./WV. MARRIAGE BOOK 1, 1853-1874   245

MILLER, Jane   book 01 page 02 line 08
born Brooke Co., Virginia, resides Wellsburg, Virginia,
age 37 yrs. single, child of Nicholas & Sarah MILLER,
married 12 Jan 1854   VA. to Cyrus H. CUNNINGHAM,
born Washington Co., PA., resides Wellsburg, Virginia,
age 43 yrs. widow, child of Hugh & Christine CUNNINGHAM,
married by E. QUILLEN. remarks : married house of S. REIDLER.

MILLER, Robert   book 01 page 19 line 03
born Wheeling, Virginia, resides Brooke Co., WV. farmer,
age 22 yrs. single, child of Robert & unknown MILLER,
married 19 Mar 1868   WV. to Sallie NAYLOR,
born Wellsburg, Virginia, resides Brooke Co., WV.
age 19 yrs. single, child of Jos. & Hester C. NAYLOR,
married by David POOR. remarks : none.

MILLER, Robert L.   book 01 page 16 line 12
born Wash. Co., PA., resides Brooke Co., WV. farmer,
age 24 yrs. single, child of George & Jane MILLER,
married 01 Jan 1867   WV. to Catharine M. HENDRICKS,
born Brooke Co., Virginia, resides Brooke Co., West Virginia,
age 20 yrs. single, child of Edward & Rebecca HENDRICKS,
married by James C. CAMPBELL. remarks : none.

MILLER, Rosann   book 01 page 20 line 08
born Belmont Co., Ohio, resides Bethany, WV.
age 30 yrs. single, child of Wm. & Mary MILLER,
married 21 Jul 1870 Bethany, WV. to Isaac DOW,
born Morgan Co., Ohio, resides Bethany, WV.
age 45 yrs. widow, child of Isaac & Rebecca DOW,
married by William K. PENDLETON. remarks : none.

MILLER, Sarah   book 01 page 05 line 01
born Ohio Co., Virginia, resides Wellsburg, Virginia,
age 20 yrs. single, child of Nicholas & Rebecca MILLER,
married 09 Jul 1856 Wellsburg, VA. to Isaac DUVALL,
born Wellsburg, Virginia, resides Peoria, Illinois,
age 24 yrs. single, child of Gabriel & Nancy DUVALL,
married by A.J. ENDSLEY. remarks : none.

MILLER, Unity   book 01 page 08 line 21
born Brooke Co., Virginia, resides Brooke Co., VA.
age 57 yrs. widow, child of John & Martha MUNCY,
married 29 Dec 1859 Wellsburg, VA. to George COX,
born Brooke Co., Virginia, resides Brooke Co., VA.
age 68 yrs. widow, child of George & Susannah COX,
married by T. HUDSON. remarks : Mrs.Unity MILLER

MILLIGAN, Mary Ann   book 01 page 09 line 09
born Jefferson Co., Ohio, resides Brooke Co., Virginia,
age 33 yrs. single, child of George & Mary MILLIGAN,
married 23 Nov 1859   VA. to Evan CONAWAY,
born Monongalia Co., VA., resides Brooke Co., VA.
age 31 yrs. widow, child of Eli & Mary CONAWAY,
married by J.M. SMITH. remarks : none.

MILLIGAN, Sarah book 01 page 15 line 68
born Ohio, resides Brooke Co., West Virginia,
age 35 yrs. single, child of George & Mary MILLIGAN,
married 21 Nov 1865 Wellsburg, WV. to David RIDDLE,
born Ohio, resides Brooke Co., West Virginia,
age 42 yrs. widow, child of John & Elizabeth RIDDLE,
married by J.A. BROWN. remarks : none.

MITCHELL, Elizabeth book 01 page 14 line 38
born Washington Co., PA., resides Wellsburg, WV.
age 25 yrs. single, child of unk. & unk. MITCHELL,
married 16 Nov 1864 WV. to George W. MURPHY,
born Washington Co., PA., resides Wellsburg, WV.
age 28 yrs. widow, child of Thomas & Eliza. MURPHY,
married by G.W. CHESTER. remarks : married Wellsburg.

MITCHELL, Mary book 01 page 19 line 13
born Washington Co., PA., resides Brooke Co., WV.
age 19 yrs. single, child of George & Mary MITCHELL,
married 15 Oct 1868 WV. to Lewis WILLQUES,
born Westmoreland Co., PA., resides Brooke Co., WV.
age 25 yrs. single, child of Wm. & Parthenia WILLQUES,
married by A.R. CHAPMAN. remarks : none.

MITCHELL, William H. book 01 page 08 line 12
born Belmont Co., Ohio, resides Madison Co., IL. scaler,
age 41 yrs. widow, child of James & Eliza. MITCHELL,
married 10 Feb 1859 VA. to Lydia M. BARNES,
born Brooke Co., Virginia, resides Brooke Co., Virginia,
age 27 yrs. single, child of Ephraim & Eliza. BARNES,
married by J. BEACOM. remarks : married BARNES house.

MONTGOMERY, Joseph book 01 page 17 line 07
born Ohio Co., Virginia, resides Brooke Co., WV. saddler,
age 31 yrs. widow, child of Abram & Nancy MONTGOMERY,
married 13 Oct 1867 Wellsburg, WV. to Sophia PILLINGS,
born Allegheny Co., PA., resides Brooke Co., West Virginia,
age 25 yrs. widow, child of James & Rebecca LAUGHEAD,
married by A.E. ANDERSON. remarks : none.

MONTGOMERY, Joseph E. book 01 page 11 line 19
born Ohio Co., Virginia, resides Brooke Co., VA. saddler,
age 24 yrs. single, child of Abram & Nancy MONTGOMERY,
married 22 Dec 1861 Wellsburg, VA. to Sarah PILLINGS,
born Brooke Co., Virginia, resides Brooke Co., Virginia,
age 20 yrs. single, child of Charles & Sarah PILLINGS,
married by R.B. WATKINS. remarks : none.

MONTGOMERY, Mary E. book 01 page 19 line 27
born Brooke Co., Virginia, resides Brooke Co., West Virginia,
age 27 yrs. single, child of Daniel & Julia MONTGOMERY,
married 28 Jan 1868 WV. to Ewing T. CARTER,
born Brooke Co., Virginia, resides Brooke Co., West Virginia,
age 28 yrs. single, child of L.W. & Martha A. CARTER,
married by L. SOUTHMAY. remarks : none.

BROOKE CO., VA./WV. MARRIAGE BOOK 1, 1853-1874   247

MOOKLAR, Jas. Phillips   book 01 page 15 line 70
born Mason Co., KY., resides Covington, KY. student,
age 25 yrs. single, child of Wm. B. & S.M. MOOKLAR,
married 30 Dec 1865 WV. to Alexandria C. PENDLETON,
born Brooke Co., Virginia, resides Bethany, West Virginia,
age 24 yrs. single, child of Wm. K. & S. PENDLETON,
married by Charles Louis LOOS. remarks : married Bethany.

MOORE, Asbury S.   book 01 page 14 line 44
born Hancock Co., VA., resides Lee Co., Iowa, farmer,
age 27 yrs. single, child of John & K. T. MOORE,
married 18 Jan 1865 WV. to Lorinda LAZEAR,
born Brooke Co., Virginia, resides Brooke Co., WV.
age 26 yrs. single, child of Asa & Mary LAZEAR,
married by William K. PENDLETON. remarks : none.

MOORE, Elizabeth   book 01 page 06 line 12
born Brooke Co., Virginia, resides Brooke Co., Virginia,
age 51 yrs. widow, child of John & Jane MOORE,
married 10 Nov 1857 Wellsburg, VA. to James PALMER,
born Washington Co., PA., resides Brooke Co., Virginia,
age 58 yrs. widow, child of Samuel & Mary PALMER,
married by E. QUILLEN. remarks : Mrs. Eliza. WAUGH.

MORENTZ, Hannah   book 01 page 14 line 54
born Ireland, resides Brooke Co., West Virginia,
age 23 yrs. widow, child of John & Ann MORENTZ,
married 05 May 1865 Wellsburg, WV. to Wm. KELLY,
born Ireland, resides Brooke Co., West Virginia,
age 33 yrs. single, child of William & Bridget KELLY,
married by S. HUBER. remarks : Hannah HULLIHAN.

MORGAN, Henry C.   book 01 page 10 line 11 B
born unknown, resides Wheeling, Virginia,
age 32 yrs. widow, child of John & Catherine MORGAN,
married 18 Jun 1861 VA. to Cynthia A. HUDSON,
born Brooke Co., Virginia, resides Brooke Co., Virginia,
age 23 yrs. single, child of Thomas M. & S.E. HUDSON,
married by Thomas M. HUDSON. remarks : none.

MORGAN, John   book 01 page 12 line 59
born Wheeling, VA., resides Wheeling, WV. telegraph,
age 22 yrs. single, child of John & Catherine MORGAN,
married 21 Jul 1863 WV. to M. Belle HUDSON,
born Allegheny Co., PA., resides Brooke Co., WV.
age 19 yrs. single, child of Thomas M. & S.E. HUDSON,
married by T. HUDSON. remarks : married HUDSON house.

MORGAN, McCullough   book 01 page 16 line 08
born Brooke Co., VA., resides Ohio Co., WV. farmer,
age 20 yrs. single, child of Edward & Marg't MORGAN,
married 01 Jan 1867 WV. to Clara B. COLEMAN,
born Brooke Co., Virginia, resides Brooke Co., WV.
age 20 yrs. single, child of David & Mary J. COLEMAN,
married by W. HOWE. remarks : married COLEMAN house.

BROOKE CO., VA./WV. MARRIAGE BOOK 1, 1853-1874

MORGAN, Wm. Finley book 01 page 12 line 52
born Lanc. Co., PA., resides Rural Valley, PA. minister,
age 40 yrs. widow, child of Isaac & Margaret MORGAN,
married 25 Aug 1863 WV. to Mary HERVEY,
born Washington Co., PA., resides Brooke Co., WV.
age 30 yrs. single, child of David & Dora HERVEY,
married by D. HERVEY. remarks : married HERVEY house.

MORLEY, Evander book 01 page 21 line 46
born NY., resides Sioux City, Iowa, lumber merchant,
age 36 yrs. single, child of Russell & Betsey MORLEY,
married 17 Sep 1872 WV. to Alice U. BRIGGS,
born New Hampshire, resides Brooke Co., WV.
age 26 yrs. single, child of James & Nancy BRIGGS,
married by Robert R. MOORE. remarks : none.

MORROW, William book 01 page 19 line 07
born Ohio Co., Virginia, resides Bethany, WV. tailor,
age 57 yrs. widow, child of John & May MORROW,
married 23 Jul 1868 Wellsburg, WV. to Nancy KEESEY,
born Fayette Co., Pennsylvania, resides Wellsburg, WV.
age 50 yrs. widow, child of unknown & unknown (...),
married by R.T. PRICE. remarks : none.

MORTON, Amanda J. book 01 page 20 line 39
born Brooke Co., Virginia, resides Brooke Co., WV.
age 30 yrs. single, child of Thomas & Eliza. MORTON,
married 16 May 1871 WV. to George W. BROWN,
born Jefferson Co., Ohio, resides Montgomery Co., IL.
age 52 yrs. widow, child of Nichodemus & Eliza. BROWN,
married by J.C. CASTLE. remarks : married Wellsburg.

MORTON, Elizabeth book 01 page 13 line 22
born unknown, resides Brooke Co., West Virginia,
age - - yrs. unknown, child of unk & unk MORTON,
married 16 Mar 1864 WV. to Greer M. CAMPBELL,
born unknown, resides unknown,
age - - yrs. unknown, child of unk. & unk. CAMPBELL,
married by UNKNOWN. remarks : none.

MORTON, J.C. book 01 page 22 line 08
born Beaver Co., PA., resides Wellsburg, WV. blacksmith,
age 46 yrs. widow, child of Wm. & Maryann MORTON,
married 13 Feb 1873 Wellsburg, WV. to Elisabeth LAKE,
born England, resides Wellsburg, West Virginia,
age 45 yrs. widow, child of unk. & unk. LAKE,
married by S.H. CRAVENS. remarks : none.

MOSS, William Rose book 01 page 20 line 24
born Guernsey Co., Ohio, resides Cambridge, Ohio, clerk,
age 25 yrs. single, child of James R. & Mary A. MOSS,
married 22 Dec 1870 WV. to Amy H. JONES,
born Brooke Co., Virginia, resides Brooke Co., WV.
age 17 yrs. single, child of Charles E. & A.A. JONES,
married by Robert R. MOORE. remarks : none.

BROOKE CO., VA./WV. MARRIAGE BOOK 1, 1853-1874   249

MOURLAND, Margaret   book 01 page 14 line 37
born County Clare, Ireland, resides Brooke Co., WV.
age 35 yrs. single, child of unk. & unk. MOURLAND,
married 13 Nov 1864 Wellsburg, WV. to Hugh JESTY,
born Liverpool, England, resides Brooke Co., WV.
age 37 yrs. widow, child of Henry & Rose JESTY,
married by Stephen HUBER. remarks : none.

MULLANY, Thomas   book 01 page 14 line 31
born Ireland, resides Benwood, West Virginia, clerk,
age 31 yrs. single, child of Thos. & Bridget MULLANY,
married 11 Sep 1864 Wellsburg, WV. to Ellen MAGEE,
born Ireland, resides Brooke Co., West Virginia,
age 20 yrs. single, child of Bernard & Nancy MAGEE,
married by Stephen HUBER. remarks : none.

MUNCY, Unity   book 01 page 08 line 21
born Brooke Co., Virginia, resides Brooke Co., VA.
age 57 yrs. widow, child of John & Martha MUNCY,
married 29 Dec 1859 Wellsburg, VA. to George COX,
born Brooke Co., Virginia, resides Brooke Co., VA.
age 68 yrs. widow, child of George & Susannah COX,
married by T. HUDSON. remarks : Mrs. Unity MILLER

MURCHLAND, David H.   book 01 page 12 line 37
born Brooke Co., VA., resides Brooke Co., VA. farmer,
age 37 yrs. widow, child of Rob't & Sallie MURCHLAND,
married 01 Jun 1862 VA. to Josephine BUCKALEW,
born Wellsburg, Virginia, resides Brooke Co., Virginia,
age 19 yrs. single, child of Garrett & unk. BUCKALEW,
married by Edward A. BRINDLEY. remarks : none.

MURCHLAND, Elizabeth   book 01 page 19 line 19
born Brooke Co., Virginia, resides Brooke Co., West Virginia,
age 19 yrs. single, child of Andrew & Eliza. MURCHLAND,
married 24 Dec 1868 WV. to John W. BOWLES,
born Washington Co., PA., resides Washington Co., PA.
age 21 yrs. single, child of James & Isabella BOWLES,
married by David HERVEY. remarks : none.

MURCHLAND, Nancy   book 01 page 18 line 24
born Brooke Co., Virginia, resides Brooke Co., WV.
age 20 yrs. single, child of Andrew & Eliza. MURCHLAND,
married 24 Mar 1868 WV. to Samuel HINDMAN,
born Brooke Co., Virginia, resides Brooke Co., WV.
age 30 yrs. single, child of William & Betsy HINDMAN,
married by James C. CAMPBELL. remarks : none.

MURPHY, Bridget   book 01 page 22 line 22
born Ireland, resides Brooke Co., West Virginia,
age 30 yrs. unknown, child of unk. & unk. MURPHY,
married 04 Nov 1873 WV. to Timothy COLLINS,
born Ireland, resides Brooke Co., West Virginia,
age 32 yrs. unknown, child of unk. & unk. COLLINS,
married by Stephen HUBER. remarks : none.

MURPHY, Elizabeth book 01 page 11 line 30
born Washington Co., PA., resides Brooke Co., Virginia,
age 18 yrs. single, child of Thomas & Eliza. MURPHY,
married 02 Jan 1863 Wellsburg, VA. to Joseph STARR,
born Washington Co., PA., resides Brooke Co., Virginia,
age 21 yrs. single, child of William & A. STARR,
married by George W. CHESTER. remarks : none.

MURPHY, George Wash. book 01 page 12 line 57
born Wash. Co., PA., resides Brooke Co., WV. laborer,
age 24 yrs. single, child of Thomas & Eliza. MURPHY,
married 20 Jul 1863 WV. to Nancy J. STARR,
born Pennsylvania, resides Washington Co., PA.
age 19 yrs. single, child of William & A. STARR,
married by G. CHESTER. remarks : married Wellsburg.

MURPHY, George Wash. book 01 page 14 line 38
born Wash. Co., PA. resides Wellsburg, WV. miner,
age 28 yrs. widow, child of Thomas & Eliza. MURPHY,
married 16 Nov 1864 WV. to Elizabeth MITCHELL,
born Washington Co., PA., resides Wellsburg, WV.
age 25 yrs. single, child of unk. & unk. MITCHELL,
married by G. CHESTER. remarks : married Wellsburg.

MURPHY, James F. book 01 page 19 line 01
born Wash. Co., PA., resides Wellsburg, WV. printer,
age 20 yrs. single, child of Joseph & Edith MURPHY,
married 05 May 1868 WV. to Sallie E. REEVES,
born Wellsburg, Virginia, resides Wellsburg, West Virginia,
age 19 yrs. single, child of Nathan & Rachel A. REEVES,
married by J.A. PIERCE. remarks : married Wellsburg.

MURPHY, Matilda book 01 page 03 line 35
born Brooke Co., Virginia, resides Brooke Co., Virginia,
age 24 yrs. single, child of William & Eliza. MURPHY,
married 01 Jun 1855 Wellsburg, VA. to David RIDDLE,
born Jefferson Co., Ohio, resides Brooke Co., Virginia,
age 28 yrs. single, child of John & Elizabeth RIDDLE,
married by Ezekiel QUILLEN. remarks : none.

MURRAY, Eleanor J. book 01 page 18 line 07
born Brooke Co., Virginia, resides Brooke Co., WV.
age 19 yrs. single, child of James & Jane MURRAY,
married 08 Dec 1867 WV. to Henry NEDENGARDEN,
born Allegheny Co., PA., resides Jefferson Co., Ohio,
age 21 yrs. single, child of Geo. & Mary NEDENGARDEN,
married by Edward A. BRINDLEY. remarks : none.

MURRAY, James A. book 01 page 20 line 07
born Simpson Co., Kentucky, resides Palmyra, MO. literary,
age 27 yrs. single, child of William & Nancy MURRAY,
married 08 Jul 1870 Bethany, WV. to Anna B. POSTON,
born Newry, Ireland, resides Bethany, West Virginia,
age 27 yrs. widow, child of Archibald & Anne CAMPBELL,
married by A. CAMPBELL. remarks : marriage 08 Jul 1850?

MYERS, Mary book 01 page 12 line 53
born Pennsylvania, resides Brooke Co., West Virginia,
age 36 yrs. widow, child of Henry & Jane BUKER,
married 28 Oct 1863 WV. to Salathiel HILL,
born Pennsylvania, resides Brooke Co., West Virginia,
age 45 yrs. widow, child of George & Alice Ann HILL,
married by J. CAMPBELL. remarks: married BUKER house.

NALLINGER, Rosena book 01 page 22 line 16
born Coshocton Co., Ohio, resides Wellsburg, WV.
age 26 yrs. unk., child of unk. & unk. NALLINGER,
married 24 Jul 1873 WV. to Asbury PERKINS,
born Brooke Co., Virginia, resides Wellsburg, WV.
age 21 yrs. unknown, child of unk. & unk. PERKINS,
married by W.H. MARTIN. remarks: married Wellsburg.

NANGLE, Elizabeth book 01 page 08 line 13
born Wellsburg, Virginia, resides Wellsburg, Virginia,
age 23 yrs. single, child of Thomas & Eliza. NANGLE,
married 13 Feb 1859 Wellsburg, VA. to John D'FOSSIT,
born France, resides Wellsburg, Virginia,
age 32 yrs. widow, child of David & Marg't D'FOSSIT,
married by S. HUBER. remarks: mother Eliza. (MATHEWS).

NANGLE, Samuel G. book 01 page 13 line 15
born Wellsburg, VA. resides Wellsburg, WV. stonemason,
age 23 yrs. single, child of Thomas & Susan NANGLE,
married 02 Jan 1864 WV. to Mary BRASHEARS,
born Brooke Co., Virginia, resides Brooke Co., West Virginia,
age 21 yrs. single, child of George & Eliza. BRASHEARS,
married by W.M. ROBINSON. remarks: married Wellsburg.

NASMITH, Mary/Nancy book 01 page 15 line 71
born Massillon, Ohio, resides Massillon, Ohio,
age 26 yrs. single, child of Henry & Mary NASMITH,
married 02 Jan 1866 WV. to Ralph DEIGHTON,
born Massillon, Ohio, resides Massillon, Ohio,
age 39 yrs. widow, child of unk. & unk. DEIGHTON,
married by G. CHESTER. remarks: married Wellsburg.

NAYLOR, Elizabeth T. book 01 page 21 line 25
born Brooke Co., Virginia, resides Brooke Co., WV.
age 19 yrs. single, child of Jos. R. & Harriet NAYLOR,
married 26 Feb 1872 WV. to J.A. SCARBOROUGH,
born South Carolina, resides Little Rock, Arkansas,
age 24 yrs. single, child of W. & M. SCARBOROUGH,
married by Joshua COUPLAND, JR. remarks: none.

NAYLOR, Sallie book 01 page 19 line 03
born Wellsburg, Virginia, resides Brooke Co., WV.
age 19 yrs. single, child of Jos. & Hester NAYLOR,
married 19 Mar 1868 WV. to Robert MILLER,
born Wheeling, Virginia, resides Brooke Co., WV.
age 22 yrs. single, child of Robert & unk. MILLER,
married by David POOR. remarks: none.

NAYLOR, Samuel G. book 01 page 12 line 43
born Brooke Co., VA. resides Wellsburg, VA. co. clerk,
age 20 yrs. single, child of J.R. & Hester C. NAYLOR,
married 13 Feb 1862 Wellsburg, VA. to Addie MELVIN,
born Beaver Co., PA., resides Brooke Co., Virginia,
age 20 yrs. single, child of Henry & Alzina MELVIN,
married by Charles Louis LOOS. remarks : none.

NEDENGARDEN, Henry book 01 page 18 line 07
born Allegh. Co. PA., resides Jeff. Co., Ohio, boilermaker,
age 21 yrs. single, child of Geo. & Mary NEDENGARDEN,
married 08 Dec 1867 WV. to Eleanor MURRAY,
born Brooke Co., Virginia, resides Brooke Co., WV.
age 19 yrs. single, child of James & Jane MURRAY,
married by Edward A. BRINDLEY. remarks : none.

NELSON, John M. book 01 page 14 line 42
born Wellsburg, VA., resides Wellsburg, WV. engineer,
age 23 yrs. single, child of Andrew & Rachel NELSON,
married 28 Dec 1864 WV. to Rebecca V. ANTILL,
born Wellsburg, Virginia, resides Wellsburg, WV.
age 21 yrs. single, child of unk. & unk. ANTILL,
married by J. PIERCE. remarks : married Wellsburg.

NELSON, Nathaniel book 01 page 54 line 77
born unknown, resides Wellsburg, Virginia,
age -- yrs. unknown, child of unk. & unk. NELSON,
married 10 Aug 1858 Independence, PA. to K.A. FITCH,
born unknown, resides Wellsburg, Virginia,
age -- yrs. unknown, child of unk. & unk. FITCH,
married by J. MC CONAUGHY. remarks : Nancy BEARD, wit.

NICHOLLS, Alexander C. book 01 page 19 line 34
born Wellsburg, VA., resides Wellsburg, WV. laborer,
age 32 yrs. single, child of Robert & Ellen NICHOLLS,
married 27 Apr 1869 Wellsburg, WV. to Mary A. HAYS,
born unknown, resides Wellsburg, West Virginia,
age 27 yrs. single, child of unk. & unk. HAYS,
married by A.R. CHAPMAN. remarks : none.

NICHOLLS, Mary Eliza. book 01 page 18 line 08
born Brooke Co., VA., resides Wellsburg, West Virginia,
age 16 yrs. single, child of Rob't & Mary A. NICHOLLS,
married 28 Dec 1867 WV. to Shepley BARNES,
born Washington Co., PA., resides Wellsburg, WV.
age 23 yrs. single, child of Thomas & Mary BARNES,
married by Edward A. BRINDLEY. remarks : none.

NIXON, James book 01 page 15 line 57
born Belmont Co., Ohio, resides Short Creek, WV. farmer,
age 22 yrs. single, child of Robert & Elizabeth NIXON,
married 15 Aug 1865 WV. to Emily MC LAUGHLIN,
born Holmes Co., Ohio resides Short Creek, West Virginia,
age 25 yrs. single, child of Peter & Eliza. MC LAUGHLIN,
married by E.C. WAYMAN. remarks : none.

NOAH, Margaret Ellenor book 01 page 12 line 41
born Pennsylvania, resides Brooke Co., Virginia,
age 18 yrs. single, child of James & unknown NOAH,
married 02 Jan 1863 VA. to James BUXTON,
born Brooke Co., Virginia, resides Washington Co., PA.
age 21 yrs. single, child of Amos & Mary A. BUXTON,
married by T. HUDSON. remarks : married F. KLEIN house.

NOBLE, Westley book 01 page 21 line 20
born Jefferson Co., Ohio, resides Jeff. Co., Ohio, farmer,
age 24 yrs. single, child of Wm. & Narcissa NOBLE,
married 09 Jan 1872 WV. to Elizabeth BEERBOWER,
born Jefferson Co., Ohio, resides Brooke Co., WV.
age 21 yrs. single, child of Reed & Anna BEERBOWER,
married by Robert MOORE. remarks : married Wellsburg.

NOLAND, Richard book 01 page 11 line 20
born Ireland, resides Wheeling, Virginia, coal digger,
age 22 yrs. single, child of John & Johanna NOLAND,
married 22 Sep 1861 VA. to Margaret MC GEE,
born Ireland, resides Wellsburg, Virginia,
age 20 yrs. single, child of Bernard & Nancy MC GEE,
married by Stephen HUBER. remarks : married Wellsburg.

NUNEMAKER, William book 01 page 05 line 15
born Wash. Co., PA., resides Brooke Co., VA. carpenter,
age 30 yrs. single, child of Daniel & Cath. NUNEMAKER,
married 19 Feb 1857 VA. to Julia Ann LEE,
born Brooke Co., Virginia, resides Brooke Co., VA.
age 25 yrs. single, child of Thomas & Rachel LEE,
married by G.W. CRANAGE. remarks : none.

O'BRIEN, Simpson book 01 page 05 line 03
born Wellsburg, VA., resides Cosmopolotan, ompolypist,
age 24 yrs. single, child of Thomas & Anne O'BRIEN,
married 30 Sep 1856 VA. to Catharine MC KINZIE,
born Brooke Co., Virginia, resides Wellsburg, Virginia,
age 17 yrs. single, child of James & Teonas MC KINZIE,
married by A.J. ENDSLEY. remarks : married Wellsburg.

O'HARA, Anne book 01 page 05 line 21
born Co. Down, Ireland, resides Brooke Co., Virginia,
age 23 yrs. single, child of Samuel & Mary O'HARA,
married 01 Sep 1857 VA. to James MC CONNELL,
born Co. Down, Ireland, resides Brooke Co., Virginia,
age 23 yrs. single, child of Peter & Sendas? MC CONNELL,
married by J.F. BRAZILL. remarks : married Wheeling.

O'HARA, Bernard book 01 page 20 line 37
born Ireland, resides Steubenville, Ohio, laborer,
age 25 yrs. single, child of Andrew & Rose O'HARA,
married 09 May 1871 WV. to Margery CONNERS,
born unknown, resides Brooke Co., West Virginia,
age 30 yrs. widow, child of unk. & unk. CONNERS,
married by R.R. MOORE. remarks : married Wellsburg.

O'HARA, Margaret book 01 page 05 line 06
born Wellsburg, Virginia, resides unknown,
age 18 yrs. single, child of Samuel & Mary O'HARA,
married 15 Oct 1856 VA. to Charles DEVINNEY,
born County Kerry, Ireland, resides unknown,
age 28 yrs. single, child of Charles & Sarah DEVINNEY,
married by John F. BRAZILL. remarks : married Wellsburg.

O'HARE, John book 01 page 10 line 03A
born Ireland, resides Bethany, Virginia, laborer,
age 24 yrs. single, child of Denis & Mary (HENRY) O'HARE,
married 09 Dec 1860 Bethany, VA. to Rosanna DOWNEY,
born Ireland, resides Bethany, Virginia,
age 23 yrs. single, child of Terrance & Mary DOWNEY,
married by Stephen HUBER. remarks : John O'HEIR.

O'NEAL, William J. book 01 page 15 line 69
born Ohio, resides Ohio, engineer,
age 23 yrs. single, child of George & Eliza. O'NEAL,
married 05 Dec 1865 WV. to Harriet INGLEBRIGHT,
born Ohio, resides Ohio,
age 21 yrs. single, child of Wm. & Sarah INGLEBRIGHT,
married by J. WAUGH. remarks : none.

O'SHANDER, Jacob Charles book 01 page 09 line 11
born Amboy, New Jersey, resides Jeff. Co., Ohio, farmer,
age 30 yrs. single, child of Wm. & Henrietta O'SHANDER,
married 18 Feb 1860 Wellsburg, VA. to Susan JOHNSTON,
born Ohio Co., Virginia, resides Jefferson Co., Ohio,
age 18 yrs. single, child of John & Nancy JOHNSTON,
married by George W. CHESTER. remarks : none.

O'WESNEY, James book 01 page 09 line 10
born Steubenville, Ohio, resides Steubenville, Ohio,
age 21 yrs. single, child of Valentine & unk. O'WESNEY,
married 16 Apr 1860 VA. to Rose Ann MC CHRISTAL,
born Beaver Co., Pennsylvania, resides Steubenville, Ohio,
age 21 yrs. single, child of Henry & Rose MC CHRISTAL,
married by G.W. CHESTER. remarks : married Wellsburg.

OBNEY, James book 01 page 05 line 18
born Jeff. Co., Ohio, resides Jeff. Co., Ohio, laborer,
age 21 yrs. single, child of James & Sarah OBNEY,
married 03 Mar 1857 VA. to Tabitha MENDEL,
born Jefferson Co., Ohio, resides Wellsburg, Virginia,
age - - yrs. single, child of Valentine & Roselane MENDEL,
married by A.J. ENDSLEY. remarks : married Wellsburg.

ORAM, Addie book 01 page 20 line 29
born Brooke Co., Virginia, resides Brooke Co., WV.
age 19 yrs. single, child of George & Catherine ORAM,
married 23 Feb 1871 WV. to Mathew HINDMAN,
born Wetzel Co., Virginia, resides Brooke Co., WV
age 23 yrs. single, child of James & Hester HINDMAN,
married by D.W. CALDERWOOD. remarks : none.

ORAM, Nancy book 01 page 05 line 08
born Brooke Co., Virginia, resides Brooke Co., VA.
age 20 yrs. single, child of George & Cath. ORAM,
married 30 Oct 1856 VA. to Adam BOWERS,
born Washington Co., MD., resides Brooke Co., VA.
age 21 yrs. single, child of Jacob & Mary BOWERS,
married by Ezekiel QUILLEN. remarks : none.

ORAM, Philip C. book 01 page 11 line 25
born Brooke Co., VA., resides Brooke Co., VA. farmer,
age 30 yrs. single, child of George & Catherine ORAM,
married 25 Nov 1862 VA. to Elizabeth HUKILL,
born Brooke Co., Virginia, resides Brooke Co., VA.
age 21 yrs. single, child of William & Mary HUKILL,
married by Charles Louis LOOS. remarks : none.

ORANGE, Sarah book 01 page 22 line 14
born Co. Tipperary, Ireland, resides Wellsburg, WV.
age 30 yrs. unknown, child of unk. & unk. ORANGE,
married 17 Jun 1873 WV. to Robert TAYLOR,
born Manchester, England, resides Wellsburg, WV.
age 36 yrs. unknown, child of unk. & unk. TAYLOR,
married by J. COUPLAND remarks : married Wellsburg.

ORR, Maggy B. book 01 page 18 line 04
born Brooke Co., Virginia, resides Brooke Co., WV.
age 21 yrs. single, child of George G. & Elisa. ORR,
married 21 Oct 1867 WV. to T.F. ANDERSON,
born Hancock Co., Virginia, resides Hancock Co., WV.
age 23 yrs. single, child of Thos. & Martha ANDERSON,
married by John B. GRAHAM. remarks : none.

ORR, Mary book 01 page 16 line 11
born Brooke Co., Virginia, resides Brooke Co., WV.
age 22 yrs. single, child of George G. & Elisa. ORR,
married 05 Jan 1867 WV. to Levi W. INGLEBRIGHT,
born Jefferson Co., Ohio, resides Belmont Co., Ohio,
age 26 yrs. single, child of Wm. & Sarah INGLEBRIGHT,
married by J.B. GRAHAM. remarks : none.

OWEN, George book 01 page 12 line 56
born Jeff. Co., Ohio, resides Jeff. Co., Ohio, farmer,
age 23 yrs. single, child of Joshua & Rachel OWEN,
married 16 Dec 1863 WV. to Margaret C. BRANDON,
born Brooke Co., Virginia, resides Wellsburg, WV.
age 21 yrs. single, child of William & Jane BRANDON,
married by G. CHESTER. remarks : married BRANDON house.

OWENS, Elizabeth book 01 page 14 line 41
born Brooke Co., VA., resides Brooke Co., WV.
age 23 yrs. single, child of C.W. & H. OWENS,
married 29 Dec 1864 WV. to William RALSTON,
born Hancock Co., Virginia, resides Hancock Co., WV.
age 26 yrs. single, child of Samuel & Eliza. RALSTON,
married by D. LAVERTY. remarks : OWENS/OWINGS.

OWENS, Helen　　　　book 01 page 10 line 07A
born Brooke Co., Virginia, resides Brooke Co., Virginia,
age 23 yrs. single, child of Ephraim & Blanche OWENS,
married 15 Feb 1860 VA. to John A. GRIFFITH,
born Hollidays Cove, VA., resides Hollidays Cove, VA.
age 30 yrs. single, child of A.W. & Nancy A. GRIFFITH,
married by J.Y. CALHOUN. remarks: none.

OWINGS, Verlinda　　　　book 01 page 08 line 06
born unknown, resides unknown,
age -- yrs. unknown, child of unk. & unk. OWINGS,
married 27 Jan 1859 VA. to Henry FULLERTON,
born unknown, resides unknown,
age -- yrs. unknown, child of unk. & unk. FULLERTON,
married by J. CAMPBELL. remarks: married OWINGS house.

PADEN, Ella　　　　book 01 page 18 line 02
born Wellsburg, Virginia, resides Wellsburg, WV.
age 23 yrs. single, child of Wm. & Rebecca PADEN,
married 24 Nov 1867 WV. to Lewis C. HALL,
born Lagrange, Ohio, resides Wellsburg, WV.
age 27 yrs. single, child of Sewell & Susan HALL,
married by Edward A. BRINDLEY. remarks: none.

PALMER, Arthur Stone　　　　book 01 page 12 line 58
born Fayette Co., PA., resides WV. 1st Lt., 1st WV.,
age 28 yrs. single, child of Thos. & Tanyia PALMER,
married 03 Aug 1863 WV. to Sallie C. WRIGHTMAN,
born Allegheny Co., PA., resides Wellsburg, West Virginia,
age 21 yrs. single, child of Alex. & Cath. WRIGHTMAN,
married by W. ROBINSON. remarks: repeated pg.13, line 59.

PALMER, Caroline A.　　　　book 01 page 04 line 39
born Brooke Co., Virginia, resides unknown,
age 20 yrs. single, child of James & Salina PALMER,
married 07 Feb 1856 VA. to James WAUGH,
born Brooke Co., Virginia, resides Brooke Co., VA.
age 22 yrs. single, child of Richard & Eliza. WAUGH,
married by Ezekiel QUILLEN. remarks: none.

PALMER, Francis　　　　book 01 page 02 line 16
born Ohio, resides Wellsburg, Virginia, farmer,
age 24 yrs. single, child of John & Elba PALMER,
married 05 Oct 1854 VA. to Nancy BROWNLEE,
born Ohio, resides Wellsburg, Virginia,
age 33 yrs. single, child of James & Mary BROWNLEE,
married by S.H. NESBITT. remarks: married Wellsburg.

PALMER, James　　　　book 01 page 06 line 12
born Wash. Co., PA., resides Brooke Co., VA. farmer,
age 58 yrs. widow, child of Samuel & Mary PALMER,
married 10 Nov 1857 VA. to Elizabeth WAUGH,
born Brooke Co., Virginia, resides Brooke Co., VA.
age 51 yrs. widow, child of John & Jane MOORE,
married by E. QUILLEN. remarks: married Wellsburg.

PALMER, John C. book 01 page 09 line 05
born Brooke Co., VA., resides Brooke Co., VA. farmer,
age 26 yrs. single, child of James & Selina PALMER,
married 16 Aug 1859 VA. to Fannie T. WAUGH,
born Brooke Co., Virginia, resides Brooke Co., VA.
age 17 yrs. single, child of Richard & Eliza. WAUGH,
married by David HERVEY. remarks : none.

PARISH, John D. book 01 page 21 line 28
born Steuben., Ohio, resides Brooke Co., WV. laborer,
age 23 yrs. single, child of Richard & Nancy PARISH,
married 02 Apr 1872 Wellsburg, WV. to Lillie BEALL,
born Jefferson Co., Ohio, resides Brooke Co., WV.
age 18 yrs. single, child of Conrad & unk. BEALL,
married by Joseph M. BERRY. remarks : none.

PARISH, Thomas B. book 01 page 22 line 09
born Jeff. Co., Ohio resides Wellsburg, WV. coalminer,
age 27 yrs. single, child of Richard & Nancy PARISH,
married 19 Feb 1873 WV. to Drusilla DORSEY,
born Brooke Co., Virginia, resides Wellsburg, WV.
age 19 yrs. single, child of Joshua & Ann DORSEY,
married by C. GOODRICH. remarks : married Wellsburg.

PARK, George M. book 01 page 21 line 33
born Brooke Co., VA., resides Brooke Co., WV. farmer,
age 18 yrs. single, child of Robert & Anne PARK,
married 02 May 1872 WV. to Jennie HESSEY,
born Brooke Co., Virginia, resides Brooke Co., WV.
age 18 yrs. single, child of Thomas & Eliza. HESSEY,
married by Robert R. MOORE. remarks : none.

PARK, Madison W. book 01 page 22 line 25
born Jackson Co., VA., resides Jackson Co., WV.
age 23 yrs. unknown, child of unk. & unk. PARK,
married 20 Nov 1873 WV. to Jennie May GREEN,
born Brooke Co., Virginia, resides Brooke Co., WV.
age 22 yrs. unknown, child of unk. & unk. GREEN,
married by Jonathan CROSS. remarks : none.

PARK, Mathew C. book 01 page 21 line 27
born Brooke Co., VA., resides Brooke Co., WV.
age 25 yrs. single, child of Robert & Anne PARK,
married 21 Mar 1872 WV. to Louisa WRIGHT,
born Brooke Co., Virginia, resides Brooke Co., WV.
age 20 yrs. single, child of James & unk. WRIGHT,
married by James C. CAMPBELL. remarks : none.

PARK, Thomas C. book 01 page 22 line 46
born Allegheny Co., PA., resides Wellsburg, WV.
age 50 yrs. unknown, child of unk. & unk. PARK,
married 03 Sep 1874 WV. to Mary MC HENRY,
born Jefferson Co., Ohio, resides Wellsburg, WV.
age 39 yrs. unk., child of unk. & unk. MC HENRY,
married by C. STILLWAGON. remarks : married Wellsburg.

PARKER, Martha E. book 01 page 13 line 26
born Long Bottoms, Ohio, resides Wellsburg, WV.
age 21 yrs. single, child of Adam & unk. PARKER,
married 02 Jun 1864 WV. to Charles N. LALLANCE,
born Racine, Ohio, resides Cincinnati, Ohio,
age 27 yrs. single, child of Peter & Mary LALLANCE,
married by J.A. PIERCE. remarks : married Wellsburg.

PARKS, Robert book 01 page 03 line 19
born Hancock Co., VA., resides Brooke Co., VA. farmer,
age 27 yrs. single, child of John & Jane PARKS,
married 30 Nov 1854 VA. to Charity HINDMAN,
born Brooke Co., Virginia, resides Brooke Co., Virginia,
age 22 yrs. single, child of James & Rebecca HINDMAN,
married by W.D. LEMON. remarks : married Wellsburg.

PARSONS, Electa M. book 01 page 16 line 13
born Ohio, resides Wellsburg, West Virginia,
age 20 yrs. single, child of John & Sarah PARSONS,
married 28 Jan 1867 WV. to James A. RUSSELL,
born Wellsburg, Virginia, resides Wellsburg, WV.
age 25 yrs. single, child of James & Sarah RUSSELL,
married by Charles Louis LOOS. remarks : none.

PARSONS, Olivia book 01 page 16 line 06
born Wellsburg, Virginia, resides Wellsburg, WV.
age 22 yrs. single, child of unk. & unk. PARSONS,
married 12 Jun 1866 WV. to James M. HANEY,
born Wellsburg, Virginia, resides Brooke Co., WV.
age 26 yrs. single, child of John & Sarah HANEY,
married by Charles Louis LOOS. remarks : none.

PARSONS, Sebrina J. book 01 page 11 line 34
born Ohio, resides Wellsburg, Virginia,
age 22 yrs. single, child of John & Sarah PARSONS,
married 12 Feb 1863 VA. to James LAZEAR,
born Wellsburg, Virginia, resides Wellsburg, Virginia,
age 23 yrs. single, child of John & Sarah LAZEAR,
married by C. LOOS. remarks : married PARSON house.

PARSONS, Susan G. book 01 page 06 line 10
born Jefferson Co., Ohio, resides unknown,
age 25 yrs. single, child of John & Sarah PARSONS,
married 25 Sep 1857 VA. to John F. DOWLER,
born Ohio Co., Virginia, resides unknown,
age 22 yrs. single, child of Joseph & Hannah DOWLER,
married by E. QUILLEN. remarks : married Wellsburg.

PATTERSON, Elizabeth book 01 page 07 line 05
born Brooke Co., Virginia, resides Brooke Co., Virginia,
age 26 yrs. single, child of Francis & Ann PATTERSON,
married 24 Dec 1857 VA. to Reason Bell POOL,
born Brooke Co., Virginia, resides Brooke Co., Virginia,
age 22 yrs. single, child of William & Elizabeth POOL,
married by M. PUGH. remarks : none.

PATTERSON, James book 01 page 20 line 12
born Jefferson Co., Ohio, resides Wellsburg, WV. courier,
age 24 yrs. single, child of Reuben & Martha PATTERSON,
married 01 Sep 1870 Wellsburg, WV. to Lena LETZKUS,
born Brooke Co., Virginia, resides Wellsburg, West Virginia,
age 19 yrs. single, child of George & unk. LETZKUS,
married by Stephen HUBER. remarks : none.

PATTERSON, Mary Eliza. book 01 page 05 line 12
born Jefferson Co., Ohio, resides unknown,
age 17 yrs. single, child of Reuben & Martha A. PATTERSON,
married 25 Dec 1856 Wellsburg, VA. to William FRANK,
born Brooke Co., Virginia, resides unknown,
age 22 yrs. single, child of Hogan & Fredirick FRANK,
married by Ezekiel QUILLEN. remarks : none.

PATTERSON, Melissa book 01 page 20 line 47
born Jefferson Co., Ohio, resides Brooke Co., West Virginia,
age 26 yrs. single, child of Reuben & Martha A. PATTERSON,
married 29 Jun 1871 WV. to Milton R. FRESHWATER,
born Brooke Co., Virginia, resides Brooke Co., West Virginia,
age 26 yrs. single, child of George & Marg't FRESHWATER,
married by Henry MATWOOD. remarks : married Wheeling.

PATTERSON, Sarah A. book 01 page 17 line 01
born Brooke Co., Virginia, resides Brooke Co., WV.
age 30 yrs. single, child of Francis & Ann PATTERSON,
married 07 Aug 1867 Wellsburg, WV. to David W. LONG,
born Jefferson Co., Ohio, resides Jefferson Co., Ohio,
age 36 yrs. single, child of Charles & Mary J. LONG,
married by Hamilton CREE. remarks : none.

PATTON, James C. book 01 page 19 line 10
born Brooke Co., VA., resides Brooke Co., WV. farmer,
age 27 yrs. single, child of Thomas & Eliza. PATTON,
married 25 Aug 1868 WV. to Mahala LINTON,
born Brooke Co., Virginia, resides Brooke Co., WV.
age 29 yrs. single, child of William & Eliza. LINTON,
married by Milton WELLS. remarks : none.

PATTON, Maria book 01 page 21 line 06
born Brooke Co., Virginia, resides Brooke Co., WV.
age 35 yrs. single, child of Wm. E. & Eliza. PATTON,
married 21 Sep 1871 WV. to Thomas WADDLE,
born Washington Co., PA., resides Jefferson Co., Ohio,
age 45 yrs. widow, child of Isaac & Elizabeth WADDLE,
married by W. PENDLETON. remarks : married Wellsburg.

PATTON, Thomas book 01 page 02 line 07
born Brooke Co., VA., resides Wellsburg, house carpenter,
age 25 yrs. widow, child of John & Elizabeth PATTON,
married 16 Mar 1854 VA. to Angeline KIMBERLAND,
born Monroe Co., Ohio, resides Wellsburg, Virginia,
age 23 yrs. widow, child of Wm. & Naomi ROMINE,
married by E. QUILLEN. remarks : married FLEMING house.

PELLY, Francine R.　　　　book 01 page 20 line 36
born Brooke Co., Virginia, resides Brooke Co., WV.
age 18 yrs. single, child of James & Margaret PELLY,
married 27 Apr 1871 WV. to John W. HOUGH,
born Ohio Co., Virginia, resides Brooke Co., WV.
age 28 yrs. single, child of James & Tabitha HOUGH,
married by J.B. WALLACE. remarks : none.

PENDEGRASS, Patrick　　　book 01 page 19 line 32
born Ireland, resides Brooke Co., West Virginia, farmer,
age 30 yrs. single, child of Pat. & Ellen PENDEGRASS,
married 18 Mar 1869 WV. to Hannah SWEENEY,
born Ireland, resides Brooke Co., West Virginia,
age 30 yrs. single, child of unk. & unk. SWEENEY,
married by S. HUBER. remarks : married Wellsburg.

PENDLETON, Alexandria C.　　book 01 page 15 line 70
born Brooke Co., VA., resides Bethany, West Virginia,
age 24 yrs. single, child of Wm. K. & S. PENDLETON,
married 30 Dec 1865 WV. to James P. MOOKLAR,
born Mason Co., Kentucky, resides Covington, Kentucky,
age 25 yrs. single, child of Wm. B. & S.M. MOOKLAR,
married by C.L. LOOS. remarks : married Bethany.

PERINE, Mary Elizabeth　　　book 01 page 16 line 04
born Brooke Co., Virginia, resides Brooke Co., WV.
age 21 yrs. single, child of unk. & unk. PERINE,
married 24 May 1866 WV. to John D. ROBINSON,
born Ohio, resides Pennsylvania,
age 25 yrs. single, child of Sam'l & Hannah ROBINSON,
married by Wm. BRIGGS. remarks : married Wellsburg.

PERKINS, Asbury　　　　book 01 page 22 line 16
born Brooke Co., Virginia, resides Wellsburg, WV.
age 21 yrs. unk., child of unk. & unk. PERKINS,
married 24 Jul 1873 WV. to Rosena NALLINGER,
born Coshocton Co., Ohio, resides Wellsburg, WV.
age 26 yrs. unk., child of unk. & unk. NALLINGER,
married by W. MARTIN. remarks : married Wellsburg.

PERKINS, Minnie　　　　book 01 page 22 line 49
born Brooke Co., Virginia, resides Brooke Co., WV.
age 19 yrs. unknown, child of unk. & unk. PERKINS,
married 09 Oct 1874 WV. to Samuel M. DAVIDSON,
born Jefferson Co., Ohio, resides Steubenville, Ohio,
age 30 yrs. unknown, child of unk. & unk. DAVIDSON,
married by D. CALDERWOOD. remarks : married Wellsburg.

PERRY, Ann Rebecca J.　　　book 01 page 14 line 48
born Brooke Co., Virginia, resides Wellsburg, West Virginia,
age 20 yrs. widow, child of David & Rebecca KERNS,
married 26 Feb 1865 WV. to Samuel H. ALEXANDER,
born Muskingum Co., Ohio, resides Muskingum Co., Ohio,
age 24 yrs. single, child of Mathew & unk. ALEXANDER,
married by J. PIERCE. remarks : married house of D. KERNS.

PERRY, John book 01 page 08 line 09
  born Jeff. Co., Ohio, resides Brooke Co., VA. farmer,
  age 29 yrs. widow, child of Henry & Eliza. PERRY,
  married 06 Jan 1859 VA. to Ann Rebecca KERNS,
  born Brooke Co., Virginia, resides Brooke Co., VA.
  age 14 yrs. single, child of David & Rebecca KERNS,
  married by Thomas M. HUDSON. remarks: none.

PETERS, William book 01 page 05 line 17
  born Fayette Co., PA., resides Wellsburg, Virginia,
  age 31 yrs. single, child of David & Eliza. PETERS,
  married 26 Feb 1857 VA. to Margarett MC INTYRE,
  born Jefferson Co., Ohio, resides Wellsburg, Virginia,
  age 25 yrs. single, child of James & Marg't MC INTYRE,
  married by E. QUILLEN. remarks: married Wellsburg.

PICKLEMAN, Julia A. book 01 page 20 line 34
  born Wellsburg, Virginia, resides Brooke Co., West Virginia,
  age 21 yrs. single, child of John & Mary A. PICKLEMAN,
  married 11 Apr 1871 WV. to John A. BLOTTAN,
  born Maryland, resides Baltimore, Maryland,
  age 23 yrs. single, child of Anton & Margaret BLOTTAN,
  married by Stephen HUBER. remarks: married Wellsburg.

PIKIRRA, Adrian book 01 page 14 line 53
  born Williamsburg, resides Brooke Co., WV. stonemason,
  age 56 yrs. single, child of Leo & A. PIKIRRA,
  married 18 Apr 1865 Wellsburg, WV. to Therisia SEILA,
  born Williamsburg, resides Brooke Co., West Virginia,
  age 48 yrs. single, child of Vinez? & B. SEILA,
  married by Stephen HUBER. remarks: none.

PILLINGS, Charles book 01 page 10 line 13A
  born Ohio, resides Wellsburg, Virginia, moulder,
  age 21 yrs. single, child of Charles & Betty PILLINGS,
  married 30 Sep 1860 VA. to Sophia LAUGHEAD,
  born Pennsylvania, resides Wellsburg, Virginia,
  age 18 yrs. single, child of James & Rebecca LAUGHEAD,
  married by Thomas HUDSON. remarks: married Wellsburg.

PILLINGS, Sarah E. book 01 page 11 line 19
  born Brooke Co., Virginia, resides Brooke Co., Virginia,
  age 20 yrs. single, child of Charles & Sarah PILLINGS,
  married 22 Dec 1861 VA. to Joseph E. MONTGOMERY,
  born Ohio Co., Virginia, resides Brooke Co., Virginia,
  age 24 yrs. single, child of Abram & Nancy MONTGOMERY,
  married by R.B. WATKINS. remarks: married Wellsburg.

PILLINGS, Sophia book 01 page 17 line 07
  born Allegheny Co., Pennsylvania, resides Brooke Co., WV.
  age 25 yrs. widow, child of James & Rebecca LAUGHEAD,
  married 13 Oct 1867 WV. to Joseph MONTGOMERY,
  born Ohio Co., Virginia, resides Brooke Co., West Virginia,
  age 31 yrs. widow, child of Abram & Nancy MONTGOMERY,
  married by Alex. E. ANDERSON. remarks: married Wellsburg.

BROOKE CO., VA./WV. MARRIAGE BOOK 1, 1853-1874

PITTMAN, Hannah   book 01 page 17 line 06
born Monroe Co., Ohio, resides Brooke Co., WV.
age 20 yrs. single, child of Thomas & Ann PITTMAN,
married 03 Oct 1867 WV. to Thomas B. LAZEAR,
born Brooke Co., Virginia, resides Brooke Co., WV.
age 21 yrs. single, child of John & Matilda LAZEAR,
married by Milton WELLS. remarks : married Wellsburg.

PLANTS, David   book 01 page 21 line 29
born Beaver Co., PA., resides Steubenville, Ohio, miner,
age 24 yrs. single, child of Joseph & Rosana PLANTS,
married 12 Mar 1872 WV. to Catherine A. CARMICHAEL,
born Brooke Co., Virginia, resides Brooke Co., West Virginia,
age 24 yrs. single, child of George & Nancy CARMICHAEL,
married by Robert R. MOORE. remarks : married Wellsburg.

POOL, Reason Bell   book 01 page 07 line 05
born Brooke Co., VA., resides Brooke Co., VA. farmer,
age 22 yrs. single, child of William & Eliza. POOL,
married 24 Dec 1857 VA. to Elizabeth PATTERSON,
born Brooke Co., Virginia, resides Brooke Co., Virginia,
age 26 yrs. single, child of Francis & Ann PATTERSON,
married by M. PUGH. remarks : none.

POOL, William   book 01 page 12 line 49
born Brooke Co., VA., resides Brooke Co., VA. farmer,
age 36 yrs. widow, child of Benjamin & Eliza. POOL,
married 07 Apr 1863 VA. to Martha Ann MAGEE,
born Washington Co., PA., resides Brooke Co., VA.
age 40 yrs. single, child of R.T. & Adaline MAGEE,
married by W. ROBINSON. remarks : married MAGEE house.

POSTON, Anna B.   book 01 page 20 line 07
born Newry, Ireland, resides Bethany, West Virginia,
age 27 yrs. widow, child of Arch. & Anne CAMPBELL,
married 08 Jul 1870 WV. to James A. MURRAY,
born Simpson Co., Kentucky, resides Palmyra, MO.
age 27 yrs. single, child of William & Nancy MURRAY,
married by A. CAMPBELL. remarks : married Bethany.

POTTER, James M.   book 01 page 19 line 45
born Clarion Co., PA., resides Cincinnati, OH. merchant,
age 25 yrs. single, child of unknown & unk. POTTER,
married 20 Jan 1870 WV. to Frances KLINEFELTER,
born Pittsburg, PA., resides Wellsburg, West Virginia,
age 22 yrs. single, child of Mich'l & Keziah KLINEFELTER,
married by Robert R. MOORE. remarks : married Wellsburg.

POTTS, Jasper   book 01 page 21 line 31
born Beaver Co., PA., resides Wellsburg, WV. tanner,
age 21 yrs. single, child of Nathan & Elizabeth POTTS,
married 04 Apr 1872 WV. to Francis LETZKUS,
born Brooke Co., Virginia, resides Brooke Co., West Virginia,
age 21 yrs. single, child of Richard & Apolonia LETZKUS,
married by Stephen HUBER. remarks : married Wellsburg.

PRATHER, Elbert book 01 page 02 line 11
born Wellsburg, VA. resides Wellsburg, VA. cabinetmaker,
age 23 yrs. widow, child of John & Elizabeth PRATHER,
married 24 Aug 1854 VA. to Mary COCHRANE,
born New York City, NY., resides Wellsburg, Virginia,
age 23 yrs. single, child of John & Agnes COCHRANE,
married by E. QUILLEN. remarks : married Wellsburg.

PRATHER, George M. book 01 page 12 line 42
born Brooke Co., Virginia, resides Wellsburg, Virginia,
age 22 yrs. single, child of John & Eliza. PRATHER,
married 08 Mar 1862 VA. to Amelia C. TAYLOR,
born Brooke Co., Virginia, resides Brooke Co., Virginia,
age 20 yrs. single, child of unknown & Ann TAYLOR,
married by E. BRINDLEY. remarks : married Wellsburg.

PRIEST, William book 01 page 20 line 17
born Brooke Co., VA., resides Christian Co., IL. carpenter,
age 60 yrs. widow, child of William & Elizabeth PRIEST,
married 26 Sep 1870 Bethany, WV. to Micha HALLIE,
born Brooke Co., Virginia, resides Brooke Co., WV.
age 35 yrs. single, child of William & unk. HALLIE,
married by William K. PENDLETON. remarks : none.

PUGH, John book 01 page 04 line 48
born Hancock Co., VA., resides Han. Co., VA. farmer,
age 22 yrs. single, child of Hugh & Nancy PUGH,
married 01 Jan 1856 VA. to Julia Ann HAYS,
born Brooke Co., Virginia, resides Brooke Co., VA.
age 21 yrs. single, child of Enoch & Nancy HAYS,
married by David HERVEY. remarks : none.

PUNTNEY, Isabelle book 01 page 13 line 60
born Jefferson Co., Ohio, resides Brooke Co., WV.
age 24 yrs. single, child of James & Polly PUNTNEY,
married 15 Oct 1863 WV. to Lewis W. CARTER,
born Brooke Co., Virginia, resides Brooke Co., WV.
age 23 yrs. single, child of Lewis & Martha CARTER,
married by G. WHARTON. remarks : none.

QUEST, Elizabeth C. book 01 page 13 line 19
born Washington Co., PA., resides Wellsburg, WV.
age 25 yrs. single, child of E.C. & unknown QUEST,
married 25 Feb 1864 WV. to William L. DURANT,
born Washington Co., PA., resides Wash. Co., PA.
age 26 yrs. single, child of Henry & Mary DURANT,
married by J.A. PIERCE. remarks : married Wellsburg.

QUEST, Mary L. book 01 page 04 line 59
born Jefferson Co., PA., resides Washington Co., PA.
age 20 yrs. single, child of Samuel & Martha QUEST,
married 12 Aug 1856 VA. to Joseph K. LAWTON,
born Washington Co., PA., resides Wash. Co., PA.
age 25 yrs. single, child of Pardon & Tabitha LAWTON,
married by E. QUILLEN. remarks : married Wellsburg.

QUEST, Melissa E. book 01 page 16 line 24
born Allegheny Co., PA., resides Brooke Co., WV.
age 23 yrs. single, child of Sam'l & Martha C. QUEST,
married 23 Jun 1867 WV. to William H. MELVIN,
born Beaver Co., PA., resides Columbiana Co., Ohio,
age 24 yrs. single, child of Henry & Alzina MELVIN,
married by Edward A. BRINDLEY. remarks : none.

QUEST, Minerva J. book 01 page 18 line 05
born Middletown, Pennsylvania, resides Brooke Co., WV.
age 21 yrs. single, child of Sam'l S. & Martha C. QUEST
married 25 Dec 1867 WV. to Joseph E. HARDING
born Lewiston, Maine, resides Brooke Co., West Virginia,
age 25 yrs. single, child of J.B. & Mary Ann HARDING,
married by Edward A. BRINDLEY. remarks : none.

RALSTON, Elizabeth book 01 page 22 line 17
born Wood Co., Virginia, resides Brooke Co., WV.
age 23 yrs. unknown, child of unk. & unk. RALSTON,
married 26 Jul 1873 WV. to Joseph J. WILKEY,
born Germany, resides Brooke Co., West Virginia,
age 23 yrs. unknown, child of unk. & unk. WILKEY,
married by S. CRAVENS. remarks : married Wellsburg.

RALSTON, Joseph book 01 page 14 line 50
born Brooke Co., VA., resides Brooke Co., WV. laborer,
age 22 yrs. single, child of Samuel & Eliza. RALSTON,
married 02 Mar 1865 WV. to Lucy MC HENRY,
born Brooke Co., Virginia, resides Brooke Co., WV.
age 22 yrs. single, child of unk. & Rachel MC HENRY,
married by J. PIERCE. remarks : married MC HENRY house.

RALSTON, William book 01 page 14 line 41
born Hancock Co., VA., resides Hancock Co., WV. farmer,
age 26 yrs. single, child of Samuel & Eliza. RALSTON,
married 29 Dec 1864 WV. to Elizabeth OWENS,
born Brooke Co., Virginia, resides Brooke Co., WV.
age 23 yrs. single, child of C.W. & H. OWENS,
married by D. LAVERTY. remarks : OWENS/OWINGS.

RAMSEY, Macky book 01 page 02 line 13
born Brooke Co., Virginia, resides Wellsburg, Virginia,
age 30 yrs. widow, child of William & Eliza. WOOD,
married 06 Aug 1854 VA. to Peter SWINER,
born Jacksonville, Ohio, resides Wellsburg, Virginia,
age 23 yrs. single, child of Peter & Mary SWINER,
married by C. HOLMES. remarks : married Wellsburg.

REED, George F. book 01 page 13 line 28
born Madison, IN., resides Chillicothe, Ohio, dentist,
age 26 yrs. single, child of John & Cath. M. REED,
married 17 Aug 1864 WV. to Anne E. WHEELER,
born Wellsburg, Virginia, resides Wellsburg, WV.
age 21 yrs. single, child of A.P. & C.H. WHEELER,
married by J.A. PIERCE. remarks : married Wellsburg.

REED, John book 01 page 10 line 01A
born Allegh. Co., PA., resides Wellsburg, VA. carpenter,
age 48 yrs. widow, child of James & Jane REED,
married 05 Aug 1861 VA. to Susan ROBERTS,
born Pennsylvania, resides Wellsburg, Virginia,
age 48 yrs. widow, child of Isaac David & Eliza. ROBERTS,
married by G.W. CHESTER. remarks : married Wellsburg.

REED, Margaret Jane book 01 page 07 line 22
born Allegheny Co., PA., resides Brooke Co., VA.
age 30 yrs. single, child of John & Elizabeth REED,
married 17 Nov 1858 VA. to Samuel KEITH,
born Brooke Co., Virginia, resides Brooke Co., VA.
age 19 yrs. single, child of Quillen & Jane KEITH,
married by E. QUILLEN. remarks : married Wellsburg.

REEVES, Cornelia K. book 01 page 04 line 47
born Brooke Co., Virginia, resides Brooke Co., VA.
age 18 yrs. single, child of Reason & Eliza. REEVES,
married 29 Nov 1855 VA. to James W. COX,
born Brooke Co., Virginia, resides Brooke Co., VA.
age 28 yrs. single, child of George & unk. COX,
married by A.J. ENDSLEY. remarks : none.

REEVES, John C. book 01 page 11 line 32
born Brooke Co., VA., resides Brooke Co., VA. farmer,
age 28 yrs. single, child of Reason & Elizabeth REEVES,
married 26 Nov 1862 VA. to Sarah B. GIST,
born Brooke Co., Virginia, resides Brooke Co., VA.
age 25 yrs. single, child of Cornelius & Isabel GIST,
married by T. HUDSON. remarks : married BEALL'S house.

REEVES, Julia C. book 01 page 21 line 09
born Brooke Co., Virginia, resides Brooke Co., WV.
age 24 yrs. widow, child of Reason & Eliza. REEVES,
married 26 Oct 1871 WV. to Isaac BICKERSTAFF,
born Beaver Co., PA., resides Brooke Co., West Virginia,
age 24 yrs. single, child of unk. & unk. BICKERSTAFF,
married by J.C. CASTLE. remarks : Julia C. (REEVES) COX.

REEVES, Sallie E. book 01 page 19 line 01
born Wellsburg, Virginia, resides Wellsburg, West Virginia,
age 19 yrs. single, child of Nathan & Rachel A. REEVES,
married 05 May 1868 WV. to James F. MURPHY,
born Washington Co., PA., resides Wellsburg, WV.
age 20 yrs. single, child of Joseph & Edith MURPHY,
married by J.A. PIERCE. remarks : married Wellsburg.

REEVES, Wheeler book 01 page 17 line 05
born Wellsburg, Virginia, resides Wellsburg, West Virginia,
age 30 yrs. single, child of Nathan & Rachel A. REEVES,
married 24 Sep 1867 Wellsburg, WV. to Jane LAZEAR,
born Wellsburg, Virginia, resides Wellsburg, West Virginia,
age 22 yrs. single, child of John & Sallie LAZEAR,
married by Thomas M. HUDSON. remarks : none.

RICHARDSON, I.L.   book 01 page 17 line 26
born Washington Co., PA., resides Marietta, Ohio, clerk,
age 25 yrs. single, child of Isaac & Nancy RICHARDSON,
married 05 Nov 1867 WV. to Drusilla GREEN,
born Brooke Co., Virginia, resides Brooke Co., WV.
age 20 yrs. single, child of Wm. E. & Elizabeth GREEN,
married by J.A. PIERCE. remarks : none.

RICHARDSON, Mary B.   book 01 page 15 line 62
born Brooke Co., Virginia, resides Brooke Co., WV.
age 26 yrs. single, child of R. & K. RICHARDSON,
married 27 Sep 1865 WV. to Albert W. CHAPLINE,
born Wheeling, Virginia, resides Brooke Co., WV.
age 30 yrs. single, child of William & Ann CHAPLINE,
married by W. PENDLETON. remarks : married Bethany.

RIDDLE, David   book 01 page 15 line 68
born Jeff. Co., Ohio, resides Brooke Co., WV. farmer,
age 42 yrs. widow, child of John & Elizabeth RIDDLE,
married 21 Nov 1865 WV. to Sarah MILLIGAN,
born Ohio, resides Brooke Co., West Virginia,
age 35 yrs. single, child of George & Mary MILLIGAN,
married by J.A. BROWN. remarks : married Wellsburg.

RIDDLE, David   book 01 page 03 line 35
born Jeff. Co., Ohio, resides Brooke Co., VA. farmer,
age 28 yrs. single, child of John & Elizabeth RIDDLE,
married 01 Jun 1855 VA. to Matilda MURPHY,
born Brooke Co., Virginia, resides Brooke Co., Virginia,
age 24 yrs. single, child of William & Eliza. MURPHY,
married by E. QUILLEN. remarks : married Wellsburg.

RIDGLEY, Horace   book 01 page 17 line 12
born Ohio Co., Virginia, resides Ohio Co., WV. farmer,
age 33 yrs. widow, child of Richard & Marg't RIDGLEY,
married 11 Sep 1866 WV. to Nancy M. SMITH,
born Ohio Co., Virginia, resides Ohio Co., WV.
age 24 yrs. single, child of Fergus & Nancy SMITH,
married by J.A. BROWN. remarks : none.

RIDGLEY, Rebecca E.   book 01 page 06 line 08
born Brooke Co., Virginia, resides Brooke Co., VA.
age - - yrs. single, child of unk. & unk. RIDGLEY,
married 15 Oct 1857 VA. to John DAVIS,
born Brooke Co., VA., resides Pomeroy, Ohio,
age - - yrs. widow, child of unk. & unk. DAVIS,
married by James CAMPBELL. remarks : none.

RIDGLEY, William C.   book 01 page 19 line 05
born Brooke Co., VA. resides Brooke Co., WV. farmer,
age 22 yrs. widow, child of Franklin & Ann RIDGLEY,
married 24 Jun 1868 WV. to Mary V. HUSTON,
born Ohio Co., Virginia, resides Brooke Co., WV.
age 28 yrs. widow, child of Samuel & Mary HUSTON,
married by William K. PENDLETON. remarks : none.

RIDOUT, John book 01 page 10 line 02A
born Allegheny Co., PA., resides Jeff. Co., Ohio, laborer,
age 23 yrs. single, child of Mark & unknown RIDOUT,
married 04 Sep 1860 VA. to Martha MAGOINGAN,
born Washington Co., PA., resides Brooke Co., Virginia,
age 23 yrs. single, child of Jas. & Prudence MAGOINGAN,
married by Watson RUSSELL. remarks: none.

RIEN, George W. book 01 page 17 line 14
born Jeff. Co., Ohio, resides Jeff. Co., Ohio, boatman,
age 22 yrs. single, child of Henry & Elizabeth RIEN,
married 30 Sep 1866 WV. to Elizabeth JOHNSON,
born Scotland, resides Jefferson Co., Ohio,
age 24 yrs. single, child of Peter & Eliza. JOHNSON,
married by J.A. PIERCE. remarks: none.

RINEHART, William S. book 01 page 16 line 19
born Green Co., PA., resides Wheeling, WV. carpenter,
age 33 yrs. single, child of unk. & unk. RINEHART,
married 25 Mar 1867 WV. to Sally SILVERS,
born Brooke Co., Virginia, resides Brooke Co., WV.
age 24 yrs. single, child of unk. & unk. SILVERS,
married by Thomas M. HUDSON. remarks: none.

RIPLEY, Lena book 01 page 21 line 34
born Pennsylvania, resides Brooke Co., West Virginia,
age 19 yrs. single, child of unknown & unknown RIPLEY,
married 02 May 1872 Wellsburg, WV. to James JOHNSON,
born Ohio Co., Virginia, resides Brooke Co., West Virginia,
age 24 yrs. single, child of John & Mary JOHNSON,
married by J. COUPLAND remarks: listed Alina CRIPLEY.

ROBERTS, Andrew J. book 01 page 03 line 33
born Brooke Co., VA., resides Brooke Co., VA. coaldigger,
age 25 yrs. single, child of Wm. & Rebecca ROBERTS,
married 01 May 1855 VA. to Rosetta DEIGHTON,
born Brooke Co., Virginia, resides Brooke Co., Virginia,
age 17 yrs. single, child of William & Sarah DEIGHTON,
married by E. QUILLEN. remarks: married DEIGHTON house.

ROBERTS, Marcellus book 01 page 05 line 07
born Wellsburg, VA., resides Wellsburg, VA. brickmaker,
age 22 yrs. single, child of Isaiah & Marg't. ROBERTS,
married 30 Oct 1856 VA. to Ann Elizabeth BUCKALEW,
born Wellsburg, Virginia, resides Wellsburg, Virginia,
age 19 yrs. single, child of Garrett & Lydia BUCKALEW,
married by Wm. GAMBLE, JR. remarks: married Wellsburg.

ROBERTS, Nancy book 01 page 02 line 02
born Ohio Co., Virginia, resides Brooke Co., Virginia,
age 36 yrs. widow, child of Wm. & Rebecca ROBERTS,
married 27 Apr 1854 VA. to William MC CREARY,
born Washington Co., PA., resides Brooke Co., Virginia,
age 50 yrs. widow, child of Thos. & Marg't MC CREARY,
married by David HERVEY. remarks: married Wellsburg.

ROBERTS, Richard T. book 01 page 07 line 03
born Brooke Co., VA., resides Brooke Co., VA. glassblower,
age 25 yrs. single, child of William & Rebecca ROBERTS
married 27 Dec 1857 VA. to Margaret V. DEIGHTON
born Brooke Co., Virginia, resides Brooke Co., Virginia,
age 21 yrs. single, child of William & Sarah DEIGHTON,
married by E. QUILLEN. remarks : married Wellsburg.

ROBERTS, Susan book 01 page 10 line 01A
born Pennsylvania, resides Wellsburg, Virginia,
age 48 yrs. widow, child of Isaac D. & Eliza. ROBERTS,
married 05 Aug 1861 Wellsburg, VA. to John REED,
born Allegheny Co., PA., resides Wellsburg, Virginia,
age 48 yrs. widow, child of James & Jane REED,
married by George W. CHESTER. remarks : none.

ROBERTS, William book 01 page 17 line 22
born Harrison Co., Ohio, resides Christian Co., IL. farmer,
age 26 yrs. single, child of James & Elizabeth ROBERTS,
married 01 Jan 1867 WV. to Emma D. COLEMAN,
born Ohio Co., Virginia, resides Brooke Co., West Virginia,
age 23 yrs. single, child of David & Mary COLEMAN,
married by William R. HOWE. remarks · none.

ROBINETT, Cath. Mary book 01 page 20 line 18
born Wellsburg, Virginia, resides Wellsburg, WV.
age 21 yrs. single, child of Allen & Marg't ROBINETT,
married 29 Sep 1870 WV. to Calvin B. BRASHEARS,
born Paris, Pennsylvania, resides Wellsburg, WV.
age 26 yrs. single, child of Bazle & Jane BRASHEARS,
married by William K. PENDLETON. remarks : none.

ROBINETT, Emma book 01 page 16 line 03
born Brooke Co., Virginia, resides Brooke Co., WV.
age 24 yrs. single, child of unk. & unk. ROBINETT,
married 28 May 1866 WV. to Joseph LETZKUS,
born Wellsburg, Virginia, resides Wellsburg, WV.
age 28 yrs. single, child of Geo. & Michelia LETZKUS,
married by E. BRINDLEY. remarks : married Wellsburg.

ROBINETT, James book 01 page 04 line 57
born Marshall Co., VA., resides Wellsburg, VA. saddler,
age 21 yrs. single, child of Allen & Marg't ROBINETT,
married 01 Jun 1856 VA. to Elmira J. STEWART,
born Maine, resides Wellsburg, Virginia,
age 19 yrs. single, child of Joseph & Dianna STEWART,
married by A.J. ENDSLEY. remarks : married Wellsburg.

ROBINETT, Mary A. book 01 page 17 line 13
born Brooke Co., Virginia, resides Brooke Co., WV.
age 28 yrs. single, child of unk. & unk. ROBINETT,
married 25 Sep 1866 WV. to Christopher WETHERELL,
born England, resides Brooke Co., West Virginia,
age 28 yrs. single, child of Aaron & Hannah WETHERELL,
married by E.A. BRINDLEY. remarks : married Wellsburg.

BROOKE CO., VA./WV. MARRIAGE BOOK 1, 1853-1874   269

ROBINSON, A.W.   book 01 page 21 line 19
born Brooke Co., Virginia, resides Brooke Co., WV. farmer,
age 22 yrs. single, child of Joseph & Eliza. A. ROBINSON,
married 31 Dec 1871 WV. to Mary Elizabeth BACHELL,
born Brooke Co., Virginia, resides Brooke Co., WV.
age 21 yrs. single, child of John & Jane BACHELL,
married by A. Ealion WARD. remarks: none.

ROBINSON, Elijah   book 01 page 11 line 26
born Brooke Co., VA., resides Brooke Co., VA. farmer,
age 31 yrs. single, child of John & Nancy ROBINSON,
married 30 Nov 1862 VA. to Sarah J. FRESHWATER,
born Brooke Co., Virginia, resides Brooke Co., Virginia,
age 15 yrs. single, child of Reuben & Lydia FRESHWATER,
married by Thomas M. HUDSON. remarks: none.

ROBINSON, Elizabeth E.   book 01 page 12 line 39
born Brooke Co., Virginia, resides Brooke Co., Virginia,
age 21 yrs. single, child of Wm. H. & Marg't ROBINSON,
married 12 Jun 1862 Bethany, VA. to Octavis YOUNG,
born Brooke Co., Virginia, resides Brooke Co., Virginia,
age 28 yrs. single, child of George & Mary YOUNG,
married by Charles Louis LOOS. remarks: none.

ROBINSON, Elizabeth Jane   book 01 page 09 line 01
born Brooke Co., Virginia, resides Brooke Co., Virginia,
age 16 yrs. single, child of Joseph S. & Eliza. ROBINSON,
married 22 Dec 1859 VA. to Isaac L. DAVIS,
born Belmont Co., Ohio, resides Brooke Co., Virginia,
age 24 yrs. single, child of James & Susannah DAVIS,
married by Thomas M. HUDSON. remarks: none.

ROBINSON, Gilbert E.   book 01 page 22 line 35
born Brooke Co., Virginia, resides Brooke Co., WV.
age 20 yrs. unknown, child of unk. & unk. ROBINSON,
married 05 Mar 1874 WV. to Dora BOWMAN,
born Brooke Co., Virginia, resides Brooke Co., WV.
age 21 yrs. unknown, child of unk. & unk. BOWMAN,
married by J. COUPLAND. remarks: married Wellsburg.

ROBINSON, John D.   book 01 page 16 line 04
born Ohio, resides Pennsylvania, engineer,
age 25 yrs. single, child of Samuel & Hannah ROBINSON,
married 24 May 1866 Wellsburg, WV. to Mary PERINE,
born Brooke Co., Virginia, resides Brooke Co., WV.
age 21 yrs. single, child of unk. & unk. PERINE,
married by William BRIGGS. remarks: none.

ROBINSON, Mary   book 01 page 11 line 17
born Pennsylvania, resides Brooke Co., Virginia,
age 25 yrs. single, child of Samuel & Mary ROBINSON,
married 28 Nov 1861 VA. to Jacob CHAPMAN,
born Pennsylvania, resides Brooke Co., Virginia,
age 25 yrs. single, child of Harry & Nancy CHAPMAN,
married by J.B. PATTERSON. remarks: none.

ROBINSON, Providence book 01 page 07 line 07
born Brooke Co., Virginia, resides Brooke Co., Virginia,
age 20 yrs. single, child of Jos. & Eliza. Ann ROBINSON,
married 28 Jan 1858 VA. to James HUKILL,
born Brooke Co., Virginia, resides Brooke Co., Virginia,
age 23 yrs. single, child of William & Mary HUKILL,
married by E. QUILLEN. remarks : married ROBINSON house.

ROBINSON, Sally A. book 01 page 19 line 37
born Brooke Co., Virginia, resides Brooke Co., WV.
age 17 yrs. single, child of Samuel & Marg't ROBINSON,
married 10 May 1869 WV. to Alexander ROUSE,
born Jefferson Co., Ohio, resides Ohio Co., WV.
age 22 yrs. single, child of Edward & Deliah ROUSE,
married by J. WARDEN. remarks : married West Liberty.

ROBINSON, Sarah Jane book 01 page 20 line 35
born Carroll Co., Ohio, resides Brooke Co., West Virginia,
age 26 yrs. widow, child of Reuben & Lydia FRESHWATER,
married 25 Apr 1871 Wellsburg, WV. to Robert T. JONES,
born Allegheny Co., PA., resides Brooke Co., West Virginia,
age 25 yrs. single, child of Jackson & Rebecca JONES,
married by I.C. CASTLE. remarks : none.

ROBINSON, Walter A. book 01 page 23 line 02
born Washtenaw Co., MI., resides Green Co., IN.
age 38 yrs. unk., child of unk. & unk. ROBINSON,
married 18 Nov 1874 WV. to Cornelia E. JACOB,
born Brooke Co., Virginia, resides Brooke Co., WV.
age 28 yrs. unknown, child of unk. & unk. JACOB,
married by J.A. PIERCE. remarks : none.

RODGERS, Mary book 01 page 22 line 13
born Brooke Co., Virginia, resides Brooke Co., WV.
age 22 yrs. single, child of William & Marg't RODGERS,
married 15 Apr 1873 WV. to George C. CURTIS,
born Bethany, Virginia, resides Bethany, West Virginia,
age 22 yrs. single, child of Jacob E. & Sarah B. CURTIS,
married by Robert R. MOORE. remarks : none.

RODGERS, Rebecca E. book 01 page 21 line 42
born Brooke Co., Virginia, resides Brooke Co., WV.
age 28 yrs. single, child of Wm. & Marg't RODGERS,
married 08 Aug 1872 WV. to C. SHRIVER,
born Fayette Co., Pennsylvania, resides Bethany, WV.
age 31 yrs. widow, child of Geo. W. & Melissa SHRIVER,
married by Robert R. MOORE. remarks : none.

RODGERS, Sarah book 01 page 08 line 01
born Brooke Co., Virginia, resides Morristown, Ohio,
age 51 yrs. single, child of Abram & Sarah RODGERS,
married 06 Oct 1858 VA. to John MC LEASH,
born Scotland, resides Barnesville, Ohio,
age 60 yrs. widow, child of John & Euphemia MC LEASH,
married by W. AIKEN. remarks : married W. RODGERS house.

ROMINE, Angeline book 01 page 02 line 07
  born Monroe Co., Ohio, resides Wellsburg, Virginia,
  age 23 yrs. widow, child of William & Naomi ROMINE,
  married 16 Mar 1854 VA. to Thomas PATTON,
  born Brooke Co., Virginia, resides Wellsburg, Virginia,
  age 25 yrs. widow, child of John & Elizabeth PATTON,
  married by E. QUILLEN. remarks : Angeline KIMBERLAND.

ROUSE, Alexander book 01 page 19 line 37
  born Jefferson Co., Ohio, resides Ohio Co., WV. farmer,
  age 22 yrs. single, child of Edward & Deliah ROUSE,
  married 10 May 1869 WV. to Sally A. ROBINSON,
  born Brooke Co., Virginia, resides Brooke Co., WV.
  age 17 yrs. single, child of Samuel & Marg't ROBINSON,
  married by J. WARDEN. remarks : married West Liberty.

RUSH, William book 01 page 15 line 63
  born Brooke Co., VA., resides Brooke Co., WV. blacksmith,
  age 26 yrs. single, child of Joseph & Mary RUSH,
  married 26 Oct 1865 WV. to Mary HYDE,
  born Wheeling, Virginia, resides Brooke Co., WV.
  age 26 yrs. single, child of John & A. HYDE,
  married by E. WAYMAN. remarks : married RUSH house.

RUSSELL, Anna M. book 01 page 14 line 47
  born Wellsburg, Virginia, resides Wellsburg, WV.
  age 28 yrs. single, child of James & Sarah RUSSELL,
  married 05 Feb 1865 WV. to Evan Fairchild LANDIS,
  born Wellsburg, Virginia, resides California,
  age 35 yrs. single, child of S.A. & A.S. LANDIS,
  married by G. CHESTER. remarks : married Wellsburg.

RUSSELL, Caroline E. book 01 page 09 line 13
  born Wellsburg, Virginia, resides Wellsburg, Virginia,
  age 25 yrs. single, child of James & Sarah RUSSELL,
  married 13 Mar 1860 VA. to Andrew D. FRITZ,
  born Grand Blanc, Michigan, resides Tiffin, Ohio,
  age 24 yrs. single, child of John & Sarah FRITZ,
  married by J. ROBISON. remarks : married RUSSELL house.

RUSSELL, Charles P. book 01 page 08 line 17
  born Tyler Co., Virginia, resides Tyler Co., VA. farmer,
  age 35 yrs. single, child of William & Betsy RUSSELL,
  married 13 Apr 1859 VA. to Ruth C. DONOVAN,
  born Brooke Co., Virginia, resides Brooke Co., Virginia,
  age 27 yrs. single, child of Thomas & Cath. DONOVAN,
  married by A.E. MYERS. remarks : marriage record reversed.

RUSSELL, George W. book 01 page 17 line 08
  born Wellsburg, Virginia, resides Wellsburg, WV. teacher,
  age 33 yrs. widow, child of Jas. & Sarah (ATKINS) RUSSELL,
  married 15 Oct 1867 Wellsburg, WV. to Anne MC CLURE,
  born Erie, Pennsylvania, resides West Middletown, PA.
  age 33 yrs. widow, child of Denison & Mary AIKEN,
  married by E. BRINDLEY. remarks : married Union Chapel.

RUSSELL, George W. book 01 page 07 line 01
born Brooke Co., VA., resides Brooke Co., VA. teacher,
age 22 yrs. single, child of James & Sarah RUSSELL,
married 23 Nov 1857 VA. to Ann Jane WRIGHTMAN,
born Brooke Co., Virginia, resides Brooke Co., Virginia,
age 20 yrs. single, child of Alex. & Cath. A. WRIGHTMAN,
married by Ezekiel QUILLEN. remarks : married Wellsburg.

RUSSELL, James A. book 01 page 16 line 13
born Wellsburg, VA., resides Wellsburg, WV. horticulture,
age 25 yrs. single, child of James & Sarah RUSSELL,
married 28 Jan 1867 WV. to Electa M. PARSONS,
born Ohio, resides Wellsburg, West Virginia,
age 20 yrs. single, child of John & Sarah PARSONS,
married by Charles Louis LOOS. remarks : none.

RUSSELL, Lucy A. S. book 01 page 20 line 15
born Brooke Co., Virginia, resides Wellsburg, WV.
age 19 yrs. single, child of James & Sarah RUSSELL,
married 23 Jun 1870 WV. to William F. YOUNG,
born Pocahontas Co., VA., resides Cedar Co., Iowa,
age 26 yrs. single, child of William & Ann YOUNG,
married by E. DRINDLEY. remarks : married Wellsburg.

RUSSELL, Samuel book 01 page 05 line 13
born Brooke Co., VA., resides Brooke Co., VA. cooper,
age 40 yrs. single, child of John & Eliza. RUSSELL,
married 25 Jan 1857 Wellsburg, VA. to Clara GOVER,
born England, resides Brooke Co., Virginia,
age 26 yrs. single, child of Jacob & Sarah GOVER,
married by E. QUILLEN. remarks : married bride's house.

RUSSELL, Travilla A. book 01 page 13 line 27
born Wellsburg, VA., resides Wellsburg, WV. cooper,
age 21 yrs. single, child of James & Sarah RUSSELL,
married 30 Jun 1864 WV. to Mary E. CHESTER,
born Wellsburg, Virginia, resides Wellsburg, West Virginia,
age 21 yrs. single, child of George W. & Eliza. CHESTER,
married by E.A. BRINDLEY. remarks : married Wellsburg.

RUTH, John book 01 page 13 line 24
born Monroe Co., Ohio, resides Brooke Co., WV. farmer,
age 25 yrs. single, child of Michael & Mary RUTH,
married 23 Mar 1864 WV. to Agnes A. MC COY,
born Brooke Co., Virginia, resides Brooke Co., WV.
age 19 yrs. single, child of William & Mary MC COY,
married by William M. ROBINSON. remarks : none.

SALMON, Cornelius B. book 01 page 22 line 42
born Jefferson Co., Ohio, resides Steubenville, Ohio,
age 26 yrs. unknown, child of unk. & unk. SALMON,
married 10 Jun 1874 WV. to Mattie SWEARINGEN,
born Brooke Co., Virginia, resides Brooke Co., WV.
age 23 yrs. unk., child of unk. & unk. SWEARINGEN,
married by C. STILLWAGON. remarks : married Wellsburg.

SANDERS, Fanny book 01 page 11 line 29
born Scotland, resides Brooke Co., Virginia,
age 33 yrs. single, child of John & Maria SANDERS,
married 01 Jan 1863 VA. to John M. WILSON,
born Washington Co., PA., resides Wash. Co., PA.
age 33 yrs. widow, child of William & Rachel WILSON,
married by E.A. BRINDLEY. remarks : married Wellsburg.

SANDERS, Frank A. book 01 page 20 line 46
born Brooke Co., VA., resides Brooke Co., WV. farmer,
age 21 yrs. single, child of Benja. & Martha SANDERS,
married 13 Jun 1871 WV. to Cornelia H. HOOKER,
born Brooke Co., Virginia, resides Brooke Co., WV.
age 23 yrs. single, child of George & Marg't HOOKER,
married by J. COUPLAND. remarks : married Wellsburg.

SANDERS, Fredus A. book 01 page 19 line 17
born Washington Co., PA., resides Wellsburg, WV. agent,
age 29 yrs. single, child of Benjamin D. & M.A. SANDERS,
married 01 Dec 1868 WV. to Melissa A. FRESHWATER,
born Carroll Co., Ohio, resides Brooke Co., West Virginia,
age 21 yrs. single, child of George & Marg't FRESHWATER,
married by T.A. CRENSHAW. remarks : none.

SANDERS, Jonathan book 01 page 22 line 30
born Brooke Co., Virginia resides Brooke Co., WV.
age 25 yrs. unk., child of unk. & unk. SANDERS,
married 16 Dec 1873 WV. to Kate E. HINDMAN,
born Brooke Co., Virginia, resides Brooke Co., WV.
age 21 yrs. unk., child of unk. & unk. HINDMAN,
married by George B. HUDSON. remarks : none.

SANDERS, Mary E. book 01 page 06 line 01
born Hollidays Cove, Virginia, resides Hollidays Cove, VA.
age 21 yrs. single, child of Benja. D. & Martha SANDERS,
married 21 Jul 1857 VA. to James C. GARDNER,
born Eldersville, Pennsylvania, resides Indianola, Iowa,
age 28 yrs. single, child of David & Nancy GARDNER,
married by S. TEAGARDEN. remarks : married Hol. Cove.

SANDERSON, James Y. book 01 page 09 line 03
born Allegh. Co., PA., resides Brooke Co., VA. coal trader,
age 30 yrs. single, child of John & Eliza. SANDERSON,
married 24 Dec 1859 VA. to Elizabeth A. STRONG,
born Brooke Co., Virginia, resides Brooke Co., Virginia,
age 18 yrs. single, child of Samuel & Rebecca STRONG,
married by J.M. SMITH. remarks : married Wellsburg.

SAUNER, Hannah book 01 page 20 line 30
born Germany, resides Brooke Co., West Virginia,
age 24 yrs. single, child of unk. & unk. SAUNER,
married 23 Feb 1871 WV. to John M. DEIGHTON,
born Brooke Co., Virginia, resides Brooke Co., WV.
age 26 yrs. single, child of William & Sarah DEIGHTON,
married by D. CALDERWOOD. remarks : married Wellsburg.

SCAMAHORN, George W. book 01 page 23 line 03
born Jefferson Co., Ohio, resides Jefferson Co., Ohio,
age 24 yrs. unk. child of unk. & unk. SCAMAHORN,
married 23 Sep 1874 WV. to Arabella V. GREEN,
born Brooke Co., Virginia, resides Brooke Co., WV.
age 19 yrs. unknown, child of unk. & unk. GREEN,
married by James F. HUDDLESTON. remarks: none.

SCARBOROUGH, J.A. book 01 page 21 line 25
born South Carolina, resides Little Rock, AR. merchant,
age 24 yrs. single, child of W.H. & M.E. SCARBOROUGH,
married 26 Feb 1872 WV. to Elizabeth T. NAYLOR,
born Brooke Co., Virginia, resides Brooke Co., WV.
age 19 yrs. single, child of Joseph R. & Harriet NAYLOR,
married by Joshua COUPLAND, JR. remarks: none.

SCHALK, Conrad book 01 page 07 line 19
born Limbach, GER., resides Wellsburg, VA. coaldigger,
age 32 yrs. single, child of John & Mary SCHALK,
married 23 Aug 1858 VA. to Lusetta EASTERDAY,
born Sillinger, Germany, resides Wellsburg, Virginia,
age 35 yrs. widow, child of Andrew & Catherine LOFFER,
married by S. HUBER. remarks: mother Mary (GORNET)

SCHELL, William H. book 01 page 19 line 09
born Bedford Co., PA. resides Ebensburg, PA. clergyman,
age 28 yrs. single, child of Henry & Maria L. SCHELL,
married 20 Aug 1868 WV. to Clara C. CRAFT,
born Wellsburg, Virginia resides near Bethany, WV.
age 22 yrs. single, child of Alexander & Jane CRAFT,
married by James DARSIE. remarks: married Bethany.

SCHUEY, Barbara book 01 page 17 line 19
born Germany, resides Wellsburg, West Virginia,
age 19 yrs. single, child of William & Frances SCHUEY,
married 29 Nov 1866 Wellsburg, WV. to George HORN,
born Germany, resides Brooke Co., West Virginia,
age 33 yrs. single, child of George & Eliza. HORN,
married by Stephen HUBER. remarks: none.

SCHUEY, Peter book 01 page 20 line 05
born Nausan, GER., resides Brooke Co., WV. butcher,
age 24 yrs. single, child of Wm. & Frances SCHUEY,
married 25 Apr 1870 Wellsburg, WV. to Mary GAUSE,
born Whitenberg, Germany, resides Brooke Co., WV.
age 22 yrs. single, child of Lorence & Magdaline GAUSE,
married by Stephen HUBER. remarks: Wittenberg ?, GER.

SCOTT, Jane A. book 01 page 18 line 20
born Brooke Co., VA., resides Brooke Co., WV.
age 21 yrs. single, child of John & Jane SCOTT,
married 12 Mar 1868 WV. to J.G. HANNA,
born Washington Co., PA., resides Brooke Co., WV.
age 30 yrs. widow, child of Richard & Mary HANNA,
married by A.J. LANE. remarks: none.

SCOTT, John S.   book 01 page 14 line 33
   born Han. Co., VA., resides Harrison Co., Ohio,
   age 38 yrs. single, child of John & Sarah SCOTT,
   married 05 Jul 1864 WV. to Mary Jane LITTLE,
   born Scotland, resides Brooke Co., West Virginia,
   age 24 yrs. single, child of Jeremiah & unk. LITTLE,
   married by J. PIERCE. remarks : married Wellsburg.

SCOTT, William   book 01 page 18 line 21
   born Wash. Co., PA., resides Wash. Co., PA. farmer,
   age 28 yrs. single, child of Charles & Marg't SCOTT,
   married 04 Mar 1868 WV. to Rachel D. HEADINGTON,
   born Brooke Co., Virginia, resides Brooke Co., WV.
   age 21 yrs. single, child of John & Jane HEADINGTON,
   married by H. LUCAS. remarks : none.

SEARS, James   book 01 page 18 line 19
   born Wash. Co., PA., resides Jeff. Co., Ohio, farmer,
   age 42 yrs. widow, child of Stephen & Eliza. SEARS,
   married 27 Feb 1868 WV. to Margaret MELCHS,
   born Brooke Co., Virginia, resides Brooke Co., WV.
   age 24 yrs. widow, child of George & Marg't MELCHS,
   married by Edward A. BRINDLEY. remarks : none.

SEILA, Therisia   book 01 page 14 line 53
   born Williamsburg, resides Brooke Co., West Virginia,
   age 48 yrs. single, child of Vinez? & B. SEILA,
   married 18 Apr 1865 Wellsburg, WV. to Adrian PIKIRRA,
   born Williamsburg, resides Brooke Co., West Virginia,
   age 56 yrs. single, child of Leo & A. PIKIRRA,
   married by Stephen HUBER. remarks : none.

SELBY, Sarah C.   book 01 page 21 line 21
   born Jackson Co., Virginia, resides Brooke Co., WV.
   age 21 yrs. single, child of Nathan & Margaret SELBY,
   married 11 Jan 1872 PA. to Milton LAZEAR,
   born Brooke Co., Virginia, resides Brooke Co., WV.
   age 23 yrs. single, child of Joseph & Eliza. LAZEAR,
   married by S.T. DAVIS. remarks : married Independence.

SENS, Ursula   book 01 page 07 line 04
   born Crisinger, Germany, resides Wellsburg, Virginia,
   age 43 yrs. widow, child of Michael & Cecelia LEHEKS,
   married 22 Dec 1857 VA. to Ferdinard WENNINGCOUGH,
   born Germany, resides Wellsburg, Virginia,
   age 42 yrs. single, child of unk. & unk. WENNINGCOUGH,
   married by S. HUBER. remarks : mother Cecelia (ROGENETINE).

SERVIS, Charles M.   book 01 page 03 line 31
   born Washington Co., PA., resides Brooke Co., VA.
   age 25 yrs. single, child of John & Catherine SERVIS,
   married 12 Jul 1855 VA. to Sarah LAUGHEAD,
   born Brooke Co., Virginia, resides Brooke Co., Virginia,
   age 22 yrs. single, child of Robert & Jane LAUGHEAD,
   married by David HERVEY. remarks : none.

SHARP, Elizabeth K. book 01 page 22 line 29
born Brooke Co., Virginia, resides Brooke Co., WV.
age 19 yrs. unknown, child of unk. & unk. SHARP,
married 23 Dec 1873 WV. to Francis L. WOLCOTT,
born Brooke Co., Virginia, resides Scranton, PA.
age 25 yrs. unk., child of unk. & unk. WOLCOTT,
married by S. CRAVENS. remarks : married Wellsburg.

SHEARER, Andrew J. book 01 page 13 line 21
born Wellsburg, VA., resides Wellsburg, WV. tobaccorist,
age 26 yrs. single, child of Robert & Mary SHEARER,
married 15 Mar 1864 WV. to Martha J. MC LAUGHLIN,
born Washington Co., PA., resides Wellsburg, West Virginia,
age 20 yrs. single, child of Andrew & unk. MC LAUGHLIN,
married by J.A. PIERCE. remarks : none.

SHIELDS, Henry T. book 01 page 11 line 31
born Belmont Co., Ohio, resides Brooke Co., VA. farmer,
age 21 yrs. single, child of William & Anne SHIELDS,
married 13 Jan 1863 Glen Higher, VA. to Samantha DOW,
born Ohio, resides Brooke Co., Virginia,
age 17 yrs. single, child of T.H. & Jane DOW,
married by W.E. WILLIAMSON. remarks : none.

SHOUP, Mary J. book 01 page 21 line 13
born Wheeling, Virginia, resides unknown,
age 24 yrs. widow, child of Lee & Mary SHOUP,
married 19 Nov 1871 WV. to William THOMPSON,
born Philadelphia, PA., resides Steubenville, Ohio,
age 30 yrs. widow, child of Wm. & Mary THOMPSON,
married by J.C. CASTLE. remarks : married Wellsburg.

SHRIMPLIN, Amanda book 01 page 21 line 18
born Brooke Co., Virginia, resides Brooke Co., WV.
age 23 yrs. single, child of John & Eliza. SHRIMPLIN,
married 20 Dec 1871 WV. to Hugh LAZEAR,
born Brooke Co., Virginia, resides Brooke Co., West Virginia,
age 22 yrs. single, child of Jerome R. & Susan J. LAZEAR,
married by Robert R. MOORE. remarks : none.

SHRIMPLIN, Ella book 01 page 18 line 16
born Brooke Co., Virginia, resides Brooke Co., West Virginia,
age 25 yrs. single, child of John & Elizabeth SHRIMPLIN,
married 19 Feb 1868 WV. to Samuel D. BARTHOLOMEW,
born Jefferson Co., Ohio, resides Brooke Co., West Virginia,
age 28 yrs. single, child of Sam'l & Mary BARTHOLOMEW,
married by J.A. PIERCE. remarks : none.

SHRINER, William book 01 page 15 line 67
born Jefferson Co., Ohio, resides Wellsburg, WV. laborer,
age 23 yrs. single, child of unknown & unk. SHRINER,
married 02 Nov 1865 Wellsburg, WV. to Caroline HALL,
born Wellsburg, Virginia, resides Wellsburg, West Virginia,
age 25 yrs. widow, child of William & Elizabeth GREEN,
married by J.A. BROWN. remarks : Caroline (GREEN) HALL.

SHRIVER, C.　　　　book 01 page 21 line 42
born Fayette Co., PA., resides Bethany, WV. physician,
age 31 yrs. widow, child of Geo. W. & Melissa SHRIVER,
married 08 Aug 1872　WV. to Rebecca E. RODGERS,
born Brooke Co., Virginia, resides Brooke Co., WV.
age 28 yrs. single, child of William & Marg't RODGERS,
married by Robert R. MOORE. remarks : none.

SHUPE, David D.　　　　book 01 page 21 line 07
born Monroe Co., Ohio, resides Bellaire, Ohio, merchant,
age 27 yrs. single, child of Jonathan & Juliett SHUPE,
married 11 Oct 1871　WV. to Emma J. MERRYMAN,
born Jefferson Co., Ohio resides Brooke Co., West Virginia,
age 21 yrs. single, child of Wm. & Joana MERRYMAN,
married by W. PENDLETON. remarks : married Wellsburg.

SICKLER, John Francis　　　　book 01 page 23 line 07
born Jefferson Co., Ohio, resides Steubenville, Ohio,
age 24 yrs. unknown, child of unk. & unk. SICKLER,
married 29 Dec 1874　WV. to Mary HELSTINE,
born Brooke Co., Virginia, resides Brooke Co., WV.
age 18 yrs. single, child of unk. & unk. HELSTINE,
married by Stephen HUBER. remarks : none.

SILVERS, Sally　　　　book 01 page 16 line 19
born Brooke Co., Virginia, resides Brooke Co., WV.
age 24 yrs. single, child of unknown & unk. SILVERS,
married 25 Mar 1867　WV. to William S. RINEHART,
born Green Co., PA., resides Wheeling, West Virginia,
age 33 yrs. single, child of unk. & unk. RINEHART,
married by Thomas M. HUDSON. remarks : none.

SIMPSON, Charles L.　　　　book 01 page 09 line 14
born Brooke Co., VA., resides Brooke Co., VA. carpenter,
age 30 yrs. single, child of James & Ann T. SIMPSON,
married 26 Apr 1860　VA. to Nannie E. FLEMING,
born Ohio Co., Virginia, resides Brooke Co., Virginia,
age 20 yrs. single, child of Coleman B. & Eliza. FLEMING,
married by G. WALTERS. remarks : married mothers residence.

SIMPSON, Isaac G.　　　　book 01 page 03 line 34
born Jeff. Co., Ohio, resides Brooke Co., VA. farmer,
age 48 yrs. widow, child of Robert & Eliza. SIMPSON,
married 31 May 1855　VA. to Mary Ann HESSEY,
born Jefferson Co., Ohio, resides Brooke Co., VA.
age 30 yrs. widow, child of Robert & Jane WHITE,
married by E. QUILLEN. remarks : married Wellsburg.

SIMPSON, Rebecca Ann　　　　book 01 page 04 line 46
born Brooke Co., Virginia, resides Brooke Co., Virginia,
age 21 yrs. single, child of James & Ann Jane SIMPSON,
married 04 Mar 1856　VA. to Oliver WYLIE,
born Brooke Co., Virginia, resides Mason Co., Virginia,
age 26 yrs. single, child of Robert & Elizabeth WYLIE,
married by Ezekiel QUILLEN. remarks : none.

SMITH, Clarence A.C. book 01 page 18 line 09
born Brooke Co., VA. resides Brooke Co., WV. farmer,
age 22 yrs. single, child of Andrew & Jane SMITH,
married 09 Jan 1868 WV. to Almira MC CREARY,
born Brooke Co., Virginia, resides Brooke Co., WV.
age 22 yrs. single, child of Wm. & unk. MC CREARY,
married by A.J. LANE. remarks: none.

SMITH, Elizabeth H. book 01 page 21 line 35
born Brooke Co., Virginia, resides Brooke Co., WV.
age 32 yrs. single, child of Andrew & Jane SMITH,
married 14 May 1872 WV. to Hiram MARS,
born Oldham Co., Kentucky, resides Galesburg, IL.
age 40 yrs. widow, child of Andrew & Eliza. MARS,
married by Thomas M. HUDSON. remarks: none.

SMITH, Francis book 01 page 05 line 11
born Brooke Co., Virginia, resides Brooke Co., VA.
age 18 yrs. single, child of T. Edward & unk. SMITH,
married 27 Nov 1856 VA. to Hiram? FOWLER,
born Brooke Co., Virginia, resides Brooke Co., VA.
age 22 yrs. single, child of John & Sarah FOWLER,
married by G. CRANAGE. remarks: T. SMITH deceased.

SMITH, George F. book 01 page 11 line 15
born Tuscarawas Co., Ohio resides Brooke Co., VA.
age 28 yrs. single, child of William & Mary SMITH,
married 10 Nov 1861 VA. to Sarah CORNELIUS,
born Brooke Co., Virginia, resides Brooke Co., Virginia,
age 36 yrs. single, child of Elijah & Lettice CORNELIUS,
married by George W. WHARTON. remarks: none.

SMITH, George W. book 01 page 15 line 66
born Brooke Co., VA., resides Brooke Co., WV. farmer,
age 29 yrs. widow, child of Andrew & Jane SMITH,
married 02 Nov 1865 WV. to Virginia MC CREARY,
born Brooke Co., VA., resides Brooke Co., West Virginia,
age 25 yrs. single, child of William & unk. MC CREARY,
married by T. HUDSON. remarks: married house of T. GIST.

SMITH, George W. book 01 page 09 line 16
born Brooke Co., VA., resides Brooke Co., VA. farmer,
age 24 yrs. single, child of Andrew & Jane SMITH,
married 01 Mar 1860 VA. to Elizabeth MC CREARY,
born Brooke Co., Virginia, resides Brooke Co., Virginia,
age 21 yrs. single, child of William & A. MC CREARY,
married by Thomas M. HUDSON. remarks: none.

SMITH, James Pursel book 01 page 15 line 58
born Brooke Co., VA., resides Brooke Co., WV. farmer,
age 27 yrs. single, child of Fergus & Nancy SMITH,
married 15 Sep 1865 WV. to Sallie/Sarah BONAR,
born Brooke Co., Virginia, resides Brooke Co., WV.
age 21 yrs. single, child of George & Ellen BONAR,
married by J. BROWN. remarks: married BONAR house.

SMITH, John P. book 01 page 10 line 06A
born Wash. Co., PA., resides Pitts., PA. steamboat capt.
age 28 yrs. widow, child of Henry & Barbara SMITH,
married 29 Aug 1860 VA. to Lina E. INGLEBRIGHT,
born Steubenville, Ohio, resides Brooke Co., Virginia,
age 22 yrs. single, child of Wm. & Sarah INGLEBRIGHT,
married by C. BEATTY. remarks: married Half Moon Farm.

SMITH, Nancy M. book 01 page 17 line 12
born Ohio Co., Virginia, resides Ohio Co., WV.
age 24 yrs. single, child of Fergus & Nancy SMITH,
married 11 Sep 1866 WV. to Horace RIDGLEY,
born Ohio Co., Virginia, resides Ohio Co., West Virginia,
age 33 yrs. widow, child of Richard & Marg't RIDGLEY,
married by J.A. BROWN. remarks: none.

SMITH, Robert book 01 page 13 line 13
born Washington Co., PA., resides Wash. Co., PA. farmer,
age 63 yrs. widow, child of Alexander & Jane SMITH,
married 17 Dec 1863 Wellsburg, WV. to Elizabeth WELLS,
born Brooke Co., Virginia, resides Wellsburg, West Virginia,
age 54 yrs. single, child of Absalom & Ellen WELLS,
married by James FLEMING. remarks: none.

SMITH, Robert N. book 01 page 11 line 24
born Wash. Co., PA. resides Jeff. Co., Ohio carpenter,
age 35 yrs. single, child of William & Rebecca SMITH,
married 16 Oct 1862 VA. to Anne BRADY,
born New Jersey, resides Brooke Co., Virginia,
age 25 yrs. single, child of Bernard & Bridget BRADY,
married by Stephen HUBER. remarks: none.

SMITH, Rose V. book 01 page 08 line 02
born Brooke Co., Virginia, resides Brooke Co., VA.
age 28 yrs. single, child of Andrew & Jane SMITH,
married 09 Nov 1858 VA. to John C. CASNER,
born Brooke Co., Virginia, resides Brooke Co., VA.
age 30 yrs. single, child of James & Eliza CASNER,
married by Thomas M. HUDSON. remarks: none.

SMOTE, Elizabeth Jane book 01 page 02 line 10
born Noble Co., Ohio, resides Wellsburg, Virginia,
age 25 yrs. single, child of John & Sarah SMOTE,
married 26 Feb 1854 VA. to William E. BROWNLEE,
born Brooke Co., Virginia, resides Wellsburg, Virginia,
age 24 yrs. single, child of Walter B. & Unity BROWNLEE,
married by Samuel H. NESBITT. remarks: married Wellsburg.

SNEARY, Stewart book 01 page 19 line 08
born Carroll Co., Ohio, resides Carroll Co., OH. farmer,
age 21 yrs. single, child of H.S. & Susan SNEARY,
married 11 Aug 1868 WV. to Elizabeth CAMPBELL,
born Carroll Co., Ohio, resides Carroll Co., Ohio,
age 23 yrs. single, child of unk. & unk. CAMPBELL,
married by A. CHAPMAN. remarks: married Wellsburg.

SNEDIKER, Clarinda L.   book 01 page 19 line 16
born Brooke Co., Virginia, resides Brooke Co., WV.
age 23 yrs. single, child of Wm. & Mary A. SNEDIKER,
married 04 Nov 1868   WV. to Samuel W. ATKINSON,
born Brooke Co., Virginia, resides Brooke Co., WV.
age 29 yrs. single, child of John & Mary ATKINSON,
married by J.W. KESLER. remarks : none.

SNEDIKER, Clay   book 01 page 19 line 28
born Brooke Co., Virginia, resides Brooke Co., WV.
age 21 yrs. single, child of Wm. & Mary A. SNEDIKER,
married 02 Feb 1869   WV. to Samuel COOK,
born Washington Co., PA., resides Wash. Co., PA.
age 24 yrs. single, child of Godfrey & Martha COOK,
married by J.W. KESLER. remarks : none.

SNEDIKER, Ellis M.   book 01 page 22 line 34
born Brooke Co., Virginia, resides Brooke Co., WV.
age 25 yrs. unk., child of unk. & unk. SNEDIKER,
married 03 Feb 1874   WV. to Hattie JONES,
born Brooke Co., Virginia, resides Brooke Co., WV.
age 21 yrs. unknown, child of unk. & unk. JONES,
married by N,B, STEWART. remarks . none.

SNEDIKER, Elvira Virg.   book 01 page 08 line 03
born Brooke Co., Virginia, resides Brooke Co., Virginia,
age 20 yrs. single, child of Wm. & Mary A. SNEDIKER,
married 14 Oct 1858   VA. to John H. BOTHWELL,
born Baltimore Co., MD., resides Ohio Co., Virginia,
age 38 yrs. widow, child of Chas. & Phoebe BOTHWELL,
married by Thomas M. HUDSON. remarks : none.

SNOWDEN, Sarah Ann   book 01 page 22 line 39
born Brooke Co., Virginia, resides Brooke Co., WV.
age 22 yrs. unk., child of unk. & unk. SNOWDEN,
married 21 May 1874   WV. to Ellson STEWART,
born Beaver Co., PA., resides Muskingum Co., Ohio,
age 22 yrs. unk., child of unk. & unk. STEWART,
married by John COWL. remarks : none.

SNYDER, Mary C.   book 01 page 07 line 15
born Hollidays Cove, VA., resides Hollidays Cove, VA.
age 18 yrs. single, child of David & Matilda SNYDER,
married 08 Jul 1858   VA. to Benjamin F. SPEAKER,
born Steubenville, Ohio, resides Steubenville, Ohio,
age 28 yrs. single, child of unk. & Hanna SPEAKER,
married by S. TEAGARDEN. remarks : married H. Cove.

SODIKE, William   book 01 page 16 line 26
born unknown, resides Bridgewater, Pennsylvania,
age -- yrs. unknown, child of unk. & unk. SODIKE,
married 13 Oct 1867   PA. to Harriet E. MC CLURG,
born unknown, resides Bridgewater, Pennsylvania
age   yrs. unknown, child of unk. & unk. MC CLURG,
married by J. WILLIAMS. remarks : married Bridgewater.

BROOKE CO., VA./WV. MARRIAGE BOOK 1, 1853-1874   281

SOULES, Washington   book 01 page 03 line 30
born Pennsylvania, resides Brooke Co., VA. farmer,
age 46 yrs. widow, child of Jacob & Sarah SOULES,
married 15 Mar 1855 VA. to Mary Jane HENNES,
born Brooke Co., Virginia, resides Brooke Co., VA.
age 24 yrs. single, child of Sam'l & Lucinda HENNES,
married by Warner LONG. remarks : none.

SPEAKER, Benja. Frank.   book 01 page 07 line 15
born Steubenville, Ohio, resides Ohio, farmer,
age 28 yrs. single, child of unk. & Hanna SPEAKER,
married 08 Jul 1858 VA. to Mary C. SNYDER,
born Hollidays Cove, VA., resides Hollidays Cove, VA.
age 18 yrs. single, child of David & Matilda SNYDER,
married by S. TEAGARDEN. remarks : married H. Cove.

SPRAGUE, Cora   book 01 page 21 line 44
born Gallipolis, Ohio, resides Hamersville, Ohio,
age 19 yrs. single, child of Benjamin & unk. SPRAGUE,
married 03 Sep 1872 WV. to W.H. THOMPSON,
born on the Atlantic Ocean, resides Hamersville, Ohio
age 28 yrs. single, child of Edward & Lucy THOMPSON,
married by J. COUPLAND. remarks : married Wellsburg.

SPRINGBORN, Frederick   book 01 page 17 line 17
born Germany, resides Jefferson Co., Ohio, tobaccorist,
age 25 yrs. single, child of Fred. & Mary SPRINGBORN,
married 11 Oct 1866 WV. to Mary LETZKUS,
born Brooke Co., Hollidays Cove, resides Wellsburg, WV.
age 17 yrs. single, child of George & Michelia LETZKUS,
married by Stephen HUBER. remarks : none.

ST. LEDGER, Mary Ann   book 01 page 02 line 14
born Pennsylvania, resides Wellsburg, Virginia,
age 22 yrs. single, child of John & Mary ST. LEDGER,
married 05 Oct 1854 VA. to Robert UHLRICH,
born Saxony, Germany, resides Wellsburg, Virginia,
age 25 yrs. single, child of Chas. Fred. & Joanna UHLRICH,
married by W. LEMON. remarks : married Wellsburg.

STANSBERRY, Daniel B.   book 01 page 14 line 46
born Brooke Co., Virginia, resides Brooke Co., WV.
age 37 yrs. widow, child of N. & K. STANSBERRY,
married 07 Feb 1865 WV. to Jane CAMPBELL,
born Brooke Co., Virginia, resides Brooke Co., WV.
age 30 yrs. single, child of R. & Marg't CAMPBELL,
married by T. HUDSON. remarks : married Hollidays Cove.

STANSBERRY, Hudson R.   book 01 page 18 line 22
born Brooke Co., VA., resides Brooke Co., WV. blacksmith,
age 26 yrs. single, child of John & Matilda STANSBERRY,
married 13 Mar 1868 WV. to Hanna CRISS,
born Brooke Co., Virginia, resides Brooke Co., WV.
age 24 yrs. single, child of Nicholas & Nancy CRISS,
married by H. LUCAS. remarks : none.

STARKEY, Mary book 01 page 07 line 13
born Ohio Co., Virginia, resides Ohio Co., Virginia,
age 16 yrs. single, child of Wm. & Isabelle STARKEY,
married 01 May 1858 VA. to George W. BORING,
born Ohio Co., Virginia, resides Ohio Co., Virginia,
age 34 yrs. widow, child of Ephraim & Marg't BORING,
married by E. QUILLEN. remarks: married Wellsburg.

STARR, Joseph book 01 page 11 line 30
born Wash. Co., PA., resides Brooke Co., VA. coaldigger,
age 21 yrs. single, child of William & A. STARR,
married 02 Jan 1863 Wellsburg, VA. to Eliza. MURPHY,
born Washington Co., PA., resides Brooke Co., Virginia,
age 18 yrs. single, child of Thomas & Eliza. MURPHY,
married by George W. CHESTER. remarks: none.

STARR, Nancy J. book 01 page 12 line 57
born Washington Co., PA., resides Wash. Co., PA.
age 19 yrs. single, child of William & A. STARR,
married 20 Jul 1863 WV. to George W. MURPHY,
born Washington Co., PA., resides Brooke Co., WV.
age 24 yrs. single, child of Thos. & Eliza. MURPHY,
married by G. CHESTER. remarks: married Wellsburg.

STEWART, Elizabeth C. book 01 page 19 line 18
born Wellsburg, Virginia, resides Wellsburg, WV.
age 22 yrs. single, child of Jackson & Mary STEWART,
married 24 Dec 1868 Wellsburg, WV. to Jacob MILLER,
born Ohio Co., Virginia, resides Wellsburg, West Virginia,
age 23 yrs. single, child of Joseph & Mary MILLER,
married by A.R. CHAPMAN. remarks: none.

STEWART, Elison book 01 page 22 line 39
born Beaver Co., PA., resides Muskingum Co., Ohio,
age 22 yrs. unk., child of unk. & unk. STEWART,
married 21 May 1874 WV. to Sarah A. SNOWDEN,
born Brooke Co., Virginia, resides Brooke Co., WV.
age 22 yrs. unk., child of unk. & unk. SNOWDEN,
married by John COWL. remarks: none.

STEWART, Elmira J. book 01 page 04 line 57
born Maine, resides Wellsburg, Virginia,
age 19 yrs. single, child of Jos. & Dianna STEWART,
married 01 Jun 1856 VA. to James ROBINETT,
born Marshall Co., Virginia, resides Wellsburg, Virginia,
age 21 yrs. single, child of Allen & Marg't ROBINETT,
married by A.J. ENDSLEY. remarks: married Wellsburg.

STEWART, Harriet book 01 page 19 line 46
born Brooke Co., Virginia, resides Brooke Co., WV.
age 24 yrs. single, child of Robert & unk. STEWART,
married 08 Feb 1870 WV. to William KLINE,
born Wellsburg, Virginia, resides Washington Co., PA.
age 30 yrs. single, child of Frederick & Marg't KLINE,
married by Walter BROWN. remarks: none.

STEWART, Henrietta book 01 page 07 line 10
born Cadiz, Ohio, resides Wellsburg, Virginia,
age 19 yrs. single, child of Jackson & Mary STEWART,
married 07 Mar 1858 VA. to William DUVALL,
born Wellsburg, Virginia, resides Wellsburg, Virginia,
age 20 yrs. single, child of Gabriel & Nancy DUVALL,
married by E. FLETCHER. remarks : married Wellsburg.

STEWART, James Clinton book 01 page 20 line 02
born Ohio Co., VA., resides Venango Co., PA. engineer,
age 23 yrs. single, child of Jackson & Mary STEWART,
married 30 Mar 1870 WV. to Georgianna CHESTER,
born Wellsburg, Virginia, resides Wellsburg, West Virginia,
age 19 yrs. single, child of George W. & Eliza. CHESTER,
married by E.A. BRINDLEY. remarks : married Wellsburg.

STEWART, John Gibson book 01 page 15 line 64
born Ohio Co., VA., resides Brooke Co., WV. boatman,
age 26 yrs. single, child of William & M. STEWART,
married 26 Oct 1865 WV. to Ellen CHAMBERLAIN,
born Brooke Co., Virginia, resides Brooke Co., West Virginia,
age 21 yrs. single, child of Daniel & Jane CHAMBERLAIN,
married by G. CHESTER. remarks : married E. GIVENS house.

STEWART, Mary book 01 page 20 line 28
born Jefferson Co., Ohio, resides Brooke Co., WV.
age 56 yrs. widow, child of David & Mary STEWART,
married 17 Feb 1871 WV. to John MC GREW,
born Jefferson Co., Ohio, resides Mason Co., WV.
age 57 yrs. widow, child of James & Sarah MC GREW,
married by Milton WELLS. remarks : none.

STEWART, Mary Ann book 01 page 04 line 41
born Maine, resides Wellsburg, Virginia,
age 17 yrs. single, child of Joseph & Dianna STEWART,
married 28 Feb 1856 VA. to John FARQUER,
born Brooke Co., Virginia, resides Brooke Co., VA.
age 21 yrs. single, child of John & Nancy FARQUER,
married by A.J. ENDSLEY. remarks : none.

STEWART, Ruemma Elen book 01 page 19 line 21
born Ohio, resides Brooke Co., West Virginia,
age 17 yrs. single, child of Wm. & Martha STEWART,
married 06 Oct 1868 WV. to Wilson L. KNIGHT,
born Allegheny Co., PA., resides Brooke Co., WV.
age 24 yrs. single, child of Phillip & Sarah KNIGHT,
married by M. WELLS. remarks : married Buff Twp.

STIETZE, Wellhemine book 01 page 04 line 60
born Curscean, Germany, resides Brooke Co., Virginia,
age 23 yrs. single, child of John & Catherine STIETZE,
married 08 Sep 1856 Wellsburg, VA. to Henry BERTRAM,
born Brunswick, Saxony, Germany, resides Brooke Co., VA.
age 27 yrs. single, child of Christian & Isabell BERTRAM,
married by Ezekiel QUILLEN. remarks : none.

STOCK, Benjamin book 01 page 04 line 53
born Ohio, resides Brooke Co., Virginia, laborer,
age 22 yrs. single, child of Benjamin & Jane STOCK,
married 01 May 1856 VA. to Rosanna MC HUGH,
born Brooke Co., Virginia, resides Brooke Co., Virginia,
age 22 yrs. single, child of Alex. & Susannah MC HUGH,
married by J.R. MEANS. remarks : none.

STRAIN, Eleazer G. book 01 page 02 line 12
born Brooke Co., VA., resides Wellsburg, VA. carpenter,
age 33 yrs. single, child of Ebenezer & Catherine STRAIN,
married 24 Aug 1854 VA. to Elizabeth MC KIM,
born Brooke Co., Virginia, resides Wellsburg, Virginia,
age 24 yrs. single, child of Thomas & Nancy MC KIM,
married by Samuel D. TOMPKINS. remarks : none.

STRINGER, Ruth Jane book 01 page 04 line 44
born Pennsylvania, resides unknown,
age 24 yrs. single, child of Robert & Ruth STRINGER,
married 08 Nov 1853 VA. to Edmund DARE,
born New Jersey, resides unknown,
age 26 yrs. single, child of Edmund & Hannah DARE,
married by G. CRANAGE. remarks : married Fowlersville.

STRONG, Elizabeth A. book 01 page 09 line 03
born Brooke Co., Virginia, resides Brooke Co., Virginia,
age 18 yrs. single, child of Samuel & Rebecca STRONG,
married 24 Dec 1859 VA. to James Y. SANDERSON,
born Allegheny Co., PA., resides Brooke Co., Virginia,
age 30 yrs. single, child of John & Eliza. SANDERSON,
married by J.M. SMITH. remarks : married Wellsburg.

SUTER, Clarinda book 01 page 14 line 36
born Bethany, Virginia, resides Bethany, WV.
age 19 yrs. single, child of unk. & unk. SUTER,
married 03 Nov 1864 WV. to Henry A. BIER,
born Wheeling, Virginia, resides Wheeling, WV.
age 21 yrs. single, child of Jacob & Mary BIER,
married by William K. PENDLETON. remarks : none.

SWEARINGEN, George book 01 page 23 line 04
born Brooke Co., Virginia, resides Brooke Co., WV.
age 27 yrs. unk., child of unk. & unk. SWEARINGEN,
married 09 Jul 1874 PA., to Sallie J. HOOKER,
born Hancock Co., VA., resides Hancock Co., WV.
age 30 yrs. unk., child of unk. & unk. HOOKER,
married by J. SHIELDS. remarks : married Bridgewater.

SWEARINGEN, John C. book 01 page 02 line 06
born Brooke Co., Virginia, resides Wellsburg, VA. farmer,
age 28 yrs. single, child of Geo. & Ruth SWEARINGEN,
married 11 Apr 1854 VA. to Ruth Ann JEFFERS,
born Brooke Co., Virginia, resides Wellsburg, Virginia,
age 25 yrs. single, child of John & Harriet JEFFERS,
married by E. QUILLEN. remarks : married JEFFERS house.

SWEARINGEN, Mattie L. book 01 page 22 line 42
born Brooke Co., Virginia, resides Brooke Co., WV.
age 23 yrs. unk., child of unk. & unk. SWEARINGEN,
married 10 Jun 1874 WV. to Cornelius SALMON,
born Jefferson Co., Ohio, resides Steubenville, Ohio,
age 26 yrs. unknown, child of unk. & unk. SALMON,
married by C. STILLWAGON. remarks : married Wellsburg.

SWEENEY, Hannah book 01 page 19 line 32
born Ireland, resides Brooke Co., West Virginia,
age 30 yrs. single, child of unk. & unk. SWEENEY,
married 18 Mar 1869 WV. to Patrick PENDEGRASS,
born Ireland, resides Brooke Co., West Virginia,
age 30 yrs. single, child of Pat. & Ellen PENDEGRASS,
married by Stephen HUBER. remarks : married Wellsburg.

SWINER, Bell book 01 page 04 line 54
born Jefferson Co., Ohio, resides unknown,
age 19 yrs. single, child of Peter & Mary SWINER,
married 28 Mar 1856 VA. to Edward FENWICK,
born Jefferson Co., Ohio, resides unknown,
age 21 yrs. single, child of James & Ann FENWICK,
married by S. NESBITT. remarks : married Wellsburg.

SWINER, Mary Ann book 01 page 03 line 27
born Jacksonville, Ohio, resides Brooke Co., Virginia,
age 20 yrs. single, child of Peter & Mary SWINER,
married 27 Dec 1854 VA. to William J. BROWNLEE,
born Wellsburg, Virginia, resides Brooke Co., Virginia,
age 20 yrs. single, child of Thos & Juliane BROWNLEE,
married by S.H. NESBITT. remarks : married Wellsburg.

SWINER, Peter book 01 page 02 line 13
born Jacksonville, Ohio, resides Wellsburg, VA. teamster,
age 23 yrs. single, child of Peter & Mary SWINER,
married 06 Aug 1854 Wellsburg, VA. to Macky RAMSEY,
born Brooke Co., Virginia, resides Wellsburg, Virginia,
age 30 yrs. widow, child of William & Elizabeth WOOD,
married by Charles A. HOLMES. remarks : none.

SWORDS, Robert M. book 01 page 18 line 15
born Jefferson Co., Ohio, resides Brooke Co., WV.
age 38 yrs. single, child of Finey & Sally SWORDS,
married 18 Feb 1868 WV. to Terrissa GLASS,
born Jefferson Co., Ohio, resides Brooke Co., WV.
age 19 yrs. single, child of Henry & unk. GLASS,
married by Stephen HUBER. remarks : none.

TARR, Mary Belle book 01 page 21 line 37
born Brooke Co., Virginia, resides Brooke Co., WV.
age 23 yrs. single, child of Campbell & Mary TARR,
married 05 Jun 1872 WV. to Edwin T. ALLEN,
born Brunswick, Missouri, resides Brunswick, MO.
age 27 yrs. single, child of Thos. & Mariah ALLEN,
married by R.R. MOORE. remarks : married Wellsburg.

TARR, Mary F. book 01 page 20 line 06
born Brooke Co., Virginia, resides Brooke Co., WV.
age 22 yrs. single, child of Campbell & Frances TARR,
married 27 Apr 1870 WV. to Robert W. GARRETT,
born Co. Down, Ireland, resides Leavenworth, Kansas,
age 24 yrs. single, child of Alex. & Eliza. GARRETT,
married by Robert R. MOORE. remarks: none.

TARR, Virginia book 01 page 04 line 42
born Brooke Co., Virginia, resides unknown,
age 20 yrs. single, child of Campbell & Mary TARR,
married 20 Nov 1855 VA. to Obediah LANGFITT,
born Hancock Co., Virginia, resides unknown,
age 35 yrs. widow, child of Wm. & Laodicy LANGFITT,
married by W. BEARD. remarks: married Wellsburg.

TAYLOR, Alice book 01 page 15 line 73
born Pennsylvania, resides Wellsburg, WV.
age 21 yrs. single, child of unk. & unk. TAYLOR,
married 27 Mar 1866 WV. to Thomas W. BAIL,
born Pennsylvania, resides Cincinnati, Ohio,
age 34 yrs. single, child of James & Eliza. BAIL,
married by J.A. BROWN. remarks: none.

TAYLOR, Amelia C. book 01 page 12 line 42
born Brooke Co., Virginia, resides Brooke Co., VA.
age 20 yrs. single, child of unk. & Ann TAYLOR,
married 08 Mar 1862 VA. to George M. PRATHER,
born Brooke Co., Virginia, resides Wellsburg, Virginia,
age 22 yrs. single, child of John & Eliza. PRATHER,
married by E. BRINDLEY. remarks: married Wellsburg.

TAYLOR, Anne book 01 page 11 line 28
born Brooke Co., Virginia, resides Wellsburg, Virginia,
age 18 yrs. single, child of Thomas & Ann TAYLOR,
married 14 Dec 1862 VA. to John S. BURGESS,
born New Jersey, resides Wheeling, Virginia,
age 26 yrs. single, child of Francis & Pheby BURGESS,
married by E.A. BRINDLEY. remarks: married Wellsburg.

TAYLOR, Robert book 01 page 22 line 14
born Manchester, England, resides Wellsburg, WV.
age 36 yrs. unknown, child of unk. & unk. TAYLOR,
married 17 Jun 1873 WV. to Sarah ORANGE,
born Tipperary, Ireland, resides Wellsburg, West Virginia,
age 30 yrs. unknown, child of unk. & unk. ORANGE,
married by J. COUPLAND. remarks: married Wellsburg.

THOMPSON, Elizabeth book 01 page 13 line 20
born Washington Co., PA., resides Wellsburg, West Virginia,
age 21 yrs. single, child of Robert & Eleanor THOMPSON,
married 25 Feb 1864 Wellsburg, WV. to Cyrus MILLER,
born Washington Co., PA., resides Washington Co., PA.
age 33 yrs. widow, child of unknown & unk. MILLER,
married by Edward A. BRINDLEY. remarks: none.

BROOKE CO., VA./WV. MARRIAGE BOOK 1, 1853-1874   287

THOMPSON, Joseph   book 01 page 03 line 36
born Ohio Co., Virginia, resides Brooke Co., VA. farmer,
age 22 yrs. single, child of Geo. S. & Mary THOMPSON,
married 04 Oct 1855 VA. to Sarah E. BOWMAN,
born Brooke Co., Virginia, resides Brooke Co., Virginia,
age 22 yrs. single, child of Abram. & Henrietta BOWMAN,
married by J.R. MEANS. remarks : none.

THOMPSON, Robert   book 01 page 20 line 03
born Wash. Co, PA., resides Wellsburg, WV. wagonmaker,
age 55 yrs. widow, child of Robert & Phoebe THOMPSON,
married 26 Mar 1870 Wellsburg, WV. to Margaret HANEY,
born Ohio, resides Wellsburg, West Virginia
age 41 yrs. single, child of unk. & unk. HANEY,
married by Charles Louis LOOS. remarks : none.

THOMPSON, S. Elizabeth   book 01 page 05 line 09
born Ohio Co., Virginia, resides Brooke Co., Virginia,
age 18 yrs. single, child of Geo. S. & Mary THOMPSON,
married 15 Nov 1856 VA. to William LINTON,
born Brooke Co., Virginia, resides Brooke Co., Virginia,
age 23 yrs. single, child of William & Elizabeth LINTON,
married by A.J. ENDSLEY. remarks : none.

THOMPSON, W.H.   book 01 page 21 line 44
born on Atlantic Ocean, resides Hamersville, OH. shoemaker,
age 28 yrs. single, child of Edward & Lucy THOMPSON,
married 03 Sep 1872 Wellsburg, WV. to Cora SPRAGUE,
born Gallipolis, Ohio, resides Hamersville, Ohio,
age 19 yrs. single, child of Benjamin & unk. SPRAGUE,
married by Joshua COUPLAND, JR. remarks : none.

THOMPSON, William   book 01 page 21 line 13
born Philadelphia, PA., resides Steuben., OH. brickmaker,
age 30 yrs. widow, child of William & Mary THOMPSON,
married 19 Nov 1871 Wellsburg, WV. to Mary J. SHOUP,
born Wheeling, Virginia, resides unknown,
age 24 yrs. widow, child of Lee & Mary SHOUP,
married by J.C. CASTLE. remarks : none.

THOMPSON, William R.   book 01 page 13 line 09
born unknown, resides Louisville, Kentucky, lawyer,
age - - yrs. single, child of unk. & unk. THOMPSON,
married 26 Oct 1863 WV. to Virginia A. CAMPBELL,
born unknown, resides Brooke Co., West Virginia,
age - - yrs. single, child of Alex. & Selina H. CAMPBELL,
married by W. PENDLETON. remarks : married Bethany.

THORP, Mary   book 01 page 04 line 61
born Westmoreland Co., PA., resides Wellsburg, VA.
age 32 yrs. widow, child of Aaron & Cath. THORP,
married 12 Sep 1856 Wellsburg, VA. to John COGAN,
born Cumberland Co., PA., resides Wellsburg, Virginia,
age 30 yrs. single, child of John & Martha ? COGAN,
married by W. GAMBLE. remarks : Mary (THORP) BARBER.

TIERMAN, Thomas　　　　book 01 page 05 line 05
born Co. Dublin, Ireland, resides Wellsburg, VA. laborer,
age 27 yrs. single, child of Michael & Rosa TIERMAN,
married 02 Oct 1856   VA. to Margarett DEMPSEY,
born Co. Tipperary, Ireland, resides Wellsburg, VA.
age 21 yrs. single, child of John & Mary DEMPSEY,
married by J. BRAZILL. remarks : married Wellsburg.

TILTON, Joseph　　　　book 01 page 20 line 32
born Belmont Co., Ohio, resides Bel. Co., Ohio, farmer,
age 27 yrs. single, child of Joel & Cynthiann TILTON,
married 07 Mar 1871   WV. to Valinda J. COOPER,
born Belmont Co., Ohio, resides Brooke Co., WV.
age 23 yrs. single, child of Francis & Eliza. COOPER,
married by R. MOORE. remarks : married Wellsburg.

TRUAXE, Ann　　　　book 01 page 09 line 23
born Brooke Co., Virginia, resides Wellsburg, Virginia,
age 26 yrs. single, child of William & Martha TRUAXE,
married 09 Sep 1860 Wellsburg, VA. to Josiah JONES,
born Wellsburg, Virginia, resides Wellsburg, Virginia,
age 42 yrs. widow, child of Isaac & Ann Maria JONES,
married by George W. CHESTER. remarks : none.

TUCKER, William　　　　book 01 page 22 line 41
born Monongalia Co., VA., resides Martins Hill, WV.
age 34 yrs. unk., child of unk. & unk. TUCKER,
married 26 May 1874   WV. to Sarah P. HOOKER,
born Brooke Co., VA., resides Brooke Co., WV.
age 33 yrs. unk., child of unk. & unk. HOOKER,
married by Robert R. MOORE. remarks : none.

TWEED, Mary　　　　book 01 page 10 line 3 B
born Washington Co., PA., resides Brooke Co., VA.
age 45 yrs. single, child of Robert & Eliza. TWEED,
married 10 Jan 1861   VA. to Samuel LINDSAY,
born Baltimore Co., MD. resides Brooke Co., Virginia,
age 54 yrs. widow, child of Joshua & Cath. LINDSAY,
married by T. HUDSON. remarks : married Wellsburg.

UHLRICH, Emma F.　　　　book 01 page 22 line 43
born Germany, resides Brooke Co., West Virginia,
age 39 yrs. unknown, child of unk. & unk. UHLRICH,
married 23 Jun 1874   WV. to Frederick HOFFMAN,
born Germany, resides Wayne Co., Ohio,
age 26 yrs. unk., child of unk. & unk. HOFFMAN,
married by C.L. LOOS. remarks : married Bethany.

UHLRICH, Robert　　　　book 01 page 02 line 14
born Saxony, Germany, resides Wellsburg, VA. bricklayer,
age 25 yrs. single, child of Chas. F. & Joanna UHLRICH,
married 05 Oct 1854   VA. to Mary ST. LEDGER,
born Pennsylvania, resides Wellsburg, Virginia,
age 22 yrs. single, child of John & Mary ST. LEDGER,
married by W.D. LEMON. remarks : married Wellsburg.

UTZ, Rachel Marg't book 01 page 15 line 60
born Rappa. Co., Virginia, resides Brooke Co., WV.
age 26 yrs. single, child of John & Margaret UTZ,
married 07 Sep 1865 WV. to James Newton KNOX,
born Rappa. Co., Virginia, resides Brooke Co., WV.
age 26 yrs. single, child of Wm. & Margaret KNOX,
married by M. WELLS. remarks : married J. UTZ house.

VANSICKLE, Ellie book 01 page 22 line 37
born Brooke Co., Virginia, resides Wellsburg, WV.
age 18 yrs. unknown, child of unk. & unk. VANSICKLE,
married 20 Feb 1874 Wellsburg, WV. to Robert GLASS,
born Brooke Co., VA., resides Wellsburg, West Virginia,
age 23 yrs. unknown, child of unknown & unk. GLASS,
married by C.K. STILLWAGON. remarks : none.

VERMILLION, C. A. book 01 page 16 line 16
born Jeff. Co., Ohio, resides Jeff. Co., Ohio, farmer,
age 26 yrs. single, child of C. & E. VERMILLION,
married 31 Jan 1867 WV. to Ella I. CUNNINGHAM,
born Brooke Co., VA., resides Brooke Co., West Virginia,
age 21 yrs. single, child of Cyrus & Jane CUNNINGHAM,
married by R.T. PRICE. remarks : none.

VIRTUE, William book 01 page 16 line 18
born Wash. Co., PA., resides Wash. Co., PA. farmer,
age 19 yrs. single, child of James & unknown VIRTUE,
married 28 Mar 1867 WV. to Margaret Jane HINDMAN,
born Brooke Co., VA., resides Brooke Co., West Virginia,
age 22 yrs. single, child of William & unk. HINDMAN,
married by James C. CAMPBELL. remarks : none.

WABLE, Samuel book 01 page 05 line 16
born Westmor. Co., PA., resides Har. Co., Ohio, farmer,
age 41 yrs. widow, child of Samuel & Joanna WABLE,
married 24 Feb 1857 VA. to Melissa MC MILLEN,
born Brooke Co., Virginia, resides Wellsburg, Virginia,
age 37 yrs. single, child of Hugh & Martha MC MILLEN,
married by W. GAMBLE, JR. remarks : married Wellsburg.

WADDLE, Thomas book 01 page 21 line 06
born Wash. Co., PA., resides Jeff. Co., Ohio, farmer,
age 45 yrs. widow, child of Isaac & Elizabeth WADDLE,
married 21 Sep 1871 Wellsburg, WV. to Maria PATTON,
born Brooke Co., Virginia, resides Brooke Co., WV.
age 35 yrs. single, child of William E. & Eliza. PATTON,
married by W. PENDLETON. remarks : record reversed.

WALDRON, Joseph book 01 page 15 line 56
born Hardy Co., ? VA., resides Wellsburg, WV. farmer,
age 28 yrs. single, child of Elias & Eliza. WALDRON,
married 14 Aug 1865 WV. to Sarah Eliza. CHESTER,
born Wellsburg, Virginia, resides Wellsburg, West Virginia,
age 26 yrs. single, child of Geo. W. & Eliza. CHESTER,
married by G. CHESTER. remarks : married Wellsburg.

WALKER, Anne M. book 01 page 22 line 38
born Brooke Co., Virginia, resides Brooke Co., WV.
age 35 yrs. unknown, child of unk. & unk. WALKER,
married 24 Mar 1874 WV. to John C. WALLACE,
born Washington Co., PA., resides Nebraska,
age 37 yrs. unk., child of unk. & unk. WALLACE,
married by J.C. CAMPBELL. remarks : none.

WALKER, Catherine T. book 01 page 07 line 16
born unknown, resides Brooke Co., Virginia,
age 28 yrs. single, child of unk. & unk. WALKER,
married 06 Jul 1858 VA. to James M. GOURLEY,
born unknown, resides Brooke Co., Virginia,
age 28 yrs. single, child of John & unk. GOURLEY,
married by J. CAMPBELL. remarks : none.

WALKER, Ella J. book 01 page 19 line 47
born Brooke Co., Virginia, resides Brooke Co., WV.
age 19 yrs. single, child of Mont. & Jane WALKER,
married 17 Feb 1870 WV. to Ebenezer Z. MC COLLOCH,
born Ohio Co., Virginia, resides Ohio Co., West Virginia,
age 24 yrs. single, child of Ebenezer & Sarah MC COLLOCH,
married by Robert R. MOORE. remarks : none

WALLACE, John C. book 01 page 22 line 38
born Washington Co., PA., resides Nebraska,
age 37 yrs. unk., child of unk. & unk. WALLACE,
married 24 Mar 1874 WV. to Anne M. WALKER,
born Brooke Co., Virginia, resides Brooke Co., WV.
age 35 yrs. unk., child of unk. & unk. WALKER,
married by J.C. CAMPBELL. remarks : none.

WALTERS, Lucas book 01 page 19 line 38
born Wittenberg, GER., resides Brooke Co., WV. stonecutter,
age 21 yrs. single, child of Marcus & Rheann WALTERS,
married 25 Jul 1869 WV. to Magdaline EASTERDAY,
born Prussia, resides Wellsburg, West Virginia,
age 21 yrs. single, child of Christian & Agnes EASTERDAY,
married by Stephen HUBER. remarks : married Wellsburg.

WARD, Mary A. book 01 page 20 line 23
born unknown, resides Bethany, West Virginia,
age -- yrs. widow, child of unk. & unk. WARD,
married 15 Dec 1870 WV. to James M. ADAMS,
born Bethany, Virginia, resides Bethany, West Virginia,
age -- yrs. single, child of Richard & unk. ADAMS,
married by A. CAMPBELL. remarks : married Bethany.

WATKINS, Harriet book 01 page 20 line 20
born Jefferson Co., Ohio, resides Brooke Co., WV.
age 40 yrs. widow, child of Benja. & Mary WATKINS,
married 08 Nov 1870 WV. to William T. BAILEY,
born Belmont Co., Ohio, resides Brooke Co., WV.
age 46 yrs. widow, child of John & Margaret DAILEY,
married by R. MOORE. remarks : Harriet KIMBERLAND.

WATSON, Green book 01 page 21 line 38
born Monroe Co., VA., resides Brooke Co., WV. barber,
age 29 yrs. widow, child of Samuel & Nancy WATSON,
married 19 Jun 1872 Wellsburg, WV. to Leanna BEALL,
born Culpeper Co., Virginia, resides Brooke Co., WV.
age 24 yrs. unknown, child of unk. & unk. BEALL,
married by J. COUPLAND remarks : listed as colored.

WAUGH, Amanda book 01 page 20 line 11
born Washington Co., PA., resides Brooke Co., WV.
age 19 yrs. single, child of unk. & Sarah W. CRAFT,
married 01 Sep 1870 WV. to Leonard D. MC FADDEN,
born Cadiz, Ohio, resides Bethany, West Virginia,
age 22 yrs. single, child of David & Eliza. MC FADDEN,
married by William K. PENDLETON. remarks : none.

WAUGH, David book 01 page 17 line 02
born Brooke Co., VA., resides Brooke Co., WV. farmer,
age 23 yrs. single, child of James & Mary WAUGH,
married 03 Sep 1867 WV. to Ethelinda HUKILL,
born Brooke Co., Virginia, resides Brooke Co., WV.
age 19 yrs. single, child of William & Sallie HUKILL,
married by R.T. PRICE. remarks : none.

WAUGH, Elizabeth book 01 page 06 line 12
born Brooke Co., Virginia, resides Brooke Co., Virginia,
age 51 yrs. widow, child of John & Jane MOORE,
married 10 Nov 1857 Wellsburg, VA. to James PALMER,
born Washington Co., PA., resides Brooke Co., Virginia,
age 58 yrs. widow, child of Samuel & Mary PALMER,
married by E. QUILLEN. remarks : none.

WAUGH, Fannie T. book 01 page 09 line 05
born Brooke Co., Virginia, resides Brooke Co., VA.
age 17 yrs. single, child of Richard & Eliza. WAUGH,
married 16 Aug 1859 VA. to John C. PALMER,
born Brooke Co., Virginia, resides Brooke Co., VA.
age 26 yrs. single, child of James & Selina PALMER,
married by David HERVEY. remarks : none.

WAUGH, James book 01 page 04 line 39
born Brooke Co., VA., resides Brooke Co., VA. miller,
age 22 yrs. single, child of Richard & Eliza. WAUGH,
married 07 Feb 1856 VA. to Caroline A. PALMER,
born Brooke Co., Virginia, resides unknown.
age 20 yrs. single, child of James & Salina PALMER,
married by Ezekiel QUILLEN. remarks : none.

WAUGH, James book 01 page 10 line 10A
born Brooke Co., VA., resides Brooke Co., VA. miller,
age 27 yrs. widow, child of Richard & Eliza. WAUGH,
married 18 Dec 1860 VA. to Elizabeth HAMMOND,
born Brooke Co., Virginia, resides Brooke Co., Virginia,
age 22 yrs. single, child of Talbott & Hannah HAMMOND,
married by David HERVEY. remarks : none.

WAUGH, Jane　　　　book 01 page 06 line 06
born Hopewell Twp., VA., resides Brooke Co., VA.
age 26 yrs. single, child of David & Mariah WAUGH,
married 15 Sep 1857 VA. to Thomas DODDS,
born Hopewell Twp., VA., resides Brooke Co., VA.
age 37 yrs. single, child of John & Sally DODDS,
married by David HERVEY. remarks : none.

WAUGH, Michael J.　　　book 01 page 18 line 23
born Brooke Co., Virginia, resides Brooke Co., WV.
age 21 yrs. single, child of James & Mary WAUGH,
married 26 Mar 1868 WV. to William L. MC KINLEY,
born Gallipolis, Ohio, resides Brooke Co., West Virginia,
age 27 yrs. single, child of Wm. & Ellen MC KINLEY,
married by J.A. BROWN. remarks : none.

WAUGH, Sarah　　　　book 01 page 15 line 65
born Brooke Co., Virginia, resides Brooke Co., WV.
age 26 yrs. single, child of James & Mary WAUGH,
married 26 Oct 1865 WV. to John W. MC KINLEY,
born Gallipolis, Ohio, resides Brooke Co., West Virginia,
age 29 yrs. single, child of Wm. & Ellen MC KINLEY,
married by M.A. ATKINSON. remarks : none.

WAUGH, Sarah Ann　　　book 01 page 09 line 04
born Washington Co., PA., resides Brooke Co., Virginia,
age 47 yrs. single, child of Wm. & Sarah Ann WAUGH,
married 26 Oct 1859 VA. to Charles H. CRAFT,
born Washington Co., PA., resides Brooke Co., Virginia,
age 64 yrs. widow, child of George M. & Sarah CRAFT,
married by J.M. SMITH. remarks : none.

WAY, William　　　　book 01 page 21 line 03
born Brooke Co., VA., resides Brooke Co., WV. farmer,
age 27 yrs. single, child of Abel & Elizabeth WAY,
married 30 Aug 1871 WV. to Mary E. DEULEY,
born Ohio Co., Virginia, resides Brooke Co., WV.
age 23 yrs. single, child of Wm. & Marg't. DEULEY,
married by J.C. CASTLE. remarks : none.

WEAR, James　　　　book 01 page 06 line 05
born St.Clairsville, OH. resides Wheeling, VA. papermaker,
age 21 yrs. single, child of Wm. & Comfort WEAR,
married 13 Sep 1857 VA. to Susan FARQUER,
born Wellsburg, Virginia, resides Wellsburg, Virginia,
age 18 yrs. single, child of Thomas & Eliza. FARQUER,
married by E. FLETCHER. remarks : married Wellsburg.

WELLS, Bazil, Jr.　　　book 01 page 21 line 12
born Brooke Co., VA., resides Brooke Co., WV. farmer,
age 37 yrs. widow, child of Bazil & Nancy WELLS,
married 14 Nov 1871 WV. to Nancy COOPER,
born Belmont Co., Ohio, resides Brooke Co., WV.
age 31 yrs. single, child of Francis & Eliza. COOPER,
married by Robert R. MOORE. remarks : none.

WELLS, Bazil, Jr. book 01 page 13 line 17
born Brooke Co., VA., resides Brooke Co., WV. farmer,
age 30 yrs. single, child of Bazil & Nancy WELLS,
married 01 Feb 1864 WV. to Harriet HOGG,
born Brooke Co., Virginia, resides Brooke Co., WV.
age 21 yrs. single, child of George & Sarah HOGG,
married by R.S. HOGUE. remarks : none.

WELLS, Elizabeth book 01 page 13 line 13
born Brooke Co., Virginia, resides Wellsburg, WV.
age 54 yrs. single, child of Absalom & Ellen WELLS,
married 17 Dec 1863 WV. to Robert SMITH,
born Washington Co., PA., resides Wash. Co., PA.
age 63 yrs. widow, child of Alexander & Jane SMITH,
married by J. FLEMING. remarks : married Wellsburg.

WELLS, John Dusty book 01 page 11 line 35
born Brooke Co., VA., resides Brooke Co., VA. farmer,
age 23 yrs. single, child of Bazil & Nancy WELLS,
married 21 Feb 1863 VA. to Rebecca E. ANDERSON,
born Brooke Co., Virginia, resides Brooke Co., Virginia,
age 17 yrs. single, child of William & unk. ANDERSON,
married by C. LOOS. remarks : married S. LINDSAY house.

WELLS, Josephine book 01 page 19 line 31
born Brooke Co., Virginia, resides Brooke Co., WV.
age 19 yrs. single, child of Milton & Mary WELLS,
married 16 Mar 1869 WV. to Oscar J. BECKWITH,
born Jackson Co., Virginia, resides Jackson Co., WV.
age 26 yrs. single, child of Louis & Esther BECKWITH,
married by Charles L. LOOS. remarks : married Wellsburg.

WELLS, Mary book 01 page 19 line 02
born Brooke Co., Virginia, resides Brooke Co., WV.
age 20 yrs. single, child of Nath'l & Rebecca WELLS,
married 14 May 1868 WV. to Richard MAHON,
born Brooke Co., Virginia, resides Brooke Co., WV.
age 31 yrs. single, child of Thos. & Judith MAHON,
married by L. SOUTHMAY. remarks : none.

WELLS, Richard T. book 01 page 19 line 42
born Brooke Co., VA., resides Brooke Co., WV. farmer,
age 28 yrs. widow, child of Bazil & Nancy WELLS,
married 30 Dec 1869 WV. to Rebecca J. LONG,
born Brooke Co., Virginia, resides Brooke Co., WV.
age 18 yrs. single, child of Lorenze & Marg't LONG,
married by Walter BROWN. remarks : none.

WELLS, William B. book 01 page 18 line 03
born Brooke Co., VA., resides Brooke Co., WV. farmer,
age 23 yrs. single, child of Bazil & Nancy WELLS,
married 10 Dec 1867 WV. to Amanda J. HEDGES,
born Brooke Co., Virginia, resides Brooke Co., WV.
age 18 yrs. single, child of James & Louisa HEDGES,
married by Charles Louis LOOS. remarks : none.

WELSH, Edward   book 01 page 08 line 20
born Ireland, resides Bethany, Virginia, laborer,
age 39 yrs. widow, child of Thomas & Bridget WELSH,
married 17 Jul 1859 Wellsburg, VA. to Catharine HEALY,
born Ireland, resides Bethany, Virginia,
age 26 yrs. single, child of Patrick & Ellen HEALY,
married by S. HUBER. remarks : Bridget (O'CONNER).

WENNINGCOUGH, Ferdinand   book 01 page 07 line 04
born Germany, resides Wellsburg, Virginia, laborer,
age 42 yrs. single, child of unk. & unk. WENNINGCOUGH,
married 22 Dec 1857 Wellsburg, VA. to Ursula SENS,
born Crisinger, Germany, resides Wellsburg, Virginia,
age 43 yrs. widow, child of Michael & Cecelia LEHEKS,
married by S. HUBER. remarks : Cecelia (ROGENETINE).

WEST, Elisha   book 01 page 21 line 47
born New Jersey, resides Belmont Co., Ohio, laborer,
age 39 yrs. single, child of Thomas & Charity WEST,
married 21 Sep 1872 WV. to Elizabeth BROWNLEE,
born Brooke Co., Virginia, resides Brooke Co., WV.
age 35 yrs. single, child of Thos. & Juliane BROWNLEE,
married by Robert R. MOORE. remarks : married Wellsburg.

WETHERELL, Christopher   book 01 page 17 line 13
born England, resides Brooke Co., WV. coalminer,
age 28 yrs. single, child of Aaron & Hannah WETHERELL,
married 25 Sep 1866 Wellsburg, WV. to Mary A. ROBINETT,
born Brooke Co., Virginia, resides Brooke Co., West Virginia,
age 28 yrs. single, child of unk. & unk. ROBINETT,
married by Edward A. BRINDLEY. remarks : none.

WETHERELL, Mary Ann   book 01 page 09 line 08
born Pennsylvania, resides Wellsburg, Virginia,
age 18 yrs. single, child of Wm. & Elisa. WETHERELL,
married 03 Nov 1859 VA. to Jos. Grafton MC CONKEY,
born Wellsburg, Virginia, resides Wellsburg, Virginia,
age 21 yrs. single, child of Jos. & Mariane MC CONKEY,
married by W.H. MARTIN. remarks : married Wellsburg.

WHEELER, Anne E.   book 01 page 13 line 28
born Wellsburg, Virginia, resides Wellsburg, WV.
age 21 yrs. single, child of A.P. & C.H. WHEELER,
married 17 Aug 1864 WV. to George F. REED,
born Madison, Indiana, resides Chillicothe, Ohio,
age 26 yrs. single, child of John & Catherine M. REED,
married by J.A. PIERCE. remarks : married Wellsburg.

WHEELER, Sallie   book 01 page 22 line 36
born Wellsburg, Virginia, resides Wellsburg, WV.
age 33 yrs. unk., child of unk. & unk. WHEELER,
married 17 Feb 1874 WV. to T.H. MARKS,
born Wellsburg, Virginia, resides Wellsburg, WV.
age 51 yrs. unk., child of unk. & unk. MARKS,
married by J. CROSS. remarks : married Wellsburg.

WHEELER, Zachariah C.   book 01 page 03 line 29
born Brooke Co., VA., resides Brooke Co., VA. farmer,
age 27 yrs. single, child of Thos. H. & Honor WHEELER,
married 15 Feb 1855   VA. to Elizabeth A. AMSPOKER,
born Brooke Co., Virginia, resides Brooke Co., Virginia,
age 21 yrs. single, child of Geo. & Rebecca AMSPOKER,
married by John THOMAS. remarks : none.

WHELAN, Michael   book 01 page 20 line 43
born Ireland, resides Brooke Co., West Virginia, laborer,
age 25 yrs. single, child of Michael & Mary WHELAN,
married 29 May 1871   WV. to Mary COTINGHAM,
born Belmont Co., Ohio, resides Brooke Co., West Virginia,
age 17 yrs. single, child of Geo. & Winford COTINGHAM,
married by Stephen HUBER. remarks : married Wellsburg.

WHETZELL, Everett   book 01 page 02 line 09
born Wash. Co., PA., resides Wellsburg, VA. laborer,
age 23 yrs. single, child of John & Emma WHETZELL,
married 03 Jan 1853   VA. to Catherine MC NAIR,
born Brooke Co., Virginia, resides Wellsburg, Virginia,
age 17 yrs. single, child of Samuel & Elizabeth MC NAIR,
married by E. QUILLEN. remarks : married MOODY house.

WHICKERLY, Mary   book 01 page 21 line 45
born Marshall Co., VA., resides Wellsburg, West Virginia,
age 20 yrs. single, child of Mich'l & Francis WHICKERLY,
married 12 Sep 1872   WV. to Charles W. DAUGHERTY,
born Germany, resides Wellsburg, West Virginia,
age 22 yrs. single, child of Chas. & Ethelinda DAUGHERTY,
married by Stephen HUBER. remarks : married Wellsburg.

WHITE, James   book 01 page 19 line 40
born Petersburgh, VA., resides Wellsburg, WV. service,
age 45 yrs. widow, child of John & Tempe WHITE,
married 27 Sep 1869 Wellsburg, WV. to Sarah BOWMAN,
born Brooke Co., Virginia, resides Wellsburg, West Virginia,
age 40 yrs. single, child of unknown & unknown BOWMAN,
married by A. CHAPMAN. remarks : mother Tempe (ROBINSON).

WHITE, James M.   book 01 page 20 line 27
born Brooke Co., VA., resides Wellsburg, WV. gutterman,
age 21 yrs. single, child of Isaac & Grace WHITE,
married 02 Jan 1871 Wellsburg, WV. to Mary BAKER,
born Virginia, resides Wellsburg, West Virginia,
age 21 yrs. single, child of unknown & unk. BAKER,
married by J. COUPLAND. remarks : both listed colored.

WHITE, Mary   book 01 page 21 line 23
born unknown, resides Brooke Co., West Virginia,
age 19 yrs. single, child of unk. & unk. WHITE,
married 18 Jan 1872   WV. to James GUNION,
born Jefferson Co., Ohio, resides Brooke Co., WV.
age 23 yrs. single, child of Henry & Eliza. GUNION,
married by J.W. KESLER. remarks : none.

WHITE, Mary Ann book 01 page 03 line 34
born Jefferson Co., Ohio, resides Brooke Co., VA.
age 30 yrs. widow, child of Robert & Jane WHITE,
married 31 May 1855 VA. to Isaac G. SIMPSON,
born Jefferson Co., Ohio, resides Brooke Co., Virginia,
age 48 yrs. widow, child of Robert & Eliza. SIMPSON,
married by E. QUILLEN. remarks : Mary Ann HESSEY.

WHITE, Mattie J. book 01 page 21 line 43
born Brooke Co., Virginia, resides Brooke Co., WV.
age 23 yrs. single, child of Thomas & Sarah WHITE,
married 08 Aug 1872 WV. to William P. FULTON,
born Licking Co., Ohio, resides Pittsburgh, PA.
age 24 yrs. single, child of Robert & Eliza. FULTON,
married by H. FULTON. remarks : married Wellsburg.

WHITE, Samuel K. book 01 page 19 line 23
born Wash. Co., PA., resides Wash. Co., PA. farmer,
age 34 yrs. single, child of Wm. & Elizabeth WHITE,
married 31 Dec 1868 WV. to Jennie M. MAHAN,
born Washington Co., PA., resides Brooke Co., WV.
age 24 yrs. single, child of John & Mary MAHAN,
married by T. CRENSHAW. remarks : married Wellsburg.

WHITE, William book 01 page 09 line 22
born Delaware, resides unknown,
age 70 yrs. widow, child of James & Eliza. WHITE,
married 26 Aug 1860 VA. to Rebecca L. HUNTER,
born Baltimore Co., Maryland, resides unknown,
age 42 yrs. single, child of Nath'l & Rachel HUNTER,
married by Thomas M. HUDSON. remarks : none.

WIGGINS, Margaret book 01 page 02 line 15
born Brooke Co., Virginia, resides Wellsburg, VA.
age 21 yrs. single, child of John & Marg't WIGGINS,
married 26 Oct 1854 VA. to Silas MAGEE,
born Washington Co., PA., resides Wellsburg, VA.
age 25 yrs. single, child of John & Amy MAGEE,
married by S. TOMPKINS. remarks : none.

WILKEY, Joseph J. book 01 page 22 line 17
born Germany, resides Brooke Co., West Virginia,
age 23 yrs. unk., child of unk. & unk. WILKEY,
married 26 Jul 1873 WV. to Elizabeth RALSTON,
born Wood Co., Virginia, resides Brooke Co., WV.
age 23 yrs. unk., child of unk. & unk. RALSTON,
married by S. CRAVENS. remarks : married Wellsburg.

WILKINSON, Anne book 01 page 12 line 36
born Canada, resides Brooke Co., Virginia,
age 26 yrs. single, child of Thos. & Eliza. WILKINSON,
married 06 Feb 1862 VA. to Robert E. LARGE,
born Jefferson Co., Ohio, resides Jefferson Co., Ohio,
age 28 yrs. single, child of Robert W. & Nancy LARGE,
married by Charles C. BEATTY. remarks : none.

WILKINSON, James book 01 page 07 line 08
born Ireland, resides Brooke Co., Virginia, miner,
age 23 yrs. single, child of Wm. & Mary WILKINSON,
married 16 Feb 1858 VA. to Sarah DEIGHTON,
born Brooke Co., Virginia, resides Brooke Co., Virginia,
age 23 yrs. single, child of William & Sarah DEIGHTON,
married by E. QUILLEN. remarks: married DEIGHTON house.

WILLIAMS, Frank book 01 page 22 line 44
born Brooke Co., Virginia, resides Wellsburg, WV.
age 24 yrs. unk., child of unk. & unk. WILLIAMS,
married 26 Jun 1874 WV. to Lucy GRIMES,
born Brooke Co., Virginia, resides Wellsburg, WV.
age 22 yrs. unk., child of unk. & unk. GRIMES,
married by T. HUDSON. remarks: married Wellsburg.

WILLIAMSON, Anne G. book 01 page 10 line 5 B
born unknown, resides unknown,
age -- yrs. unknown, child of unk. & unk. WILLIAMSON,
married 07 Mar 1861 VA. to James GLASS,
born unknown, resides unknown,
age -- yrs. unknown, child of unknown & unk. GLASS,
married by James C. CAMPBELL. remarks: none.

WILLIAMSON, E.A. book 01 page 16 line 20
born Brooke Co., Virginia, resides Brooke Co., WV.
age 30 yrs. single, child of Wm. & Sarah WILLIAMSON,
married 10 Apr 1867 WV. to Robert BOYD,
born Washington Co., PA., resides Brooke Co., WV.
age 46 yrs. widow, child of James & Mary BOYD,
married by James C. CAMPBELL. remarks: none.

WILLIAMSON, James book 01 page 12 line 44
born Wash. Co., PA., resides Brooke Co., VA. farmer,
age 26 yrs. single, child of Jas. & Sarah WILLIAMSON,
married 01 Jan 1862 VA. to Mary Ann BAXTER,
born Brooke Co., Virginia, resides Brooke Co., Virginia,
age 27 yrs. single, child of William & Ellen BAXTER,
married by I. MORSE. remarks: married BAXTER house.

WILLIAMSON, Mary book 01 page 03 line 32
born Washington Co., PA., resides Brooke Co., Virginia,
age 22 yrs. single, child of James & Sarah WILLIAMSON,
married 26 Apr 1855 VA. to Samuel BOSLEY,
born Brooke Co., Virginia, resides Brooke Co., Virginia,
age 24 yrs. single, child of William & Susannah BOSLEY,
married by Ezekiel QUILLEN. remarks: none.

WILLIAMSON, Mathew H. book 01 page 22 line 48
born Brooke Co., Virginia, resides Brooke Co., WV.
age 33 yrs. unk., child of unk. & unk. WILLIAMSON,
married 14 Oct 1874 WV. to Mary A. HALSTED,
born Washington Co., PA., resides Brooke Co., WV.
age 20 yrs. unk., child of unk. & unk. HALSTED,
married by W.T. WILSON. remarks: none.

WILLOUGHBY, Alice   book 01 page 20 line 33
born England, resides Brooke Co., West Virginia,
age 25 yrs. widow, child of John & unk. GELSTHORPE,
married 19 Mar 1871 WV. to William FORBES,
born Ireland, resides Brooke Co., West Virginia,
age 35 yrs. single, child of Thomas & Nancy FORBES,
married by D. CALDERWOOD. remarks : married Wellsburg.

WILLQUES, Lewis   book 01 page 19 line 13
born Westmor. Co., PA., resides Brooke Co., WV. miner,
age 25 yrs. single, child of Wm. & Parthenia WILLQUES,
married 15 Oct 1868 WV. to Mary MITCHELL,
born Washington Co., PA., resides Brooke Co., WV.
age 19 yrs. single, child of George & Mary MITCHELL,
married by A.R. CHAPMAN. remarks : none.

WILSON, Adam   book 01 page 03 line 25
born Brooke Co., VA., resides Brooke Co., VA. farmer,
age 26 yrs. single, child of Samuel & Nancy WILSON,
married 19 Apr 1854 VA. to Amanda BANE,
born Brooke Co., Virginia, resides Brooke Co., VA.
age 20 yrs. single, child of John & Mary BANE,
married by Ezekiel QUILLEN. remarks : none

WILSON, Andrew J.   book 01 page 02 line 05
born Ohio Co., VA., resides Wellsburg, VA. farmer,
age 23 yrs. single, child of Jos. & Rebecca WILSON,
married 28 Mar 1854 VA. to Margaret BANE,
born Brooke Co., Virginia, resides Wellsburg, VA.
age 21 yrs. single, child of Robert & Maria BANE,
married by E. QUILLEN. remarks : married BANE house.

WILSON, Florence K.   book 01 page 18 line 06
born Brooke Co., Virginia resides Brooke Co., WV.
age 22 yrs. single, child of James & Micha WILSON,
married 25 Dec 1867 WV. to Winfield M. WILSON,
born Brooke Co., Virginia, resides Brooke Co., WV.
age 21 yrs. single, child of William & Nancy WILSON,
married by Charles Louis LOOS. remarks : none.

WILSON, George A.   book 01 page 17 line 23
born Ohio Co., VA., resides Ohio Co., WV. farmer,
age 21 yrs. single, child of John & Sarah WILSON,
married 01 Jan 1867 WV. to Mary E. CRUSON,
born Jefferson Co., Ohio resides Brooke Co., West Virginia,
age 18 yrs. single, child of Coleman & Eliza. CRUSON,
married by J. PIERCE. remarks : George A. or W. WILSON.

WILSON, John   book 01 page 22 line 03
born Brooke Co., VA., resides Brooke Co., WV. farmer,
age 22 yrs. single, child of Jonathan & Eliza. WILSON,
married 28 Nov 1872 WV. to Hannah J. BRADY,
born Brooke Co., Virginia, resides Brooke Co., WV.
age 21 yrs. single, child of Bernard & Bridget BRADY,
married by Stephen HUBER. remarks : married Wellsburg.

WILSON, John M. book 01 page 11 line 29
born Wash. Co., PA., resides Wash. Co., PA. farmer,
age 33 yrs. widow, child of William & Rachel WILSON,
married 01 Jan 1863 VA. to Fanny SANDERS,
born Scotland, resides Brooke Co., Virginia,
age 33 yrs. single, child of John & Maria SANDERS,
married by E. BRINDLEY. remarks : married Wellsburg.

WILSON, John M. book 01 page 19 line 29
born Brooke Co., VA., resides Brooke Co., WV. farmer,
age 28 yrs. single, child of James & Michael WILSON,
married 11 Feb 1869 Wellsburg, WV. to Leah LEWIS,
born Brooke Co., Virginia, resides Brooke Co., WV.
age 23 yrs. single, child of Job & unknown LEWIS,
married by A.R. CHAPMAN. remarks : none.

WILSON, Joseph B. book 01 page 22 line 11
born Ohio Co., Virginia, resides Ohio Co., WV. farmer,
age 39 yrs. single, child of Joseph & Rebecca WILSON,
married 19 Mar 1873 WV. to Sarah Jane BANE,
born Brooke Co., Virginia, resides Brooke Co., WV.
age 30 yrs. single, child of Robert & Maria BANE,
married by J.A. BROWN. remarks : none.

WILSON, Mary/Rebecca book 01 page 18 line 11
born Brooke Co., Virginia, resides Brooke Co., WV.
age 17 yrs. single, child of Abraham & Eliza. WILSON,
married 01 Jan 1868 WV. to William B. HEDGES,
born Brooke Co., Virginia, resides Polk Co., Iowa,
age 22 yrs. single, child of James & Louisa HEDGES,
married by William F. POOR. remarks : none.

WILSON, Robert Bane book 01 page 23 line 01
born Brooke Co., Virginia, resides Brooke Co., WV.
age 22 yrs. single, child of unk. & unk. WILSON,
married 04 Nov 1874 WV. to Marg't Jennie LEWIS,
born Brooke Co., Virginia, resides Brooke Co., WV.
age 21 yrs. single, child of unk. & unk. LEWIS,
married by Charles Louis LOOS. remarks : none.

WILSON, Winfield M. book 01 page 18 line 06
born Brooke Co., VA. resides Brooke Co., WV. farmer,
age 21 yrs. single, child of Wm. & Nancy WILSON,
married 25 Dec 1867 WV. to Florence K. WILSON,
born Brooke Co., Virginia, resides Brooke Co., WV.
age 22 yrs. single, child of James & Micha WILSON,
married by Charles Louis LOOS. remarks : none.

WINESBURG, Elizabeth book 01 page 21 line 39
born Brooke Co., Virginia, resides Brooke Co., WV.
age 20 yrs. single, child of George & Jane WINESBURG,
married 23 Jun 1872 Wellsburg, WV. to Eli JOHNSON,
born Jefferson Co., Ohio, resides Jefferson Co., Ohio,
age 19 yrs. single, child of John & Nancy JOHNSON,
married by Joshua COUPLAND, JR. remarks : none.

WOLCOTT, Francis L. book 01 page 22 line 29
born Brooke Co., Virginia, resides Scranton, PA.
age 25 yrs. unk., child of unk. & unk. WOLCOTT,
married 23 Dec 1873 WV. to Elizabeth K. SHARP,
born Brooke Co., Virginia resides Brooke Co., WV.
age 19 yrs. unknown, child of unk. & unk. SHARP,
married by S. CRAVENS. remarks : married Wellsburg.

WOLCOTT, William M. book 01 page 21 line 40
born Akron, Ohio, resides New Brighton, PA. lawyer,
age 24 yrs. single, child of Christ. R. & Philis WOLCOTT,
married 25 Jun 1872 WV. to Sallie CROTHERS,
born Brooke Co., Virginia, resides Brooke Co., West Virginia,
age 23 yrs. single, child of Hugh W. & Ann H. CROTHERS,
married by Joshua COUPLAND remarks : married Wellsburg.

WOOD, Macky book 01 page 02 line 13
born Brooke Co., Virginia, resides Wellsburg, Virginia,
age 30 yrs. widow, child of William & Elizabeth WOOD,
married 06 Aug 1854 VA. to Peter SWINER,
born Jacksonville, Ohio, resides Wellsburg, Virginia,
age 23 yrs. single, child of Peter & Mary SWINER,
married by C. HOLMES. remarks : Macky RAMSEY.

WOODY, Tarlton book 01 page 04 line 49
born Winchester, Virginia, resides unknown, laborer,
age 27 yrs. single, child of Tarlton & Eliena WOODY,
married 04 Oct 1856 VA. to Rachel DAVIS,
born Ohio Co., Virginia, resides Castlemen's Run, VA.
age 28 yrs. single, child of Alexander & Sarah DAVIS,
married by UNKNOWN. remarks : none.

WORSTELL, Mary L. book 01 page 21 line 01
born Washington Co., PA., resides Brooke Co., WV.
age 24 yrs. single, child of Isaac & Eliza. WORSTELL,
married 04 Jun 1871 WV. to Leander B. FLEMING,
born Brooke Co., Virginia, resides Brooke Co., WV.
age 24 yrs. single, child of Coleman & Eliza. FLEMING,
married by A.E. WARD. remarks : none.

WRIGHT, Amelia book 01 page 21 line 02
born Brooke Co., Virginia, resides Brooke Co., WV.
age 21 yrs. single, child of John & Sofiah WRIGHT,
married 17 Aug 1871 WV. to S.P. BOLES,
born Washington Co., PA., resides Wash. Co., PA.
age 23 yrs. single, child of Jacob & Rachael BOLES,
married by J.B. LUCAS. remarks : none.

WRIGHT, Louisa book 01 page 21 line 27
born Brooke Co., Virginia, resides Brooke Co., WV.
age 20 yrs. single, child of James & unk. WRIGHT,
married 21 Mar 1872 WV. to Mathew C. PARK,
born Brooke Co., Virginia, resides Brooke Co., WV.
age 25 yrs. single, child of Robert & Anne PARK,
married by James C. CAMPBELL. remarks : none.

WRIGHT, Nancy J.   book 01 page 16 line 10
born Brooke Co., VA., resides Brooke Co., WV.
age 30 yrs. single, child of John & Edie WRIGHT,
married 16 Jan 1867   WV. to Jonathan COX,
born Brooke Co., VA., resides Brooke Co., WV.
age 32 yrs. single, child of Isreal & Ruth COX,
married by James FLEMING. remarks : none.

WRIGHT, Nancy Jane   book 01 page 15 line 74
born Brooke Co., Virginia, resides Brooke Co., WV.
age 23 yrs. single, child of unk. & Nancy Jane WRIGHT,
married 15 Mar 1866   WV. to John HINDMAN,
born Brooke Co., Virginia, resides Brooke Co., WV.
age 33 yrs. single, child of John & unknown HINDMAN,
married by A. CAMPBELL. remarks : married house of father.

WRIGHTMAN, Ann Jane   book 01 page 07 line 01
born Brooke Co., Virginia, resides Brooke Co., Virginia,
age 20 yrs. single, child of Alex. & Cath. WRIGHTMAN,
married 23 Nov 1857   VA. to George Wash. RUSSELL,
born Brooke Co., Virginia, resides Brooke Co., Virginia,
age 22 yrs. single, child of James & Sarah RUSSELL,
married by E. QUILLEN. remarks : married Wellsburg.

WRIGHTMAN, Ella V.   book 01 page 21 line 41
born Allegheny Co., PA., resides Wellsburg, WV.
age 23 yrs. single, child of unk. & unk. WRIGHTMAN,
married 05 Sep 1872   WV. to Francis C. GLASS,
born Armstrong Co., PA., resides Wellsburg, WV.
age 24 yrs. single, child of Alfred & Eleanor GLASS,
married by E. MATHEWS. remarks : married Wellsburg.

WRIGHTMAN, Sallie C.   book 01 page 12 line 58
born Allegheny Co., Pennsylvania, resides Wellsburg, WV.
age 21 yrs. single, child of Alex. & Cath. WRIGHTMAN,
married 03 Aug 1863   WV. to Arthur Stone PALMER,
born Fayette Co., Pennsylvania, resides Wellsburg, WV.
age 28 yrs. single, child of Thomas & Tanyia PALMER,
married by William M. ROBINSON. remarks : none.

WYLIE, Oliver   book 01 page 04 line 46
born Brooke Co., VA., resides Mason Co., VA. farmer,
age 26 yrs. single, child of Robert & Eliza. WYLIE,
married 04 Mar 1856   VA. to Rebecca Ann SIMPSON,
born Brooke Co., Virginia, resides Brooke Co., Virginia,
age 21 yrs. single, child of James & Ann Jane SIMPSON,
married by Ezekiel QUILLEN. remarks : none.

YOUNG, Caroline   book 01 page 20 line 40
born Germany, resides Wellsburg, West Virginia,
age 21 yrs. single, child of Peter & Eliza. YOUNG,
married 22 May 1871   WV. to Jacob BROWN,
born Germany, resides Wellsburg, West Virginia,
age 23 yrs. single, child of Jacob & Phoebe BROWN,
married by R.R. MOORE. remarks : married Wellsburg.

YOUNG, Lucy A. book 01 page 22 line 40
born Brooke Co., Virginia, resides Brooke Co., WV.
age 23 yrs. unknown, child of unk. & unk. YOUNG,
married 24 May 1874 WV. to Abram M. DAUGHERTY,
born Monroe Co., New York, resides Barry Co., Michigan,
age 31 yrs. unknown, child of unk. & unk. DAUGHERTY,
married by C. STILLWAGON. remarks : married Wellsburg.

YOUNG, Octavis book 01 page 12 line 39
born Brooke Co., VA., resides Brooke Co., VA. teamster,
age 28 yrs. single, child of George & Mary YOUNG,
married 12 Jun 1862 VA. to Elizabeth E. ROBINSON,
born Brooke Co., Virginia, resides Brooke Co., Virginia,
age 21 yrs. single, child of Wm. H. & Marg't ROBINSON,
married by Charles L. LOOS. remarks : married Bethany.

YOUNG, William F. book 01 page 20 line 15
born Pocahontas Co., VA., resides Cedar Co., IA.
age 26 yrs. single, child of William & Ann YOUNG,
married 23 Jun 1870 WV. to Lucy A. S. RUSSELL,
born Brooke Co., Virginia, resides Wellsburg, WV.
age 19 yrs. single, child of James & Sarah RUSSELL,
married by E. BRINDLEY. remarks : married Wellsburg.

When ordering original Marriage records Book 1, they are recorded by book, page and line number. There are two pages to a record in ledger column format. Many of the pages are not sequential or have two page numbers assigned to them. The page number I have cited is a handwritten number from the second page, in the upper right corner. Some of the pages may have two lines, listed as #1. I have accounted for this problem by unsing "A" for above, "B" for bottom. Expressed as "line 1 A or 1 B." All records are handwritten and presented in the original register by year. Many of the marriages and names are not listed on any of the indexes, but do appear in the register. The years of 1853 thru 1857 were not listed on the marriage index. One line handwritten across two pages, giving the names of the bride and groom, date of marriage, city or county, age, place of birth, residence, parents, occupation for grooms and person performing the marriage. A word of caution, many of the parents listed may not be the biological parents, people remarried and the wife at the time of the event, was sometimes listed as the mother. In some cases personal information was not given, "unknown" was used to show no information was recorded. The marriage index for this book is handwritten and many of the pages were skipped and not recorded. The above records shown in this book in a paragraph style format. Their corresponding marriage licenses are presented in a two line format, as books 3A and 4A.

Marriage and licenses Book 1A, pages 01 thru 083, years 1797 to 1815, appear on the combined marriage and license indexes. Marriage licenses are combined with the marriage records at random. All records are handwritten and presented in the original register, and recorded by person performing the marriage ceremony and county clerk. Usually one paragraph giving the names of the bride and groom, date of marriage, marriage license date and person performing the marriage in a random format.

Marriage records Book 2A, pages *01 thru *017. This appears to be a lost volume with it's own index. All records are handwritten and presented in the original register, recorded by person performing the marriage ceremony, covering the years 1848 to 1854. Not shown on any of the combined book indexes. Usually one handwritten line, giving the names of the bride and groom, date of marriage and the person performing the marriage in a random format. Some have marriage licenses shown in book 3A. The records have been shown in a two line format.

Marriages and licenses, Book 2A, pages 01 thru 094, years 1815 to 1848, do appear on the combined marriage/marriage license indexes. Marriage licenses are combined with the marriage records at random. All records are handwritten and presented in the original register, recorded by person performing the marriage ceremony and county clerk. Usually one handwritten line or paragraph, giving the names of the bride and groom, date of marriage, marriage license date and person performing the marriage in a random format. Hancock Co., Virginia was created in 1848, from Brooke Co., Virginia. Records after 1848 should be found in Hancock Co., VA., and are not included in this book. The records have been shown in a two line format.

Marriage license Books 3A and 4A, covering the years 1852-1874. Certificates listing date of license, bride and groom, county clerks name as recorder. Two certificates to a page. Top right corner page numbering.

Special care has been given to list all females by their maiden, married and remarried surnames, and to indicate a mothers maiden surname. Additional information will sometimes be given under these different listings. A few of the marriages took place in other counties or states, they are listed in the Brooke Co. registers and have been included.

BROOKE COUNTY
VIRGINIA / WEST VIRGINIA
RELIGIOUS DENOMINATIONS
AND MARRIAGE OFFICIALS

Baptist

Baptist Church - Twelfth and Main, Wellsburg, organized 1815.
Ebenezer Church - Short Creek, organized 1794.

Disciples of Christ Church/Christian Church

Christian Church - Wellsburg, organized 21 August 1823.
Disciples of Christ Church - Bethany, organized 1827.
Disciples of Christ Church - Hollidays Cove, organized 1830.
Disciples of Christ Church - New Cumberland, Hancock Co., organized 1840.

Episcopalian

Asbury Chapel - Methodist Episcopal, Grant Dist., Hancock Co., organized 1818.
Christ Church - Wellsburg, organized 1830.
Methodist Episcopal Church - corner of Charles & Walnut St., Wellsburg, organized about 1816.
Methodist Episcopal Church - New Cumberland, Hancock Co., organized about 1849.
St. John's Episcopal - Eldersville Road, 5 miles east of Wellsburg, organized 1793. The first Episcopal Church west of the Allegheny Mountains.
Trinity Church - Wellsburg, organized 1800.

Methodist Church

Castlemens Run Methodist Church - Castlemens Run, organized 1814. Church and school in 1856.
Kadesh Chapel - Apple Pie Ridge, Beech Bottom, organized on Redstone Circuit, 20 Jul 1786. The first church built in Brooke Co.
Franklin United Methodist - Franklin community, organized Aug 1832.
Stone Church Chapel - Methodist Prostestant, Fairview, Hancock Co., also known as Nessly Chapel, organized about 1830.
United Methodist - Colliers, organized 1834.
United Methodist - Wellsburg, organized 18 Oct 1853.
United Methodist - Bethany, organized 1871-1872.
Union Chapel Methodist Protestant Church - Freeman's Landing, Hancock Co., organized 1835.
Union Chapel Methodist Protestant Church - Wellsburg, s.w. corner of Charles & Prospect St., organized in 1854, built in 1864.

Non-Denominational Church

Stone Church Chapel - Fairview (Pierces Run), Hancock Co., organized about 1790's in a log cabin. Chapel built in 1826, by Jacob Nessly. Also known as "Nessly Chapel." Used as a school, church and meeting house by the Baptists, Episcopalians, Methodist, and Presbyterians over the years.

Presbyterian

Cross Creek United - Tent Church Road, organized 1795.
Fairview Presbyterian Church - Pughtown, Hancock Co., formerly known as Flats Presbyterian Church.
First Presbyterian Church - north side of Queen St., Wellsburg, organized 29 Nov 1839.
Flats Presbyterian Church - Fairview (New Manchester), Hancock Co., built 1794.
Holliday's Cove Presbyterian Church - Holliday's Cove, Hancock Co., also known as Three Springs Presbyterian, organized 1846.
Presbyterian Church of New Cumberland - New Cumberland, Hancock Co., organized 7 May 1851.
Three Springs Presbyterian Church - Weirton Heights, Hancock Co., built 1790, moved to Cove Hill in 1804.

Roman Catholic

St. John the Evangelist - corner of Commerce & Union St. (fourth), Wellsburg, organized 1854, as a mission station of the Diocese of Wheeling, which had been formed from the Diocese of Richmond, VA. just before the Civil War.

BROOKE CO., VA./WV. MARRIAGE OFFICIALS 309

MARRIAGE	OFFICIAL	CHURCH AFFILIATION
ADAMS	J.A.	Minister
AIKEN	William	Minister
ALLISON	Thomas	Minister, Cross Creek United Presbyterian
ANDERSON	Alexander E.	Minister, Disciples Church
	John	Minister, Cross Creek United Presbyterian
ATKINSON	M.A.	Minister
AULD	L.J.W.	Minister
BABCOCK	Samuel E.	Minister, Methodist Episcopal Church
BAINBRIDGE	J.	Minister, Methodist Episcopal Church
BAKER	Thomas	Minister, Methodist Episcopal Church
BEACOM	James	Minister
BEARD	W.P.	Minister, Methodist Episcopal Church
BEATTY	Chas.Clinton	Minister
	John	Minister, Methodist Protestant Church
BEEKS	Thomas	Minister
BERRY	Joseph M.	Minister, Disciples Church
BEST	Charles C.	Minister, German Methodist Episcopal
BETISE	Morse	Justice of the Peace, Bucks Ck., Fulton, OH.
BIRKETT	E.	Minister, Franklin United Methodist Church
BLAKE	G.W.	Minister, Ebenezer Church, Baptist
BOYD	David	Justice of the Peace, Washington Co., PA.
BOYLE	Joseph	Minister, Methodist Episcopal Church
BRAZILL	John F.	Priest, St. John the Evangelist, Wellsburg
BRICE	John	Minister, Presbyterian Church
BRIGGS	William	Minister
BRINDLEY	Edward A.	Minister, Union Chapel Methodist Protestant
BROCKUNIER	Samuel R.	Minister, Methodist Episcopal Church
BROWN	George	Minister, Methodist Protestant Church
	J.A.	Minister, Presbyterian Church
	Richard	Minister, Presbyterian, Hollidays Cove
	Walter K.	Minister, Franklin United Methodist Church
BROWNING	Lewis	Minister, Methodist Church
BROWNING,JR.	Jonathan	Minister
BUCHANAN	George	Minister, Associate Reformed Church
BURGESS	Robert	Minister
BURTON	L.	Minister, Meth. Episcopal, Wellsville, Ohio
CALDERWOOD	D.W.	Minister, Disciples Church
CALHOUN	J.Y.	Minister
CAMPBELL	Alexander	Minister, V.D.M. Christian Church, Bethany
	Archibald W.	Minister, Christian Church, Bethany
	James C.	Minister, Cross Creek United Presbyterian
	Thomas	Minister, V.D.M. Christian Church
CARVER	J.D.	Minister
CASTLE	J.C.	Minister
CAZAD	Jacob	Minister, L.B. Congregation
CHAPMAN	A.R.	Minister, Methodist Episcopal Church
CHESTER	George W.	Minister
CHRISTIAN	Edmund	Minister, Protestant EP Church
CHURCHILL	–	Minister, Presbyterian Church, Hancock Co.
CLARK	John	Minister, Methodist Protestant Church
COLEMAN	Andrew	Minister
CONNELL	John	Brooke County Clerk

310 BROOKE CO., VA./WV. MARRIAGE OFFICIALS

MARRIAGE	OFFICIAL	CHURCH AFFILIATION
COUPLAND,JR.	Joshua	Minister, also listed J. COPELAND P.E.
COWL	John	Minister, Methodist Protestant Church
COX	William	Minister, Franklin United Methodist Church
CRANAGE	George W.	Minister, Franklin United Methodist Church
CRAVENS	S.H.	Minister
CREE,JR.	Hamilton	Minister, Methodist Episcopal Church
CRENSHAW	T.A.	Minister, Disciples Church
CROSS	Jonathan	Minister, Presbyterian Church
DALLAS	Israel	Minister, Methodist Episcopal Church
DARSIE	James	Minister
DAVIDSON	W.A.	Minister, Methodist Episcopal Church
DAVIS	John	Minister, Ebenezer Church, Baptist
	S.T.	Minister, Methodist Protestant Church
DAWSON	John B.	Minister
DEMPSEY	D.L.	Minister, Franklin United Methodist Church
DODDRIDGE	Joseph	Minister, Methodist Episcopal Church
DUNLAP	S.B.	Minister
ENDSLEY	A.J.	Minister
FLEMING	James	Minister
FLETCHER	E.L.	Minister
FOUTCH	W.K.	Minister, Franklin United Methodist Church
FULTON	Henry	Minister
	Samuel	Minister
GALLOWAY	John M.	Minister
GAMBLE,JR.	William	Minister, Franklin United Methodist Church
GIST	Cornelius	Minister, Franklin United Methodist Church
GLASS	G.W.	Minister, Ebenezer Church, Baptist
GOODRICH	C.P.	Minister
GOODWIN	James B.	Minister, P.E. Church
GRAFTON	Samuel	Minister
	W.H.	Minister, Disciples Church, Hancock Co.
GRAHAM	John B.	Minister, Presbyterian Church
GUNION	Y.M.	Minister
GUTHRIE	Francis	Minister, Methodist Episcopal Church
HALES	John	Minister, Presbyterian Church, Hancock Co.
HAMMOND		Minister, Cross Creek United Presbyterian
HARRISON	J.L.	Minister, St.John's Episcopal/Christ Church
HATTEN	Robert C.	Minister, Methodist Church
HEADINGTON	Nicholas	Minister, Ebenezer Church, Baptist
HENLEY	Robert Y.	Minister, Christian Church, Bethany
HERBERT	John	Minister, V.D.M. Methodist Protestant
HERVEY	David	Minister, First Presbyterian Church
	James	Minister, V.D.M. Presbyterian Church
HODGESON	T.	Minister, Franklin United Methodist Church
HOGUE	R.S.	Minister, Ohio
HOLLINGSHEAD	James	Minister, Franklin United Methodist Church
HOLMES	Charles A.	Minister, Franklin United Methodist Church
	George S.	Minister, Methodist Episcopal Church
HOPKINS	Robert	Minister, Methodist Church
HOWE	William R.	Minister, Methodist Episcopal Church
HUBER	Stephen	Priest, St. John the Evangelist Church
HUDDLESTON	James F.	Minister, Methodist Episcopal Church

MARRIAGE	OFFICIAL	CHURCH AFFILIATION
HUDSON	George B.	Minister, Franklin United Methodist Church
HUDSON, SR.	Thomas M.	Minister, Franklin United Methodist Church
HUGHES	James	Minister, V.D.M.
HUNT	William	Minister, Castlemens Run Methodist Church
HUNTSMAN	John	Minister, Methodist Protestant Church
IRWIN	J.L.	Minister, Methodist Episcopal Church
JACKSON	Cornelius H.	Minister, Methodist Episcopal Church
JENNINGS	Obediah	Minister, First Presbyterian, Steuben., OH.
JONES	E.H.	Minister
	Garret	Minister
	P.H.	Minister, Disciples Church
	S.F.	Minister, Franklin United Methodist Church
JORDON	L.H.	Minister, Methodist Episcopal Church
KERR	N.P.	Minister, Franklin United Methodist Church
KESLER	J.W.	Minister, Methodist Episcopal Church
KOCH	Henry	Minister, German Methodist Episcopal
LANE	A.J.	Minister, Methodist Episcopal Church
LATIMER	J.W.	Deputy Brooke County Clerk
	William P.	Brooke County Clerk
LAUCK	Simon	Minister, Methodist Church
LAVERTY	D.H.	Minister, Presbyterian Church
LAWS	James	Minister
LEE	Samuel	Minister, Franklin United Methodist Church
LEMON	William D.	Minister, Franklin United Methodist Church
LONG	Warner	Minister, Franklin United Methodist Church
LOOS	Chas. Louis	Minister, Disciples Church/Christian Church
LOWMAN	G.A.	Minister, Methodist Episcopal Church
LUCAS	H.	Minister, Methodist Episcopal Church
	J.B.	Minister, Methodist Protestant Church
MACURDY	Elisha	Minister, Presbyterian Church
MAGILL	Thomas F.	Minister
MARTIN	W.H.	Minister
MATHEWS	Ebenezer	Minister, Methodist Protestant Church
MATWOOD	Henry	Minister
MAYBERRY	William B.	Minister, Ebenezer Church, Baptist
MC CASHEY	George	Minister, Methodist Episcopal Church
MC CLEARY	Thomas	Minister, Methodist Episcopal Church
MC CLURE	J.T.	Minister, Methodist Protestant Church
	T.C.	Minister, Franklin United Methodist Church
MC CONAUGHY	J.R.	Justice of the Peace, Washington Co., PA.
MC GAN	John E.	Minister, Methodist Episcopal Church
MC KENNAR	James W.	Minister, West Liberty, VA./WA.
MC LEASH	James	Minister
MEANS	J.R.	Minister, Franklin United Methodist Church
MEEK	James	Minister
MELVIN	Charles E.	Deputy Brooke County Clerk
	Henry	Brooke County Clerk
MERRYMAN	D.C.	Minister
MILLIGAN	Robert	Minister, Christian Church, Bethany
MINOR	S.F.	Minister, Methodist Episcopal Church
MOFFITT	John	Minister, Methodist Episcopal Church
MONROE	Joshua	Minister, Methodist Episcopal Church

312 BROOKE CO., VA./WV. MARRIAGE OFFICIALS

MARRIAGE	OFFICIAL	CHURCH AFFILIATION
MOORE	Robert R.	Minister
MORSE	Intrepid	Minister, Protestant EP Church, Ohio
MURRAY	Charles	Minister
MYERS	A.E.	Minister, Disciples Church
NAYLOR	J.S.	Deputy Brooke County Clerk
	Joseph R.	Brooke County Clerk
	S.G.	Deputy Brooke County Clerk
	William H.	Deputy Brooke County Clerk
NESBITT	Samuel H.	Minister, Methodist Episcopal Church
NEWELL	Thomas M.	Minister, Presbyterian Church
NICHOLLS	R.	Deputy Brooke County Clerk
NICHOLSON	E.G.	Minister, Wheeling, VA./WV.
PARKER	H.	Minister, Steubenville, Ohio
PATTERSON	J.B.	Minister
PENDLETON	William K.	Minister, Disciples/Christian Church
PETTY	A.L.	Minister, Methodist Episcopal Church
PICKETT	J.D.	Minister, Christian Church, Bethany
PIERCE	J.A.	Minister, Methodist Episcopal Church
PINKERTON	E.Y.	Minister, Disciples Church
POMEROY	Joseph L.	Minister, Presbyterian Church, Hancock Co.
POOR	David	Minister, Methodist Episcopal Church
	William F.	Minister, Methodist Episcopal, West Liberty
PRICE	R.T.	Minister, Presbyterian Church
PRITCHARD	John	Minister, Ebenezer Church, Baptist
PUGH	M.L.	Minister, Methodist Episcopal Church
PURDY	James	Minister, Cross Creek United Presbyterian
QUEST	John	Minister
	S.S.	Brooke County Clerk
QUILLEN	Ezekiel	Minister, Presbyterian Church
REED	Samuel	Minister, Presbyterian, Three Springs & Flats
REEVES	William	Minister, Methodist Protestant Church
REGAL	Eli	Minister, Disciples Church
RICHARSON	Robert	Minister, Christian Church
ROBERTS	Jepton	Minister
ROBINSON	D.	Minister
	George W.	Minister, West Liberty, VA./WV.
	William M.	Minister
ROBISON	James	Minister
ROSELL	Joseph	Minister, Ebenezer Church, Baptist
SCOTT	George M.	Minister, V.D.M. Presbyterian Church
	John W.	Minister, Presbyterian Church
	William	Minister, Ebenezer Church, Baptist
SCULL	William M.	Minister, St.John's Episcopal/Christ Church
SEDGWICK	G.C.	Minister, Ebenezer Church, Baptist
SEEMAN	Daniel	Minister, Ebenezer Church, Baptist
SHAMPSON	David	Minister, Presbyterian Church
SHEPHERD	H.C.	Brooke County Clerk
SHIELDS	James M.	Minister, Bridgewater, Pennsylvania
SIMONTAIS	R.T.	Minister, Methodist Protestant Church
SLADE	George	Minister, Disciples Church
SMITH	Edward	Minister, Methodist Episcopal Church
	J.M.	Minister

MARRIAGE	OFFICIAL	CHURCH AFFILIATION
SMITH	Joseph	Minister, Presbyterian Church
	Wesley	Minister, United Meth., Franklin & Colliers
SNYDER	Henry	Minister, Methodist Episcopal Church
SOUTHMAY	L.	Minister, Disciples Church
SPENCER	John	Minister, German Meth. Episcopal Church
STEIRSHCOMB	Thomas	Minister
STEVENS	William	Minister, Methodist Church
STEVENSON	Josias	Minister
STEWART	N.B.	Minister, Methodist Episcopal Church
STILLWAGON	C.K.	Minister, Methodist Church
STOCKTON	John	Minister, V.D.M.
SUMMERS	William	Minister, Methodist Episcopal Church
SWAYZE	John J.	Minister, Methodist Episcopal Church
SWEENEY	M.M.	Minister
TEAGARDEN	S.B.	Minister, Disciples Church
TELCHENELL	Moses	Minister, Methodist Episcopal Church
THOMAS	John	Minister, Ebenezer Church, Baptist
THOMPSON	David E.	Minister, Presbyterian Church
TOMPKINS	Samuel D.	Minister, Christ Church/Methodist Church
TURNER	C.B.	Brooke County Clerk
WALLACE	J.B.	Minister
WALTERS	George G.	Minister, Franklin United Methodist Church
WARD	A. Ealion	Minister, Methodist Episcopal Church
WARDEN	James M.	Minister, Methodist Episcopal Church
WATERMAN	John	Minister, United Methodist Church
WATKINS	R.B.	Minister
WAUGH	Joseph	Minister
WAYMAN	E.C.	Minister, Methodist Episcopal Church
WEAVER	J.W.	Minister, Franklin United Methodist Church
WEIRICK	C.E.	Minister
WELLS	Milton	Minister, Baptist Church/Disciples Church
WHARTON	George W.	Minister, Ebenezer Church, Baptist
WHITE	R.J.	Minister
	Robert M.	Minister, Presbyterian Church
	W.H.	Brooke County Clerk
WILLIAMS	John	Minister, Bridgewater, Pennsylvania
WILLIAMSON	W.E.	Minister, Reformed Episcopal Church
WILLSON	William	Minister, L.S.
WILSON	W.T.	Minister, Methodist Protestant Church
WOODWARD	Enos	Minister, Methodist Protestant Church
WORTHINGTON	Samuel G.J.	Minister, Methodist Episcopal Church
WYLIE	William	Minister, Presbyterian Church
YATES	Charles	Minister, Castlemens Run Methodist Church
YOUNG	Aleinous	Minister

BROOKE COUNTY
VIRGINIA / WEST VIRGINIA
DISTRICTS, TOWNS, TOWNSHIPS AND PLACE NAMES

MAP OF BROOKE AND HANCOCK COUNTIES, VA./WV.
Districts, Place Names, P.O. Box, Towns and Townships

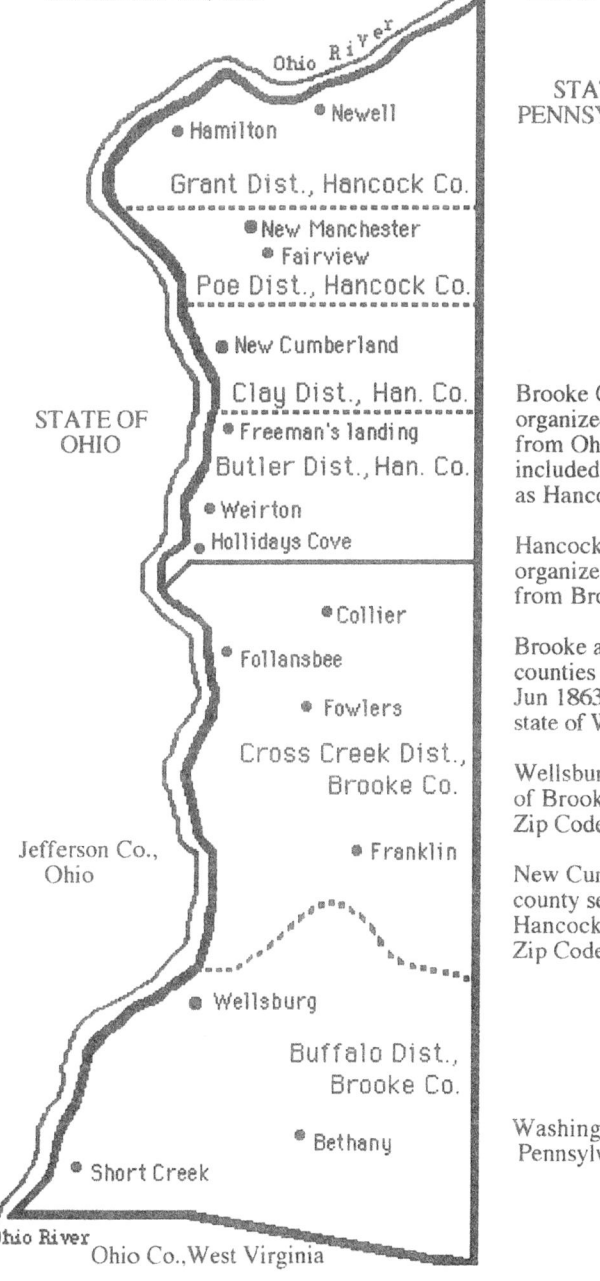

Brooke Co., Virginia organized May 1797 from Ohio Co., VA. included the area shown as Hancock Co., WV.

Hancock Co., Virginia organized 15 Jan 1848 from Brooke Co., VA.

Brooke and Hancock counties organized 20 Jun 1863, into the new state of West Virginia.

Wellsburg county seat of Brooke Co., WV. Zip Code : 26070

New Cumberland county seat of Hancock Co., WV. Zip Code : 26047

PLACE NAME/TOWN	DISTRICT	COUNTY	STATE
Anderson	Butler District	Hancock Co.	VA./WV.
Archer Heights	Cross Creek District	Brooke Co.	VA./WV.
Arroyo	Grant District	Hancock Co.	VA./WV.
Beech Bottom	Buffalo District	Brooke Co.	VA./WV.
Bethany	Buffalo District	Brooke Co.	VA./WV.
Blair	Clay District	Hancock Co.	VA./WV.
Brownsdale	Grant District	Hancock Co.	VA./WV.
Buffalo District		Brooke Co.	VA./WV.
Butler District	created 09 Apr 1872	Hancock Co.	VA./WV.
Butler Township	Butler District	Hancock Co.	VA./WV.
Carnegie		Brooke Co.	VA./WV.
Castlemen's Run	Buffalo District	Brooke Co.	VA./WV.
Charlestown (bef.1816)	sames as Wellsburg	Ohio/Brooke	VA./WV.
Chester	Grant District	Hancock Co.	VA./WV.
Chestnut Hill	Poe District	Hancock Co.	VA./WV.
Clay District	created 09 Apr 1872	Hancock Co.	VA./WV.
Clay Township	Clay District	Hancock Co.	VA./WV.
Cliftonville	Cross Creek District	Brooke Co.	VA./WV.
Collier	Cross Creek District	Brooke Co.	VA./WV.
Congo	Grant District	Hancock Co.	VA./WV.
Cross Creek District		Brooke Co.	VA./WV.
Cuppy Town	same as New Cumberland	Hancock Co.	VA./WV.
East Steubenville	Cross Creek District	Brooke Co.	VA./WV.
East Toronto	Butler District	Hancock Co.	VA./WV.
Fairview	Poe District	Hancock Co.	VA./WV.
Follansbee	Cross Creek District	Brooke Co.	VA./WV.
Fowlers	Cross Creek District	Brooke Co.	VA./WV.
Franklin	Cross Creek District	Brooke Co.	VA./WV.
Freeman's Landing	Butler District	Hancock Co.	VA./WV.
Grant District	created 09 Apr 1872	Hancock Co.	VA./WV.
Grant Township	Grant District	Hancock Co.	VA./WV.
Hamilton	Grant District	Hancock Co.	VA./WV.
Hollidays Cove	Butler District	Hancock Co.	VA./WV.
Hooverson Heights	Cross Creek District	Brooke Co.	VA./WV.
Kenilworth	Grant District	Hancock Co.	VA./WV.
Lawrenceville	Grant District	Hancock Co.	VA./WV.
Louise	Cross Creek District	Brooke Co.	VA./WV.
Marland Heights	Cross Creek District	Brooke Co.	VA./WV.
Mc Kinleyville	Buffalo District	Brooke Co.	VA./WV.

DISTRICTS, TOWNS, TOWNSHIPS & PLACE NAMES

PLACE NAME/TOWN	DISTRICT	COUNTY	STATE
Mingo Bottom	Cross Creek District	Brooke Co.	VA./WV.
Moscow	Poe District	Hancock Co.	VA./WV.
New Cumberland	Clay District	Hancock Co.	VA./WV.
New Lexington	Poe District	Hancock Co.	VA./WV.
New Manchester	Poe District	Hancock Co.	VA./WV.
Newell	Grant District	Hancock Co.	VA./WV.
Oak Run	Grant District	Hancock Co.	VA./WV.
Pleasant Valley	Grant District	Hancock Co.	VA./WV.
Poe District	created 09 Apr 1872	Hancock Co.	VA./WV.
Poe Township	Poe District	Hancock Co.	VA./WV.
Power	Buffalo District	Brooke Co.	VA./WV.
Pughtown	Poe District	Hancock Co.	VA./WV.
Rockdale	Cross Creek District	Brooke Co.	VA./WV.
Short Creek	Buffalo District	Brooke Co.	VA./WV.
Tomlinson Run	Grant District	Hancock Co.	VA./WV.
Vernon	same as New Cumberland	Hancock Co.	VA./WV.
Virginia	Cross Creek District	Brooke Co.	VA./WV.
Virginville	Buffalo District	Brooke Co.	VA./WV.
Weirton	Butler District	Hancock Co.	VA./WV.
Weirton Heights	Cross Creek District	Brooke Co.	VA./WV.
Wellsburg (27 Dec 1816)	Buffalo District	Brooke Co.	VA./WV.
White Oak Run	Grant District	Hancock Co.	VA./WV.
Windsor Heights	Buffalo District	Brooke Co.	VA./WV.

BIBLIOGRAPHY

The following sources were consulted by the author

Brooke Co., Virginia/West Virginia Register of Marriage License Index. Original Records from the Clerk of the County Court. Combined Index: Books 1, 1A, 2A, 3A, 4A. Male and Female Indexes. Typewritten and alphabetical.

Brooke Co., Virginia/West Virginia Register of Marriages and Licenses, Book 1A. [1797-1815] Original Records from the Clerk of the County Court. Handwritten pages 01 thru 083.

Brooke Co., Virginia/West Virginia Register of Marriages and Licenses, Book 2A. [1815-1848] Original Records from the Clerk of the County Court. Handwritten pages 01 thru 094, covering years 1815-1848.

Brooke Co., Virginia/West Virginia Register of Marriages, Book 2A. Original Records from the Clerk of the County Court. Handwritten pages *01 thru *017, covering the years 1848-1854.

Brooke Co., Virginia/West Virginia Register of Marriages Index, Book 2A. Original Records from the Clerk of the County Court. Handwritten index for pages *01 thru *017, covering years 1848-1854.

Brooke Co., Virginia/West Virginia Register of Marriage License. Original Records from the Clerk of the County Court. Book 3A. Handwritten certificates, by year, pages 01 thru 167, covering the years 1852-1866.

Brooke Co., Virginia/West Virginia Register of Marriage License. Original Records from the Clerk of the County Court. Book 4A. Handwritten certificates, by year, pages 01 thru 148, covering the years 1865-1874.

Brooke Co., Virginia/West Virginia Register of Marriages, Book 1. [1853-1897] Original Records from the Clerk of the County Court. Handwritten ledger by year, pages 01 thru 023, covering the years 1853-1874.

Brooke Co., Virginia/West Virginia Register of Marriages Index, Book 1. Original Records from the Clerk of the County Court. Handwritten, alphabetical male and female.

Brooke Co., Virginia/West Virginia County Order Books, Marriages. [1799-1899] Historical Records Survey. Typewritten and alphabetical by groom.

History of The Pan-Handles; being Historical Collections of the Counties of Ohio, Brooke, Marshall and Hancock, West Virginia. Compiled and written by J.H. Newton, G.G. Nichols, and A.G. Sprankle. Published by J.A. Caldwell, Wheeling, WV. [1879].

A History of Brooke County. By Nancy Lee Caldwell. Published by Brooke County Historical Society. [1976]

Map, Colton's Delaware, Maryland, Virginia and West Virginia [1886].

West Virginia, Her Counties, Her Townships, Her Towns. The Researchers, Indianapolis, IN.

BIBLIOGRAPHY

Hinton & Simpkin & Marshall, London, England [01 Sep 1831] steel engraving, Map of Virginia and Maryland. Reproduced by Jonathan Sheppard Books, Albany, N.Y.

Map of Brooke and Hancock Counties, VA./WV. By Renee Britt Sherman [Jan 1991].

United States Postal Service [1991] Standard abbreviations for states.

History of Hancock County, West Virginia. By Jack Welch. [1963].

BROOKE COUNTY
VIRGINIA / WEST VIRGINIA
MARRIAGE RECORDS
1853 - 1874

BOOK 1
INDEX

BROOKE CO., VA./WV. MARRIAGE BOOK 1 INDEX 325

ABRAHAMS	Matilda	135,216,	BARCLAY	James T.	139,140,157,
	Robert	135,216,		Jillian	140,157,
ACKERMAN	Abraham	135,163,	BARNES	Elizabeth	140,141,227,246,
	Margaret	135,163,		Ephraim	140,246,
ADAMS	Ann	135,153,		John	141,146,227,
	John	135,195,		Mary	141,252,
	Maria	135,195,		Rachel	141,146,
	Richard	135,290,		Thomas	141,252,
	Thomas	135,153,	BARTH	Fidel	141,223,
AGNEW	John	135,231,		Martha	141,223,
	Mary	135,231,	BARTHOLOMEW	Mary	141,150,276,
AIKEN	Denison	136,233,272,		Noah	141,150,
	Mary	136,233,272,		Samuel	141,276,
ALEXANDER	Mathew	136,217,260,	BAXTER	Daniel	142,236,
ALLEN	Amos	136,156,		Ellen	141,142,151,
	Elizabeth	136,156,		Ellen	210,297,
	Mariah	136,285,		Mary	142,236,
	Thomas	136,285,		William	141,142,151,
ALLISON	John	136,158,		William	210,297,
	Mary	136,158,	BEALL	Aaron	142,172,
AMSPOKER	George	136,176,295,		Bazil	190,265,
	Rebecca	136,176,295,		Conrad	142,257,
ANDERSON	Martha	137,255,		Jane	142,172,
	Thomas	137,255,	BEARD	Nancy	183,252,
	William	137,293,	BEATER	Ann	142,143,
ANTILL	Mary	137,194,		Mingus	142,143,
	Thomas	137,194,	BEATTY	Rachel	143,164,
ATKINS	Sarah	136,233,272,		Thomas	143,164,
ATKINSON	John	137,138,146,156,	BECKWITH	Esther	143,293,
	John	280,		Louis	143,293,
	Margaret	137,146,156,	BEDILLION	Abraham	143,164,
	Mary	138,280,		Margaret	143,164,
ATWELL	Elizabeth	138,183,	BEERBOWER	Anna	143,253,
	John	138,183,		Reed	143,253,
BACHELL	Jane	138,194,269,	BEITER	Francis	143,223,
	John	138,194,269,	BELL	Aaron	144,225,
BAIL	Elizabeth	138,286,		Jane	144,225,
	James	138,286,	BENCE	Justina	144,185,239,
BAILEY	John	138,145,218,290,		Richus	144,185,239,
	Margaret	138,145,218,290,	BENTZ	Justina	144,180,
BAIR	James	139,179,238,		Richus	144,180,
	Sarah	139,179,238,	BERTRAM	Christian	144,283,
BALLENTINE	Joseph	139,169,		Isabell	144,283,
	Rosa	139,169,	BIER	Jacob	145,284,
BALLETT	C.	139,190,		Mary	145,284,
	P.	139,190,	BLAIR	Rachael	138,145,
BANE	John	139,298,		Walter	138,145,
	Maria	139,140,298,299,	BLANKENSOP	Ellen	145,203,214,
	Mary	139,298,		Joseph	145,203,214,
	Robert	139,140,298,299,		Peter	145,157,192,244,
BANNON	Anne	140,178,237,		Susan	145,157,192,244,
	Thomas	140,178,237,	BLAYNEY	Charles	137,146,

326 BROOKE CO., VA./WV. MARRIAGE BOOK 1 INDEX

BLAYNEY	Elizabeth	141,146,	BROWN	Hanna	141,151,
	Nancy	137,146,		Jacob	151,301,
	Richard	141,146,		James W.	141,151,
BLOTTAN	Anton	146,261,		Joseph	151,171,190,
	Margaret	146,261,		Leanetta	151,155,
BOLES	Jacob	146,300,		Nichod.	151,248,
	Rachael	146,300,		Phoebe	151,301,
BONAR	Ellen	146,278,		Rachel	151,171,190,
	George	146,278,		Robert	151,155,
BORING	Ephraim	146,282,	BROWNING	Arnold	151,199,
	Margaret	146,282,		Catherine	151,199,
BOSLEY	Jane	147,156,		Lewis	152,230,
	Susannah	147,297,		Margaret	152,230,
	William	147,156,297,	BROWNLEE	James	152,256,
BOTHWELL	Charles	147,280,		Juliane	152,153,160,178,
	Phoebe	147,280,		Juliane	215,285,294,
BOWERS	Jacob	147,255,		Mary	152,256,
	Mary	147,255,		Thomas	152,153,160,178,
BOWLES	Isabella	147,249,		Thomas	215,285,294,
	James	147,249,		Unity	152,279,
BOWMAN	Abraham	147,148,243,287,		Walter B.	152,279,
	Elizabeth	148,159,	BUCHANAN	John	153,200,
	Henrietta	147,148,243,287,		Sarah J.	153,226,
	John	148,154,159,		William	153,226,
	John	185,194,	BUCKALEW	Garrett	135,153,249,267,
	Sarah	148,154,185,194,		Lydia	135,153,267,
BOYD	James	148,297,	BUCKEY	Elizabeth	153,154,183,189,
	Mary	148,297,		Elizabeth	212,235,
BRACKEN	Sarah	149,182,		John	154,189,212,235,
	Solomon	149,182,		Volentia	153,183,
BRADLEY	Frances	149,161,	BUCY	Joshua	148,154,
	John	149,161,		Margarett	148,154,
BRADY	Bernard	149,279,298,	BUKER	Henry	154,203,251,
	Bridget	149,279,298,		Jane	154,203,251,
	Hannah	149,233,	BULLOCK	Charles	154,220,
	William	149,233,		Harriet	154,220,
BRANDON	Jane	149,255,	BURGESS	Francis	154,286,
	William	149,255,		Pheby	154,286,
BRANNON	Jane	149,195,	BURGOYNE	Joshua R.	155,201,
	William	149,195,	BURT	Martha	151,155,
BRASHEARS	Bazle	150,268,		William	151,155,
	Elizabeth	150,251,	BUXTON	Amos	155,253,
	George	150,251,		Mary A.	155,253,
	Jane	150,268,	CAGLAND	Ann	177,
BRIAN	Farnum	150,186,	CAIN	Ellen	155,192,
BRIGGS	James	141,150,166,		James	155,192,
	James	197,248,	CAIRNES	Anne	156,159,
	Nancy	141,150,166,		James	147,156,159,
	Nancy	197,248,		Nancy	147,156,
BRINDLEY	Benjamin	151,202,	CALDERWOOD	Samuel	156,186,
	Eleanor	151,202,		Sarah	156,186,
BROWN	Elizabeth	151,248,	CALDWELL	Andrew	156,187,

BROOKE CO., VA./WV. MARRIAGE BOOK 1 INDEX   327

CALDWELL	Elizabeth	137,156,	CHRISTIAN	William	162,181,
	Isabel	156,187,	CHURCHMAN	Jacob	162,228,
	John	137,156,		Mary	162,228,
CALENDINE	Henry	156,177,	CLARK	Ruhanna	162,209,
	Maria J.	136,156,		Samuel L.	162,209,
	Samuel	136,156,	CLENDENEN	Rachel	146,163,
CAMPBELL	Alex.	140,157,158,287,		William	146,163,
	Anne	157,205,250,262,	CLERKIN	Julia	163,177,
	Archibald	145,157,205,		Peter	163,177,
	Archibald	250,262,	CLOSE	John	135,163,
	Lousia	145,157,		Nancy	135,163,
	Margaret	157,281,	CLOW	Susannah	163,165,
	R.	157,281,		Thomas	163,165,
	Selina H.	140,157,158,287,	COATES	Esther	163,179,
CARBINTUR	Ellen	201,		John	163,179,
CARIENS	Elliott	158,181,221,	COCHRANE	Agnes	163,263,
	James	136,158,		John	163,263,
	Mary	136,158,	COGAN	John	140,163,287,
	Sarah	158,181,221,		Martha	140,163,287,
CARMICHAEL	George	158,159,184,262,	COLE	Catherine	164,194,
	Nancy	158,159,184,262,		William	164,194,
CARSON	Elizabeth	148,159,	COLEMAN	David	164,225,247,268,
CARTER	Catharine	159,183,		Mary	143,164,225,247,
	Joseph	159,183,		Mary	268,
	Lewis W.	156,159,200,		Richard	143,164,
	Lewis W.	246,263,	CONANT	Lot	143,163,164,165,
	Martha A.	156,159,200,		Mary	143,163,164,165,
	Martha A.	246,263,	CONAWAY	Eli	165,245,
CASNER	Elizabeth	160,279,		Mary	165,245,
	James	160,279,	CONE	Elizabeth	165,169,
	Mary	160,244,		Patrick	165,169,
	William	160,244,	CONNELL	Elizabeth	165,241,
CASSIDY	Isabel	160,200,		Harrison	165,241,
	Robert	160,200,	CONNELLY	Ellen	165,172,
CAVANAUGH	Elizabeth	160,179,		William	165,172,
	Thomas	160,179,	COOK	Godfrey	165,280,
CEATH	Susan	152,160,215,		Martha	165,280,
CHALLENCE	B.D.	160,242,	COOPER	Elizabeth	166,201,288,292,
	M.A.	160,242,		Francis	166,201,288,292,
CHAMBERLAIN	Daniel	149,161,283,	CORNELIUS	Elijah	166,278,
	Jane	149,161,283,		Lettice	166,278,
CHAPLINE	Ann	161,266,	COTINGHAM	George	166,295,
	William	161,266,		Winford	166,295,
CHAPMAN	Harry	161,269,	COULBURN	James C.	150,166,
	Nancy	161,269,		Zepporah	150,166,
CHEEK	Amanda	161,167,	COWAN	Mary	166,176,
	Oscar	161,167,		Micheal	166,176,
CHESTER	Elizabeth	161,162,272,	COX	Abraham	167,177,
	Elizabeth	283,289,		Elizabeth	167,177,
	George	161,162,272,		George	167,245,249,265,
	George	283,289,		Isreal	167,301,
CHRISTIAN	Ruth	162,181,		James	167,208,

BROOKE CO., VA./WV. MARRIAGE BOOK 1 INDEX

COX	Nancy	161,167,	DAVIS	Mary V.	173,194,
	Ruth	167,208,301,		Morgan	173,194,
	Susannah	167,245,249,		Sarah	142,172,300,
	William	161,167,		Susannah	172,269,
CRAFT	Alex.	168,274,	DAWSON	Amelia	173,181,
	George	168,292,		Nathaniel	173,181,
	Jane	168,274,	DEGARMO	John	173,175,216,
	Sarah	168,237,291,292,		Parthenia	173,175,216,
CRIDER	Jane	168,201,	DEIGHTON	Sarah	174,175,198,229,
	Obediah	168,201,		Sarah	232,267,268,273,
CRISS	Nancy	168,281,		Sarah	297,
	Nicholas	168,281,		William	174,175,198,229,
	Polly	168,203,		William	232,267,268,273,
	William	168,203,		William	297,
CROTHERS	Ann H.	168,300,	DEMPSEY	John	175,288,
	Hugh W.	168,300,		Mary	175,288,
CRUSON	Coleman	169,298,	DEULEY	Margaret	173,175,292,
	Elizabeth	169,298,		William	173,175,292,
CRUTH	Andrew	169,234,238,	DEVINNEY	Charles	175,254,
	Jane	169,238,		Sarah	175,254,
	Lou	169,234,	DEVORE	John	175,210,
CUNNINGHAM	Christine	169,245,		Sarah	175,210,
	Cyrus	169,289,	DINSMORE	Nancy	166,176,
	Hugh	169,245,		Patrick	166,176,
	James	165,169,	DODDS	John	176.292,
	Jane	169,289,		Sally	176.292,
	Susan	165,169,	DONNELLY	Margaret	176,218,236,
CUPPLES	Esther	170,236,		Owen	176,218,236,
	Joseph	170,236,	DONOVAN	Catherine	136,176,271,
CURRAN	Stephen	170,238,		Thomas	136,176,271,
CURTIS	Jacob E.	170,270,	DORLAND	Elizabeth	176,220,
	Sarah B.	170,270,		Garrett	176,220,
D'FOSSIT	David	170,251,	DORSEY	Ann	177,257,
	Margaret	170,251,		Edward	163,177,
DAILY	Martin	170,198,		Elizabeth	163,177,
	Mary	170,198,		Joshua	177,257,
DANNER	Lewis	155,170,	DOUBLAZIER	Henry	156,177,
	Sabrina	155,170,		Nancy	156,177,
DARE	Edmund	171,284,	DOUGHERTY	Andrew	177,237,
	Hannah	171,284,		Ann	177,237,
DARRAH	James	171,215,		George	177,228,
DAUGHERTY	Charles	171,295,	DOW	Isaac	177,245,
	Dolly	171,216,		Jane	178,276,
	Ethelinda	171,295,		Rebecca	177,245,
	George	171,216,		T.H.	178,276,
DAUMONT	P.	171,190,	DOWDLE	Charlotte	152,178,
	Z.	171,190,		Jonas	152,178,
DAVIN	John	165,172,	DOWLER	Hannah	178,196,258,
	Mary	165,172,		Joseph	178,196,258,
DAVIS	Alex.	172,300,	DOWNEY	Mary	178,254,
	Jacob	142,172,		Terrance	178,254,
	James	172,269,		Thomas	140,178,

Surname	Given	Pages	Surname	Given	Pages
DOWNEY	Turns	160,179,	FORBES	Nancy	158,159,184,189,
DUNCAN	Ellen	179,184,		Nancy	298,
	Norris M.	179,184,		Thomas	158,159,184,189,
DUNLAP	Ann	179,229,		Thomas	298,
	Hugh	179,229,	FORBS	Ann Beth	185,211,
DUNWELL	Margaret	163,179,		Thomas	185,211,
	William	163,179,	FORSE	David	185,240,
DURANT	Henry	180,263,		Margaret	185,240,
	Mary	180,263,	FORSYTHE	Margaret	185,195,
DURRETT	Nancie	180,242,		Thomas	185,195,
	Richard	180,242,	FOSTER	Elisabeth	144,185,
DUVALL	Gabriel	180,245,283,		Jacob	144,185,
	Nancy	180,245,283,	FOWLER	John	185,278,
EASTERDAY	Agnes	144,180,290,		Sarah	185,278,
	Christian	144,180,290,		Susannah	162,185,201,
EBBERT	Charlotte	181,196,		William	162,185,201,
	John	181,196,	FRANK	Fredirick	148,185,186,259,
EBERLINE	Catherine	173,181,		Hogan	148,185,186,259,
	Johanes	173,181,	FRATER	George	186,195,
ELLIOTT	Elizabeth	162,181,		Susan	186,195,
	James	162,181,	FRAZIER	Alex.	186,215,231,
ELSESSER	Catherine	181,		Hiram	186,193,
	John	181,		John	150,156,186,240,
ELSON	Alex.	158,181,		Lucinda	186,193,
	Charlotte	158,181,		Mary	186,215,231,240,
EMIG	Christ.	181,		Nancy	156,186,
	Mary	181,	FRESHWATER	George	187,259,273,
EVERETT	Martha	149,182,		Lydia	156,187,214,269,
	Thomas	149,182,		Lydia	270,
FARQUER	Elizabeth	182,228,292,		Margaret	187,259,273,
	John	182,283,		Reuben	156,187,214,269,
	Nancy	182,283,		Reuben	270,
	Thomas	182,228,292,	FRIKE	Mary	187,212,
FENWICK	Ann	182,285,	FRITZ	John	187,271,
	James	182,285,		Sarah	187,271,
FINK	Catherine	182,232,	FULTON	Elizabeth	188,296,
	Henry	182,232,		Robert	188,296,
FINLEY	Alex.	183,243,	GAFFNEY	Mary	188,207,
	Ann	183,243,		Matthew	188,207,
FISHER	Beth Ann	153,159,183,	GARDNER	David	188,202,273,
	Henry	153,159,183,		James	188,238,
FITZ-PATRICK	James	183,205,		Mary	188,238,
	Mary	183,205,		Nancy	188,202,273,
FLEMING	Coleman	138,183,184,	GARRETT	Alex.	189,286,
	Coleman	277,300,		Elizabeth	189,286,
	Elizabeth	138,183,184,	GAUSE	Eve	189,196,
	Elizabeth	277,300,		Joseph	189,196,
	Joseph	179,184,		Lorence	189,224,274,
	Mrs. J.	217,218,223,259,		Magdalin	189,224,274,
	Naomi	179,184,	GELSTHORPE	John	184,189,298,
FORBES	Christina	184,198,	GEORGE	Sarah	154,189,190,218,
	Donald	184,198,		Sarah	244,

330 BROOKE CO., VA./WV. MARRIAGE BOOK 1 INDEX

GEORGE	Thomas	154,189,190,218,	HALL	F.P.	193,196,244,
	Thomas	244,		Grace	189,196,
GIFFORD	Hannah	190,209,		John	178,196,
	Philip	190,209,		Lewis	181,196,197,239,
GILBERT	Charles	139,190,		Mary	192,196,
	H.	139,190,		Matthew	189,196,
GIST	Cornelius	151,171,190,265,		Sallie	197,239,
	Isabel	151,171,190,265,		Sarah	181,196,
	Mary	155,191,		Sewell	197,256,
	Thomas	155,191,235,278,		Susan	197,256,
GIVENS	E.	161,283,	HALLIE	William	197,263,
GLASS	Alfred	191,301,	HAMILTON	William	197,230,
	Eleanor	191,301,	HAMMOND	Hannah	197,291,
	Henry	191,285,		Talbott	197,291,
	James	191,222,236,	HANEY	Jane	150,197,
	Sidney	191,222,236,		John	150,197,198,258,
GLENN	Sarah	192,211,		Mary	170,198,
	William	192,211,		Michael	170,198,
GORDON	Anthony	155,192,		Sarah	198,258,
	David	192,196,	HANNA	Mary	198,274,
	Elizabeth	192,196,231,		Richard	198,274,
	Mary	155,192,	HAPNER	Caroline	174,198,
	William	192,231,		Fredirick	174,198,
GORNET	Mary	227,274,	HARCUM	Denis	184,198,
GOUDY	Nancy	145,192,		Isabella	184,198,
	Robert	145,192,	HARDING	J.B.	198,199,217,264,
GOURLEY	John	192,290,		Mary A.	198,199,217,264,
GOVER	Jacob	193,272,	HARVEY	Alina	199,218,
	Sarah	193,272,		Jane E.	199,226,
GRANT	Margaret	218,236,		William	199,218,226,
GREEN	Eli	173,194,	HAYS	Abraham	199,232,
	Elizabeth	137,138,193,194,		Enoch	199,200,210,263,
	Elizabeth	196,266,276,		Nancy	199,200,210,263,
	Henry	148,194,		Sarah	199,232,
	John F.	186,193,	HEADINGTON	Jane	153,159,160,
	Nancy	148,186,193,194,		Jane	200,275,
	Priscilla	173,194,		John	153,159,160,
	William	137,138,193,194,		John	200,275,
	William	196,227,266,276,	HEALY	Ellen	201,294,
GRIFFITH	A.W.	194,256,		Patrick	201,294,
	F.	164,194,	HEDGES	James	201,293,299,
	M.E.	164,194,		Joseph	162,166,185,201,
	Nancy A.	194,256,		Louisa	201,293,299,
GRIMES	Catharine	185,195,		Margaret	166,201,
	Darius	185,195,		Mary	168,201,
GUNION	Elizabeth	135,149,195,295,		Nancy	162,185,201,
	Henry	135,149,195,295,		Samuel	168,201,
HAGGERTY	Sarah	186,195,	HELMICK	Joseph	155,201,
	William	186,195,		Mary	155,201,
HALL	Abba	178,196,	HELMS	Mary	151,202,
	Barbara	193,196,		Samuel	151,202,
	Clarkson	192,196,	HENDRICKS	Edward	202,245,

BROOKE CO., VA./WV. MARRIAGE BOOK 1 INDEX 331

HENDRICKS	John	188,202,	HUKILL	Sallie	207,291,
	Mary	188,202,		William	167,207,208,244,
	Rebecca	202,245,		William	255,270,291,
HENNES	Lucinda	202,281,	HUMBLE	Benjamin	202,208,
	Samuel	202,281,	HUNTER	Catharine	208,229,
HENRY	Mary	178,254,		Nathaniel	208,209,229,296,
HERON	John	202,208,		Racheal	209,296,
HERVEY	David	202,248,	HUPP	Isaac	190,209,
	Dora	202,248,		Mary A.	190,209,
HESSEY	Elizabeth	203,257,	HUSTON	Mary	209,266,
	James	168,203,		Samuel	209,266,
	Mary A.	168,203,	HYDE	A.	209,271,
	Thomas	203,257,		John	209,271,
HICKMAN	Jacob	203,212,	INGLEBRIGHT	Sarah	162,209,210,254,
	Nancy	203,212,		Sarah	255,279,
HILL	Alice A.	154,203,251,		William	162,209,210,254,
	George	154,203,251,		William	255,279,
HINDMAN	Amelia	203,206,	JACK	David	199,210,
	Betsy	205,249,		Jane	199,210,
	Elizabeth	205,231,	JACKSON	John	210,215,
	Hester	204,254,		Mary	210,215,
	James	204,233,254,258,	JACOB	Benjamin	142,210,
	John	203,204,206,301,		Jacob	210,243,
	Rebecca	204,233,258,		Jane	142,210,
	William	204,205,231,249,		Kate	210,243,
	William	289,	JAMES	Elizabeth	155,185,211,216,
HINES	Ellen	183,205,		John	155,185,211,216,
	Patrick	183,205,	JAMISON	Elizabeth	211,
HITCHCOCK	Elizabeth	217,234,		John	211,
HOGG	George	205,293,		Nancy	211,
	Sarah	205,293,		Richard	211,
HOLLEY	Isabel	205,218,	JEFFERS	Harriet	192,211,284,
	William	205,218,		John	192,211,284,
HOLTON	Sally P.	157,205,	JENKINS	David	212,214,
	William	157,205,		Elizabeth	212,214,
HOOKER	George	206,219,273,	JESTER	Andrew	154,212,239,
	Margaret	206,273,		Elizabeth	154,212,239,
	Mary	206,219,	JESTY	Henry	212,249,
	Sarah J.	203,206,		Rose	212,249,
	Tallman	203,206,	JOHNS	Mark	187,212,
HORN	Elizabeth	206,274,		Mary	187,212,
	George	206,274,	JOHNSON	Elizabeth	213,267,
HOUGH	James	206,260,		John	213,267,299,
	Tabitha	206,260,		Margarett	203,212,
HOW	Mary	188,207,		Mary	213,267,
	Michael	188,207,		Nancy	213,299,
HOWARD	Catherine	207,234,		Peter	213,267,
	Daniel	207,234,		William	203,212,
HUDSON	S.E.	207,247,	JOHNSTON	John	213,254,
	Thomas	207,247,		Nancy	213,254,
HUKILL	Mary	167,207,208,244,	JONES	A.A.	213,248,
	Mary	255,270,		Ann M.	214,288,

JONES	Charles	213,248,	KUHN	Priscilla	206,219,223,
	Emeline	212,214,244,	KUNTZES	Elisabeth	185,
	Isaac	214,288,		Margaret	170,
	Jackson	187,214,270,	LALLANCE	Mary	220,258,
	Rebecca	187,214,270,		Peter	220,258,
	William	212,214,244,	LANDIS	A.S.	220,271,
KEITH	Aquilla	186,215,231,		Charlotte	176,220,
	Jane	215,265,		David	176,220,
	Quillen	215,265,		S.A.	220,271,
	Sarah	186,215,231,	LANGHTT	Laodicy	220,286,
	Susan	152,160,215,		William	220,286,
KELLY	Andrew	171,215,	LANNUM	Margaret	220,228,
	Bridget	208,216,247,		Samuel	220,228,
	Elizabeth	210,215,241,	LARGE	Nancy	221,296,
	Ellen	173,216,		Robert	221,296,
	Esther	216,	LATIMER	David	221,225,
	John	173,216,		Nancy	221,225,
	Mary	216,	LAUGHEAD	James	221,246,261,
	Owen	210,215,241,		Jane	221,275,
	Whit	171,216,		Rebecca	221,246,261,
	William	208,216,247,		Robert	221,275,
KEMP	Adam	135,155,211,216,	LAWTON	Pardon	221,263,
	Adam	217,234,		Tabitha	221,263,
	Elizabeth	135,216,217,234,	LAZEAR	Asa	222,247,
	Rachel	155,211,216,		Elizabeth	222,275,
KENEDY	Ann	217,230,		Jerome R.	191,222,276,
	Phillip	217,230,		John	222,258,262,265,
KERNS	David	136,217,260,261,		Joseph	222,275,
	Rebecca	136,217,260,261,		Mary	222,247,
KIMBERLAND	Henry	190,199,217,218,		Matilda	222,262,
	Henry	226,		Sallie	222,265,
	Mary	190,199,205,217,		Sarah	222,258,
	Mary	218,223,226,		Susan J.	191,222,276,
	William	205,218,223,	LEMOYNE	F. Julius	219,223,
KINDRICKS	Edward	176,218,236,		Madalene	219,223,
	Margarett	176,218,236,	LEE	Rachel	223,253,
KIRKER	Mary C.	199,218,		Thomas	223,253,
	W.C.	199,218,	LEHEKS	Cecelia	223,275,294,
KLEIN	F.	155,253,		Michael	223,275,294,
KLINE	Christian	144,218,	LEMMON	M.	218,223,
	Francis	144,218,		S.	218,223,
	Frederick	219,282,	LETZKUS	Apolonia	170,224,225,262,
	Margaret	219,282,		Catherine	180,227,
KLINEFELTER	Keziah	219,262,		George	141,189,223,224,
	Michael	219,262,		George	259,268,281,
KNIGHT	Phillip	219,283,		John	224,243,
	Sarah	219,283,		Justina	144,
KNOX	Margaret	219,289,		Mary	189,224,
	William	219,289,		Michelia	141,223,224,268,
KUHN	Adam	206,219,223,		Michelia	281,
	Barbara	154,220,		Millie	143,223,
	Peter	154,220,		Richard	143,170,223,224,

BROOKE CO., VA./WV. MARRIAGE BOOK 1 INDEX 333

LETZKUS	Richard	225,262,	MARION	Elizabeth	230,231,
LEWIS	Ann	226,230,	MARKES	Margarett	218,
	Douglass	144,225,	MARS	Andrew	231,278,
	Henry	199,217,226,		Elizabeth	231,278,
	Job	164,225,236,299,	MARSH	Elizabeth	192,231,
	John	153,221,225,226,		James	205,231,
	Leah	153,221,225,226,		John	230,231,
	Margaret	164,225,236,		Sarah A.	205,231,
	Mary	144,225,		Thomas	192,231,
	Oliver	226,230,	MARSHALL	Sarah	135,231,
LIAS	George	224,226,		Thomas	135,231,
	Mary	224,226,	MATHEWS	Elizabeth	251,
LINDSAY	Catharine	226,288,	MATTHEWS	James	199,232,
	Joshua	226,288,		Lavinia	199,232,
	Samuel	137,293,	MAY	Catherine	182,232,
LINTON	Ann	194,227,		Jacob	182,232,
	Benjamin	194,227,	MAYHALL	Jane	174,232,
	Elizabeth	226,227,259,287,		William	174,232,
	William	226,227,259,287,	MC BRIDE	Rosa	139,169,
LITTLE	Jeremiah	227,275,	MC BURNEY	John	228,232,
LLOYD	Susannah	227,243,		Mary	228,232,
	William	227,243,	MC CHRISTAL	Henry	233,254,
LOFFER	Andrew	180,227,274,		Rose Ann	233,254,
	Catherine	180,227,274,	MC CLEARY	Ewing	149,233,
LONG	Charles	227,259,	MC CLURG	John	204,233,
	Lorenze	141,227,228,293,		Nancy	204,233,
	Margaret	141,227,228,293,	MC COLLOCH	Ebenezer	233,290,
	Mary J.	227,259,		Sarah J.	233,290,
LUCAS	Rebecca	162,182,220,228,	MC CONKEY	Joseph	207,234,294,
	Rebecca	232,		Maria	207,234,
	Samuel	162,182,220,228,		Mariane	234,294,
	Samuel	232,	MC CONNELL	Elizabeth	169,234,
LYONS	Benjamin	177,228,		Mary	178,
	Jermy	179,229,		Peter	234,253,
	Mary	166,179,229,		Sendas	234,253,
MACKEY	Alex.	174,229,		William	169,234,
	Rosa	174,229,	MC CONVILLE	Arthur	217,234,
MAGEE	Adaline	229,262,		Bridget	217,234,
	Amy	229,296,	MC COY	Mary	235,272,
	Bernard	140,229,237,249,		William	235,272,
	John	229,296,	MC CREA	Mary	235,237,
	Martha	208,229,		Robert	235,237,
	Nancy	140,229,237,249,	MC CREARY	A.	154,235,278,
	R.T.	229,262,		Margaret	236,267,
	William	208,229,		Thomas	236,267,
MAGOINGAN	James	229,267,		William	154,235,278,
	Prudence	229,267,	MC DUGAN	Mary	142,236,
MAHAN	John	230,296,		William	142,236,
	Mary	230,296,	MC ELFRESH	Zacharia	170,236,
MAHON	Judith	152,197,230,293,	MC ELROY	James	225,236,
	Thomas	152,197,230,293,		Mary	225,236,
MARION	Edward	230,231.	MC FADDEN	David	237,291,

MC FADDEN	Elizabeth	237,291,	MELVIN	Alzina	242,252,264,
MC GEE	Bernard	140,237,253,		Henry	242,252,264,
	Nancy	140,237,253,	MENDEL	Ann	160,180,242,
MC GLAUGHLIN	Elizabeth	185,240,		John	160,180,242,
MC GREW	James	237,283,		Roselane	242,254,
	Sarah	237,283,		Valentine	242,254,
MC GROUERTY	James	177,237,	MERRYMAN	Catherine	183,227,243,
	Martha	177,237,		Joana	243,277,
MC GUIRE	Catherine	235,237,		John	183,227,243,
	Jane	188,238,		William	243,277,
	Luke	188,238,	MEYERS	Christian	210,243,
	Thomas	235,237,		Mary	210,243,
MC HENRY	Rachel	170,238,264,	MILELECH	Eva	224,243,
	William	170,238,	MILLER	Elizabeth	196,214,244,
MC HUGH	Alex.	169,238,284,		Ellen	189,244,
	Susannah	169,238,284,		George	145,160,202,244,
MC INTIRE	Ann	139,179,238,		George	245,
	Robert	139,179,238,		James	189,214,244,
MC INTYRE	James	239,261,		Jane	202,245,
	Margarett	239,261,		Joseph	244,282,
MC IVID	Martha	237,		Mary	177,244,245,282,
MC KEE	Adaline	212,239,		Nicholas	147,169,180,208,
	Matilda	197,239,		Nicholas	243,244,245,
	Melvin	197,239,		Rebecca	145,147,180,208,
	R.T.	212,239,		Rebecca	243,244,
MC KIM	Felix	144,239,		Robert	196,244,245,251,
	Mary	144,239,		Sarah	169,245,
	Nancy	239,284,		Susan	160,244,
	Thomas	239,284,		William	177,245,
MC KINLEY	Ellen	239,292,	MILLIGAN	George	165,245,246,266,
	Nancy	176,		Mary	165,245,246,266,
	William	239,292,	MITCHELL	Elizabeth	140,246,
MC KINZIE	James	240,253,		George	246,298,
	Teonas	240,253,		James	140,246,
MC LAUGHLIN	Andrew	185,186,240,276,		Mary	246,298,
	Elizabeth	240,252,	MONTGOMERY	Abram	221,246,261,
	Mary	185,240,		Daniel	159,246,
	Peter	240,252,		Julia	159,246,
MC LEASH	Euphemia	240,270,		Nancy	221,246,261,
	John	240,270,	MOODY	Mrs.	241,295,
MC MANIS	John	215,241,	MOOKLAR	S.M.	247,260,
	Mary	215,241,		William	247,260,
MC MILLEN	Hugh	241,289,	MOORE	Jane	247,256,291,
	Martha	241,289,		John	222,247,256,291,
MC NAIR	Elizabeth	241,295,		K.T.	222,247,
	Samuel	241,295,	MORAN	Nancy	237,
MC NALLY	Bernard	165,176,241,	MORENTZ	Ann	208,216,247,
	Mary	165,176,241,		John	208,216,247,
MEEKER	Isaac	235,241,	MORGAN	Catherine	207,247,
	Mary	235,241,		Edward	164,247,
MELCHS	George	242,275,		Isaac	202,248,
	Margaret	242,275,		John	207,247,

MORGAN	Margaret	164,202,247,248,	NUNEMAKER	Catherine	223,253,
MORLEY	Betsey	150,248,		Daniel	223,253,
	Russell	150,248,	O'BRIEN	Anne	140,240,253,
MORROW	John	214,248,		Thomas	240,253,
	May	214,248,	O'CONNER	Bridget	294,
MORTON	Elizabeth	151,248,	O'HARA	Andrew	165,253,
	Maryann	220,248,		Mary	175,234,253,254,
	Thomas	151,248,		Rose	165,253,
	William	220,248,		Samuel	175,234,253,254,
MOSS	James R.	213,248,	O'HARE	Denis	178,254,
	Mary A.	213,248,		Mary	178,254,
MULLANY	Bridget	229,249,	O'HEIR	John	254,
	Thomas	229,249,		Mary	144,239,
MUNCY	John	167,245,249,	O'NEAL	Elizabeth	209,254,
	Martha	167,245,249,		George	209,254,
MURCHLAND	Andrew	147,205,249,	O'SHANDER	Henrietta	213,254,
	Elizabeth	147,205,249,		William	213,254,
	Robert	153,249,	O'WESNEY	Valentine	233,254,
	Sallie	153,249,	OBNEY	James	242,254,
MURPHY	Bridget	234,		Sarah	242,254,
	Edith	250,265,	ORAM	Catherine	147,204,207,254,
	Elizabeth	246,250,266,282,		Catherine	255,
	Joseph	250,265,		George	147,204,207,254,
	Thomas	246,250,282,		George	255,
	William	250,266,	ORR	Elisabeth	137,209,255,
MURRAY	James	250,252,		George	137,209,255,
	Jane	250,252,	OWEN	Joshua	149,255,
	Nancy	157,250,262,		Rachel	149,255,
	William	157,250,262,	OWENS	Blanche	194,256,
NANGLE	Elizabeth	170,251,		C.W.	255,264,
	Susan	150,251,		Ephraim	188,194,256,
	Thomas	150,170,251,		H.	255,264,
NASMITH	Henry	174,251,	OWINGS	Ephriam	188,256,
	Mary	174,251,	PADEN	Rebecca	197,256,
NAYLOR	Harriet	251,274,		William	197,256,
	Hester C.	242,245,251,252,	PALMER	Elba	152,256,
	J.R.	242,252,		James	256,257,291,
	Joseph R.	245,251,274,		John	152,256,
NEDENGARDEN	George	250,252,		Mary	247,256,291,
	Mary	250,252,		Salina	256,257,291,
NELSON	Andrew	137,252,		Samuel	247,256,291,
	Rachel	137,252,		Tanyia	256,301,
NICHOLLS	Ellen	200,252,		Thomas	256,301,
	Mary A.	141,252,	PARISH	Nancy	142,177,257,
	Robert	141,200,252,		Richard	142,177,257,
NIXON	Elizabeth	240,252,	PARK	Anne	203,257,300,
	Robert	240,252,		Robert	203,257,300.
NOAH	James	155,253,	PARKER	Adam	220,258,
NOBLE	Narcissa	143,253,	PARKS	Jane	204,258,
	William	143,253,		John	204,258,
NOLAND	Johanna	237,253,	PARSONS	John	178,222,258,272,
	John	237,253.		Sarah	178,222,258,272,

336 BROOKE CO., VA./WV. MARRIAGE BOOK 1 INDEX

PATTERSON	Ann	227,258,259,262,	REED	Catherine	264,294,	
	Francis	227,258,259,262,		Elizabeth	215,265,	
	Martha	186,187,224,259,		James	265,268,	
	Reuben	186,187,224,259,		Jane	265,268,	
PATTON	Elizabeth	217,226,259,271,		John	215,264,265,294,	
	Elizabeth	289,	REEVES	Elizabeth	144,167,190,265,	
	John	217,259,271,		Nathan	222,250,265,	
	Thomas	226,259,		Rachel A.	222,250,265,	
	William	259,289,		Reason	144,167,190,265,	
PELLY	James	206,260,	REIDLER	Mrs. S.	169,245,	
	Margaret	206,260,	RICHARDSON	Isaac	193,266,	
PENDEGRASS	Ellen	260,285,		K.	161,266,	
	Patrick	260,285,		Nancy	193,266,	
PENDLETON	S.	247,260,		R.	161,266,	
	William	247,260,	RIDDLE	Elizabeth	246,250,266,	
PERRY	Elizabeth	217,261,		John	246,250,266,	
	Henry	217,261,	RIDGLEY	Ann	209,266,	
PETERS	David	239,261,		Franklin	209,266,	
	Elizabeth	239,261,		Margaret	266,279,	
PFIFFER	Martha	141,		Richard	266,279,	
	Michelia	223,	RIDOUT	Mark	229,267,	
PICKLEMAN	John	146,261,	RIEN	Elizabeth	213,267,	
	Mary A.	146,261,		Henry	213,267,	
PIKIRRA	A.	261,275,	ROBERTS	Elizabeth	164,265,268,	
	Leo	261,275,		Isaac D.	265,268,	
PILLINGS	Betty	221,261,		Isaiah	153,267,	
	Charles	221,246,261,		James	164,268,	
	Sarah	246,261,		Margaret	153,267,	
PITTMAN	Ann	222,262,		Rebecca	174,236,267,268,	
	Thomas	222,262,		William	174,236,267,268,	
PLANTS	Joseph	158,262,	ROBINETT	Allen	150,268,282,	
	Rosana	158,262,		Margaret	150,268,282,	
POOL	Benjamin	229,262,	ROBINSON	Elizabeth	138,172,208,269,	
	Elizabeth	229,258,262,		Elizabeth	270,	
	William	258,262,		Hannah	260,269,	
POTTS	Elizabeth	224,262,		John	187,269,	
	Nathan	224,262,		Joseph	138,172,208,269,	
PRATHER	Elizabeth	163,263,286,		Joseph	270,	
	John	163,263,286,		Margaret	269,270,271,302,	
PRIEST	Elizabeth	197,263,		Mary	161,269,	
	William	197,263,		Nancy	187,269,	
PUGH	Hugh	200,263,		Samuel	161,260,269,270,	
	Nancy	200,263,		Samuel	271,	
PUNTNEY	James	159,263,		Tempe	295,	
	Polly	159,263,		William	269,302,	
QUEST	E.C.	180,263,	RODGERS	Abram	240,270,	
	Martha	198,221,242,263,		Margaret	170,270,277,	
	Martha	264,		Sarah	240,270,	
	Samuel	198,221,242,263,		William	170,270,277,	
	Samuel	241,	ROGENETINE	Cecelia	275,294,	
ROSSION	Elizabeth	238,255,264,	ROMINE	Naomi	217,259,271,	
	Samuel	238,255,264,		William	217,259,271,	

ROUSE	Deliah	270,271,	SHRIVER	George	270,277,
	Edward	270,271,		Melissa	270,277,
RUSH	John	209,271,	SHUPE	Jonathan	243,277,
	Joseph	209,271,		Juliett	243,277,
	Mary	209,271,	SIMPSON	Ann Jane	277,301,
RUSSELL	Betsy	176,271,		Ann T.	184,277,
	Elizabeth	193,272,		Elizabeth	203,277,296,
	James	136,162,187,220,		James	184,277,301,
	James	233,258,271,272,		Robert	203,277,296,
	James	301,302,	SMITH	Alex.	279,293,
	John	193,272,		Andrew	160,231,235,278,
	Sarah	136,162,187,220,		Andrew	279,
	Sarah	233,258,271,272,		Barbara	210,279,
	Sarah	301,302,		Fergus	146,266,278,279,
	William	176,271,		Henry	210,279,
RUTH	Mary	235,272,		Jane	160,231,235,278,
	Michael	235,272,		Jane	279,293,
SANDERS	Benjamin	187,188,206,273,		Mary	166.278,
	John	273,299,		Nancy	146,266,278,279,
	Maria	273,299,		Rebecca	149,279,
	Martha	187,188,206,273,		T. Edward	185,278,
SANDERSON	Elizabeth	273,284,		William	149,166,278,279,
	John	273,284,	SMOTE	John	152,279,
SCARBOROUGH	M.E.	251,274,		Sarah	152,279,
	William	251,274,	SNEARY	H.S.	157,279,
SCHALK	John	180,227,274,		Susan	157,279,
	Mary	180,227,274,	SNEDIKER	Mary A.	138,147,165,280,
SCHELL	Henry	168,274,		William	138,147,165,280,
	Maria L.	168,274,	SNYDER	David	280,281,
SCHUEY	Frances	189,206,274,		Matilda	280,281,
	William	189,206,274,	SOULES	Jacob	202,281,
SCOTT	Charles	200,275,		Sarah	202,281,
	Jane	198,274,	SPEAKER	Hanna	280,281,
	John	198,227,274,275,	SPRAGUE	Benjamin	281,287,
	Margaret	200,275,	SPRINGBORN	Frederick	224,281,
	Sarah	227,275,		Mary	224,281,
SEARS	Elizabeth	242,275,	ST. LEDGER	John	281,288,
	Stephen	242,275,		Mary	281,288,
SEILA	B.	261,275,	STANSBERRY	John	168,281,
	Vinez?	261,275,		K.	157,281,
SELBY	Margaret	222,275,		Matilda	168,281,
	Nathan	222,275,		N.	157,281,
SERVIS	Catherine	221,275,	STARKEY	Isabelle	146,282,
	John	221,275,		William	146,282,
SHEARER	Mary	240,276,	STARR	A.	250,282,
	Robert	240,276,		William	250,282,
SHIELDS	Anne	178,276,	STEWART	David	237,283,
	William	178,276,		Dianna	182,268,282,283,
SHOUP	Lee	276,287,		Jackson	161,180,244,282,
	Mary	276,287,		Jackson	283,
SHRIMPLIN	Elizabeth	141,222,276,		Joseph	182,268,282,283,
	John	141,222,276,		M.	161,283,

BROOKE CO., VA./WV. MARRIAGE BOOK 1 INDEX

Surname	Name	Pages
STEWART	Martha	219,283,
	Mary	161,180,237,244,
	Mary	282,283,
	Robert	219,282,
	William	161,219,283,
STIETZE	Catherine	144,283,
	John	144,283,
STOCK	Benjamin	238,284,
	Jane	238,284,
STRAIN	Catherine	239,284,
	Ebenezer	239,284,
STRINGER	Robert	171,284,
	Ruth	171,284,
STRONG	Rebecca	273,284,
	Samuel	273,284,
SWEARINGEN	George	211,284,
	Ruth	211,284,
SWINER	Mary	153,182,264,285,
	Mary	300,
	Peter	153,182,264,285,
	Peter	300,
SWORDS	Finey	191,285,
	Sally	191,285,
TARR	Campbell	136,189,220,285,
	Campbell	286,
	Frances	189,286,
	Mary	136,220,285,286,
TAYLOR	Ann	154,263,286,
	Thomas	154,286,
THOMPSON	Edward	281,287,
	Eleanor	243,286,
	George	148,227,287,
	Lucy	281,287,
	Mary	148,227,276,287,
	Phoebe	198,287,
	Robert	198,243,286,287,
	William	276,287,
THORP	Aaron	140,163,287,
	Catherine	140,163,287,
TIERMAN	Michael	175,288,
	Rosa	175,288,
TILTON	Cynthian	166,288,
	Joel	166,288,
TRUAXE	Martha	214,288,
	William	214,288,
TWEED	Elizabeth	226,288,
	Robert	226,288,
UHLRICH	Charles	281,288,
	Joanna	281,288,
UTZ	John	219,289,
	Margaret	219,289,
VERMILLION	C.	169,289,
VERMILLION	E.	169,289,
VIRTUE	James	204,289,
WABLE	Joanna	241,289,
	Samuel	241,289,
WADDLE	Elizabeth	259,289,
	Isaac	259,289,
WALDRON	Elias	162,289,
	Elizabeth	162,289,
WALKER	Jane	233,290,
	Mont.	233,290,
WALTERS	Marcus	180,290,
	Rheann	180,290,
WATKINS	Benjamin	138,218,290,
	Mary	138,218,290,
WATSON	Nancy	142,291,
	Samuel	142,291,
WAUGH	David	176,292,
	Elizabeth	197,256,257,291,
	James	207,239,291,292,
	Mariah	176,292,
	Mary	207,239,291,292,
	Richard	197,256,257,291,
	Sarah A.	168,292,
	William	168,292,
WAY	Abel	175,292,
	Elizabeth	175,292,
WEAR	Comfort	182,292,
	William	182,292,
WELLS	Absalom	279,293,
	Bazil	137,166,201,205,
	Bazil	228,292,293,
	Ellen	279,293,
	Mary	143,293,
	Milton	143,293,
	Nancy	137,166,201,205,
	Nancy	228,292,293,
	Nathaniel	230,293,
	Rebecca	230,293,
WELSH	Bridget	201,294,
	Thomas	201,294,
WEST	Charity	152,294,
	Thomas	152,294,
WETHERELL	Aaron	268,294,
	Elisabeth	234,294,
	Hannah	268,294,
	William	234,294,
WHEELER	A.P.	264,294,
	C.H.	264,294,
	Honor	136,295,
	Thomas	136,295,
WHELAN	Mary	166,295,
	Michael	166,295,

BROOKE CO., VA./WV. MARRIAGE BOOK 1 INDEX

Surname	Given	Pages
WHETZELL	Emma	241,295,
	John	241,295,
WHICKERLY	Francis	171,295,
	Micheal	171,295,
WHITE	Elizabeth	209,230,296,
	Grace	139,295,
	Isaac	139,295,
	James	209,296,
	Jane	203,277,296,
	John	148,295,
	Robert	203,277,296,
	Sarah	188,296,
	Tempe	148,295,
	Thomas	188,296,
	William	230,296,
WIGGINS	John	229,296,
	Margaret	229,296,
WILKINSON	Elizabeth	221,296,
	Mary	175,297,
	Thomas	221,296,
	William	175,297,
WILLIAMSON	James	142,147,297,
	Sarah	142,147,148,297,
	William	148,297,
WILLIQUES	Parthenia	246,298,
	William	246,298,
WILSON	Abraham	201,299,
	Elizabeth	149,201,298,299,
	James	225,298,299,
	John	169,298,
	Jonathan	149,298,
	Joseph	139,140,298,299,
	Micha	298,299,
	Michael	225,299,
	Nancy	139,298,299,
	Rachel	273,299,
	Rebecca	139,140,298,299.
	Samuel	139,298,
	Sarah	169,298,
	William	273,298,299.
WINESBURG	George	213,299,
	Jane	213,299,
WOLCOTT	Christ.	168,300,
	Philis	168,300,
WOOD	Elizabeth	264,285,300,
	William	264,285,300,
WOODY	Eliena	172,300,
	Tarlton	172,300,
WORSTELL	Elizabeth	183,300,
	Isaac	183,300,
WRIGHT	Edie	167,301,
	James	257,300,
	John	146,167,300,301,
	Nancy J.	204,301,
	Sofiah	146,300,
WRIGHTMAN	Alex.	256,271,301,
	Catherine	256,271,301,
WYLIE	Elizabeth	277,301,
	Robert	277,301,
YOUNG	Ann	272,302,
	Elizabeth	151,301,
	George	269,302,
	Mary	269,302,
	Peter	151,301,
	William	272,302,

www.ingramcontent.com/pod-product-compliance
Lightning Source LLC
Chambersburg PA
CBHW071954220426
43662CB00009B/1122